Edward A. Tenenbaum and the Deutschmark

German industry had survived Allied bombing largely unscathed. Currency reform was necessary to provide incentives for capital owners and workers to produce. The abundance of old Reichsmarks had to be replaced with a scarce supply of Deutschmarks that users would expect to retain value. It was Edward A. Tenenbaum, currency expert of the US military government in Berlin since 1946, who, in 1948, managed the exceptionally successful currency reform in West Germany that was implemented by the legislative powers of the three Western Allies against opposition from West German financial experts. It was the foundation of West Germany's "economic miracle." The West German currency conversion is part of the founding myth of the Federal Republic of Germany. Yet Tenenbaum's pivotal role is largely unknown among the German public. Besides providing a full-blown biography of the true father of the currency reform, this book elevates Tenenbaum to his proper place in German history.

CARL-LUDWIG HOLTFRERICH is Professor of Economics and Economic History at the John F. Kennedy Institute for North American Studies of the Free University of Berlin. He is the author of *The Great German Inflation 1914 to 1923* (1986) and has published extensively on business and banking history as well as domestic and foreign economic-policy issues. He is the recipient of The Financial Times/Booz-Allen & Hamilton Global Business Book Award and the Helmut Schmidt Prize in German–American Economic History at the German Historical Institute in Washington, DC. He is a member of the Berlin-Brandenburg Academy of Science.

T0384228

STUDIES IN NEW ECONOMIC THINKING

The 2008 financial crisis pointed to problems in economic theory that require more than just big data to solve. INET's series in New Economic Thinking exists to ensure that innovative work that advances economics and better integrates it with other social sciences and the study of history and institutions can reach a broad audience in a timely way.

Recently published:
Power and Inequality: A Reformist Perspective by Alessandro Roncaglia

Money and Empire: Charles P. Kindleberger and the Dollar System by Perry Mehrling 2022

Titles forthcoming in the series:
Economics without Preferences: Microeconomics and Policymaking beyond the Maximizing Individual by Michael Mandler

Edward A. Tenenbaum and the Deutschmark

How an American Jew Became the Father of Germany's Postwar Economic Revival

CARL-LUDWIG HOLTFRERICH

Free University of Berlin

CAMBRIDGE
UNIVERSITY PRESS

CAMBRIDGE
UNIVERSITY PRESS

Shaftesbury Road, Cambridge CB2 8EA, United Kingdom

One Liberty Plaza, 20th Floor, New York, NY 10006, USA

477 Williamstown Road, Port Melbourne, VIC 3207, Australia

314–321, 3rd Floor, Plot 3, Splendor Forum, Jasola District Centre, New Delhi – 110025, India

103 Penang Road, #05–06/07, Visioncrest Commercial, Singapore 238467

Cambridge University Press is part of Cambridge University Press & Assessment, a department of the University of Cambridge.

We share the University's mission to contribute to society through the pursuit of education, learning and research at the highest international levels of excellence.

www.cambridge.org
Information on this title: www.cambridge.org/9781009492812

DOI: 10.1017/9781009492829

© Carl-Ludwig Holtfrerich 2024

This publication is in copyright. Subject to statutory exception and to the provisions of relevant collective licensing agreements, no reproduction of any part may take place without the written permission of Cambridge University Press & Assessment.

When citing this work, please include a reference to the DOI 10.1017/9781009492829

First published 2024

A catalogue record for this publication is available from the British Library

A Cataloging-in-Publication data record for this book is available from the Library of Congress

ISBN 978-1-009-49281-2 Hardback
ISBN 978-1-009-49280-5 Paperback

Cambridge University Press & Assessment has no responsibility for the persistence or accuracy of URLs for external or third-party internet websites referred to in this publication and does not guarantee that any content on such websites is, or will remain, accurate or appropriate.

Dedicated to

Charles P. Kindleberger (†)

OSS comrade, fellow economist, and friend of Edward A. Tenenbaum.

After Hitler had declared war on the United States, they were both called to arms to defend their country against German aggression and to liberate Europe from fascism.

Helmut Schmidt (†)

Former chancellor of the Federal Republic of Germany, who wrote in his memoirs:

"One of the figures behind the German [currency] reform, the young American Edward A. Tenenbaum, was unfairly ignored in Germany. ... Lieutenant Tenenbaum from New York was the son of Jewish emigrants from Poland. He deserves a monument in German economic history."

Jorge Semprun (†)

Prisoner of Buchenwald concentration camp after anti-fascist resistance in Paris. Celebrated novelist of the post-war period.

Driving around in a jeep on April 11, 1945 Tenenbaum and his civilian OSS colleague Egon Fleck by chance ran into a large formation of inmates marching on a road to Weimar. Still dressed in prisoner clothing they carried weapons, some of them, including Semprun, even bazookas. In his posthumous Exercises de Survie: récit *(Paris 2012), Semprun puts many questions as to the irony of history that two Jews of all people were the first Americans to come across Buchenwald and how their lives went. This book answers them all.*

Tenenbaum's children: Anne, Mark, Joan, and Charles (†)

Contents

Figures

I Introduction

> For the great enemy of truth is very often not the lie – deliberate, contrived, and dishonest – but the myth – persistent, persuasive, and unrealistic. Too often we hold fast to clichés of our forebears. We subject all facts to a prefabricated set of interpretations. We enjoy the comfort of opinion without the discomfort of thought.
>
> John F. Kennedy, <u>Yale University Commencement Address</u> June 11, 1962, twenty years after Edward A. Tenenbaum's graduation at Yale.

I am pursuing two goals with this book: First, I want to debunk the myth that Ludwig Erhard was the originator of the West German currency reform of June 20, 1948, and do justice to the historical truth that Edward Adam Tenenbaum was the key figure in shaping and implementing that reform. Second, contrary to my original intention to write only an introduction to the publication of some Tenenbaum documents on the 1948 currency reform, I have decided to write a biography of Tenenbaum. This is because during my initial review of his papers at the Harry S. Truman Presidential Library in Independence MO in November 2017, I came across Tenenbaum's many exciting rendezvous with world history throughout his "Life and Fate."[1]

Before recounting Edward Tenenbaum's life story in the following chapters, I want to make readers aware of three points. First, I divert from the traditional design of a biography. I not only put the puzzle pieces together that I collected in the process of my research. But at times the finding of such pieces was so unusual and thrilling that I want to share such search experiences with my readers.[2]

Second, a secret service wouldn't deserve its name, if information on its agents and their tasks would freely be disseminated by their employers, the media, and other channels of communication. Even in scholarly publications on institutional structures, activities, and histories of secret services, authors seem to be reluctant to attach name tags, the more so the less distant the object of study is away from the present. Therefore, in order to reconstruct Tenenbaum's life I will make extensive use of early postwar publications on the Organization of Strategic Services (OSS), the wartime US secret service in Washington, DC, by which Tenenbaum was employed from June 1942, and on the battlefield in North Africa and Europe, as well as on military outfits in which Tenenbaum served, but where his name and his specific tasks are not mentioned. Likewise, I make use of biographies of people with whom he shared war and postwar professional experiences on a personal level, like Lucius D. Clay, or of those who played an important role in shaping the policy framework in which Tenenbaum acted. Examples of the latter case are the memoirs and published papers of George F. Kennan as well as biographies by others about Kennan and his contribution to the unfolding of the Cold War. After all, progressive postwar disruption of the wartime alliance of the Western Powers with the Soviet Union proved to be the breeding ground for the partition of Germany as a result of West Germany's currency reform, shaped and managed by Edward A. Tenenbaum.

Third, Charles P. Kindleberger and his activities during World War II play a large role in Section 3.2. His and Tenenbaum's common denominator was not only brilliance in economics and finance, but also their parallel careers in OSS. Kindleberger was so close a friend of Edward Tenenbaum that he continued to keep contact with his widow Jeanette Kipp Tenenbaum after Edward's early death in 1975. Likewise, Kindleberger and I were not only economic-history colleagues, but also close friends between our first acquaintance in Cambridge MA in 1975 until his death in 2003. Sometime during the 1990s he made me aware of the rich Tenenbaum Papers, which widow Jeanette Kipp had donated to the Harry S. Truman Presidential Library in Independence MO. He urged me to make use of it in a scholarly publication on Tenenbaum's largely unknown key role in shaping and executing West Germany's currency reform of June 20, 1948. He tried to whet my appetite by giving me a copy of forty-two single-spaced pages of verbatim minutes of a whole-day meeting of Tenenbaum (and his British counterpart Bernard C. A. Cook) with German financial experts on November 20, 1947. During the previous month, the latter had started working under Ludwig Erhard's chairmanship on a currency-reform plan in the *Sonderstelle Geld und Kredit* (Special Agency for Money and Credit) at Bad Homburg.[3]

Kindleberger's efforts to make academia and the public aware of the crucial role his friend Tenenbaum had played in the introduction of the Deutschmark in West Germany is also evidenced in an article published in the *Jüdische Allgemeine* on the sixtieth anniversary of the currency reform in 2008. The two coauthors explicitly state that they are particularly obliged to Kindleberger for information on important sources of their Tenenbaum story.[4] And Kindleberger himself contributed a scholarly piece on the 1948 currency reform to a conference at Princeton University in April 1998. It was coauthored by F. Taylor Ostrander, who as part of the Office of Military Government, United States (OMGUS) for Germany in Berlin had eye-witnessed the planning and the execution of the reform.[5]

In the following paragraphs I will share with my readers some information of a more private nature about my friendship with Charlie Kindleberger. The reason is that I owe to him my deep interest in Tenenbaum's invaluable contribution to postwar German economic history. Our friendship started during my research year in Cambridge MA 1975–1976.

There he told me about some of his wartime roles in Europe. Among others, he had interrogated German prisoners of war (PWs). As a member of the Psychological Warfare Division of General George Patton's Third US Army, Edward Tenenbaum had done the same. They both belonged to General Omar Bradley's 12th US Army

Group. Their goals were to collect information on the German *Wehrmacht's* military capacity to defend against immediate tactical or more long-term strategic targets of the US Army and its Air Force during the advance from the beaches of Normandy into the center of Germany. Charles Kindleberger asked me in Cambridge whether I had any recollections of World War II. I told him that my father as a civilian had been wounded, not fatally, in a daylight bombing raid on Münster in Westphalia in November 1944. When hospitalized he was infected by gas gangrene. He died a week after being wounded, as there was no penicillin available in provincial hospitals in Germany at the time. This narrative, including my last visit with her at the hospital bed, where my father surprised me with chocolate, had been what my mother tried to keep alive in my memory. I told Kindleberger that even for the following months I hardly had any recollections since I was only three years and two months old when my home town Telgte, not far from Münster, was liberated by US troops on April 3, 1945.[6] My mother and I were evicted from our four-room apartment. GIs were billeted there for about one week. On this occasion my mother saw Black people for the first time in her life. My mother and I stayed across the street with a neighbor and her two children. This lady's husband had not yet returned from the war, but did so unscathed shortly after its end. A few weeks later, carrying a can of milk he had fetched from a farmer for his children, he was killed when a British military vehicle crashed into his bicycle.. He was on his ride home after curfew had started.

Charles Kindleberger was a compassionate man. Therefore, after what he had learned about my war experience he held back to tell me about his most important role in World War II in Europe which he would freely share with his students in classes at MIT.[7] I ran across information on that part of his life only during my research for this book. He was the head of the Enemy Objectives Unit (EOU), stationed in a wing of the US embassy building in London. It consisted of America's best and brightest young economists and mathematicians. Their task was – by using cost-benefit analysis and detailed knowledge of production chains – to supply the US Strategic Air Force with information on bombing targets. The selection was based on solving equations to determine an optimum of damage to the German war machine in relation to own aircraft and pilot losses. While Kindleberger performed this job from February 1943 until May 1944, targets were mainly attacked in daylight for precision bombing of factories, railroad bridges, airplane production sites, oil supplies and refineries etc. The technically less well-equipped British bombers, in contrast, flew attacks at night to destroy cities with area bombing. Toward the last months of the war, the US Strategic Air Force, however, joined with the British Royal Air Force for area bombardment, like in the case of Münster in November 1944 and the notorious Dresden case in mid-February 1945.

By holding back on his EOU activities Kindleberger had been very considerate not to hurt my feelings. Instead, we kept up and deepened our friendship by correspondence and meetings in Cambridge MA and Princeton, in Berlin and Bad Homburg near Frankfurt am Main, and once in Paris where he invited me to give a paper in his seminar, cochaired by Fernand Braudel.

His EOU team's role in World War II had been crucial in virtually drying up Germany's oil supplies and thereby immobilizing the German Army and Air Force. He also urged me to embark on my Tenenbaum project. For these two reasons it is not a haphazard digression from my main subject that in Section 3.2 I will also deal with Charles Kindleberger's leading roles in EOU and subsequently on the battlefield in Continental Europe. There he also ran into his secret-service colleague Edward Tenenbaum again after they had first met and as economists cooperated on estimating Germany's economic and war potential at OSS headquarters in Washington, DC during the second half of 1942.

What impressions of Edward Tenenbaum's expertise in currency-reform matters and of his role not only in American military government under General Lucius Clay, but also in his relations to the financial experts of British and French military governments did German currency experts gather? A good source for answering these two questions is a treatise that Erwin Hielscher wrote after he had left early the so-called *Conclave of Rothwesten* on May 21, 1948. The Conclave comprised a group of eleven German financial and currency experts and a few more persons as support staff. Eight of the Bizone experts and the support staff had been summoned in Bad Homburg, near Frankfurt, transported to an unknown destination in a military bus with frosted glass windows, and lodged in a US Air Force barracks building in Rothwesten near Kassel on April 20, 1948.[8] (For more details see Section 4.3). By leaving prematurely, Hielscher protested against the little say that the Allies had granted the German experts over the substance of currency reform. He wrote his treatise after having left and before sending it off to his publisher in a sealed envelope on June 18, 1948, two days before currency reform was started. He obliged the publisher to delay publication for about three months so that his harsh criticism of the reform plan would not contribute to weaken the public's confidence in the new Deutschmark currency.[9]

Hielscher's treatise is an especially good source for several reasons. The author was the chairman of the group of German experts in meetings with Tenenbaum and the financial experts of the two other Western Allies. As such he had a special relationship with Tenenbaum, including many informal discussions on a one-to-one basis. He belonged to the minority of the German group that adamantly argued for a harsh conversion rate of only 5 percent as opposed to the 10 percent conversion rate of the Allied plan that Tenenbaum started out with. And last but not least, the treatise was written with a fresh memory of positions, proceedings, and personalities represented in the Conclave of Rothwesten.

Hielscher entitles the last one of his four chapters *The currency strategy of Mr. Tenenbaum*. This in itself is a recognition of the central role that Tenenbaum played in devising the currency-reform plan before and during the Conclave. To document further Hielscher's high esteem of Tenenbaum, I quote from the introduction to this chapter:

> Since I will be taking a critical look at Tenenbaum's currency strategy in this chapter, I would like to start by saying something personal. Certainly the names of the people actually responsible are different: [Jack] Bennett the American, Sir Eric Coats the English and Leroy Beaulieux the French. It was, of course, not the intention or the task of the German experts to determine which part of the Allied designs could be attributed to this or that Ally or to this or that of the Allied experts. There can be no doubt, however, and nothing is taken away from the merits of the other experts involved, if the presumably large share of Tenenbaum is emphasized. In [Bad] Homburg [where Hielscher had been part of the Special Agency for Money and Credit, the German financial expert group appointed by the two Anglo-Saxon military powers, at first as deputy and eventually as chairman], the idea was often discussed that Tenenbaum was a Morgenthau man, that he wanted to use currency policy to try to make Germany an economically impotent and unviable entity. It is one of my great fears that the money reform of Rothwesten, because of its overall construction and because of particularly ingenious ideas, could create this impression among the German people, that this reform program could be seen as a punitive action against the German people. Once again the lack of understanding [on the German side] of the inevitability of a hard currency policy will take its revenge, once again the illusions artificially maintained and nurtured by the frivolous illusionists will take their revenge. I am in complete agreement with Dr. [Ludwig] Erhard [chairman of the Special Agency until he became the director of the Economic Administration of the Bizone on March 1, 1948] that the toughest currency reform is the best, also with regard to social justice. ... The German people would do themselves no service if they were to regard the currency measures of the Allies, and especially the

> rigorous monetary-theory view of Mr. Tenenbaum, as hostile to
> Germany. Even within our group of German experts I have isolated
> myself to a large extent through my frank and open cooperation
> with Mr. Tenenbaum in particular. I have assumed that American
> and German interests run parallel on this point. I would like to
> testify that Tenenbaum wants nothing other than what I too
> wanted: the restoration of orderly monetary conditions at all costs.
> My personal relationship with Tenenbaum was very good. In some
> conversations with him, he was able to develop his ideas more
> openly than in plenary sessions. ... Right to the end we were both
> in agreement on the basic line of our views; it may be due to the
> difference in age and to psychological facts that I did not succeed in
> convincing him completely in a core part of my opinion.[10]

This quote from one of the two chairmen[11] of the German expert
group who had prematurely left the Conclave of Rothwesten in protest, contains the answers to the two questions posed above, namely
what weight did Tenenbaum carry among the German experts, as to
his role and to his expertise. Of all the Allied financial experts
involved, including on the next level up, namely the financial advisers
of Western military governments, Hielscher leaves no doubt about
Tenenbaum's central role.

The same is true of Hans Möller. Born June 12, 1915, he was the
youngest German expert at the Conclave. But Tenenbaum was still
six and a half years younger than him. Möller writes on his experience
at Rothwesten:

> During the 49 days of the Conclave, meetings with representatives
> of the military governments were held for about 20 days, with the
> main work on the Allied side being done by Tenenbaum (USA),
> while his colleagues Lefort (France) and Cook (UK) took a back seat.
> Tenenbaum, in addition to his intensive discussions with the
> German experts, did an immense amount of travel between Berlin
> (the seat of the military governments for Germany), Rothwesten
> and Frankfurt (the seat of the bizonal authorities on the German

and Allied sides) in order to organize the necessary coordination between the three military governments and between them and their home governments. Coordination with the French played a decisive role in this process, as they delayed the decision on their participation in the currency reform until the last minute.[12]

Moreover, Hielscher's clear endorsement of Tenenbaum's basic conception of a harsh currency reform – although differing from his own in some details – proves how highly Tenenbaum's expertise was recognized on the German side. Hielscher's premature departure from Rothwesten, after Tenenbaum had obtained clearance for this move from higher authorities, does not seem to have been directed against the lead person of the Allied experts. It looks like it has been primarily in protest of a currency-conversion conception softer than his own and Tenenbaum's by the majority of his German colleagues. Hans Möller alludes to this by explaining Hielscher's ostentatious premature departure "as a step which was also due to differences of opinion with his colleagues in the Conclave."[13]

Another Conclave member was Otto Pfleiderer. He later served as long-term president of the Land Central Bank of Baden-Württemberg. Twenty-five years after currency reform, he published some of his recollections of the Conclave discussions between the German experts and the representatives of the three Western Allies, Edward A. Tenenbaum for the US, Bernard C. Cook for the British, and Charles Lefort for the French military government. Here is what Pfleiderer wrote: "The most important spokesman on the side of the military governments was Edward Tenenbaum, a still young man who for years had been dealing practically full time with all questions connected with the reform of the German currency."[14]

Michael Budczies, the son of Wolfgang Budczies, another German expert at the Conclave of Rothwesten, reports on his father's impressions of Tenenbaum's constructive role:

The importance of the task, the trusting and friendly cooperation between the German experts, who had already grown together into a team at the Special Agency, and probably also the isolation from the outside world soon created an extremely pleasant atmosphere that was very conducive to the progress of the work. // Colonel Stoker, who took great care of the physical and mental well-being of the camp inmates, and Edward A. Tenenbaum, who was only 26 years old, primarily contributed to this, as my father told me. The latter, despite his young age and the skepticism he initially encountered, succeeded in winning the respect of the German experts through his tireless efforts, his outstanding intelligence, his professional competence and his fairness, even though he was often unable to meet their expectations. On him lay the main burden of work on the Allied side. From time to time, his superior [plagued by health problems] Jack Bennett, who had succeeded Joseph Dodge as Clay's financial advisor, attended the meetings at the Conclave. The representatives of the French and British occupying powers essentially acted only as listeners and observers for their governments. // [... Tenenbaum initially had] great reservations about the Germans .... As his widow told me in 1998 at the commemoration of the 50th anniversary of the currency reform in Rothwesten, in 1945, as a lieutenant, he was one of the first American soldiers to enter the Buchenwald concentration camp and liberate the inmates who were still alive. What he had seen there had shaken him terribly. In 1948, he was still under this impression. On the additional barbed wire around 'Haus Posen' in the Rothwesten barracks there was a warning in German and English that anyone climbing the fence would be shot on sight. The sign had been put up there – as his widow told me – on Tenenbaum's orders. Whether this order is still due to the memory of Buchenwald, I do not know. It would be understandable. It is all the more to be acknowledged that Tenenbaum did not let these feelings show in his very objective work with the Germans.[15]

2 Ludwig Erhard, Who Took Credit for Edward A. Tenenbaum's Success*

The West German currency reform of 1948 is considered the most successful in modern economic history. One can suppose that if it had failed, Tenenbaum would have become much better known in Germany – as a scapegoat. In the memory of the older generation in Germany, who experienced Erhard as the Federal Minister of Economics from 1949 to 1963 and then as Konrad Adenauer's successor in the Chancellery until 1966, the myth of Erhard as the Father of the Deutschmark and the currency reform of 1948 is firmly anchored. It has also been cultivated by the media. During the years of the so-called economic miracle [*Wirtschaftswunder*], there was no reason to call it into question. And yet it would have been easy to see that, in 1948, no such thing as the Federal Republic of Germany existed, and that only the occupying powers with their legislative competence could have carried out such a sovereign task as the creation of a new currency. And as to the monetary policy proposals of Erhard and other German experts, the occupiers were largely indifferent.

But Erhard had become the embodiment of West Germany's spectacular economic resurgence in the 1950s and 1960s. In elections, he was a stronger magnet for the Christian Democratic Union (CDU) than Adenauer, partly because of his superior rhetorical skills and sonorous voice. And this despite the fact that he was not a member of the CDU or of any other party. Indeed, like the 1954 World Cup soccer champions, he was virtually worshipped by a fan community. For a long time, even I belonged to the club. The fact that someone else, an employee of the American military government, moreover of Jewish descent and twenty-five years younger than Erhard, had laid the primary foundation for such rapid economic growth, namely a stable German currency, was a disturbing thought even to those who knew.

The memory of the first postwar years – in the ignominy of defeat and under foreign rule, with hunger and housing shortages to boot – was repressed during the "economic miracle" as much as the memory of being on the fronts or under a hail of bombs at home.

My project began with the goal of singling out the central role and decisive contributions of the true "founding father" of the Deutschmark and manager of the 1948 West German currency reform, Edward A. Tenenbaum. He was the preeminent currency expert of the American military government (Office of Military Government for Germany, United States, OMGUS) under General Lucius D. Clay in Berlin. Since his departure from active military service on March 23, 1946, coinciding with his promotion from first lieutenant to captain, he remained in the US Army Air Forces as a reserve officer. For OMGUS, he worked as a civilian. He had worked for the Office of Strategic Services (OSS), the US intelligence agency, from June 1942 until after the end of the war as well as serving as a US Army conscript since December 1942. To this day, he remains virtually unknown to the German public. Even among historians he is widely unknown or ignored, including for his key role in shaping and enforcing the currency reform. He is not mentioned once in the following key publications:

- the document collection *Records of the Prehistory of the Federal Republic of Germany, 1945–1949* [*Akten zur Vorgeschichte der Bundesrepublik Deutschland 1945–1949*], published by the German Federal Archives and the Institute of Contemporary History in five volumes, some of them double volumes;[1]
- the *OMGUS Handbook: The American Military Government in Germany, 1945–1949* [*OMGUS-Handbuch. Die amerikanische Militärregierung in Deutschland 1945–1949*], also published in a series by the Institute of Contemporary History;[2]
- History of the Federal Republic of Germany, Vol. 1: *The Years of Occupation, 1945–1949* [Geschichte der Bundesrepublik Deutschland, Vol. 1: *Jahre der Besatzung 1945–1949*];[3]
- Hans-Ulrich Wehler, *German Social History* [*Deutsche Gesellschaftsgeschichte*];[4]

- Henry C. Wallich, *Mainsprings of the German Economic Revival*;[5] nor
- the contribution of Christoph Buchheim, "The Establishment of the Bank deutscher Länder and the West German Currency Reform," to a Bundesbank *Festschrift*.[6]

Indeed, the name Tenenbaum does not appear in the economics thesis submitted to the University of Hamburg in 1949 by Helmut Schmidt, Minister of Finance and Economics in the early 1970s and chancellor of Germany from 1974 to 1982.[7] In his thesis, Schmidt compared the failed Japanese currency reform of 1946 with the West German one of 1948. The thesis was deemed "good," a grade that was rarely given at the time and hardly ever with the addition of "very." That is to say, the author knew a lot about currency reform. In his 1987 memoirs, Schmidt pays tribute to Tenenbaum with the following words: "One of the figures behind the German [currency] reform, the young American Edward A. Tenenbaum, was unfairly ignored in Germany. He was the intellectual link between the American military government and the German experts. Lieutenant Tenenbaum from New York was the son of Jewish emigrants from Poland. He deserves a monument in German economic history."[8]

Otmar Emminger, while still vice president of the Deutsche Bundesbank (he later served as president from 1977–1979), telegraphed Edward Tenenbaum's widow, Jeanette Kipp Tenenbaum, after Edward's fatal car accident on October 14, 1975: "His eminent services in ending the disastrous inflation and establishing a new and firm currency are not forgotten in the Deutsche Bundesbank."[9] With the invitation of Tenenbaum's widow and her daughter Anne to attend the fiftieth anniversary celebrations of the currency reform as guests of the Bundesbank, Emminger's appreciation became known to a wider public for the first and last time via media coverage. In his memoirs, Emminger mentions Tenenbaum only briefly: "Here, at least one sentence should stand to commemorate the young American expert Tenenbaum, to whom the principal credit is due within the American military government for the preparation of the currency transition, but who soon fell into oblivion after his return to the U.S."[10] As if to demonstrate this oblivion, Emminger does not include Tenenbaum in the book's index of names. In contrast, there are thirty-two pages in that index referring to the name Ludwig Erhard.

This one-sided German culture of remembrance is also expressed in the following fact: In Germany, around 110 streets and squares are named after Ludwig Erhard, not to mention a great number of schools, buildings, assembly halls, foundations, medals, prizes, and scholarships. In contrast, there were no streets in Germany bearing the name of Edward Tenenbaum until recently – in Fuldatal, near Kassel, one can now be found on the grounds of the former barracks in the Rothwesten district, where the Museum of the 1948 Currency Reform [Museum Währungsreform 1948] is now located in the Posen House. It was here, together with eleven West German currency experts, in seven weeks of total seclusion – the *Konklave* ["conclave"], as the German participants called it – that Tenenbaum worked out the administrative details of the West German currency reform, following the blueprint provided by the Americans.

The museum came into being as a result of a private initiative, initially that of Alfons Kössinger, who had been stationed at the Rothwesten Air Base as a Luftwaffe pilot.[11] It was only a few years prior to the fiftieth anniversary of the Konklave and the currency reform of 1948 that the Deutsche Bundesbank began providing financial and advisory support to the institution, only to withdraw its support a few years later. Nevertheless, I take the conduct of the Bundesbank to be an important step toward recognition of the historical truth: that Tenenbaum laid the foundation for the West German "economic miracle" and thus made a decisive contribution to stabilizing parliamentary democracy in the Federal Republic of Germany (FRG), founded in 1949.

Konklave member Otto Pfleiderer also saw it this way. In 1953, on the occasion of the fifth anniversary of the currency reform, he wrote that this reform had been one of the most significant events in

West German postwar history. This reform was getting more and more recognition. "In any case, it marked the decisive turning point for economic life in West Germany." It was only through the creation of the German Mark, he said, that the conditions for a functioning market were established, "without which the astonishing upswing in production, labor productivity, and the general standard of living would not at all have been possible."[12]

Two events were held in June 1998 to mark the fiftieth anniversary of the currency reform: "50 Years of the Konklave," a celebration in the officers' mess at the Rothwesten Air Base to mark the reopening of the expanded Currency Reform Museum on June 15, 1998;[13] and "50 Years of the Deutsche Mark," a ceremony in the Paulskirche in Frankfurt am Main on June 20, 1998. In each case, Bundesbank President Hans Tietmeyer gave the keynote address. At the invitation of the Bundesbank, Jeanette Kipp Tenenbaum and her eldest daughter, Anne, who was born in Berlin in 1947, traveled from the United States to attend both events. Family friend Christel G. McDonald, along with her husband, US ambassador John McDonald, were also among the Bundesbank's guests at both ceremonies. For years, Christel McDonald had provided advice and support to Alfons Kössinger in designing the Currency Reform Museum. She had completed an MA in history at the University of Iowa in 1990 with a thesis on Tenenbaum's key role in the preparation and implementation of the West German currency reform.

In the presence of German Chancellor Helmut Kohl, who also gave a speech, as well as German President Roman Herzog and ECB President Wim Duisenberg,[14] Tietmeyer said in his keynote address at the *Paulskirche* that the favorable conditions for the success of the currency reform were mainly attributable to the influence of the American military authorities. "In particular, the contributions made by the officer and scientist Edward A. Tenenbaum, who was still young at the time and who sadly passed away much too early, have not been forgotten."[15] And in his speech five days earlier in the officers' mess at Rothwesten Air Base, Tietmeyer had said, "The

Konklave was not a marginal event. It was a decisive factor in the successful implementation of the currency reform." Tenenbaum "stretched the German 'Council of Eleven' of Rothwesten to its limits, drove it to be efficient."[16]

In 1998, a well-researched, accessible book by journalist Werner Meyer also helped to bring Tenenbaum's role in introducing the Deutschmark to the attention of a wider public.[17] Initiatives by the Currency Reform Museum and the municipality of Fuldatal as well as funding from the federal government and private donors also contributed to educating the public about Tenenbaum's crucial role in German economic history. In the window of time between the Bundeswehr's relinquishment of the barracks (then known as *Fritz-Erler-Kaserne*) and the federal government's conveyance of the Posen House to the nonprofit Museumsverein Währungsreform 1948 on February 15, 2013, the new street leading to the building was named Edward-Tenenbaum-Str. by the municipality of Fuldatal on April 25, 2012.[18]

Some years earlier, on June 22, 1990, in the lead-up to German reunification, *Die Zeit* had published a lengthy article on the occasion of the German monetary union written by the American historian David Schoenbaum, entitled "Mentor of the Deutschmark: Edward A. Tenenbaum's still unpublished, highly topical recollections of the currency reform." In it, he addresses a few assessments and opinions contained in Tenenbaum's unpublished memoirs.

In 2016, there was another public recognition of Tenenbaum's fundamental contribution to the successful development of the FRG. After consulting with several professors of economic history, two journalists, one from the *Handelsblatt* and one from the *Wirtschaftswoche*, published *Made in Germany: Great Moments in German Economic History*, a collection of twenty articles on important figures in German economic history, from Friedrich List to Birgit Breuel. Ludwig Erhard is not included. But Edward Tenenbaum is one of the twenty. He is acknowledged there for his central role in introducing the Deutschmark as the basis for the West German "economic miracle."[19]

Ludwig Erhard, of course, was also aware that Tenenbaum had played the key role in designing and implementing the currency reform. After Tenenbaum's fatal car accident, Erhard sent a telegram to his widow:

> Dear Mrs. Tenenbaum! // Although I haven't had the honor of meeting you personally, the memory of your husband, who died recently in his fatal accident, has stayed with me since 1948. I will always think of him fondly and with great respect. I believe I can say that the deceased and I, on the American and German sides, were in complete intellectual and scientific agreement when creating the conditions for the successful implementation of the German currency reform. Keeping his memory alive in Germany will always be a special concern of mine. I mourn the death of this excellent man and convey to you my sincere condolences, with the wish that you may quickly recover from the consequences of the accident. // In faithful remembrance // Yours // Ludwig Erhard.[20]

In this telegram, Erhard at least concedes that Tenenbaum had a hand in creating the conditions for the success of the currency reform. In Germany, by contrast, the first Federal Minister of Economics always claimed the exclusive status of Father of the Deutschmark. It is true that, in an interview after Tenenbaum's appearance at the meeting of the Special Agency for Money and Credit on November 20, 1947 (headed by Erhard), he gave the following assessment of Tenenbaum: "A young man, smart as a whip, scientifically trained, and cut out for questions of monetary policy."[21] Yet in spite of this assessment and of his assurance to Tenenbaum's widow that keeping her husband's memory alive in Germany was a matter of personal concern, he did nothing to that end. Erhard did not make the contents of his telegram public. I made inquiries to *Die Zeit, Frankfurter Allgemeine Zeitung, Frankfurter Rundschau, Süddeutsche Zeitung, Die Welt*, and *Mannheimer Morgen* as to whether an obituary had appeared in the weeks following Edward A. Tenenbaum's accidental death in October 1975. All inquiries drew a blank.

Having found no mention of Tenenbaum by name in any of Erhard's published books, I finally came across a short contribution by Erhard to an issue of the *Zeitschrift für das gesamte Kreditwesen* in June 1973, on the occasion of the twenty-fifth anniversary of the West German currency reform. There, Erhard recalled the following: "More and more, on the American side, a young, rather brilliant macro-economist – generally called only Mr. Tenenbaum – came into the picture, with whom I found myself in agreement on almost every question."[22] This mention of his name – in parenthesis, without a first name – indicates how much Erhard would have liked to leave it out again, as he had ten years earlier in a television interview with Günter Gaus on April 10, 1963. When Gaus asked how large a part the Germans had played in shaping the currency reform and how much the Americans had ultimately decided on their own, Erhard replied: "Of course, that can't be measured in percentages. But there was a very close connection between the Allied experts, especially the American representative, and the Special Agency for Money and Credit and above all with me."[23] Before a television audience of millions, Erhard chose to conceal the name of the American representative, with whom he alleged to have worked "very closely." If it had been a complicated English name, this might have been pardonable given Erhard's poor command of English. But Edward Adam Tenenbaum is a German name in all its components, and it certainly had not vanished from Erhard's memory.

Erhard probably mentioned Tenenbaum in the above-mentioned article in *Zeitschrift für das gesamte Kreditwesen* only because fellow witnesses to the currency reform explicitly acknowledged the key role of Tenenbaum in their contributions to the same issue: the first President of the Landeszentralbank [State Central Bank] of Württemberg-Baden, Otto Pfleiderer; and the first President of the Bank deutscher Länder [Bank of German States], Wilhelm Vocke, who was particularly full of praise. Erhard would therefore have compromised himself if he had omitted Tenenbaum not only from his books but also from his contribution to the journal. But he could assume that an article in the *Zeitschrift für das gesamte Kreditwesen* would be read by a negligible fraction of those who had read his books, in particular the bestseller *Prosperity for All* [*Wohlstand für Alle*].[24]

The second thing that comes to mind when reading Erhard's praise of Tenenbaum – the only such instance in his many publications – is the image of a deadly embrace: "with whom I found myself in agreement on almost every question." Erhard had neither Tenenbaum's financial expertise nor his power to shape currency reform. But by claiming to agree with Tenenbaum on almost all issues, he appropriated Tenenbaum's skills as his own.

The way the media have sustained the myth of Erhard as father of the currency reform, thus advancing a politics-of-history agenda in Germany, is exemplified by Figures 2.1 and 2.2.

In 1957, the first edition of Erhard's book *Prosperity for All* was published. Erhard had asked the journalist economist Wolfram Langer to write the first draft. Langer was initially head of the Frankfurt office of the business newspaper *Handelsblatt*, then took charge of the Bonn office after the founding of the Federal Republic in 1949. He had thus always been in close contact with Erhard. In 1958, he was appointed department head [*Ministerialdirektor*] in the Federal Ministry of Economics under Erhard, and in 1963, state secretary.[25] Was this a reward for Langer's successful politics-of-history contribution to the shaping of Erhard's public image? Inside the paperback edition of 1962 (p. 17), which was a commercial success, Erhard included the caricature shown in Figure 2.3. He also styles himself as the creator of the Deutschmark on the cover of the paperback (Figure 2.4).

This raises questions about Erhard's character, in particular his honesty and rectitude. In this chapter, I will treat the strengths and weaknesses of Erhard's character from three points of view: Was Erhard a two-time political turncoat? How candid was his treatment of historical truths? Did he have his act together in his roles as economics minister and federal chancellor or was he just a talented self-promoter and communicator?

FIGURE 2.1 *Phoenix from the Ashes* caricature of Ludwig Erhard by Rolf Peter Bauer, 1959 in *Hamburger Abendblatt*

FIGURE 2.2 Photo of Ludwig Erhard, with cigar in his right hand, behind a giant Deutschmark coin, taken 1959 by Sven Simon

The relevance of these questions will emerge from the discussion that follows. They have been debated at length and controversially in the extensive literature on Erhard. This literature can be roughly divided into hagiographic and apologetic writings on the one hand and more scholarly ones on the other. The authors in the former group often worked closely with Erhard, were active in the management, staff, and committees of the Ludwig Erhard Foundation in Bonn or the Ludwig Erhard Zentrum (LEZ) in Fürth, Erhard's birthplace, or were otherwise associated with these institutions.[26] The authors of scholarly historiographical works attempt to elucidate Erhard's personal, scientific, and political development and significance by means of archival sources unattached to the Foundation in Bonn, which was founded by Ludwig Erhard himself in 1967. They aim to demythologize both Erhard as a figure and his economic policies. With two exceptions, this research work essentially began after Erhard's death on May 5, 1977.[27]

FIGURE 2.3 Caricature of Ludwig Erhard by Rolf Brinkmann, *The Face of the D-Mark*

FIGURE 2.4 Title page of Ludwig Erhard, *Wohlstand für Alle* (paperback edition 1962)

2.1   ERHARD'S VITA IN SHORT

Before I discuss those three questions, I will briefly outline Erhard's life up to the time he took office as Federal Minister of Economics on September 20, 1949.[28] Ludwig Erhard was born in Fürth on February 4, 1897, the third of four children. At the age of three, he contracted spinal polio. This left him with a lifelong limp. After graduating from the Royal Bavarian Secondary School in Fürth and completing a commercial apprenticeship, he volunteered for military service with the 22nd Royal Bavarian Field Artillery Regiment in 1916. He was trained as a gunner and rose to the noncommissioned rank of technical sergeant. In the fall of 1918, on the Ypres Front in Flanders, a bullet went through his left shoulder. The wound was so severe that, before his discharge from a hospital in Recklinghausen in June 1919, Erhard had to undergo surgery seven times. Because his arm came out shortened, he was not yet capable of physical work in his father's textile business. He thus enrolled at the newly founded commercial college [*Handelshochschule*] in Nuremberg near Fürth in October 1919, initially as an observer, then as a full-time student, which was still possible without an *Abitur* (the general qualification for university entrance). On campus, he met Luise Schuster, née Lotter, a war widow, who was four years his senior and a fellow student of business administration. She had also grown up in Fürth and had been the best friend of Erhard's sister. The two were married on December 11, 1923.

What influenced him most in Nuremberg were the basic economics courses taught by the young rector of the college, Wilhelm Rieger, a student of the famous monetary theorist Georg Friedrich Knapp. With a thesis on "The Macroeconomic Significance of Cashless Payments" [*Die volkswirtschaftliche Bedeutung des bargeldlosen Zahlungsverkehrs*], Erhard graduated at the same time as his future wife with a "very good" mark in economics. Rieger then put Erhard in contact with Franz Oppenheimer, the "liberal socialist," at the University of Frankfurt am Main. There he earned his PhD with a dissertation on "The Essence and Content of the Value Unit" [*Wesen und Inhalt der Werteinheit*] in December 1925, which received a 3 ("sufficient").

With respect to this grade, the first examiner Oppenheimer was in agreement with the chair holder Fritz Schmidt, who was renowned in business administration.[29] Erhard then returned to his father's textile business in Fürth. The plan was for him to take it over. But the business had been in trouble since the Great Inflation 1914 to 1923. And contrary to his father's expectations, Erhard, with all his academic training, was unable to save it. Despite the economic rebound in 1927 and 1928, the business fell into bankruptcy, which was ultimately filed on February 13, 1929.

Erhard was again drawn to the Nuremberg School of Commerce. At the beginning of 1929, he took up a part-time position there as a research assistant at the Institute for Economic Observation of German Manufactured Goods [*Institut für Wirtschaftsbeobachtung der deutschen Fertigware*], which was affiliated with the college. As a married man with two children, he received a monthly salary of 150 Reichsmark (RM).[30] Amid the worldwide Great Depression, together with Institute director Professor Wilhelm Vershofen, he developed the thesis that by stimulating the production of consumer goods, the state could bring about an overall economic upswing. Erhard summarized this in a 141-page study entitled "Overcoming the World Economic Crisis through the Influence of Economic Policy" [*Die Überwindung der Weltwirtschaftskrise durch wirtschaftspolitische Beeinflussung*]. It is not known whether this study was given much attention in political circles, nor whether it was ever published. Hohmann discusses four smaller articles of Erhard, written before Hitler's seizure of power – two in *Das Tagebuch* and one each in *Der Deutsche Ökonomist* and in *Wirtschaftsdienst* – with which Erhard intervened with his own proposals for getting out of the deep depression, which in his view the government's misguided economic policy had helped catalyze.[31]

In 1933, Professor Vershofen took on Erhard and his colleague Dr. Erich Schäfer as his deputies in the management of the Institute. In 1934, the three founded the Society for Consumer Research [*Gesellschaft für Konsumforschung*], headquartered in Nuremberg and Berlin, and occupied the executive board as a trio. After Associate

Professor Erich Schäfer's move to the Leipzig School of Commerce in 1936, Erhard advanced to the post of Vershofen's first deputy. By 1939, he was in charge of 80 to 100 market researchers.[32] As early as 1933, Erhard had been urged – to no avail – to join the National Socialist Lecturers' League [NS-Dozentenbund], in part to further his academic career. And during World War II, when the pressure on Erhard to join any Nazi organization increased, he refused to join even the most harmless, by comparison, the German Labor Front.[33]

Below, in discussing the three main questions, I will expand on Erhard's personal adaptation to the economic and racist ideologies of the Nazis and on his professional involvement in the criminal activities of Nazi leaders. Of course, these activities and changes in attitude are also part of his biography, but I will continue first with Erhard's career during Germany's time under occupation rule.

A few days after the US Army occupied his hometown of Fürth, which occurred on April 18–19, 1945, Erhard began working for the US city commandant there, Captain John Daly Cofer. On May 24, 1945, as promised, he delivered his report to Cofer on the status of Fürth's industry and its potential for development. I will discuss how this cooperation came about later in this chapter. In any case, Cofer liked the report so much that he recommended Erhard for larger assignments in the Bavarian region of the US occupation zone. As a result of this recommendation, Erhard was put to work as an economic adviser to a higher US office for Central and Upper Franconia. The American military government regarded him as a politically untainted economic expert and held him in high esteem.[34] At its suggestion, on October 22, 1945, he was appointed Minister of Economics in Bavaria's second postwar cabinet, that of Minister-President Wilhelm Hoegner of the Social Democratic Party (SPD). Erhard held this office until a new Bavarian government was formed on December 21, 1946, under Minister-President Hans Ehard (CSU, the Bavarian sister party of the CDU).

After that, Erhard kept his head above water with teaching assignments at the University of Munich. His patron there was Professor Adolf Weber, an economist of some importance. Erhard had been active in Weber's working group on monetary issues since shortly after the war.[35] The Faculty of Political Sciences at the University of Munich had already decided on February 2, 1946, to apply to the Bavarian Ministry of Culture for Erhard's appointment as honorary professor. After approval by the US military government on March 26, 1946, he was given two teaching assignments "on contemporary economic policy issues, though he only carried out the first [assignment] on account of his ministerial workload."[36] When Erhard lost his post as Bavarian Minister of Economics, the Faculty gave him another teaching assignment. But it was not until November 7, 1947, that he was officially awarded the appointment as honorary professor of the University of Munich's Faculty of Political Sciences.[37]

As Volker Hentschel has shown, Adolf Weber and the Faculty of Political Sciences were aware that Erhard's scientific merits were insufficient to justify this appointment. In exchanges with the Ministry of Culture, they therefore emphasized Erhard's practical experience "in all areas of the Bavarian economy." It was precisely the aim of the Faculty, they wrote, to train its students "in all matters of the Bavarian economy." They would like to "tie the proven expertise of Dr. Erhard more closely to the Faculty. ... He is to train the students for practical work in the field of the Bavarian economy."[38]

Still, considering the insufficiency of Erhard's scientific qualifications, the Bavarian Ministry of Culture hesitated for a long time before reaching a decision on the application by the Faculty of Political Sciences. Moreover, the decision was put on hold because of an ongoing investigation of Erhard's conduct as Minister of Economics by a fact-finding committee of the Bavarian parliament. Only after the committee's report had absolved Erhard of any personal guilt for the abuses in the Bavarian Ministry of Economics did the Ministry of Culture approve the award of honorary professorship. However, it was granted on the condition that Erhard was permitted to assume the title of professor only "for the duration of his membership in the teaching staff of the University of Munich," as Volker Hentschel discovered verbatim in Erhard's personnel file in the archives of the

Ludwig Maximilian University of Munich.[39] Surprisingly, this time limit on the permission to use the title is not mentioned in other accounts of how the honorary professorship was awarded – neither by the authors Volkhard Laitenberger and Daniel Koerfer, who are sympathetic to Erhard, nor by Ulrike Herrmann,[40] who is very critical of him. When Erhard stopped teaching in the summer semester of 1948, his permission to use the title expired. But he illegally, and unabashedly, continued to go by it as if it were his first name.[41]

With the favor and official consent of the US military government, Erhard headed the Special Agency for Money and Credit [*Sonderstelle Geld und Kredit*],[42] established by the Economic Council [*Wirtschaftsrat*], precursor to the Bundestag, on July 23, 1947. After appointing its members, the Special Agency convened for its first meeting in Bad Homburg on October 10, 1947. There, nineteen German experts[43] took part in the creation of a central banking system by the American and British occupying powers and worked on a plan for currency reform. The consultations with the Western military governments on the design of the Bank deutscher Länder, which was founded on March 1, 1948, coincided with Erhard's time at the Special Agency.[44] He also exerted great influence on the drafting of the "Homburg Plan" of that Agency. At the beginning of February 1948, the German monetary experts had already submitted a first draft to the two powers of the "Bizone" (the fusion of British and American occupation zones). Immediately after his election as director of the Economic Administration on March 2, 1948, Erhard handed over the chairmanship of the Special Agency to his deputy, Erwin Hielscher. But since he did not take up his new post in Frankfurt-Höchst until April 6,[45] he was able to help draft the plan until practically the end. He also personally spoke at the fifty-first meeting of the Special Agency on March 31, 1948, as recorded in the minutes.[46] The Homburg Plan was completed on April 8, 1948, and handed over to joint administrations of the Bizone.

It was also in the interest of the US military government that Erhard, who had no party affiliation, was elected by the Economic Council to succeed Johannes Semler (CSU) as director of the

Economic Administration [*Verwaltung für Wirtschaft*] on March 2, 1948.[47] This was done with the votes of the CDU/CSU at the suggestion of the FDP (*Freie Demokratische Partei*). At an internal CSU event in Erlangen on January 4, 1948, Semler had given an impassioned speech against the conditions of American food aid during the famine of 1947. His accusation was twofold. For one, the Bizone had to pay for this aid itself, either with foreign exchange earned from exports or through cash from interest-bearing loans. Second, he denounced the fact that corn had been delivered, claiming the Germans were being fobbed off with "chicken feed."

The Economic Administration, precursor to the Federal Ministry of Economics, had originally been founded as the Administrative Office for Economics [*Verwaltungsamt für Wirtschaft*] in Minden in early 1946. It had been renamed before Erhard's election and relocated to the confiscated buildings of the Höchst Dye Works in Frankfurt before he took office on April 6.[48] In an editorial about Ludwig Erhard in the 28 October, 1957 edition of *Time* – with Erhard on the cover page – this early career is described as follows:

> At 60 Ludwig Erhard's plump cheeks fairly glisten with the new German look of wellbeing. But nine years ago he was to be found, in frazzled pepper-and-salt suit and dirty shirt, in a little hole-in-the-wall office in flaking, bomb-scarred barracks near the imposing Frankfurt headquarters from which Allied commanders bossed the US and British zones of occupied Germany. 'There sat the economics adviser to the conquerors,' recalls one caller, 'almost like a dog on a chain.' The professor was a torrential talker. To all comers he talked and talked, in the midst of Frankfurt's flattened wreckage, of free private enterprise and the mechanism of Marktwirtschaft, the free-market economy. // ... U.S. experts laughed after listening to Erhard's spouting, or felt sorry for the pathetic figure so obviously lost amid the realities around him.[49]

Together with members of the Economic Council's currency committee and Alfred Hartmann, director of the Bizonal Financial

Administration, Erhard took part in the consultations of the Konklave at the US Air Force barracks in Rothwesten on only one day, May 11, 1948.[50] German monetary experts, mainly members of the Special Agency for Money and Credit, had been brought there from Bad Homburg on April 20, 1948, in a military bus with frosted glass windows. For seven weeks, under the strictest secrecy, they discussed the modalities of the planned currency reform among themselves and with the currency experts of the three Western Allies. At the helm was Edward A. Tenenbaum, the Special Assistant for Currency Reform of the US military government in Berlin, headed by General Lucius Clay.

2.2 WAS ERHARD A TWO-TIME POLITICAL TURNCOAT?

In Erhard's lifetime, there were three fundamental political regime changes in Germany: the transitions a) from the German Empire [*Kaiserreich*] to the Weimar Republic in 1918/19, b) from the Weimar Republic to Hitler's dictatorship in 1933, and c) from Hitler's dictatorship to the occupation regime in 1945 by constitutional democracies – the USA, England, and France – in the three Western zones and in the Soviet occupation zone by the communist USSR, with its model of a dictatorship of the proletariat.

The first historical turning point was experienced by Erhard in the fall of 1918, while seriously wounded from combat. Historical research has not yet uncovered anything about his political views at that time. But as to the second and third regime changes, a great deal of evidence has been produced in this regard.

In a television interview on ZDF on April 10, 1963, six months before he was elected to succeed Konrad Adenauer as Chancellor, Ludwig Erhard claimed that he had voted for the left-liberal DDP (*Deutsche Demokratische Partei*) during the Weimar Republic.[51] One biographer, Volkhard Laitenberger, believes that Erhard most likely leaned toward the Social Democrats during the Great Depression.[52] This does not necessarily contradict Erhard's statement. Together with the SPD and the Catholic Center Party, the DDP belonged as a junior partner to the coalition of parties underpinning the Weimar Republic. But in the Reichstag elections of 1930 and 1932, like other smaller parties of the center, it was pulverized between the two extremes of the Communist and Nazi parties, while the SPD and the Center Party held their own relatively well.

Since Erhard began working at the Institute for Economic Observation of German Manufactured Goods in Nuremberg in 1929, his boss had been Wilhelm Vershofen, its director. As a DDP member of the National Assembly, Vershofen had helped design the Weimar Constitution in 1919. As a consequence of the Institute's task, namely to represent the export interests of the medium-sized consumer goods industry, its staff tended toward the left-liberal side of the political spectrum, whereas right-wing parties were more aligned with the interests of large-scale industry and agriculture. The long-standing, exceedingly good relationship between Vershofen and Erhard – as well as Erhard's rapid advancement in Vershofen's Institute – likely owed a lot to this shared anti-fascist sentiment.

Erhard's last public expression of repugnance to the rise of the Nazi Party came in 1932. To this end, he wrote a review of Hjalmar Schacht's bestselling *Principles of German Economic Policy* [*Grundsätze deutscher Wirtschaftspolitik*] (1932) in the left-liberal anti-fascist weekly *Das Tagebuch*.[53] Since his resignation from the post of Reichsbank President in connection with the Young Plan negotiations of March 1930, Schacht had been a supporter of Hitler. He delivered a widely acclaimed speech on economic policy at the meeting of the Harzburg Front. On the initiative of Alfred Hugenberg, chairman of the right-wing conservative DNVP (*Deutschnationale Volkspartei*) since 1928, the "National Opposition" had convened for a mass rally in Bad Harzburg on October 11, 1931, to demonstrate its unity in the struggle against the Weimar Republic and Reich Chancellor Heinrich Brüning's emergency decree-based deflationary policy. One year later, Schacht's book would serve as the model for the economic policy of the Nazi Party.

A digression on the irony of history: In November 1918, Schacht had been a founding member of the left-liberal DDP. He resigned from the party in May 1926 to campaign for a more conservative position on budgetary policy than that advocated by the DDP. Despite their initial divergence on the rise of the Nazis, Schacht and Erhard shared a reluctance to join the NSDAP. Schacht was reappointed Reichsbank President in 1933 and also Reich Economics Minister in 1934. On January 30, 1937, the fourth anniversary of the seizure of power, Hitler awarded Schacht and the other Reich ministers the NSDAP's Golden Party Badge [*Goldene Parteiabzeichen*] – or rather imposed it on them. Erhard likewise was not spared such an award under National Socialism. In January 1943, he was decorated with the War Merit Cross 2nd Class [*Kriegsverdienstkreuz 2. Klasse*] for his expert opinions, which he himself had always considered crucial to the war effort. It was the highest wartime distinction for civilians who were not involved in acts of war.

At any rate, Erhard's review of Schacht's book is polemical and full of spleen. In this way, he distances himself from right-wing extremism in 1932. In the introduction he writes: "... whoever calls these fundamentally meaningless sentences 'economic policy principles' should never again – in a country that is halfway normal – be addressed as an expert." I take up only one substantive point made by Erhard, namely how Schacht, of all people, the "capitalist and big interest collector [*Grosszinsbezieher*]," parrots Hitler's distinction between "moneygrubbing" [*raffende*] and "hardworking" [*schaffende*] capital and partly accepts and justifies this distinction:

> It is delightful to watch the worm wriggle. ... This whole chapter on interest consists of general, meaningless phrases. It is a bastard of the perverse affair with both Hitler and Hugenberg in that, for the time being, since fully breaking the yoke of interest finds no approval in the whole Harzburg Front, one carries on propaganda for a halfway break.

Erhard concludes his review with a scathing verdict: "Such a book cannot be discussed at all in the usual sense, not even criticized – it is beyond the realm of the discussable; one can only throw it down, enraged and embittered by this rape of thought itself, of economic thought in particular, for the advancement of a political career."[54]

On the one hand, the quotes prove Erhard's tendency toward the verbose and the redundant. On the other hand, they prove how strongly Erhard still rejected the "National Opposition" mentioned above (and Schacht's economic policy ideas in particular) three months before Hitler took over. This changed quickly after the German nationalists and the Nazis assumed power on January 30, 1933. His childhood friend Walter D. Klugmann, a Jewish emigrant, wrote to him in 1948 from his US exile: "I still remember very well how, on one of our streetcar rides from Fürth to Nuremberg in 1933, you drew my attention in a whisper to the madcap and fraudulent economic measures of the Nazis, and how at the time I still couldn't really wrap my head around it …."[55] At that point, Erhard must have still been in the train of thought of his vehement response to Hjalmar Schacht's principles of German economic policy.

"As a matter of fact, after 1933 Erhard rapidly transformed into a supporter of National Socialist economic policy," Karl Heinz Roth noted in 1995. He substantiates this with numerous previously undiscovered documents from the period of Nazi rule. As early as 1934, Erhard wrote in a publication that the "National Socialist ideology had always" found "the strongest resonance" within the middle-class circles served by the Nuremberg Institute, and that their "affirmative stance on the new state and the new economy" was therefore "more than lip service."[56] In 1998, in the second part of his publications, Roth wrote that Ludwig Erhard "stands before us as an economic adviser who unreservedly affirmed the Nazi economy from 1933 onward and made a significant mark in the service of its 'market-ordering' regulatory systems, annexation strategies, and post-war planning."[57]

On May 10, 1933, Nuremberg University was renamed "Hindenburg University (University of Economic and Social Sciences)." After that point, a lecture on "Race and the People" [Volk und Rasse] was also offered there. After 1933, Erhard published articles not only on issues of market regulation and price formation, but also on the "relationship between the economy and the state as well as the dialectic of freedom and order." His opinion at the time was that the "liberal principle" had failed. In Volker Hentschel's account, Erhard's assessment of 1930s (pre–World War II) Nazi economic policy was as follows:

> *The backbone [Träger] of the modern national economy can only be the state.* [verbatim Erhard] The German state of the present has heeded this insight in a most welcome and consistent manner. *The political goals have been set; it is now a matter of hoisting the nation to the sort of physical and mental development of strength that will ensure success.* [verbatim Erhard 1938] To this end, the state must not only order the economy but also steer it; in other words, socio-economic order and state direction form a conceptual unity. The more effectively the state steers the economy, the more smoothly economic events may unfold. The market price must therefore be set aside as a means of control. . . . For the market price is unjust, creates social tensions, and disturbs the life of society. [Nevertheless,] *the example offered by the communist world is the best guarantee that the German economy will always remain a free market economy in its basic features.* [verbatim Erhard][58]

Erhard's display of anti-communism and rejection of classical liberalism are in agreement with important elements of the Nazis' conception of economic policy. But the agreement extended further. He also shared their ideas about the primacy of national policy goals, to which the economy always had to be subordinated. Indeed, he even called for state control of the economy, with interventions into the price formation and distribution of goods that would arise in free markets.[59]

After the Nazis came to power at the end of January 1933, Erhard underwent a Damascene conversion. From 1934 on, he was committed to the restriction of competition through an estate-like economic structure based on the Führer principle and facilitated by coercive cartels, to price monitoring, price controls, and ultimately price freezes, and explicitly to the Nazi slogan "public interest comes before self-interest" [*Gemeinnutz geht vor Eigennutz*]. Private interests, in other words, must always take a back seat to politically set goals. From this, he also deduced that, if war became the political goal, the profitability of the consumer goods industry could lag behind that of the armaments industry. The only element of Nazi economic policy that he rejected was the autarky program, because the consumer goods industry formed the regular clientele of his Institute for Economic Observation, and this industry, which accounted for easily the largest share of German exports, had developed its most important markets abroad.[60]

Horst Friedrich Wünsche, who was a close associate of Erhard's in the 1970s and who subsequently worked for the Ludwig Erhard Foundation, does take up these Nazi-era writings by Erhard in his 1986 book. He likewise admits that they stand in contradiction to the views that Erhard became known for after the war's end. But he gives Erhard a pass: "On the basis of the expectations of a political public – the public of the present moment – it would hardly be appropriate to judge these writings now."[61]

In 1988, Wünsche came out with a carefully and comprehensively edited, 1,104-page anthology of Erhard's speeches and writings, which covers the period before Hitler's chancellorship and picks up again in 1944, when Erhard prepared his memorandum "War Financing and Debt Consolidation" [*Kriegsfinanzierung und Schuldenkonsolidierung*] commissioned by the Reichsgruppe Industrie (RI) in view of the looming military defeat.[62] The fact that none of Erhard's numerous publications between January 1933 and 1944 were reprinted in Wünsche's edition is a giveaway. Had Wünsche done otherwise, Erhard's turncoat behavior – twice in one decade – would have been recognizable at first glance. But this revelation was in the interest of neither the Ludwig Erhard Foundation nor its and Erhard's loyal cooperators.

Erhard had already delivered a memo on war finance to the Reich's Ministry of Economics around the turn of the year 1940.

In it, he fully supports the "silent war funding" that the Nazi government had practiced since the start of their colossal rearmament program in the 1930s. It was reinforced after Hitler initiated World War II with the invasion of Poland. This led France and Great Britain to declare war on Germany, as they had guaranteed (on March 31, 1939) the independence and security of Poland, which had been recreated as a state as a consequence of World War I. Erhard correctly enumerates Germany's three options for funding the war: tax increases, war bonds, or the silent use of private savings, the volume of which was increasing due to the introduction of economic controls that forced German income earners to accumulate savings in banks. And although he admitted that it posed an inflationary danger, he fully supported and recommended the last of the three methods, which was what the German government had chosen anyway: the silent capture of private savings on the liabilities side of financial institutions' balance sheets through a regulation that obliged those institutions to fund savings accounts with government debt securities on the asset side.

In retrospect, knowing the war's outcome and the gist of Erhard's memorandum of 1944, one might be tempted to assume that Erhard laid the foundation in 1939/40 for his 1944 employment by the *Reichsgruppe Industrie* and by the Reich's Ministry of Economics. Already from the very early stages of the war, he was a believer in the necessity of total concentration on efforts to win the war. He committed himself to the strengthening of Germany's military readiness. Here are some excerpts of Erhard's 1939/40 memo on war financing:

> Total war requires the strongest concentration of all economic forces. ... Insofar as the budgetary resources of the public sector are not sufficient to cover such expenditures and an increase in taxes and the issuance of bonds are to be dispensed with for other considerations, the state can add to its purchasing power by availing itself – to the extent available – of the non-expendable portions of

income resulting from market-economy paralysis. In this case, however, there can be no doubt that the fictitious purchasing power accumulated in private hands will actually be spent [by the government] in market terms, and that therefore, in consequence, it appears to be a matter of total indifference whether the affected income bearers immediately and conclusively relinquish their claim now or whether they are to become aware of these necessary sacrifices only at a later point in time. Psychologically speaking, there is undoubtedly much to be said for the latter way ....[63]

In other words, Erhard fully supported the course of silent war financing taken by the Reich government. Toward the end of the war, however – after the German defeat in the tank battle at Kursk in the summer of 1943 – an opportunistic change in thinking became necessary, this time for Erhard's survival and advancement in postwar Germany.

On top of this, Wünsche completely hides Erhard's cooperation with SS General Josef Bürckel, which I discuss now. In 1986, Volkhard Laitenberger, then head of the archives of the Ludwig Erhard Foundation in Bonn, published a biography of Erhard. In it, he not only discusses Erhard's publications during the Third Reich, but also briefly reports on his cooperation with Bürckel, though only to the extent it concerned Austria and Lorraine. In Lorraine, Erhard had supervised the local glass industry at Bürckel's behest. In reality, the assignment was much broader in scope. But in referring to Erhard's numerous trips to Lorraine and neighboring Alsace, which "earned him many a personal friendship, such as that with Albert Schweitzer's family,"[64] Laitenberger glosses over Erhard's activity there. He does not say a word about Erhard's work for the Main Trusteeship Office East (*Haupttreuhandstelle Ost*, HTO), with all the crimes committed in its domain of responsibility.

The beginning of the German Reich's territorial expansion with the annexation of Austria in March 1938 also marked the beginning of a close cooperation between the Nuremberg Institute, especially its deputy director Erhard, and leading men of the SS. Since the outbreak of the Great Depression, Erhard had ensured the survival of the Institute mainly by obtaining practical – rather than scientific – commissions from business and politics. In the territories either annexed to the German Reich or otherwise conquered and occupied, leadership positions were filled with SS men especially. They needed advice on how to integrate the enterprises of these territories into the economic area controlled by Germany. In 1938, Erhard had organized a course on consumer research in Vienna – his first outside Nuremberg – where he personally gave a lecture on "Sales Problems of the Austrian Economy – Ways and Means to Solve Them" [*Absatzprobleme der österreichischen Wirtschaft – Mittel und Wege zu ihrer Lösung*]. Josef Bürckel, an elementary school teacher by profession, was present as Reich Commissioner and Gauleiter and was highly impressed by Erhard's lecture. A year-long collaboration ensued. Bürckel supported Erhard and protected him from war service and the impositions of the Nazi Party. The fact that both had fought in Royal Bavarian Field Artillery Regiments – though not the same one – during World War I may have contributed to their mutual understanding.

Bürckel had been Reich Commissioner for the reincorporation of the Saar region in 1935/36. In 1937 he was appointed SS major general, then on January 30, 1942, SS lieutenant general, both ranks corresponding to generalships in the *Wehrmacht*. From 1938 on he held the office of "Reich Commissioner for the Reunification of Austria with the German Reich" in Vienna and as Gauleiter of the *Ostmark* (the term used for Austria postannexation), and from 1940 on in Saarbrücken as Reich Governor of the *Westmark* (comprising the Saar region, Rhenish Palatinate, and Lorraine) and as Chief of Civil Administration [*Chef der Zivilverwaltung*] of Lorraine. Bürckel had already joined the NSDAP in 1921. He was a proponent of antiSemitism. In his respective areas of operation, he was responsible for the early deportations of Jews starting in 1939. Five days after Bürckel's natural death on September 28, 1944, Hitler awarded him the German Order, the NSDAP's highest honor.

After engaging Erhard as an adviser to the Austrian consumer goods industry, Bürckel called him to Lorraine in 1940. He did so not only for Erhard's assessment of the local glass industry; above all, Bürckel needed advice on the general integration of Lorraine's industry into the German armaments industry. Erhard himself emphasized this in his correspondence with Nuremberg mayor Willy Liebel and his successor Walter Eickemeyer. This concerned the approval of secondary employment for Erhard under Bürckel in the Westmark and the legal admissibility of a remuneration of 1,200 Reichsmark per month for one and a half days of work per week on site.[65] Allegedly, after the war, the French inhabitants of Lorraine provided the Allied investigating authorities with the best testimonies about Erhard's behavior. It had been irreproachable, they reported.

Whether Bürckel or other Nazi heavyweights had arranged for Erhard to receive the War Merit Cross 2nd Class in January 1943 is an open question. The fact seems to be, however, that Josef Bürckel had been an adherent of the Strasser faction of the Nazi Party and, even after its elimination in 1934, considered sociopolitical goals more important than racial ones.[66] The degree of power held by Bürckel in Lorraine becomes clear from a seven-page note dated November 20, 1940, concerning a business trip by a certain Mr. Koch from Berlin to Metz between November 9 and 14 of that year. From the contents it can be inferred that the document came from the Central Office of Land [*Zentralbodenamt*], a bureau of the Reich Commissioner for the Consolidation of German Nationhood [*Reichskommissar für die Festigung deutschen Volkstums*], headquartered on Friedrichstr. 110/112 in Berlin NW 7:

> Lorraine has not yet been incorporated into the territory of the Reich. All authority is currently in the hands of Gauleiter Bürckel, appointed by the Führer as C.d.Z. [Chief of Civil Administration], who is not bound by instructions from any Reich agencies, but derives his formal powers from the Führer's mandate. ... // On the

basis of agreements, Bürckel is representative of the Reich
Commissioner for the Consolidation of German Nationhood.[67]

The Reich Commissioner in question was Reichsführer-SS Heinrich
Himmler. And as Chief of Civil Administration, Bürckel had been
personally appointed by Adolf Hitler. Thus, as the appointee of
Bürckel, his confidant and benefactor, Erhard showed himself to be
the political grandson of both the Führer and Himmler in the power
structure of the Third Reich. Erhard's work under Bürckel in Lorraine
could not have been as harmless as Erhard or others later portrayed it.
The Chief of Civil Administration for Lorraine, in an "Order on Assets
Inimical to the People and the Reich in Lorraine of August 7, 1940,"
determined, among other things, the following:

> In order to prevent assets in Lorraine which have served or serve
> ambitions inimical to the people or the Reich from being used to
> those ends, such assets shall be confiscated for the benefit of the
> Reich. ... This includes all the assets of: a) all political parties as
> well as their subsidiary, auxiliary, and substitute organizations, b)
> the lodges and lodge-like associations, c) the Jews, d) interior French
> people [*Innerfranzosen*] who have acquired property in Lorraine
> after November 11, 1918, e) the members of the other enemy states.
> // The commander of the Security Police [*Sicherheitspolizei*] shall
> decide which other property is to be regarded as inimical to the
> people and the state. The same applies to uncertain cases. // The
> administration of the confiscated property is incumbent on the
> "Trustee for Assets Inimical to the People and the Reich"
> [*Treuhänder für das volks- und reichsfeindliche Vermögen*], whom
> I shall appoint.[68]

Bürckel then appointed himself as said "Trustee." In this capacity, he
ordered the following in an executive order of November 6, 1940:

> Assets inimical to the people and the Reich belonging to
> individuals and legal entities located in Lorraine, insofar as they are
> confiscated – pursuant to numbers I and II of the order of August 7 –

for the benefit of the Reich, are to be secured, administered, and disposed of in favor of the reconstruction of Lorraine in accordance with my detailed instructions.

Above all, three main types of assets are distinguished: assets of the French state and other public institutions, agricultural assets, and "commercial assets, with the exception of Lorraine's metallurgical industry and ore and coal mines, insofar as their administration is under the jurisdiction of specially commissioned general agents."[69]

In a circular dated November 11, 1940, the "Higher SS and Police Leader as Deputy Representative of the Reich Commissioner for the Consolidation of German Nationhood" in Metz laid down the distribution of tasks for the "forced emigration or resettlement campaign ...: // Determination and inventory of the persons to be resettled to unoccupied France in accordance with the instructions of the Gauleiter ... // will be carried out by "details of the Security Police" and the SD."[70] Following this, responsibilities are assigned to specific agencies and individuals.

Daniel Koerfer[71] has described how the cooperation between Bürckel and Erhard developed, and that it was probably due to Bürckel's intercession that Erhard, and through him the Nuremberg Institute, received a well-paid commission from the Nazi HTO in the summer of 1940. The HTO had been established by the October 19, 1939 decree of Hermann Göring (Chairman of the Ministerial Council for Reich Defense [*Ministerrat für die Reichsverteidigung*] and Plenipotentiary of the Four-Year Plan), published in the Reich Law Gazette on November 1, 1939. Its purpose was the confiscation, administration, and utilization of Jewish and Polish property in the areas of western Poland (including the Free City of Danzig) that were being reintegrated into the German Reich. Agricultural assets were not the responsibility of the HTO but of Heinrich Himmler, the Reich Commissioner for the Consolidation of German Nationhood, because he was tasked with the settlement of ethnic Germans living abroad (*Volksdeutsche*) and, after a victorious conclusion to the war, domestic Germans (*Reichsdeutsche*). The decree of the Reichsführer-SS and Chief of the German Police as Reich Commissioner for the Consolidation of German Nationhood of November 10, 1939, and corresponding circulars of the head of the HTO set out the delimitation of responsibilities.[72]

Under the direction of Erhard, a report was to be prepared on the economic reintegration of former German territories that, under the Treaty of Versailles after World War I, had been ceded to Poland or, in the case of the Free City of Danzig, separated from the German Reich and placed under League of Nations administration. Erhard visited those areas several times. In the report, as in other statements, he made no mention of the mistreatment and forced confinement of Jewish Poles in ghettos, although he must have observed this in conquered Poland.[73] In contrast, his report recommended a peaceable coexistence in those areas between Germans and Poles, whose role in the workforce was indispensable to local economic development, and who were also expected to further this development as consumers.

Indeed, kowtowing to Nazi racism and Aryan pride, he also wrote the following in the expert report: The Polish worker had proven to be eager and hardworking, though his performance could not be measured by German standards. This was due to a lack of education and to racially conditioned attributes. Erhard speaks approvingly of "evacuating the so-called Polish intelligentsia" – although in reality they were murdered. And he welcomes the elimination of Polish business leaders from economic life.

Dr. Max Winkler, head of the HTO (according to the letterhead "Representative for the Four-Year Plan – Main Trusteeship Office East"[74]), was so enthusiastic about Erhard's 164-page study, "Preliminary and Interim Report on the Market and Corporate Structure of the New German East" [*Vor- und Zwischenbericht über die Markt- und Betriebsstruktur des neuen deutschen Ostraumes*], delivered in June 1941, that he forwarded it to an extraordinarily long list of recipients. In an abridged version of fifteen closely written pages, it was sent to Minister-President and Reich

Marshal Hermann Göring as well as to eighteen Reich ministers, five state secretaries, Heinrich Himmler, the Office for the Four-Year Plan, the Office of Military Economics and Armaments, Governor-General of Poland Hans Frank, the Reich Court of Auditors, and to numerous offices in the incorporated Eastern territories – a total of ninety-one addressees.[75] Many of the recipients responded approvingly. Even Hermann Göring expressed his praise in a letter to Erhard, which was a particular point of pride for him.[76]

Unlike Erhard's complete "Preliminary and Interim Report," this summary has survived and was published by Christian Gerlach in 1997.[77] The relatively short final report of the Nuremberg Institute for Economic Observation of German Manufactured Goods, titled "The Economy of the New German East" [*Die Wirtschaft des neuen deutschen Ostraums*] and dated April 1943, has likewise been found. Because Erhard had already left the Institute almost a year before, however, he no longer had any influence on this report. Karl Heinz Roth discovered it in the Federal Military Archives in Freiburg and published excerpts.[78] The final report refers in many places to Erhard's lost preliminary report in an attempt to empirically substantiate its statements on regulatory policy and demographic economics.[79]

Many Nazi heavyweights shared Erhard's opinion that expelling Polish workers from the reintegrated Polish occupied territories – let alone exterminating them through a combination of hard labor and insufficient rations – was an incomprehensible, senseless measure in light of the major labor shortage in Germany caused by wartime conscription.

In contrast, Heinrich Himmler, the head of the extermination policy, criticized the lack of reference in Erhard's report to the fact that, at a certain point in time, the Poles would have to be "eradicated from the body of the German population [*aus dem deutschen Volkskörper*] and from the German economy."[80] Despite this criticism, in May 1943, Himmler's office requested Erhard to provide a "supplementary report." Approved by all the main departments of

Himmler's office, it was supposed to depict how the Warthegau could be developed economically, "taking as a starting point the demand that the Eastern territories are completely populated by German people."[81] Erhard was highly interested in this assignment, among other things because the fee was 6,000 Reichsmark (RM).

A memo dated June 4, 1942, reports a discussion on June 3, 1942, between Erhard and the two coauthors of the report, Dr. Holthaus and Dr. Kerschbaum, and three officials of the headquarters of Himmler's Reich Commissariat for the Consolidation of German Nationhood (Berlin-Halensee, Kurfürstendamm 140–142): Dr. Stier of Main Department I, Dr. Eggers, and State Councilor Schaefer of Main Department III (the lead department). The Himmler side made it clear that the area in question had to be cleared of all Poles for reasons of national identity. The note on the meeting states:

> I [Schaefer] countered that the problem could only have been solved in a manner deemed satisfactorily usable by the Reich Commissioner [Himmler] if, conversely, the necessities for economic reconstruction had been considered from the standpoint of the demand that the Poles be regarded as foreign-born, i.e., as people who would have to be eradicated from the body of the German people and the German economy at a certain point in time. // ... It could only be of value to find out what result the investigations would lead to if the stated political demand were taken as the immutable starting point of consideration. Dr. Erhard offered to prepare such a study and quoted the sum of 6,000 RM as a non-binding price for it. It would take about 6 months to complete.[82]

On June 8, 1942, Erhard wrote to State Councilor Schaefer, the responsible aide in Himmler's Reich Commissariat, who strongly advocated for giving Erhard the commission: "The more I consider the idea you have put forward, the more I am tempted by the assignment, all the more as I am convinced that looking at it from another fixed pole [i.e., the expulsion of the Poles from the annexed Polish territories] will provide insights that are no less interesting" than those in the preliminary report.[83] In Erhard's letters of the following months, he virtually begged Himmler's office for this commission, which was not officially given until May 1943.[84] This was two months before the failure of the last major German offensive on the Eastern Front in the Kursk Bulge, the largest tank battle of the war. This was the second military disaster of the Wehrmacht in 1943, after Stalingrad in the winter, and indicated that the war in the East was lost. The great resettlement of Germans to the conquered "living space" [*Lebensraum*] in the East no longer made much sense.

In one of the pleading letters (written on January 11, 1943) to his sponsor in the Himmler authorities, State Councilor Schaefer, who shortly thereafter would be called up to the Wehrmacht, Erhard began and ended as follows: "Allow me first of all to convey to you my best wishes for your personal welfare and your success at work in a happy and victorious 1943. ... with kind regards and *Heil Hitler!* Your very devoted [signature]." On January 11, 1943, shortly before the final defeat of the Sixth Army, which was trapped in Stalingrad, at the turn of the month of February, Erhard was thus still nurturing hopes for a victorious campaign in the East. After the second crushing defeat of the Wehrmacht in the tank battle at Kursk, he had a change of heart. With the moral and financial support of the *Reichsgruppe Industrie* (RI), he turned his attention to planning for the postwar economy. Erhard never completed or delivered the report with its racist provisos to Himmler's office.

After this account of Erhard's questionable activities for the HTO, it is certainly interesting to note that Alfred Müller-Armack, later Erhard's department head and subsequently his State Secretary, was fully behind the Nazi economic policy in the East. His support took the form of a study on the forced emigration and resettlement policy by one of the research units he had headed since 1940, the year of his appointment to a full professorship at the University of Münster.[85] In his case, there was also the fact that he had joined the NSDAP immediately in 1933 and professed his faith in National

Socialist ideology with the publication of *Idea of the State and Economic Order in the New Reich* [*Staatsidee und Wirtschaftsordnung im neuen Reich*] (Berlin 1933). Even Leonard Miksch, the student of Eucken in Freiburg, who was Erhard's closest adviser since his tenure in the Economic Administration, was by no means an anti-Nazi – though, like Erhard, he also wasn't a party member. He was placed in a key position in the Economic Administration by Erhard, and played an instrumental role in preparing and formulating the June 1948 Guiding Principles Act [*Leitsätzegesetz*]. In 1949, Erhard took him on as department head in the Federal Ministry of Economics. Miksch died relatively young in 1950, whereupon Erhard appointed Müller-Armack as his successor. During the Nazi period, Miksch had endorsed and praised Nazi economic policy through his publications, especially in the journal *Die Wirtschaftkurve* from 1939 onward. Ralf Ptak, having thoroughly researched the publications and activities of Erhard and his closest postwar associates during the Nazi period, comes to the following conclusion:

> It remains to be noted that Erhard, Müller-Armack, and Miksch, who held prominent positions after 1945 and, as such, saw to the political implementation of the social market economy [*Soziale Marktwirtschaft*] in West Germany, were not resistance fighters. On the contrary, they cooperated with the Nazi system as scientists and publicists. In some areas, this even resulted in active support for government policy.[86]

The RI funded Erhard for three years beginning in 1943 with a generous 450,000 RM, topped up by another 180,000 RM in 1944,[87] for the purpose of founding and expanding his Institute for Industrial Research [*Institut für Industrieforschung*]. Once Erhard recognized that there was no prospect of a German victory (a recognition he shared with the RI leadership), he preferred to shift the focus of his report to the transition from a wartime to a peacetime economy rather than complete his assignment from Himmler's office.

On the one hand, Ulrike Herrmann has called Ludwig Erhard a "profiteer of the Nazi regime" because he was paid by the Nazi state to carry out assignments. This is not in itself dishonorable behavior. After all, all contractors of the state profited from the Nazi regime – not only the owners, managers, and employees of armaments factories but also, for example, the construction industry and typewriter manufacturers, building cleaners and undertakers, and, in light of the autarky policy, agricultural enterprises and synthetic gas manufacturers. In this context, it is interesting to note the findings of the CIA with regard to Erhard's income: "He had an income of RM 10–25,000 per year between 1933 and 1941, including his salary at the Institute for Economic Observation and fees as an economic adviser. In 1942 he earned RM 40,000 as an independent economic expert, and in 1943 and 1944 his income was RM 40–50,000 annually (head of Institute for Industrial Research)."[88]

On the other hand, Herrmann claims, "Erhard thought in the Nazi ethnic categories [völkische Kategorien]."[89] In contrast to Daniel Koerfer, I can only agree with her on this. For how else can one understand Erhard's above remarks on the inferiority of Polish workers in his 1941 interim report for the HTO, or the way he begged Himmler's office to commission a study that took as its starting condition (on ethnopolitical grounds) the expulsion of all Poles from the economic area in question? Erhard's silence about the ghettoization of Jewish Poles, for example, in Lodz/Litzmannstadt, also speaks volumes. During his numerous stays in Poland to conduct research in 1940/41, this played out before his eyes.

At the end of the war, Erhard again showed his incredible ability to adapt very quickly to new political circumstances: from SS General Josef Bürckel to US General Lucius Clay. Erhard had lost the protection and support of the former after his falling-out with Hitler in early September and his surprising death on September 28, 1944. In May 1945, Erhard sought political protection and a career-boost from the Clay-led US military government. The first report that he submitted in service of the Americans, instead of the Nazis, concerned the status and development potential of industry in Fürth and was accompanied by a May 24, 1945 letter (quoted in full below) to the US town commander there, Captain John Daly Cofer, the son of a Texas senator and in civilian life an accomplished lawyer. Cofer had arrived there on April 22, 1945, three days after the capture of Fürth, and had probably been pointed in Erhard's direction by Germans in the town who had opposed the Nazis.[90]

These fellow Fürth citizens may have known that Erhard had not belonged to any Nazi organization or political party. But Erhard's "strategically important" cooperation with SS General Josef Bürckel in the incorporation of Saarland, Austria, and Lorraine into the German Reich as well as his contract work for HTO in the East starting in 1940 were most likely unknown to them, just as they were initially to the US occupation forces. Unlike Adenauer, Erhard had not been taken into account by the Western Allies before the war's end as a potential candidate for higher political office in postwar Germany, and had not been vetted for his attitudes and activities during the Nazi era. But soon enough, with the aid of confiscated German files (probably in Fürth, Nuremberg, Bayreuth, and perhaps earlier in Saarland and Lorraine), the intelligence agencies of the US Army were onto him.

In any case, a German-language report dated November 9, 1945, from the Office of Special Investigations (OSI) in Fürth – signed Schmidt, to CIC, concerning Ludwig Erhard, as a "supplement to our reports of 10/4/45 and 10/19/1945" – proves that by then the US military government was well aware of Erhard's work for SS General Bürckel and was in possession of the appropriate documents.[91]

Erhard's four-page letter to Captain Cofer goes beyond what we now call an "unsolicited application." In parts, it reads like a letter of recommendation and denazification certificate, only in each case from his own pen and not by a third party.[92] The English version in the OMGUS files is a translation of Erhard's German draft of May 23, 1945,[93] which he asked someone to produce for him, perhaps an English teacher in Fürth. This is supported on the one hand by the

fact that the English version ends with Erhard's original signature, and
on the other hand by the relatively poor English. In any case, a native
speaker in the US military government with a sound knowledge of
German would have produced a much better translation. Because this
letter was the cornerstone of Erhard's career in postwar Germany
(Erhard: I am an "American discovery"[94]), I quote the contents in full:

> Dr. Ludwig Erhard // Manager of the // Institute of // Economical
> Research // Fürth May 24 1945 // To the // Military Government //
> Captain C o f e r // F ü r t h / Bay. // Sir: // In connection with the
> delivery of a preliminary report concerning the state of Industry of
> the town of Fürth, I take the liberty to present before the Military
> Government a relation rendering political and professional
> opinions as are being entertained by my person. As I am convinced,
> on the foundation of a thorough education, acquired knowledge and
> ability, to be capable of accomplishing essential tasks of high order
> and also being prepared, on the basis of my mental conviction, to
> offer my services for the reconstruction of the German economics
> under the conduction of the Military Government, I consider it to
> be my duty, in spite of existing obstructions, to speak for myself
> and in my own interests. // After studying Trade Economies and
> having graduated from Commercial High School [for *Hochschule*,
> which in English is college or university] in Nürnberg thus
> acquiring a diploma, I devoted myself to the study of National
> Economies at the University of Frankfurt, graduating there and
> acquiring the title of a Dr. rer. pol. under Professor Franz
> Oppenheimer (1925) with whom close connections and a cordial
> friendship was entertained until he departed from Germany. (This
> may be verified by letters). //
>
> After several years of practical activity had passed, I entered the
> Institute for Economic Research (1929) as an assistant, there
> gradually promoting to the conducting position of this Institute of
> Research. My intensions were then to dedicate myself to the career
> of a High School Teacher and to acquire a professorship. I was,

however, obliged to refrain from such aspirations, since the acquisition of a professorship was leashed with the obligation of entering the Party of National Socialism, which I strictly rejected. // When the desire to found an own Scientifical Institute of Economical Research became vividly felt in the circles of the German industry, and, in accordance with my suggestions, voluntary means were offered for this purpose, I founded and overtook the conduction of the Institute of Industrial Research and have retained this activity unto this day. // I have in this capacity, being assisted by a staf of highly qualified collaborators, executed thorough examinations concerning problems of structure, costs and distribution for almost all branches of the German industry and can therefore designate myself with full authority as one of the best experts of German Industrial Economics and its problems. // It is to be mentioned in this connection that I was obliged to transfer the staf of the previously mentioned Institute, which is to be regarded as a scientifically researching body, performing its elaborations upon a basis of own responsibility only and without any bindings of organizational character, from Nürnberg to Bayreuth, owing to political persecution (refusal of U K [*Unabkömmlich*, meaning exemption from compulsory military service due to war-related tasks in civilian occupations] applications and assignment of personnel.) // Within the last few years I have been dedicating my entertained deliberations almost exclusively to the economical problems emerging from the to be expected German collapse and have laid out my standpoint in detailed scientifical memoirs and discourses. In this manner actual and essential preparatory work has been accomplished [(] strictly prohibited here-to-far), whereby I wish to distinctly add that these considerations pertaining to finances, currency, and general economics are at the possibility of studying the Anglo-Saxon Literature, relating to this matter, during the war, so that I am conscious of the fact not only to be agreeing with these real plans and trains of ideas, moreover, in a world-contemplationing way [*weltanschaulich*] also. // For a period of many years my professional occupation had lead to close connections with the former major of Leipzig, Mr. Goerdeler, with whom I had been exchanging formed deliberations and publications up to the time of his arrest in July 1944. Correspondance confirming this statement is at disposal. // In spite of the fact that I had never denied my political opinions, I have, considered to be one of the most prominent experts by the German industry, always been engaged by Official Boards and the industry for drawing up expert evidence, perhaps exactly for the reason, that my always maintained incorruptible bearing has never left room for political compromising and considerations. In this capacity I had frequently been induced to engage all of my influence to safeguard politically oppressed persons. This has especially been possible in Lorraine, taking an example for many others, whose names could possibly be mentioned, one case, the brother of the famous philosopher and investigator Albert Schweizer – Paul Schweizer [*sic*: misspelling of Schweitzer] – General Manager of the "Glashütten von Vallerystal und Portieux", whom I could guard against political persecution and banishment. These explanations erect a case of self evidence and it is thus only natural, that I have never been a member neither of the party of National Socialism nor the SA, SS or any other organization of the Party. I have even refused to become a member of the party-bound occupational organisations such as the "Arbeitsfront." // The Military Government may rest assured to recognize in my person a man, who is absolutely reliable in political respect and capable of achieving tasks of highest order in the sphere of Scientifical Economics and Organizing. // I have offered my services to the Military Government immediately after the garrison and at present occupied honorary at the Country Board of Economy in special commission for elaborating plans for reactivating the industry of Fürth. I believe, however, not to be able to utilize my knowledge and ability to the full extent in this dependent position and it is my eager desire to get into connection with an Instance of the American Military Government which is competent for regulation of territorially wide ranging and fundamental problems, (eventually for the Country of Bavaria). I should be highly indepted to the Military Government of Fürth for a mediation in this sense, i.e. for transmitting this letter to the competent instance, considering the task for which I wish to render my services. Until then I wish to gladly offer my services to the Military Government in Fürth and also my advice at any time. // After the demon of National Socialism has been rejected I have the only desire to collaborate in the purification of Germany. I confess myself to the opinion, perhaps with few Germans at the present, that it is to be regarded as fortunate, that Germany is not being <u>compelled</u> to expiate for the evil deeds of its Government, moreover, that it is being <u>permitted</u> to do so, thus once more being deemed as an honest Nation by all other Nations of the World. // Most respectfully // [original signature of] Ludwig Erhard.[95]

Since the German military defeats at Stalingrad in February 1943 and at Kursk in July 1943, both Erhard and the sponsors of his Institute for Industrial Research in the RI considered the war a lost cause. In the summer of 1943, after Germany's defeat in the tank battle of the Kursk Bulge, Erhard got commissioned by the RI to analyze the structure and production capacities of the German economy and to suggest ways to return to a peacetime economy. In March 1944, he submitted his memorandum "War Financing and Debt Consolidation" [*Kriegsfinanzierung und Schuldenkonsolidierung*] to the RI. It was considered lost after the war until its discovery in 1976. The following year, it was published in a facsimile print.

The first historian to take a close look at the contents of this memorandum was Ludolf Herbst.[96] In a 1977 article, Herbst states that Erhard already "sharply distanced himself from the economic policy followed in the Third Reich" in his memorandum.[97] Herbst neglects the fact that, with the exception of the autarky program in the prewar period, Erhard had expressly approved of this policy until 1942, as shown above. But he does correctly note that, in his 1944 memorandum, Erhard pointed to the danger of an impending social-ization of the German economy and insisted on maintaining market-economy conditions and private ownership of the means of produc-tion at all costs. To this end, he said, a consolidation of the enormous debt burden from war financing was the decisive prerequisite. Only in this way could the citizens' trust in the state and the traditional economic system be restored. "Only on the basis of orderly state finances will the private economy be able to regain that degree of free movement which will allow it to take responsibility as master of its own destiny."[98] Herbst summed up Erhard's opinion in the memoran-dum on the role of debt consolidation, that is, currency reform, thus: It was the necessary starting point and precondition of the market economy and thus would have to play first fiddle. If this starting point could not be established, the path would lead alternatively to chaos or a command economy.[99]

In his letter to the US military authorities, Erhard traces his dissociation from National Socialist economic policy back to before the war's end. Until 1942, he had praised this policy for its prioritiza-tion of political objectives over the market-based control of prices, wages, resources, and investments. But as early as 1943, anticipating defeat in the war, he did an about-face. Now he advocated the priority of the market economy and curtailment of the political role of the state, and documented this opinion in his memorandum. Perhaps Erhard was not merely catering to the preferences of German indus-try. It is possible that he was already thinking ahead. The Western Allies would presumably occupy at least West Germany. That is, under their rule, economic reconstruction would take place under the sign of the capitalist market economy. In any case, it was not politically unwise to make a pledge while Hitler was still in power. For Hitler's Führer Decree of January 25, 1942, and increasingly severe follow-up instructions, decrees and orders through April 13, 1942, had forbidden any postwar planning under threat of severe penalties, right up to execution.[100] To violate this prohibition anyway – of course, under the aegis of the highest authorities of the SS – could give him the aura of a resistance fighter in the eyes of the Western Allies and thus open up career opportunities. And this is exactly what happened.

This dialectical reasoning is sometimes interpreted to mean that Erhard was already a Keynesian at that time.[101] But at the height of Keynesianism in the Federal Republic, from the beginning of the work of the German Council of Economic Experts [*Sachverständigenrats zur Begutachtung der gesamtwirtschaftlichen Entwicklung*] in 1964, Erhard launched his concept of a "formed society" [*formierte Gesellschaft*] as Chancellor in 1966. It aimed at combating group interests in favor of an economic and social policy oriented toward the common good.[102] This marked the resurfacing of his doctoral supervisor Franz Oppenheimer's "liberal socialism." The "formed society" differed little from the aspect of Nazi policy that Erhard had praised in his publications from 1938 to 1942, that is, the repression of group interests.

Gerhard Schröder (CDU), a member of the cabinet without interruption from 1953 to 1969 as Federal Minister of the Interior, Foreign Affairs, and Defense, claimed – in the widely read commemorative volume that Schröder coedited for Erhard's seventy-fifth birthday – that "without a doubt, his high morality, his pronounced sense of justice" had shaped Ludwig Erhard's political actions.[103] This assertion is refuted by Erhard's disregard for Tenenbaum's key role in shaping and implementing the West German currency reform. As Erhard's 1975 condolatory telegram to Tenenbaum's widow attests, he was well aware of Tenenbaum's importance. Tenenbaum laid the stable footing without which Erhard's (more accurately, Alfred Müller-Armack's[104]) social market economy could not have functioned. Without Tenenbaum and his currency reform, the implementation of Erhard's program to dismantle state controls would have come at the cost of high inflation. Politically, he probably would not have survived. And the founding of the Federal Republic in 1949 would have taken place under conditions similar to those at the beginning of the Weimar Republic.

I do not know what Gerhard Schröder understood by high morality and a pronounced sense of justice. As is customary in sports,

I prefer the Anglo-Saxon term "fairness." Referees would be completely at a loss if they had to apply morality and a sense of justice as standards for decision-making. But athletes and referees know which behavior corresponds to the rules of fairness. In this sense, Ludwig Erhard behaved unfairly toward Edward Tenenbaum. He bragged about accomplishments that belonged to Tenenbaum. He knew about Tenenbaum's central role in the currency reform, but did nothing to make it known to the German public.

Lucius Clay paid tribute to Erhard's economic policy achievements in the aforementioned commemorative volume, calling him the "master architect."[105] Why did Erhard refrain from publicly acknowledging Tenenbaum's historic achievement with a similar tribute? Why did he allow Tenenbaum to slip through the collective memory of the Germans, to be deprived of a place befitting his achievement in the German culture of remembrance? Erhard's cover-up can probably be explained by the fact that he enjoyed the appearance of having achieved it himself, as if he laid the monetary cornerstone upon which his subsequent policy rested. But why did the whole German political establishment and the media (with few exceptions) fail to take public note of Tenenbaum's historic contribution until nearly the end of the twentieth century? Erhard was showered with honorary doctorates. Meanwhile, the star student of Yale University, despite his impact on the course of German economic history, was not awarded a doctorate *honoris causa* by a single German university.

In biographies of Ludwig Erhard penned by his admirers, most of them employed by or otherwise affiliated with the Ludwig Erhard Foundation, there are indeed reports of Erhard's advisory activities for Nazi heavyweights during World War II. But even these authors omit Erhard's activities for the HTO in Poland, where, in contrast to Lorraine, the gravest crimes against humanity were committed by the Germans and their local accomplices.

In each consecutive transition – from the Weimar Republic to the even shorter-lived Third Reich, and from the Third Reich to the period of occupation after Germany's unconditional surrender in May 1945 – Ludwig Erhard behaved like those citizens of the GDR who after reunification in 1990 were labeled turncoats [*Wendehals*]. This is evidenced above all by his promotion of American-style economic liberalism in his cooperation with the American as well as with the British occupiers since the founding of the Bizone at the beginning of 1947, while, during the Nazi era, he had advocated price controls and rationing of goods as well as cartels. To deepen his knowledge of Anglo-Saxon market economies, which the British and Americans clearly considered necessary, Erhard traveled to England in December 1948 "to study the economic system." At the invitation of General Clay, he visited the United States for two weeks in April 1949, where he "appeared before a committee appointed by Secretary of the Army Royall to study decartelization and decentralization in Germany."[106]

Moreover, Erhard was a master of adorning himself with borrowed plumes. This is demonstrated not only by the way he took credit for Tenenbaum's achievements in currency reform. Erhard also tried to steal a bit of General Clay's thunder for the successful organization of the Berlin Airlift, as evidenced by his following statement:

> "After all, it was General Lucius D. Clay himself who, after a long, one-to-one conversation, cut the Gordian knot [Erhard's controversial decontrolling of prices] and stood behind me. The amount of credit due to him cannot be overstated. And when Clay himself repeatedly testified that he could proudly boast of having been responsible for two decisions, referring to the [Berlin] Airlift and to 'letting me have my way,' I certainly do not want to contradict him."[107]

So far, I have not found any source before 1973 (the date of Erhard's statement) in which Clay held up the significance of his decision to underwrite Erhard's policy of decontrolling markets in West Germany's Bizone as comparable to his initiation and organization of the Berlin Airlift. Is Erhard here giving his reputation yet another face-lift by ranking Clay's support for his decontrol policy on an even keel with Clay's renown for the Berlin Airlift?

Erhard even tried to share in the glory of a world-famous figure whom he had never met personally. Albert Schweitzer, born in 1875, was a great philosopher, writer, musician, Protestant minister, and established physician based (after 1913) in Lambaréné in French Equatorial Africa. He was the prototype of a cosmopolitan who devotes his life to a humanitarian cause. His fame extended across the world, and he received not only a great many accolades and honors but also generous financial support for his clinic in Lambaréné. Although Erhard could not spell the last name of the brothers Paul and Albert Schweitzer correctly, he tried to siphon off prestige and fame from the latter by claiming that he had guarded Paul, a glass manufacturer in occupied Alsace-Lorraine, "against political persecution and banishment." (See above Erhard's letter to Captain Cofer of May 24, 1945!)

As managing director of the Ludwig Erhard Foundation, Karl Hohmann – former department director of the Ministry of Economics under Erhard as well as head of Erhard's Chancellor's Office – in his article "From the Life of Ludwig Erhard: The Years up to 1945" [*Aus dem Leben Ludwig Erhards: Die Jahre bis 1945*], published in 1982 in the journal of that foundation, conceals all activities that Erhard had performed in occupied territories for the highest leaders of the SS. Neither Erhard's close collaboration with SS General Josef Bürckel in Austria after the *Anschluss* (annexation) to Germany nor his work in Lorraine and Alsace after the victorious campaign in France of the German *Wehrmacht* is mentioned. Nor is Erhard's activity for the HTO in occupied Poland. Erhard's personal contact with one of the worst German war criminals and criminals against humanity, the highly educated lawyer and economist Otto Ohlendorf, is also concealed.[108] This historic–political concealment of Erhard's incriminating activities during the Nazi period is continued by Hohmann in his 1997 publication.[109]

In contrast, in a 2018 online publication of the Ludwig Erhard Foundation, Horst Friedrich Wünsche, a former research associate of

Ludwig Erhard and managing director of the Foundation from 1991 to 2007, no longer concealed that Erhard personally met Ohlendorf in his function as Deputy State Secretary in the Reich Ministry of Economics (RWM) and Nazi currency and economic expert on November 16, 1944. Wünsche writes that Erhard had had no objections when

> "Rudolf Stahl, who maintained contact with the Reich Ministry of Economics on behalf of the Reich Industry Group (RI), appealed to Ohlendorf in a letter on November 10, 1944, to have a conversation with Erhard. Along with his request, Stahl enclosed an excerpt from Erhard's memorandum that he had himself prepared. Stahl's initiative resulted in Erhard being summoned to a discussion with Ohlendorf at the Reich Ministry of Economics on November 16, 1944. ... Erhard met Ohlendorf for the first time on this day, and it was on this day that Ohlendorf first got to see the complete version of Erhard's memorandum. Whether Ohlendorf hinted, in his conversation with Erhard, at the prospect of cooperation between Erhard and the Reich Ministry of Economics or called this a desirable prospect is unlikely, but also insignificant, because this cooperation did not come to pass. Ohlendorf handed Erhard's writings over to one of his advisors, Karl Günther Weiss, and never met Erhard again. An appointment blocked off by Ohlendorf's secretariat for another meeting with Erhard on January 7 [Weiss 1996 and Koerfer 2020 agree on January 12], 1945, was not attended by Ohlendorf but by Weiss. ... Weiss was the only one who heard anything from Ohlendorf about his one-on-one conversation with Erhard. Weiss believed he could vouch for the fact that Erhard's visit had been short, very short, and could hardly have lasted a quarter of an hour, for the gentlemen had obviously gotten along well: They had realized that they were born on the same day, but ten years apart. Ohlendorf had commented that the age difference between them also explained their different educational paths, by which Ohlendorf had implied – such was Weiss's assumption – that he knew Erhard had been conferred his doctorate by a Jew, Franz Oppenheimer.[110]

To understand this connection of the RI with Ohlendorf in the RWM, on the one hand, and with Erhard, whose Institute for Industrial Research had been generously financed by the RI since 1942, on the other hand, one should consider the following: In the fall of 1943, Ohlendorf had commissioned the RI and the Reich Group Banking [*Reichsgruppe Banken*] "to consider in a joint working group the transition from a wartime to a peacetime economy."[111] Neither the representatives of the RI nor Ludwig Erhard could have known anything about Ohlendorf's crimes as commander of one of the four *Einsatzgruppen* ("task forces" of the SS) in the Soviet Union.[112]

With the above-quoted remarks, Wünsche attempts to defend the public's high regard for Erhard's role in the West German currency and economic reform of 1948 against attacks that had appeared in the press on the seventieth anniversary of that reform, especially by Michael Brackmann. The latter, in contrast to Wünsche, is a proven expert on the history of currency reform.[113] Brackmann had claimed in the *General-Anzeiger Bonn* and in the *Handelsblatt*[114] that the main features of such a reform had not only been put down in Erhard's memorandum "War Financing and Debt Consolidation" of March 1944, but that Otto Ohlendorf, as a promoter of Ludwig Erhard, had also been among the masterminds of the 1948 reform. In Brackmann's account, Erhard and Ohlendorf were in no way concerned with social justice in their conception of a monetary and economic reform. Rather, by eliminating monetary debts and assets – two sides of the same coin – and protecting real assets, they had one-sidedly represented the interests of capital. The "social market economy," he writes, was a chimera. In making it a reality, Erhard took encouragement from Ohlendorf, who had also fought centralized economic management during the Nazi era and had advocated for a more market-driven economy. Thus, Brackmann claims, SS General Ohlendorf, who had held the highest offices in Heinrich Himmler's Reich Security Main Office [*Reichssicherheitshauptamt*, RSHA; led first by Reinhard Heydrich, then by Ernst Kaltenbrunner] until the very end, had also been one of the intellectual fathers of the 1948 reforms attributed to Erhard.[115]

I consider this interpretation by Brackmann to be exaggerated, with the exception of the origin of the term "social market economy," as I show below. In my view, Brackmann overestimates Erhard's memorandum and his other expert activities for the RWM as scaffolding for the West German currency reform of 1948. He underestimates the meticulous preparatory work done by two Jewish Germans in American exile, Gerhard Colm and Raimund Goldschmidt, as authors of the Colm–Dodge–Goldsmith (CDG) plan of May 1946, a template for the currency reform that followed. Colm had lost his office as professor at the Institute for World Economics at Kiel University in 1933. Goldschmidt, who completed his *Abitur* in Berlin and earned his doctorate at Berlin University, assumed the name Raymond Goldsmith in the United States. It is possible that Joseph Dodge, financial adviser in General Clay's OMGUS, had at his disposal a copy of Erhard's memorandum, which US intelligence agencies discovered after the occupation of Germany and may have provided to the Colm-Dodge-Goldsmith (CDG) trio. It is possible that they had been informed that a copy of the memorandum had been sent by Erhard to resistance fighter Carl Friedrich Goerdeler before Colonel Claus Schenk Graf von Stauffenberg's assassination attempt on Hitler of July 20, 1944. Erhard had, after all, communicated this in his letter to Captain Cofer, the town commander of Fürth, in his "unsolicited application" of May 24, 1945. But CDG were most likely unaware that Erhard had presented the memorandum to Otto Ohlendorf, SS general and Deputy State Secretary in the RWM, in an intimate one-on-one conversation on November 16, 1944. At best, Erhard's memorandum was one of multiple currency reform proposals – one of many, especially in the postwar period – that CDG took into account.

In contrast to Erhard's memorandum and the Homburg Plan, which was developed under Erhard's chairmanship, Brackmann underestimates the weight of the CDG plan as the basis for the West German currency reform, even though the plan had been developed for an all-German currency reform. After all, this was the reason why Konklave members, after failing to push through their vision (as per the Homburg Plan) in the consultations beforehand, rejected any responsibility for the success of the currency reform in a letter to the three West German military governments on June 8, 1948, the last day of the Konklave. In any case, the work of the RWM's policy department (headed by Otto Ohlendorf, one of the worst Nazi criminals against humanity) can be ruled out as a source for the CDG plan, if only because its authors were Jews who had fled from the Nazis into American exile in 1933 and 1934.

The fact is that Ohlendorf was head of Office III, responsible for domestic intelligence, in Himmler's agency throughout the war, even after he assumed his position in the RWM in November 1943. What is correct about Wünsche's above-quoted account is that Ohlendorf's conversation with Erhard in the RWM was one-on-one and on amicable terms. Ohlendorf was well informed about Erhard, not only through his contact in the RI, deputy RI director Rudolf Stahl, but also through his own domestic intelligence service. Thus, he knew not only Erhard's date of birth but also where Erhard had studied – that he had received his doctorate in economics under the Jewish professor Franz Oppenheimer at the University of Frankfurt. Wünsche explicitly refers here to the 1996 autobiography of Ohlendorf's personal adviser, Karl Günther Weiss. It is also true that Erhard and Ohlendorf never met again.

What is concealed is that Ohlendorf reserved a second meeting with Erhard in his appointment book for January 12, 1945. But Ohlendorf had to appear for a different meeting at such short notice that there was not enough time for him to inform Erhard and to ask to reschedule before the latter left Bayreuth for Berlin. Therefore, he instructed his young, recently hired adviser Weiss (who was supposed to attend the meeting anyway because he was responsible for maintaining contact with scientific institutions) to hold the meeting with Erhard alone and to attempt to engage Erhard and his Institute for a paid expert opinion on questions of the postwar economic order.[116] Thus, in Wünsche's quoted account, it is untrue that

Ohlendorf expressed no interest in cooperating with Erhard. The opposite is the case.

This is shown not only by the agreement on a date for another meeting (January 12, 1945) but also by the following fact: During their conversation, Ohlendorf spontaneously invited Erhard to a RWM sociology conference in Berlin-Wannsee on December 1, 1944. The infamous Wannsee Conference of January 20, 1942, at which the "Final Solution of the Jewish Question" [*Endlösung der Judenfrage*] had been agreed, had taken place in the same building. Erhard initially accepted Ohlendorf's invitation. But because he feared that Ohlendorf would expect him to identify himself with Nazi racial ideology, he cancelled by telephone shortly after his return to his Institute.

Further evidence: On November 24, 1944, Ohlendorf ordered his new adviser Weiss to report to him in person for the first time. Because Ministerial Councilor Wilhelm Lautenbach, whom Hjalmar Schacht had dismissed after taking over the RWM in 1934 and who had been rehired by Ohlendorf, had recommended Weiss as "imaginative," Weiss received a very warm welcome. Ohlendorf instructed him to attend the sociological conference in place of Erhard. He told Weiss that he would have liked Erhard to be there with him at the conference "to discuss the idea of an ethnic [*völkisch*] conception of economics with the sociologists, but Erhard had excused himself by saying that he was unavailable that day because his Institute was relocating from Nuremberg to Bayreuth." Ohlendorf also told Weiss the following:

> "As your evaluation states, you are by nature a courteous and reliable person, and thus ideally suited to take over the supervision of Erhard at the Ministry. With your help, he will gain the necessary trust and his institute will receive the requisite backing. Since you are Franconian on your father's side, you should also get along with him in other respects. As you know, we have already awarded a contract to Vershofen's Institute in Nuremberg, where Erhard worked for a long time. I have arranged another meeting with him

at the Ministry for the beginning of January, which you are to attend. // Until then, I need from you an excerpt, suitable for the Ministry, from his work *War Financing and Debt Consolidation*, which he handed to me during his visit. ... But in addition to this, you should also give thought to how the Ministry can come to a reasonable agreement with him the next time he is in Berlin, because of all the professors [Erhard did not yet carry this title], his economic ideas are the clearest. All I want from him are the basic principles and the corresponding concepts for a future economic order. If I get such an expert opinion from him, he can simply leave the associated ideological questions to my discretion."[117]

This text from Weiss's autobiography blatantly contradicts the statement by Horst Friedrich Wünsche quoted above, which I repeat here: "Whether Ohlendorf hinted, in his conversation with Erhard, at the prospect of cooperation between Erhard and the Reich Ministry of Economics or called this a desirable prospect is unlikely." Wünsche is familiar with Weiss's book and claims, "Weiss believed he could vouch for the fact that Erhard's visit had been short, very short, and could hardly have lasted a quarter of an hour, for the gentlemen had obviously gotten along well." In Weiss's autobiography, I have not been able to find any evidence for the alleged brevity of the conversation. Wünsche's reasoning also renders the claim implausible. If they got along so well, why should this have resulted in a very brief conversation?

But first, another word on Ohlendorf! I already gave an account of Ohlendorf's leading role in the domestic secret service of the SS, the SD. Furthermore, he belonged to the SS elite, which "proved and distinguished itself" abroad by committing crimes against humanity. From June 1941 to June 1942, Ohlendorf was commander of *Einsatzgruppe D*, which, trailing behind the front in Ukraine and the Crimea during the Wehrmacht's invasion of the Soviet Union, killed some 90,000 people. For this, a US military court sentenced Ohlendorf to death by hanging in Nuremberg on April 10, 1948. He was executed in the US prison at Landsberg am Lech in Bavaria on June 7, 1951.[118]

Wünsche's charge against Brackmann is that, apart from the sole historical fact of a one-on-one conversation between Erhard and Ohlendorf at the RWM on November 16, 1944, his claim is derived from "insinuations, conjecture, and speculation." What speaks against this and in favor of Brackmann's thesis, however, is the auto-biography of Ohlendorf's young adviser Dr. jur. Karl Günther Weiss, to whom Wünsche refers several times in the above quotation. In it, Weiss claims that he himself, and by extension Ohlendorf, had coined the term "social market economy."

As Weiss describes in his autobiography, the meeting between him and Erhard at the RWM on January 12, 1945, despite Erhard's initial disappointment that Ohlendorf could not make it, took place in an excellent conversational atmosphere. A contributing factor was that Weiss, in response to Erhard's question, confirmed that Director Carl Weiss was his father, a Franconian from Sonneberg and the German representative of Woolworth – an American company that was then under German trusteeship as enemy assets. Erhard had spent many pleasant evenings with Carl Weiss in Sonneberg and also in the Grand Hotel in Nuremberg. By way of the RI, Erhard had already offered the RWM an expert report on the subject of "Full Employment and Economic Stabilization" [*Vollbeschäftigung und Konjunkturstabilisierung*], which was still in progress. Weiss prom-ised him the commission from the RWM for this study "under the usual conditions." With a March 3, 1945 stamp of receipt, Erhard's study, now entitled "Full Employment, Economic Stabilization, and Monetary Order" [*Vollbeschäftigung, Konjunkturstabilisierung und Währungsordnung*], was delivered to the RWM.[119]

Together with other documents from the RWM (either by or concerning Erhard), it was packed in a box and sent for safekeeping to Ohlendorf's alma mater, the University of Göttingen. Among other things, it contained Erhard's memorandum, a copy of which would not reappear until 1976. Because it also contained material from the RWM's cooperation with various research institutes as well as foreign literature, for example, by Röpke from Geneva, Weiss had the contents of this box labeled "Social Market Economy" instead of "Erhard." After the war, though they remained in storage in Göttingen in West Germany, these documents were considered lost.[120]

In his conversation with Erhard on January 12, 1945, Weiss had suggested to Erhard that he use the term "social market economy" rather than "democratic market economy" [*demokratische Marktwirtschaft*] because this would be a step toward the National Socialist ideology of Ohlendorf, who wanted to return from a controlled to a market economy anyway.[121] Erhard was grateful for this suggestion and, according to Weiss, supposedly replied:

> What was that you said? "Social market economy" – there's a term I like. One can never quite trust you lawyers, but I must admit, you're useful when it comes to coining terms [*Begriffsbildung*]. I'll think it over. If you still have a glass of that good burgundy, let's toast to it: "Social market economy," that's a sensible way to connect the past with the future. Coming up to your office has paid off after all.[122]

Erhard was scared stiff by the possibility that the origin of the term "social market economy," in Ohlendorf's economic policy department of the RWM, would be uncovered. On October 1, 1946, the main war crimes trial in Nuremberg concluded with twelve death sentences, seven prison terms of varying lengths, and five acquittals. Since January 1946, Ohlendorf's frank and detailed testimony about the approximately 90,000 civilian murders committed under his command, primarily of Jews and communist officials, had provided crucial evidence in the prosecution's favor. Erhard foresaw that Ohlendorf would also be indicted in one of the planned Nuremberg follow-up trials. Erhard feared that, because he was held in high esteem by the US occupation forces, Ohlendorf would call on him as a witness for the defense to testify that the two of them had been in agreement about a postwar return from the controlled Nazi economy to an American-style market economy. For the first time since the end of the war, Erhard, now Bavarian Minister of Economic Affairs, contacted Karl Günter Weiss to get his advice. The former RWM adviser, who was now working as a lawyer in Munich, accepted Erhard's invitation to dinner.

The dinner took place in November 1946 at the Naturweinhaus Schwarzwälder in Munich. Weiss gave the following account in his autobiography: After the wine had loosened their tongues, Erhard reportedly said that he had been friends with Professor Alfred Müller-Armack since 1940. Müller-Armack had formerly preferred to handle religious topics, but was now trying to make a name for himself in economics.

> [Müller-Armack] was working at the University of Münster, but also had a house at Chiemsee, so that the two of them could meet on the way there, especially in summer. As per his [Erhard's] request, the professor had "thoroughly taken care of the matter." // In doing so, he had found the aforementioned material in good order, though not inside a box with his [Erhard's] name on it. His acquaintance [Müller-Armack] would publish the documents, whose contents mustn't contain a word about Erhard or the Reich Ministry of Economics, with a brief reference to the still-valid concept of the *social market economy*, in Hamburg right away.[123]

On this basis, Weiss concludes that Alfred Müller-Armack's 1946 *Economic Order and Economic Policy* [*Wirtschaftsordnung und Wirtschaftspolitik*], the second chapter of which was titled "Social Market Economy," was nothing other than a review of the "intellectual preparatory work done in the Reich Ministry of Economics, which was in such convenient proximity to him [at the University of Münster] in the British zone [at the University of Göttingen]. Ultimately, he never claimed to have developed such a concept himself."[124] "The compilation that it contained coincided almost word for word with the documents he [Weiss], as the Reich Ministry's liaison to the economic science institutes, had compiled and prepared for Erhard."[125]

Indeed, Ralf Ptak does not dispute Weiss's claim that he had recommended the term "social market economy" to Ludwig Erhard at their meeting at the RWM in January 1945. But he points out that the term represented "a conceptual trend in the economic policy of the 1930s" that

> was promoted by substantial sections of the establishment in the National Socialist state and, not least, had a noteworthy following in the public economic administration. Precisely this fact can explain the relatively widespread use of the term "social market economy" starting roughly in the mid-1940s, or of similarly interpretable word-structures that had already been around since the early 1940s.[126]

In the interest of bolstering his chances for a postwar career, Erhard not only embellished his résumé, as in his letter to Captain Cofer in Fürth of May 24, 1945. With the assistance of his Chiemsee-crony Alfred Müller-Armack, he also obliterated the documentary traces that could have proved that the term "social market economy" originated in the RWM Policy Department under the leadership of Otto Ohlendorf, an SS general and criminal against humanity later sentenced to death in Nuremberg. It was a matter of shifting the perceived origin of the term from the Third Reich to the postwar period, and Müller-Armack's publication was useful to this end.

A much more comprehensive attempt than that of Horst Friedrich Wünsche to vindicate Erhard can be found in the book *Ludwig Erhard: The Road to Freedom, Social Market Economy, Prosperity for All [Der Weg zu Freiheit, Sozialer Marktwirtschaft, Wohlstand für Alle]*, released by the Ludwig Erhard Zentrum in 2018. Here, it is no longer concealed that Erhard accepted and carried out reprehensible assignments – duties antithetical to human and civil rights – as an adviser to the highest-ranking personalities of the SS, such as SS General and Gauleiter Bürckel in annexed Austria or in conquered Alsace-Lorraine, as well as to the highest SS offices for the Germanization of conquered Eastern territories, such as the Haupttreuhandstelle Ost and Himmler's office in Berlin. His conversation with human rights violator Otto Ohlendorf upon Ohlendorf's personal invitation to the RWM is also mentioned. But all these contacts are glossed over, while the collegial, mainly epistolary contact – with the exception of a few personal meetings – with Carl Friedrich Goerdeler is inflated and even equated to participation in the civil resistance to the Hitler regime. Yet Erhard knew nothing of Goedeler's resistance activities until his arrest or the preceding manhunt. Therefore, it is a historical misrepresentation to portray Erhard as someone who was threatened with arrest after the Hitler assassination attempt on July 20, 1944, and thus indirectly as a participant in Goerdeler's resistance circle.

Erhard himself planted the seeds of this legend with his letter of May 24, 1945, quoted above, to Captain Cofer, the US town commander in his hometown of Fürth. The Ludwig Erhard Zentrum in Fürth still stands by this distortion of history in its 2018 publication.[127] Karl Günther Weiss, Ohlendorf's adviser in the RWM, who was responsible for keeping contact with scientific institutes and therefore with Erhard, probably gave a correct assessment of the danger posed to Erhard at the time when he wrote in his autobiography: "It was certainly true that Erhard had also sent a copy of his memorandum to … Goedeler, but this could be explained by the latter's reputation as a longtime Price Commissioner [*Preiskommissar*] of the Third Reich. Almost everyone of any importance at that time possessed some connection with the men of July 20th."[128]

It is true that Erhard's support of central components of Nazi economic policy, which went back to the prewar years, and his willingness to accept SS-backed, inhuman commissions after the annexation of Austria and the start of the war, are also acknowledged in the 2018 publication. But they are downplayed with this concise statement: "Over the years, Ludwig Erhard came to terms with the political circumstances and advised a large number of companies and authorities."[129] Erhard's two-time turncoat behavior in the transitions from the Weimar Republic to the Third Reich and in turn to the rule of US occupation forces in his hometown of Fürth, in Franconia, part of Bavaria, in the greater US occupation zone, and in the Bizone are historically obscured and concealed with that statement. After a detailed analysis of Erhard's positions and publications during the Nazi period, the historian Ralf Ptak comes to the following assessment: "Erhard had a certain feel for adapting his thoughts and actions to the respective political requirements without blocking his own path to a later change of position."[130] I fully agree with this as an explanation for Erhard's turncoat behavior.

What did the CIC, the American military secret service, know about Erhard's turncoat behavior after Erhard offered his services to the American military government? This is revealed in a memo titled "SUBJECT: Ludwig Erhard" by Peter Deubel, Special Agent CIC, Fürth Field Office, of September 13, 1946. I quote at length:

> 2. A party membership of SUBJECT could not be proved, although his work and associations suggest that he was quite close to the NSDAP. // 3. SUBJECT worked with the Institute of Economical Observation from 1929 until 1941 [sic]. He then founded and headed the Institute for Industrial Research until April 1945. This Institute was financed by big industry under the guidance of NSDAP and was politically absolutely in line with the party. It operated under Reichsgruppe Industrie which was headed by Dr. Guth (Brother-in-law of SUBJECT) as business manager. Several leaders of this organization have been arrested as War Criminals (Voegeler, Reemtsma, Poensgen). // 4. On information received from reliable sources, a Staatssekretar Oehlschlaege [sic, he obviously alludes to Otto Ohlendorf], SS Gruppenfuehrer and Sicherheitsdienst agent in the Reichsministry of Economics also worked on this project, and the close cooperation between Oelschlaeger [sic] and SUBJECT is generally known. // 5. SUBJECT is the author of a book titled: War Financing and Debt-Consolidation, dated March 1944, which was written with a German victory in view. This agent points out the following remarks: // I. Comments favorable to the National Socialist Governmental system: // a. On p. 233, where the author points out

that the National Socialist Government stabilized the German economy through the use of generous and therefore efficient expenditures for large projects (Autobahn) and rearmament program, in comparison to the democratic Government of 1929–1933 which used totally insufficient financial means. // b. On page 234 he states that "the efficiency of the work-creating methods used by the national-socialist Government" has been practically and historically proven. // II. On page 222 SUBJECT made a completely wrong prediction for postwar Germany when he stated: Above all will the complete depletion of private and national economic stocks (stores) warrant the quickest mobilization of all productive powers, and under these conditions it is the greatest contradiction imaginable to hold the danger of unemployment as a possibility. // 6. It seems like the author could see the end of the war only as victorious for Germany. // 7. It is of interest to note that on page 252 he recommends "Reichsgruppe Industrie as an organized head of the German Industrial Manufacturing (production) organization in its specialized far-reaching structure," especially since the author is a relative of the head-business manager of this Reichsgruppe. // 8. SUBJECT also worked in the capacity of economic adviser to Gauleiter Buerckel (Saar). // SUBJECT had been in correspondence with Dr. Goerdeler, the former Burgermeister of Leipzig who was sentenced to death because of his part in the Hitler-Putsch of 20 July 1944. SUBJECT supposedly is now using this connection as a means to convince higher authorities of his friendly political standing. // Agents notes: In view of the facts uncovered it is doubtful whether this man is as good as can be found for the responsible position for which he is considered.[131]

In a Letter of Appreciation from October 21, 1946, the Commanding Officer of CIC Headquarters Region VI in Frankfurt wrote: "This Headquarters received a telephonic message from Major Hess of the Office of Director of Intelligence, Office of Military Government for

Germany (U.S.), in which he complimented Special Agent Deubel for the completeness and effort expended on the above referred report."[132]

2.3 HOW CANDID WAS ERHARD'S TREATMENT OF HISTORICAL TRUTHS?

Erhard failed in his pursuit of an academic career.

In his interview with Günter Gaus in April 1963, Erhard stated that he had not been able to habilitate (to qualify as a professor) because he had not joined the Nazi Lecturers' League: "I wanted to habilitate and wanted to become a university teacher, but to do so I would have had to join the NS Lecturers' Guild. The possibility never entered my mind. I made no compromises at the time, no compromises that I could not have defended before my own conscience and honor."[133]

But this is not true. His alma mater, the Nuremberg School of Commerce, had been renamed the School of Economics and Social Sciences in 1929. It was granted the right to confer doctorates in 1930 and, in 1931, the right to confer habilitations. The 141-page study mentioned before, "Overcoming the World Depression through the Influence of Economic Policy," which has been preserved in Erhard's papers, was the prelude to his habilitation attempt. In Volker Hentschel's opinion, the paper was only proof that its author lacked the rigor of thought and formulation demanded of a university professor. Whether as a result of self-awareness or of Vershofen's benevolent advice, Erhard did not submit the paper. He was thus spared the embarrassment of an officially failed habilitation attempt.[134] Daniel Koerfer assesses Erhard's scientific abilities as follows: "Comprehensive treatises on economic theory were not his strong suit and thus, including from his late phases, he left no record of such."[135]

Shortly after the end of the war, Erhard also claimed that his intention to become a university professor had failed because of the Nazis' seizure of power. This was because the offer of a professorship had since been linked to the obligation to join the Nazi Party. According to him, he categorically refused to do so.[136] The latter point is true. Nevertheless, the account in his letter to John D. Cofer of May 24, 1945, is just as bogus as his self-styled image as Father of the Deutschmark: For Erhard's pursuit of a habilitation with the afore-mentioned 141-page paper would have taken place before the Nazis came to power, as had the successful habilitation proceedings of his younger colleague and rival Erich Schäfer.

In his letter of May 24, 1945, Erhard made another bid for the confidence of Captain Cofer and furthermore of the US military government. During the war, he wrote, while working on financial and monetary policy papers for the RI – most likely, he is referring mainly to his memorandum on war financing and debt consolidation, which he had completed in March 1944 – he had had the chance to study the relevant Anglo-Saxon literature, and as such knew himself to be in agreement, not only in factual but in ideological terms, with the ideas developed therein. It may be true that he had gained access to economic studies in English through the RI and that he had come to favor the market-oriented Anglo-Saxon economic model at the time of writing his letter. But he conceals the fact that he had spoken approvingly of Nazi economic policies in publications and expert opinions from 1934 up to the German defeat in the Kursk Bulge tank battle in the summer of 1943, the last major German offensive on the Eastern Front (see Section 2.2). In contrast to the basic principles which he advocated from the time of his above-mentioned memorandum until the end of his life, he had previously approved and praised the Nazi government's centralizing political interventions in economic processes and its restrictions on competition by promoting cartels and mergers of entire branches of industry into Reich groups, among other things.

It appears that, in the postwar period, Erhard developed a way to craft an image of himself as a Nazi opponent by adopting some of his regime-persecuted acquaintances as close friends. The most outstanding examples were his Jewish doctoral adviser Professor Franz

Oppenheimer and the leading civil resistance fighter Carl Friedrich Goerdeler.

It is true that Oppenheimer, as a Jew, left Germany in 1938. It might also be true that Erhard had personally said goodbye and farewell to him, as the Ludwig Erhard Zentrum maintains.[137] But it is untrue that by meeting Oppenheimer in person, Erhard was putting himself in danger and that Oppenheimer fled the Gestapo. In fact, 74-year-old Oppenheimer was allowed to emigrate legally in December 1938. His passport was procured by a personal aide of SS-chief Heinrich Himmler, albeit under the condition that he give up his pension rights. In 1929 the University of Frankfurt had given emeritus status to Oppenheimer, and he kept receiving his full salary of monthly 902.55 RM until the end of 1933. On January 1, 1934, he lost his emeritus status. He was forced into retirement. But this meant he kept receiving an old-age pension of monthly 571.33 RM (employees in Germany earned on average 179 RM a month in 1934)[138] until he had emigrated from Germany following the Nazi-organized pogrom against synagogues, Jews, and their institutions during the night of 9 to 10 November 1938. This means that he enjoyed the privilege of living personally unharmed and under comfortable financial conditions for almost six years under and among the Nazis in Germany. It was only after his emigration that his numerous books, which till then were still available in German bookstores and public libraries, were destroyed by order of the Gestapo.[139]

In his letter to Captain Cofer of May 24, 1945, Erhard refers to "close connections with the former major [sic] of Leipzig, Mr. Goerdeler, with whom I had been exchanging formed deliberations and publications" (see text of the letter in Section 2.2). Carl Friedrich Goerdeler (DNVP), originally an arch-conservative supporting Hitler, was appalled at the Nazis' practice of anti-Semitism. As an expression of his opposition to such excesses, he personally broke the boycott of Jewish shops in Leipzig on April 1, 1933. When he was out of town, a hoard of Nazis, probably SA, tore down the memorial of the Jewish composer Felix Mendelssohn Bartholdy in front of the famous Leipzig

Gewandhaus in a night-and-fog action in November 1936. In April 1937, this prompted him to resign as mayor of Leipzig and start working as a consultant for the Robert Bosch electric company.

From 1934 to 1935, Goerdeler had also served as Hitler's appointed Price Commissioner of the Third Reich, a post he had held already from 1931 to 1932 during the reign of Reich Chancellor Heinrich Brüning. Because of this function, Goerdeler had come into contact with the Vershofen Institute and with Erhard personally in 1934/35. Erhard had invited him. And Goerdeler gave this one lecture in Nuremberg during the first *Absatzwirtschaftlicher Kurs* (marketing course) of the *Institut für Wirtschaftsbeobachtung der deutschen Fertigware* from June 28 to July 6, 1935.[140] After the war Erhard interpreted his first meeting with Goerdeler in person for the lecture, the ensuing professional correspondence with him on economic questions, and further personal meetings with Goerdeler in Berlin during the war as a bond of friendship which, if detected by the Gestapo, would have put his own life in jeopardy.

In Berlin "we mostly met in his lodging house, the '*Hospiz am Askanischen Platz*.' There Goerdeler also introduced me to General Beck, who appeared casually in civilian clothes, English style. In this conversation, questions of Germany's future were discussed in a matter-of-fact style."[141] This is another case of Erhard's postwar habit of presenting himself in close contact with leading resistance members who lost their lives as a result of the Nazi purge after Colonel Stauffenberg's failed assassination attempt on Hitler on July 20, 1944. But Erhard at the time did not know that General Ludwig Beck was part of the conspiracy. And he was unaware of Goerdeler's central role in organizing the civil resistance movement in Germany until he received news of the search for Goerdeler through a wanted poster, published August 1, and of Goerdeler's arrest on August 12, 1944.

Goerdeler, to whom Erhard had sent his March 1944 memorandum by regular mail, recommended Ludwig Erhard as an expert on economic issues in a final letter to the resistance circle from his hiding place. He did so without Erhard's knowledge. Had the Gestapo discovered this letter, Erhard would probably also have been arrested after the assassination attempt of July 20, 1944, and tried before the People's Court. But neither the Gestapo nor Erhard knew of the existence of this letter. It remained unknown until 1954, when the famous historian Gerhard Ritter discovered it.[142] Nevertheless, with the Goerdeler name-drop, Erhard tries to give the US military government the impression that he was working closely with the anti-Hitler resistance.

After his resignation as mayor of Leipzig, Goerdeler had developed into the central figure of the civil resistance against the Nazi regime. In parallel, with the increasing hopelessness of the war effort, a military resistance movement had also emerged, which was likewise supported by conservative-minded former supporters and acolytes of Hitler. Goerdeler played a mediating role between the civil and military resistance movements. However, he opposed plans on the military side to trigger the overthrow with an assassination. Even during his imprisonment, he considered his influence over Hitler to be so great that, given the chance to talk things out with the *Führer*, he could bring about a change of course. With the failed assassination attempt on Hitler on July 20, 1944, carried out by Colonel Claus Graf Schenk von Stauffenberg, the resistance to Nazi rule reached its peak. At Stauffenberg's urging, Goerdeler had already gone into hiding before that date, as there were signs that he was being shadowed. Stauffenberg had also demanded of Goerdeler that both break off all telephone contacts to avoid blowing the cover on the military conspiracy. Nevertheless, Goerdeler was arrested, sentenced to death, and executed before the war ended.[143]

After the assassination attempt, the pursuit of suspected members of any resistance movement was the top priority of the Gestapo, which offered cash rewards for information. Goerdeler was betrayed by 42-year-old Helene Schwärzel in exchange for a reward of one million Reichsmark. In 1916, at the age of 14, she had moved with her family to the seaside resort of Rauschen in East Prussia. At the time, Goerdeler was mayor of this small town. He had been in hiding in West and East Prussia from the assassination attempt on July 20, 1944, up until his arrest on August 12. Schwärzel recognized Goerdeler in a restaurant in Konradswalde, West Prussia. At the time, she was compulsorily employed by the German Air Force and lodged in the payment office of a nearby air base. She reported this to the two paymasters working there, who searched for Goerdeler on their bicycles. Though he had already left the restaurant, they managed to find and then deliver him to the Gestapo. Helene Schwärzel was summoned to the Führer's headquarters, the *Wolfsschanze* in East Prussia, at the end of August. There, Hitler personally presented her with a check for the advertized reward of one million RM.[144]

In January 1946, after a warrant had been issued for her arrest, Schwärzel herself was given away by an informant. In November of that year, after confessing, she was sentenced as an informant [*Denunziant*] to fifteen years in prison, a $100,000 fine, and the loss of her civil rights for ten years by the first-instance jury court of the Berlin Regional Court System. In the subsequent appeal proceedings, her sentence "for crimes against humanity" was set at six years' imprisonment, loss of her civil rights for the same period, and confiscation of her assets in Dresdner Bank accounts. The full period of her pretrial detention was deducted. Schwärzel was the first of 490 informants to be sentenced in the postwar period. No one else was convicted in connection with the judicial murder of Goerdeler.[145]

In 1977, Erhard exaggerated his closeness to Carl Goerdeler even more than in his letter to Captain Cofer on May 24, 1945:

First and foremost, this manuscript ["War Financing and Debt Consolidation"] was intended for Carl Goerdeler, whom I had in mind in my deliberations most of all. When I wrote this study, however, it was not actually on his personal behalf. By that time, a friendly collaboration with Goerdeler had been in place for many years already, and in many conversations and through lively correspondence, it had led to such a high degree of intellectual and moral agreement that, in factual questions pivotal to the direction of our future, the two of us grew closer and closer. // Special circumstances had it that German men in the business sector who had likewise grown pensive approached me with the request that I give some thought to the economic situation and the resulting necessities for the time after the collapse.[146]

In 1977, Erhard passed himself off as a former member of the resistance circle around Goerdeler:

Quite understandably, after 20 July 1944, there was an oppressive silence and suspense in my family and a close circle of friends, because I actually had to reckon with being called to account under certain circumstances as well. As a precaution, my wife had found temporary emergency quarters in a small village near her hometown with farmer friends in their barn, which, almost to my surprise, I never needed to make use of. My only explanation, in fact, was that Goerdeler, in a kind of premonition or perhaps even knowledge of the approaching disaster, was able to destroy particularly incriminating correspondence, in the same way that I myself, in view of the veritable rampage of the most brutal Nazis, had shed this burden.[147]

This is contradicted by Erhard's own statement that he did not know until after the war that he had been recommended to the resistance circle by Goerdeler, who told them Erhard had written a very good paper on wartime debt consolidation and that he would "advise you well."[148] Erhard thus stylizes his general correspondence with Goerdeler on economic topics as if these letters had concerned a political conspiracy and could have brought him under suspicion as a member of the resistance or even as one of those behind the assassination attempt of July 20, 1944.

It may well be true that Erhard disposed of his correspondence with Goerdeler after his role as head of the civil resistance circle had become known. For someone who had been unaware of Goerdeler's highly treasonous activities until then, this news must have come as a shock, and a panicked disposal of the correspondence is not implausible. But Erhard's assumption that Goerdeler had similarly considered this correspondence to be potentially incriminating and therefore, in order to spare Erhard, destroyed it, is absurd. Goerdeler had corresponded about economic matters with numerous people, and there is no possibility that they all came under suspicion as co-conspirators. Goerdeler had more important connections to protect him from persecution than Erhard or other such correspondents of his. It is therefore very unlikely that Goerdeler also destroyed his correspondence with Erhard, which Erhard cites as a reason why the Nazi authorities never gave him trouble. The idea that Goerdeler had been his guardian angel against Nazi henchmen is nothing but a self-dramatization.

Toward the end of the war, however, Erhard may have destroyed a much more extensive correspondence, namely that with SS General Bürckel, the Himmler authorities, the managing director of the Southeast Europe Society [*Südosteuropa-Gesellschaft*] in Vienna, August Heinrichsbauer,[149] and Max Winkler (Representative for the Four-Year Plan – HTO) and his office. Erhard also probably disposed of a letter from Hermann Göring praising his "Preliminary Report" for the HTO. The occasion, however, was probably not the "veritable rampage of the most brutal Nazis," but the advance of General George Patton's Third US Army on Nuremberg and Fürth.

In the Günther Gaus television interview of April 10, 1963, Ludwig Erhard went one step further in associating himself with the resistance fighter Goerdeler. Erhard claimed: "At the time, in a thick manuscript, *in collaboration with Goerdeler* [my emphasis], I set down the ideas for a policy that [was] necessary to overcome all the misery in the economic and financial domains and to once again dare a new fruitful beginning."[150] Erhard did have collaborators in his Institute for Industrial Research who had followed him from Vershofen's Institute and who were most likely involved in the drafting of his memorandum. But the idea that he wrote the "thick manuscript" together with Goerdeler is a fantasy. As with the name-dropping of Albert Schweitzer, whose brother Paul he had met as a factory owner in Alsace, Erhard wanted to ensure that something of Goerdeler's high reputation as a resistance fighter rubbed off on him, too.

But as we have seen, Erhard was skilled in cover-up methods. He never commented on, let alone confessed to, what he had published during the Nazi period. What he had found correct or praiseworthy about Nazi economic policy in those years, with the exception of the autarky policy, he never explained. Nor did he ever mention – either to the Allied occupying powers or to the German public – the work he did as an adviser to SS General Bürckel in Austria after its annexation and in conquered Alsace-Lorraine, or the human rights violations that he observed there. This applies also to the far more severe crimes against humanity that he had observed in occupied Poland during his expert activities for the HTO (which reported to Hermann Göring) and for Himmler's office.

Most likely, the occupying powers were soon informed by their intelligence services about Erhard's activities for the highest Nazi and SS authorities and the human rights violations he had observed in his areas of operation. But it was not until after Erhard's death on May 5, 1977, by way of painstaking historical work, that more and more fragments of these activities came to the attention of the German public. Throughout his life, at any rate, Erhard was a master of concealment.

2.4   DID ERHARD HAVE HIS ACT TOGETHER OR WAS HE JUST A TALENTED SELF-PROMOTER?

It has been said of Erhard that he was a dilettante in the field of monetary theory. Nevertheless, he unabashedly claimed credit for the currency reform. For "he did indeed possess one talent: He could draw attention to himself without a hint of shame. Useful in this regard was his utter lack of self-doubt."[151] In her later book, Ulrike Herrmann devotes an entire chapter to Ludwig Erhard under the heading "A Talented Self-Promoter" [Ein talentierter Selbstdarsteller].[152]

It was not only in the field of money and finance that West Germany and West Berlin were blessed with good leadership. Indeed, they were lucky to have Edward Tenenbaum on this count, a man appreciated and recognized by the Western Allies, the German monetary experts, and the decision-makers in Washington, DC and who furthermore enjoyed the full confidence of military governor Lucius Clay and his financial adviser, Jack Bennett. Another godsend for West Germany, right up to the reunification with East Germany in a liberal-democratic system of government, was General Clay himself. He and his OMGUS team laid the foundations of this system during his four years as military governor in Berlin. He helped inculcate the ideologically saturated German public with Western values, and prevented the spread of the dictatorship of the proletariat into West Germany and especially into West Berlin, with its exposed location in the middle of the Soviet occupation zone. He accomplished this by mobilizing the strong financial and military power of the United States, as seen most clearly in the case of the Berlin Airlift. The character traits that Clay brought to this success story – differing markedly from those of Erhard – were so aptly described by Don D. Humphrey, former deputy director of the OMGUS Economic Division in Berlin, that I quote his 1983 text here in full:

> Lucius Clay is destined to remain a controversial figure. Blunt soldier and shrewd diplomat; democrat and autocrat; administrator and policy maker; world figure and citizen of Georgia. Clay defies summing up. // One remembers of Clay the aquiline features and the piercing eyes. He looks like a Roman emperor, and some have added that he acts like one. The first part is apt; the second is good enough for an aphorism. Yet it is equally misleading, for the General is the antithesis of all that is pompous and pretentious. Clay ruled by his intelligence, his energy, and the vehemence of his convictions, and not by rank. He was, in fact, a most unmilitary general, a statement that may be contradicted by those who have heard only the precision of his speech, have witnessed the speed of

his decisions, and, on occasions, the hauteur of his manner. Clay lived and operated in a goldfish bowl. He never cloaked his remarks in the anonymity of the uniform or sought protection in the privilege of rank. He took responsibility, he ruled, he answered criticism, and, when necessary, slugged it out – with or without gloves. It is Clay the man, not Clay the general, who was so intimately identified with every aspect of the German occupation. // Clay's failures are mainly those of American policy – the negative objectives; the failure to reshape the German mind by encouragement and support of the constructive forces; the failure to restore Ruhr coal and European trade; the maintenance of an economic wilderness bounded by dollar rule in the heart of Europe for four critical years. I know of no one who, under the circumstances, could have done so well as Clay. But Clay was the occupation and history does not measure success and failure in the light of circumstances. // Clay gave all of himself to the job. In his selflessness, in his courage, in his devotion to his country and to peace, he was truly a great man. But more was required than the capacities of a single man. Clay fell short in his incapacity to use the perception and wisdom of others fully. // Hostile critics do not question Clay's penetrating intelligence or his extraordinary competence. He would not have claimed for himself that he was easy to get along with. The post he held for four years was among the most trying and thankless jobs in history. Lesser men would have come home under the criticism thrown at Clay. No one outside the President carried a greater load of responsibility. The support that he gained he made for himself. The people who did not like Clay, whether in Washington or among our European Allies, were mainly those who did not deal with him directly. Those who worked directly with him or faced him across the table know his irascible strength, but they feel also the warmth and wealth of his magnetism. // Whether in the counsels of the American element or at the council tables of Europe, Clay was truly a formidable opponent. Intelligent, resourceful, tough, articulate – he brought to bear on an issue a mastery of detail and, excepting money matters, a profound sense of larger values. The quality, however, which carried the punch, and which threw people off balance in dealing with and in appraising him, was Clay's intensity. Having lived so deeply with a job so serious, he was outraged by criticism or opposition by neophytes. The seeming contradictions in Clay were many. Humility was not his particular virtue. Yet I believe that Clay's greatest quality, and the one that enabled him to lead when there was no leadership, and to survive where generals were expendable, was his utter selflessness. The capacity for policy and the stability to administer are a unique combination. Add to this, selflessness, and there emerges something rare in public figures. General Clay is such a man.[153]

It is true that Clay and Erhard had one thing in common: in matters of money, they were out of their depths. But unlike Erhard, General Clay was characterized by selflessness and, as head of his military government in Berlin, displayed willpower and assertiveness as well as organizational talent. During World War II, he had distinguished himself as an exceptionally tough and disciplined workhorse and become known for setting things straight in messy circumstances. This again became evident in the organization of the Berlin Airlift in 1948–49. Erhard was known for the opposite. Scholarly research has found the following evidence for this:

In the fall of 1941, Prof. Wilhelm Vershofen made up his mind: He would turn over the management of the Institute for Economic Observation of German Manufactured Goods to someone younger for health reasons, which he proceeded to do soon after his sixty-third birthday on December 25, 1941. As his successor, he did not recommend his deputy, Ludwig Erhard, to the responsible university and foundation committees, but preferred Professor Erich Schäfer, who was four years younger and had previously worked together with Erhard – not always in perfect harmony – in leading positions at the Institute. Schäfer had obtained his habilitation at the Nuremberg

School of Commerce in 1931. In 1936, primarily for political reasons, he had gone to the Leipzig School of Commerce as a lecturer. There he was appointed associate professor of business administration in 1937 and full professor in 1940. At the time of his appointment as Vershofen's successor, he was simultaneously appointed to a professorship at his alma mater, the School of Commerce in Nuremberg, renamed Hindenburg University in 1933. He began teaching there in the winter semester of 1942/43.

It is not known to what extent political considerations played a role in the choice of Schäfer as Vershofen's successor in the administration of the Institute. In any case, Associate Professor Erich Schäfer, together with Wilhelm Vershofen and seven other colleagues at Hindenburg University, had cosigned the "Declaration of Faith [*Bekenntnis*] in Adolf Hitler and the National Socialist State by Professors at German Universities and Colleges" on November 11, 1933.[154] To commemorate the fifteenth anniversary of the Compiègne Armistice, the ceremonial presentation of the list with more than 900 signatories took place that day in the Alberthalle in Leipzig. Erhard was not among them. Presumably impressed by the German military successes in the first months of the war and in view of his appointment as a full professor, Schäfer had joined the NSDAP on February 1, 1940. In contrast, Erhard, with his skepticism toward political parties – a skepticism that remained in evidence during the postwar period – stuck to his persistent refusal to join any Nazi organization.

Erhard was so hurt by the fact that Vershofen had passed him over that he resigned from the Institute on July 1, 1942. Erhard then founded his own private research institute, the Institute for Industrial Research, with headquarters in Nuremberg (Comeniusstr. 6/III)[155] and Berlin. He was helped financially by friends in industry, in particular the husband of his sister Rose, Karl Guth, chief executive of the Reichsgruppe Industrie (RI), and Philipp Reemtsma, head of a large tobacco company in Hamburg and a member of the advisory group of the RI. At the instigation of its chairman, Wilhelm Zangen, and of

Rudolf Bingel, chairman of the board of Siemens-Schuckert, the RI founded the Association for the Promotion of German Industry (*Förderergemeinschaft der Deutschen Industrie*) in November 1942 with an endowment of more than 22 million RM.[156] From these assets, Erhard's newly founded Institute was sponsored by his brother-in-law Dr. Karl Guth.

It was also the RI which, in the summer of 1943, commissioned Erhard's Institute to draw up plans for the necessary steps to convert Germany's wartime economy to peacetime economy. As repeatedly mentioned above, in March 1944, Erhard submitted his 268-page memorandum "War Financing and Debt Consolidation" to his clients. It remained lost for a long time and was not published until 1977. Karl Heinz Roth composed a five-page summary with the outline of this memorandum and excerpts of its core theses. In addition, he published statements on the memorandum by senior RI staff.[157]

Erhard was also partly responsible for Schäfer's decision to move from Nuremberg to Leipzig. I quote Daniel Koerfer on this: "Schäfer, of all people, Erhard must have thought, as the two had been bound to each other in mutual antipathy – it was not by chance that Schäfer had justified his departure from the Institute to Vershofen in 1938, among other things, with the 'completely unscrupulous professional sloppiness of Dr. Erhard.'"[158]

During his tenure as Bavarian State Minister of Economics in the Hoegner cabinet from October 3, 1945, to December 16, 1946, Erhard came under heavy domestic political fire. This came mainly from the SPD, which rejected Erhard's liberal economic approach and backed planned economy concepts. With the support of the CSU, which had won an absolute majority with 52.3 percent (SPD: 28.6 percent) in the first Bavarian state election on December 1, 1946, a committee was set up by the State Parliament (*Landtag*) on January 31, 1947, to investigate abuses in the Bavarian Ministry of Economics. The issue was corruption and embezzlement in Erhard's area of responsibility. The investigations led to the dismissal of thirteen people, including ten senior officials. Regarding Erhard, the final report states:

> Minister (ret.) Dr. Erhardt [sic] cannot, in the conviction of the Committee, be reproached with regard to the integrity of his person. ... If Minister Erhardt [sic] was denied success, the Committee is convinced that this was due in particular to the fact that he was too much of a theorist, that he lacked the necessary administrative experience to run a ministry, and that he did not know how to look for employees to make up for what he lacked.[159]

Erhard's severe organizational weaknesses were also observed in political negotiating sessions during the course of his postwar career. In one of his weekly commentaries in the magazine *Stern*, Sebastian Haffner, after listing several mishaps in June 1964, comes to the following conclusion:

> It is embarrassing to say, but it is obvious: Erhard cannot govern. He lacks the most elementary prerequisite, the ability to stay on top of business. // Adenauer, who was able to observe his popular economics minister from close quarters for many years, never left any doubt that he considered him unfit to lead a government. Many of those who refused to listen will now ask the old man – who made serious political mistakes, but was an undeniable master of his craft all the same – for an apology. After all, the Erhard government is like a school class where firecrackers and stink bombs fly through the air and students pour ink into the teacher's chemistry set.[160]

In his memoirs, Heinz Reintges, then executive board member of the German Coal Association (*Gesamtverband des deutschen Steinkohlenbergbaus*), reports on an important coal policy meeting chaired by Chancellor Erhard with representatives of the federal government and state (North Rhine-Westphalian) government on the one hand and representatives of the coal industry and the Federation of German Industries (*Bundesverband der Deutschen Industrie*) on the other on March 29, 1966:

The meeting has stuck with me less for its coal-policy significance than for the depressing impression I took away from it as a citizen. The conduct of negotiations and the course of the meeting showed every sign of the development that led to the failure of the Erhard cabinet in November of that year. One had to wonder what result, if any, the meeting would have produced if it had not been virtually a foregone conclusion.[161]

Reintges's impression of Chancellor Adenauer was an exact counterpoint:

> I personally experienced Adenauer only once in a small group, during a conversation between him and Helmuth Burckhardt [chairman of the Ruhr Mining Association] in December 1959, to which Adenauer called in his State Secretary, Hans Globke, and to which Burckhardt allowed me to come as his accompaniment. I remember three things from this meeting: the concentrated way in which Adenauer conducted the conversation, relying on an extremely small piece of paper that actually seemed to include all the essential keywords. Then his famously undogmatic attitude toward economic policy: // When he asked Burckhardt for a "program of effective measures to preserve the German coal industry," he added with emphasis that what mattered to him "was not the adherence to any theories but the practical result."[162]

The latter can easily be interpreted as a dig at Erhard. It is possible that Adenauer's experience both with Erhard's theoretical (rather than practical) orientation and his organizational weakness contributed to the first Chancellor's unswerving, but ultimately futile, attempt to prevent Erhard from succeeding him in the chancellorship. To his longtime State Secretary Ludger Westrick, Erhard once described the stark contrast between his own temperament and that of Adenauer by saying Adenauer's personality was more Gothic in style, while his own was more baroque.[163] In his biography of Ludwig Erhard, Alfred C. Mierzejewski describes Erhard's style of working as follows:

In contrast to Adenauer, Erhard shunned desk work. He avoided reading memoranda. He was interested in the big philosophical and theoretical issues concerning the overall direction of the economy. He let his subordinates handle the paperwork, the details of reports and memoranda, and staff meetings. He was not interested in preparing programs, studies, and organizational plans. His philosophy steered him away from these things. Not only did Erhard have no inclination or aptitude for micromanagement; he thought that it was wrong. Erhard valued freedom for the individual. Therefore, plans were unnecessary. Because he thought that government planning must lead to economic disaster, he saw no need to prepare such plans himself and avoided technocratic and econometric methods of reporting and planning. If government planning had been the cause of the German economy's problems, then why continue it? Erhard wanted to reduce government planning to the minimum and allow individual households and companies to plan for themselves. Erhard's critics, both at the time and later, never understood that his seeming incompetence or indolence had sound philosophical roots. State planning was the problem, not the solution. It was far better for him to spend time propagating his free market message to the public rather than wasting his time reading reports.[164]

Last but not least, what information had the CIA, the successor of OSS as US secret service, collected on Erhard that it used during the 1950s and 1960s as background updates for the administration in Washington, DC, mainly in preparation of the West German economics minister's and chancellor's visits to the USA? These files have only recently been declassified. They are now researchable at the National Archives at College Park MD in textual form and part of them in digitalized format also online.

Dated May 27, 1952, Walter J. Mueller, Reporting Officer of HICOG, Bonn/Germany, had produced a biographical memo "Confidential Security Information" of eight pages on Ludwig

Erhard, "Federal Minister of Economic Affairs": It contained such usual data as birth date and place, education, professional career, and "Languages: School knowledge of English and French." But it also described: "Appearance: Stout, medium height, thinning blond hair parted on left, somewhat florid complexion and porcino features, Light blue eyes, Always neatly groomed and not displeasing in appearance;" Erhard's postwar political orientation; his activities during the Nazi regime, including his cooperation with SS General Joseph Bürckel in Alsace-Lorraine as well as SS General and war criminal Otto Ohlendorf in the Reich Ministry for Economic Affairs in December 1944 on planning Germany's postwar economic and financial order. However, the biographical memo remains mute on Erhard's work for the HTO (*Haupttreuhandstelle Ost*) and other departments of the Heinrich Himmler ministry concerning the Germanization of industry and the racial purification in what is now Poland and the Ukraine. On a completely different topic, Erhard's character, the memo is very outspoken and according to my own findings very apposite:

> Not intentionally devious, he is subject to being influenced by the last person he has met, hence promises made on one day may, a short time later, undergo startling alterations. Considered quite intelligent, his weaknesses are psychological rather than mental. He is not flexible or creative in his thinking, but adept at using other people's ideas when they fit in with his own, and presenting them as his own. He is egotistical and has a capacity for self-delusion. A good talker and a poor listener, he is always convinced of the rightness of his ideas. // A late 1945 Military Government evaluation of Erhard read in part as follows: "A good mixture of the thinker, planner, and executive, he is, however, primarily the thinker. He has the rare ability of inciting extreme loyalty and cooperation among his associates. He would make an excellent deputy and prefers that job to the top spot." // US officials who have observed Erhard in Bonn, on the other hand, regarded him as a poor

administrator, a bon vivant who does not like hard work, and a man who keeps irregular office hours and spends much time attending public functions.[165]

The incomplete and partially embellished information that Erhard had sent with his letter of May 24, 1945 to Captain Cofer in Fürth was not questioned in this long biographical document or in much shorter ones written during the 1950s, which were based on the 1952 memo and are contained in the first file mentioned in the source note. In the fall of 1946, however, CIC had checked Erhard's description of his activities in occupied Alsace-Lorraine while working for SS General Bürckel. In June 1946 it had asked the secret service of the French element of the Allied Control Authority for help in this matter and received detailed information by letter of October 29, 1946. Statements by interrogated glass manufacturers, including Paul Schweitzer, were also passed on from the French secret service to CIC. All French sources had rated Erhard as anti-Nazi and as protecting their glass-manufacturing companies in Alsace-Lorraine against pressure to sell or lease their enterprises to Germans.[166]

How well informed Mueller was of Erhard's personal weaknesses is documented in a written note of July 21, 1950 by CIC on Ludwig Erhard after having spoken with Jakob Kaiser (CDU) about the conduct of the Economics Ministry. Kaiser would consider it "to be absolutely disorganized due, mainly, to the fact that its Minister, Prof. Dr. Ludwig Erhard (CDU [sic]), behaves more like a traveling salesman than a minister of economics, in addition to showing a complete disinterest in his own ministry." Even Erhard's State Secretary would have to make a three-day advance appointment with his boss in the same building in order to be able to just see him for a few short moments on matters of state.[167] Already in 1950 Adenauer wanted to get rid of Erhard, as a CIC note of December 8, 1950 documents: "On 13 Nov 50, Chancellor Dr. Adenauer conferred with the Bavarian Minister of Economics, Dr. Seider. They discussed the possibility of replacing during the next few months the present Minister of Economics, Prof. Erhard."[168]

In a memo of December 11, 1957, the FBI (Federal Bureau of Investigation) of the US Department of Justice informed the CIA of the gap in Erhard's bio as to his work for the Nazis in occupied Poland during World War II. Prompted by a *Time Magazine* cover story on Ludwig Erhard of October 23, 1957, a reader, Joseph Anthony Gwyer of Washington, DC, had informed the FBI that he knew Erhard from November 1939 to May 1940. He had met him twice. First at Kolo on the Warta River at the home of his uncle Stanislav Swiasdzinski, the half brother of his father. Erhard had been charged with the economic development and exploitation of this area on behalf of the Nazis and had – after he had evicted his uncle with his family – moved into his uncle's house. At that time Erhard had worn the uniform of the German Forest Service. Gwyer reported further that his two meetings with Erhard were casual, the first merely on a perfunctory basis, "while on the second occasion he spoke with Erhard about a half-hour on various conversational matters. // Gwyer stated he merely desired to bring attention to Erhard's affiliation with the Nazis during the period November 1939–May 1940 and the lack of personal or historical data concerning Erhard during the period of World War II."[169]

Four months before Erhard was sworn in as Chancellor of the Federal Republic, the CIA reports on another clue to Erhard's activities in German-occupied areas in Eastern Europe. This is documented in a dispatch of June 10, 1963 from "Chief, EE" to "Chief of Base, Frankfurt; Chief of Base, Bonn; Chief of Station, Germany; Subject: Derogatory allegation re CASPHERE." In a separately sent identity sheet the code name CASPHERE is identified as Ludwig Erhard. The dispatch reads as follows:

> 1. An American adviser to ODACID has submitted the following information on CASPHERE (Identity-1) to ODACID and also to KUBARK: "CASPHERE then a professor of economics, was charged by 'Hitler' (it is not clear whether this means Hitler himself or 'The Government') with the detailed planning for the German-occupied territory, and those yet to be occupied in the East, especially the

Ukraine. The resultant project is composed of a compendium slightly under 500 pages long, of which only six to eight copies were produced." This information comes from the wife (Identity-2) or widow of Identity-3 and was sent to me by a mutual friend – a French woman. Since Identity-3 was the collaborator of CASPHERE in this scheme, I am inclined to give it some credence. //
2. Information received from KUPALM, a HICOG report dated 27 May 1962, states that CASPHERE was commissioned in 1944 by the Reich Ministry of Economic Affairs to do a paper on reorganization of economic affairs in postwar Germany. A perusal of extensive KUPALM files does not further expand this information. Our own files contain an unevaluated ODENVY report which states CASPHERE was charged with the economic development and exploitation of the Kolo on the Warta area in Poland on behalf of the Nazis during WW II [see above]. CASPHERE's denazification file, in summary, indicates CASPHERE has a blameless record regarding the Nazi Government before and during WW II and contains no material which lends substance to the above charges. // 3. ... We do not have enough information to trace Identity-3 and therefore suggest that the Field can gain pertinent information through a check on Identity-2 who is said to reside in Wetzlar. // 4. We would also appreciate your querying [name deleted] on the general subject of CASPHERE's activity during WW II with special attention to any economic functions performed for the Ministry of Economic Affairs of the Third Reich. In discussing this with [name deleted] defer to the Field as to how much detail should be provided him. We shall await the results of your action.[170]

Besides CASPHERE, cryptonym for Ludwig Erhard 1963 to 1966, other code names used in this dispatch stand for the following institutions: ODACID = State Department; KUBARK = CIA; EE = East European Division of the State Department; ODENVY = FBI; KUPALM is not deciphered as such. But all cryptonyms beginning with "KU" refer to CIA offices.[171] A Progress Report for May 1, to June 1, 1963 contained an answer to the dispatch of June 10:

> 5. b. [name deleted] has been briefed on the derogatory allegations concerning CASPHERE which were contained in EGFW-15321, 10 June 1963. He found the substance of this dispatch very interesting since he had learnt from CASPHERE's personal secretary that CASPHERE had travelled to Poland at least once during WW II. He had found CASPHERE's secretary reluctant to divulge details about this trip and remarked that CASPHERE had not mentioned it to him at all. [name deleted] will attempt to uncover sufficient information on this matter through his own research to allow him to ask CASPHERE direct questions about this alleged activity. We will keep headquarters informed as information is developed.[172]

Most probably the "name deleted" is Jess M. Lukomski. At the time he was writing a biography of Erhard, which was published in 1965 in German and a year later in Italian.[173] Lukomski was an American who had grown up in Leland, Michigan. He had studied economics, in 1948–49 also in West Germany. He made his career in economic journalism. Since 1955 he worked as foreign correspondent in Europe, at first for *Business International* and then for the *Journal of Commerce*. But beyond that he seems to have cooperated with CIA. Since 1958 he lived in Bonn. Writing Erhard's biography was obviously a door-opener into Erhard's Economics Ministry, to Erhard himself, and to his secretary.

As my book is not primarily on Erhard, but on Tenenbaum's life story, I want to cut a longer research story short. The CIA must have collected more information on Erhard's role and activities in German-occupied territories in Eastern Europe than I have here reported on. CIA and other secret service archives were closed to researchers. Therefore, Congress passed the Nazi War Crimes Disclosure Act in 1998 and the Japanese Imperial Government Disclosure Act in 2000. After an Interagency Working Group had screened and declassified the records, it released them for use by researchers in the National Archives and Records Administration at College Park MD (NARA II). In tandem with declassification progress, copies of the records were passed on to NARA II in digital format, while the originals remain in the archives of the respective secret service. NARA II has made CIA records, collected in RG 263, available online. Releases included summary lists of persons who had been under CIA investigation in connection with war crimes. On the following list Ludwig Erhard appears in between Germany's and other countries' famous war criminals:

> Major subjects who came under investigation include Zsolt Aradi, Hungarian press attaché to the Vatican; Andrija Artukovic (AKA Andrew Artukovic) who committed war crimes in Croatia; Klaus Barbie, the "Butcher of Lyon"; Hildegard Beetz (AKA Hildegard Purwin) who worked for the Reich Central Security Office (Reichssicherheitshauptamt or RSHA), and with Italian Foreign Minister Galeazzo Ciano; Otto von Bolschwing, who committed war crimes in Austria and Romania; Martin Bormann, who was head of the Nazi Party Chancellery and private secretary to Adolf Hitler, before disappearing at the end of the war; Arturs Brombergs, who was accused of committing war crimes in Latvia; Ernst Brueckner, who served as an anti-aircraft officer during the war, and who became the Vice President of West Germany's Federal Office for the Protection of the Constitution (Bundesamt fuer Verfassungsschutz or BfV); Hans Max Clemens, a former Security Service (Sicherheitsdienst or SD) officer who worked for the BND before being unmasked as a Soviet spy; Paul Dickopf, who defected from the Nazis to the Allies, and who became Chief of the West German Criminal Police, and President of the International Criminal Police Organization, Interpol; Ivan Docheff, head of Bulgaria's Department for Oral and Practical Propaganda during the war, who became a leader of the Bulgarian émigré community; Ferdinand Durcansky, who was accused of committing war crimes in Czechoslovakia; Adolf

Eichmann, Chief of the Jewish Office of the Gestapo, the Nazi secret state police; *Ludwig Erhard* [my emphasis], the Director of the Institute for Industrial Research during the war, who became Chancellor of West Germany; Heinz Felfe, a former SS (Schutzstaffel or Defense Squadron) officer who rose to be deputy chief of the BND before being unmasked as a Soviet spy; Nazi and West German intelligence chief Reinhard Gehlen; . . .

This quotation covers only the first third of the complete list, whose alphabetical order places Erhard next to Adolf Eichmann. But Erhard was, of course, not the same type of war criminal as Eichmann. The Interagency Working Group distinguished between two categories of people on the list:

Axis personnel accused of committing war crimes, or of belonging to criminal organizations, during World War II; and former Axis personnel who were used by the U.S. or West Germany as intelligence sources during the Cold War. The series also includes files relating to people who were never accused of war crimes or of belonging to criminal organizations, but who may have been associated with war crimes as victims, witnesses, investigators, sources, or officials.

Until further research finds out more on Erhard's activities in Eastern Europe during World War II, pick your choice between the two categories! One document that I found might contain a clue, a letter in German [my translation] from Chancellor Ludwig Erhard to the director of CIA, John A. McCone (1961–1965), of May 28, 1965:

Dear Mr. McCone, // I thank you obligingly for your letter of April 28, informing me that you are giving up your post and retiring. I think back fondly on your visits to Bonn and on our conversations, and I appreciate very much the collaboration you had with your German colleagues. // For your future welfare I send you my best wishes // With sincere compliments and kind regards // [signed] Ludwig Erhard.[174]

3   Edward A. Tenenbaum's Family Roots, Adolescence, and Military Experience until 1946

This part of the book covers his parents' roots in Austria; their education up to PhD for both of them; his father's military service in the Austrian Army; their emigration in 1920 to New York where Edward was born as their first of three sons; his father's leading role in New York's medical circles, in the American and World Jewish Congress as well as in organizing a campaign for boycotting German imports during the Nazi period. It also deals with Edward's formative years in New York; his excellent education, including a year in the world's first international school at Geneva; his four years in Yale College; his employment immediately afterward at the newly founded secret service Office of Strategic Services (OSS) in Washington, DC; and his military service in America, England, France, Belgium, and Germany, where he became the first American officer to enter the Buchenwald concentration camp on its liberation day April 11, 1945.

3.1   FAMILY ROOTS AND ADOLESCENCE UNTIL BA GRADUATION AT YALE IN JUNE 1942

As the first of three children Edward Adam Tenenbaum (Social Security Number SSN 577460475) was born into a highly educated Jewish family on November 10, 1921 in New York City (NYC). His younger brothers were also born in NYC, Bertrand April 25, 1923 (SSN 067247056, died December 28, 2003) and Robert Felix May 30, 1926 (SSN 124209238, died October 24, 2006 with his assumed last name Tannenbaum).[1] Like Edward, both would serve in World War II, Bertrand in the US Army and Robert in the US Navy.

More information is available on Bertrand, which also tells us something about the way Edward grew up. ... "he grew up going to concerts & operas on Saturday matinees. As a young boy of five he had meningitis and nearly succumbed. He went to Cornell then on to graduate & medical schools in Lausanne, Switzerland. After fighting in World War II he returned to the USA for his internship and residency. He eventually went into private practice in San Luis Obispo, CA. First wife, Janine, he met in France and one child, Margie, was born to them. In 1959 he married Annie Denny Donohoe and left her his widow in 2003."[2] He died as Dr. Bertrand Tenenbaum in San Luis Obispo, California. He was cremated and his ashes were scattered at sea.[3]

Here are some impressions that Tenenbaum's son Mark shared with me about his father's two brothers in an interview on November 10, 2018:

> I saw Robert last time in 1993. And he was still the same kind of a wisecracker. He was a perpetual student. He had been working on a PhD for 50 years. We made it down here [our interview took place in Washington, DC] with my fiancé at the time and kind of had some laughs. I understand he passed away. But we never found out where he was or what happened. He was a humorous sort, smaller than my father, much shorter, well like my grandfather [Joseph], and a real wisecrack and quick-witted, kind of arrogant, nothing like my father's personality, completely opposite. And Bertrand I never met.

In our interview on October 29, 2018, the Tenenbaum's younger daughter Joan reported:

> Robert was an academic bum, that was his words. He was a historian. I never forgot, he once took me to the Metropolitan Museum. He was full of knowledge. He took me through the Egyptians and told me everything there was to know about Egyptians and artefacts and things. So he was really a very scholarly guy. But he worked for many universities around the world and in this country. He never kept his job long. I don't know if he got to be a professor or anything like that. But he did write a book about the

secular Jesus, you know, as if Jesus had been just a guy, just a man. [And as to Edward's other brother:] Bertrand became a psychiatrist in California. But they [Bertrand and Robert] were not on speaking terms . . . I never met Bertrand. I know he had a daughter named Margery. I have no idea, never met her.

Their father Joseph Leib Tenenbaum had been born on May 22, 1887 in Sassow, Eastern Galicia, Poland,[4] today Sasiv, Ukraine. That part of Poland had belonged to the Habsburg Empire since 1772 until the Peace Treaty of Saint-Germain-en-Laye, near Paris, came into force on July 16, 1920. The Treaty had been signed on September 10, 1919 by the Allied powers and Austria.[5]

As a young man Josef [as his first name was officially spelled in Europe] Tenenbaum was attracted to the Austrian capital, where he studied at the medical faculty of the University of Vienna from 1908 to 1911. His enrollment certificates, made available to me by the University of Vienna archive, lists professors he studied with and courses he took. They reveal that his mother tongue was Hebrew and that he was of Mosaic faith. He also listed Berisch Bienstock living in Sassow as his father as well as legal guardian and his father's and guardian's occupation as day laborer. We are also informed by this source that Josef had been awarded his maturity certificate at the K. K. VI. Gymnasium in Lemberg, that during his student years in Vienna he lived in the 14th district, Reindorfgasse 13 and that for one semester he was also enrolled at Vienna University for the study of law.

As a student, he became involved in the Hashahar student youth organization.[6] In 1914 he completed his medical doctorate (MD) at the University of Lemberg. The city of Lemberg was also situated in the Polish area under Habsburg rule.[7] It was the capital of Eastern Galicia and after Vienna, Prague, and Trieste the fourth largest city of the Habsburg Empire.[8] After the World War I Eastern Galicia became part of the newly created independent state of Poland. Lemberg was renamed Lwow under Polish rule. Due to the Hitler–Stalin Pact of August 23, 1939, Germany's occupation of the larger part of Poland starting a week later, and the Soviet Union's annexation of the eastern part of Poland, Lemberg/Lwow became part of the Ukraine and adopted the name Lviv. Today the former University of Lemberg is called Ivan Franko National University of Lviv.

Adolf Hitler, born two years later than Joseph Tenenbaum in Braunau am Inn, Austria, had also been attracted to his capital. He lived in Vienna for some months during the second half of 1907. He went back to Linz to take care of his dying mother during her last days and settle her affairs. He returned to Vienna in January 1908 to live there until 1913.[9] A year before the outbreak of World War I he emigrated to Munich to escape the draft of the Habsburg monarchy which he hated for the multinational mixture of its population. He saw it as a betrayal of *Germanness*. Ambitious to be educated as a painter, Hitler flunked his first entrance exam at Vienna's Academy of Fine Arts in October 1907, despite some attested talent. He gave it a second try in 1908, but was unsuccessful again. In Vienna he made a living not only from taking occasional jobs, but also from painting postcards and selling them. Hitler had Jewish friends who sold his postcards on commission.[10] He had not yet developed into that anti-Semitic maniac as which he presented himself in Germany early after World War I and throughout his political career until his suicide on April 30, 1945.

Did young Joseph Tenenbaum and Adolf Hitler ever run into each other in the bohemian world of Vienna? It's not impossible, but very improbable. Here is well-educated Joseph, speaking several languages, with admission to the University of Vienna and there is Adolf, speaking nothing but German, who after several repetitions of classes had dropped out of his middle school at Steyr/Austria in 1905 never finishing a degree. He twice failed with his application to Vienna's Academy of Fine Arts. It is true that during the World War I Joseph as officer of the Austro-Hungarian Army and Adolf as private of the German Army were fighting on the same side. During that time Adolf, had he known Joseph, would have despised him primarily for being of Polish origin.[11] As we will later see, Adolf's post–World War I antisemitism, which according to latest research seized Hitler in the summer of 1919,[12] will explain why Joseph fought Adolf and the Nazis with his literary and organizing power as much as he could during World War II from New York City.

If Adolf had been accepted by Vienna's Academy of Fine Arts and had established some private stability in his life by marrying at the usual age and having children, world history might have taken quite a different course. Thomas Weber (*Hitler's First War*) offers a clue to that question by comparing Hitler's career with that of his revered List Regiment comrade Lieutenant Albert Weisgerber who from teenage years had also aspired to be a painter. They both had grown up in small towns and were mediocre students in school. Both went to Munich, then Germany's metropolis for artists. Upon the outbreak of World War I, both enthusiastically followed the call to arms and were fully committed to the war. But otherwise Weisgerber's life and entourage was very different from Hitler's. He had been accepted by and studied in Munich's Academy of Fine Arts and became a painter of fame. Among his friends were such towering figures of German Liberalism as Theodor Heuss, West Germany's first president. Before the war he repeatedly had spent time in Paris, where he became acquainted with Henri Matisse. Hitler, in contrast, had never traveled beyond a small section of German-speaking Austria and southern Bavaria. Weisgerber was married to a woman that the Nazis should later define as half-Jewish.[13] Only one day before their common suicide did Hitler marry his long-time girlfriend Eva Braun. They never had children.

For Hitler the Bavarian Reserve Infantry Regiment 16, called the List Regiment, especially his fellow dispatch runners in regimental headquarters, had been his foster family during the war. Here Hitler found respect, trust, friendship and even love. He had no other family, profession, and life to return to. This is the reason why he clung tenaciously to military service when the German Army was demobilized in 1919, unfortunately without success. No wonder that Hitler tried to enlist the support of his comrades and friends in List Regiment, when after discharge he had started his political career in Munich in 1919 and again when his National Socialist German Workers' Party had become the strongest party in the Weimar Republic's parliament in 1932. In some cases, he succeeded, but in most cases he didn't.

On January 30, 1933 President Paul von Hindenburg took Hitler's oath of office as chancellor of Germany, ironically upon the constitution of the Weimar Republic that the new chancellor had hated so much throughout his prior political career. The discrimination of Jewish German citizens was launched already in April 1933 by legislation and by Nazi boycott campaigns against Jewish shop owners. It intensified during the 1930s and reached its climax in the Holocaust after Hitler had started World War II and the initial German military successes were stalled in front of Moscow in the late fall of 1941.[14] This drove even some of Hitler's List Regiment comrades to contribute to resistance against Hitler and the Nazis.[15]

On September 21, 1914 Joseph Tenenbaum married Otilia Jon; she was Jewish like him. She had been born in Lemberg/Lwow/Lviv on February 11, 1891. At the age of eighty-four she would die in May 1975 in Brooklyn, Kings County, New York State.[16] She had also completed her studies with a PhD.[17] I assumed that she, too, received it at the University of Lemberg. So I contacted the University of Lviv archive to find out when and in what field. Unable to detect such early alumni records as that of Otilia's undergraduate and postgraduate studies, the archivist referred me to the State Archive in Lviv. But the search there also produced no result. My interviews with Otilia's grandchildren couldn't clarify the matter either.

More than a year later I tested a different hypothesis: During World War I when Joseph did his military service Otilia might have moved from Lemberg to Vienna and might have studied and finished her PhD there. I contacted the University of Vienna asking for traces of Otilia's doctorate there. Within a week I received links to her enrollment documents. These had already been digitalized like those of all students in the faculty of philosophy which until 1975 also comprised the natural sciences. They are available online. For a small fee I was offered scans of Vienna University's file on her PhD studies and completion.

Otilia's field of study was botany and zoology. On July 21, 1920 she was awarded her doctoral degree by the Faculty of Philosophy of Vienna University. This was after her husband had left Vienna, embarking on a boat at the port of Le Havre, France, on March 20, 1920 to sail for New York City, as we will later see. *Otylia* Tenenbaum, born *John*, as she spelled her first and maiden name before her own emigration to New York City at the end of 1920, is listed as the 783rd woman in the register of female doctorates of the University of Vienna 1897 to 1923.[18]

Otylia's enrollment certificates and her PhD file contain – besides the courses she took and the professors she studied with as well as the fact that her mother tongue was Hebrew and that she was of Mosaic faith – a wealth of information on family roots, her own living quarters in Vienna, and on her education before she started university. She had studied the first eight semesters of her undergraduate education at the University of Lemberg. After the outbreak of World War I and her marriage with Joseph in September 1914, she moved to Roten Löwengasse 9/27 in the 9th district of Vienna and enrolled for the winter semester of 1914/15 at the Faculty of Philosophy of the University of Vienna, her ninth semester of botany. Her father is listed as Markus John, a merchant at Lemberg.[19] The description of the same source counts only twenty-nine women as being enrolled in the almost all-encompassing Faculty of Philosophy. During her prior studies at the University of Lemberg she was probably even more a female solitaire in her field of study and at the university as a whole. One could even say that Otylia John Tenenbaum belonged to the very first pioneers of female university students in Europe.

Her enrollment certificate for the summer semester 1915 shows a change of address to Seegasse 5/17 in Vienna's 9th district.[20] She then evidently interrupted her studies at the University of Vienna for a year. She came back from Lemberg, at whose university she was evidently enrolled for her eleventh semester, to continue studies with her twelfth semester during the winter term of 1916/17. Her address then was Bechardgasse 19/8 in Vienna's 3rd district.[21] Living at the same address, she finished her undergraduate studies in her thirteenth semester during the summer term 1917.[22]

On July 14, 1917 Otylia addresses the *Löbliches Dekanat der philosophischen Fakultät der K. K. Universität in Wien* [Laudable deanery of the philosophical faculty of the K. K. University in Vienna] in her own beautiful handwriting:

> *Die ergebenst Gefertigte bittet um Zulassung zu den strengen Prüfungen behufs Erlangung des philosophischen Doktorgrades aus Botanik in Verbindung mit Zoologie und legt bei: 1) Geburtschein 2) Reifezeignis 3) Absolutorium 4) Curriculum 5) Dissertation.* [The most devoted undersigned asks to be admitted to the rigorous examinations for the award of a doctorate in philosophy for botany in conjunction with zoology and encloses 1) Birth certificate 2) Matriculation certificate 3) Graduate degree 4) Curriculum 5) Dissertation].

Evidently, Otylia had completed her doctoral dissertation at this point in time. It was entitled *Beitrag zur Mikrochemie der Suberinlamelle* [A contribution to the microchemistry of the suberinlamella]. She paid the usual fee of forty Austrian Crowns for the evaluation of her dissertation. On June 16, 1917 her first adviser, Professor Dr. Molisch, from whom she had taken most of her courses at Vienna University, handwrote a one-page assessment of her thesis and approved its academic quality. By countersignature Otylia's second adviser, Hofrat Dr. Ritter von Wettstein, agreed with the report.

It is not clear to me why it took Otylia three more years to complete her doctorate. To be sure, in addition to the acceptance of her dissertation by the faculty she was required to pass a number of oral exams. I spotted two: a two-hour exam on June 30, 1920, and a one-hour exam on July 9, 1920, each one with two examiners other than Prof. Molisch. All four graded her *ausgezeichnet* [excellent], which corresponds to *summa cum laude* in the academically more common Latin grading system.

But Vienna University's file on Otylia's doctoral degree also contains information on her earlier education in Lemberg. Until the age of thirteen she attended the local *Volksschule und Bürgerschule* [elementary school and citizen school]. After passing the entrance exam, she was admitted to the *Privates Mädchengymnasium mit Öffentlichkeitsrecht und polnischer Umgangssprache* of Frau Sophie Strzatkowska. There, on June 7, 1910, she received her maturity certificate. And as we already know, she studied at the University of Lemberg from 1910 to the summer semester of 1914.

During the World War I Joseph served in the Austro-Hungarian Army as a captain of the medical corps.[23] For this service he was awarded the Golden Cross donated by Franz Joseph I, Emperor of Austria-Hungary. By Poland he was granted the *Commander Cross Polonia Restituta*. In the USA he was given the status of a *Diplomate American Board Urology*.[24] In 1919 he participated as a representative from Eastern Galicia in the Jewish delegation to the Paris Peace Conference.[25] In 1920 the Tenenbaum couple emigrated separately to the United States, where they were naturalized in New York City in 1926.

More detailed information on their passage from Europe and on their start in New York City is available. The immigration records of Ellis Island in the mouth of the Hudson River between New York and New Jersey, the gateway for millions of immigrants to the United States between its opening in 1892 and closure in 1954, are researchable, even online.[26] Joseph left from Vienna to the French port of Le Havre, where he embarked on the French passenger liner *SS La Lorraine*, which departed from there on March 20, 1920 to cross the Atlantic.[27] Before the boat had reached Ellis Island on March 30, 1920, Joseph – like all other passengers – was questioned by a crew member who took note of his answers on a large sheet designed by USA

Immigration with thirty lines for thirty passengers and thirty columns for questions to answer. The passengers' names and the answers had to be typewritten. "The master or commanding officer of each vessel" was obliged to deliver these lists to the immigration officer upon arrival. Such officers would check it, put their own questions to each person, make additions or changes in handwriting on the list and, of course, would have the last word on permitting or rejecting immigration. In the latter case the ship on which he or she had arrived would have to take him or her back to Europe free of charge.

Joseph was on a list for "first-cabin passengers only." His height was put down as 5 feet 6 inches, the color of his hair and his eyes as brown. He affirmed that he had paid for the passage himself, was in possession of at least fifty dollars, and had not been in the United States before. As to the length of time he would stay in the USA he replied "unknown." Like all the others, he assured that he was not a polygamist or an anarchist and that he could read and write in a language of his choice – he chose Polish. Asked for the nearest relative or friend in the country where he came from, he answered "Wife, Mrs. Tenenbaum at Vienna." Obviously Joseph wanted to sound out his opportunities for work and renting a family home, before Otilia would join him in New York City.

Joseph was also asked whether he would join a relative or friend in the United States and, if yes, to give the name and exact address. Here he didn't list a person's, but an organization's name: "Federation of Galic[i]an Jews, 66 Second Av. New York." This is evidence of his international, in this case transatlantic, connections that Joseph had established when playing prominent roles in Jewish organizations back home in Galicia and as Eastern Galicia's representative within the Jewish delegation to the Paris Peace Conference in 1919.[28] His role in Paris must have been a prominent one, as the following paragraph will show.

When the Habsburg Empire had collapsed, both the Ukraine and the newly created Polish state rivalled over the annexation of Eastern Galicia with its capital Lemberg, to which both Otilia and Joseph had been attached from growing up in Eastern Galicia since birth and later from studying at the University of Lemberg. Civil war–like conditions developed in early November 1918, after the Ukrainian state had assented to the claim of the Eastern Galicia's Jewish leadership for a sort of national autonomy for the particularly large share of Jewish population in that region, especially in Lemberg, also called *Jerusalem of Europe*. The Poles had not only refused to acknowledge such minority rights, but a wave of antisemitism and even pogroms had erupted in Poland. After Polish troops had ousted their Ukrainian counterparts, they and Polish civilians carried out a pogrom in the Jewish quarter of Lemberg, a sort of vendetta for the Jewish community's favoring of political ties with the Ukraine over those with Poland. News and reports were spread quickly worldwide. Especially Jewish citizenry and Jewish national and international organizations in Western countries rose up in protest and organized large demonstrations, for example, a *weep in sympathy with the persecuted Jews in Galicia and Poland* with 8,000 participants in NYC's Madison Square Garden. Together with other mass protests in Berlin, London, Paris, The Hague, Vienna, and Zurich, it put so much pressure on the heads of state negotiating at the Paris Peace Conference after January 1919 that the issue of protecting minority rights in peace settlements and in the charter of the League of Nations could no longer be ignored.[29] As representative of Eastern Galicia Joseph Tenenbaum must have played a central role in the Jewish delegation to the Paris Peace Conference.

Otylia (spelling on the passenger list) Tenenbaum, arriving on the same *SS La Lorraine* on October 11, 1920, came to join him in NYC. She was on a list for "steerage passengers only." But there she, at age twenty-nine, (by that time Joseph was thirty-three) traveled in the company of another married Jewish woman from Lemberg, Adela Lempert (age thirty-two), who was accompanied by her two children Abraham (nine years) and Simon Leib (seven years). It looks like they had already known each other in Lemberg and had planned the trip together.

Where Joseph had put down "surgeon" as his "Calling or occupation," Otylia had specified "labor." The immigration officer changed it to "wife" in his handwriting. Otylia's height was registered as 5 feet 7 inches, one inch taller than Joseph. Other notable differences from his data were: her birthplace "Poland, Lemberg" and her given address of a relative or friend to join in the USA "Dr. Tenenbaum Sea Gate, Coney Island." Sea Gate at the southwestern tip of Brooklyn NY was a thriving Jewish, and America's first gated, community, where well-to-do New Yorkers spent their summer vacation. It was and is run by the Sea Gate Association. It looks like Joseph's friends of the Federation of Galician Jews in New York had offered him one of the mostly single-family houses there to join with his wife in a decent home.

The Tenenbaum couple had emigrated to the United States just in time, that is, a year before a Republican Congress and newly elected President Warren G. Harding severely restricted immigration, especially from eastern European countries, such as Poland, and southern European countries, such as Italy. First the Emergency Quota Act of May 19, 1921 and later a tightened version, the National Origins Act of 1924, limited the number and nationality of immigrants allowed into the United States. These laws effectively ended the era of mass immigration into New York and the United States altogether. They were aimed at countering the tide of uneducated, working-class immigrants. Professionals continued to be allowed to enter the United States with few restrictions, regardless of their nations of origin. Therefore, the highly educated Tenenbaums might not have been affected by this new policy, had they emigrated later.

After having settled in New York in 1920 Joseph's and Otilia's war-torn married life and uncertain professional future in Vienna or in the newly created Polish state came to an end after six years of nothing but turmoil in Europe. As a urologist and surgeon, obviously with English-language skills, Joseph had no problem in New York City to find employment and to make a living. The time had finally come for creating a family with children. And Edward Adam was the first addition to the family in late 1921.

I couldn't find out how long the Tenenbaum family lived in Sea Gate on Coney Island. But the fifteenth US census of 1930 reveals a different abode for April 2, 1930: 29 Edgewood Park, New Rochelle City, Westchester County, NY. And it delivers more details on living conditions. The household comprised Joseph and Otilia, their three sons Edward, Bertrand, and Robert as well as the German "servant" Margaret Hammer. The dwelling was rented at a monthly price of $100. Another of the eleven houses recorded on the same enumeration sheet for that neighborhood was rented for $105. Six houses were registered as owner-occupied. Their values – as listed – ranged between $9,000 and $25,000. The question for rent or owner-occupancy was not answered for three households. Six of the eleven households were recorded as having a radio set, among them the Tenenbaums. On April 24, 2019 an online search for 29 Edgewood Park, New Rochelle NY, delivered the following results: home type: multi-family residence; lot size: 13,939 square feet; home value: $612,000; bus transportation to Manhattan between 30 and 60 minutes. At this stage, I drew the conclusion that the Tenenbaum family in not even ten years after immigration had socially advanced to the upper middle class in the New York area.

I interpret Margaret Hammer's membership of the Tenenbaum household in 1930 along the following lines. Apart from helping Otilia in managing the daily chores, her role might well have been to let the kids grow up with a native speaker of German around them, especially so as the parents would probably have spoken Yiddish among themselves and English with their children. This would help to explain Edward Tenenbaum's fluency in the German language which would prove to be so valuable for both his first job after BA graduation in June 1942 and later for his engineering of the West German currency reform in June 1948. An essential ingredient of Edward's language education was probably provided by Margaret Hammer, native of Graz/Austria.

But I wanted to find out more about the "servant" of the family. On the 1930 Census sheet Margaret Hammer was registered as twenty-eight years old and single, immigration from Germany in 1929, able to speak English. The language spoken at home before immigration was recorded as *German*, while for Joseph and Otilia Tenenbaum it was *Jewish*, probably a misunderstanding of *Yiddish* by the interviewer. With the above information on the "servant" of the Tenenbaum family in New Rochell NY I went online into the immigration records of Ellis Island. Margaret Hammer crossed the Atlantic on SS *Columbus* departing from the port of Bremen on August 25, 1928 and arriving at the port of New York on September 3, 1928. On an Alien Passengers List "for steerage passengers only," I could find quite a bit more information on Margaret Hammer, some of it deviating from the US 1930 Census data, for example, her age was noted as only twenty years. Under *race or people* she was recorded as German, but for her *nationality* as Austrian. Graz in Austria was listed as her birthplace. As *calling or occupation* she declared "servant." Her father was put down as her nearest relative: Valentin Muster, Graz/Austria, Scheidenberg. Margaret Hammer declared that she had paid for the passage herself and that she doesn't intend to return to Europe, but wants to become a US citizen. After answering the "funny" questions with "no," such as whether being a polygamist or anarchist, she is attested to be in "good" mental and physical health condition and 5 feet 6 inches tall, to have a "fair" complexion, brown hair, and gry eyes.

And then I was surprised by the unexpected: Her visa had been issued May 9, 1928 in Washington, DC, not in Europe. And her last permanent residence was recorded as New York/USA, having lived there from 1925 to 1928. Her home address to which she returned was given as 202 East 104th Street, New York NY. Evidently, on September 3, 1928, Margaret Hammer had returned from a vacation trip to Europe, started sometime after May 9, 1928, the day her visa for re-entry into the USA had been issued in Washington, DC. She probably had visited her family in Graz/Austria and friends elsewhere. I again went online into the immigration records of Ellis Island to find out when she first had immigrated into the USA. The records show that she had been issued a visa on August 3, 1925 in Vienna and had departed from Antwerp September 3, 1925 on SS *Belgenland*, arriving in New York, date missing on the source document, about ten days later at the age of eighteen. Here she was listed on an Alien Passengers List "for second-cabin passengers only." She attested that she wanted to stay in the USA and named her father Valentin Muster, Graz/Ausrria as her *nearest relative or friend* of her home country. She declared that her father had paid for the passage and that she was in possession of $25. As *calling or occupation* she had put down "cook." As *final destination* she was registered with "NJ Maple Shade." She named her aunt Christine Vetter as a relative living there.

After the initial result of my search in the US Census for the Joseph Tenenbaum family in 1930 had led me to 29 Edgewood Park, New Rochelle, Westchester County NY, I stepped – when searching the birth date of son Robert Tenenbaum, Edward's youngest brother – upon a second listing of the same Joseph Tenenbaum family in the 1930 US Census, this time in New York City, 956 Fifth Avenue at corner of East 77th St., right across Central Park.[30] All of the seven apartments on the same sheet were rented. The Tenenbaums paid $300 monthly, while all of the other six lodgers paid higher rents up to a maximum of $1,000. The household in NYC did not include Margaret Hammer, the "servant" in New Rochelle. But besides the five family members proper it comprised 44-year-old Elisabeth S. McGee as Virginia-born unmarried "servant/lodger." Her occupation was listed as "governess." This means that she would care for and teach the Tenenbaum kids privately at home. In addition, Elisabeth K. Noren as a 23-year-old Sweden-born just-married "servant" was listed. She was attested to speak English.

I conclude from this evidence that Joseph Tenenbaum and his wife Otilia not only belonged to the upper middle class as I had assumed after rating his abode in New Rochelle. But actually they had made true the *American Dream*, that is, from poor beginnings when they immigrated to the USA in 1920 to their US census–recorded situation ten years later.

From the mid-1930s on until Joseph's death at the age of seventy-four years on December 10, 1961, addresses are known, because *Who's Who in America,* volume 18 (1934–1935), started to list him, including his home and office addresses.[31] In the 1934–1935 edition Joseph Tenenbaum's home address is stated as 106 E. 85th St., New York NY and his nearby office address as 115 E. 82nd St. At the time he probably still lived with his wife and their three sons. In the 1936–1937 edition the address given is this: *"Home-Office*: 115 E. 82nd St., New York, NY," the same for 1938–1939.[32] Around the mid-1930s he had obviously separated from his family by moving into his office apartment. Both locations are situated in the Upper East Side of New York City, two blocks from 5th Avenue and Central Park and until today a very fancy and well-to-do neighborhood.

In the sixteenth US census of 1940 in early April 1940 Joseph and Otilia were registered as divorced and were living in two separate households. Asked for the number of hours he had worked during the last week of March 1940, Joseph had sixty-five listed. Of the forty persons enumerated on the same sheet this was surpassed only by seventy hours for another medical doctor and seventy-two each for a nurse in a doctor's office and an office manager in the paper industry. The 1940 Census also reveals that the three sons stayed in Otilia's household, where Edward was registered "AB" for absent, as he already went to college out of town. The downsized family had moved from the family's home (see above), to 427 East 89th Street in New York City. This is confirmed by Edward Tenenbaum himself on his application form for government employment in Washington, DC filled out sometime after July 1950 and before July 1952. Asked for dates and places of residence for the last ten years he states the same address for the period "1935 to June 42,"[33] the month he graduated from Yale College, moved to Washington, DC, and took up employment there with the newly founded OSS. The move of Otilia Tenenbaum and her three sons into the above address, probably smaller than the previous family apartment for economy reasons, must have taken place before April 1, 1935, because Otilia affirmatively answered the census question whether she had lived there already on that date. In combination with Edward Tenenbaum's noted residence there for "1935 to June 42" it is safe to assume that the separation of the family and the move to 427 East 89th Street took place during the first quarter of 1935.

The 1940 Census records Otilia as a housewife without other employment. For all four, zero weeks worked in 1939 and nil "Amount of money wages or salary received" are noted. As to the question in Column 33, also pertaining to 1939: "Did this person receive [annual] income of $50 or more from sources other than money wages or salary?" Otilia is recorded with a "No," while for each of the three sons a "Yes" is noted. Adjusted for inflation $50 was worth $1,060 in 2023 money. The children's income was certainly paid by father Joseph Tenenbaum as child support. As Otilia didn't earn or receive any income, it might well be that her former husband also paid the rent for her household. According to the census in 1940 it amounted to $65 per month, which is worth almost $1,378 in 2023.

At the time of the 1940 US Census Joseph Tenenbaum was registered as living in 505 Ocean Avenue, Brooklyn (= Kings County) NY. He is listed as having already resided there on April 1, 1935. Therefore, we might safely conclude that the marriage had broken up before the latter date, that is, when the three sons were still children. His occupation is noted as a medical doctor, Class of worker "OA," that is, working on own account. Each for 1939, he is recorded with fifty weeks of work, nil money wage or salary, but "Yes" as to the above-cited question under Column 33. His hours of work during the last week of March 1940 were noted as sixty-five. Evidently he was a hardworking man.

For Joseph Tenenbaum I could spot some address changes thereafter. The 1940–1941 edition of *Who's Who in America* lists the home-office address as 55 E. 86th St. and the 1942–1943 and the next two editions as 70 E. 83rd St., where he obviously lived with his second wife Sheila Tenenbaum, born Schwartz. They were married on January 23, 1943.[34]

Joseph Tenenbaum was not only a highly esteemed urologist and surgeon, as his different positions in reputed hospitals, like the one on Welfare Island and two NYC Jewish hospitals, prove. He had also been an instructor in urology at Columbia University 1922–1924. He was a fellow of the NY Academy of Medicine. In addition, he was active in leading roles in Jewish organizations: American Jewish Congress (1929–1936), World Jewish Congress (member of the administrative committee 1936), 1933–1941 founder and chairman of the Joint Boycott Council of the American Jewish Congress and the Jewish Labor Committee, and vice-chairman of the Federation of Polish Jews (1928–1936). As president of the American and World Federation of Polish Jews, he traveled to Poland after World War II to bring and distribute aid to Jewish survivors there.[35] He was an active member of the Workmen's Circle, of the Zionist Organization of America, of the American Hebrew-Speaking Medical Association, and of the Jewish Academy of Arts and Sciences. He also belonged to the Club of Jewish Writers and was himself a very prolific author of books and contributions to magazines.

I only mention his books and monographs. In German: *Unsere Friedensfrage, von einem Zionisten* (1917); and under pseudonym "Josef Bendow" *Der Lemberger Judenpogrom* – November 1918 – Jänner 1919 (1919).[36] In Polish: *Jewish Economic Problems in Galicia* (1918). In French: *La Question Juive en Pologne* (1919).[37] In Hebrew: *Galicia, My Old Home* (1952); *Between War and Peace: Jews at the Peace Conference after WW I.* In English: *In Fire: Stories from the Field of Battle of a Doctor in the former Austro-Hungarian Army* (1926); *The Riddle of Sex: The Medical and Social Aspects of Sex, Love and Marriage* (1929); *Mad Heroes: Skeletons and Sketches of the Eastern Front* (1931); *Races, Nations and Jews* (1935); *The Riddle of Woman* (1936); *The Third Reich in Figures: Present Economic Conditions in Germany* (1938); *Can Hitler Be Stopped?* (1938); *The Economic Crisis of the Third Reich* (1939); *American Investments and Business Interests in Germany* (1940); *The Road to Pan-Americanism* (1941); *Peace for the Jew* (1945); *The Road to*

Nowhere (1947); (in collaboration with Sheila Tenenbaum, his second wife) *In Search of a Lost People: The Old and the New Poland* (1948); *Underground: The Story of a People* (1952); *Race and Reich: The Story of an Epoch* (1956).[38] At the time of his death in 1961 Joseph Tenenbaum had finished a manuscript on Jewish rescue operations during the Holocaust, which was never published.[39] In his obituary the *New York Times* reported: "The Nazis denounced him over their radio network in World War II as an enemy of the Third Reich."[40] This time they indeed spoke the truth.

His 1936 book *The Riddle of Woman: A Study in the Social Psychology of Sex* probably originated from Joseph Tenenbaum's urge to come to terms with the trauma that his family's breakup and divorce had caused in him. In one of the top academic journals a

FIGURE 3.1 Dr. Joseph Tenenbaum (left) stands with Fiorello LaGuardia NYC mayor (center) and Rabbi Stephen S. Wise (right) in front of a medical field unit sponsored by the United Jewish War Effort that is being sent to the Soviet Union, 1943

reviewer "regretted that Dr. Tenenbaum was not prevented from falling into numerous errors of fact and judgment."[41] This indicates that the book was written in haste, as if to get something not only off the desk, but also off the soul. Probably due to its title the book and its author were broadly popularized all over the USA in provincial news media. His views on the role of woman in society and in marriage are concisely summarized there. I quote from an article that has appeared in numerous provincial newspapers:

> The men folk had better step spryly to regain ground lost to women, says Dr. Joseph Tenenbaum. ... Otherwise ... America is likely to see a return to the Age of Amazons. ... At the rate things are going today, he says, it seems inevitable that men will soon do little more than take orders. ... The schools, he says, teach girls how to make a living, but never how to make a home. They are adding yearly to the increasing number of spinsters. Marriage is the biggest, most difficult job in the world, yet girls are given no preparation at all for it. ... Home life, he says, has suffered and is suffering – and we see the consequences everywhere. Men, with all the substitutes they can get elsewhere, need a home, a place to relax, where there is someone to understand and encourage them.[42]

In another article, also published in different journals in the Midwest and South, the following quote of Joseph Tenenbaum serves as an appetizer:

> Modern woman has enslaved man. If you make a slave of someone, you give him the psychology of slavery. It weakens him. What type of woman has enslaved man? Women of leisure. Their demands are terrific. The woman who does not work cannot be a friend to the man who is absorbed by his work. Nor is the fatigued husband, who must work harder than ever to foot the bills, a suitable companion for an idling leisure-loving woman.[43]

By today's standard and may be even by that of the 1930s Joseph Tenenbaum preached Macho views. His black-and-white vision of either dominance or slavery, his one-sided attribution of perhaps undesirable social developments to the female sex, and his yearning for a traditional home with an understanding, encouraging, and caressing wife under male dominance is often a typical result of men's frustration and suffering from divorce. It's a pity that Otilia Tenenbaum never published a companion volume entitled *The Riddle of Man* after divorce. Was it because she – although educated enough – was an *idling leisure-loving woman* that Joseph complained about and, therefore, didn't possess the necessary work ethic for writing and publishing a book? Or was it because she experienced separation and divorce as liberation, not as frustration and trauma?

For teenager Edward the family's residence in in the Upper East Side of Manhattan meant quite a distance from his Stuyvesant High School ("Stuy"), at that time in the Eastern Village area down south at 345 East 15th Street.[44] It had been founded in 1904. It developed into being the best public high school in NY City and one of the best nationwide. Its mission is contained in its logo: *Pro Scientia Atque Sapientia* (For science and wisdom). For more than 100 years the school has specialized in Science, Technology, Engineering, and Mathematics (STEM).[45] Admission began to be restricted based on scholastic achievement in 1919 and since 1934 an entrance exam is required.[46] In Stuy's yearbook of 1937 Edward is imaged only twice: individually like all his other classmates and on a group photo of the Spectator staff. The Spectator is a biweekly newspaper, founded in 1915 and published by students of Stuy.[47] The individual yearbook photo comes – behind Tenenbaum's name – with a comparatively short list of his extracurricular activities: "Service Squad, Spectator Staff, NYU" and with a self-chosen wise saying. Edward chose: "The greatest men are the simplest." This choice foreshadows a characteristic trait that he would display throughout his life: modesty. His oldest daughter Anne described this trait in her father in a letter to me: "... my father was really a rather modest man (albeit, obviously, with a sense of humor), and never really an attention seeker ... He was a very practical man."[48]

After Edward's graduation from Stuy in 1937 at the unusually young age of fifteen, he studied for a year at the École Internationale (Ecolint) in Geneva, Switzerland, which on a much larger scale is still in operation today. The remote cause of the school's founding in 1924 was the Versailles Peace Treaty of 1919, according to which the League of Nations (LoN) and the International Labor Office (ILO) established their headquarters in Geneva in 1920 and 1921. Senior members of the two organizations founded this private school in 1924, jointly with educators from Geneva's Institut Jean-Jacques Rousseau.[49] From the beginning, the school's aim was to educate for peace, for humanitarian values and for intercultural respect and understanding, values that LoN and ILO also stood for. Ecolint's website states until today: "Resolutely not-for-profit, mankind is the only beneficiary of our work, not corporate shareholders or private equity firms." Until today Ecolint is considered one of the best international schools in the world. It was and is a bilingual school, with instruction primarily in French and English.[50] It was there that Edward acquired his fluency in French. He must have learned German fluently from his parents and their German-speaking servants and maybe additionally from German language courses in his NYC high school. The teacher and archivist of Ecolint described Edward's performance there in the following words:

> Tenenbaum turns out to have been creatively active and successful . . . the contribution he submitted to the school's annual literary competition at the time won the first prize within the English language category, and was published in the annual magazine *Ecolint*. I think that it reveals both a developed socio-economic awareness and an ability to identify with the lives of others (as well as some narrative panache) that are unusual in a 16 year-old.[51]

The essay is short. Because it can be seen as revealing Edward Tenenbaum's cultural imprint and seems to presage some of the Tenenbaums' decisions later in life, e.g., to settle down in the countryside outside of Washington, DC on farmland, I reproduce it here:

Mackleborough, Pa., U.S.A.

Tuesday. Six-thirty-seven P.M. In a bit the sun would be down, and he could go back. He would have liked to work on a while. What would plowing be like if you didn't have to push your way through mucky layers of heat? Besides, when he got back, there would only be milking, stabbing the mare, and firewood to be cut awaiting him.

He didn't mind plowing. It was hard, a day-long strain on your guts. But you were way from the house with only the horse to remind you of the rest of the family. There was peace. You weren't bothered by yells to hurry or to drop this and run to that, finish that and return on the double to this.

Here he just kept going from one end of the field to the other. All he had to worry about was to follow the contours and keep an eye open for a few boulders. The horse stopped at the fence, you swung the plow around, pushed the dirt-streaked share into the earth, and began again.

Automobiles from New York, Florida, California, and all points west whizzed past on the state road. Sometimes one stopped at the pop stand, and he would run down to pull purple raspberry, or purple grape, yellow lemon or green lime, orange orange or strawberry strawberry, out of the cool water in the box. Then he would get a 'deng yoo' or a 'tha-inks' or a 'much oblaged' or sometimes something queer, like the Californian family who called out 'blessu'lord' in unison before driving off. Twice this summer tourists had bought one of his hand-whittled Souvenirs of Penna, but one had been obviously drunk.

They reminded him of the time two years ago when Pop took a week off and drove the family to New York to visit some cousins. Millions of windows ablaze in the sun, or gazing fixedly into the murk (like fishes' eyes seen through the scum of the west pond).

Millions of people hurling themselves about like flies over a manure pile at mid-day. So many and so much that they had been almost glad to find refuge in their cousin's flat.

A trailer skimmed up behind a new Chevy. It reminded him of movie he'd seen a couple of months ago. He wished, he wished he could flee away from work and chores, never ending, never altering for days, weeks, months, years, a lifetime. So off to a stately city, in a foreign country. See and be in a new, glamorous world of deeds and rewards.

Edward Tenenbaum

Américain, S.B., $16^{1/2}$ ans.[52]

In the course of my account of Edward Tenenbaum's real life story, I will present my interpretation of this teenage blueprint of actual decisions taken by him and his wife Jeanette during later life.[53]

Edward's nickname at Ecolint was "Charli," as is evidenced by the description of the following sketch of his head in the rediscovered scrap book of Ecolint for the class of 1938.

Milein Cosman's Jewish family had left home in Düsseldorf/ Germany shortly after the *Kristallnacht* in 1938, first for the Netherlands and shortly before the outbreak of World War II for England, where Milein had already moved to in June 1939 after finishing her school education 1937–1939 at Ecolint and L'École d'Humanité at Geneva.

FIGURE 3.2 Edward A. Tenenbaum 1938 at École Internationale de Genève (Ecolint)

FIGURE 3.3 Sketch of Edward A. Tenenbaum, nicknamed "Charlie" by later famous Ecolint classmate Milein Cosman 1938

Two months after graduation and departure from Ecolint in July 1938,[54] 16-year-old Edward started his BA studies at Yale, the third oldest university in America, founded in 1701 in New Haven, Connecticut. Yale remains one of the best Ivy League members today. There he was nicknamed *Charlie*.[55] A train ride from there to New York City took just one hour and a half. It is very probable that Edward spent quite some weekends in his home city, either to enjoy its rich cultural offers and otherwise entertaining facilities, to visit his family or to consult his father about the Nazis and their economic system in Germany and in countries occupied by them, such as his parents' homeland Poland.

But Yale was also a breeding ground for innovative entertainment. In late November 1939 the freshmen of the class of 1943 were asked to vote not only on the desirability of a Prom, but also on the orchestra they would prefer of those available nearby. Out of 531 votes cast, 507 voted for a Prom. On the preferred band each voter was asked to give five points for first place, three for second and one for third. On this basis Glenn Miller of Glen Island – about sixty miles southwest en route to New York City – came out first with 1,174 points. The other choices tracked far behind him: Jimmy Dorsey 313, Tommy Dorsey 246, Jan Savitt 140 and Artie Shaw 137.[56] In an interview in December 1940, in which Glenn Miller was already called "the number one band leader of the nation," he also stated: "College students set the music tastes for the nation. They are the first to spot the new tunes and new bands." He recalled playing "at several Yale house parties" over the last six or seven years.[57] When the Japanese attack on Pearl Harbor had happened and half of Yale' s campus was taken over by the US Army for military training, Glenn Miller like so many others was also inducted to the army. But ranked captain he and the members of his orchestra became the official Army Air Corps Band on Yale campus, where they often played. Many of their performances were transmitted over the radio nationwide. And they also were commissioned by the Air Corps to tour the country and form Air Corps bands in various large centers.[58] This was a stepping stone in big-band history and the breakthrough of swing music.

During freshman year Edward had roomed in Wright College.[59] The *Yale Daily News* reported on March 6, 1939 that he had been allocated to Yale's Davenport College unit.[60] Later he was assigned to Pierson College from where he graduated.

FIGURE 3.4 Pierson College on Yale campus. Tenenbaum and his best friend John A. Kneubuhl lived here for three years

FIGURE 3.5 Edward A. Tenenbaum and his best friend at Yale John A. Kneubuhl at graduation time 1942

In his Stuyvesant High School in New York City Edward had made it into the top 20 percent. At Yale the ranking was much more differentiated. He belonged to the top students of the college from the beginning. On October 6, 1939, The *Boston Globe-NYHerald Tribune* published an article entitled "Yale Awards 13 Prizes for High Freshman Marks." Edward A. Tenenbaum won two of them. In a group of ten freshmen he received "Charms to the Highest General Average of 89.4 and above." And among the three prizes for "Highest Stand" he won the second endowed with $75, while the first one of $125 went to his classmate Sidney Rosen.[61] Yale yearbook class of 1942 lists the following prizes and scholarships: in freshman year the Andrew D. White Prize and a New York Yale Club Prize and Charm, in junior and senior years the William R. Godfrey Scholarship.[62] In senior year he was also awarded the Warren Memorial High Scholarship Prize for the highest rank in scholarship.[63] He was one of the ten juniors who were elected to the Yale chapter of Phi Beta Kappa, Yale's oldest and most honored society, on November 13, 1940.[64] This was a special honor, because the selection of most new members took place when they were seniors. Membership was reserved for about 10 percent of the class of 1942, amounting to forty-five students. Only ten of them had been selected already in their junior year as a special distinction of their scholarly achievements.[65]

The other side of the coin was Tenenbaum's lack of interest in extracurricular activities in physical sports, as seen already during his education in Stuyvesant High School in NYC. I could spot only two voluntary activities, in which Tenenbaum needed a modest amount of physical movement. 1.) Yale Daily News of February 17, 1940 listed Tenenbaum as one of six participants in an Outing Club event, to spend the weekend in Pittsfield MA, a skiing resort.[66] If he did ski there, it might have been due to learning it in Switzerland, while he had been attending *Ecolint*. 2.) Immediately after the Japanese surprise attack on Pearl Harbor on December 7, 1941, Tenenbaum and fifteen other juniors and seniors spontaneously followed a call by Richard S. Jackson (Yale 1934), a member of the Connecticut Committee for Civilian Defense, and volunteered for defense work on December 9,

1941 in case of an air raid. Yale Daily News printed their names in a call on others to follow suit.[67] For Pierson College we know that by the end of the academic year 1941–1942 205 of the 209 student members had likewise volunteered as air raid wardens, while the remaining four students would sit in and take care of the air raid shelters. In February 1942 Pierson's first black-out drill assembled everyone in the cellar playing bridge by candlelight.[68] The fear of a Japanese surprise bombing raid even on the East Coast of the USA was so intense that the following notice was part of the printed program of the commencement exercises of June 9, 1942: "INSTRUCTIONS IN CASE OF AIR RAID [:] When alarm sounds remain seated. Be calm. Lights in the hall will be dimmed but not turned out."[69]

Yale Yearbook Class of 1942 has more to report on Tenenbaum's activities in intellectual sports: "He belongs to the Political Union and ... was an editor of the *Freshman Weekly* and in junior and senior years served on the Kohut Forum board."[70]

The Yale Political Union (PU) had been founded in 1934 during the academic year 1933/34, about a year after secular changes in political power had occurred in the USA as well as in Germany. Hitler had assumed the chancellorship in Germany on January 30, 1933 shifting the country's power center to the far right and Franklin D. Roosevelt with his New Deal policies had been inaugurated to the US presidency on March 4, 1933 shifting the leadership of the country to the left. PU was organized as a model parliament discussing and voting on controversial resolutions of current importance in US policies and sometimes in university policies. This model parliament was first limited to about 300 members divided into three political parties, Labor, Liberal, and Conservative.

> Each has a floor leader and a whip who 'gets out the vote' at the crucial moment. The Labor Party, sitting on the left, represents the point of view of the working man and the extreme "New Dealers." The Liberals maintain the balance of power, swinging sometimes with the Conservatives, but more often with the Laborites. The

> Conservative policy is to stand pat on the principles of
> Republicanism. Of course, no one is obliged to vote as his party
> leader tells him and anyone is free to stray from the straight and
> narrow path of partisanship.[71]

It is further reported that election of members in a competitive process is left exclusively to the discretion of the party leaders and the
President of the Union. The fee for membership was $5 for nonbursary
students and $3 for bursary students. Freshmen could not apply.
Applicants would first have to decide which party they wished to join
and then would be obliged to visit their party leader personally. The
leaders in September 1939 when Tenenbaum applied were: for the
Conservatives E. A. Ballard , for the Liberals McGeorge Bundy, who
would later become John F. Kennedy's and Lyndon B. Johnson's
National Security Adviser, and for Labor S. L. Cox, all class of 1940.

When PU did not listen to and discuss a lecture by an invited
prominent guest speaker, like Senator Robert A. Taft (Yale 1910),
meetings would be opened by the presentation of a resolution on a
controversial subject. Then a representative of each party would be
given ten minutes to speak for or against it before the floor was opened
for debate. The sessions concluded with a vote. Parliamentary rules of
order similar to those in the US Senate were observed.[72]

Tenenbaum was selected from the pool of 108 applicants
together with fifty-five other new PU members. The unsuccessful
applicants would be put on a waiting list from which they had a
chance to be selected during the course of the year to fill vacancies.
Twenty-one were assigned to the Liberals, twenty to the
Conservatives, and fifteen to the Laborites. They were allowed to join
their respective parties already in the first PU meeting on October 11,
1939 to debate the most-up-to-date proposition: "Resolved, That this
house favors the exportation of munitions of war on a cash and carry
basis to belligerents." [73] The meeting was on for two hours. The
following day Yale Daily News covered in detail the arguments
exchanged and the outcome of the vote during this first PU session

of the new academic year under the headline: "Resolution for Cash and Carry Plan Defeated in Political Union, 52–34."[74] Essentially it was a debate on how the USA could best keep out of war. "Despite their raging harangues, opposing speakers reflected the sentiment of the country by agreeing on one point – that the advancement of peace was the primary concern of any legislation."[75] In his closing remarks for the position of the Liberals McGeorge Bundy expressed himself in support of the resolution, while E.A. Ballard for the Conservatives attacked it sharply and won the vote.

Tenenbaum was reportedly outspoken at a meeting of the New Haven chapter of the American Student Union (ASU) in the PU House on January 25, 1940. "I am glad the American Student Union has been called 'red,' seditious, and Moscow-controlled by the big-business press," said Ms. Toni Grose, a graduate student of Smith College[76] 1938 and New England district secretary of ASU,[77] in defense of resolutions that the national meeting of ASU had unanimously passed.

> At this meeting the delegates refused to pass an amendment censuring Russia, though condemning the English, French, Germans and Japanese for fighting "imperialist wars." ... Attacks on Russia and communism by Snowden Herrick, 1940, Spencer Coxe, 1940, and Edward Tenenbaum, 1942, were followed by equally strong replies from other members. ... Resolutions were passed, however, condemning the proposed loan to Finland, the three-billion-dollars war budget, and favoring the anti-lynching bill.[78]

After Germany's occupation of Denmark and Norway and the invasion of the Netherlands, Belgium, and France ending in victory in the first half of 1940, the sentiment among the American public, Yale undergraduates in general and members of PU in particular changed. The isolationist position was weakened and the interventionist–isolationist issue moved to center stage and resulted in "stormy sessions." For the first time PU membership passed the 400 mark during Tenenbaum's senior year. The balance of voting tipped in favor of the interventionist cause, not along but strongly cutting across party lines. And the eloquent debates found a wide audience as they were broadcasted by Yale's radio station WOCD.[79]

However, opinions voiced on Yale and other Ivy League campuses on the interventionist–isolationist issue differed quite a bit from the sentiment of American society as a whole. One study dug into attitudes and actions at Ivy League universities and their Seven Sisters (i.e., elite universities for women only, until 1938). It found that their presidents, administrators, student leaders, and alumni were "indifferent to Nazi Germany's terrorist campaign against the Jews and assisted the Nazis to gain acceptance in the West."[80] In her "impressively researched and nuanced book" Michaela Hoenicke Moore is drawing a broader picture by focusing "on the interactions and debates among American government officials, public intellectuals, journalists, pollsters, German émigrés, and other American experts on Nazi Germany before and during World War II."[81] Hoenicke Moore questions the seemingly monolithic American view that previous historians have constructed of Germans, namely that they were good people trapped by bad government. In her prologue on "Thomas Wolfe and the Third Reich" she displays how much Wolfe, as evidenced in his correspondence and in two of his posthumously published novels[82] contributed to that image. She also finds that the pogrom against German citizens of Jewish race on November 9, 1938 caused abhorrence among Americans and that this was not directed at the German people, but at their Nazi government.[83] Before then there was a widespread "reluctance to identify Germany as a threat."[84] And as to attitudes in academia during the 1930s she notes: "American academics were well informed about conditions in Nazi Germany but tried to maintain ties in the spirit of 'academic internationalism.'"[85] By classifying Americans into discursive groups she discovers much more complexity for the 1930s.[86] She concludes that by mid-war "Germany's self-chosen special path had ended in disaster for itself and others and that the German people could not be exculpated by collectively being declared victims of their regime."[87]

The Kohut Forum, of which Tenenbaum was a board member during his Junior and Senior years at Yale, was a completely different institution. It was initiated by Jewish students at Yale and founded in January 1936.[88] "This was contrary to the basic policy of the counsellorship which was against an isolation of the Jews from the rest of the students. Nevertheless Jewish student interest was sufficient to pursue the idea."[89]

As to its precursors, during the 1880s Yale had about five Jewish students in each year's class of about 600. Especially after Arthur Twining Hadley had been appointed as the first lay president of Yale in 1899, more and more local students from the Jewish quarter in New Haven were admitted to the traditionally Christian Yale University. When their percentage had reached the 10 percent quota limit set by the Yale administration, the Jewish students felt the need for a formal Jewish organization on campus. A first attempt was made in 1909 with the founding of a Hebraic Club. But it didn't last, just like four other Jewish organizations that were founded afterward.[90]

The Kohut Forum derived its name from holding its first meetings in Yale Library's Alexander Kohut Memorial Collection section, then housed in Lawrence Hall.[91] It had been established following the first donation of Judaica to Yale by George Alexander Kohut in 1915. It consisted of the very large Judaica collection of his father Rabbi Alexander Jacob Kohut (1842–1894). The son also created the *Kohut Endowment* in order to maintain and improve the Kohut Memorial Collection.

In 1936 the Kohut Forum replaced the Jewish Club that had existed on Yale campus since 1934.[92] Its purpose was to establish status and credibility to Jews on campus "to show that Jews weren't all beasts," by this formal organization. [93] Officially organized bad treatment of Jews in Germany played an important role. Like in other Ivy League colleges there was subtle discrimination not only against Jews, but also against other minorities like the Twentieth-Century Yale Catholics and "Protestant religionists" at Yale.[94] All the while Ivy League colleges officially and the large majority of their student bodies turned a blind eye to political developments in Germany.

Instead they were eager to maintain academic exchange and relations with German academic institutions as usual.

The minority organizations on Yale campus supported each other. The Protestant Young Men's Christian Association (YMCA) opened its Dwight Hall campus building for events of the Kohut Forum soon after its foundation.[95] It was the Common Room of Dwight Hall where the Kohut Forum met, mainly for lectures of invited speakers, but also for panel discussions.[96] The student Kohut Forum had a leading board and officers, but no membership rolls or dues.[97] The board consisted of fourteen members that elected new members each year to replace those lost due to graduation.[98]

Among the invited speakers during Tenenbaum's years at Yale was the noted Zionist leader Dr. Louis I. Newman of Temple Rodeph Sholem in New York City. He argued that a Renaissance in Jewish learning and religion was underway in the USA. A new unity among Jews had developed which was laying the basis for a renewed and deepening interest in Judaism. He "contradicted the popular notion that the Jews are dependent on persecution for their survival. Rather the positive, spiritual message of Judaism is the true source of its eternity. . . . [He] urged the entry of more Jews into Palestine . . . He concluded by urging the Jewish college students to prepare for leadership in later life by combining with their regular work a knowledge of Jewish history."[99]

On October 25, 1939, there was another prominent speaker, Professor James Grafton Rogers (Yale 1905), Master of Timothy Dwight College. He conveyed his impressions from a trip to Germany in the summer of 1939, evidently before Germany's attack on Poland. His purpose had been to learn about the viewpoint of the 'man-in the street' on various controversial subjects, in particular the Jewish situation. Half of the Jews had emigrated. For the other half "'Constant small raids' on groups of Hebrews tend to make them 'keep their heads down,' was the way a German expressed the situation to Professor Rogers in a casual conversation."[100] Rogers also reported of the "mystical quality which the average German associates with Hitler, of the warmth felt for the large, smiling Goering, and of the dislike held for Goebbels. He found that none of the Germans with whom he spoke thought there would be a war. They all felt that Great Britain would back down at the last minute."[101]

As further example of invited guests speaking on topics related to Jewish questions I refer to a lecture by Dr. Harold Korn of New York City, "Jews in American History" on February 29, 1940[102] and by John Tepfer, visiting professor from the New York Institute of Religion, "Is there a Racial Mind and Character?" on January 28, 1942.[103]

I spotted only one lecture of the Kohut Forum that covered a non-Jewish topic of general political interest. On October 23, 1940 Associate Professor Harry Rudin spoke on The Decline and Fall of Internationalism. "My feeling is that Internationalism was killed by the first World War."[104] He attributed the then existing world state to excessive nationalism caused by the collapse of free trade. He argued that the trade embargo against Germany during World War I induced all countries thereafter to strive for economic self-sufficiency by erecting tariff barriers. Conflict between wealthy nations and countries that had been discriminated against had inevitably resulted in a renewal of conflict. Rudin presented the formation of a federation of countries as his only hope for creating a lasting peace. This would depend on a reduction of economically caused national rivalries. If intelligent policy could not form such a union, "'brutality and fanaticism' would; and if it were formed through German victory, the transition period would be 'terrible.'"[105]

Like its precursors the Kohut Forum didn't last either. In July 1941 the B'nai B'rith Hillel Foundation at Yale was established for Jewish students. It was the 56th unit in the national Hillel organization. "As far as the students were concerned, the only real change was in the name" from Kohut Forum to Hillel Foundation.[106] The Kohut Forum dissolved itself. Yale Hillel, in contrast, has been present on campus until today.

In 1936 Yale students founded not only the Kohut Forum, but also – two years later than other universities around the nation – the Peace Council (PC). It protested against militarism and war, like the Japanese occupation of Manchuria in 1931 and of large parts of northeastern China 1937, the Italian war against and occupation of Ethiopia 1935 to 1941, the Civil War in Spain 1936 to 1939, and aggressive postures by Germany leading to conquests of neighboring countries such as Austria and Czechoslovakia. PC organized Annual National Peace Strikes, always in April. Students and even faculty would leave their classes at 11 a.m. for one hour[107] rallying for anti-war demonstrations. The first nationwide Peace Strike had taken place on April 13, 1934.[108] Only about 5,000 students participated. A year later the number had jumped to 25,000. In 1936 already half a million marched out of their classes and rallied for peace. In April 1937 more than a million participants were expected. A national US Student Peace Committee had been formed in 1937 all the while supporting organizations were spreading both in scope and in number.[109]

The belated start of the peace movement at Yale might have signaled the same lack of enthusiasm there as the relatively low turnout in the first two local rallies for peace. In April 1936 more than 300 persons had gone on Peace Strike.[110] On Thursday, April 22, 1937, the turnout was down to only "more than 200 persons."[111] "The Big Three were half-hearted backers of the strike with five hundred at Harvard, three hundred at Princeton, and a scant two hundred at New Haven."[112] A poll taken with Yale undergraduates at Friday dinner, at the beginning of the Peace Week the previous week, displayed a turnout of 1,200 Yale undergraduates. Only 10 percent declared themselves die-hard isolationists, while 60 percent favored a policy of collective security.[113] The outcome is representative for the sentiment of these Yale students: "... the Peace Poll registered large majorities in favor of United States' present neutrality program as well as 'cooperation among nations for the prevention of war,' as opposed to isolation."[114] This was exactly the foreign policy line that Franklin D. Roosevelt's Secretary of State Cordell Hull had been pursuing with his Reciprocal Trade Agreements Act of 1934. His trade policy aimed and succeeded at building an alliance of countries opposing militarily aggressive countries in Europe, like fascist Germany and Italy, and in East Asia, in particular Japan.

Yale PC was initially composed of members of four campus organizations: the Kohut Forum, Graduate Forum , Dwight Hall, and the Yale chapter of the American Student Union. Until retiring President Spencer L. Coxe Jr. announced a basic restructuring of its organization in early 1940, students interested in the work of the council had elected its executive body. From 1940 on the governing board was formed by six official delegates of the following Yale extra-curricular activities: the Political Union. the Kohut Forum, Dwight Hall, News, the (Catholic) More Club, and the Yale chapter of the American Student Union.[115] Tenenbaum was neither the delegate of the Kohut Forum nor of the Political Union, the two student organizations in which he was active. But he was indirectly involved in PC. As a board member of the Kohut Forum he must have participated in selecting and guiding the Forum's delegate.

In his freshman year at Yale Tenenbaum encountered or participated in a Peace Strike on April 20, 1939 for the first time. In preparation of it, A. J. Muste gave a lecture at Yale's Divinity School on April 19, 1939. It is quite possible that Tenenbaum belonged to the audience of Muste, who came forward with a most unusual contention: "If we had stayed out of the last war, there might have been a United States of Europe, but as it was we lost four billions and thousands of lives."[116] In other words, Germany would have won the war and created a United Europe dominated by it. Consequently, he sketched and advocated a plan for keeping the USA out of another war. That Muste would have preferred a United States of Europe dominated by Germany to American participation in World War I, is a most remarkable opinion against his personal backdrop. He lectured at Yale as pastor of the New York Labor Temple and associate of the pacifistic Fellowship of Reconciliation, as such a Christian pacifist. But formerly he had been associated with the Communist Party and other radical movements.[117] Thus he embodied traits of communists, Socialists, and Christians, which is not unusual. But preferring German victory and the formation of a United Europe under authoritarian German rule to victory by the democratically legitimated

Allied countries is a very conservative position that doesn't match with his above-mentioned personal traits.

On graduation day, June 9, 1942, William Gardner White addressed the class and its faculty on "Class History" from its arrival at Yale in 1938 to the present. His speech was very witty and eloquent, full of anecdotes, sublime sense of humor, and erudition of the finest quality. Here is how he described the prevailing sentiment when the class students returned to Yale for their junior year in the fall of 1940 after the Fall of France on June 22, 1940:

> As it seemed plain to us that the world was not behaving itself properly and was in need of enlightened leadership, we lent our services to all manner of organizations which broke out like the strawberry rash all over the face of the campus. They ranged from the ASU (SSR) to the Council for Knick-nacks for the Nazis, or knitten mittens for the Britains, and Moose Chandler started the Lone Eagle off on his speaking tour, recently cancelled.[118]

"Moose" was the nickname of classmate Kent Chandler Jr. He served on the executive committee of Yale Political Union during Junior year. Throughout his four years at Yale he was also active in tough sports (hockey, crew squad, and football). He enlisted in the Marine Corps Reserve in June 1941.[119] Taking the US state of war as a point of departure John T. Pigott Jr. in a more serious tone delivered the Class Oration. In his farewell address he reminded his classmates that they were "the Greatest Class ever to leave New Haven. For a century or more the even succession of classes has brought with it … the prospect of an ordered and familiar civilization, containing no problems the educated man could not face with equanimity. … We, in contrast, emerge from our comparatively static life to view a world incomprehensible by the standards we have accepted. … The sophistries of civilization have fallen away …. To adapt ourselves to the altered world does not imply renunciation of any of the standards we have accepted. … 'To do justly and to love mercy' have ever been the criteria of our [American] society."[120] During and after World

War II Tenenbaum stood fast by these criteria. After having looked squarely into the face of brutality of Germans vis-à-vis all kinds of people in general and Jews in particular, he didn't deviate from calmness and equanimity. Instead he wrote a highly reputed analytical report on the inner hierarchical structure of the inmates of the Buchenwald concentration camp.[121] And his central role in introducing the Deutschmark via West Germany's currency reform of June 20, 1948 – against opposition by West German currency experts with a very low, but for West Germany's economic future extremely successful conversion rate[122] – is testimony of Tenenbaum's unwavering "love of mercy." Even in times of extreme temptation to fall prey to basic instinct like revenge Tenenbaum in Germany lived up to the high civilization standards his Yale education had instilled in him and in his classmates.

While for almost all other classmates the yearbook states with whom they had been sharing a room, Tenenbaum "roomed in Wright Freshman year and subsequently in Pierson."[123] In both cases no mate is listed. His daughter Joan described him as "extremely shy and studious."[124] But he had made a friend at Yale who also graduated class of 1942: John Alexander Kneubuhl. John was born in Pago Pago, the US-held eastern part of Samoa, on July 2, 1920. He had majored in English and like Tenenbaum also been a member of Pierson College.[125] "I think Johnny Kneubuhl was a friend of my father's because they kept in touch, at least distantly."[126] He "went on to write Grade B horror movies. One was called The Screaming Skull [released 1958 in black and white[127]] and there was a character in it who was a creepy misfit ... allegedly patterned after my Dad in college."[128] "It was something of a joke in our family. ... I remember one night we watched it on TV and laughed our heads off when we saw this character."[129]

Kneubuhl is a German name. In both parts of Samoa, the eastern US territory and the independent mini-state of Samoa west of it, German family names are very numerous, because German male settlers had married Samoan native wives. This was the result of German efforts to colonize the Samoan islands in the South Pacific. Since 1855 Hamburg merchants explored these islands and established branches of their German firms there. But the USA and UK rivaled with the Germans for commercial settlements there. It escalated into gunboat diplomacy in the 1870s and again in 1988/89. Thanks to a cyclone rampaging from March 13–17, 1889, the German and American warships anchored in Samoan ports were destroyed. This prompted the Samoa conference and *Treaty of Berlin* of June 1889 between Germany, the UK and the USA. It was agreed that Samoa would be a formally independent kingdom under the protectorate of the *three powers*. After Samoa's first and only king Malietoa Laupepa had died in 1898, rivalries between the *three powers* again erupted over the successor question. A compromise was found in 1899 with the *Samoa Treaty*. It stipulated the division of the Samoan islands into a German and an American territory. The British were compensated by granting other Pacific islands to them.[130] The German Samoan colony was conquered by New Zealand three weeks after the outbreak of the World War I in 1914. The former German colony remained under New Zealand rule until Samoa was granted independence on January 1, 1962.[131]

Why do I present details on this issue? Intellectually Tenenbaum towered Kneubuhl by far. In freshman year Tenenbaum had won the Andrew D. White Prize and a New York Yale Club Prize and Charme. And in junior and senior years he held the William R. Godfrey Scholarship.[132] Kneubuhl had received no such distinctions at Yale. It seems to me that Tenenbaum's friendship with Kneubuhl had to do with the latter's non-WASP appearance, visible on his yearbook photo. During World War II racial prejudice was still rampant in US society. Blacks and Whites were separated even in the US Army. Antisemitism was also still an undercurrent of American society. Therefore, Kneubuhl and Tenenbaum might both have felt outcasts of mainstream American society despite their success at admission to the prestigious Yale education.

Edward A. Tenenbaum's Yale College Scholarship Record - Class of 1942

Freshman 1938–1939	Grades Feb.	Year	Sophomore 1939–1940	Grades Feb.	Year	Junior 1940–1941	Grades Feb.	Year	Senior 1941–1942	Grades Feb.	Year
English 11	85	90	Econ. 10	A+	A+	Econ. 21	A	A	Econ: 20	A	--
History 14	80	90	French 56	B	A	Econ. 105	A	A	Econ: 23	--	B
Zoology 10	92	95	Governm. 10	B	A	Econ. Dept.	A	A	Econ: GradC.	A	A
French 42	80	96	History 20	A	A	English VIII	A+	A+	Econ. Essay	--	A+
Mil. Sci. 10	96	96	History 35	A+	A+	History 36	A	A	Governm. 36	A	A
Classics 10	85	90	Mil. Sci. 20	A	A						

FIGURE 3.6 Yale College – From scholarship record card of Edward A. Tenenbaum

But there might be a simpler explanation for their enduring friendship. Theodor Ernst Mommsen was instructor in history at Pierson. He was the "guiding genius" of a regular German table there. Both being second-generation migrants with their parent's roots (in German-speaking Austria and Germany respectively) they had inherited German-speaking abilities. In all probability both participated in Mommsen's German table. For John A. Kneubuhl we know this for sure due to the following report on Pierson College in Yale 1942 yearbook. During Christmas vacation Mommsen's familiar Dachshund Waldi I was run over by a car. "Slaves [nickname for all members of Pierson College] are no longer treated to the common sight of Mr Mommsen strolling with his pet. . . . Howie Holtzmann and Johnny Kneubuhl . . . are the prime movers of the plan among the residents of Slave Quarters to give Mr. Mommsen, their Master, a new and lively *Waldi*. Consequently as a testimony of esteem and affection, he is presented with *Waldi II*."[133]

Other Yale professors were also revered by class-1942 students. On Class Day as part of graduation ceremonies, William G. White mentioned in his *Class History* address Nicholas J. Spykman, Mr. Gabriel, and Mr. Haggard as intellectually especially stimulating. He reported further that his adviser in junior year took him aside one day and said: "Son, if you have a spark of genius, water it."[134]

On June 9, 1942 Edward A. Tenenbaum, at the age of twenty, graduated from Yale College. The title of his BA thesis was "National Socialism vs. International Capitalism." Yale's Committee on Undergraduate Prize Essays chose Tenenbaum's thesis as the best of his class of 1942. According to the tradition established in 1940 the prize consisted of immediate publication of the thesis as a book with Yale University Press and its joint publishing houses in England, namely Humphrey Milford in London and Oxford University Press, all in 1942. The dice had been cast on April 26, 1942, because the following day *Yale Daily News* reported that a day earlier the three winners of the Charles Heber Dickerman Memorial Prize for senior essays in economics had been announced. "This year the prize was divided into three separate prizes of $35 each. Tenenbaum won the grant for Yale College seniors who elected the four-course plan in junior year."[135] On February 18, 1942 Edward's name had already appeared on the Dean's Honor List of Upperclassmen.[136]

In his introduction Edward presents his study's content in a nutshell: "It concerns itself with the revolutionary negation of the tenets of free enterprise by Germany after 1933, largely as a result of her experiences with the system of free enterprise before 1933. This is the tale of the circumstances within international capitalism which made of Germany an unparalleled challenge to its very existence. It has as its subject matter stupidity, lack of foresight, selfishness, blind jealousies, and megalomania. It is, indeed, as unpleasant as our time."[137] This rings a bell of the dangers that the recent spreading of anti-globalism and our-nation-first policies pose for the international division of labor. Demanded and backed by populist movements in highly developed countries, the recent rollback on the long post–World War II process of progressive integration of the world economy with unprecedented advances in economic productivity, growth, and welfare inadvertently puts at risk living and income standards we have proudly attained all over the world. Think only of the breathtaking advances in China since the 1980s to gauge what integration into the world economy can do for a country. A much earlier example is the spectacular *economic miracle* of West Germany following Edward Tenenbaum's currency reform of 1948 in tandem with Ludwig Erhard's – but in fact General Lucius Clay's and his American military government's[138] – audacious quick return from public price controls and rationing to liberalized market conditions.

The study deals extensively with the National Socialist economic system, focusing mainly on its bilateral foreign trade in its theoretical design and in practice. Of the 127 pages of the book the first 112 are devoted to the study of conditions in Germany. On the remaining pages the author concludes with a discussion of the challenge that such a system poses to international capitalism.

Apart from professional brochures that he would later release through his financial consulting firm Continental-Allied Company

Ltd., which he founded in 1954 in Washington, DC, his Yale University Press book remained the only book he published until his early death in 1975. How deeply grateful and attached to his parents Edward still seemed to have been at age twenty, when his undergraduate prize essay was published, might be evidenced by the book's dedication: "To my mother and father, without whom I would never have written this." When I asked his daughter Joan during my interview with her on October 29, 2018, whom Edward was more attached to, his mother or his father, she interpreted this dedication as an example of his humor. His mother had been hospitalized for mental disorders for quite some time during the 1930s. To put the two of them on an even keel, she said, the meaning behind Edward's dedication simply was: "If my mother and father would not have procreated me, I could never have written this." It is nevertheless quite interesting that the presentation of Edward's book in "The Yale Bookshelf" of the Yale Alumni Magazine of February 1943 reveals that the publication "was made possible by a generous gift of an anonymous donor."[139] The donor might well have been his father Joseph.

As to the reception of Tenenbaum's study in the academic community I quote from a book review in the *American Political Science Review:* The book

> records the negation of free enterprise by Germany after 1933, and the resulting challenge to international capitalism. To explain how Germany enmeshed much of the world in an economic prison, which developed generally into military as well as economic exploitation, the Nazi methods of economic warfare are surveyed. Tenenbaum concludes therefrom that dissolution of international capitalism can be prevented by economic concordance among nations for control of the business cycle, with automatic regulation inherent in international trade; that without such agreement, some one nation will dominate by political means. His premise that full economic freedom existed under international capitalism, and that cooperation can be achieved by solely economic means, is ingenuous, and non-recognition of politico-economic concentaneity based on a system

other than capitalism or fascism stems from circumscribed classical thinking. However, his analysis of the German weapons of economic warfare is well delineated and presents some hitherto unpublished information to which the author had access through the confidential files of the Joint Boycott Council. This factual survey is a well-organized addition to the literature about the Nazi economy.[140]

As mentioned above Edward's father Joseph L. Tenenbaum was chairman of the Joint Boycott Council of the American Jewish Congress and the Jewish Labor Committee during World War II. Beyond letting the son use the confidential files of that council for his BA thesis, one might safely assume that Joseph Tenenbaum played the role of an unofficial adviser of his son's most successful study.

Did Edward like it at Yale? When I interviewed his son Mark on November 10, 2018, he told me: "He didn't really like the people at Yale. He had a couple of friends [among them Kneubuhl, whom Mark explicitly mentioned]. But other than that he didn't like it. He told me that."

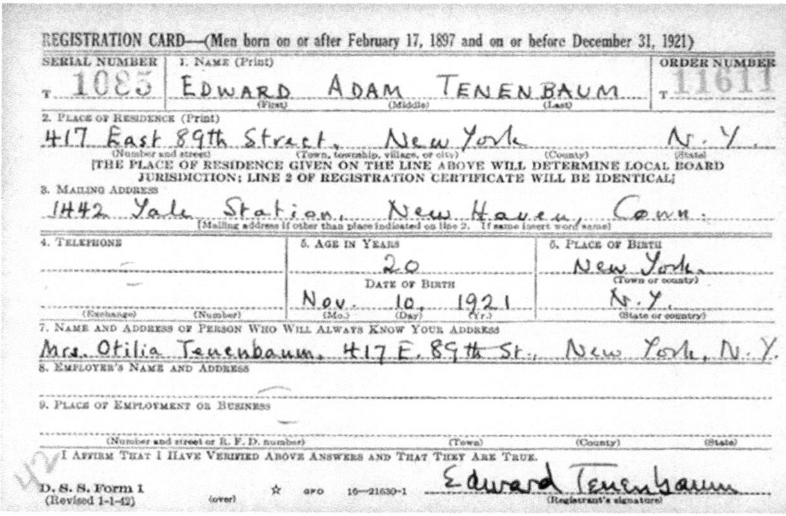

FIGURE 3.7 Edward A. Tenenbaum's draft registration card and report of February 16, 1942

REGISTRAR'S REPORT

DESCRIPTION OF REGISTRANT

RACE		HEIGHT (Approx.)	WEIGHT (Approx.)	COMPLEXION	
White	✓	6' 0"	175	Sallow	
		EYES	HAIR	Light	✓
Negro		Blue	Blonde	Ruddy	
		Gray	Red	Dark	
Oriental		Hazel	Brown ✓	Freckled	
		Brown ✓	Black	Light brown	
Indian		Black	Gray	Dark brown	
			Bald	Black	
Filipino					

Other obvious physical characteristics that will aid in identification_____

_____

_____

I certify that my answers are true; that the person registered has read or has had read to him his own answers; that I have witnessed his signature or mark and that all of his answers of which I have knowledge are true, except as follows:

_____

_____

James G. Leyburn
(Signature of registrar)

Registrar for Local Board____ *8 A Pierson Coll.* ____ *Yale* ____ *New Haven, Conn.*
 (Number)   (City or county)   (State)

Date of registration ____ *Feb. 16, 1942* ____

LOCAL BOARD . . 42
1058 . . . . nue
New York, N. Y.

(STAMP OF LOCAL BOARD)

(The stamp of the Local Board having jurisdiction of the registrant shall be placed in the above space)

16—21630–1

FIGURE 3.7 *(cont.)*

Not only Yale, but also Uncle Sam had confronted Edward with consequences of the American involvement in World War II after the Japanese surprise attack on Pearl Harbor and Hitler's declaration of war against the USA a few days later in December 1941. In preparation of his call to arms, Local Board No. 42 of the Selective Service System, located 1632 York Avenue, New York NY, registered him for the draft on February 16, 1942. Tenenbaum lists his mother's address (417 East 89th Street in New York City) as his own place of residence. His mailing address, however, is noted as 1442 Yale Station, New Haven, Conn. But his temporary residence in Pierson College at Yale is also registered. It is perhaps revealing for Edward's relative attachment to his divorced parents that he names Mrs. Otilia Tenenbaum as the person who will always know his address. Some physical characteristics of Edward Tenenbaum for identification purposes are also listed on the Registrar's Report: approximate height: six feet zero inches; approximate weight: 175 pounds; eyes: brown; hair: brown; complexion: light.[141] In the next chapter we will be able to compare some of this with Edward's features in a thorough medical examination in September 1943.

3.2   IN OSS AND MILITARY SERVICE 1942–1946

As this chapter is long, due to the extremely exciting events surrounding Tenenbaum during the war period, I have divided this section into four parts, covering the United States, Western Europe, wartime Germany, and postwar Germany.

3.2.1   In the United States

By the time of Tenenbaum's graduation at Yale on June 9, 1942, the United States had been at war with Germany and Japan for half a year. The class of 1942 was the last one to run the full program of a four-year college education with two-term years. The class of 1943 after a three-term year in 1942 already graduated just half a year later in 1942. Yale History Timeline records for 1942: "July 1, 1942 Year-round program for undergraduates began. ... 1942 Yale campus converted into wartime training school."[142]

At war with both Japan and Germany as well as their Allies, the USA was in great need of military personnel. Uncle Sam was looking not only for the ordinary GI, but also for exceptionally smart people for special intelligence war assignments.[143] And where could he better recruit and train the best and the brightest than on an Ivy League college campus. In the second half of 1942 the US Army had taken over about half of Yale campus' premises to establish an Officer Candidate School (OCS) there. Other specialized training for the armed forces was started in July 1943, such as engineering, medical training, area and language studies, a Military Intelligence School, and a Civil Affairs Specialist Training School.[144] When, in 1945, the armed forces study programs on Yale campus were terminated, 14,000 Air Corps cadets, 3,650 officers and enlisted men in other Army schools, and 4,000 members of Navy units had received training at Yale. The three-term year in the undergraduate schools during the war was finally restored to the traditional two terms per year in September 1946.[145]

FIGURE 3.8 Military training on Yale campus 1942–1943

As we will see in more detail below, Tenenbaum was assigned to OCS at Yale in December 1943. He had been drafted and inducted to the US Army Air Forces on December 14, 1942. With his service number 11611, he had initially been assigned to basic military training until February 1943 at Air Base in Sioux Falls, South Dakota. Afterward at the same place, he received shortwave radio training in Army Radio Operator-Mechanical Training School there until June 1943. From July to December 1943 he served as an instructor, also for the Morse Code, at Seymour Johnson Air Force Base in Goldsboro, North Carolina, and at the US Army Air Forces training center on Yale campus. From December 1943 to April 1944 he was assigned to New Haven's "Army Air Force Officer Training School, Communications Officer; maintenance and operations of Air Force Communication:"[146]

Between his graduation at Yale on June 9, 1942 and his induction to the army in mid-December 1942 Tenenbaum was employed as a civilian by the OSS in its Research & Analysis (R&A) branch in Washington, DC. He listed 1905 Biltmore Street NW in Washington, DC as his residence for this period on his application form for reemployment by the US government, specifically by the Mutual Security Agency (MSA), filled out in late 1951 or early 1952.[147] While serving in the US Army Air Forces (AAF)[148] throughout the war, he remained on the OSS membership roster, mainly with special assignments in R&A on financial matters and in psychological warfare. In Europe Tenenbaum would be serving in the OSS R&A branch in London as a research analyst from mid-July to mid-November 1944 and thereafter in addition to his OSS activities as an intelligence officer with the Psychological Warfare Division (PWD) of 12th US Army Group on the European continent in France, Belgium and Germany from mid-November 1944 to July 1945.[149] In the final months of the war in 1945 he was attached to the Fourth Armored Division of General George S. Patton's Third US Army. I will report on the roles he played there further below.

Who initiated *America's First Intelligence Agency*,[150] how did it develop, what did its organizational structure look like, what were its goals and assignments, and what did it accomplish? I will treat these questions before I come back to Tenenbaum's specific role and personal development during his serving for OSS and the US AAF.

Like so often in political and military history – as in techno-logical, economic, and social developments – innovative break-throughs result from both the emergence and recognition of a new problem and the initiative of a person with a plan to cope with the problem and at the same time with enough personal clout to win the consent of decision-makers in order to implement his idea. The new problem was the Fall of France in June 1940. The person initiating an innovative countermeasure with clout in the White House to have it implemented was William J. Donovan.

Germany had started its invasion of France and the Low Countries on May 10, 1940. In early June 1940 Germany had overrun the four neighboring countries on its Western border, namely the Netherlands, Belgium, Luxembourg, and France. This was Germany's third Blitzkrieg after the conquest of Poland in September 1939 and the occupation of Denmark and Norway starting in early April 1940. In the summer of 1940 Germany had become a much enlarged European Power that could threaten vital American interests from the European Atlantic coast.

The quick capitulation of France only six weeks after the start on May 10, 1940 of the German invasion took the US government by surprise. It is true that it had begun to increase its military expend-itures already shortly before the outbreak of World War II. As a reaction to the Fall of France the pace of military spending was speeded up and the US government reintroduced the draft by the *Selective Training and Service Act* of September 16, 1940. But US foreign policy still acted more or less blindfolded, as America was the only major power that had never used a secret intelligence service, neither in peace- nor in wartime.[151] After the Fall of France it was William J. Donovan who managed to gradually draw the attention of the US government, especially of President Franklin D. Roosevelt, to this missing instrument of modern foreign policy and to the essential part that secret intelligence could play in modern warfare.

Donovan had been born on January 1, 1883 in Buffalo NY into a relatively poor Catholic family of Irish descent. He studied in college at Niagara University, transferred from there to Columbia University for the fourth year, graduating BA in 1905. He continued with law school there. One of his classmates was Franklin D. Roosevelt. But due to their opposite social backgrounds they did not take much notice of each other. Because Donovan had combined his final college year with prelaw studies, he graduated from law school in 1907.[152] He went back to Buffalo, was undecided what to do with his education until he started practicing law in Buffalo in 1909.[153]

In 1916 he served as an elected captain of a newly formed cavalry group of the New York National Guard, called to federal service for patrol duty along the Mexican border in southern Texas during the Pancho Villa raids. Due to his strenuous drills and forced marches his men nicknamed him "Wild Bill."[154] On the battlefield in France with the US Army's 165th Infantry Regiment (still called the New York 69th from Civil War–times) since November 1917 he kept up his training methods and his nickname just the same.[155] Donovan returned from US military service in Europe on April 21, 1919 with the rank of a colonel. He was the only officer decorated with the three highest awards of the US Army in World War One: the Distinguished Service Cross, the Oak Leaf Cluster for that Cross, and the Congressional Medal of Honor.[156] He was appointed US district attorney for western New York in 1922 and prosecuted especially bootleggers, all the while still being a partner of his law firm in Buffalo. In 1924 he was promoted to Assistant Attorney General in charge of the Justice Department's Criminal Division, a position he resigned from in 1929 because Herbert Hoover, whom Donovan had vigorously supported during his presidential election campaign, did not ask him to become a member of his cabinet as Attorney General or as Secretary of War.[157] Having severed connections with his Buffalo law firm he set up a law firm of his own in New York City. His business on Wall Street developed into the prestigious partnership Donovan, Leisure, Newton, and Irvine during the 1930s. All the while Donovan maintained his political connections both within the USA and abroad.

His successful corporation law firm enabled Donovan to travel in Europe and East Asia, collecting first-hand information useful for his partnership and for interested parts of US military forces and the US government. He also assessed strength and weaknesses of countries, including those under totalitarian rule (Italy, Germany, Soviet Union). He predicted that another Great War was in the offing. Donovan first came to the attention of Franklin D. Roosevelt when in 1932 he ran as Republican candidate in the election campaign for governor in the State of New York, the position that Roosevelt had held before. But Donavan lost the election to his Democratic opponent Herbert Henry Lehman by a wide margin.

The Warner Bros. film *The Fighting 69th*, released on January 26, 1940, about the actual heroic World War I fighting in France of the 1st battalion, 165th Regiment of the 42nd Division – in the tradition of the Civil War nicknamed the New York City's 69th Infantry Regiment – under the command of Major Donovan boosted his popularity. Donovan's friend Frank Knox, Secretary of the Navy since June 1940, made President Roosevelt aware of Donovan's outstanding career as a military officer in combat on French soil and of his nationally useful information gathering around the world during the 1930s. Roosevelt, himself thereby participating in Donovan's acquired popularity from the movie, gave him a number of increasingly important assignments.

After the Fall of France, Donovan traveled from mid-July to August 3, 1940 as an informal diplomat to the United Kingdom (UK). He had been urged by Knox and Roosevelt to gauge Britain's ability to withstand the German air force's bombardment, the German submarine fleet's significant inroads into Britain's supply lines from overseas, and especially a German invasion.[158] Acting US ambassador to the UK, Joseph P. Kennedy, the father of John F., Robert and Edward Kennedy, had favored appeasement toward Germany, because he expected the Allies to be beaten.[159] Donovan, after personal consultations with like-minded Winston Churchill, was given open access to classified British secret service material. His analysis was that the UK stood a good chance to withstand German aggression, if the USA would fully support and supply them with needed military equipment.[160]

Donovan was most welcome and in private exchanges taken into complete confidence by Churchill about Britain's war strategy when he undertook his second mission to London and afterward to many other capitals in Europe and the Middle East from mid-December 1940 to March 18, 1941. From Churchill's viewpoint this mission's purpose was to bring the USA to join the UK in the war in Europe and to craft a US secret service modeled after the long-established and experienced British one.[161] Upon his return Donovan started to work on the establishment of a central US secret service. He was still a conservative corporation lawyer without an official position in government. He initiated the founding of the position of Coordinator of Information (COI) to overcome the fragmentation of eight different secret services in military and government institutions[162] with his *Memorandum of Establishment of Service of Strategic Information* of June 10, 1941, "Prepared for the President Roosevelt by Donovan."[163] During the preceding weeks Donovan had convinced President Roosevelt of the urgent need of collecting the knowledge of the existing different intelligence units, government departments, and directly collected intelligence to be then reported to the president as commander in chief. Roosevelt followed his advice.

By executive order of July 11, 1941 *Designating a Coordinator of Information* he created America's first intelligence agency and appointed William J. Donovan as COI reporting directly to the White House. He supplied Donovan with the power to recruit the necessary personnel "and make provisions for the necessary supplies, facilities, and services."[164] Harvard professor of diplomatic history William L. Langer and president of Williams College in

Massachusetts James Phinney Baxter III, along with other highly qualified World War I comrades, belonged to his first staff members. Baxter headed the Research & Analysis Branch of COI. It was appropriately located in the Library of Congress, as Donovan was convinced that most of the useful military and civilian information for fighting and occupying enemy countries could be gained from sifting already collected printed material like books, journals, magazines, and newspapers.[165] In addition, intercepted radio broadcasts provided a valuable free source of information on enemy countries.

In his autobiography Langer describes the difficulties Donovan and his cofounders of the Research & Analysis Branch of COI had to overcome when initially recruiting staff and finding customers for its intelligence reporting.[166] David K. E. Bruce was one of the early recruits and started work as head of the newly created Secret Intelligence (SI) of COI on October 10, 1941. Bruce had married Ailsa Mellon in 1926, the daughter of Treasury Secretary Andrew W. Mellon who contributed significantly to his career as a businessman. After the war in Europe had broken out and especially when after the Fall of France Britain's military situation seemed hopeless, Bruce, like Donovan, fought against widespread isolationism in the USA and pleaded for support of the British cause in the war with Hitler. He became a member of the war relief committee of the American Red Cross and embarked on an ocean liner in New York harbor on June 28, 1940 for an inspection tour to England until autumn. In London he witnessed the harassment by the German *Blitz*. "The spirit of the people is very high indeed. ... Personally, I believe that England is impregnable against a German invasion," he wrote to his mother Louise E. F. Bruce on July 29, 1940.

Donovan and Bruce had personally come close when during the summer of 1940 they both stayed in the house of a common friend. In early 1941 Bruce visited London again and gathered similar impressions of Britain's prospects. After his return he joined a new pressure group, the Fight for Freedom committee, to which Donovan belonged, too. Its purpose was to combat isolationist opinion in the USA and engage the USA in war on the side of Britain to defend Western civilization. Before this movement reached its goal, Hitler's declaration of war on America four days after the Japanese attack on Pearl Harbor brought about its windfall success. In the summer of 1943 Donovan sent Bruce to London to expand OSS's activities there. The latter would head OSS in European Theater of Operations USA (ETOUSA) at first from London, shortly after D-Day almost continually from the battlefield on the Continent.[167] After the war, he worked side by side with Jean Monnet on European integration via the Marshall Plan and became as ambassador in the most important positions one of the top American diplomats.

David Bruce's London OSS outpost was in sixty-eight Brook Street, catercornered from Claridge's, a block away from the location of the US embassy in London at Grosvenor Square.[168] He later described how much COI "was harassed and badgered by the jealousy of the Army, Navy, and State Departments. Temporarily they forgot their internecine animosities and joined in an attempt to strangle this unwanted newcomer at birth."[169] The Joint Chiefs of Staff were initially very skeptical of the value of COI, the "egghead" organization in Washington, DC, with personnel far remote from any battlefield experience. War Department generals scoffed at a "fly-by-night civilian outfit headed up by a wild man [Donovan] who was trying to horn in on the war."[170] Charles Lindbergh who crusaded the country to keep the USA out of the war in Europe, refused an invitation by Donovan to join COI accusing it to be "Full of politics, ballyhoo, and controversy."[171] When the Nazis got wind of the establishment of COI (25th and E Street NW in Washington, DC), they did likewise not take it seriously. Propaganda Minister Joseph Goebbels' Berlin radio mocked it as the home of "Fifty professors, ten goats, twelve guinea pigs, a sheep, and a staff of Jewish scribblers."[172]

COI's R&A diminished its problems with customers by launching the regular series *The War This Week*, succinctly gathering the latest information from around the world. It was in great demand among high officials of the government who were the only ones allowed to receive it. But the Joint Chiefs of Staff ordered its discontinuance on the grounds that important secret information was spread about town. Also other agencies in Washington questioned the usefulness of COI and demanded its abolition. But the Japanese attack on Pearl Harbor on December 7, 1941, followed by Hitler's declaration of war against the USA four days later, changed the situation completely.[173]

The Joint Chiefs of Staff learned to appreciate the essential role R&A played in preparing the landing and invasion of US forces in North Africa. After the German expeditionary North Africa Corps under the later legendary General Erwin Rommel had landed in Tripoli, Libya, in February 1941 to reinforce the battered Italian forces there, Churchill and Donovan were in agreement that North Africa was the soft front of the Axis powers. When the Joint Chiefs of Staff was formed as a result of Pearl Harbor and started strategic planning for military action against the Axis powers, it came to the same conclusion. But it lacked specialized knowledge of all kinds, such as language, geography, polity, economy, history, mentality, and culture.

Faced with conceding defeat and signing the Franco-German Armistice, French Prime Minister Paul Reynaud, who with his cabinet had left Paris for Bordeaux, resigned. He left the signing of the armistice to his vice premier, 84-year-old Marshal Henri Philippe Pétain, famed as a hero of World War One.[174] In the first half of July 1940 Pétain would become the new head of state on the basis of an authoritarian constitution approved by more than two-thirds of the legislators on July 10, 1940. They had already been assembled in Vichy, traditionally a spa with about 30,000 permanent residents and facilities for about 100,000 tourists during peak season. The town was to be the new capital of temporarily unoccupied France until the liberation of Paris August 19, 1944. Vichy-France comprised more than one-third of French territory in the southeastern part of the country. Hitler had granted an unoccupied semi-independent status not only to continental Vichy-France itself, but also to all of France's African empire.

For his cabinet there, Pétain chose another World War I celebrity, General Maxime Weygand, seventy-three years old, as Minister of National Defense. Weygand reluctantly accepted, but soon wanted to escape from Vichy government's political intrigues. He persuaded Pétain to create a new position for him as Delegate General of French Africa with supreme authority there, including command of French forces; he was appointed on September 9, 1940. [175] The US ambassador in France William C. Bullitt, an outspoken anti-Nazi, asked Washington to relieve him from his post. On June 30, 1940 he left Paris by motorcade, accompanied by his personal assistant Carmel Offie, his military and naval attachés, and the career diplomat Robert Murphy. The latter had worked in the US embassy in Paris continuously for ten years since 1930, after he had gathered experience and German-language skills in Germany as a consular officer in Munich for almost four years since November 1921. Bullitt would make his inaugural visit to the new head of state of the Vichy government before his return to Washington immediately thereafter. Murphy would fill his post as US chargé d'affaires in Vichy-France until mid-September 1940, when he was recalled to Washington for a new assignment to French Africa. Murphy and Weygand had, of course, taken notice of each other during their simultaneous presence in Vichy, but they had not really met in person then. [176]

Back in Washington it turned out that the president who had become aware of the strategic importance of French North Africa wanted to see Murphy. He sent him on an exploratory expedition to that region to find out what the generals in command of French forces there, especially Weygand, were up to, whether loyal to the Vichy government collaborating with the Germans or inclined to support the war effort of Britain and its Allies. The mission was so secret that Roosevelt demanded that Murphy should bypass his superiors in the State Department and send his reports to the president directly.

"Thus I became one of President Roosevelt's 'personal representatives,' assigned to carry out secret missions under his orders during World War II."[177]

Murphy was stationed in the US consulate in Algiers, where he arrived December 18, 1940.[178] The next day he started for his first trip, which took him to Dakar, a large port on the Atlantic coast of Senegal, where French naval forces had withdrawn to escape seizure by the German occupiers. He met with General Weygand there who – as Roosevelt had expected – was under certain conditions willing to support the Allied cause. After some negotiation there and during the following weeks the *WeygandMurphy Accord* of February 1941 was concluded. It was agreed that the USA would send certain essential materials and supplies to French North Africa conditioned on use there. Reshipping to continental Europe was excluded, because the Axis powers might benefit. It was understood, however, that the USA would send some diplomatic officials to French North Africa to oversee that this proviso was respected and not evaded.

But in fact their main task would be to collect intelligence on North Africa in preparation for military action there. After the Fall of France Roosevelt – in contrast to Hitler – had this region on his radar as a top strategic priority for opening a possible US military crusade against the Nazis in Europe. Usually the State Department was in charge of sending diplomatic personnel abroad. But it did not have specialists for intelligence jobs that would involve irregular and possibly dangerous activity. Murphy and State turned to the chiefs of Army and Navy Intelligence sections for recruiting twelve "control officers" for Morocco, Algeria, and Tunisia to be stationed in Casablanca, Algiers, Oran, Tunis, and Rabat as regular vice-consuls. The first allotment of these men arrived by boat in Algiers on June 10, 1941. As carefully selected persons all of them had had experience in France and spoke French, but not Arabic. They were responsible to Robert Murphy in Algiers.

On April 24, 1941 Murphy, then back in Washington, DC after his scouting tour in preparation for the *Weygand–Murphy Accord*, had been assigned to Algiers "as a sort of High Commissioner for French Africa,"[179] although officially still listed as a Counselor of the US embassy to (Vichy) France. Apart from an intermission from the end of August to mid-October 1942[180] in Washington, DC and in General Dwight D. Eisenhower's newly established Allied Force Headquarters in London during the planning phase of the landings in French North Africa, Murphy remained at his post in Algiers until Eisenhower was about to leave for London in December 1943 in order to assume his role as commander in chief for the planning and execution of the cross-channel invasion of France of June 6, 1944. From the landing of US troops in North Africa on November 8, 1942, Murphy had served as political adviser of commanding General Eisenhower who headquartered first in Gibraltar for a short time around the landing date, followed by twenty months in Algiers. Roosevelt had designated Murphy verbatim Operating Executive Head of the Civil Affairs Section and Adviser for Civil Affairs under General Eisenhower.[181]

Soon after the invasion at Salerno near Naples in Italy's southern mainland, a new Allied Force Headquarters was established at Caserta in October 1943 for Italian military matters without giving up the one in Algiers. After around that time the USA, following the UK, had diplomatically recognized General De Gaulle's French Committee of National Liberation in North Africa as the Government of France and sent a representative with the rank of an ambassador, Murphy saw his mission as accomplished and asked Roosevelt to relieve him. The president consented, but gave him a new assignment as his personal representative in Italian affairs. At Caserta he served on the Advisory Council for Italian and Balkan Affairs, together with his UK counterpart already at Algiers, Harold Macmillan, and on this four-power council now also with Couve de Murville for France and Alexander Bogomolov for USSR.[182] Murphy's Mediterranean assignments came to an end when the State Department notified him on August 14, 1944 that he would be transferred to Supreme Headquarters Allied Expeditionary Force (SHAEF) in France, this time as Eisenhower's political adviser on German affairs. On September 4, 1944 he came by plane from Italy to Washington, DC to be briefed on his new assignment for two weeks. Thereafter he reported for duty at Eisenhower's headquarters in the castle of Versailles.[183]

In occupied Germany Murphy would serve as political adviser of General Lucius D. Clay's US military government in Berlin. There he would give political advice also to Edward A. Tenenbaum and cooperate with him on the currency-reform project.

Immediately after Pearl Harbor, Colonel William A. Eddy, who had a distinguished record with the Marines in the World War I and spoke Arabic fluently from his growing up in the Middle East, was designated as Naval Attaché to the important US consulate in Tangier in December 1941. He was also given authority over the "control officers" to collect intelligence in cooperation with Murphy and to work jointly with British secret service people there. Two men with ample experience in the Arab world received special training to serve Eddy in Special Operations, that is, organizing unconventional warfare with local resistance groups.[184]

Before Eddy's departure for Africa in January 1942, he was briefed on his mission's purpose which was devised by Donovan: "That the aid of native chiefs be obtained, the loyalty of the inhabitants cultivated, fifth columnists organized and placed, demolition materials cached, and guerrilla bands of bold and daring men organized and installed."[185] Murphy was also engaged in Fifth-Column activities in French North Africa, but by means of diplomacy. He was trying to induce French military leaders there to defect from the Vichy government's resolve to combat against any attack on French North African territories. Instead they should regard and support the landing of US troops as reinforcements in the fight to liberate Europe from Nazi occupation and rule.[186]

Operation Torch, the US landing and invasion, with British support, in Morocco and Algeria took place November 8, 1942. It was a first US attempt to take on the Axis powers and to support the British with fighting troops. The Brits had stopped the advance of the joint German–Italian Tank Force Africa under the command of German General Erwin Rommel through North Africa in Egypt in the first battle of El Alamein already in July 1942. In the second battle of El Alamein during the weeks immediately preceding the American invasion in the Western part of North Africa, the British, now under the command of Bernard Montgomery, forced General Rommel's North Africa Corps and his Italian Ally to retreat westward. Rommel was caught in a pincer attack. The joint German–Italian Tank Force Africa, which had withdrawn to Libya, finally capitulated on May 12 and 13, 1943.

After a number of memoranda and a letter from Donovan to the president between January 3, and May 16, 1942,[187] Roosevelt's military order of June 13, 1942 split COI into the Office of War Information (OWI), which served war information and propaganda functions, and the Office of Strategic Services (OSS), which took over the secret service parts. It appointed William J. Donovan as OSS director and subjected it to the command and supervision of the Joint Chiefs of Staff.[188] Thus close cooperation between the military high command and the secret service of the USA was firmly established for the duration of World War II. Top officials of COI would constitute the core personnel of OSS. While serving as OSS director, Colonel Donovan was promoted to brigadier general on April 1, 1943 and to major general on November 10, 1944.[189]

On September 20, 1945, that is, after the end of World War II, President Truman ordered the dissolution of OSS to be effective as of October 1, 1945. OSS was dismembered. The Research & Analysis (R&A) branch was attached to the State Department. Secret Intelligence (SI) and Counterespionage (X-2) branches were merged and integrated into the War Department as its Strategic Services Unit.[190] On January 22, 1946, President Truman – after having realized that a central intelligence body was necessary also in peace time – created the Central Intelligence Group (CIG). By the spring of 1946, the *Strategic Services* Unit of the War Department was transferred to CIG, thus giving it the remnants of the OSS clandestine collection capability. "This led to the formation of the Office of Special Operations (OSO), which was responsible for espionage and counter-espionage. By June 1946, CIG had a strength of approximately 1,800, of which about one-third was overseas with OSO."[191] Finally, the National Security Act of July 26, 1947 renamed CIG Central Intelligence Agency (CIA) and transformed it into an independent entity.

After R&A of COI had been integrated into OSS as its Research & Analysis Branch, Langer succeeded Baxter, who had to withdraw from directing R&A for reasons of health, in September 1942.[192] Edward Tenenbaum was part of the staff then, assigned to the Central European Section headed by Walter L. Dorn, a University of Chicago historian whose special field had been Prussian history of the eighteenth century and who had also belonged to the early staff members of COI.[193] The research staff of the R&A branch of COI in October 1941 had amounted to scarcely 200 employees,[194] but kept expanding, especially after OSS had taken over. R&A reached its peak in employment in 1945 with a staff of close to 2,000, of which 1,500 worked in Washington, DC and 450 overseas.[195] OSS as a whole reached its apogee in personnel in December 1944 with 13,000 on its staff, of which 5,500 were working within the USA, the remainder – like Tenenbaum – overseas.[196] During the last year of the war about 2,000 OSS members, comprising all fourteen branches of R&A included, were stationed in London. It was the largest and most important outpost of OSS.[197]

Tenenbaum did not work for COI. During the eleven months it existed he was still a student at Yale. He joined OSS, employed as a civilian, a week after its founding. I will, therefore, skip details of COI's organizational structure. In more detail I will present only the one of OSS in general and the two branches Tenenbaum worked for during his belonging to OSS.

First, how did OSS recruit its personnel and what made employment by this secret service attractive to possible candidates from Ivy League universities? Here is an answer by the eminent historian of intelligence in World War II in his contribution to the National Archives conference on OSS in Washington, DC July 11–12, 1991:

> The OSS offered an opportunity to do what was widely regarded, at least in university circles, as an important job, which drew upon a candidate's education, experience, and general background, with a whiff of danger (and sometimes a good bit more than a whiff). A job with the OSS most likely assured a posting to an interesting and cosmopolitan place, such as London, Bern, Paris, later Milan, or even Cairo or Istanbul, and an escape from the assumed tedium of spending the war typing up supply requisitions in some overheated stateside military post. The OSS appealed to a good number of men of action who had excelled on the football field, but any examination of photographs of groups of OSS men shows a disproportionate number who wore glasses. These were 'the bad eyes brigade,' people not lacking in courage or a desire to contribute to the war effort but acutely aware that a simple matter of a heavy rain might incapacitate them at a crucial moment. They composed disproportionately the largest unit, the Research and Analysis Branch (R&A).[198]

Edward A. Tenenbaum belonged to 'the bad eyes brigade.' Due to his considerable short-sightedness (see data of his medical examination below) he had been dependent on wearing glasses since his early youth.

The following description of the structures of OSS and R&A is instructive:[199]

The Research and Analysis Branch

When the OSS was created in 1942, its leader Gen. William J. Donovan had not intended for it to be an organization of spies. Donovan originally wanted OSS to support military operations in the field. However, he soon realized the value of clandestine human reporting. The OSS consisted of five branches:

- Secret Intelligence (SI) Branch
- Research and Analysis (R&A) Branch
- Special Operations (SO) Branch
- Morale Operations (MO) Branch
- X-2 Branch [= Counterespionage]

The R&A Branch was one of the first branches established, and its purpose was to find Axis strengths and vulnerabilities using all open sources available. Donovan believed that valuable information for the Allies could be found in such open sources, including:

- Libraries,
- Newspapers, and
- Government and industry information.

Utilizing these resources, the R&A Branch became a force to be reckoned with. The work of R&A analysts was able to win over even its harshest critics, and won many allies for the OSS. The R&A Branch was held in such high esteem that when the OSS was disbanded in 1945, it was one of the few components that was salvaged and handed over to the State Department.

The Best and Brightest

The R&A Branch was headed by Dr. James Phinney Baxter, president of Williams College. Harvard historian William Langer later replaced Baxter as director.

The R&A Branch was composed of 900 scholars from many different disciplines, including:

- Historians,
- Economists,
- Political Scientists,
- Geographers,

- Psychologists,
- Anthropologists, and
- Diplomats.

Many famous names made contributions to the R&A Branch, such as Arthur Schlesinger, Jr., Sherman Kent, and Ralph Bunche. R&A veterans included seven future presidents of the American Historical Association, five of the American Economic Association, and two Nobel Laureates.

Axis Vulnerabilities in Europe: German Oil Production

The most important contribution the R&A Branch made to the war was supporting the Allied bombings in Europe. The Enemy Objectives Unit (EOU) – a group of R&A economists posted in London – were able to pinpoint German oil production as a major vulnerability in the Nazi effort. This analysis by the EOU sent Allied bombers toward German aircraft factories. The idea was to weaken the Luftwaffe first, and then begin bombing German oil facilities.

There is a book out with detailed accounts of B-17 (Flying Fortress) and B-24 (Liberator) bombing runs, their dates and targets, their effectiveness, their damage achieved, and their often high costs in terms of own carrier and crewman losses. So we have more precise information on when the strategic bombing of refineries, synthetic oil plants and other oil production and storage centers started and was further carried out later. The book reports May 12, 1944 as the beginning:

> 886 B-17s and B-24s, with 980 escorting fighters, took part in the first attack on oil production centers in the Reich. Five main plants in central Germany and Czechoslovakia were bombed. ... After some tactical pre-invasion raids in France the Eighth US AAF on May 28, 1944 had] 1,341 bombers pound oil targets in Germany, and 32 'heavies' went down. VIII Fighter Command claimed 27 fighters destroyed for the loss of nine of its own. On the 29th 993 B-24s and B-17s were launched – some 888 of them carried out visual attacks on aircraft plants and oil installations in Germany.[200]

But actually General Carl Spaatz, commander of US Strategic Air Forces (USSTAF) in Europe since January 1944, whom EOU had convinced of the priority of oil over transportation-system targets before Eisenhower and the British Charles Portal, Marshal of the Royal Air Force, fell in line, undertook bombing raids on oil targets by sleight of hand. In April 1944 the Fifteenth US Air Force stationed in Italy "began a number of raids against the Romanian oil-producing city of Ploesti, nominally against 'marshalling yards.' In fact the raids hit the oilfield, as was intended."[201] After successful US air strikes since July 1943 on German aircraft production sites concentrated in central Germany had forced the Germans to disperse and hide such production sites, German fighter production recovered strongly and even reached a maximum in 1944. Since May 1944 oil production and storage sites in German-controlled territory had officially become prime targets of US Air Forces and later on also of British Bomber Command. Walt W. Rostow reports:

> when German aircraft production began to rise in dispersed
> factories later in 1944, there was insufficient aircraft fuel to train
> the pilots and fly the planes. From a peak of 180,000 metric tons
> production in March 1944 – before the insubordinate attack on
> Ploesti – aircraft fuel production was down to an incredible 10,000
> tons by September. (Overall, oil supplies were reduced from 981,000
> to 281,000 tons.)[202]

The heaviest raids on oil installations, mainly by Eighth US Air Force stationed in Britain, but also by General Arthur Harris' British Bomber Command, took place in the autumn of 1944, from October to December 1944. Richard Overy reports this and its results. From its peak in March 1944 to December 1944 synthetic oil production in Germany dropped from 542 to 164 thousand tons and the production of German aviation fuel by 95 percent during 1944.[203]

This is corroborated by George C. Marshall's report to the Secretary of War shortly after the end of World War II: "In late spring of 1944, synthetic fuel plants and crude oil refineries became prime targets. Captured documents now show that the bombing campaign succeeded in reducing production between May and October 1944 to five percent of the former monthly output."[204]

Let me give you two examples of what this meant for the fighting capacity of the *Wehrmacht* as seen from the German side. Albert Praun, commanding general of the *Wehrmacht*'s telegraph and telecommunication service, writes in his memoirs that after the American capture of the Remagen Bridge he himself was waiting five miles north in Bad Honnef for a meeting with the commander of the Western Front, General Field Marshal Walter Model. The latter had given orders to the 11th German Tank (*Panzer*) Division for a counterattack to recapture the Remagen Bridge. While already on the move on the Autobahn (highway) the advance of the tank division was stalled due to lack of fuel.[205] The second example: Besides in production sites in Southern Germany, the world's first jet fighter Me 262 was during the last months of the war mass-produced in underground bombproof tunnels under the Walpersberg mountain near Kahla in Thuringia. This was the most effective German weapon against bombing raids by Allied air forces. But sorties of altogether a little more than one thousand Me 262s delivered to the German air force were very limited due to lack of aviation fuel among other problems.[206]

In the fall of 1944, Arthur Harris and his British RAF Bomber Command only reluctantly and belatedly fell in line with the US Strategic Air Forces' priority-targeting of German oil installations. Here is how in his memoirs Harris judged his participation in the US bombardment of German oil installations:

> the success of which was far from assured. In the event, of course, the offensive against oil was a complete success, and it could not have been so without the co-operation of Bomber Command, but I still do not think that it was reasonable, at the same time, to expect that the campaign would succeed; what the Allied strategists did was to bet on an outsider, and it happened to win the race.[207]

Even more revealing about the success of bombing German oil instal-
lations are postwar memoirs of Germans in leading positions. Albert
Speer, Minister of Armaments and War Production and close friend of
Hitler, stated in his memoirs:

> On May 8, 1944, I returned to Berlin to resume my work. I shall
> never forget the date May 12, four days later. On that day the
> technological war was decided. Until then we had managed to
> produce approximately as many weapons as the armed forces
> needed, in spite of their considerable losses. But with the attack of
> nine hundred and thirty-five daylight bombers of the American
> Eighth Air Force upon several fuel Plants in central and eastern
> Germany, a new era in the air war began. It meant the end of
> German armaments production. ... As a result of the losses in the
> fuel industry it was no longer possible even in December 1944 and
> January 1945 to make use of the reduced armaments production in
> the battle. The loss of fuel had, in my opinion, therefore, a more
> decisive effect on the course of the war than the difficulties in
> armaments and communications.[208]

The highly decorated German flying ace and commander of the
German fighter forces, General Adolf Galland, summarized in his
postwar memoirs: "The most successful operation of the entire
Allied strategical air war was against German fuel supply. This was
actually the fatal blow for the Luftwaffe. ... The raids of the Allied air
fleets on the German petrol supply installations was the most important of the combined factors which brought about the collapse of
Germany."[209]

In his autobiography Langer describes his plane trip to Europe in
September 1942, just after he had succeeded Baxter as head of the
R&A branch. To get a sense of how uncomfortable transatlantic air
travel was in those days, I quote Langer:

> Our transportation was a great lumbering seaplane operated by the
> American Export Airlines. It was equipped to sleep sixteen

individuals on the long, tiresome trip to Newfoundland and thence to Ireland, whence a less monstrous machine would take us, with all windows sealed, to the Bristol airfield. Instead of sixteen passengers we numbered twenty-six, mostly Army officers. Under the circumstances we drew lots for the upper berths, while the losers (I among them) stretched out and sometimes slept head to foot on the lower bunks.[210]

But I doubt that R&A boss Langer would have preferred the transatlantic crossing by boat which one of the economists on his staff, Charles P. Kindleberger, has described for February 1943: "that trip, in a six-knot convoy, twenty-two days from New York to Cardiff in February gales, with four locomotives aboard as deck cargo, threatening to break loose in the storms and sweep away the ship's superstructure and her fifteen passengers."[211]

Correspondence between OSS and Local Board No. 42 of the Selective Service System in New York City reveals a lot of details on Tenenbaum's specific position and job with OSS in 1942. He had entered the Office in Washington, DC on June 20, 1942 and was employed as a P-1 Analyst in the Central European Section, Division of Special Information. OSS operated under authority of the Joint Chiefs of Staff (JCS). Tenenbaum drew an annual salary of $2,000. This is equivalent to $36,920 in 2023 money. On a form "Affidavit to Support Claim for Occupational Deferment" Tenenbaum's job description was: "Mr. Tenenbaum is a German labor analyst of the Central European Section. In addition, he is now making a comprehensive study of the German electric power industry for OSS" The Office justified its demand for deferment (classification II-A instead of I-A[212]) with the following arguments. No one in OSS could finish off the study of the German electric power industry but Tenenbaum himself. All attempts to find a substitute with Tenenbaum's skill and knowledge had not been successful. And "Skilled students of German wartime economy not already engaged in some Government agency are extremely difficult to find, particularly as well-trained and versatile a student as Mr. Tenenbaum."[213]

Attached to his OSS Interoffice Memo of October 13, 1942 Walter L. Dorn, the head of the Central European Section, had sent a copy of completed Form DSS 42A, the "Affidavit," to Robert L. Wolff, for approval.

Dorn had been teaching history at the University of Chicago. He was a specialist of Prussian history. During the 1930s he had come to Berlin several times to do research in the *Geheimes Staatsarchiv* [Secret State Archive] of Prussia. Of course, he had then also gathered first-hand observations of life in Nazi Germany. In 1943 his deputy Eugene N. Anderson, also a specialist of German history from the University of Chicago, succeeded him as head of R&A's Central European Section. Dorn had proven to be too academic and averse to quick decision-making for an undertaking that needed reports produced speedily without lengthy back-and-forth and tight administrative barriers.[214] In 1947 he resumed teaching as professor of modern European history at Ohio State University. After 1956 he taught at Columbia University. Wolff was an academic historian as well, with special expertise on the Balkans. After the war he would teach for four years at the University of Wisconsin and after 1950 as professor in the Harvard history department.

In his memo mentioned above, Dorn points out to Wolff that deferment is demanded for two or three months only, no more than is necessary for Tenenbaum to finish his study on the German electric power industry. He estimates that with all the material already collected Tenenbaum could finish it in about eight weeks. Dorn again praises Tenenbaum's unique knowledge: He "has become Washington's best-informed man on this subject … only he can complete it. There is no other person either in the Central European Section or in the Economics Division who can do so." In closing Dorn points out that Tenenbaum is only twenty years old and that he is "excellent soldier material." But he added that his task was important enough to justify the deferment request "for this very short period."[215]

The initial deferment request was sent to the chairman of Local Board No. 42 of the Selective Service System in New York City on October 17, 1942. In his covering letter, with Form DSS 42A as enclosure, James B. Opsata, OSS personnel officer, wrote:

> The Office of Strategic Services is engaged 100% in the war effort, its main functions being to collect and analyze such strategic information and plan and operate such special services as may be directed by the Army and Navy Chiefs of Staff. Mr. Tenenbaum ... has collected and familiarized himself with a vast amount of material on industrial conditions in Germany and is currently preparing an extensive report on German power facilities. Twelve weeks will be required to finish this report. At the present time we consider Mr. Tenenbaum an irreplaceable person since he alone is the only one acquainted with and, therefore, capable of successfully completing this particular project.[216]

George C. Thornson, member of Local Board No. 42, replied by letter to OSS, Att: James B. Opsata, of October 26, 1942 informing that the deferment had been denied.[217] Tenenbaum's induction at that time must have been imminent, because OSS appealed the decision successfully. In a letter of November 17, 1942 Edward W. Bourne, Government Appeal Agent of Local Board No. 42, reported to James B. Opsata that his discussions with the Board did not result in a change of Tenenbaum's classification from I-A to II-A. However, he would not be inducted until the December induction date, namely December 14, 1942. And he would be granted one week of furlough immediately after his induction. [218] So in practice, Tenenbaum was not granted the full twelve weeks of deferment Opsata of OSS had asked for in his initial request to Local Board No. 42 of October 17, 1942. But he got a little more than the eight weeks that Dorn in his OSS Interoffice Memo of October 13, 1942 had regarded as sufficient for Tenenbaum to finish his study.

The study is most probably the one that was filed as IR [Intelligence Report] 184 by the Economics Division of OSS. It was entitled "The Electric Power System of the German Altreich," dated February 20, 1943, and classified as "Confidential." In contrast to other IRs it does not show the author's name. This might be due to the fact that Tenenbaum at that date was part of the US Army, not of the Washington Office of OSS any more. The first sentence states the study's result: "The German electricity supply system is not at present a limiting factor in the German war economy." In the 12-page document this is substantiated by many numbers and tables for the supply of electricity by the various domestic power plants plus imports minus exports and its consumption by industry as a whole and its individual branches, by households, electrified transportation, and even further down to agriculture and public street lighting.[219]

Tenenbaum himself described his tasks with OSS Washington, DC from June to December 1942 in his "Application for Federal Employment" of September 1948 as follows:

> Development of information and reports on Germany. Major topics
> were the organization, operation and resources of the electric power
> and long-distance gas industries, and the organization, composition
> and efficiency of the German labor force. Available material was
> almost exclusively in German. Work required fairly high degree of
> ability to interpret and evaluate, as well as to discover sources of
> material in ordinary publications despite the German censorship.
> Reports had to be prepared in non-technical language for the
> inclusion in Military Government briefing material.[220]

During his six-month stint as a civilian employee with the R&A branch of OSS in Washington, DC, Tenenbaum met Charles P. Kindleberger ("Charlie") for the first time. The latter one was employed by OSS in Washington, DC as a civilian since August 6, 1942 and worked as chief of the Military Supplies Unit in R&A's Europe–Africa Division, Economic Capabilities Subdivision[221] until February 1943 (see below). His former colleagues at the Federal Reserve Board, Emile Depres and Chandler Morse, had already been hired by OSS and offered him to join them.[222] But while Tenenbaum was assigned to the Central European Section, Kindleberger was part of the Economics Division[223] (at times called Economics Group or Section), where together with Harold Barnett, Edward Mayer, and two BAs from Columbia University, he analyzed the military supply situation in enemy countries,[224] more precisely in Kindleberger's own words: "to analyze intelligence on German production of war materiel."[225] On detached service of OSS Washington, DC, being paid his regular Washington salary of $5,600 per annum and, in addition, a living and quarters allowance of $2,520 per annum as of February 28, he arrived in London on February 27, 1943.[226] There he became the head of the Enemy Objectives Unit (EOU).[227] It had been created the previous fall on a small scale as a subsection of the US Board of Economic Warfare (BEW) representation in London. Its first head had been Chandler Morse who played a crucial role in recruiting the economists of which EOU consisted.[228] It had been instigated by the American Army Air Corps' new strategy of "daylight precision bombing," conceptualized already during the interwar period. It stood in sharp contrast to the Royal Air Force's strategy of "nighttime area bombardment" regardless of the collateral destruction of housing and lives of civilians. Charles P. Kindleberger, who should play an important role in implementing the American strategic concept of bombing, criticized the British approach with his characteristically dry humor: "all hammer and no anvil."[229]

The first American Flying Fortresses (B 17s) were stationed in England in the fall of 1942. They were heavier and larger, better armed, faster than the British Lancaster and Halifax, and carried the more accurate Norden bombsights.[230] Therefore, they were better suited for daylight precision bombing than their British counterparts. Air Corps Colonel Richard D. Hughes, senior target planning officer for the US Army Air Forces in Europe, vigorously pursued the American strategic doctrine in the European Theater of Operations (ETO) for the US Strategic Air Force (USSTAF), including the US 8th Air Force, headquartered in England at Wydewing.[231] He supported Carl A. Spaatz

Charles Kindleberger, "an intensely serious and hostile young man" (left, seated), with the Enemy Objectives Unit. Seated next to Kindleberger are Roselene Honerkamp and Irwin Nat Pincus; standing, left to right, are the economists William Salant, Walt W. Rostow, (?) Selko, and Edward Mayer.

FIGURE 3.9 Charles P. Kindleberger, head of the Enemy Objectives Unit (EOU) 1943–1944 in London, with a part of his team relaxing from work

(who in contrast to the British Air Force Commander Arthur Harris was a strong advocate of daylight bombing raids) to negotiate the first joint Anglo-Saxon directive for the Combined Bomber Offensive, dubbed *Pointblank*, approved at the summit meeting of Churchill and Roosevelt as well as their Combined Chiefs of Staff in Casablanca January 14–24, 1943. It laid down five primary targets in the following order of priority: submarine construction yards, aircraft industry, transportation, oil, and other war industries.

Colonel Hughes was the one who had had and pushed the idea of recruiting able economists for selecting enemy target "systems" according to precise calculations of the input-output structure of the

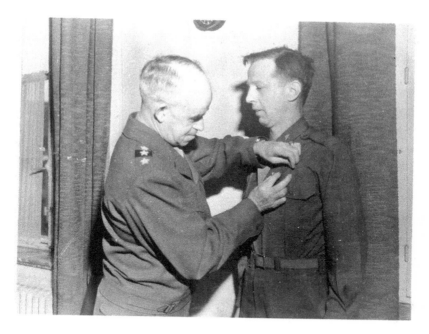

FIGURE 3.10 General Omar N. Bradley awards the Bronze Star to Captain Charles P. Kindleberger 1944 for his work in World War II with OSS, especially as head of the Enemy Objectives Unit (EOU) in London from February 1943 until May 1944

German war economy and on that basis of targets with the widest margin between costs (own input and losses) and benefits (disruption of enemy chains of production).[232] Captain Kindleberger left his position as chief of EOU in May 1944.[233] Colonel Hughes and Kindleberger seem to have stayed professionally and personally closely attached. Sometime after reactivated Captain Kindleberger had been sent from England to France shortly after the Normandy invasion, Colonel Hughes was transferred from the Strategic Air Forces in England to the US 9th Air Force as A-2 (Intelligence, Air Force) which moved to the Continent in company with Omar Bradley's 12th Army Group.[234] As Captain (on July 15, 1944 promoted to Major) Kindleberger was G-2 (Intelligence) of 12th Army Group; he and Hughes were bound to have been cooperating closely during the last part of the war. Kindleberger treats Colonel Hughes with great admiration and respect in his autobiography.[235] Their mutual respect and trust, if not friendship, is evidenced by the colonel's invitation of the major in mid-April 1945 to accompany him to inspect near Nordhausen in Thuringia the *Mittelbau* SS underground military production facilities, especially for the V-2 missiles, and the adjacent concentration camp Dora. There thousands of inmates had been worked to death. On that trip they also visited a one-fourth completed tunneling construction planned to be another headquarters (*Führerhauptquartier*) for Hitler and his staff and for underground armaments production in the middle of Germany close by the village of Ohrdruf, where Johann Sebastian Bach grew up. The village is near Arnstadt, where Bach from 1703 to 1707 gained his first employment as a church organist.[236]

Edward S. Mason, an economics professor from Harvard, became part of the OSS Research & Analysis Branch, where his innovative microeconomic thinking shaped the analytical foundation of the Economics Division in Washington, DC as well as in London. Chandler Morse, a more practical man with management talent, was instrumental in recruiting the EOU team. The first EOU-contingent – Chandler Morse, the unit's chief; Roselene Honerkamp, its secretary; and Walt Rostow – arrived in London on September 13, 1942, "after a languid Sikorsky flying boat journey from New York to Bottwood Bay (Newfoundland) to Shannon harbor in Ireland – and then on to London in a plywood DeHaviland."[237] All the while the London detachment of OSS grew from its tiny beginnings in 1942 to an "increasingly professional shadow warfare organization of some 2,000 people and 14 branches,"[238] R&A being one of those. The maximum was probably reached in the summer of 1944, before the London OSS staff started to move to liberated parts of continental Europe in September 1944, that is, after the Normandy bridgehead had been opened in Operation Cobra at the end of July and Paris had been liberated on August 19, 1944.

Even earlier some London OSS personnel were integrated into the US Army as field detachments. In Captain Kindleberger's case this happened shortly after June 19, 1944,[239] when he was sent to France to serve in G-2 (Intelligence), headed by Brigadier General Edwin L. Sibert,[240] of General Omar Bradley's 12th US Army Group. Lieutenant Tenenbaum kept working for R&A in London from his arrival in England in July 1944 until November 1944. This means that "Charlie" and Edward, whose nickname in Yale College had also been "Charlie,"[241] could not have met again in London.

The bread and butter issues R&A London worked on were "specific intelligence requests for the continental operations of the Office of War Information and of other American (and British) agencies." It included "interviews with German prisoners-of-war who were often able – wittingly or otherwise – to yield important clues on such matters as the effects of Allied bombardment on civilian morale." And the London branch of R&A "was responsible for maintaining regular contacts with the welter of German émigré groups in London. The specific projects ... particularly after the Normandy invasion in June and the failed assassination attempt [on Hitler] in July, corresponded to the changing priorities of the final months of the war and preparations for the close of hostilities in Europe." In most of 1944 the German–Austrian section of R&A London, to which Tenenbaum after his arrival in July was attached with all his expertise on Germany's economy and finance, was headed by the German-American historian Felix Gilbert, Jewish émigré from Nazi Germany. With a fellow officer from the Geographic Section Gilbert was involved in planning for the zonal administration of Berlin and made an enduring contribution to German history: "I pointed to the Grunewald and Dahlem area on the map and jokingly said, 'This is where my relations had houses; this ought to be the American section.' The lines they drew have stood ever since."[242] Except that the Grunewald area would become part of the British Sector in Berlin.

In one of his later "Applications for Federal Employment" Tenenbaum described his OSS tasks in London: "Analysis of intelligence and other information ... on German wartime clearing and trade agreements. Work involved use of German-language material and contacts with Allied agencies having similar functions (such as British Ministry of Econ. Warfare and Ministry of Information)."

The task of the London branch of R&A comprised maintaining contacts with German émigrés in London. Therefore, Tenenbaum with all his exceptional knowledge of Germany's economy and finance as well as his German-language skills is bound to have been in contact with one particular Jewish émigré from Berlin, Jürgen Kuczynski. The latter was a political economist of communist persuasion and party affiliation. In his memoirs on the post-1945 period he described himself as a "loyal dissident" of the communist regime in the German Democratic Republic (GDR), which like the Federal Republic of Germany was founded in 1949. What is more, he was even a colleague of Tenenbaum in collecting information on the German economy from the US outpost in London with a salary of a lieutenant colonel. He was not part of R&A, but had been hired as an anti-Nazi expert for the functioning of the German industry and economy, especially its labor component.

His background: He was born September 17, 1904 in Elberfeld, nowadays a part of Wuppertal, into a well-to-do family. He studied philosophy, statistics, and political economy at the universities of Erlangen, Berlin, and Heidelberg. After arriving in the USA September 17, 1926, he did postgraduate studies for one year at the Brookings School which was attached to the Brookings Institution in Washington, DC. There he met Marguerite Steinfeld. They married in September 1928. From 1927 until the return of the couple to Germany in 1929, Kuczynski worked as the chief statistician for the American Federation of Labor. On July 14, 1930 he became a member of the German Communist Party. He kept working for it underground for three years after Hitler's accession to power, before in 1936 he and his family emigrated to England and lived in London.[243]

In September 1944 he was recruited for the staff of the US Strategic Bombing Survey (USSBS). In chief positions were also several other nonmilitary persons, especially among them the nominal head

Franklin D'Olier, chairman of Prudential Insurance Company, and the main driving force behind the project, the Chicago lawyer George Ball. The latter recruited two of his friends, the young Wall Street financier Paul H. Nitze as survey director and economist John Kenneth Galbraith.[244] Nitze later became a reputed politician. The later famous Harvard economist Galbraith was USSBS' mastermind. The report summarized that the bombardment of German industrial production plants had not achieved the expected results. In 1944 German production had been three times of what it had been at the beginning of the war and no traces could be found that the bombing had impaired the morale of citizens and soldiers in Germany. But successes were recorded in two fields: "attacks on railroad lines and oil depots had greatly slowed German troop movements and curtailed training. By keeping German planes in the air, the bombing also helped deplete the Nazi air force."[245]

Kuczynski was clad in a US Army uniform, like other civilians who worked for the army, although they never went through military training. In London the USSBS team worked in the same building as the R&A branch of OSS there. Kuczynski's first task was to work on calculations of Germany's national income, later of its workforce (i.e., topics that Tenenbaum might well have treated for R&A). Working in the same building on similar economic problems of the German economy, they must have known each other quite well. In his memoirs Kuczynski does not mention Tenenbaum, of OSS's personnel only Richard Ruggles and the Norwegian Ohlin, who both by smart thinking found easy ways to obtain information on the extent of German armaments production (Ruggles) and on all transports by freight trains, including oil (Ohlin). Kuczynski also mentions that he had unrestricted access to all information of OSS on German armaments output and to even the most secret information on the economic situation in Germany.[246]

On December 18, 1944 Jürgen Kuczynski and Richard Ruggles were flown to Paris in preparation for field work to be done for USSBS in occupied parts of Germany. But due to the last German offensive, the Battle of the Bulge, the mission was stalled. Kuczynski and his unit were flown back to London on January 5, 1945. It wasn't until March 27, 1945 that his group of civilian scientists in uniform, under the military command of Major Ellis H. Wilner and First Lieutenant Robert C. Stern, were again ordered to travel to Paris. From there the unit proceeded to Strasbourg where it arrived on March 31. This was its starting point for touring Germany in convoys of jeeps with a large measure of leeway in selecting its itinerary. Kuczynski's official task on this mission was to collect statistical information on the effects of bombing in Germany, especially on industrial production. From the second half of May to the end of August 1945 the USSBS team settled in Bad Nauheim to write the report. Kuczynski was one of the authors under a pseudonym. My economic history colleague Rainer Fremdling has found circumstantial evidence that the man behind the listed coauthor of the USSBS summary report Samuel J. Dennis was probably Jürgen Kuczynski.[247] After finishing the report, one part of the USSBS team was transferred to East Asia for investigating the bombing effects on the Japanese war economy. The other part, to which Kuczynski belonged, was decommissioned.[248]

Kuczynski returned to his family in London. There he was demobilized from the US Army and received the information that the commander in chief of the Soviet military government, Marshal Zhukov, on July27, 1945 had issued order No. 17 appointing Jürgen Kuczynski director of the administration for finance for all four occupation zones of Germany. Walter Ulbricht, who had returned from his exile in Moscow to Berlin and became the party leader, strongly supported him. The German Communist Party considered Kuczynski as its economic and financial expert. Tenenbaum played a comparable role in OSS, US Army, and US military government (OMGUS) in Berlin. This fact makes it very unlikely that Kuczynski and Tenenbaum did not maintain close relations with each other, first in London and later in Berlin.

Demobilized in London, Kuczynski tried to return to Berlin as soon as possible. Soviet help didn't lead anywhere. Therefore, he mobilized American friends who managed to get him to Berlin in November 1945 with a job in OMGUS. As living quarters, he was lucky to settle next to his family's mansion overlooking the lake in Berlin-Schlachtensee. His neighbor and friend Hans Gaffron had emigrated to the USA.

In London he had successfully made top secret reports for Roosevelt, Churchill, and their top military advisers on German armaments' production and oil supplies. In his memoirs he is proud of having made them available to Stalin and his chief of staff by way of his sister Ruth Werner, an important Soviet spy under her code name *Sonja*. In an interview on July 24, 1998 Galbraith, the chief economist on the USSBS team, admitted that he had known about these connections of Kuczynski with the Soviet Union and that USSBS had even used this informal communication channel to the Soviet Ally consciously.[249] Because he had been a useful channel for top secret information collected by USSBS, the Soviet Secret Service (NKWD, later named KGB) demanded from Kuczynski to continue spying on his OMGUS job instead of assuming the position of director of the administration for finance. Kuczynski's counter-argument that his OMGUS job was so unimportant that he would not be able to deliver useful information, was of no avail. Therefore, somewhat consoled by the disappointment of Walter Ulbricht and Marshal Zhukov, Kuczynski grudgingly kept working for OMGUS. His boss there was Chandler Morse, who had been the first chief of EOU in London and had recruited its members, including Charles Kindleberger who had succeeded Chandler Morse as EOU chief in February 1943. Walt W. Rostow devoted this eulogy to Kindleberger:

> His character and style suffused the outfit to the end. His rule in exercising authority was: "Tough upwards, soft downwards." Despite our modest military ranks, we spoke our minds to higher authority. We all learned that one could debate quite amicably with general officers if advocacy was interspersed with a sufficient

number of "Sirs." But beneath the fraternal spirit that marked EOU and the texture of humor which suffused virtually all talk in the family, Kindleberger quietly exercised discretion and compassion on behalf of his subordinates when required. Above all he is, as I once wrote, a man of "fierce integrity." He insisted on a self-critical integrity among us, perhaps best illustrated by his insistence in the autumn of 1944 [sic, probably a typo instead of 1943], after a sustained period of advocacy, that we pause, draw back, and reexamine skeptically our logic and the factual evidence for the policy positions we held.[250]

But finally in April 1946 NKWD allowed Kuczynski to leave his OMGUS job, because his spy material, as he had predicted, had not been high-yield. On April 13, Chandler Morse staged a "charming farewell," as Kuczynski noted in his diary. He then took up a professorship in economics at the rich-in-tradition Berlin University, located in the Soviet sector of Berlin. He claims to have been the first Marxist faculty member there.[251] His appointment as director of the administration of finance had been vetoed by the Western occupying powers and thus had failed anyway.

> In my military days, I had cultivated many a good acquaintance with progressive left-wing American citizens. And the circle of these acquaintances was partly maintained and partly expanded during my OMGUS time. // This also made my material life easier. Of course I had a cold or barely heated room at home, of course not enough to eat. But at least once a week I was invited to dinner, often combined with a warm bath, at the home of my American acquaintances, who now sometimes became friends.[252]

Tenenbaum was certainly not one of them, because he started working for OMGUS in Berlin not before the fall of 1946. But it might well be that due to their London acquaintance they met again in Berlin between the fall of 1946 and 1948.

FIGURE 3.11 Lieutenant Edward A. Tenenbaum in military uniform

Tenenbaum had already been transferred to France in November 1944 to continue work for R&A of OSS, all the while also being attached to the Psychological Warfare Division of 12th Army Group. He also seems to have been part of G-2, headed by Brigadier General Oscar W. Koch,[253] of General Patton's Third US Army, which was part of the 12th US Army Group. Koch's G-2 staff proved to be superior to G-2 units of other US Armies and Army Groups. Among other achievements,[254] the outstanding one was that it correctly spotted the German concentration of troops in preparation of a counteroffensive during the weeks preceding the opening of the Battle of the Bulge on December 16, 1944. On December 9, 1944 Koch briefed Patton and his command staff that his capability analysis clearly showed that a German offensive was imminent. Patton took him seriously, but Eisenhower and Bradley did not.[255]

The reason is that their G-2 Intelligence relied mainly on ULTRA, the intercepted radio messages between German military units. The codes of the German ciphering *Enigma* machines had been progressively broken since 1940. On the German side there had been no knowledge that the British had deciphered *Enigma.* But still for the German preparation of the Ardennes offensive leading to the Battle of the Bulge, Hitler had forbidden using radio messages for communication between troops as a mere precaution. Patton's G-2 General Koch also received all the ULTRA information. But he kept using all available sources for intelligence.[256] "ULTRA picked up very little of the information that Koch gleaned from other sources – including heavy reliance on air reconnaissance and POW interrogations. He also gained crucial information from the OSS detachment at his command."[257]

Edward Tenenbaum belonged to the OSS detachment of General Koch's G-2 staff. With his T-Force activity he might well have contributed to General Koch's correct assessment of German capabilities for an Ardennes offensive. On December 12, 1944 Patton was alarmed enough to order his staff to plan what Third Army could do if called upon to counterattack a German breakthrough as suspected in the First Army's zone north of Third Army.[258]

Since March 1944 US Third Army had been newly formed and trained under General Patton's command with its original headquarters in historic Peover Hall in Knutsford, Cheshire, in northwest England.[259] It was here in March 1944 Patton bought for himself Punch, a white fifteen-months-old bull terrier, and renamed him Willie after William the Conqueror. His former owner had been a Royal Air Force pilot who was killed in action over continental Europe. The dog had had combat experience himself as his former owner had taken him along in his aircraft on a raid over Berlin.[260]

Patton's prowess in assault warfare was not only highly recognized among the Allies, but it was also feared by the Germans.[261] Everything was done to keep the Third Army built-up and Patton's new command hidden from the Germans, because the General was officially commanding a fake First US Army Group right across the Channel from Pas-de-Calais, the shortest cross-channel route for an invasion and much closer to Germany's industrial heartland, the Ruhr district, than the Normandy beaches. During the first days after the Normandy invasion Hitler still believed that the main attack would happen in the Pas-de-Calais area by Patton's feigned First US Army Group. Therefore, he had German forces in that area released only belatedly as reinforcements of German troops fighting the Allies in Normandy.

On D-day the personnel strength of the US Army, which included the Air Force, numbered 1,533,000 in ETOUSA. At the same time the US AAF had 3,000 heavy bombers and 6,500 first-line planes of other types stationed in England on D-day. On January 1, 1944 the Eighth US Air Force was combined with the Fifteenth, which was operating from Italy, to form the US Strategic Air Forces in Europe with Lieutenant General Carl Spaatz in command. "From the time of the Eighth Air Force's first heavy bomber attack on 17 August 1942 until V-E Day, United States airmen had dropped more than 1,550,000 tons of bombs on western European targets."[262] Despite the success of the German troops to keep the Allied armies contained within the beachhead until the American breakout in *Operation Cobra* during the last days of July 1944 and before Patton's Third Army started operations making use of that breakthrough on August 1, 1944, 2,086,000 Allied soldiers and 3,446,000 tons of military equipment had been unloaded in France by September 5, (D-day + 90). And in late November, when the port of Antwerp had been put in operation for supplying the Allied troops, more than 3 million soldiers were on the Continent for the final blow into Germany.[263]

Patton's Third US Army was not to be involved in the planning of and assault on D-Day. It was designated to be a follow-up force entering the Normandy battlefield thirty days later when the beachhead would have been enlarged, secured, and maybe even opened. Patton, Third Army's chief of staff, his personal aides, and his dog Willie left England by plane on July 6, 1944 at exactly 10:25 a.m. They flew into Normandy, inspected Omaha Beach, and drove on to General Bradley's 12th Army Group Headquarters south of Isigny, where they spent the first night. The following day Patton and his entourage drove to Third Army's first headquarters on continental Europe in an old apple orchard at Nehou, southeast of the Château Bricquebec. In the morning of July 31, headquarters was moved to a place north of the Granville-St.Sever-Lendelin road. On August 12, Patton's command post changed again to six miles northwest of Le Mans. On August 25, it was moved to a place somewhere between

Orléans and Pithiviers, on August 29, to La Chaume, near Sens, in early September to a place southeast of Chalon, and in mid-September to a location five miles south of Etain, on October 13, to Nancy, and to Luxembourg on December 19, 1944, three days after the Germans had started their counteroffensive leading to the Battle of the Bulge.[264]

From Luxembourg Patton commanded attacks on the Siegfried Line, strong fortifications along the Western border of Germany from the Netherlands to Switzerland, consisting of tank traps and thousands of bunkers and pillboxes. One especially fortified portion protected the city of Trier. The First US Army attack on the *Siegfried Line* had led to the capture of Aachen, the most Western of German cities, in September 1944. In October/November 1944 troops of the First US Army also attacked the Siegfried Line in Hürtgenwald, a forest about thirteen miles away from Aachen. Inexperienced in fighting in such terrain where heavy weapons were of no use, the US Army suffered the bloodiest defeat of the whole war in Europe losing about 35,000 men, among them 12,000 dead, about three times the losses of the German defenders. This reinforced fears among Allied troops and headquarters of the *Westwall*, as the Germans called the Siegfried Line.

However, Patton with his Third Army learned quickly that the Siegfried Line with dragons' teeth, anti-tank ditches, and bunker and pillbox installations provided no real barrier to Allied armor when attacked at places where armored and infantry divisions could operate in tandem. When the 10th Armored Division supported by an infantry division was moving toward the city of Trier on February 28, 1945, Patton's superior, General Bradley, gave instructions to bypass the city, "since it would take four divisions to capture it."[265] Patton took the city of Trier on March 1, 1945 anyway.[266] Then he responded to Bradley: "Have taken Trier with two divisions. What do you want me to do? Give it back?"[267] Like Edward Tenenbaum, Patton was full of cynicism and black humor. Here is another example. When on November 19, 1944 his Third Army had encircled Metz and street fighting had begun, a German general commanding his troops in the city sent a message to the Americans that his men would fight to the last man. Patton's reply: "We are trying to satisfy him."[268]

He often ridiculed believers in fixed-installation defenses as well as military education and strategic planning more concentrated on defense rather than offense. The French Army had done this in the interwar years. During the 1930s it invested huge funds to construct the Maginot Line on the French eastern border instead of building up mobile tank units for assault purposes. Despite Maginot the French quickly fell victim to the German Army's attack in 1940. "In war, the only sure defense is offense," was Patton's belief and slogan.[269]

But there was also a dark side of Patton's personality, which overshadowed his months after the end of combat action in Europe until his death on December 21, 1945, from injuries to his spinal column in a car crash on December 9. After VE-Day he pronounced delusional ideas, even in public. He was not firm regarding denazification, feared that Germany and possibly all of continental Western Europe would fall prey to communist expansionism, and he held the view that Germany and its brave soldiers should replace the Red Army as an ally of the Western powers. United they should march right on to exorcise Bolshevism from the Soviet Empire.[270] In his eyes the liberated German inmates of concentration camps and prisons were nothing but communists, labor leaders, and Jews. The latter ones he hated most of all. When Eisenhower came to visit Patton's camps for displayed persons, Patton told him that Jews had "no sense of human decency." He was of the opinion that they "are lower than animals."[271] It is revealing in a wider sense that such racial antisemitism was not incompatible with the fact that Patton was a believing and practicing Catholic. Even during his military campaigns from Normandy to the end of the war he attended Sunday Mass regularly, unless the situation on the battlefield required him to skip it.

By July 1, 1944 the US Army and Navy, aided by the British elite force No. 30 Commando, had broken all German resistance in Cherbourg, the port in the north of the Cotentin peninsula whose capture was essential for supplying and reinforcing the Normandy beachhead. In late July the Third Army and most probably Tenenbaum with it was moved from England through Cherbourg into Normandy. It became operational at noon on August 1, 1944 and started pouring its troops southward.[272] Its spectacular military successes during the first two weeks of August are well documented in Patton's diary and his letters to his wife Beatrice.[273] On August 13, 1944 Patton wrote to his wife: "This is probably the fastest and biggest pursuit in history."[274] Why Patton and his Third Army, for which the general chose the code-pseudonym Lucky, operated so efficiently and how their courageous quick drives for the liberation of France and Germany developed is described in detail by eyewitness Colonel Robert S. Allen.[275] With secret and ULTRA[276] clearance he had been serving as G-2 Assistant Chief under Patton's G-2 Chief Oscar W. Koch during Third Army's campaign in ETOUSA.[277]

Famous economists served on Kindleberger's EOU team: Walt W. Rostow, later Charlie's MIT colleague and President Lyndon B. Johnson's national security adviser; Robert V. Roosa, John F. Kennedy's Under Secretary of the Treasury for monetary affairs; Charles J. Hitch, later president of the University of California; and Carl Kaysen, who would serve as director of the Institute for Advanced Study at Princeton 1966–1976.[278] Further OSS members of EOU were the following economists and secretaries: Harold Barnett, Warren Baum, Phillip Coombs, Russell Dorr, Roselene Honerkamp, Nancy House, Mark Kahn, Edward Mayer, Chandler Morse, William Salant, and James Tyson; the BEW contributed John de Wilde, Ruth Ellerman, and Irwin Nat Pincus.[279] In their rivalry for control over EOU, BEW had lost out to OSS due to the latter's better qualified economists (probably because BEW was a government agency with typically lower pay and less flexibility than the OSS institution which – although financed by Treasury – was operating like a private business with probably higher productivity than BEW could have delivered).

EOU-recommended targets were backed by General Carl A. Spaatz, Commander of US Strategic Air Forces in Europe, but not always by other commanders in SHAEF, including commander-in-chief

General Eisenhower and his deputy, the British Air Chief Marshal Arthur Tedder. The three main controversies over bombing targets were: 1.) nighttime area bombing practiced by the Royal Air Force versus daylight precision bombing preferred by the US Air Forces; 2.) strategic targeting of marshaling yards versus oil production and refineries to disrupt the German economy; 3.) tactical bombing of marshaling yards versus bridges over the Seine and Loire in preparation of the Normandy invasion to impede transport of German reinforcements from the Pas-de-Calais area to the Normandy battlefield. Despite temporary setbacks the recommendations of Kindleberger's EOU – sometimes belatedly – prevailed.[280]

The unit was stationed at the US embassy in London, then situated at Grosvenor Square. But it actually worked in an auxiliary building, at 40 Berkeley Square in the West End of London.[281] Kindleberger describes the contrast between his wartime and early postwar occupations in these words: "From 1942 to 1945 I was engaged in helping to take the German economy apart; from 1945 to 1947 I was busy helping put it back together again."[282] For the latter task he worked in the State Department, first as chief of the Office of German and Austrian Economic Affairs (GA) (with EOU-colleague John C. de Wilde as his deputy) from June 1945 until June 1947 and then as an adviser to the European Recovery Program (ERP) until the end of July 1948, before he switched to the academic world as economics professor at MIT in August/September 1948.[283]

From a few days after the Normandy invasion of June 6, 1944 to VE-Day 1945 Kindleberger had served as captain and major in the 12th Army Group under the command of General Omar Bradley.[284] Why and how did he get there from his civilian OSS status as chief of EOU in London? In his autobiography he has given the answer himself. In preparation of the invasion EOU was asked by the US Army how the Strategic Air Forces could be used in support of the invasion,

> we inevitably learned something about how to attack by air enemy
> supply and transport, and especially to force opposing ground troops

to detrain far from the battle and proceed by road, exposing them to strafing attacks. Using this skill I served in a combined headquarters during the invasion in June, and was thereafter transferred from OSS to [G-2 (Intelligence)] 12th Army Group, as an army captain, to help the American ground forces formulate intelligent requests for air support to the accompanying Ninth Air Force commanded by General Hoyt Vandenberg.[285]

G-2 and thus Kindleberger were stationed wherever 12th Army Group headquarter moved.

On July 19, 1944, shortly after Tenenbaum's transfer from Washington, DC to England, General George S. Patton's Third Army joined the 12th Army Group. At the end of the war in Europe 12th Army Group numbered over 1.3 million men. As part of an OSS field detachment Lieutenant Tenenbaum was assigned to the Psychological Warfare Division of Patton's Third Army, also a G-2 position attached to headquarters. Patton's and Bradley's headquarters were often at the same place, for example, in Luxembourg City and Wiesbaden. One can assume that Kindleberger and Tenenbaum, who had first met as OSS economists in Washington, DC in 1942, had been in close contact within the relatively small circle of military intelligence officers of the 12th US Army Group. They developed their friendship on the European battlefield in France, Belgium, Luxembourg, and Germany. After the end of the war in Europe they parted company. While Tenenbaum, urged by his wife Jeanette Kipp who was eager to join him in Germany, stayed on, Kindleberger left from headquarters in Wiesbaden on June 5, 1945 to go home. Airborne with a number of intermediate stops and waiting times, even days, he arrived in the USA on June 9, and in Washington, DC on June 11, 1945.[286] After only one week of vacation he was obliged to work in the State Department to prepare the economists on the US delegation for the Potsdam Conference in July/August 1945.[287]

In his own words Edward Tenenbaum described his career after finishing college as follows: "Immediately after graduation, a job was found for me by a generous '42 classmate, working in Washington for OSS. After six months I was drafted, training as a radioman, and sent back to Yale to OCS. These were my only unhappy months at Yale. Upon my second graduation, I was returned to OSS, and shipped overseas, where I never saw another radio for the duration."[288] Before leaving the States he had been trained in psychological warfare, especially in war propaganda aimed at weakening the enemies' military strength.

But the real reason for his unhappy months at Yale might not have been the training in OCS. While working with OSS in Washington, DC during the second half of 1942 Edward had met the woman of his life, herself an exceptionally talented economist, Jeanette Kipp. She had been born June 2, 1919 in Chicago, Illinois, and had been adopted by Myrtle and Warren Kipp of Rockford, Illinois. At the time of the census in April 1940 Myrtle Kipp was fifty-two. Accordingly, she had been born 1887 or 1888. She lived 627 Mulberry Street, Winnebago, Illinois, a village which is part of the Rockford metropolitan area, with her adopted son William, aged twenty-four, her adopted daughter Jeanette, aged twenty, and two lodgers, aged twenty-four and twenty-five. They lived in a house or apartment rented for $30 per month. The two lodgers and the place of residence suggest that the Kipp family lived in very modest circumstances. Myrtle had received no college education. Her highest schooling was recorded as elementary school, sixth grade. Myrtle Kipp did not specify any occupation in the census. But when asked for income from other sources she replied "yes," probably referring to family support from her husband. At the time of the 1940 Census Warren Kipp, her husband, aged fifty-eight, lived separated from Myrtle and their two adopted children at 730 W State Street, also in Winnebago, Illinois, in a residence rented for $20 per month. This was in walking distance just around the corner from Myrtle's address (0.2 miles). In this sense he remained close to his wife and two kids. He also had no college education, but had finished elementary school, 8th grade. He was working as a machinist in a machine shop. His annual income in 1939 was recorded as $1,544 [= $33,417 in 2023], a very modest amount for supporting a family of four.

Both of them must have been very proud of their adopted daughter Jeanette. She had graduated, class of 1940, from private liberal arts Rockford College. There she had written for the Rockford Review and had been a member of the International Relations club. In her senior year she had been listed in *Who's Who* among American college and university students. She had played the violin, also as a member of the Mendelssohn club and of the Rockford Symphony Association Orchestra. After graduation she had been a member of the society department of the newspaper *Rockford Register-Republic*. In April 1942 she had left her home town and had started working in the Treasury Department in Washington, DC. By March 1943 she was serving as a junior economist with the Treasury's monetary research department.[289]

During Edward's short period of employment with OSS in Washington, DC from June to December 1942 love seems to have gripped them both like a stroke of lightning. Their daughter Joan relayed to me the family story about their first encounter: "He was definitely socially awkward at a young age. My mother used to tell the story of how they met at a party in Washington. He didn't say any-thing to her, but he kept bringing her things to eat."[290]

What an emotional disaster it must have been for them that he was inducted into military service in mid-December 1942, stationed first for basic combat training with the 4s (AAF) radio school in Sioux Falls, South Dakota. Facing complete uncertainty about the future of their relationship Jeanette and Private Edward decided to marry before he would possibly be shipped offshore to the battlefield. The wedding took place in Sioux Falls, South Dakota, on March 31, 1943. Jeanette's separated parents Myrtle and Warren Kipp had come from Rockford, Illinois, a distance of 500 miles, and Edward's divorced parents, Joseph and Otilia, from New York City, an even farther distance.[291] It was clear at the wedding and even before then after Edward's induction to the army that there might possibly not be much of a normal intimate relationship between the couple as long as the war would last, except the longing of their souls for each other, the precious feeling of belonging to and supporting each other from a distance by mail.

After his basic training in Sioux Falls, South Dakota, had ended and after intermediate stationing at Seymour Johnson Air Force Base in Goldsboro, North Carolina and perhaps at other AAF locations, Edward Tenenbaum ended up at Yale for his "second graduation" on the premises of the Yale campus which had been requisitioned for OCS. This turned him into a second lieutenant in uniform on April 6, 1944.

At this point it is time to inform my readers that it would have been easy to display details of Edward Tenenbaum's military career if the catastrophic fire on July 12, 1973 at the site of the "National Personnel Records Center" (NPRC) in St. Louis MO had not destroyed his personnel file. All military personnel records from early on in American history were and are stored at NPRC as part of the national heritage of the USA. The fire destroyed approximately 16–18 million Official Military Personnel Files. The records affected: Army, Personnel discharged November 1, 1912 to January 1, 1960 estimated loss 80 percent, and Air Force, Personnel discharged September 25, 1947 to January 1, 1964 (with names alphabetically after Hubbard, James E.) estimated loss 75 percent.[292] The catastrophe happened – with the exception of the faraway Vietnam War – in peacetime and before the age of terrorism. When I called NPRC to order NPRC *Auxiliary Records* collected from numerous series of records for reconstruction of at least some basic information, I asked about the cause of the fire. The answer was that it was probably a security guard on the premises who had smoked a cigarette; at the time the storage facilities were not equipped with up-to-date-fire-protection devices. The lesson was learned – alas – too late. Today NPRC in St. Louis MO is located in a building equipped with fire-protection according to up-to-date standards.

How long Tenenbaum served in the AAF can be approximately calculated. We know for sure that the "Report of Physical

Examination" on Tenenbaum of September 10, 1943 was issued by two officers of the Medical Corps at Station Hospital, Seymour Johnson Air Force Base in North Carolina.[293] So Edward must have been stationed there for a while. We also know for sure that Tenenbaum's last day of duty for AAF 999th Technical School Squad at Yale in New Haven CT was April 5, 1944. Along with seventy-nine others he had "successfully completed the Communications Course, C1 23–44-C" and was thereby graduated and discharged from duty at Yale University. He ranked second lieutenant from April 6, 1944,[294] and on the same day he departed from Yale. As ordered he reported for duty at OSS headquarters, "Room 107 North Bldg, 25th and E Streets" in Washington, DC on April 7, 1944.[295] During World War II, Basic Combat Training lasted ten weeks, OCS until graduation seventeen weeks.[296] This adds up to twenty-seven weeks. But between Tenenbaum's changeover from OSS in Washington, DC to military service in mid-December 1942 and his "second graduation" at Yale, which turned him into a second lieutenant, sixty-seven weeks had elapsed, that is, forty weeks more than Basic Combat Training and OCS schooling would normally require. So he must have been charged with extra assignments, such as teaching or financial and economic research. Or he received extensive extra training, before he reached the rank of officer. But definitely he was not trained as a pilot, on account of his vision impairment and perhaps due to his most precious expertise in economics and finance.

From one source in his OSS personnel file we know that Tenenbaum had been released from duty from "999th Tech School SQ Yale U New Haven Conn." on April 5, 1944 to join OSS in Washington, DC on April 7, 1944,[297] actually to the headquarters of AAFs within OSS.[298] SQ stands for "Squadron," it conforms to the notation of "Sqd. L" (= Squadron Leader) in Tenenbaum's medical report of September 10, 1943, while he was stationed at Seymour Johnson Air Force Base in North Carolina. In his Final Pay Voucher of May 1944 his rank is listed as Squad Leader "comm."[299] It seems that Tenenbaum spent his military service outside of basic combat and officer candidate training mainly as a teacher in technical schooling at Yale campus in New Haven and at Seymour Johnson Air Force Base in Goldsboro, North Carolina,[300] before returning from Yale University to OSS in Washington, DC on April 7, 1944. The following day OSS Special Orders No. 83 assigned him to "R&A (ET) [Research & Analysis (European Theater)]."[301]

For private life, return to OSS in Washington, DC meant in practice that Kipp (she didn't like to be called Jeanette, a name she regarded as "provincial"[302]) and Edward Tenenbaum were allowed almost three months of regular marriage life before he was transferred from OSS in Washington, DC to OSS in Europe in early July 1944, four weeks after the Normandy invasion of the Allies on June 6 (D-Day). In Washington, DC Edward had even been granted a leave of absence for seven days beginning May 15, 1944, more than the other four officers listed on OSS Special Orders No. 111 were allowed to take.[303]

On June 14, 1944 OSS, located at 24th and F Streets NW, Washington, DC, issued confidential travel orders. Instructions said:

> Upon call of the port commander the following named personnel are relieved from their present station and duty and directed to proceed by rail to the New York Port of Embarkation, Brooklyn, New York, reporting upon arrival to the Commanding General thereat for instructions and water transportation to an overseas destination under Shipment IJ-900-CN, and upon arrival at overseas destination personnel will report to the Commanding General thereat for duty with the Office of Strategic Services.[304]

The order referred to only four persons: Private first class Stanley Rubint, Private Arthur B. Johanson, Private Sevellon Brown and Second Lieutenant Edward A. Tenenbaum, who was put in charge of the three enlisted men. Detailed instructions were also given as to their clothing, equipment and guns. Two sentences are noteworthy: "Pfc. Rubint and Pvt. Johanson are authorized to wear civilian clothing in the performance of this mission."[305] Does this mean that they would be performing the proverbial cloak-and-dagger work as spies? Nevertheless, Private Brown and also Private Johanson were entitled to "1 Pistol, auto. .45 cal. M1911" and all the necessary accessories. In contrast: "LT. Tenenbaum and Pfc. Rubint are technical specialists and their duties overseas will be of such nature that it will not be necessary for them to be armed with a weapon."[306] This probably indicates that they were meant to be the brains in the back area analytically processing information gathered by personnel in the field. As to intergovernmental relations one more statement in this OSS Travel Order is remarkable: "Reimbursement for the expenses incurred in connection with the travel will be made to the War Department by the Office of Strategic Services."[307]

On June 15, 1944 one of the chiefs of the R&A Branch of OSS, Lt. Col. Infantry Preston E. James, delivered upon request of the OSS the "Manner of Performance Rating" of Second Lieutenant Edward A. Tenenbaum as "Research Analyst, Transportation Section, Geographical Subdivision, Europe-African Division" for the period of April 7, 1944 to June 30, 1944 as "Excellent." The form also states the purpose of the rating: "for entry on officer's Qualification Card."[308]

On June 24, 1944, Tenenbaum had signed a

Certificate, I, the undersigned about to depart for duty overseas, hereby certify that I have 1. Fired the prescribed course in marksmanship with the arm I have been issued. 2. Completed all inoculations and immunization required. 3. Drawn the equipment as described in my orders. 4. Obtained the clothing in accordance with T/BA 21 and as prescribed for my theater. 5. Been advised to prepare my Will, Power of Attorney, Allotments, Insurance, Statement of Service. 6. Obtained correct identification tags, Identification card, Passport, Pay Data card, Statement of Service. 7. Been properly relieved of accountability and/or responsibility for all property and funds for which I am custodian.[309]

The call of the port commander must have reached Edward Tenenbaum and his three enlisted men on June 26, 1944. Under that date Edward A. Tenenbaum "2nd Lt., Air Corps" signed the Officers

Clearance Sheet of OSS. He named his wife Jeanette as "Person to be notified in case of emergency" and as person to whom "Lost or mislaid personal property to be shipped to," each with the address 2500 K Street NW in Washington, DC.[310] This obviously was Jeanette Kipp's address, since she had begun working for the Treasury Department in Washington, DC in 1942 and Edward was serving in the US Army Air Forces. Another source in the same OSS personnel file reports that Tenenbaum was "Reld fr asgmt & dy OSS Wash DC & asgd to sta outside continental limits" [= Released from assignment and duty OSS Washington, DC and assigned to station outside continental limits] and indeed departed from Washington, DC for shipment IJ-900-CN to Europe on June 26, 1944.[311] Asked for his residences in the last ten years on application and other forms required for federal employment after the war, Tenenbaum noted his address from May to June 1944 as 2500 K Street NW, Washington, DC It doesn't seem that he was on furlough from his military and OSS duties to be together with his wife before departure to the battlefield in Europe. Asked for his employment history on the above-mentioned forms, Tenenbaum notes OSS research analyst in Washington, DC and London, England, for the entire period from April to November 1944.

3.2.2 In Western Europe

On July 18, 1944 "HQ & HQ Detachment/Office of Strategic Services/ ETOUSA" informed the director of OSS in Washington, DC that Edward A. Tenenbaum, among numerous others, had reported to headquarters in Europe and that he was assigned to the Research and Analysis (R&A) Branch of OSS in ETOUSA.[312] This was located in London. Tenenbaum's and his OSS companions' transport from the Brooklyn port in the USA to England must have taken place between June 27, and July 17, 1944. Assuming that it took a few days for assembling at the New York Port of Embarkation, Brooklyn NY, all passengers for shipment IJ-900-CN, the actual crossing of the Atlantic probably took place in early July 1944. He then worked in the massively enlarged OSS branch in London directed by David K. E. Bruce.

From there he was transferred to the OSS branch in Paris under Harold Deutsch in mid-November 1944. In his double function as OSS member and army-trained lieutenant he became part of the Psychological Warfare Division (PWD) of General Omar Bradley's 12th US Army Group and was specifically attached to General Patton's Third Army. It is uncertain whether, before his move from London to Paris, he also touched base with the American–British German country unit in London which prepared plans for military government in Germany after the end of hostilities, including the *SHAEF Handbook for Germany*.[313]

Office of Strategic Services, 79 Champs-Élysées, Paris. Seated: Lt. (jg) Vernon Munroe; Mr. Ross Finney; Lt. Commander Dwight C. Baker; Pvt. Arthur M. Schlesinger, Jr.; Mr. Ralph Carruthers; Ensign Lawrence Stevens; Mr. Harold C. Deutsch; Lt. William Koren; Lt. (jg) Just Lunning. Standing: Cpl. Chat Paterson; Lt. Fred Foster; Cpl. Robert I. Kull.

FIGURE 3.12 Meeting of Tenenbaum's OSS colleagues in liberated Paris. The second European OSS R&A branch office after London was headed by Harold C. Deutsch

D-Day marked the launch of a mass relocation of OSS personnel from Washington, DC to London. One of them was Arthur Schlesinger Jr., later famous historian of twentieth-century US politicians and policies. As he and Tenenbaum must have known each other and must have shared experience in OSS during the last year of World War II, his recollections of OSS on a NARA conference in 1991 helps to fill gaps in the Tenenbaum story. Schlesinger, four years older than Tenenbaum, had been recruited for the R&A branch of OSS in Washington, DC in May 1943 at "the munificent salary of $3,800 a year. ... My job was to edit a classified publication of strictly limited circulation called *The PW Weekly* – PW standing for psychological warfare." PW was also a specialty of Tenenbaum, who, however, during 1943 and further until April 1944 was on military duty outside Washington, DC.

> In February 1944 the economist Chandler Morse was appointed head of R&A/London ... [He assumed the position at the end of March followed by a tenfold expansion of its professional staff.[314]] The arrival of Harold Deutsch in February [1944] greatly strengthened R&A political analysis. ... In late June [1944] I set sail on the old *Queen Elisabeth*, crossing out of convoy in zigzag course in 6 days from New York to Greenock, a Scottish port on the Clyde near Glasgow. There were 16,000 persons on board: Army, Red Cross, a smattering of civilians and Glenn Miller's band. Twelve of us slept in a stateroom built for two.[315]

It is probable that Tenenbaum and Schlesinger, who later also worked under Harold Deutsch in OSS/Paris, crossed the Atlantic as members of a large contingent of OSS personnel, together with Glenn Miller's band, which had grown to fame by majority student voting for bands at Yale during Tenenbaum's study years there.

Edward Tenenbaum had turned twenty-two years old on November 10, 1943 and was still twenty-two when he was shipped to Europe in early July 1944. This age, as "nearest birthday" was noted on a form 184. A/C (= Aviation Cadet[316]) was listed as his "Grade,"

Sqd. L (= Squadron Leader) as "Organization and arm or service." For the nature of the medical examination "TAC (EC)" was noted. The acronyms stand for Tactical Air Command and, probably, Electronic Combat. Tenenbaum's height measured 71.5 inches (= 1.82 m), his weight 184 pounds (= 83.5 kg). Today's body mass index, accordingly, was 25.2. This means he was only minimally above the upper end of normal weight. Tenenbaum's chest measured 36.5 inches in rest, 38.5 inches after inspiration and 34.5 inches after expiration. His abdomen measured 31 inches. These measurements stand for a well-built stature.

Under medical history the doctors noted: "Usual childhood deseases [sic]. Tonsillectomy and Adenoidectomy, 1931. No Sequelae. Seasick. Denies any other operations, injuries, or serious illnesses. Family history negative. Denies fear of flying. Denies all else." The examination of the eyes, otherwise normal and no red–green color blindness, revealed a considerable short-sightedness: -2.75 = 125 X 15 for the right eye and even -4.75 = -1.00 X 30 for the left eye. Otherwise his health status was impeccable: ears, nose, and throat functioned normally. His teeth didn't show any defect at all. His cardiovascular and respiratory systems were all normal. The x-ray of the chest was negative. A scar on his left knee was noted. His endocrine system, bones, joints, muscles, feet, abdominal viscera, genito-urinary and nervous systems were normal. His urine analysis and examination for hernia were negative. In sum, on October 25, 1943 the Assistant Surgeon of "HQS. AAFETTC [= Army Air Forces Eastern Technical Training Command][317] Greensboro, NC," captain of the Medical Corps L.G. Hoag, grades Tenenbaum as "physically qualified as aviation cadet, ground duty."[318]

What is the nature of psychological warfare? I quote from an American publication on PWD's operations from the Normandy invasion June 6, 1944 to the end of the war in Europe. It was printed in October 1945 in Bad Homburg, Germany. Judging by the quality of about 100 oversized pages of descriptive text and of almost 200 pages of documents and exhibits, it must have been authored and compiled by experienced PWD personnel waiting for new assignments or for a ticket home to the States

> The aims of psychological warfare are to destroy the fighting morale of our enemy, both at home and at the front, and to sustain the morale of our Allies. In the case of both, the ultimate aim is to build up a background of acceptance of what we say to the point where, when the time arrives, the instructions of the Supreme Commander can be transmitted quickly to the audiences for which they are intended, with some hope that these instructions will be acted upon. // In its simplest terms, modern psychological warfare is a vast operation in the field of publicity. Every possible medium of expression must be mobilized in order to achieve the broadest possible coverage. ... [Psychological warfare is] similar in many ways to modern advertising.[319]

This is followed by a list of examples: not only fixed radio transmitters like BBC, but also mobile radio transmitters and public address vans; leaflets dropped by bombers, fired over the front lines by artillery, and carried into enemy positions by patrols and agents; newspapers, wall news bulletins, and posters published for liberated areas to fulfill the people's need for information and instructions. As to leaflets: "Between D-Day and the German surrender, PWD disseminated, or supervised the dissemination of, more than three billion leaflets."[320]

But, of course, the Germans also made use of psychological warfare, especially after the US Army had crossed the border into German territory:

> as we approached the Palatinate. The route was littered with large cardboard placards warning us of the American defeat that lay ahead. ... "Stop!" said one, "Death is Ahead." Another one read, "This Is Our Ballpark Now," a worthy effort, to be sure, to communicate with the enemy in his own vernacular. The funniest one was a five- or six-foot rhomboid sign which was printed, in oversized, shockingly red letters, the simple words, "You Will

Bleed"// ... Indeed, the fact that the enemy would warn us against
our own eventual destruction – such a patently absurd suggestion –
actually worked against them; they were only reminding us of how
inevitable our victory was. In that sense this propaganda effort
boosted rather than demoralized our spirits. // Yet there was a slight
truth to the German bullshit. It didn't really matter that the
Americans had it all in the bag; these signs could have been true,
were true, for some of us. ... "You Will Bleed"was true, not for the
American army, but for some small percentage of it – and we knew
that when we read the sign, we knew it as we laughed. The only
thing we didn't know were the names comprising the you in "You
Will Bleed." So I'd be less than honest if I said that these German
efforts were wholly ineffective; there were twinges of fear, taciturn
comprehensions of the abyss, somewhere beneath the surface of our
self-assured derision.[321]

An actual proposal for psychological warfare originating inside PWD
with a mixture of white (source truly indicated) and black (origin
falsified) propaganda might best explain what PWD aimed at and how
truth and deception were mingled to achieve the aim of demoralizing
German citizens. Since January 1944 General Carl A. Spaatz was commanding not only the Eighth US Air Force stationed in England, but the
combined *US Strategic Air Forces* (USSTAF) in Europe, including the
12th US Air Force and the Fifteenth US Air Force, both based in Italy.
It was in Spaatz's headquarters where in the summer of 1944:

> the deputy director of intelligence, Colonel Lowell P. Weicker,
> promoted a psychological warfare bombing plan. Weicker wanted
> to broadcast warnings that particular German towns and cities
> were about to be destroyed, then issue black propaganda, purporting
> to originate with the Nazi government, that would tell the
> inhabitants that the Americans could not harm them. Finally,
> American planes would bomb the designated places, showing the
> German people that their government could no longer defend
> them.[322]

Spaatz turned the plan down, because he preferred US precision day-light bombing to nighttime area bombing with many civilian casual-ties, which the British Royal Air Force under the command of Air Marshal Sir Arthur Harris practiced. Harris had hoped to break the morale of German civilians, thereby shortening the war. This turned out to be a miscalculation on the part of Harris, while Spaatz's deci-sion against bombing civilians turned out to be just right.

3.2.3   In Wartime Germany

As a soldier Tenenbaum would also participate in combat when General George S. Patton's Third Army moved deeper into Germany. After the US Army had stopped the last German offensive in the *Battle of the Bulge*, which lasted from December 16, 1944 to January 25, 1945,[323] Patton's tanks in tandem with air force, artillery, and troops started their advance within Germany toward the Rhine, the last great natural barrier to overcome before conquering Germany. The 347th regiment of the Infantry Division of General Patton's Third US Army entered Coblenz on March 17, 1945 after heavy aerial and artillery bombing and in fierce street fighting. By March 19, at 8:30 a.m. the Americans had crushed resistance in all parts of the town.[324]

It must have been between March 8, 1945 (blowing-up of the Adolf Hitler Bridge, see Figure 3.14) and the especially heavy artillery bombardment of Coblenz on March 16, 1945 and the start of the taking of the old town by the 87th US Infantry Division of General Patton's Third Army the following day[325] that *Tiger Patrol*, com-manded by Lieutenant Edward Tenenbaum, was sent across the Moselle to set foot on the eastern bank of the river in old-town Coblenz. Other evidence corroborates this time span and even allows to narrow it down a bit. The daily situation report of the German commander in chief for the Western Theater of Operations notes for March 10, 1945 that the enemy took Lützel, a district of Coblenz northwest of the Moselle.[326] It was connected with the old town of Coblenz by three bridges: The Balduin bridge, a railroad bridge, and the Adolf Hitler Bridge. Tenenbaum's patrol must have come

across the Moselle from the Lützel bank of the river at the earliest
during the night March 10–11, 1945, but more probably after the
87th US Infantry Division had in strength arrived in that area on
March 13.[327]

In careful preparation of the capture of Coblenz Third Army G-
2 had during the week before collected information on the strength
of German defenses in the town.[328] An interim report of March 14,
1945, summarizing intelligence so far collected, came to the conclusion: "There is no evidence for a concentration of troops in defense of
the town."[329] On this date Patton's Third Army began its advance on
Coblenz by crossing the River Moselle from west to east at two
locations and successfully formed bridgeheads southwest of
Coblenz.[330] Another summarizing G-2 report on the defenses of
Coblenz on March 15, 1945 came to essentially the same conclusion
as the one a day earlier.[331] The date of Tenenbaum's daring, but
failed patrol across the Moselle into the old town of Coblenz can
be narrowed down to three days when following the eyewitness
history of the 87th US Infantry Division. It reports that "On
March 13, the 346th RCT [of the 87th Division] moved to a new
sector [the town of Lützel] on the west side of the Rhine and Moselle
Rivers, opposite the historic city of Koblenz .... With the 346th on
the left flank and the 347th on the right, patrols crossed the Moselle
during the next three days to probe the city and vineyard-covered
mountains to the south."[332] Assuming that the taking of Lützel took
place very early on March 13, Tenenbaum's patrol could have taken
place between 13 and 17, or even in the nightly hours of
March 17, 1945.

A reconnaissance patrol behind enemy lines had also been
among the daring missions during that one week of secret information
gathering. Some GIs of German origin in German uniforms equipped
with captured military papers and a captured German military vehicle
were ferried across the Moselle probably by night. This must have
taken place around March 10, 1945. The patrol returned unscathed
with an abundance of useful information.[333]

An intelligence unit of the Sixth SS Mountain Division Nord (*6. SS-Gebirgs-Division Nord*) had reinforced the German defenses of Coblenz on March 12, 1945. Raiding patrols of this unit also crossed the Moselle, but in the opposite direction. They did capture GIs and thereby obtained information that an attack on Coblenz was imminent.[334] As against that, an Operation Report of the Third US Army for March 13, states that in the XII US Corps zone two enemy patrols were repulsed after crossing the Moselle in amphibious jeeps during the night from March 12–13, 1945.[335] The SS Mountain Division's deployment in and around Coblenz didn't change the course of the war. Instead it contributed to the destruction of the Sixth SS Mountain Division Nord.[336]

This was the state of my knowledge before, during the second week of December 2019, I searched for and found the original after-action report on Tenenbaum's raiding patrol from Lützel into the old city of Coblenz in the G-2 *Journal of Headquarters* of the 87th Infantry Division. From March 15, 1945 23:30h to March 16, 07:15 four after-action reports on raiding patrols from the Regimental Combat Team (RCT) 346 reached division headquarters in Bassenheim, about six miles West of Coblenz. Tenenbaum's patrol report came in as the last one at 07:15 on March 16. We now know exactly that his and the other patrols took place during the night from March 15 to 16. Tenenbaum's report reads as follows:

Patrol No. 2, Lt Tannenbaum [*sic*] & 5 men in two boats (rubber rcn [= reconnaissance]). At 2030 discovered German patrol, shot at this patrol, no obsvd [= observed] results, went back for more ammo, returned back at river bank at L881965 [= geographical code] at 0030. Rptd [= Reported] that current in that place is swift. Patrol landed at L886966. Moves SE fr [= southeast from] this point to a Bldg [= Building] at L885964 where they were challenged. More than one German around as some were in fox holes,
Lt Tannenbaum tried to talk to them re [= regarding] regular army

functions, while patrol made get away, en [= enemy] had ambush patrol set, and then fire fight followed, one man got to where boat was and took off in boat alone to railway bridge at L896962.
Lt Tannenbaum couldn't get to boat so he swam the river and landed at N [= North] end of highway bridge. He states that current is very swift. Infod [= Informed] that where they landed the slopes were gentle, land not muddy. Did not rpt [= report] any underwater obstacles nor obstacles on shore. // There are 4 men of this patrol missing, PFC [= Private First Class] Cummings seen to be wounded and Lt Tannenbaum is sure 1 man was killed in ambush fight.[337]

The official history of the 87th Infantry Division in World War II reports that shortly before its taking of Coblenz:

> Psychological Warfare made an attempt to persuade the enemy defenders of the city to surrender but was unsuccessful. Koblenz now began to feel the explosive force of medium and heavy artillery shellings. Division Artillery, with attached units, prepared the city for the coming attack with nearly a full week of steady bombardment. // On the morning of March 16 at 0345 the First and Third Batallions, 347th Regiment, assaulted and successfully crossed the Moselle against light opposition.[338]

Since Lt. Tenenbaum belonged to the PWD of General Omar Bradley's 12th US Army Group, it is quite probable that he was sent to the Coblenz area and attached to the 87th Infantry Division to execute the PWD's unsuccessful attempt to persuade the German defenders of the city to surrender in order to avoid bloodshed and destruction. His raiding patrol mission the night before the assault of the 87th Infantry Division on March 16 might have simply served reconnaissance purposes in preparation of the attack. But it might also have been a second unsuccessful attempt of PWD's Lt. Tenenbaum to convince the German defenders of the city of Coblenz to spare them the imminent fighting of a losing battle.

The newspaper of Jeanette Kipp Tenenbaum's original home-town Rockford IL reported on Tenenbaum's raiding patrol mission more than a month later:

> The six-man patrol ferried across the Moselle river in two rubber boats, landing near the Adolph [sic] Hitler highway bridge in Coblenz. They encountered an enemy soldier and were about to take him prisoner when they were fired upon by enemy machine gunners. One man was hit. Returning to the boats, Lt. Tenenbaum had his boat punctured by enemy fire after he had sent the other boat into midstream. The lieutenant swam to the friendly shore about 100 yards away. // Boat Upset // While the second boat was crossing the river, the machine gunners directed their fire on it. It capsized, and three of its occupants were wounded. One of the men escaped after trying unsuccessfully to rescue his companions.[339]

I have seen a copy of an article with similar content, namely a report on Tenenbaum's failed "Tiger Patrol" mission across the Moselle river, in one of the different overseas editions of the US Army news-paper *Stars and Stripes* of late March or early April 1945.[340] Unfortunately, I didn't copy it, assuming that *Stars and Stripes* would be researchable online and I would this way spot the article not only with its exact date, but also with information regarding in which of the different European editions it had been published. But, alas, *Stars and Stripes*, is only accessible online via *Ancestry* and not the way almost all other American newspapers are.

My colleague and friend Irwin Collier shared two useful news-paper articles pertaining to Tiger Patrol with me. One article of an anonymous journalist, embedded in the 87th Infantry Division of General Patton's Third Army, reports not only on a different six-man Tiger Patrol mission, which had been successful, also in combat with German soldiers, and had returned safely. From that article we also learn that Tiger Patrol was a generic term for all reconaissance mission of the 87th Division, also called Golden Acorn infantry division, across the Moselle in preparation for the taking of Coblenz. And we are informed that Brigadier General Frank L. Culin from Tucson AZ was the division's commander. The six men of the successful mission all belonged to the 2nd battalion, 346th regiment under the command of Lt. Colonel William B. Aycock. (This might also be a clue to the command of Tenenbaum's unsuccessful Tiger Patrol mission.) The Golden Acorn division "has fought the Germans successfully through five major engagements. It has advanced a total of 109 kilometers; breached a heavily fortified section of the Siegfried Line; destroyed or captured 326 concrete pillboxes, and captured 3,467 prisoners of war."[341]

The second much longer article, a sort of mood survey of the 87th Infantry Division in front of Coblenz, carries also a report on Tenenbaum's Tiger Patrol and records its crossing of the Moselle river precisely "in the early morning hours of March 17." As reported, on order of Lt. Colonel Perry E. Conant of Care MI, commander of the 1st battalion of 346th regiment of 87th Division, three other successful Tiger Patrols crossed the river that night, but not, like Tenenbaum's, directly into the city. Therefore, the opening statement was: "The first American soldiers to set foot in Coblenz during this war were members of a 'Tiger Patrol' of this division under the leadership of Lieut. Edward Tannenbaum [sic] of Silversprings, Md., consisting of six men." The author knew of only two men who had returned safely when he wrote the article on March 17, 1945: Lt. Tenenbaum and Private 1st class Lester L. Snider of Hennessy OK. Only in this report about Tenenbaum's mission did I find the following information:

As the second boat, in which Private Snider was riding, reached mid-stream the machine gunners directed fire on that. It capsized as it was hit and three of its occupants were wounded. Snider, after trying unsuccessfully to rescue his three companions, swam to his own shore. Here he met two Germans who were from a scout patrol sent over by the enemy. Almost exhausted from the ordeal he had just been through and armed with nothing but a hand grenade that had clung to his combat jacket, Snider challenged the patrol, threatening to heave the grenade unless they surrendered. // The 87th Division starts its new operation of crossing the Moselle to capture Coblenz this morning with some valuable enemy information, thanks to the "Tiger Patrols" and Snider's two prisoners of war.[342]

So, Tenenbaum's Tiger Patrol wasn't unsuccessful after all. Private Snider's valor saved it from total failure.

Tenenbaum's daughter Joan reported in our interview of October 29, 2018 how US soldiers on the friendly side of the Moselle river made sure that her father was not a German spy: Lt. Edward Tenenbaum had to enumerate New York City subway stops.

The *Adolf-Hitler-Brücke* had a lane width of 12 meters between two pedestrian walkways of 3 meters each. It had been opened and dedicated to Hitler on April 22, 1934. Before Tenenbaum's patrol crossed the Moselle river to land near the bridge, it had been blown up by special forces of the German Army on March 8, 1945 in order to hold up the advance of the American Forces.[343]

The day before, the famous Bridge of Remagen (*Ludendorff-Brücke* in German[344]), some twenty-five miles northwest of Coblenz, had been unexpectedly captured – damaged, but for ten days still usable – by units of the 9th Armored Division of the US First Army. A few minutes before the German defenders of the bridge were trying to blow it up, a grenade of a US tank had cut through the main ignition cable, an unintended, extremely improbable lucky strike. A fallback, less powerful blow-up of the bridge did function, but it only lifted the bridge a bit from its pillars whereupon it fell back.[345] Ironically it collapsed the same day as US units entered Coblenz on March 17. During the ten days in between, thousands of troops and their materiel speedily crossed over to form a first strong bridgehead on the eastern side of the Rhine. From there the advance to conquer the Ruhr district, then Germany's industrial heartland, was launched. By means of pontoon bridges, assault boats, other watercrafts, and

FIGURE 3.13 The Adolf Hitler Bridge across the Moselle in Coblenz on a postcard 1939

FIGURE 3.14 Destroyed bridges of Coblenz, with the Adolf Hitler Bridge in the foreground after its blasting by the German defenders of Coblenz on March 8, 1945. Tenenbaum almost lost his life here

amphibious trucks all of the four US armies on the left of the Rhine had made it across Germany's main river before the end of March.

On March 22 at 10:30 p.m. the 5th Infantry Division spear-headed the Rhine-crossing of Patton's Third Army at Oppenheim even without a real or pontoon bridge. A Navy Detachment (Naval

Unit   N-2)   consisting   of   twelve   Landing   Craft,   Vehicle, Personnel (LCVP), also called Higgins boats, and their crew were attached to the Third Army. Oppenheim was chosen, because it had a barge harbor. The transport of the assault boats through the town could not be sighted from either side of the Rhine. And the LCVPs could be slipped into the Rhine water of the harbor quietly. German awareness of what had happened was a day late and so was German resistance. Patton also notes in his memoirs that he had figured correctly the enemy would assume that the first Third Army Rhine-crossing would take place at Mainz. To reinforce that assumption, Third Army smashed artillery fire for days at Mainz.[346] Therefore, German defenses had been concentrated there with two regiments. In order to reinforce the enemy's assumption, GIs covered both sides of the Rhine at Mainz with a smoke screen as if the crossing was imminent. In fact, it took place at the same time at Oppenheim and Nierstein without resistance to speak of. [347]

The Third Army pushed ahead to Frankfurt, which was cap-tured March 27, 1945. On the same day Patton moved his head-quarters from Luxembourg City to Idar-Oberstein thirty miles east of Trier, until he moved again on April 3 to Hanau, Frankfurt's catchment area. From these two places he commanded the speedy advance of his army in force into the middle of Germany, Thuringia. On April 10 Patton again moved his headquarters for-ward to Hersfeld,[348] about ninety miles northeast, but like Frankfurt still in Hesse. Eisenhower and Bradley ordered him not to capture Berlin and therefore not to cross the Elbe river, but instead to halt at the Werra river and from there later to turn south into Czechoslovakia.

The signing by General Alfred Jodl of Germany's unconditional surrender in General Eisenhower's Headquarters SHAEF in Reims on May 7, 1945 and on May 9, 1945 at 0:16 a.m. in Marshal Georgy Zhukov's Red Army headquarters in Berlin-Karlshorst by Field Marshal Wilhelm Keitel for the Supreme Command of the German *Wehrmacht* and Army, Admiral Hans-Georg von Friedeburg for the

	Third Army		Enemy
Human Losses			
Killed	21,441		144,500
Wounded	99,224		386,200
Missing	16,200	Prisoners of War	956,000
Total	136,865		1,486,700
Non-battle casualties	111,562		
Grand Total	248,427		
Matériel Losses			
Light tanks	308	Medium tanks	1,529
Medium tanks	949	Panther and Tiger tanks	858
Guns	175		3,486

FIGURE 3.15 Third US Army's final casualty report as compared to enemy losses for the whole campaign from Normandy to Czechoslovakia.
Source: George S. Patton, Jr., *War As I Knew It*, Boston: Houghton & Mifflin, 1995, p. 331

Navy and Colonel General Hans-Jürgen Stumpff for the Air Force ended the war on May 8 at 11:01 p.m.

The Third Army's final casualty report as compared to enemy losses is contained in Figure 3.15.

This tally list speaks not only for the superiority of Third Army in battle strength and tactics, but also for Patton's comparative success in minimizing own losses of men and matériel.

The habits of Patton about the setup of his headquarters are worth mentioning, because his G-2 officers, like Tenenbaum as well as his and Third Army G-2 boss Oscar W. Koch, mostly attached to headquarters, would have to accustom themselves to Patton's idiosyncrasies. The editor of the 1995 edition of Patton's memoirs, Rick Atkinson, describes them in a long footnote:

> While in the field and when at home in Army Headquarters, General Patton lived and worked in two truck trailers. // His parlor, bedroom, and bath was a converted Ordnance Trailer, entered from the rear after climbing a steep set of steps. The steps were corrugated iron and were a great hazard to Willie, the General's dog. After Willie had lost several of his toenails in the corrugation, it

became necessary to cover the steps with boards. // ... A radio was installed in an upper panel inside the truck, which the General used frequently in listening to broadcasts. He never used radio in talking to his commanders. Even during the most rapid advances, the Signal Corps usually kept up with wire communications. Once in a while it was necessary to use radio telephone, but this was handled over the regular telephone system installed in the truck. One of the two telephones – incidentally it had a green receiver – was a direct line to General Bradley and General Eisenhower. This particular telephone had a device supposed to scramble the words as they passed over the wire and come out as spoken on the other end. Most of the General's oaths were used at this device. It seemed he could never get it in phase and complained that it scrambled his own words before he uttered them. // All the electric devices were run by a mobile generator that furnished electricity for the Headquarters group. // The office trailer was a long, moving-van type of truck, fitted inside with a desk, map-boards, and telephones. It was located in camp close to the General's living trailer and was used frequently for conferences. // The General preferred to use the two trailers for living and work, and it was not until the winter set in that he moved inside. When spring came in 1945, while moving through Germany, he favored his truck-house for sleeping and used it even though his office was in a building and his meals served indoors.[349]

Interrogation of prisoners of war and of civilians to obtain information on the enemy's forces, their strength and location and on targets of special importance and value is a common practice in wars. This was part of Edward Tenenbaum's job in Psychological Warfare Division and of G-2 officers and enlisted men of US Armed Forces. Compared to this routine it is unusual that an enemy defector voluntarily offers valuable secret information to support the cause of the other side or to aid in shortening the war. A most peculiar example of this sort which even led to changes in the planning of Third Army advance toward the

Elbe river happened to General Patton and, as far as the goal of taking Berlin by US forces was concerned, to the Allied commander in chief, General Eisenhower.[350]

On March 19, 1945 a German officer defected and contacted elements of Third Army at Alzey, a small town West of the Rhine in the state of Rhineland-Palatinate. It was 32-year-old First Lieutenant Helmut Arntz[351] who happened to be apprehended by Patton's Fourth Armored Division. It was this Division that two weeks later would spearhead the extra advance of Third Army from the river Werra into the state of Thuringia to capture Gotha and Ohrdruf (a small town about seven miles south of the much larger district town of Gotha and about thirty-five miles Southwest of Weimar), near which the defector had pointed out a tunnel construction site for underground production facilities and a new *Führerhauptquartier* (Führer Headquarters), code-named *Olga*. Since the end of 1943 Arntz had been attached to the headquarters of the telegraph and telecommunication service of the *Wehrmacht* commanded by Colonel, later General Albert Praun.[352] The headquarters' and therefore Arntz' service location was that of the German Army high command (*Oberkommando des Heeres*). It was attached to the Führer Headquarters *Wolfsschanze* in East Prussia. When toward the end of 1944 the Red Army was approaching and the *Wolfsschanze* had to be given up, it was moved to the bomb-proof underground military installations in Zossen, some twenty-five miles south of Berlin. When the Red Army approached this area, most of the personnel of telegraph and telecommunication outfit was relocated to the town of Gotha in Thuringia on March 1, 1945 and General Praun undertook an inspection tour of the Western German front from March 2 to 10, 1945. Thereafter Praun traveled a lot short-distance in Thuringia for inspection purposes, also to Ohrdruf to visit the already completed telegraph and telecommunication exchange for Hitler's never-completed last headquarters *Olga*.[353] When experts of the US Army found the underground telecommunication center after occupying Ohrdruf on April 4, 1945, they were amazed at its technical modernity and monetary worth.

First Lieutenanat Arntz informed the Americans that he, who obviously had been left behind in Zossen, had been commissioned from there around mid-March to inspect and check on military tele-communications units in West Germany. He claimed that he had first reported to Supreme Commander West in Castle *Ziegenberg*, which was part of Führer Headquarters *Adlerhorst,* and that from there he had fled on a bicycle to where he turned himself in to elements of Patton's Third Army. But actually he had reported to Castle Ziegenberg only by phone announcing that he would travel directly from Gießen to the area of Remagen, to which he had been ordered to proceed. Arntz also claimed he had been part of the conspiracy against Hitler. But he turned out to be unfamiliar with names of prominent participants in the July 20, 1944 putsch. "On the other hand, it must be acknowledged that, wherever PW's answers could be checked, they have been found correct."[354]

After his orchestrated surrender to Fourth Armored Division, the German First Lieutenant contended that he possessed very vital information for the Western Allies which would help to speedily end the war; this would be in his patriotic interest. But he would give it only to General Patton. According to Colonel Oscar W. Koch, chief of Patton's G-2, Patton's chief of staff General Robert Gay would inter-view the German officer, whom Koch mistakenly took for a German major, in Patton's office making him believe that he, Gay, was the commander in chief of the Third US Army. This ploy worked because – it is true – Patton's name was famous in German military circles, but in most cases not his physical features. Koch and an interpreter were also present. First Lieutenant Arntz asserted that he approached Patton due to his reputation as "a doer." But before divul-ging his material, he asked for a favor in return: Could the Commander guarantee protection of his home and family which was on the way Third Army would probably advance? General Gay, in disguise of Patton, declined, pointing out the impossibility of such a guarantee in times of war. But he would listen if the prisoner wanted to talk anyway. Otherwise the interview would be over.

Then Arntz decided to open up. He explained that his duties in German headquarters had been concerned with construction of proposed military installations. He spread out a current map on which symbols marked the locations of communication centers housed in bombproof underground shelters. Work in progress was indicated by a color code. General Gay recognized the potential value of the map not only to Third Army, but to higher headquarters as well. Therefore, after his interrogation he immediately dispatched the prisoner to the G-2 section of General Bradley's 12th Army Group. At the same time a check on the credibility of the German officer was urgent. Some of the locations shown on the map were in the area of Third Army's planned advance. They would soon prove or disprove the defector's credibility. Until then the information obtained from the prisoner would be disclosed to only a few persons, among them, of course, Patton.[355]

"The information given to Patton's G-2 section that day was highly significant. It is quite possible it changed the entire course of the war. Prior to this time, the [Western] allied armies' objective was to take Berlin. As of March 20, 1945, it was still to take Berlin. That would soon change."[356] Actually on March 27 the Allied commander in chief Eisenhower took the decision to leave the taking of Berlin to Stalin's Red Army. Instead US troops – after encircling and cracking German resistance in the Ruhr district – would take their time to skim the cream from the multiple secrets that the Thuringia area promised to hold. Thereafter they would turn south to the Regensburg-Linz area to prevent the consolidation of German resistance in an Alpine redoubt in Southern Germany. The *Alpenfestung* was believed to be a real threat. However, in reality it turned out to be as soft as a soap bubble.[357]

The German officer's information was definitely verified after the Fourth Armored Division had taken not only Gotha, but also Ohrdruf on April 4, 1945. Both towns as such surrendered peacefully to Fourth Armored Division, but before each handover of control of the towns there was heavy German military resistance:

A whole company of German tanks decorated with leaves and branches and two small airfields hidden in the brush guarded the outskirts of Gotha. These panzers gave us the toughest resistance we had seen in weeks, though they seemed too tired to charge, or perhaps they preferred to stay as close to the airfields as possible. In any case it was a desperate defense; their fire was almost hysterical, as if they must have known that we'd eventually run them over. .... We took Gotha ... and we set our sights for the town of Ohrdruf. // We took it without significant incident, though a heavy German artillery barrage slowed our progress. A neat line of dead German infantrymen pointed the way from the outskirts to the center of the town. It was like following a row of tombstones to some dark destination – and little did we foresee how appropriate those signposts would prove and how dark that destination would turn out to be![358]

The Fourth Armored Division first found the underground telecommunication site, which the defector, the German First Lieutenant Helmut Arntz, had revealed to Patton's Third Army and afterward on March 29, 1945 in his interrogation by the office of the assistant chief of staff of the G-2 Section of 12th Army Group Headquarters, APO 655. There the interview was entitled *Interrogation of Oberleutnant Dr. Helmut Arntz.*[359] In any case, the underground telecommunication site at Ohrdruf turned out to be equipped with the most modern telephone and telegraph technology and luxurious designs of offices and living space, all very valuable. It was only thereafter that Fourth Armored Division discovered Ohrdruf's deadly labor camp.[360]

The advance of Patton's Third Army came to a halt for about two weeks to have different secrets that this area of Thuringia was supposed to hold investigated by among others Colonel Allen, assistant chief of Patton's G-2. The secrets comprised the so-called S-III tunnel system for bombproof underground construction sites (twenty-five tunnels under construction since November 1944) and possibly the new Fuehrer Headquarters as well as dislocations for the German military high command and the political government in Berlin.[361]

An unknown German POW had reported to Third Army G-2 in March 1945 that he had been working on a new and unusual weapon in Thuringia and that he had been witness of a terrific explosion which could not possibly have resulted from a regular bomb. At the time, the credibility of this prisoner remained in doubt, but after decades the story gained in credibility.[362] In 2005 economic historian Rainer Karlsch published his book *Hitler's Bombe* with his research results on it.[363] Although he had made use of sources in Moscow and Washington archives, his book was not well received. The Red Army findings, however, comprised only the remainders of the original findings by Third US Army, including the German atomic research installation in Stadtilm, not far from Ohrdruf in Thuringia. The German documents Third Army and its attached special technical task forces captured from there and its reports on those findings had not been fully declassified when Rainer Karlsch consulted them in NARA in the process of his research for his book of 2005. And until today they have remained classified. Historians or physicists are therefore unable to solve the puzzle of whatever super-bomb was tested on the Ohrdruf military training area on March 4 and 12, 1945.

However, in 2019 a team of three Anglo-Saxon authors published a biography of SS-General Hans Kammler, Hitler's and Himmler's manager for all secret and largely underground weapons production and development during the last phase of the war. The authors used the Freedom of Information Act to get access to some classified documents on the matter in the US National Archives. But even they could not penetrate into such classified documents deep enough to come up with a definite answer on what kind of super-bomb explosion had taken place on the Ohrdruf military training ground on March 4 and 12, 1945.[364]

From ULTRA intelligence (i.e., an intercepted German message) the commanders of the Western Allies learned already on March 4, that the Germans had tested a new extraordinary powerful weapon that day. We know it from a diary entry of Captain Kay Summersby on that day. She was General Eisenhower's Private Secretary and his lover during World War II. Therefore, she was part of a meeting of the top brass on that day when the ULTRA briefing took place. She noted: "Apparently the Germans have got some kind of a new weapon. – Whether it is a rocket or some kind of gas that we know nothing about. [Field Marshal Albert] Kesselring[365] is supposed to have sent a message saying that he would refuse to use its new weapon, as it wouldn't bring victory, but only a blood bath on both sides."[366]

For the relatively small state of Thuringia it is amazing how many secret underground armament production and research facilities as well as underground depots for storage of valuables were concentrated there during the last phase of World War II. The state became a cluster for turning the most advanced technologies worldwide into the most advanced products for military use. The most important of them have been collected and described in a book by Ulrich Brunzel on Hitler's secret installations in Thuringia.[367] The author covers:

- the already mentioned S-III tunnel system near Ohrdruf;
- the nuclear reactor research at Stadtilm under Dr. Kurt Diebner, while a larger group of leading physicists under Professor and Nobel laureate Werner Heisenberg was doing similar research in Haigerloch near Hechingen in the Württemberg part of postwar Germany's most southwestern state of Baden-Württemberg;
- the preparatory construction of the new *Führer* Headquarters *Olga* and other military command posts evacuated from Berlin under the command of SS-General (*Obergruppenführer*) Dr. Hans Kammler, an architect and engineer;[368]
- the tunnel system *Mittelbau-Dora* near Nordhausen, where slave laborers produced V-2 rockets (and V-1 cruise missiles) under the technical director of the German missile project and SS officer Dr. Wernher von Braun;
- and the *Reichsmarschall Hermann Göring* (REIMAHG) works near Kahla, code-named *Lachs*, where toward the end of World War II – also under the command of SS-General Dr. Hans Kammler – the world's first jet fighter Me 262 was mass-produced underground.

Besides Colonel Robert S. Allen's mission, numerous specialized technical task forces flooded into Third Army occupied Thuringia to probe the many hints for research on and production of most modern weapons. These had plentifully been collected by US Army intelligence from interrogations of German PWs or civilians. While in action, for example in Thuringia, the different most secret task forces operated largely on their own without coordination.[369]

One of the most important task forces was an American–British special team of atomic, biological, and chemical (ABC-weapons) scientists as well as intelligence and military personnel, code-named *Alsos*, the Greek word for "grove." This outfit had been created in late 1943 after the Allied invasion in Italy. The Alsos mission on German territory in general and in Thuringia in particular was the last one on the European battlefield. Under Colonel Boris T. Pash, a former Manhattan Project security officer, and Samuel Goudsmit, chief scientific adviser, it aimed at collecting as much information and records on the German atomic-weapon program and at capturing as many of the German nuclear scientists as possible.[370] The Alsos mission came to the conclusion that German scientists did not come close to developing a nuclear device. This served as the base for the near-unanimity among historians of World War II that due to lack of suitable moderator material, like heavy water, Germany was far from having an atomic bomb of the type, nuclear fission, that was dropped over Hiroshima and Nagasaki on August 6 and 9, 1945.

But the most recent research on *Nuclear Secrets* in Nazi Germany brings to light a lot of evidence that German scientists, especially Kurt Diebner and Erich Schumann, had experimented with nuclear fusion technology, first in Gottow near Berlin and toward the end of the war in Stadtilm in Thuringia. They were ardent Nazis which they did not disclaim even after the war when they kept on acquiring numerous patent rights in their fields of expertise. Toward the end of the war they were trusted and supported by SS-General Kammler who had been empowered by Heinrich Himmler, the

infamous SS leader, with command over all secret-weapon developments in German and German-occupied territory. Through Kammler
they had access to scarce research material. Schumann was the head
of Germany's Institute for Physics of Explosives. And

> Diebner was a specialist in hollow charge explosives, or shaped
> charges, which concentrate the explosive energy of a conventional
> explosive into a single point. The shaped charge was first
> weaponized by the Germans in 1942, in the form of the *panzerfaust*
> ("tank fist"), the first disposable anti-tank weapon operated by a
> single soldier. The shaped charge warhead of the *panzerfaust* was
> ingenious: impacting at a little over the speed of a baseball, it could
> penetrate every armored fighting vehicle of the era, killing all crew
> members inside.[371]

Diebner and Schumann were on the path to produce the world's first
hydrogen bomb. As compared to the enriched-uranium fission bomb,
it not only needed much less heavy water to produce it. But the heavy
water also served a different purpose, not as a moderator in the process
of enriching uranium, but as the active ingredient of the bomb. Here is
a summary description of the nuclear fusion technology:

> In a gross over-simplification of the science, for thermonuclear
> fusion reactions to occur – for two hydrogen atoms to become
> "fused" together to make a single helium atom – the hydrogen
> needs to be exposed to extremely high temperatures and pressures.
> In addition to producing helium, another product of a
> thermonuclear fusion reaction is the creation of a large pulse of
> energy – the same energy that drives the stars, including our sun. //
> Schumann and Diebner ... understood that for nuclear fusion to
> occur, the hydrogen atoms must overcome the repulsion forces (the
> Coulomb Barrier) to get close enough for the attractive nuclear
> forces to take over. They reasoned that any array of shaped charges
> exploding simultaneously around a central core of heavy water
> hydrogen would be sufficient to overcome the Coulomb Barrier and

create a high number of thermonuclear fusion reactions in the heavy water fuel – an atomic explosion. // ... Interestingly, the same early experimental methods employed by Schumann and Diebner during World War II would ultimately lead to the development of today's small tactical nuclear weapons (of a size that might have fit in a German rocket). Their experiments may have been responsible for the small tactical nuclear explosions rumored to have happened in central Germany near the end of the war.[372]

Reuter, Lowery and Chester link Schumann's and Diebner's research on and development of an atomic fusion (hydrogen) bomb to the parallel development since 1943 by the *Rheinmetall* company and production since 1944 of a new type of rocket, namely the *Rheinbote* (Rhine Messenger), also called V 4. In both cases, as for other wonder weapons, SS-General Hans Kammler was in charge and in command. In contrast to the V-2 missile, which could carry a payload of one ton of explosives, it was a solid-fuel rocket, which provided for more dependability and stability on the launch pad as well as in flight. The more slender four-stage *Rheinbote* could, according to different sources, carry only 20 or 40 kilograms. Loaded with conventional explosives more than 200 were aimed at the port of Antwerp and other targets from November 1944 to the end of the war. Due to the small warhead and the imprecision of the missile on its ballistic course, it was of little military utility bearing no relation to its production costs. The three authors conclude that the production of this rocket was promoted by Kammler for the purpose of having launch vehicles ready for carrying small hydrogen bombs that the physicist teams around Diebner and Schumann, also under Kammler's command, were about to push forward to the production stage.[373]

Another very important task force with activities in Thuringia was the Enemy Equipment Intelligence Service (EEIS) directly attached to the Supreme Commander of the US Army. Other outfits for specialized intelligence collection were: Combined Intelligence Objective Subcommittee(CIOS), Technical Industrial Intelligence Committee (TIIC) of the US Navy, Ordnance Technical Intelligence Team (OTIC), Combined Advanced Field Team (CAFT), US Strategic Bombing Survey (USSBS) under the leadership of later famous Harvard economics professor John Kenneth Galbraith, as well as other technical teams in direct support of secret services or branches of the armed forces.[374]

We know that First Lieutenant Edward Tenenbaum was an eyewitness of the discovery of Ohrdruf. However, I could not find evidence that he as PWD attachment to Fourth Armored Division of Patton's Third Army was involved in searching for or detecting the secrets mentioned above. Colonel Allen's search for secrets included an ambush of his whole detachment at the small village of Apfelstädt on April 7, 1945. He was taken prisoner by German soldiers and, severely wounded in his right arm, taken to a German military hospital at Weimar. An Austrian surgeon saved his life first by amputating his arm and second by declaring him not transportable when the SS wanted to have this secret service officer immediately transferred to headquarters in Berlin for a possibly deadly interrogation. Three and a half days later Third Army captured the hospital and liberated Colonel Allen alive.[375]

After its halt in Thuringia Third Army was ordered to turn south into Czechoslovakia and Bavaria. To the chagrin of Patton, the taking of Berlin by the Third Army had been dropped. It was left to the Red Army instead. General Omar Bradley, commanding 12th US Army Group, to which Third Army belonged, visited General Patton's headquarters at Bad Hersfeld on April 4 in the afternoon to deliver news on the new directive SHAEF was about to issue. "I know you don't like being slowed down ... and there isn't very much in the way of organized resistance to stop you. But at the same time, we don't want to take any unnecessary chances on getting a bloody nose at this late stage of the game. It's only a matter of a few weeks now before it's over."[376] Patton protested slowing down arguing that it might mean increased casualties. It would provide time for the Germans on the run to regroup and organize more resistance. Bradley retorted that "a lot of high-level politics are involved" in relations with the Russians.[377]

A German officer deserter had been apprehended West of the Rhine by Fourth Armored Division of Patton's Third US Army. This division received permission to advance further into Thuringia to capture the town of Ohrdruf near Arnstadt on April 4, 1945 and the unfinished underground tunnel system in the *Jonastal* (Jonas Valley) between the two towns on April 12, 1945.[378] As expected, it found a communication tunnel system early on:

> an immense underground communications center set up in deep concrete tunnels, with radio facilities, cables, and telephone switchboards large enough to serve a small city. It had been constructed as a headquarters for the Armed Forces High Command (OKW) during tense days preceding the Czechoslovakian crisis in 1938, but [was] never used. In recent weeks the Reichsfuehrer SS, Heinrich Himmler, had ordered the facilities expanded as a possible retreat for Hitler and his entire entourage, to be presented to the Fuehrer for his birthday on 20 April.[379]

The tunnel system was planned to be used as Hitler's underground headquarters code-named *Olga* in case he would want to escape from Berlin.[380]

But Fourth Armored Division found something else which it had not expected: the adjacent concentration camp. The inmates there had been worked to death on expanding the tunnel system. Tenenbaum participated in the liberation of Ohrdruf, as not only the description of his papers in the US Holocaust Memorial Museum reveals.[381] Interviewed for an article in the German weekly *Stern* published on March 1, 1964, he disclosed his attachment as a lieuten-ant to the Fourth Armored Division[382] during Patton's Third US Army *Blitz* advance from the Rhine into Thuringia. Needless to say, his role was Intelligence while he was attached from PWD of the 12th

US Army Group to Fourth Armored of Patton's Third Army. As Ohrdruf was the first concentration camp liberated by the US Army, the military top brass, namely Generals Eisenhower, Bradley, Patton, Eddy, Middleton, and Walker, came on April 12, 1945 to inspect the unbelievable atrocities committed there. More than 4,000 inmates had been starved, clubbed, and burned to death during the preceding eight months, claims the documentary of this visit.[383] The official history of the US Army in World War II reports on the generals' inspection of the camp:

> At Ohrdruf ... soldiers came upon the first of the notorious concentration camps to be uncovered by the advancing Allied armies. Small by the standards of others to be discovered later, the camp nevertheless contained enough horror to make the American soldier and even his Supreme Commander, General Eisenhower, pale. Patton, when he saw it, vomited. Forced by the XX Corps

FIGURE 3.16 On April 12, 1945 Generals Dwight D. Eisenhower, Omar Bradley, and George Patton, Jr. as well as other high brass of the US Army visited camp Ohrdruf, an outpost of the Buchenwald concentration camp

commander, General Walker, to tour the camp, the burgomaster of Ohrdruf and his wife went home and hanged themselves.[384]

Patton, as tough as he acted, had a habit of vomiting when tenseness grabbed him shortly before his army started an attack.[385]

Walker also ordered the citizens of Ohrdruf to visit the camp and bury the corpses. Before then Lt. Colonel James H. Van Wagenen, the Fourth Armored Division's military government officer (G-5: civil affairs), had taken a tour of the camp with Albert Schneider, mayor of Ohrdruf. He had been a Nazi Party member since 1933,

> but he had been an honest and conscientious mayor, and he had not skipped town ahead of the Americans as other Nazi officials were doing. He was shocked by what he saw. Admitting there had been rumors in the town, he claimed simply not to have believed Germans capable of such atrocities. On Van Wagenen's orders, he agreed to summon twenty-five prominent men and women who were to be taken to view the camp the next morning. In the morning, a soldier who had been sent to fetch him after he failed to appear at the stated time found him and his wife dead in their bedroom, their wrists slashed. G-2 investigators concluded the Schneiders' suicides were motivated by sincere shock and regret over what had happened in their town.[386]

Eisenhower's later recollection of Ohrdruf was this: "The things I saw beggar description ... the visual evidence and the verbal testimony of starvation, cruelty, and bestiality were so overpowering. ... I made the visit deliberately, in order to be in a position to give first-hand evidence of these things if ever, in the future, there develops a tendency to charge these allegations to propaganda."[387]

Patton described his impressions of his visit of Ohrdruf in more detail. Among these was the following observation:

> A man who said he was one of the former inmates acted as impresario and showed us first the gallows, where men were hanged for attempting to escape. ... Our guide then took us to the

whipping table ... [and] claimed that he himself had received twenty-five blows ... It later developed that he was not a prisoner at all, but one of the executioners. General Eisenhower must have suspected it, because he asked the man very pointedly how he could be so fat. He was found dead next morning, killed by some of the inmates.[388]

Tenenbaum certainly saw what every US Army member from top general to private could see and what Third Army's Signal Corp documented with photos, among them Margaret Bourke-White.

FIGURE 3.17 Margaret Bourke-White, US Army photographer of unspeakable atrocities at Buchenwald concentration camp after its liberation on April 11, 1945

Block 56 im Kleinen Lager. Stehend: Simon Toncman, untere Pritsche 1. v. l.
Miklos Grüner, 4. v. l. Max Hamburger, 2. Reihe, 3. v. l. Willi Kessler, 4. v. l. Hermann
Leefsma, 7. v. l. Elie Wiesel, 3. Reihe, 3. v. l. Paul Argiewicz, 5. v. l. Naftali Fürst, 6. v.
l. Leonardus Groen, 4. Reihe, 4. v. l. Mel Mermelstein.
Harry Miller, U.S. Signal Corps, 16. April 1945
National Archives at College Park, Maryland

FIGURE 3.18 Lieutenant Edward A. Tenenbaum and other soldiers of the
US Army were confronted with this and even worse scenes, like piles of
dead bodies, after they had liberated 21,000 inmates of concentration
camp Buchenwald near Weimar on April 11, 1945

When certified and passed by SHAEF Censor, the US Office of
War Information (OWI) in London would send them by wire to the
USA for the press to publish them freely in daily newspapers and
weekly magazines, such as *Life*, *Time*, and *Newsweek*.

To one of the photos the following background information was
relayed:

American soldiers who seized the camp found the courtyard
littered with the bodies of Czechoslovakian, Russian, Belgian and
French slave laborers, slain because they were too weak to be

evacuated. In a shed, they found a stack of 44 naked and lime-covered bodies. // According to survivors, 3,000 to 4,000 prisoners had been killed by SS troops, 70 being slain just before the Americans reached the camp. The 80 survivors had escaped death or removal by hiding in the woods. They reported that an average of 150 died daily, mainly from shooting or clubbing. The Nazi system was to feed prisoners a crust of bread a day, work them on tunneling until they were too weak to continue, then exterminate them and replace them with another 150 prisoners daily. // Led by Colonel Hayden Sears of the Fourth Armored Division, prominent German citizens of the town of Ohrdruf saw with their own eyes the horrors of SS brutality during a conducted tour of the Ohrdruf charnel house April 8, 1945. As they stood over the slain prisoners, Colonel Sears said: 'This is why Americans cannot be your friends.' ... The enforced tour of the Germans ended with a visit to a wood where ten bodies lay on a grill, made of railway lines, ready for cremation. Colonel Sears asked a uniformed German medical officer: "Does this meet with your conception of the German master race?" The officer faltered and at last answered: "I cannot believe that Germans did this."[389]

From ULTRA and interrogations of POWs the leadership of the US Army knew that Thuringia, which had already been chosen to become part of the later Soviet zone of occupation, was replete with hidden Nazi secrets. Besides the huge tunnel system at Ohrdruf there were reports on the testing of a new huge weapon on the nearby military training area on March 4 and 12, 1945, either an atomic bomb or some other device much more powerful than a conventional bomb. Furthermore, there also were huge gold, silver, and banknote assets (foreign and domestic) of the Reichsbank as well as art treasures from Berlin's first-class museums hidden in a salt mine.[390]

Before visiting Ohrdruf, Generals Eisenhower, Bradley, and Patton had visited the Nazi's treasure trove near Merkers in the morning.[391] On April 4, 1945 the town had been taken by Patton's

90th Infantry Division. In the morning of April 6, two military policemen (MP), Pfc Clyde Harmon and Pfc Anthony Kline, were enforcing the customary orders against civilian circulation. On a road outside Merkers they stopped two women. They were displaced persons (DP) from France, one of them pregnant. Rather than arrest them, the MPs decided to escort them back to Merkers. On the way they passed the entrance to the Kaiseroda potassium salt mine. This inspired the women to talk about gold that the Germans had stored in the mine. They said that local civilians and DPs were used as labor and it had taken them seventy-two hours to unload it.

> By noon the story had passed from the MP first sergeant to the chief
> of staff and on to the division's G-5 officer, Lt. Col. William
> A. Russell, who in a few hours had the news confirmed by other
> DPs and by a British sergeant who had been employed in the mine
> as a prisoner of war and had helped unload the gold. Russell also
> turned up an assistant director of the National Galleries in
> Berlin who admitted he was in Merkers to care for paintings
> stored in the mine. The gold was reportedly the entire reserve of
> the *Reichsbank* in Berlin, which had moved it to the mine after the
> bank building was bombed out in February 1945.[392]

On April 6, 1945 at 5:05 p.m. General Eddy, the commander of the XX Corps, had called Patton to report that his 90th Division had captured the German gold reserves in a salt mine near Merkers. Patton asked him to keep it a secret. The following day at 3:00 p.m. Eddy called Patton again and said that he had descended into the Kaiseroda Mine to enter the gold reserve vault and had found paper marks worth a billion dollars and a steel door behind which, if actually gold was stored in that mine, it would be behind that safe door. Patton ordered him to blow it up and also stated that he had two Reichsbank members in custody. On blowing up the steel door, Eddy found about 4,500 gold bars weighing 35 pounds a piece with an alleged total worth of 57 million US-dollars. At this point Patton informed Bradley, who must have informed Eisenhower.[393] Here is Patton's description of what he saw during his visit in the salt mine:

> In addition to the paper money [the equivalent of a billion dollars in Reichsmark] and gold bricks, there was a great deal of French, American, and British gold currency; also a number of suitcases filled with jewelry, such as silver and gold cigarette cases, wrist-watch cases, spoons, forks, vases, gold-filled teeth, false teeth, etc. These suitcases were in no way labeled, and apparently simply contained valuable metal gleaned by bandit methods. General Eisenhower said jokingly that he was very much chagrined not to find a box full of diamonds. We found no precious stones in this particular hideout. We examined a few of the alleged art treasures. The ones I saw were worth, in my opinion, about $2.50, and were of the type normally seen in bars in America.[394]

In fact, the treasures of the Berlin art museums and Nazi-looted art pieces stored in the bombproof Merkers salt mine were of great value and are shown in leading art museums around the world today. Patton certainly was a great military commander, but his understanding of art was obviously on the level of the Nazis who organized the Munich exhibition of *Entartete Kunst* (Degenerate Art) in 1937.

On Sunday, April 8, 1945:

> 90th Infantry Division engineers blasted a hole in the vault wall to reveal on the other side a room 75 feet wide and 150 feet deep. The floor was covered with rows of numbered bags, over 7,000 in all, each containing gold bars or gold coins. Baled paper money was stacked along one wall; and at the back – a mute reminder of nazism's victims – valises were piled filled with gold and silver tooth fillings, eyeglass frames, watch cases, wedding rings, pearls, and precious stones. The gold, between 55 and 81 pounds to the bag, amounted to nearly 250 tons. In paper money, all the European currencies were represented. The largest amounts were 98 million French francs and 2.7 billion *Reichsmarks*. The treasure almost

FIGURE 3.19 Reichsbank gold reserves detected by US troops in a salt
mine near Merkers/Thuringia on April 8, 1945

made the 400 tons of art work, the best pieces from the Berlin
museums, stacked in the mine's other passages seem like a
routine find.[395]

After the Reichsbank building in Berlin had been bombed out in
February 1945, its entire reserve was moved out to the Kaiseroda salt
mine near Merkers. Just like this operation had been a job for the
Reichsbank's financial experts, the safeguarding of the treasures
found by the 90th US Infantry Division became a matter of the top
financial experts of SHAEF. They learned about the spectacular find
when on Sunday April 8 Lt. Colonel Bernard Bernstein, Deputy Chief
of the Financial Branch of G-5 (Civil Affairs) of SHAEF read an article
about it in the New York *Herald Tribune*, Paris edition. In the afternoon he checked the story with Lt. Colonel R. Tupper Barrett, Chief of
the Financial Branch of G-5 of General Bradley's 12th Army Group.

FIGURE 3.20 On April 12, 1945 Generals Dwight D. Eisenhower, Omar Bradley, and George Patton, Jr. inspect art treasures stolen by Nazis and hidden in a salt mine near Merkers/Thuringia

Bernstein flew into Germany on Monday. At noon he arrived at Patton's Third Army Headquarters, now with instructions from General Eisenhower to check the mine's valuable content and to remove it to a depository farther back in the SHAEF zone.[396]

> Bernstein and Barrett spent Tuesday looking for a site and finally settled on the *Reichsbank* building in Frankfurt. Wednesday, at Merkers, they planned the move and prepared for distinguished visitors by having Germans tune up the mine machinery. The next morning, Eisenhower, Bradley, Patton, and Maj. Gen. Manton S. Eddy

took the 1,600-foot ride down into the mine. When they stepped out at the foot of the shaft, the private on guard saluted and, in the underground stillness, was heard by all to mutter, 'Jesus Christ !' // The move began at 0900 on Saturday morning, 14 April. In twenty hours, the gold and currency and a few cases of art work were loaded on thirty ten-ton trucks, each with a 10 percent overload. Down in the mine, jeeps with trailers hauled the treasure from the vault to the shaft, where the loaded trailers were put aboard the lifts and brought to the surface. At the vault entrance an officer registered each bag or item on a load slip, and at the truck ramps an officer and an enlisted man checked the load slips and verified that every item that left the vault was loaded on a truck. Finally, the officer recorded the truck number and the names and serial numbers of the driver, the assistant driver, and the guards assigned to the truck. // The convoy left Merkers on Sunday morning for the 85-mile trip to Frankfurt with an escort of five rifle platoons, two machine gun platoons, ten multiple-mount antiaircraft vehicles, and Piper cub and fighter air cover. All this protection, however, was not enough to prevent a rumor, which surfaced periodically for years after, that one truckload of gold (or art work) disappeared on the way to Frankfurt. On Sunday afternoon and throughout the night the trucks were unloaded in Frankfurt, each item being checked against the load lists as it came off a truck and again when it was moved into the *Reichsbank* vault. Two infantry companies cordoned off the area during the unloading. // The same procedures, except that a hundred German prisoners of war did the work, were followed in loading the art objects aboard a second truck convoy on Monday, and a similar security guard escorted the trucks to Frankfurt the next day. After the main treasure was removed, the mine was still a grab bag of valuables. Reconnaissance of the other entrances had turned up four hundred tons of German patent office records, *Luftwaffe* material and ammunition, German Army high command records, libraries and city archives (including 2 million books from Berlin and the

Goethe collection from Weimar), and the files of the Krupp, Henschel, and other companies. The patent records in particular were potentially as valuable as the gold; but Third Army needed its trucks, and Bernstein had to settle, on 21 April, for a small seven-truck convoy to move the cream of the patent records, samples of the Krupp and Henschel files, and several dozen high quality microscopes. // Leads found in the *Reichsbank* records at Merkers also helped uncover a dozen other treasure caches in places occupied by US forces that brought into the vault in Frankfurt hundreds more gold and silver bars, some platinum, rhodium, and palladium, a quarter of a million in US gold dollars (the Merkers mine set the record, however, containing 711 bags of US $20 gold pieces, $25,000 to the bag), a million Swiss gold francs, and a billion French francs.[397]

The gold in the vault of the Reichsbank remained under control of the US Army until January 24, 1946. On that day control and responsibility for it was passed on to the Inter-Allied Reparations Agency (IARA) in Brussels.[398] This agency was in charge of distributing not only reparations from dismantling war and other unnecessary industries in the three Western occupation zones, but also the gold on a pro rata basis to governments having claims on it. But according to a later agreement of June 14, 1946 $25 million in monetary gold plus all nonmonetary gold and all heirless funds had to be made available to nonrepatriable victims of German action. These funds were mostly used to compensate and resettle Jewish victims of Nazism. The USSR was not participating in the distribution, because in the Potsdam Agreement Stalin had consented to: "The Soviet Government makes no claims to gold captured by the Allied troops in Germany."[399]

It is certain that also the art treasures were removed from the *Reichsbank* vault in Frankfurt. For, since December 1947, Edward A. Tenenbaum, under top secret conditions, would be in charge of storing 23,000 wooden boxes there, for camouflage reasons labeled with *doorknobs* as their content. They contained about six billion nominal worth of Deutschmark banknotes. Tenenbaum had used all the influence he could muster in OMGUS, Berlin, and personally on the scene in the decision-making process in Washington, DC to have them printed in America at US government expense beginning in mid-October 1947. I could not determine where OMGUS moved the art treasures which from their Nazi hiding places, mostly in underground bombproof mines and shelters, had fallen into the control of the US Army and after the war into the hands of a sub-branch of OMGUS' Economics Division, called Monuments, Fine Arts, and Archives (MFA&A).[400] On a few pages Earl Ziemke describes some of the activities of MFA&A.[401] According to plans from early 1944, SHAEF and 12th US Army Group had MFA&A sections in their G-5 (= civil affairs-military government section), each equipped with one officer. Some of them were very critical of the senseless destruction of historical monuments by bombing raids on cities during the last months of the war. One example is what Captain Louis B. LaFarge, MFA&A officer of the Ninth US Army, wrote when after the taking of Münster in Westphalia on April 2, 1945 he himself saw the destruction of the city caused by the last severe bombing raid on Sunday March 25, 1945:

> The greater part of the old city of Muenster is gone for good. It is little better than rubble with the towers of the medieval churches alone standing to mark what the city once was. All the fine fourteenth to eighteenth century buildings are gone. // The cathedral sustained direct hits on the western porch and the nave, and an unexploded bomb lies near the sacristy door. … There is little that can be done at present. The *Domprobst* (prior) responsible for the treasure is dead, and a new one has not been appointed. The architect is old, ill, absent, and useless; and a new appointment must be made. The bishop and the vicar general have migrated to the village of Sendenhorst, and the only resident canon who had concern in the matter is an old man of somewhat defeatist views.[402]

As to the safeguarding, the British military government had already established a central storage facility for fine-art findings in its zone of occupation in a castle located at Celle in Lower Saxony a few days before the war ended.[403] Though the 12th US Army Group had also established collecting sites at Marburg, Wiesbaden, and Munich, its art-treasure findings were so large that transportation capacities became a bottleneck and the safekeeping of fine-art treasures and archival records took place mainly on a decentralized basis. Ziemke reports that

> At the time of surrender, although they did not know it yet, the US armies held the contents of all the major German art repositories except the Hamburg museums and, apparently, nearly all the art work the Nazis had looted in the countries occupied by Germany. The march into the south had uncovered dozens of cages, among them *Einsatzstab* Rosenberg loot at Neuschwanstein, the Rothschild collections at Herrenchiemsee, Nazi Foreign Minister Joachim von Ribbentrop's collection at Gailbach, and, in Austria, mines at Laufen and Alt Aussee – the first mine containing the collections of the Vienna *Kunsthistorischesmuseum*, and the other holding the best of the *Einsatzstab* Rosenberg loot, probably intended originally for the great museum Hitler had planned to build in his hometown Linz. // In neighboring salt mines at Heilbronn and Kochendorf, Seventh Army made finds that rivaled those of Third Army at Merkers. When MFA&A officer, Lt. James J. Rorimer, went into the mines in late April, he saw, in cavernous galleries 700 feet below the surface where the temperature never varied from 67° Fahrenheit in winter or in summer, thousands of paintings and works of sculpture, millions of books, all the stained glass from the Strassburg Cathedral, the crown jewels and throne of the Grand Duchy of Baden .... // On into June, depositories came to light almost daily. By the end of the month, the number reported to Headquarters, 12th Army Group, came to 849. ... Maj. Louis B. LaFarge estimated that just moving the contents of the Alt

Aussee mine to Munich would take the sixteen trucks at his disposal six weeks.[404]

The gold mine at Merkers was not the only treasure trove the US Army found in Thuringia. On April 11, 1945 First US Army's VII Corps took the town of Nordhausen on the Southern edge of the Harz mountains including the nearby underground V-1 and V-2 missile factory in *Mittelwerk*. This was located in an extensive bombproof tunnel construction into the Harz mountains. Attached to it was its deadly forced-labor concentration camp *Mittelbau-Dora*, which matched the horrors of *Ohrdruf*.[405] In contrast to that, VII Corps also detected the Benterode salt mine southwest of Nordhausen. On the one hand, they found it full of ammunition produced by the ammunitions factory on the premises. On the other hand, it contained historical and art treasures that had been stored there for protection from war damage. It contained:

> the remains of Frederick the Great, Frederick Wilhelm I of Prussia, and Paul von Hindenburg and his wife; the Prussian royal regalia, scepter, orb, crowns, helmet, broadsword, and seal; over two hundred regimental standards; the best books from the Prussian royal library; several dozen palace tapestries; and 271 paintings, all valuable, among them several by Lucas Cranach.[406]

Also on April 11, 1945 the much larger Buchenwald concentration camp near Weimar, of which Ohrdruf had been an outpost, was detected by elements of Patton's Third US Army's Fourth Armored Division, which was passing by it.[407]

The first US Army members to enter the Buchenwald camp were First Lieutenant Emmanuel Desard and Sergeant Paul Bodot on April 11, 1945. They were Frenchmen. Before the Normandy invasion they had belonged to French resistance groups, Desard to Organisation de Résistance de l'Armée (ORA) and Bodot to the Forces Françaises de l'Intérieur (FFI), which after its creation on February 1, 1944 united three important resistance groups including

ORA. The Fourth Armored Division of Patton's Third US Army assimilated the two French resistance fighters in Normandy. From there the two advanced with the Fourth Armored Division through France, Belgium, Germany, and finally down to Czechoslovakia and Austria. First Lieutenant Desard was in charge of the Fourth Armored vehicle fleet reserve. He and Bodot had been supplied with an army jeep which on the right fender they had equipped with a small French flag in blue-white-red with the cross of Lorraine on its white in the middle. This was the coat of arms of the FFI. What follows is based on a joint diary of Bodot and Desard.[408]

April 11, 1945: Sergeant Bodot describes himself as being part of the Military Intelligence Interpretation / MII of B Corps of the Fourth Armored Division. He and First Lieutenant Desard left their last billet in Gotha/Thuringia rather late due to thick fog in the morning. Their orders for that day allowed them room for maneuver to choose their itinerary, as on that day the combat troops spearheaded the advance. So they distanced themselves from the troops and took side roads.

There they noticed a group of prisoners who were guarded by armed civilians. They were greeted by a person who gave orders to a prisoner of Belgian nationality. This person in authority, also a Belgian, informed them of the existence of the concentration camp Buchenwald a few kilometers away. He told them that about 22,000 prisoners were seeking protection there and that the prisoners had liberated themselves by attacking their Nazi guards. From their own ranks they had formed armed groups and sent them out on foot with the order to capture SS men and guards under their command who had fled the camp. The person declared himself ready to guide the two French soldiers to the Buchenwald camp and seated himself on the hood of their jeep. After having passed agricultural fields and driven through a forest, they reached the camp and the Belgian guide roared in full voice: that the Allies had arrived and that the French were the first. Thereafter a flood of human skeletons ran to the multiple barbed-wired fence to take a view of the jeep as if to verify the announcement of the Belgian guide. Once they had driven into the camp they were greeted by leaders of the committee for the liberation of the camp which consisted of prisoners of different nationalities. The reception was indescribable, Bodot writes.

The emaciated and often beaten prisoners were a pain to look at. But at least they were living. Bodot and Desard had been somewhat prepared to cope with sights of misery when a week earlier they had seen the pile of corpses killed with shots in the neck in the forced-labor camp at Ohrdruf. The leaders of the committee for the liberation of the Buchenwald camp had already prepared lists of the most urgent provision needs for the camp's inmates, like medicine, food etc. First Lieutenant Desard used the camp's communication lines to inform his higher ranks of the urgency of sending such provisions along with physicians and medics as well as to relay that the estimated number of prisoners was 20 to 22 thousand.

Meanwhile, Sergeant Bodot was guided by some inmates through barracks with sick prisoners, including a Frenchman on the verge of dying. He was so happy to be addressed in his mother tongue that he asked Bodot for permission to hug him in the name of all present in the shack, which the sergeant conceded. Despite warnings by his guides of the risk of infection, he also shook hands. Many just touched his uniform as if to ascertain that they were not dreaming. Bodot let all this happen in order to lift their spirits.

Desard and Bodot did not spend more than one hour inside the camp, because they were in a hurry to catch up with their unit. To their great surprise, after having driven a few hundred meters away from the camp, they ran into a road on which US Army vehicles drove, unaware that they were so close to a large concentration camp. The moment Desard and Bodot had left the camp a jeep with American soldiers arrived. It must have been the one with Tenenbaum and Fleck. It is true that the two Frenchmen Bodot and Desard were the first soldiers of the Allies to enter Buchenwald. But it is also true that Tenenbaum was the first American officer to enter the camp.

A big step toward liberation had occurred after the roll-call officer at 12:10 p.m. had announced over the camp's loudspeaker system his last command: "All SS men leave the camp immediately!"[409] And they, almost 3,000, actually did so. The approaching battle noise of Third US Army's Fourth Armored Division, the appearance at 11:45 a.m. of low flying fighter bombers, and lots of heavy bombers heading east high above Buchenwald camp in the morning hours had prompted the SS to flee from the camp. But guards with their weaponry still remained in and between the watch towers around the camp. They, too, became scared of the Americans' approach in the early afternoon.[410] Most of them also fled into the woods around the camp. "The lead tanks of the American unit were visible from the camp at 13:00. About 14:30, American tanks were attacking the immediate vicinity."[411] The remaining guards on and between towers on the outer side of the fence had also seen, how American fighter aircraft was flying:

> low over the heads of the fleeing SS men, firing at them. The planes repeated their passes several times, and flew over the tower in which two SS guards were manning a heavy caliber machine gun. As long as they were there, any movement in camp was extremely dangerous. // ... Tension grew as the two SS men stayed at their post and continued to dominate the camp ominously with their fearsome weapons. Then the action shifted to the right of the barracks near a forest, where a large group of SS troopers suddenly appeared on the run. The Allied planes spotted them and opened fire until they disappeared from sight among the trees. They had either escaped or were dead. // Soon after, I saw two inmates with rifles in their hands crawling towards the guard tower. A shouted order went up to the two SS men to give up and lay down their arms. One of them pulled a white handkerchief from his pocket, tied it to the end of a stick and waived it in the air. That simple sign marked the end of Nazi power in Buchenwald! ... On April 11, 1945, at 2:30 p.m., misery, torture, starvation and death were to come to an end in Buchenwald.[412]

In the morning, inmates had caught the attention of American fighter aircraft by an ingenious action. Medical prisoners dressed in their usual white clothing had moved out into the open and grouped themselves to form the three letters SOS as a signal of their wishes and hopes to the low flying American planes. The answer came in the form of continued fighter sorties and strafing of fleeing SS men in areas outside the camp.[413] And US Air Force responded with an ingenious action, too. In order to encourage hope among the desperate lot of emaciated, sick, and depressed prisoners, one of the planes dropped a loaf of bread into the camp assuming correctly that starved inmates would run for it and break bread together. They would then find the written message inside: "Hold on; the Allies will soon be in the camp to liberate you." Typhus-stricken inmate Mel Mermelstein, already transferred to the Little Camp where the unfit for work were sorted out of the main camp in preparation for death, reports this:

> I felt that the bread itself was the message. The fact that they even thought of using a loaf of bread to communicate with us was both natural and intriguing. Bread was heavy enough to serve as a good missile, and would land where aimed. But it was a soft and non-explosive one that carried both the energy and promise of life within it. Bread would certainly be picked up and not neglected, and it would certainly be broken to reveal the note. // For me it seemed an inspiration that a loaf of bread from the skies – manna from heaven – should proclaim our imminent liberation. Bread had been the staple of our diet. If I had bread, I could survive.[414]

But the inmates kept swaying back and forth between hope and despair, even after the SS men had left the camp shortly after noon. Mel Mermelstein:

> Then another rumor was heard: dynamite had been planted throughout the entire camp, and as soon as the order was issued from Weimar, the camp would be blown to bits. // Indeed, it seemed more than plausible that the Nazis would want to destroy as much

of their handiwork as possible, together with the living witnesses against them. We heard rumors that the order did come through, and the fuse was lit, but the dynamite failed to go off.[415]

Mel (officially Moric) Mermelstein was born on September 25, 1926 in the Jewish community of Munkács in the Carpathian region of Czechoslovakia into a Jewish family with eventually four children. He was trained as a machine fitter and worked as an automobile mechanic and engine fitter in that same community. He lived with his family at Oroszveg 272. Before the outbreak of World War II, the Carpathian region was occupied by Hungarian military forces known as Magyars and ruled by Regent Horty Miklos. In March 1944 German armed forces, including SS and Gestapo, cooccupied the region. On April 19, 1944 the whole Mermelstein family with their four children was rounded up by the Hungarian militia. After being detained in a local gathering camp called *Kalus Telep* for about one month, they were loaded into railroad boxcars and were sent on a trip with, for them, an unknown destination. At Kassa, Slovakia, the guards on the train were changed from Hungarian militia to German SS. After three days and two nights of travel the train reached Auschwitz-Birkenau on May 21, 1944. This was part of the campaign in which from May 15 to July 9, 1944 Hungarian gendarmerie officials, under the guidance of German SS officials, deported around 440,000 Jews from Hungary and the occupied Carpathian region, mostly to Auschwitz. When the train with the Mermelstein family had arrived at the Auschwitz station, men fit for work were separated from women, children, ill, and elderly. Father Mermelstein and his two sons were grouped with the men fit for work. The last time Mel saw his mother and his two sisters, nineteen and fifteen years old, was when they were driven into the alleged disinfection hall, which he later learned was the gas chamber at Birkenau, at dawn on May 22, 1944. Mel's father and his elder brother had been assigned for work at the Jaworzno coal mines. As it turned out Mel's father, poorly fed and working hard in the hope of survival, fell dead in the coal mine from exhaustion. Mel's brother who had worked with him in the coal mine was shot dead by SS guards. Long before Auschwitz-Birkenau was liberated by the Red Army on January 27, 1945, Mel Mermelstein, after six weeks there, was transported from Auschwitz to one of its four sub-camps at Gleiwitz, probably due to his expertise as an engine fitter. The Gleiwitz IV camp worked at facilities that converted army truck engines to run on wood gas from gasifiers. With the Red Army approaching, Mel Mermelstein must have been transferred to the concentration camp Gross-Rosen approximately forty miles south-west of Wroclaw [the formerly German city of *Breslau*] in today's Poland. When this camp was threatened to be taken by the Soviet Army, he was again evacuated, this time to Buchenwald. He arrived there with a group of other prisoners from Gross-Rosen on February 10, 1945. At Buchenwald he was assigned his new prisoner number 130508. Infected with typhus, he was transferred on February 24, 1945, to barracks number 56 in the Little Camp, the lousy hospice for those expected to die. The healthier, fit-for-work inmates called such a walking-dead person *Muselmann* (= Musselman). Mermelstein found out that he had lost his whole family, as to his father and his brother already in Buchenwald, and as to his mother and two sisters after the liberation of Buchenwald or after the end of the war.

UNRRA paved his way for emigration to the USA with a war-ship ticket on SS (=Steamship) *Marine Perch*, which left the port of Bremerhaven on August 22, 1946 for New York. After ten days Mermelstein arrived there on August 31, 1946 at the age of nineteen. The ticket price had been $142. He served in the Korean War 1950–1953 and later became a businessman in California, and in 1980 was living at 708 Gladys Ave., Long Beach CA 90815. After publication of his book *By Bread Alone. The Story of A-4645*, he took the anti-Semitic *Institute for Historical Review* at Torrance CA 90505 at their word when the Institute had publicly offered a reward of $50,000 to anyone who would prove that the Nazis had killed Jews in gas chambers at Auschwitz. The Institute's purpose was to propagate their contention that the Holocaust, for example, mass-murders of Jews by gassing, were a hoax, a Zionist plot. He submitted his evidence, including his book, but the Institute didn't reciprocate by paying out the reward. He then filed lawsuits for 17 million and 50,000 dollars at the Superior Court of California against the Institute and some of its supporters and affiliates. The judges didn't have any doubt that the Holocaust was a matter of historical fact. Mermelstein won his cases, some by court settlement with the defendants, others by court sentences.[416]

Militarily well-organized inmates had already liberated themselves from the remainder of their guards and torturers, when shortly after 4:00 p.m.

> the first American armored scout car arrived [with Desard and Bodot], followed by the first tanks, which drove up in front of the camp. A comrade who had been imprisoned for twelve years greeted the Americans and gave them the directions they asked for. For three hours, without interruption, the tanks, motorized artillery, and motorized infantry rolled by the camp in an easterly direction. ... At 5:30 p.m. a car with two American officers [Tenenbaum and Fleck, the latter actually being a civilian employee of OSS] arrived at the camp and was greeted by the representatives from all nations on the camp committee. Captured SS men [78 altogether[417]] and even some Wehrmacht soldiers were constantly being brought in. But the command area and the surrounding territory of the camp had already been cleaned up. The battle for Buchenwald concentration camp had been fought and won.[418]

Communist inmates whom the SS had put in charge of running the camp in self-administration and who had skillfully also organized means of resistance, including a small collection of weapons, created the narrative that the prisoners themselves, not elements of Patton's Fourth Armored Division, had liberated the camp on April 11, 1945. This version became part of the historical account of Buchenwald in the communist German Democratic Republic (GDR), which used anti-fascist ideology to legitimize itself.[419]

But historians in West Germany and the USA, often based on testimony of inmates, regarded the thesis as a myth. Surely, well-organized and disciplined groups of inmates had taken control of the camp. But this was only in the afternoon of April 11, after the SS at noon had been ordered to leave the camp immediately. The day before food had been prepared for 2,792 SS men and on each of the previous two days for just under 3,100.[420] Had the SS not left the camp on its own initiative the inmates with their few small arms would never have been able to stand a chance fighting them. It was the battle noise closing in on the Buchenwald camp that prompted the SS to hurriedly run away.[421] Therefore, liberation is considered to have been a process rather than a single act.[422] The inmates played an important contributing role, but certainly a smaller one than the fighting Fourth Armored Division, supported by Air Force, of Patton's US Third Army. This is corroborated by a report of an anonymous author on the course of events on April 11, 1945 in Buchenwald: "When it became clear that the American tanks had broken through on all sides, the prisoners' military action in support of the approaching American troops began. The first measure was to take control of the command tower at the camp gate."[423] This happened at 3:00 p.m.[424]

Like the two French soldiers who had entered the Buchenwald camp about one hour before them, First Lieutenant Edward A. Tenenbaum and civilian Egon W. Fleck were also attached to the Fourth Armored Division. They were both members of OSS and served in the Psychological Warfare Division (PWD) of Omar Bradley's 12th Army Group. Their arrival in the Buchenwald camp is documented in an online document with shocking photos of heaps of corpses they found there.[425] Within two weeks since their arrival they coauthored the famous Buchenwald Report on the internal inmate governing structure of the camp. Fleck was a specialist of PWD, together with Tenenbaum hunting for militarily useful information for the US Army, for example, through interrogation of German prisoners of war (Charles Kindleberger was also doing this, as he once told me) and German civilians. And they applied means of psychological warfare to weaken the fighting spirit of the German troops and the resistance morale of German civilians, for example, by dropping leaflets and broadcasting. Tenenbaum himself stated: "The most interesting part of my military career consisted of interviewing German civilians as background for propaganda broadcasts. I got to see several interesting concentration camps and other tourist attractions and became rather hard-hearted about Germans in the process."[426]

Egon Fleck had been born on June 30, 1902 in Vienna, Austria. On September 6, 1932 he had married his wife Hedwig there. She was born February 24, 1907. After the annexation of Austria by Germany in March 1938 they had emigrated together from Antwerp, Belgium, to the USA on SS [= Steamship] *Westernland* to arrive in New York on December 21, 1938. The American authorities recorded their race in both cases as "Hebrew." They delivered their Declaration of Intention to become US citizens in the US District Court of Southern California for Egon on August 16, and for Hedwig on November 9, 1939. The latter date was the first anniversary of the pogrom against citizens of Jewish race in Germany and in annexed Austria. Hedwig may have chosen this date intentionally. In any case, their address of residence was recorded as 7622 Hampton Avenue, Los Angeles CA. His occupation was recorded as office-clerk, hers as housewife, his height as 5 feet 4 inches, hers as 5 feet 6 inches, weight 145 pounds in both cases.[427] I mention these bodily measures, because there is such a huge difference with those of Edward Tenenbaum who measured 6 feet 1 inch and weighed 184 pounds, as we know from his above-mentioned medical report. To the inmates of Buchenwald, Tenenbaum in his officer's uniform must have looked much more important than Fleck in probably civilian clothing. Fleck had been registered for the draft in California in 1942 at the age of forty. But it seems that he was never drafted. He entered OSS on March 3, 1944. He was assigned the role of a Field Representative. He left the USA for transfer to the European Theater of Operations (ETO) on April 5, 1944 and returned on August 26, 1945. His annual salary amounted to 3,800 US dollars. He died at the age of eighty in July 1982 in Des Moines, Iowa.[428]

The concentration camp Buchenwald, located in the vicinity of Weimar, was first detected by the above-mentioned two French scouts Bodot and Desard and about one hour later by the two American OSS members 1st Ltd. Tenenbaum and civilian Fleck in the late afternoon of April 11, 1945. All four were attached to General Patton's Fourth Armored Division. It wasn't until two days later, on April 13, that the American troops took control of the camp, including the prisoners of the inmates: SS men, guards, and *Wehrmacht* soldiers.

As mirrored in an inmate's eyewitness account of April 11, 1945[429] and in the diary of the German inmate Ernst Thape,[430] this very day was at the same time the most dangerous and exciting as well as the most longed-for and happy day for the inmates of camp Buchenwald. In the morning before the SS abandoned the camp around noon, the danger loomed large that the remaining 21,000 inmates of the originally 48,000 prisoners would suffer the same fate as the 27,000 that had been removed from the camp during the previous eight days.[431] They had been forced by the SS to move out of Buchenwald on long marches, called "death marches," into not yet liberated concentration camps in the South of Germany (Dachau and Flossenburg in Bavaria) and Theresienstadt in Czechoslovakia.[432] As during the eight days before, the weak and sick would be killed inside the camp before the march, and everybody who would collapse exhausted on the march would likewise fall victim to the unscrupulous SS murderers. On April 3, 1945, a first evacuation of 1,500 Jewish inmates on route to Theresienstadt took place; prisoner Ernst Thape recorded in his diary: "We knew that evacuation would mean death for every second person of us."[433] But when after the command of the SS roll-call officer at noon the SS men had left the camp without evacuating inmates, the inmates' weathering of highest danger reached its climax in tandem with the sun for that day. The further approaching battle noise then transformed itself slowly from warning sirens of extreme danger into the loveliest music played for the festival of their impending liberation.

However, the inmates learned of another fatal danger looming over the camp in the morning only after the event. Camp commander Hermann Pister told Senior camp inmate Hans Eiden around 10:30 a. m. on April 11, 1945: "I hereby turn the camp over to you. Give your word of honor that you will not let this fact be known until the Americans are here, to prevent a panic in the camp. From my side nothing will happen to you."[434] But shortly before that, Pister had demanded that the German air force bomb or strafe the camp. Unknowingly, the inmates were most lucky when the commander of the air field at Nohra rejected the order.[435]

When Tenenbaum and Fleck were arriving in the camp at 5:30 p.m., they were introduced to

> the Camp Commandant, a German inmate ... That evening the interrogators [Tenenbaum and Fleck] attended a meeting of the Camp Directorate and of the Council. Then they were provided with beds in Block 50, the Typhus Experiment Laboratory, where victims of typhus injections were observed as they died. In the morning they were awakened by a brass band, which serenaded them until they appeared at the windows, to be cheered by several thousand inmates. Later they were present at a huge parade of part of the camp's inhabitants, and addressed them over a loudspeaker system. It was an incredible experience, as hard to forget as the sight of the camp's crematorium, the fresh corpses, and the living dead of the so-called "small camp." It was the rebirth of humanity in a bestial surrounding.[436]

One of the German inmates witnessing the first "freedom roll call in Buchenwald," which lasted from 8 to 10 a.m. on April 12, noted in his diary that during that event speeches were held by the camp elders, Czechs, Frenchmen, and Germans. He continues:

> The American lieutenant and another officer [the latter must have been Egon Fleck] participated and marched together with the action committee, consisting of about 20 men, as the last on. Lieutenant

Tannenbaum [*sic*] spoke in limited American-German some words in which he said that he was glad that the camp inmates helped to do everything quickly, and that one would see things through to the end. The other speeches were more powerful and spoke of the extermination of the fascist brood.[437]

This is a testimony to the character of Edward Tenenbaum. Himself being Jewish, he would have had every reason to express hate for the fascist brutality that he had just been confronted with in the Buchenwald camp. Yet he remained analytical and disciplined in judgment, pragmatic, and reason-, result-, and future-oriented. He instinctively displayed precisely those qualities that had given American citizens the edge over other countries in developing their respective polity, society, and economy to a leading position in the world. In today's times of bitter political confrontation in the USA instead of compromise and respect for the opponent, American citizens could learn from Tenenbaum how valuable their traditional qualities are.

Buchenwald was full of traces of unimaginable atrocities and war crimes committed by SS men, their mercenaries on the guard towers, and by some of their *Kameradschaftspolizei* (Kapo) members.[438] On April 14, General Patton learned about the detection of Buchenwald. He immediately called Eisenhower to whom he suggested to send senior media people and photographers to document the atrocities. Eisenhower not only did this, but also managed to get Congressmen over. "This was the camp where we paraded some fifteen hundred citizens of Weimar to give them a first-hand knowledge of the infamy of their own government. In honesty, I believe that most of them were ignorant of much that had gone on there."[439]

Patton visited the camp on April 15, in company of General Walker. He devotes considerable space in his memoirs to describe his impressions, in part seemingly drawing on the Tenenbaum-Fleck report:

a large number of political prisoners [in other parts of this text Patton calls them "slaves," see below] were assembled at this camp and fed eight hundred calories a day, with the result that they died at the rate of about one hundred each night. I walked through two buildings, each with two tiers of bunks on a side. The bunks were at right angles to the gangway and were built so that they sloped slightly towards the front, and so that the fecal matter and other refuse left by the prisoners trickled down under their chins onto the floor, which was at least three inches deep in filth when I went through. Strange to say, the smell was not particularly bad; it was more musty than putrid. // The inmates looked like feebly animated mummies and seemed to be of the same level of intelligence. If a sufficient number did not die of starvation or if, for other reasons, it was desirable to remove them without waiting for nature to take its course, they were dropped down a chute into a room which had a number of hooks like those on which one hangs meat in a butcher shop, about eight feet from the floor. Each of these hooks had a cord of clothesline thickness with a grommet at each end. One grommet was passed through the other and the loop put over the slave's head, while the other grommet was fastened over the hook and the man was allowed to hang there until he choked to death, except that if he took too long they had a club, very like a large potato masher, with which they beat out his brains. The club must have been considerably used because it was splintered on one side. // One of the most horrible points about this place was that all these executions were carried on by slaves. There was a further devilish arrangement of making the various groups select those who had to die. Each racial group had a certain number of men who represented it. These men had to select those from their group who would be killed locally, or sent to camps like Ohrdruf, which were termed "elimination camps." // In this camp there were a number of allegedly eminent physicians whose professional rectitude had been so completely destroyed that they had been persuaded to perform some very abominable experiments on their fellow inmates. One case was reported in which eight hundred slaves had been inoculated with anti-typhus vaccine and

then inoculated with the typhus bug. Of the eight hundred, some
seven hundred died, and the experiment was considered
unsatisfactory. Colonel Odom asked some of these doctors if there
was anything he could do for them. One said yes, that he was
making a very interesting experiment on a human brain and needed
some carbon black. The human brain, apparently, was still alive. //
From the execution room in the Buchenwald set-up there was an
elevator, hand operated, which carried the corpses to an incinerator
plant on the floor above. Here there were six furnaces. The corpse
was placed on a loading tray similar to those used in the 155 mm.
guns and at the command "Ram home!" the end of the tray hit
against the stopper on the door and the body shot forward into the
oven, where it was shortly burnt up. The slave in charge of this took
great pride and kept rubbing his hand on the floor and then showing
me how clean it was.[440]

Heinrich Himmler's SS had established the camp in 1937 and
remained in command of it until his underlings abandoned it shortly
before the Americans arrived. Apart from prisoners of war inside, First
Lieutenant Edward Tenenbaum was the first American military
person to enter the camp on April 11, 1945. Together with Egon
Fleck, a civilian employee of OSS, he delivered the highly appreciated
report, dated April 24, 1945, not even two weeks later,[441] on the
governing structure of the camp below the SS, namely self-
administration by inmates. Buchenwald and Weimar, rock bottom
and shining highlight of German history, side by side. History is
obviously capable of black humor of its own making.

For the sake of brevity, I refer to the Fleck–Tenenbaum single-
spaced 18-page report by naming only Tenenbaum as its author.
In addition, for their first freedom roll call on April 12, 1945, the
leadership of the inmates introduced Tenenbaum as speaker for the
two Americans whom they had so enthusiastically welcomed and
hosted since their arrival the previous day. Further, it was
Tenenbaum who received the accolade for the Buchenwald report,

among other esteemed reports on Germany in preparation of G-5 civil affairs policy, by being awarded the Bronze Star Medal.

Tenenbaum subdivided his Buchenwald analysis into the following headings: A. Introduction, B. Evacuation, C. Present Government, D. Control of Buchenwald, E. Method of Organization, F. Groups Other Than Communist, G. Atrocities, H. The Small Camp, I. The Transports, and Annex A.

I quote the introduction in full:

1. The full truth about BUCHENWALD will never be known.
   To approach it a large staff of interrogators would be necessary, as well as some means of protecting witnesses. The look of terror in the eyes of inmates when certain questions were asked was not lost on the writers. Names of informants are not given in this report. They are still in BUCHENWALD, and would undoubtedly be in the grave gravest danger if what they have said ever becomes known there. The major informants are two Allied intelligence agents who were caught by the Germans.

2. The writers first learned of the liberation of BUCHENWALD as they were riding down a forest road with an American column. They turned a corner onto a main highway, and saw thousands of ragged, hungry-looking men, marching in orderly formations, marching East. These men were armed, and had leaders at their sides. Some platoons carried German rifles. Some platoons had PANZERFAUSTS on their shoulders. Some carried "potato masher" hand grenades. They laughed and waved wildly as they walked. Or their captains saluted gravely for them. They were of many nationalities, a platoon of French, followed by a platoon of Spaniards, platoons of Russians, Poles, Jews, Dutch, mixed platoons. Some wore striped convicts suits, some ragged uniforms of the United Nations,[442] some shreds of civilian clothes. These were inmates of BUCHENWALD, walking out to war as tanks swept by at 25 miles per hour.

3. They were ordered to return to their camp by a tank officer. They did so, though many seemed disappointed. They wanted to

know where the Germans were. They wanted to kill. The interrogators turned back towards BUCHENWALD, which lay close on the main road. At the gates of the camp were sentries. In the camp was a Camp Commandant, a German inmate. In the camp were 21,000 survivors who cheered at the sight of an American uniform, rushed out to shake hands, and threw valuable binoculars from their slave workshops at the passing troops. Yet in the camp there reigned order. Meals were served. Armed guards – inmates – patrolled the somber grounds, and wildly excited groups of men calmed at a word from those in authority.

4. That evening the interrogators attended a meeting of the Camp Directorate and of the Council. Then they were provided with beds in Block 50, the Typhus Experiment Laboratory, where victims of typhus injections were observed as they died. In the morning they were awakened by a brass band, which serenaded them until they appeared at the windows, to be cheered by several thousand inmates. Later they were present at a huge parade of part of the camp's inhabitants, and addressed them over a loudspeaker system. It was an incredible experience, as hard to forget as the sight of the camp's crematorium, the fresh corpses, and the living dead of the so-called "small camp." It was the rebirth of humanity in a bestial surrounding.

5. The immediate problems of BUCHENWALD are food and medicine. When American troops entered, there had been no bread for three days. The Nazis removed most of the food supply before leaving. Regular sources of supply are being visited by an inmate driving a car, who already has an MG pass. But those in the neighborhood cannot suffice. Five or six thousand of the survivors are critically ill. Dysentery, typhus and phlegmenia [*sic*] are the most important diseases. Medical supplies are very low.[443]

Under *B. Evacuation* Tenenbaum reports about such events which occurred from April 3 to 10, 1945, altogether 27,000, marching on foot accompanied by SS guards and held together by death threats, many of them carried out. The communist inmates were largely in control of the self-administration of the camp, including the "trustees," as Tenenbaum called the Kapos, and the internal police force consisting of inmates. Over some years they had prepared themselves for mutiny and self-liberation by stealing all sorts of weapons from the SS or weapon factories that prisoners were forced to work in. Tenenbaum realistically judged their weaponry as no match for that of the SS guards. But Tenenbaum acknowledged that the communist "trustees" of the SS sabotaged the complete evacuation of the camp by all sorts of delaying tactics. He takes note of the claim by the communist leadership of the camp that armed prisoners had liberated the camp from SS guards and their guns on and between the watch towers outside the fence of the camp by storming those. But he also writes "that there was no actual fighting between inmates and SS until American troops had seized control of the area."[444]

Tenenbaum juxtaposes this claim with what had been

worked out by certain Western European nationals independently, which played some part in the survival of the remaining prisoners. This consisted of playing on the feelings of the camp commander [as of January 1, 1942 Hermann Pister], to encourage him to continue delaying the evacuation. On Sunday morning, April 8, an inmate[445] left the camp and donned the uniform of a German Air Force EM. He went to WEIMAR and mailed a letter. The letter was based on information to the effect that Allied parachute agents had been dropped between EISENACH and ERFURT, and had not been captured. It was addressed to the commandant of Buchenwald, and stated: "A special mission has been dropped in your area. We know of the scandal and terrors at OHRDRUF. We also know that there has been an improvement in your camp since the time of KOCH (PISTER's predecessor). At the moment our tank commanders are on the way to bring you to account. You must cease sending evacuation transports from BUCHENWALD. You must cease at

once. You have one more chance." // The letter was received by
PISTER on Monday, and appears to have had a great effect on him.
However, an order arrived from BERLIN, insisting on evacuation
and threatening that if he disobeyed, he would be turned over to the
Security Police (SICHERHEITSDIENST). The Commandant
continued evacuating but did not make use of the harsh measures
which lay within his power, and which would have resulted in the
speedy removal of all inmates.[446]

A much more detailed account of the tug of war over evacuation
during the two weeks before liberation between Himmler and Pister
on the one hand and between Pister and his Buchenwald prisoners on
the other is contained in memoirs of the British inmate Christopher
Burney, originally published in the autumn of 1945.[447]

Here is some information on Christopher Burney's background.
Born 1917 and having run away from school at age sixteen, he had
mainly lived in France until the war broke out. After French defeat he
had been dropped into France as a Special Operations Executive (SOE)
working with the French Resistance. In 1942 he was captured by the
Gestapo, the German Secret Police. Until the end of 1943 he was held
in *Solitary Confinement* by the Gestapo in France and then was
transferred to Buchenwald in a train load of Frenchmen, which he
describes as follows: "I came to Buchenwald in a convoy of two
thousand Frenchmen. We spent four days in wagons (40 hommes,
8 chevaux en long), 110 men in a wagon, with no water and two small
holes for air, which were almost completely blocked by wire."[448] So he
never experienced the worst of Buchenwald under its first commander
Karl Otto Koch, his sadistic wife Ilse, and the German criminal
inmates whom Koch had put into positions of power within the self-
administration of the camp by inmates. Koch and his wife were first
arrested in 1941. He was removed from his commanding post in
Buchenwald. He was finally sentenced to death by an SS-Nazi court
for murder, receiving stolen goods, fraud, and embezzlement, while Ilse
Koch was acquitted.

As if murderous SS-Nazis wanted to express their sense of black humor shortly before their ultimate downfall, Karl Otto Koch was finally executed in the Buchenwald camp on April 5, 1945 (i.e., about a week before the camp's liberation on April 11, 1945). His sadistic wife Ilse was sentenced for murder charges to life-long imprisonment in the Buchenwald trials in former concentration camp Dachau/ Bavaria, US occupation zone, in 1947 and again in a German court in Bavaria in January 1951. She hanged herself in her prison cell in September 1967.

Burney also reproduces "as nearly as I can remember" the text of the forged letter of April 8, 1945 to Pister. Its content is in essence identical with what Tenenbaum reports. But Burney relates some more information which Tenenbaum left out. Burney's text is fake undersigned by "James Macleod, Major, War Office, London." Its heading is "Weimar, April 8th, 1945." As on that date Weimar had not yet been taken by Patton's Third Army, Burney's text contains an explanation for the writing and mailing of the letter in Weimar on April 8: "Dropped from the air with a special mission," in combination with "Stop it [evacuations], Commandant, stop it at once! ... You have one more chance!" The special mission to contact him, Pister, was meant to be as flattering for Pister as the opening paragraph of the letter: "Hitherto you have earned for yourself the reputation of being one of the best commandants of a concentration camp. We, the Allies, know this as well as your prisoners."[449]

The letter, in short, is a psychological masterpiece of a carrot-and-stick approach to entice Buchenwald commander Pister to handle evacuations in the prisoners' interest. Burney reveals that he himself was involved in planning the subversive action and drafting the letter. But he praises, even reveres his German noncommunist fellow prisoner who during the night from April 7 to 8, 1945 proposed the idea for such a forged letter, took the lead in planning the whole operation, inspired reliable fellow noncommunist prisoners, among them Burney, to cooperate and adopt the plan, and finally in a German air force uniform carried the letter to Weimar for mailing it there to Pister. Burney names Emil Kalman,

> head and shoulders above all, ... a Viennese journalist. ... Emil had, in August 1944, saved two British and one French officer from certain execution. It was at this time that I came to know him, though our relations were for security reasons restraint, and to appreciate his unbelievable clarity and coolness of mind and his ability to take risks which would have daunted most ordinary heroes. ... Emil had been in Buchenwald since the early days of the war. He was, in Austrian politics, known to be a Rightist and a Catholic, and for this reason came in for much persecution at the hands of the Communists. He escaped two of their traps, but one day, finding himself scheduled to leave for Auschwitz for liquidation, took a bold step and persuaded the SS major in charge of the Hygiene Institute to employ him as secretary. ... Emil was virtually in safety from his fellow prisoners. ... Working for [*Sturmbannführer* = major] Ding he studied him, learned his connections with Himmler, of whom he was a special protégé, read his correspondence and established himself in his confidence. Often Ding would take him down to Weimar, where he met the major's family and even became known to the children as 'Onkel Emil,' and in a short time he had so far mastered his subject that he was in effect master of the Institute, Ding and all. When he was approached in the matter of the three [Allied] officers, he never hesitated, but agreed to save them, and proved his mastery by virtually forcing Ding into committing himself. It was the first important use he had made of his power and it was such a complete success that, when one of the three was called for by the executioners before he had time to die, Ding made a personal assurance to the Commandant that he had executed him himself and a certificate to that effect was sent to Gestapo Headquarters.[450]

We know from another source that it was Eugen Kogon who in a German air force uniform carried the forged letter of April 8 to

Weimar and mailed it there.[451] We also know that Christopher Burney had been an agent of the British Secret Service whose members are accustomed to cover up real names and instead use pseudonyms. Therefore, it is easy to surmise that Emil Kalmann is in fact Eugen Kogon, identical initials. The information that Burney provides on Emil Kalmann's background, "in Buchenwald since the early days of the war. He was in Austrian politics"[452] etc., corroborates this identification. Christopher Burney's adoration for Eugen Kogon, alias Emil Kalmann, stems from the fact that Burney was one of the Allied officers whose lives Kogon had saved.[453]

Four prominent non-German inmates of Buchenwald had already approached Pister by letter on April 3, 1945 with the same intention as that the forged letter of five days later aimed at, namely to stop or at least delay the evacuations of the camp with their extremely high death toll. The foursome consisted of:

> the Belgian cabinet member Soudain, the French under-secretary of state, Marie, Captain Burney, and the Dutch naval officer, Cool.
>
> The letter, in clever fashion, certified the Commandant's loyal and correct behavior and expressed the hope that the four signers, once they had returned to their countries, might find the opportunity to call this to public attention. The Commandant's barber transmitted the letter, which had its effect. Pister took it to be a safe-conduct for himself and his family. "One can always delay carrying out an order!" he remarked.[454]

A very good portrayal of the different styles of the two commanders of concentration camp Buchenwald has also been provided by Christopher Burney. The first one was Karl Otto Koch, the most brutal commander of Buchenwald, from mid-July 1937 to his first arrest in November 1941. At that time Himmler intervened and enforced his release. But Koch's loss of the command of Buchenwald remained in place. He was transferred to concentration camp Majdanek in occupied Poland as its commander. After more evidence of his wrongdoings even against SS-standards had been collected, he – together with his wife Ilse, the bitch of Buchenwald – was arrested again in August 1943. He was sentenced to death for murder and corruption by a special court for Himmler's police- and SS men in Kassel. It was headed by SS judge Konrad Morgen in December 1944. Burney's judgment of Koch's personality is as follows:

> He was a sadist who had been rewarded for faithful service in the name of brutality and Nazidom by the gift of a plaything for his twisted, foaming mind; and he played with an abandoned wantonness, a care-free fiendishness which astounded even his masters and in the end brought about his downfall. No cruelty was foreign to him, no single cell of his brain had not at some time or other contributed to the planning of new refinements of anguish and death for the rats in his trap. He viewed his subject from every angle and sought variety in his methods. He liked the open crimson blood-bath, gloated over the slow white squeezing of life out of a single man, and rested content when he knew that at each moment of the night and day his scheme of death and torture was being faithfully executed by subordinates who perfectly understood his most delicate intentions.[455]

Since his second arrest Koch had remained imprisoned in Buchenwald. He was executed there on April 5, 1945. Since Burney arrived in Buchenwald after Koch had been removed from his position as camp commander, his recollection must have been based on what he had been told by other inmates. But during the fifteen months Burney was imprisoned in Buchenwald he collected himself the following impressions of Hermann Pister, the successor of Koch since December 1941:

> He was a blunt man, rough and without education, but had learned in his party career enough of the twists and turns of politics to realize that it was not enough to be a brute, but that a fox could serve both himself and his masters at the same time. Perhaps he already reckoned with the possibility of a Nazi defeat when he

came to the camp; what is certain is that he not only increased the profits of the camp to the SS, but at the same time won for himself the reputation among the prisoners of being one of the mildest concentration camp commanders in history. ... Execution for the pettiest offences continued as before, but an order was issued to the effect that the SS supervisors were no longer to beat the prisoners. ... Moreover, some of the worst NCOs were sent to the front as a punishment for corruption and were replaced by others who were in many cases half-hearted Nazis and unwillingly in the SS. Even the food improved for a short while, and by the spring of 1944 the behavior of the SS seemed to have undergone a radical change.[456]

Under *C. PRESENT GOVERNMENT* Tenenbaum starts out by describing his impressions of a meeting of the Camp Council, which took place in the evening of his and Egon Fleck's arrival and to which "the interrogators" were invited. This is how in the report he consistently referred to himself and Fleck as a duo. The Council was composed of about fifty delegates, one

for each thousand inmates of the same nationality, or fraction thereof. ... German was the predominant language. But each group had its own interpreter. ... Apart from the surroundings, this could have been a meeting of a committee of the League of Nations. The business of the evening was the organization of the camp. Commissions had been appointed to take charge of Security (police and guards), Food, Sanitation, Clothing, Administration and Information. As the interrogators entered a report was being rendered by one of the Committees: "Comrades, tomorrow will be the first holiday in the history of BUCHENWALD. We will have real goulash for lunch!" The announcement was met with applause.[457]

Then followed a period of complaints or questions by delegates of different nationalities, which were answered by the chairmen of the

Council. Thereafter, deviating from the agenda of the meeting, it was interrupted to give "a short summary of the Organization progress" to the two American interrogators:

> Besides the large committee, there is a directorate consisting of five men from the biggest national groups, a German, Russian, Frenchman, Czech and "Roman," representing the Italians, Spaniards and Belgians. (Note: The absence of a Pole is perhaps significant, the number of Poles in the camp being very large.)
> In addition, the camp's prisoner-trustee [= Kapo] system has been retained as the executive branch of its government. At its head is the Camp Eldest One (LAGER-AELTESTE EINS), a German Communist named Hans EIDEN, who has taken over the duties of Camp Commander. As the SS left, EIDEN emerged from his hiding place to issue the first order over the loudspeaker system: "Attention! Attention! This is the Camp Elder. All are to remain in the blocks. The gates remain closed. Further instructions follow."[458]

Tenenbaum quotes further instructions that, indeed, followed, such as: "Representatives of all nations have formed a Camp Leadership. Their orders are to be obeyed *unconditionally* [my emphasis]."[459] The government by prisoners for prisoners actually functioned almost perfectly even before the US Army took command of Buchenwald on April 13. Inmates followed the orders, a sign of trust in the internationally constituted internal government body. The upper long quotation conveys the impression that the postwar unification of Europe under principles of freedom, equality, democracy, rule of law, and human rights was given birth in Buchenwald, albeit after tremendous pain and suffering. Tenenbaum draws the following most interesting conclusion on the internal government structure:

> Thus, instead of a heap of corpses, or a disorderly mob of starving, leaderless men, the Americans found a disciplined and efficient organization in BUCHENWALD. Credit is undoubtedly due to the

self-appointed Camp Committee, an almost purely Communist group under the domination of the German political prisoners. They have made themselves almost indispensable to the American authorities who will have the task of managing the 21,000 survivors of BUCHENWALD. Earlier in the history of the camp these same people made themselves indispensable to the SS in managing the 60,000 prisoners normally kept at this focal center of the concentration camp system.[460]

Under *D. CONTROL OF BUCHENWALD*, Tenenbaum explains the predominance of German communists within the inmates' self-administration and evaluates its significance. He refers to the fact that Buchenwald was established in 1937, then only for German prisoners of three types: Jews, criminals, and political prisoners. Among the latter the communists constituted the major portion. When foreigners from countries occupied by Germany began to arrive and increased the number of inmates the SS could no longer handle the running of the camp alone. It then created a system of self-administration. It culminated "early in 1943 in the appointment of police-trustees (LAGERSCHUTZ) from among the inmates."[461]

All trustees (= Kapos) were equipped with wide powers. Until 1942 the SS entrusted such positions almost exclusively to German criminals. But the SS noticed that the criminals had little group cohesiveness. They were simply out for their own individual benefit. The communists, in contrast, had been detained in concentration camps longer than any other group. "They clung together with remarkable tenacity ... maintained excellent discipline, and received a certain amount of direction from outside the camp. They had brains and technical qualifications for running the various industries estab-lished in the camp. They made themselves indispensable."[462]

What is not mentioned in the Tenenbaum report are the com-plaints of the two industrial firms right next to the main camp itself whom Buchenwald supplied with laborers: the *Deutsche Ausrüstungs-Werke* (= German Equipment Works) specialized in investments close by concentration camps and the *Wilhelm-Gustloff-Werke* II (= Gustloff arms factories) which by March 1943 had established its factory in Buchenwald outside the main camp. They complained to the SS commander, by that time Hermann Pister, that the laborers the ruling German criminals sent into the factories were unskilled and unproductive. The communists, in turn, had mostly been skilled industrial workers. Christopher Burney writes:

> It was these men, then, who found their entry to power in their better training in industry and they used the opening adroitly. They started by impressing the civilian staffs of the factories with their good-will. The latter, finding that work was done and the stream of invective from the head office dammed, out of gratitude filled the air with a chorus of praise for these prisoners who, even if they had different and foolish ideas on the Government of Germany, were at least honest and painstaking workers. The chant was heard by the SS, and did much to overcome their feeling that the worst of all men after the Jew was the Communist. ... The Communists were organized just for this opportunity and had chosen the men to fill these positions long before they were offered. ... although some of these positions offered could have been very lucrative to any one of them, it stands to their credit that there was extraordinarily little bickering over their choice. That was eliminated by the rule that all profits must be divided among the whole of the party leadership. So the one who controlled the tobacco saw to it that the others smoked all they wanted before using his surplus for his own ends or friends.[463]

From 1942 on the communists gradually gained control of the trustee system. Resistance from the criminals was overcome, "partly by intimidation, partly with the aid of the SS. Numbers of the criminals were killed by beatings, hangings, or injections of phenol into the heart, or of air or milk into the veins. The injections were a specialty of the camp doctor, who became a partisan of the communist faction."[464] Large numbers of Poles from Auschwitz arrived in 1943, where they had been accustomed to running the camp. They developed the same ambition in Buchenwald. The German communist group averted this challenge to their privileged positions. "According to one informant their effort was crushed by the killing of large numbers in the typhus experiment station."[465]

Starting toward the end of 1942 large transports of French and Belgians arrived in Buchenwald and again posed a threat to the ruling positions of the German communists. Almost all of the arrivals in the first convoys were immediately selected to be transferred to subcamp Mittelbau-Dora as forced laborers in the underground production of V-2 and V-1 missiles. This meant almost certain death. Tenenbaum reports further that anyone of the remainder who dared to complain was put on the list for transport there. Later, the ruling German communists selected a French communist by the name of Marcel Paul, a town council member from Paris; they empowered him as the representative of the French prisoners. Paul, in turn appointed a French Committee, mostly composed of former deputies of French parliament. Colonel Mankes, a resistance leader captured by the Germans was made the French Committee's president.

To demonstrate how the French Committee favored the German communist group instead of the interests of their French fellow inmates, Tenenbaum reports on the Red Cross parcel scandal. The French Red Cross, in contrast to most other national Red Cross organizations, kept sending thousands of parcels to their compatriots. But the German communist leadership of the camp decided that all prisoners were comrades and should share the content of all parcels arriving in the camp. The SS camp commander agreed and henceforth passed all incoming Red Cross parcels on to the communist Camp Elder No. One. French inmates receiving private parcels addressed directly to them were also forced to "voluntarily" add these to the pool. Those who protested or refused were put on the transport lists. The communist Camp Elder No. One was supposed to distribute the parcels among the block leaders. These, in turn, were supposed to divide them up among the block's inmates. Radio Eriwan: In principle it was a fair distribution system, but

> The German trustees [= Kapos] always seemed to have more than the ordinary inmates. ... The Germans had more to smoke and more to eat than any others, provided they belonged to the ruling party. Even now, they may be distinguished from the rest of the inmates by their rosy cheeks and robust health, though they have been in concentration camps for much longer periods than the others.[466]

Under *E. METHOD OF ORGANIZATION*, Tenenbaum starts out to describe that in the hierarchy of self-administration by inmates there was a group of "mystery men" above the ostensible leaders of the trustee [= Kapo] system. It acted as a political directorate, but stayed in the background. These men were Buchenwald's link to the outside world, to German communists in other concentration camps and to the undercover organization of the German Communist Party. The latter "maintained an extraordinarily effective organization, covering the whole country. From BUCHENWALD an inmate went out regularly to establish contact with a communist courier bringing news and instructions. Bound by his loyalty to his Party, the contact man never made use of his opportunity to escape personally." Orders and information from outside the camp were passed on to the communist inmates.[467]

As a practical example of Buchenwald's external linkage with the outside world, Tenenbaum then reports about a conspiracy of Buchenwald's communist inmates to establish a new German government. As he was told the story, it began in September 1944, the month the US Army had set foot on German territory in Aachen. Gustav Wegerer was the leading figure in the plot. He was aided by then Camp Elder No. one, Roeschke, and by other Austrians and Germans, mainly employed around the property room (*Effektenkammer*), a communist stronghold. Wegerer managed to establish contact with the communist cells at the Mittelbau-Dora and Sachsenhausen concentration camps. On a drinking party in the property room the planning of a plot was indiscreetly talked about. An Austrian relayed what he had heard to a prisoner belonging to the group of criminals. He, in turn, informed the SS. Men involved, including the Kapo of the property room, were arrested and sent to the Gestapo, the Nazi secret police, in Weimar. They were dismissed from their privileged positions as Kapos. While arrested communist fellow-conspirators in camps Mittelbau-Dora and Sachsenhausen were mostly killed, a number of the men arrested from Buchenwald were later returned alive to the camp, reason unknown. But it could have been due to Buchenwald camp commander Pister's efforts to later present himself to the Allies as somebody who protected lives of his inmates. He was at that time by far not the only one in Germany who after the German Army's disastrous defeats in Stalingrad and in the tank battle of Kursk in the East and, furthermore, after the Normandy invasion of the Western Allies – in tandem with the war aim "unconditional surrender" of Germany, previously agreed on by all three big military powers – saw the occupation of Germany in the offing.

Tenenbaum also identifies key communist power positions in the camp's self-administration besides the top positions in the Kapo hierarchy:

One was the food supply organization, through which favored groups received reasonable rations while others were brought to the starvation level. A second was the hospital (REVIER), staffed almost exclusively by Communists. Its facilities were largely devoted to caring for members of their party. All scarce drugs (and many were scarce at BUCHENWALD) were reserved for Communist patients, and hospital food was available for members of the Party even if not absolutely necessary. Another Communist stronghold was the property room (EFFEKTENKAMMER). Here came all the personal property of new prisoners going through the disinfection plant, down to their religious medallions, as well as of inmates who died at BUCHENWALD. Money and gold (including gold teeth from the dead or dying) was placed in a safe, and was carted away by the SS in suitcases a few nights ago. Other goods of lesser value were distributed by the Communists. Each Russian PW, for example, received a wrist-watch as a token of solidarity. Each German trustee obtained good clothing and numerous other valuables: the Communists of BUCHENWALD, after ten or twelve years in concentration camps, are dressed like prosperous business men. Some affect leather jackets and little round caps reminiscent of the German navy, apparently the uniform of revolution.[468]

The key position of power, however, was the Labor Office (*Arbeitsstatistik*). Here inmates were assigned their workplaces and transport lists were put together. Officially an SS Labor Allocation (*Arbeitseinsatz*) officer was in charge. But he usually devolved his task on the Kapos working in the office. These were then instructed only as to the number of prisoners required for a particular work assignment or transport and the Kapos would choose the names themselves. The Kapo positions in the Labor Office had over time almost exclusively been taken over by German communists.[469] They had thus acquired the power over life and death of all other inmates. By their work or transport assignments they could sentence a person or a group to almost certain death on the one hand, but also to perks and benefits on the other.

Tenenbaum also found out that communist Kapos, besides SS guards, were directly responsible for a large part of the brutal beatings and killings committed at Buchenwald. He names a few persons and describes examples of their practices. "Of categories ... the following may be cited: (a) Almost all police trustees (LAGERSCHUTZ) (b) Almost all Block Chiefs in the 'small camp.' Besides personally beating their charges, these individuals sometimes forced whole blocks to stand barefoot in the snow for hours, apparently on their own initiative."[470]

On the other hand, Tenenbaum notes that not all communist leaders are bad. Hans Eiden, Camp Elder No. One, was generally respected as an honest and good man, likewise a number of other communists, including the chief Kapo for food supply. These men would follow the orders of the "mystery men" in the political directorate which had placed them in power. The shadowy directorate, in turn, received its instructions from the underground German communist Party organization outside the camp. The good Kapos were disciplined enough not to hurt their party comrades.

To Tenenbaum the Communists' excuse for their brutal conduct

> is entirely logical. The camp lived under an unspeakable reign of terror until they [the Communists] took power. (Note: Under Commandant KOCH this was true. His removal from office coincided roughly with the rise of Communist influence. Whether there is a connection between the two could not be determined.) They assumed office to make BUCHENWALD a better place to live. To be able to do so, they had to produce a certain output of work, order, and discipline. Thus their means were justified by the end. The Communists' motives, in so far as such things can be reconstructed, are entirely human. Only the fittest could survive twelve years of concentration camp. Fitness consisted of convincing the SS of one's usefulness, and in the fight for survival this trait was bound to appear. Sustained by the sacred egoism of their mission, by the thought of living to shape a Communist Germany, they lost their human idealism. They became hard, surviving not for themselves but in the name of the proletarian future of Germany, and thereby justifying many extreme means of survival. To them most of the other inmates are "bandits." They consider themselves almost the sole valuable residue of the great process of selection which was the concentration camp system.[471]

Under *F. GROUPS OTHER THAN COMMUNIST*, Tenenbaum identifies two nationalities that formed well-organized and disciplined groups: the Czechs and the Russians. The former, the so-called Protectorate Prisoners [*Protektorat-Häftlinge*] had been arrested at the outbreak of the War as possibly dangerous persons. But at Buchenwald they were granted a privileged status. At least until 1940 they were not required to work. Thereafter they were assigned to jobs of their own choice. They formed their own National Committee in a democratic manner. All political factions from left to right were represented in it.

The second disciplined and well-organized group were the Russians. If they had not been sentenced for escape attempts or refusal of work, they were in principle having PW status, distinguished by not having to wear concentration camp numbers. But mass executions, outside and inside the camp as long as Karl Koch was its SS commander until the end of 1941, and a last-minute evacuation of 1,800 Russian PWs on April 10, 1945 had reduced this group to about 800 when Tenenbaum arrived in the camp a day later. Quite a number of high officers, two to six colonels among them, maintained military discipline. "Relations between the German Communists and Russian PW's were peculiar. The senior Russian officer, as representative of the workers' fatherland, had great influence over the German Communists. His word was law. However, he made little use of this advantage," Tenenbaum reports. And he continues:

> There were thousands of non-German Communists in BUCHENWALD, particularly French, Dutch, and Spanish. To some extent these were absorbed into the German organization, and took their orders from the Germans. A vast underground system of councils and meetings was built up to integrate them. Yet many did not like their German overlords. Many Russians and foreign communists spoke of beating up the German Communists when the day of liberation arrived. Their hopes will have to be deferred. By their "coup d' état" within the camp, the German Communists remain masters over all the inmates, with rifles in their own hands to replace the support once offered by the SS.[472]

Under *G. ATROCITIES*, Tenenbaum differs less from other reports on concentration camps than under his previous headings, which contain his analytical findings on the ruling system that led to the unspeakable sufferings. The monstrosity of atrocities fully absorbed the attention of most authors and took their breath away. They were dominated by humankind's most noble virtue: human compassion. Only few authors developed the ambition and possessed the intellectual qualifications to penetrate from perception of brutalities and maybe their proximate causes to lay bare the remote causes: the organizational structure and hierarchy on which the inhuman treatment of inmates by SS and their underlings, the Kapos, rested. For this it takes a whole lot of mental discipline, education in analytical skills, and ambition to explain instead of merely to describe. It is no wonder that only a few of the inmates of Buchenwald possessed these qualifications, prominently among them Bruno Bettelheim,[473] Eugen Kogon,[474] and Jorge Semprún.[475]

For Tenenbaum as an outsider it was probably easier than for the above-mentioned postwar authors, with all their personal experiences and observations in the camp, to write an analytical report on the ruling system that caused the modern world's greatest break with values of European civilization. In any case, he was the first one to compose an analytical report and this within two weeks after the liberation of Buchenwald. Of course, he had an unlimited number of information-delivering assistants at his disposal, ordinary and ruling inmates of the camp. They were enthusiastic to deliver information to representatives of their liberators, which previously had been impossible to communicate to the Allied nations.

Tenenbaum opens this passage of his report by pointing out that since September 1943 [in fact December 1941] "Buchenwald became the best of the German concentration camps." Karl Koch as commander of Buchenwald had been arrested then "for misuse of authority and fraudulent conversion of Party funds." Hermann Pister became his successor. But even then this camp kept sharing in the SS-inspired system of contempt of life, cruelties, and murderous killings. Tenenbaum asked the Camp Council to write a short report on atrocities. This single-spaced three-page summary was attached as

Annex A to Tenenbaum's own report, in which he himself picked up the worst of horror scenarios, like this one during Karl Koch's infamous reign of terror:

> Koch is famous as "Femme Koch." Both he and his wife were perverts, the husband a homosexual and the wife a nymphomaniac. Both satisfied their desires on the hapless inmates. The wife would walk through the camp, pick a likely partner, take him home for the night, and then invariably order him shot. She delighted in tattoos. Prisoners were regularly inspected in the hospital. Whenever a prisoner was found with a more than ordinary tattoo, he was killed, his skin was stripped, and the tattooed portion was tanned. Some extraordinary objects were made from these, including a famous lamp shade.

Tenenbaum also reports that some prisoners had told him that four days previously, that is, before the date of his report, Karl Koch, who had remained in Nazi arrest, was brought back to Buchenwald, where he was shot.

> An urn bearing his name on a piece of adhesive tape can be seen at the camp's crematorium. His successor, PISTER, tended to do only what was required to meet the demands of Berlin, and introduced relatively decent conditions in at least part of the camp. No longer, for example, was the entire camp deprived of food for three days, if the output of work slacked off. Lately the entire SS has become relatively mild, and tried to curry favor with the Communist faction, expecting an Allied victory.

Tenenbaum then identifies the physician who had helped the German communists to oust the German criminals from their power positions in Buchenwald by killing with injections those inmates from the criminal group who acted as Kapos: Dr. Waldemar Hoven. He worked under Koch from 1939. He was arrested for murder about the same time as Koch, September 1943. A Nazi court condemned Hoven to death. But he was reprieved and remained in jail for about eighteen months. Obviously due to a shortage of doctors he was reactivated and returned to Buchenwald on March 15, 1945 where he was arrested by US forces and imprisoned within the camp. Tenenbaum interrogated him or at least was present when somebody else did, because he devotes to him more than half a page of the thirteen and a half pages (without the covering note by Chief of Intelligence, Alfred Toombs, on p. 1 and without Annex A, written by inmates. on pp. 16 to 18) and because he describes details of Dr. Hoven's psychic condition.

For his killing of Kapos from the group of criminals he gave the following explanation: He could not bear to watch the criminal prisoners systematically killing off the political and racial inmates, and this even with the encouragement of commander Koch. "Prisoners confirm his story, and state that HOVEN saved numerous prisoners by declaring them sick and hiding them in the hospital. Other inmates, though agreeing to these facts, add that HOVEN also killed political and racial prisoners with his injections. ... He is known to have continued to help some prisoners" after his return to Buchenwald three weeks before its liberation.

> HOVEN gives the impression of being a psychopathic case. When the interrogators met him he cried, claiming to be overjoyed at seeing a few Jewish inmates whose lives he had saved. On the other hand, Dr. HOVEN was responsible for the cruelties committed in the typhus laboratory, where hundreds of healthy prisoners were burned with phosphorus for experimental reasons, dying in great pain. Since returning to the camp, HOVEN has renewed his friendship with the Communist faction, apparently as a form of life insurance in the event of an Allied victory. In return the Communists seem anxious to keep him alive, ostensibly because of the information he can provide. He was always considered their friend because of his dispatch of the criminal faction.[476]

Tenenbaum then describes two Experiment Stations at Buchenwald in which selected inmates were used like human "guinea pigs." This took place in Block 50, where Tenenbaum and Fleck were lodged during their two-week stay in the camp. During the years after 1942 physicians, also from the world-famous Robert-Koch-Institut in Berlin, had tried to find a cure for typhus in that particular building, but remained unsuccessful. Even those who survived the artificial infection with typhus material delivered by the Robert Koch-Institut were killed by injections from Dr. Waldemar Hoven.[477] The victims of those human experiments had been housed in Block 46, the injection block, where Hoven practiced killing besides curing. As of late, experiments had been started to find a cure for homosexuality, using prisoners with that sexual orientation, reports Tenenbaum. His last point under his heading "Atrocities" is the crematorium of the camp:

> The Crematorium BUCHENWALD boasts a large, modern crematorium, with six ovens, a tiled floor, and an elevator which brought live men to the torture chamber in the cellar, and hauled up their corpses later to be burned. The torture chamber was cleaned up by the SS before the Americans arrived. Its walls are freshly painted to cover blood stains, and the row of meat hooks along the ceiling, on which the living victims were impaled, has been removed. The holes from which the hooks were taken have been plastered over. But the evidence of the purpose of this plant is not completely gone. There are large piles of bone and ash, not yet concealed. And outside, in the courtyard, are thirty or so bodies, not yet burned. These are typical concentration camp bodies, unbelievably thin, scarred, beaten. In one corner lies a stretcher with two of these pitiful bodies on it head to foot, bulking smaller than one healthy man. On the second floor of the plant are about 1,200 sealed tin cans. These rattle when shaken. They contain the ashes of prisoners murdered in 1939 and 1940, for which there had been no claimants. After that the nicety of separate urns was no longer considered necessary, and only in rare cases were ashes of individuals preserved. Almost all remains went into a common pile, which was allowed to accumulate. When it got too large, five

or six trucks would come to haul it away to a pit in the nearby forest. 6. In the last four weeks the coal shortage forced suspension of the crematorium. About 2,500 who died in this period were simply buried near the camp's BISMARCK guard tower. Capacity of the crematorium was about 3–400 bodies every 24 hours, and sometimes even these facilities were strained. In the month of February, for example, 2,800 were cremated. The chief of the crematorium, also responsible for the torture chamber in its basement, was SS-Hauptscharfuehrer [= the SS equivalent of an Army First Sergeant] WANNSTEDT. There was also a stable near the camp, used for occasional mass shootings. Here thousands were disposed of, particularly P/W transports from the East in the early years of the war. About a week ago the SS made preparations to blow this up. The place still stands, but may be mined.[478]

Under its heading *H. THE SMALL CAMP*, the Tenenbaum report dives even deeper into the world of human abysses. The *Kleines Lager* was a barbed wire enclosure in the middle of the big camp. Originally it had been established as a quarantine center for new arrivals at Buchenwald. But during the war it had changed its function. It had developed into a "replacement center." Before being transported into death camps in Germany, such as Ohrdruf, "where undesirables were killed by beating and work," they were ghettoized in the Small Camp. This happened especially to Jews, foreign workers, or prisoners who had tried to escape or had stolen food, to gypsies, petty criminals from all over Europe, and minor political figures whom the SS or other leaders of the camp wanted to get rid of. Tenenbaum calls this arrangement "the transport system." He reports that the French tire magnate Marcel Michelin,[479] "now evacuated or dead," and Isaac, an eminent Rumanian Jew, had been there. A few months in the system had made them and the others "indistinguishable, filthy, whining, clamoring bodies, covered with sores, which seem to be without souls." Transports would return to the small camp regularly, bringing some who were still considered useful as workers back for recuperation and transporting other inmates out as replacements. Whoever was not considered fit for work was weeded out here and killed. Tenenbaum as an eyewitness:

> Even now, a trip through the little camp is like a nightmare. On the sight of an American uniform a horde of gnomes and trolls seems to appear like magic, pouring out of doorways as if shot from a cannon. Some hop on crutches. Some hobble on stumps of feet. Some run with angular movements. Some glide like Oriental genies. Almost all wear striped convict suits, covered with patches, or grey-black remnants of Eastern clothing. The universal covering is a little black skull cap. They doff these ceremoniously to the visitors. Some are crying, others shouting with joy. An old man, dirty, bearded, one eye blind, totters up and introduces himself as a French general. His son is dying here. Can help be brought? Will it come in time? A child of twelve smiles and says, "I am from Poland, I have been in concentration camps for two years now."[480]

Most remarkable would be the sight of children, six to fourteen, most about twelve, Tenenbaum reports. They would rush about, shrieking and playing, playing where the smell of death would still be thick in the air. There would be seven hundred children in Buchenwald, most in the small camp. Even a baby, three years old, was there. He goes on:

> Conditions in the small camp are incredible. In the main camp there are solid barracks, clean and well made. In the small camp are twenty-seven low wooden barns. In these are three to five tiers of wide shelves, running the length of the building. On them are sacks of rotten straw, covered with vermin. These are sleeping and living quarters. In the center of the camp are open sheds, covering deep concrete-lined pits. These are the latrines, from which pour an indescribable stench.[481]

Tenenbaum reports that the rated capacity of each block in the small camp was 450 inmates. But filled with this number the wooden barns would look like the interior of a slave ship. To make matters even worse, sometimes "1,000 to 1,200 newly arrived East Jews and Poles were crowded in here. Daily mortality was high, 20–25 per block per day. Once 160 out of 1,000 died in Block 57 within 24 hours." The Block Chiefs of the small camp are Germans, and are considered the most brutal of the inmates.

Part of the Small Camp had once been the "tent camp," consisting of canvas shelters which were later replaced by poorly constructed barracks. Tenenbaum continues: "Here 170 American aviators were brought, after being captured in France while attempting to escape. Their shoes were taken away, and in the dead of winter they slept under canvas shelters, or out in the open. One died here of pneumonia, Lt LEVITT A BECK, 0–78286. The rest went on to M.-STAMMLAGER LUFT 3, after questioning by the GESTAPO."[482]

Tenenbaum noted in his report that the gates of the Small Camp were still closed at the date of his report, two weeks after liberation of the Buchenwald main camp. Armed guards – inmates from the big camp – would still encircle the barbed wire of the Small Camp. It had not participated in the first voluntary roll call arranged on the morning after the day of liberation. "For too many of the self-styled aristocrats of the big camp these are all 'bandits'". Tenenbaum concedes that they represent a problem for the camp. Some are in fact "'bandits,' criminals from all Europe or foreign workers in Germany who were caught stealing." All prisoners of the Small Camp would be hungry, as the inmates of the big camp never were. The "bandits" would carry lice and disease to a greater extent than the inmates of the main camp. Also they would seek to break out of the terribly crowded corner of the Small Camp into the more comfortable clean blocks of the main camp.

> They are brutalized, unpleasant to look on. It is easy to adopt the Nazi theory that they are subhuman, for many have in fact been deprived of their humanity. It would be easy to continue favoring the big camp, in the distribution of food, as has been done in the

past, and, more important for the wretches of the small camp, in the distribution of medicine.[483]

Under *I. THE TRANSPORTS*, Tenenbaum reports on the origin and practice of the "transport system." It was started in October 1942 in response to the German war machine's increasing demand for raw labor. The first transport from Buchenwald was sent to Dora near the town of Nordhausen at the Southern tip of the Harz mountains. There, tunnels had been dug for an underground factory. The Buchenwald subcamp there was later called Concentration Camp Mittelbau. Its inmates were slave workers for the Mittelbau AG which ran the underground factory.

> Other transports still in German-held territory are listed in the appendix [which was compiled by representatives of all nations who formed the inmates' governing Camp Leadership under Camp Eldest One Hans Eiden], as may be seen, many of the transports served synthetic gasoline factories, a large proportion is in the area North West of BUCHENWALD, the so-called prohibited zone (SPERRZONE). The entire area centered around NORDHAUSEN and SANGERSHAUSEN is a nest of underground factories producing munitions and secret equipment. BUCHENWALD, too, had its munitions factory, located in the middle of the camp. In August, 1943 this was bombed by the Allies. The entire factory was destroyed, while the barracks lying immediately around it were virtually undamaged. This bombardment was used as an excuse for the murder of ERNST THAELMANN, the famous German Communist leader, though THAELMANN had never been in BUCHENWALD.[484]

J. OHRDRUF. This is the only subcamp Tenenbaum picks up in his report. He probably does so, because Ohrdruf was the first and only horror camp he had seen exactly a week earlier before his entering of Buchenwald. He reports:

> Eight thousand evacuated inmates of the OHRDRUF camps (OHRDRUF-NORD and OHRDRUF-SUD) arrived in

BUCHENWALD about a week ago. Hundreds died or were killed as unfit to go further when they reached BUCHENWALD, before the column proceeded East again. The OHRDRUF camps, known as TRANSPORT or KOMMANDO S-3, were established to dig tunnels. These were to [be] used as housing for the most important departments of the German government, and as emergency shelter for the train which contains HITLER'S Hq (FUEHRERHAUPT-QUARTIER). About ten days ago the FUEHRER train was at OBERHOF, south of CRAWINKEL.

Caused by the disruption of communication with Berlin, a conference was held at Ohrdruf about twelve days ago, Tenenbaum continues. Camp Commander Stiebitz, Dr. von Schuler, and a major general were present. The topic was how to dispose of the prisoners. Some proposals were made like gassing or blowing them up in the tunnels. But they were abandoned as "technically unfeasible." Two days later, a letter with instructions from Heinrich Himmler was received at camp Ohrdruf: "I leave it within your discretion to kill all criminals and perhaps certain important political prisoners." The ambiguity of the order left Commander Stiebitz confused. He finally came to the conclusion to try to evacuate the whole camp. He started the evacuation the following day.[485]

ANNEX A, three single-spaced pages entitled *Report on Concentration Camp Buchenwald (Atrocities)* was compiled by a group of five inmates who each of them represented Buchenwald's prisoners according to their nationality and at the time of liberation formed the ruling authority of the camp under its Eldest No. One, the German Hans Eiden. Besides him, the following five representatives undersigned Annex A: Walter Bartel for the Germans (he would later be East Germany's top historian for Buchenwald), Iwan Smirnow for the Russians, Josef Frank for the Czechs, Marcel Paul for the French, and Dominico Cinpoli for the Italians, Spanish, and Belgians. It is most remarkable that the many Poles and other nationalities, like the Hungarians, in Buchenwald were not likewise represented in the governing council of the self-administrated camp, probably because most of them were Jewish or gypsies. These were despised by the mostly communist representatives of inmates in power almost as much as by the Nazis, somewhat similar to the disdain the camp elders showed for the *Small Camp*, into which they – fully in line with the SS – had disposed of such elements and of their rivals, the German criminal inmates. Most indicative of this is that the Small Camp of Buchenwald, whose miserable inmates were most in need of liberation, medical care, and careful bodily recovering nutrition, much more than the inmates of Buchenwald in the main camp, was not liberated on April 11, 1945, when 1st Lt. Paul Bodot and, shortly afterward, Edward Tenenbaum entered the otherwise self-liberated main camp in the late afternoon. Its inmates did not take part in the liberation roll call on April 12 in the morning. Their liberation was executed by the US Army that took over the command of the camp on April 13, 1945. As Tenenbaum used Annex A as his quarry of information for the parts that he had written himself, I will not take up the details of this appendix.

In the introduction to his report Tenenbaum writes: "Names of informants are not given in this report. They are still in BUCHENWALD, and would undoubtedly be in the grave gravest danger if what they have said ever becomes known there. The major informants are two Allied intelligence agents who were caught by the Germans."[486] After having read Christopher Burney's account of his 15-months Buchenwald experience *The Dungeon Democracy*, first published already in the fall of 1945, I am sure that Burney was one of them, as a British SOE with the rank of a captain,[487] captured in France by the Gestapo in 1942. The parallels between the information contained in the Tenenbaum report and in Burney's *Dungeon Democracy*, especially his Parts I and III, are too obvious to be overlooked.[488]

But it speaks for Tenenbaum's analytical mind that he stayed clear of some of Burney's harsh judgments, such as:

> The Communists were merely Nazis painted red, neither better nor worse, pawning their souls and their fellows' lives for a mock

abstract power ... They were whole-heartedly amoral and had cast off in disgust such shreds of inherited morality as they found still clinging to them. "Bourgeois sentimentality," they called it, but brought from the recesses of their parrot minds unpondered gilded catch-words and the twisted sayings of half-ignorant men to replace it; words of hatred and envy, apologies for murder, theft and enslavement.[489]

Actually, reviews in 1946 of the first edition in the USA have criticized Burney's judgments, especially for his degrading and condescending descriptions of the German communists running the camp and of the national characters of other European citizens and PWs detained in Buchenwald: "he concludes that 'ideology cannot replace morality'; and that continental Europe holds little prospect of evolving a democratic way of life. ... these theoretical views are highly disputable and seem in part influenced by the author's belief in the moral superiority of the British."[490] Another reviewer states: "There is neither charity nor tolerance here – Why publish such a book? It seems neither creditable nor warranted."[491]

One of the most remarkable findings of the Tenenbaum–Fleck report was that the numerous communist inmates were entrusted by the SS to run the camp in detail on the basis of the *Kapo*, called "trustee" in the report, and block elder system. They had proven to be the best organized and accustomed to strictest discipline. The very same traits, however, allowed these communists to organize the most effective resistance network within the camp, while at the same time maintaining connections with communist resistance groups outside of the camp. While to a considerable degree they shared with the SS personnel in the power over life and death, they also proved to be capable of clandestine measures to hide small and even large groups of endangered inmates, sometimes even with cooperating SS officers.

An outstanding example is the saving of more than 600 mainly Jewish youth and children – among them 15-year-old Elie Wiesel – in the final months of Nazi Buchenwald. In the deepest part of the disease-infested *Little Camp* – outside the normal gaze of SS guards, except the one who was in charge, but actively cooperated – the underground resistance organized *Block 66* (i.e., windowless barracks to shelter and protect those teenagers and younger kids). The barracks block elder was Antonin Kalina, a Czech communist, his deputy Gustav Schiller, a Jewish communist from Poland. Other minors were hidden in Block 8 in the main camp and elsewhere while prisoners from the underground network guarded and kept care of them. When the Americans arrived they found and liberated more than 900 youths, mostly teenagers, but also younger children.[492]

When Alfred Toombs, Chief of Intelligence, distributed the Tenenbaum/Fleck confidential Buchenwald Report to a select group of recipients he wrote in his covering letter:

> it is one of the most significant accounts yet written on an aspect of life in Nazi Germany. It is NOT just another report on a concentration camp. It does not deal exclusively with the horror of life in Buchenwald, nor with the brutalities of the Nazi perverts. It is the story of wheels within wheels. It tells how the prisoners themselves organized a deadly terror within the Nazi terror.[493]

A second report on Buchenwald after its liberation by the US Army is about 400 single-spaced pages long, with 125 pages in the main and 275 pages of testimonies by inmates. It was much longer, more detailed, and finished about three weeks later than the Tenenbaum–Fleck report. But it never reached the prominence of the latter. It was compiled by a CIC team of five persons headed by Lieutenant Albert G. Rosenberg. The team arrived at Buchenwald on April 16, 1945. It soon realized that it could produce no meaningful report without an ample information supply from long-term insiders in leading positions in the camp's inmate hierarchy. Eugen Kogon was recruited. He, in turn cooperated mainly with five of his trusted friends in the camp. In fact, Kogon dictated the 125-page main report himself. Kogon was soon urged by the Western Allies to enlarge his report text for official uses and turn it into a book for the public. He did so between June 15 and December 15, 1945 for the first edition of his famous book to appear in German in 1946 under the title *Der SS Staat*.[494]

Tenenbaum was awarded the *Bronze Star Medal*. This Medal was authorized by Executive Order 9419 of President Franklin D. Roosevelt on February 4, 1944. It was to be given to any person who, after December 6, 1941, while serving in any capacity with the Armed Forces of the United States, distinguished himself or herself by heroic or meritorious achievement or service, not involving participation in aerial flight.[495]

It wasn't the above-mentioned combat action in Coblenz for which Edward A. Tenenbaum was awarded the *Bronze Star Medal*, but his excellent reports on persons, economic and political matters in Germany on the one hand and on Buchenwald concentration camp on the other. Colonel James R. Forgan, who directed OSS intelligence as commander of the *cloak-and-dagger organization* in the European Theater of Operations,[496] recommended Lieutenant Tenenbaum for the medal in a "secret" letter of May 24, 1945. It was sent from HQ & HQ Detachment/Office of Strategic Services/European Theater of Operations/United States Army to commanding general/European Theater of Operations/USA, APO 887.[497] I quote from the letter:

1. a. It is recommended that 1st Lt. EDWARD TENENBAUM, AG, 0–870114, be awarded the BRONZE STAR. Lt. TENEBAUM is now on active duty with the Research & Analysis Branch of the Office of Strategic Services, ETO.

    b. Lt. TENEBAUM was attached to the Research & Analysis Branch of the Office of Strategic Services, assigned to the Intelligence Sub-Branch, Psychological Warfare, 12 AG, for the period of service for which this award is recommended.

    c. The nearest relative is: Mrs. Edward Tenenbaum, 2500 K St. NW, Washington, DC.

    d. Entered military service from Washington, DC.

    e. No decorations have previously been awarded.

f. The entire service of Lt. TENENBAUM has been honorable since the rendition by him of the service for which this award is recommended.

g. A similar recommendation for this individual has not been submitted.

2. a. The officer recommending this award has personal knowledge of the service on which this recommendation is based.

b. This recommendation is supported by letter of recommendation, a certified copy of which is inclosed [*sic*].

3. 1st Lt. EDWARD TENEBAUM, AG, O-870114, while serving with the Armed Forces of the United States, distinguished himself by meritorious achievement in the performance of outstanding services not involving participation in aerial flight in connection with military operations against the enemy. The activities for which this award is recommended were completed between 1 March 1945 and 3 May 1945.

Lt. TENENBAUM was assigned to the Intelligence Sub-Branch Psychological Warfare 12th AG, by the Research & Analysis Branch, Office of Strategic Services, and served with that headquarters from 1 January 1945 through 8 May 1945. Lt. TENENBAUM, without previous field experience, assumed his assignment in the forward field during the crucial post-Ardennes phase of the campaign against Germany, and his entire service was performed under conditions of combat. As one of a special team of two interrogators of selected German civilians Lt. TENENBAUM prepared regular reports and analyses summarizing and interpreting the results of those interrogations and interpreting as well observations on political and economic conditions in Germany following penetration of the American troops. His biographical studies of leading German citizens and other individuals, prepared with the highest quality of technique while under mobile conditions, constitute some of the most valuable documentary material to have been gathered in Germany. Each of Lt. TENENBAUM'S numerous reports were reproduced and circulated among the various branches of the Allied Army and to the civilian agencies charged with the several responsibilities in occupied Germany. These reports are considered by PWD, Q-5 SHAEF, G-5 12th AG, and US Group GC, to have been most valuable in establishing policy for civilian control in Germany.

During the course of operation in Central Germany, largely through his own initiative, Lt. TENENBAUM arrived at the Buchenwald Concentration Camp shortly after the releasing troops and prepared the first extensive report and analysis of conditions therein. This lengthy document, based upon the immediate interrogation of hundreds of the Camp's personnel and survivors, is remarkable in that it brought to light the system of internee control and the clandestine political structure within the Camp, hitherto unsuspected in Allied intelligence offices. The findings are considered to be among the most brilliant to come out of psychological warfare headquarters and went far in anticipating many of the political problems to be faced by Allied Military Government in Germany.[498]

The same Colonel James R. Forgan, commander (CSC) of OSS intelligence in the European Theater of Operations, recommended in a letter of April 28, 1945 to the commanding General of ETO, USA, APO 887, Major Charles P. Kindleberger, Headquarters 12th Army Group, to be awarded the *Legion of Merit* for his outstanding services as chief of the Enemy Objectives Unit. The award proposal was successful on July 9, 1945,[499] that is, after Kindleberger had left ETO for home in June. It was presented to him by Colonel Quinn in a ceremony in Washington, DC on January 17, 1946.[500]

Edward A. Tenenbaum had been promoted from "temporary" First Lieutenant to permanent First Lieutenant on January 16, 1945. The card with this information shows "ETO" (= European Theater of Operation) in handwriting as header. Besides his promotion it contains information that I have already been using above: his precise assignment in Officer

Candidate School (OCS) on Yale campus, before he graduated from OCS on April 6, 1944 and was transferred back to OSS in Washington, DC, the dates of his seven-day leave of absence in May 1944 and the exact date of his shipment to England.[501]

While Tenenbaum was in Patton's Third Army G-2 (Intelligence) as part of the PWD of General Bradley's 12th Army Group, he was at the same time also an analyst under the command of OSS posts in ETO. After the Allied Armies had broken out of their Normandy pocket in early August 1944 they advanced very rapidly through Western France as they headed for the liberation of Paris. With the support of the fighting French *Resistance* inside the city, French and US troops entered the city even before the City Commander General Dietrich von Choltitz surrendered largely undamaged Paris to those Forces on August 25, 1944. Thus he refused to execute an explicit order by Hitler on August 23 that Paris must not fall into the hands of the enemy, but should it happen the city must have been laid in ruins. This not only meant tough fighting up to the last man and bullet, but also the deliberate blowing-up of the most precious cultural buildings like Notre Dame and the Louvre. The dynamite charges had already been installed.

After capitulation the German forces had left Paris in a haste. They had been unable to take with them their looted art treasures, printed material, like books and journals, as well as important military and civil documents. Nor had they been able to destroy them. A similar situation arose when Brussels was liberated by British troops, flanked by a Belgian corps, on September 3, 1944. These developments turned first Paris and not much later Brussels into treasure troves full of information for the Allies, useful for assessing military strength, strategy, and tactics of the German Army and for planning occupation policy in Germany.[502] The 12th Army Group formed special Target Forces (T-Forces) in order to find, screen, and catalog the wealth of material. They have been defined as follows: "Intelligence units with OSS representatives tasked with searching recently captured locations for material of intelligence value."[503]

At first, T-Forces were composed mainly of G-2 staff of the 12th Army Group and of its constituent armies.

A branch of London headquarters of OSS/R&A was established in Paris on September 28, 1944, headed by Harold C. Deutsch. His office was located at 79 Champs-Élysées.[504] Born in 1904, Deutsch became an eminent historian teaching at the University of Minnesota.[505] From the start in Paris, he and his staff became very active in attaching OSS personnel to the T-Forces of 12th Army Group.[506] This was probably the reason why an official report on OSS records in the National Archives at College Park MD contains the information that OSS reached the height of its wartime activities in October 1944 with about 5,500 military and 2,000 civilian personnel overseas and approximately 2,700 military and 2,000 civilian personnel in the USA.[507]

On November 11, 1944 Harold Deutsch sent a memo to Chandler Morse, chief of OSS/R&A in London, "Attention: Allan Evans ... Subject: Launching of T-Force Operations." In cooperation with London, Paris OSS office had built up a special R&A T-Force to be dispatched forward when a major military offensive would be started. Actually, on November 16, the Allies began their large-scale autumn offensive called *Operation Queen*, which made them advance to the Rhine in Southern Germany. Obviously, Deutsch was informed about the operation. He writes that the earliest date on which the R&A T-Force can be dispatched would be November 20. Therefore, its prospective members already in Paris should be alerted and others – still in London – should be sent to Paris as fast as possible.

Deutsch reports further that on November 10 he had a conference with Major Shewbridge, about cooperation forward of R&A T-Force with G-2 SHAEF Document Subsection. The Major would welcome the attachment of R&A personnel to the forward G-2 SHAEF echelon and could see no obstacle to attaching them simultaneously also to the PWD T-Force outfit. But he would not want to include more than three persons in this dual assignment. Deutsch proposed

to include Wells, Rubint, and Schmid and send them forward to
visit the various G-2 Document stations as soon as Wells and
Schmid [still in London] are here. When the other three men are
ready they can ... join the first team at the PWD T-Force outpost.
The second team would be composed ... of three of the following:
Hankin and/or Hall, an economist (Tennenbaum [sic]), Canby,
Sarlie and Kull. I hope to hold Kull back, however, until someone
can be sent to replace him here.[508]

On the same day, November 11, 1944, assistant chief of staff (AC of S)
G-2 of SHAEF, on his behalf signed by Major A. J. Marsden, issued
Standard Operating Procedures (SOP) for handling by G-2 Subdivision
of SHAEF special documents, destined for special agencies:

> 1. The term "Special documents" is defined as documents of special
> interest or import to the agencies concerned with their subject
> matter; documents whose value depends upon expeditious
> transmission of the agency/ies concerned. // 2. The term "special
> agency" is defined as any agency not part of the SHAEF Theater of
> Operations. // 3. All documents received from "T" Force will be
> handled as special documents.[509]

In my understanding special agency refers to OSS, its R&A and
other branches.

Evidently Edward Tenenbaum was chosen for the leading pos-
ition in the R&A T-Force team. On November 25, 1944 Harold
Deutsch, Chief of R&A Paris, sent a memo to "R&A T-Force, 12th
Army Group, Attention Lt. Albee, Leonard Hankin and Stanley
Rubint." They constituted the first three-man R&A T-Force sent
forward, as mentioned above. The subject of the memo was: "R&A/
London Target List for Köln." The memo text begins with: "Lt.
Tennenbaum [sic] is carrying with him a copy of the recently completed Target List for Köln compiled and assimilated by Court Canby
in London from material supplied by the Divisions there." At first
sight I thought this was a list of bombing targets in Cologne, similar to

those selected by EOU in London, headed by Tenenbaum's friend Charles P. Kindleberger before the Normandy invasion.

But then I learned that a target list of OSS differs from that of strategic bombing in two respects. 1. It wasn't aimed at inflicting damage and destruction, but rather at finding useful German documents undamaged. 2. The weapon of OSS to attain this goal was a most diligent information gathering by all methods available to the spies of the US Secret Service. The memo text ends on this note: "In the event that at any future time you receive an indication as to what target cities are likely to become available to the T-Forces, it is important to inform this office so as to make possible similar target analyses."[510]

On November 27, 1944, a week after the first R&A T-Force group had been scheduled to be sent forward from Paris, Harold Deutsch sent a note to the adjutant general of 12th Army Group requesting that the assignment of following R&A T-Force personnel "be amended to read on 'detached service' rather than 'temporary duty.'" Besides Lt. Lewis Allbee, Cpl. Leonard Hankin, Pfc. Stanley Rubint, and John Wells as a civilian, he lists 2nd Lt. Edward Tennenbaum [sic]. "The original SHAEF orders state that this contingent is to be dually assigned to the PWD/12th Army T-Force and the SHAEF, Documents Subdivision. This is to remain the same."[511]

The names of the five members of this R&A T-Force have already appeared in this text above. Tenenbaum had crossed the Atlantic in July 1944 together with Stanley Rubint on the same boat. Such a passage in those days was always exposed to the danger of attacks by German submarines. The two OSS men must have become personally close comrades-in-arms. If he didn't get to know the others while stationed in OSS headquarters in Washington, DC, Tenenbaum will have grown close to them through his R&A work in London and Paris or on the battlefield in G-2 Intelligence of Omar Bradley's 12th Army Group and of General Patton's Third US Army.

Leonard J. Hankin, who meanwhile had been promoted to lieutenant, led the R&A T-Force that four days after Cologne had been captured on March 6, 1945 and entered the city with the target list that originally Tenenbaum had carried with him on his trip from London to Paris to start R&A field work with his T-Force in Belgium in November 1944. Rubint was part of Hankin's T-Force in Cologne, which in principle was totally open field for collecting intelligence material and books. For, constantly intervening rivals of OSS T-Forces, namely G-2 (intelligence) and G-5 (civil affairs) personnel of the army, had not yet arrived. Rubint, who on the Republican side had been a veteran of the Spanish Civil War with all its brutality, summarized his first impression: "Cologne is the sorriest sight I have run across yet in any war."[512] After thirty thousand casualties from the final raid of the Royal Air Force, the city was not only covered by corpse stench, but also three-quarters of its center and thus the majority of buildings on the target list had been transformed into ruins and rubble.

Ross Lee Finney, a composer of modern music and a professor of music at Smith College in Massachusetts, joined OSS in the spring of 1944. He became a very smart and successful confiscator of books and documents for IDC, for instance, when the search was on after the liberation of Paris. There, in September 1944, he got to know and grew close to Stanley Rubint, who was fluent in several languages and would be a key T-Force member "on continual field assignments ... across the entire line of the armies." By the end of the war he had exploited more than 1,600 targets in France and Germany. On October 4, 1944, before Tenenbaum arrived in Paris for his T-Force mission with Rubint in Belgium in late November, Finney wrote to his wife about Rubint that he is "really the most brilliant guy in our outfit – even if he is only a GI."[513] For his accomplishments Pfc Stanley Rubint received the Award of Unit Commander's Certificate of Merit from Chandler Morse on June 27, 1945.[514]

Dated also November 27, 1944 "Edward A. Tenenbaum, 2nd Lt., AC" sent the first of his several reports as an R&A T-Force member in a forward position from Brussels or La Roche in Belgium to Harold Deutsch in Paris. It covered the difficulties of Belgian officials whose task was to investigate and liquidate the subsidiaries of German banks in Brussels. "Such information may be of interest (a) in supplementing any present impressions of the Belgian epuration (b) as an example of the problems to be faced by financial personnel of civil affairs." The subsidiaries under investigation were the Continentale Bank, owned by the Dresdner Bank, located at 27, Avenue des Arts and the Hansa Bank NW, owned by the Commerzbank, located at 72 A, Rue Revalo.

> About seven people were working at each bank, most of them former employees who were Belgian. The main accounts had been removed from both by the Nazis, and the first problem of the Belgian personnel was to reestablish books for the banks on the basis of files of correspondence, in order to enable their liquidation. At the same time, an effort was being made to establish lists of firms which had engaged in economic collaboration with the Germans. Since these two banks, plus the Westbank (of the Bank der deutschen Arbeit) and a Brussels branch of the Deutsche Bank had a virtual monopoly on payments from Germany through the clearing, the files of correspondence (which were virtually intact) probably covered almost all the companies of interest. Unfortunately, the Germans had been much more thorough in cleaning out the Westbank and the Deutsche Bank before departing. ... // At both banks the Belgians employed there took precautions to save some of the records when the Germans withdrew, one having rescued many items from the furnace of the building. Organized work on the available records began about a month after the liberation of Brussels. ... // The Belgians seem to have a great attachment to legality and form. Most of the documents which we wished to remove for T-Force processing had been inventoried, and we were required to sign a receipt for them, although in general they were of no possible interest to the Belgian authorities.[515]

Attached to Tenenbaum's report of November 27, 1944 was a multi-page list of publications obtained from the two banks and "sent to G-2 SHAEF Document Section in Versailles."[516]

Tenenbaum's first weekly report on November 28, 1944 sent from forward R&A T-Force in Brussels to Harold Deutsch, Chief of R&A Paris, with special attention to Lt. Lunning, temporary chief of the German unit in London, also mentions the visit to the two subsidiaries of German banks described above. Tenenbaum recommends that Lt. Poole, obviously an R&A expert on German finance like Tenenbaum himself, should keep on the lookout for the collected "very valuable material ... [on] German banking, foreign trade control, finance and taxation. ... Our own very fruitful excursion to the two German banks was prompted by the admission by G-2 Documents that they had only covered two of the four German banks in Brussels (in fact, they did not know that there were any more)."[517] This means that G-2 Documents had only sifted the above-mentioned Westbank and Deutsche Bank for useful information.

Tenenbaum finds it most surprising that such a wealth of material is still remaining in Brussels, although G-2 Documents and others have been combing sources for a long time, but evidently only the rather obvious ones. He complains about the inadequacy of target lists of G-2 Documents. He encourages Lt. Canby and his group to produce additional comprehensive target lists like the one on Cologne that he had taken with him from London to Paris.

Tenenbaum also reports that he had left London for Paris in a hurry by plane, after he had received a phone call at about 22:00 h. Assuming that he flew over early the next morning, I can date the phone call on November 22, 1944 and the flight on the following day.[518] For, Tenenbaum regrets the fact that he could stay in Paris only for less than two days and that he arrived in Brussels in the afternoon of November 25 by jeep from Paris, shared with Lt. Sawyer. He reports on one impression of his stint in Paris: "The main complaint of the Paris personnel was that they were understaffed and overworked, though they all seemed enthusiastic about the opportunities for exhausting themselves in coping with the mountains of material they had managed to collect."

His impressions of Brussels are of a quite different character: "OSS is in many ways an underground organization here, and Americans in general are second-class allies, only on sufferance in a city belonging to the British Army (this is the official condition, the individual Englishman I have had contact with are very friendly and helpful)."[519]

Tenenbaum names the composition of his R&A T-Force in Brussels: Leonard Hankin, Stanley Rubint, Lt. Allbee (on loan from X-2), a Belgian intelligence officer, and himself. "Also Raymond, our driver, who tells us all about his love-life, which is a living proof that variety is the spice of life." In Brussels R&A T-Force would work with the G-2 Documents outpost of SHAEF in Versailles and a British-staffed team through which also the American finds are transmitted to SHAEF.[520] As to plans of R&A T-Force for the immediate future, Tenenbaum lists visits to commercial and industrial firms in Brussels, a trip to the *Frontbuchhandlung* [= frontline book store], which had been evacuated and stored some fifty miles outside of the city, "and a visit to the G-2 Documents SHAEF outpost at La Roche, where we believe we can obtain some of the material taken at Aachen." And in handwriting below the typed text: "P.S. Please excuse the typewriter. We don't like it but it's all we've got."[521]

Harold Deutsch responded immediately by sending out his memo "Subject: Present Situation and Next Moves" to R&A T-Force on November 29, 1944, not from his Paris office, but from APO 413, the London OSS detachment, from where – as we saw above – he would leave the following day back to France. He expressed much appreciation for Tenenbaum's report No. 1. He explained the reason for the change of R&A T-Force personnel from TD to DS, for which he had asked the Adjutant on November 27 out of his office in Paris (see above). "... our Adjutant has informed me that otherwise we must keep all of you on our Paris T/O [Theater of Operations], which would [financially] be rather crippling to our operations." For Deutsch it didn't come as a great surprise that "Brussels is pretty well worked out. ... If you move forward to La Roche [G-2

Documents SHAEF outpost, see above], anticipate an early order to join PWD T-Force. There is a good deal of optimism here about the fall of Cologne within the next two weeks and ... it would be well for you to have a little time with your PWD colleagues before you get going on a major target." [In fact, it wasn't until the first half of March 1945 that Cologne was taken by US troops. Hitler had ordered to defend the city up to the last cartridge. It was the largest city that the US Army captured in Germany.] Deutsch wrote further that Fink, the promised clerk, had not yet arrived, "but every effort is being made to break him loose quickly. We hope he can bring a standard typewriter." He announced he would provide a second car and driver that Colonel Colby had promised him. His great appreciation for R&A T-Force in Brussels came best to the fore in his complimentary close: "Warmest greetings and good luck to you all: Harold C. Deutsch, Chief, R&A/Paris."[522]

I found a Progress Report for the second half of November 1944 from OSS ETO, US Army (Main), APO 413, R&A Branch. The report underpins the volume of documents found by G-2 Documents Subdivision and R&A T-Force and delivered to the Central Information Division (CID) of OSS since August 1944: "the number of documents supplied per month to various requestors has risen from 577 to 2,937; the Reference Section now daily takes in 150 documents."[523] The same report mentions other OSS divisions, e.g., Biographical Records Division and German Division. It also lists movements of personnel under different headings. In category *Departures to other Theaters* Tenenbaum is noted as having left for France on November 23 for a "Political" OSS Mission. This corroborates my calculations above. Cpl. Leonard Hankin is reported to have left for France on November 20 and Harold Deutsch, Chief R&A Branch Paris, on November 30, 1944. These departures were out of London, as a paragraph further down explains by differentiating the APO numbers of R&A Branch Paris and OSS/R&A London. Tenenbaum and Hankin might have been on OSS duty in London for a while; Harold Deutsch certainly only paid a short-term visit there.

And actually Deutsch writes on December 1, 1944 in his Progress Report, R&A/Paris, 16–30 November 1944 to Colonel D. K. E. Bruce, that he visited the London office from November 27 to 30 "to discuss administrative and other Branch matters and to confer on planning for future continental operations."[524] Under arrivals and departures of personnel Tenenbaum is listed as having arrived in R&A/Paris branch on November 23. Deutsch reports further that the first three members of a five-man R&A T-Force left Paris on November 24 "to join the G-2/ SHAEF Documents Subdivision (Forward) currently operating from Brussels." It had been agreed with T-Force, PWD/P&PW, 12th Army Group on the one hand and with G-2/SHAEF, Documents Subdivision on the other that the R&A team was attached to both of them. The R&A team's major efforts would consist of T-Force activities. However, it would consider itself "an advance echelon of R&A and, as such, will exercise every possible initiative in contributing to the general R&A program."[525] Deutsch also reports a great success of operational importance: the acquisition by Ross Finney, from the Interdepartmental Committee for the Acquisition of Foreign Publications (IDC), of a set of French patents and adaptation devices abstracts for V-1 and V-2 missiles and jet propulsion.

IDC was founded on William Donovan's initiative by President Roosevelt in early 1942 (after the Japanese attack on Pearl Harbor followed by Hitler's declaration of war on the USA). This had cut down US access to books, journals, and newspapers of the Axis powers even more than before, while the need for information from such sources had risen with the outbreak of World War II and even more with the entry of the USA. IDC was equipped with funds to purchase and microfilm publications, achieved mostly through representatives in neutral countries like Portugal and Sweden. This was the hour of trained US librarians in Europe. Especially after the Normandy invasion, IDC and R&A of OSS cooperated closely and even interchanged personnel.[526]

In fact, Deutsch's memo of November 29, 1944 to R&A T-Force was not sent out of his office in Paris, but from APO 413 in London, obviously in reaction to Tenenbaum's first weekly report from Brussels the day before. Progress Reports were written to OSS European headquarters in London out of the OSS/R&A Paris Branch APO 887 with its chief Harold C. Deutsch to London, and out of the OSS European (ETO) headquarters in London, R&A Branch, attached to US Army (Main), with APO 413 to OSS headquarters in Washington, DC. I mistook "Main" at first for the river in Germany which flows through Frankfurt, where the American Forces would establish their headquarters for the administration of their zone of occupation, so to speak as a goal to be reached, not a description of a goal already reached. On a second thought I realized that it meant Main headquarters of the US Army in ETO, which for the most part of US operations in World War II remained in London. APO 413 stood for OSS London headquarters.[527]

Reports of R&A T-Force came pouring into Harold Deutsch's Office in Paris. On Saturday, December 2, 1944, Private first class Stanley Rubint, R&A T-Force, 12th Army Group, wrote to the Chief R&A Paris, with special attention to "Lt. Ashcraft, Chief IDC, Paris." He addressed both with "Dear Harold and Jack." This reveals that military correctness in saluting played no role in OSS R&A and IDC circles. Brains counted more than ranks. Rubint then starts out by describing his group's detour to their forward outpost in Brussels. They had left Paris on Thursday, November 23, by car in the morning for Verdun, where they arrived in the afternoon. They were to report to Colonel Powell, who had left one hour earlier for Luxembourg, headquarters of 12th Army Group under General Omar Bradley. So Rubint and his companions also moved on to Luxembourg. But they could meet Powell only the next morning. After a short talk the Colonel assured the group that he did not have any objection to our three-week excursion to Brussels. Thereafter Rubint and his company left and arrived in the Belgian capital in the late afternoon of Friday, November 24.

Rubint briefs his addressees further about target places they had visited, especially the two banks that Tenenbaum had already reported about (see page PP 283–285). But visits that Tenenbaum had reported as planned, had by now been made. Rubint writes about these:

> Some other, less interesting material was obtained from the Deutsche Arbeitsfront Verlag (see list). We also took a trip to Bourg Leopold, where the main branch of the Frontbuchhandlung had been located in Belgium. We found only some very skimpy remainders of a stock of publications too well known to us from our visit to the Frontbuchhandlung in Paris.[528]

Rubint was one example of a person who worked for IDC and R&A at the same time, because he also reports that he has purchased about 150 books for IDC worth 13,926.60 Belgian Francs and that he would probably spend the rest of his IDC money within the next two days. He would send the first lot of books, made up of four packages, either Sunday or Monday to Paris via G-2 SHAEF Documents Subdivision. They would presumably end up in Versailles. As an enclosure Rubint attaches his IDC purchase list. He ends his letter on the following note:

> According to all the information available from various sources, Brussels and the surrounding areas have been thoroughly cleaned out, and I feel that our continued attachment to G-2 Documents in Belgium will not be of any, or at the most of very little use to R&A. // My best regards to everybody, // Stanley Rubint.[529]

We will see in the following three reports how Edward Tenenbaum judged the situation.

On December 5, 1944 Tenenbaum sent his second weekly report out of Brussels "on my part in the work of the T-Force" to Harold Deutsch, chief, R&A/Paris "Attention: Lt (jg) Just Lunning, Chief, German Unit (Tempo) R&A/London." Like Stanley Rubint he also noted that R&A T-Force in Brussels had been finding little of interest. For tackling primary targets its arrival there should have happened much earlier, before "unit G-2s, Army T-Forces and SHAEF T-Force Outposts, not to mention souvenir hunters, manage to do a thorough job on the most obvious sources of information without our assistance, and without much thought for our needs." Therefore, he continues, R&A T-Force in Brussels covered a second-best type of target, namely commercial firms, those owned by Germans and after liberation confiscated by the Belgian government, and those in Belgian ownership. He observed that the former were reluctant to give up material.

> [A] little bullying was necessary to convince subordinate personnel that the Germans would not come back and fire them after the war if they turned over part of their libraries to us. Two especially valuable collections were (or will be) obtained from the Brussels branches of Siemens and AEG. This material is largely technical and of little value to R&A, but as is known we must at all times represent the interests of all intelligence agencies: in practical terms this means that if we turn over good material to the general T-Force system, we are able to earmark other material of greater interest to us brought in by somebody else. Thus, we were able to establish a claim to some railroad material of great value which had been found by the SHAEF Outpost personnel. ... // Having found Brussels subject to the law of diminishing returns, and anticipating the early availability of a major German target [Cologne, see above] we are leaving for the Remouchamps (near Spa) area to join the PWD-12th Army Group T-Force. It is believed advisable for us to have at least a week of personal contact with the personnel of this group before attempting to operate with them on a serious project, in order to learn their personal interests and so as to be able to proceed without too much attention to formalities.

Tenenbaum further wrote that he was surprised by the many opportunities for political and economic reporting available in Brussels. Often they had been tempted to neglect their primary responsibility as members of a T-Force, namely the collection of documentary material, in order to pursue the more fascinating activity of interviewing and observing. Tenenbaum listed four specific economic reports, already dispatched or to be sent to Paris, on observations and interviews that he and his men had collected with little of their own effort on visits to commercial targets in Brussels.

But Tenenbaum shared his impressions of the Belgian political and economic situation also in a broader sense. "I arrived by jeep in the middle of the famous 'Resisistanco' (Communist) demonstration against the [Hubert] Pierlot government, and was opposite the street where the hand grenade went off when the shooting began." Monetary measures by the Pierlot government, namely the unblocking of money on bank accounts up to the amount on deposit in 1940, did spark the communist street violence. Big business did have considerable deposits in 1940, while small business didn't. The communists would present themselves as the "champions of the small bourgeoisie" and therefore would meet with a lot of sympathy in those circles. They demanded and demonstrated for the unblocking of 50,000 francs per person. This amount would be far exceeding what working-class people would have in their bank accounts. In order to show that Tenenbaum was more than an economic and financial expert, I quote his observations and analysis of the Belgian polity and society in length:

> This is part of the intransigent policy of the Belgian communists,
> which more than anything else except the presence of British
> troops, is responsible for the maintenance of Pierlot in power, since
> it has forced all other opposition elements, who hold a majority of
> the parliament, to support his government against their will. One
> other point to illustrate the implications of the financial measures
> one of the major causes of the lack of confidence in the Pierlot
> government is the fear that the collaborators and war profiteers will
> be let off easily. So far the financial measures have only intensified
> this fear, since they have not committed the government to
> anything except a gradual de-blocking of money up to a certain,
> undefined percentage of the money which has been blocked. It is
> common knowledge that the collaborators have succeeded in

putting their wealth in real estate (ranging from the individual's 'vignoble & Bordeaux' to the trust's new factory). Furthermore, the measures have warned even the most stupid profiteer that the time has come to destroy his files of incriminating papers, and the government has very kindly given plenty of time for this to be done by all but the most obvious and lest German tools or direct subsidiaries. In fact, the financial measures have become the focus for all the discontent with the government, because they are the most positive act yet undertaken by the government.

Tenenbaum ended his second report by noting that his next report should be much shorter. It should contain little or nothing about accomplishments, as his team would be occupied with orienting itself in the organization of the 12th Army Group T-Force, "and/or dodging buzz-bombs,"[530] (the German V1 cruise missile and V2 rocket as ballistic missile).

I found two more Tenenbaum reports out of Belgium, sent not from Brussels, but from La Roche. This was the location of SHAEF G-2 Documents outpost. "The La Roche outpost is similar in mission and activity to the one in Brussels: it assembles material collected by the Army and Army Group channels for shipment to Versailles."[531] The two reports were not written from the La Roche location, but from a location further advanced to the frontline. In his third weekly report to Harold Deutsch in Paris for attention of Lt. Just Lunning, temporary chief of R&A/London, of December 12, 1944 Tenenbaum wrote that more than expected the week had been full of activity. He and his team had arrived at the 12th Army Group T-Force in Remouchamps (near Spa) in Belgium on December 8, 1944. A lot of the three-page, single-spaced report describes impressions and new information gathered at the new location, such as: An Army T-Force would be

a complete military unit, including in this case an armored infantry battalion, which is designed to take over a large target city, clear mines, booby traps, snipers and protect it against counterattacks, and then exploit the intelligence possibilities. Apart from combat troops, the T-Force includes documents people, P/W interrogator teams, counter-intelligence, political warfare personnel, radio broadcast technicians, and more alphabetical abbreviations than all of Washington.[532]

Contrary to earlier expectations, the capture of an assigned target city would not be imminent, the 12th Army Group's T-Force would at present be doing nothing in its own right. But intelligence people would be loaned out to Army and Corps G-2s for specific tasks.

Here is another fact Tenenbaum reported. Without the express permission of Army and Corps G-2s "rear echelon elements (that's us)" would not be allowed to be active in their area of operations. And permissions would not be lightly given due to professional jealousy and difficult housing and food conditions in those forward areas.

Tenenbaum described their experience at Remouchamps. Their orders assigned his group to Captain Krafft, CO of Publishing and Political Warfare Advance Detachment of 12th AG, temporarily attached to 12th AG T-Force. Upon arrival Captain Krafft had left for Eupen. They drove there the next morning. Again upon arrival Captain Krafft had already left Eupen. But of the two other persons they had hoped to meet there, namely Mr. Sweet and Mr. Padover, both probably civilian OSS personnel, the R&A team had a fruitful conversation with Mr. Padover. And because this might have been Tenenbaum's first concrete encounter with Germany's monetary problem for him to solve after the war, I quote from his report:

> Mr. Padover told us a little about the state of mind of Germans in captured areas. Among the statements which I found surprising as a self-styled economist was his estimate of the German monetary situation. The Germans, he found, had no interest in money. Their most vocal economic interest was in work and in a job, even though one day's work would [not] pay for possible expenditures for a long time. The famous "inflationary psychosis," in short, seems absent, either because the Germans have mentally written off their money

holdings as worthless, or because they believe the Nazi control of prices and purchasing power will continue of its own weight after the war. This is but one indication of the fundamental surprises which may await us in Germany.

Tenenbaum's R&A team returned to Remouchamps in the afternoon and finally met Captain Krafft there. He informed them of the paucity of documents worthwhile to be analyzed in his forward area. But he would welcome "any personnel willing and able to undertake political and economic reporting (called 'civilian interrogation' or 'survey' here; reporters and analysts are 'writers') ... [They] could be introduced into forward areas under his auspices." Any reporting on results would have to go through his official channels from 12th AG to SHAEF, "but arrangement could be made to ensure delivery to R&A in Paris."

Tenenbaum expressed personal interest and enthusiasm for Captain Krafft's proposal. He regarded this as:

> an excellent opportunity for current intelligence on Germany for R&A at this time. ... As long as captured German territory remains a forward area (and there is little indication here of a break in the front in the near future) we have little chance of obtaining entry openly as R&A.

Operating under Captain Krafft, the R&A team would be part of the 12th AG and would benefit from its personal and official contacts with Army and Corps G-2:

> the ultimate and independent arbiter of any activity in the field. Thus, if we desire to observe German conditions, it will have to be done through some such arrangement as this. Capt. Krafft claims that no one else in this area is performing similar work and my now-dimmed recollections of London indicate that the need for such material is great.

Tenenbaum also echoed what Pfc Stanley Rubint had already reported to Harold Deutsch on December 2 on the first week of R&A T-Force's activities. There would not be sufficient documents to find at their position to justify the presence of a whole R&A T-Force. While he was recommending to send his team back to R&A in Paris, he was trying to convince Harold Deutsch in Paris and thereby Lt. Just Lunning in London with a broad array of arguments to leave him in his forward position.

Much more than in his weekly report of December 12, this comes out in a letter Tenenbaum wrote actually from La Roche on December 10, 1944 to Deutsch, "Subject: T-Force Assignments, 12 AG Area," before his team returned to its location in Remouchamps from a visit there with Captain Krafft. There would be no prospect of document work as originally envisaged until the opening of Cologne or another major R&A target city. Only one person of his team should stay with Captain Krafft and he recommended himself. The others should go back to R&A Paris. He would exploit occasional documents when Army and Corps authorities had cleared them. But mainly he would devote his time to reporting, as Captain Krafft's unit offered excellent opportunities for such work. On recommendation of Captain Krafft he would send reports expeditiously via the official channel (T-Force 12th AG to SHAEF) with an extra copy to R&A/Paris. Thus it would not be exclusive material, but it would be "eminently suitable for evaluation, background and processing and dissemination by R&A/Paris."

Captain Krafft had informed him that according to his knowledge his unit would be the only one along the whole frontline which aims at "thorough coverage of civilian information. On the basis of my London experience," Tenenbaum continues, such information would almost totally be lacking in London. It would be of "the greatest interest to us if we seriously propose to provide current intelligence on Germany at this time and in the near future." Captain Krafft would at that time lack qualified personnel for such work. In reciprocity the captain would certainly be receptive for proposals to expedite report delivery to R&A, as long as his unit got a copy. This arrangement would not be ideal. But it would be "the utmost obtainable in forward areas, barring a SHAEF directive for independent R&A-OSS operation in Corps and Army territory." The latter would be unlikely.

Tenenbaum claims that from his experience in London he would know that R&A London has little current knowledge of civilian affairs in Germany, "and the Economics Division in particular seems to have none." As he also states that he would not know the situation in Paris, we can conclude that Tenenbaum must have spent a lot of time with R&A London between his arrival in England in July 1944 and his flight from London to Paris on November 23, 1944. Actually he speaks of his "personal observations in the last few weeks" in London, to substantiate his claim "that the most elementary value judgements, indispensable for effective operation once it begins, cannot be made on the basis of the limited information available in London." He therefore pleaded for frontline assignments also as a training measure. In order to convince Harold Deutsch even further to let him remain with Captain Krafft's unit in advanced position, he argued that "my return to Paris might precipitate a request from Lt. Lunning for my transfer back to London."[533] So much was gleaned from Tenenbaum's letter to Deutsch on December 10. The following information is taken from Tenenbaum's third weekly report of December 12, 1944.[534]

Following the visit at SHAEF G-2 Documents Outpost at La Roche on December 10, one man of Tenenbaum's R&A team, Cpl. Leonard Hankin, was sent from La Roche to Paris "to present our collective opinion and individual aspirations to Mr. Deutsch." Upon his return Hankin brought back Deutsch's permission for Tenenbaum to accept Captain Krafft's offer. Tenenbaum announced that he would report this to the captain on December 13. The rest of the group would probably join the Sixth AG T-Force and would "attempt to participate in document work in the Strasbourg area:" For himself Tenenbaum lists the three tasks he was ordered to perform during his tenure with Captain Krafft: 1. Political and economic reporting, 2. Representation of R&A documents interests at the 12th

Army Group T-Force to prepare for future operations in this area, 3. To assist, if deemed desirable, in sending additional reporting personnel to his location for short periods.

One passage in Tenenbaum's report is most revealing as to rivalries between army and OSS in field positions. The army would require the sending of Tenenbaum's future reports through its regular channels. Under such conditions his reports would necessarily be somewhat restrained. When OSS channels are used, it would be "advisable to send an expurgated version through Army facilities at the same time." Any knowledge by the army of direct communication via OSS channels might endanger further continuance of OSS personnel in this area. Therefore, Tenenbaum maintains, any direct OSS exchange would have to be kept strictly within OSS at all times.

In closing, Tenenbaum relays another point of interest to other R&A persons who would in the future come to his area location for work similar to his own. The modes of behavior would often be strictly GI. "While allowances are made for intelligence personnel by some organizations, they are by no means universal. Small matters like failure to salute at the proper times could, in my opinion, be the difference between failure and success of operations in the field, whether conducted by officer or enlisted personnel."[535]

How well organized and prepared the OSS establishment in ETO was is especially evidenced by a memo that on March 9, 1945 Harold Starr from OSS detachment (Main), APO 413 US Army, which – as already mentioned above – was the OSS headquarters main outpost in ETO, sent to Philip Bastedo, OSS headquarters in Washington, DC. Its subject: the tentative planning of "the disposition and use of Branch personnel in Germany during the period beginning now and ending with the establishment of OSS Headquarters in the Zone of American occupation." Starr refers to the existing uncertainties which make planning very difficult. Apart from the speed of the Allied advance he mentions "(1) the demands on the R&A market, that is, the needs of those who receive R&A assistance and (2) the need to rotate personnel so that our analysts will not develop into narrow, one-sided experts." He elaborates on the options for obtaining information "through personal observation and interrogation." For, this could be used by OSS T-Forces, Field Detachments, and perhaps the PWD, to which Tenenbaum was attached while serving in Patton's Third US Army.

Starr evaluates the advantages and disadvantages of the three possible channels for use of OSS personnel. He mentions the detailed plans for document exploitation and current reporting that already existed in Harold Deutsch's memo "Field Program of the Intelligence Services Staff, R&A/ETO/Forward" of February 21, 1945 and "our own memorandum" entitled "Suggestions to OSS Field Detachment Commanders." The most revealing part in Starr's memo for the high quality of planning is the one in which in the event of US troops entering Berlin a first (Chandler Morse, Harold Starr, Harold Deutsch and four others) and second group (thirteen persons) of OSS are named. A stenographic staff is also requested for reporting out of Berlin. Starr also names personnel that was already attached or should be attached to 12th Army Group, among them 2nd Lt. Edward Tenenbaum, "Reporting, Economic" with the remark that he is already attached to PWD of that army. Lt. (jg) Just Lunning is named in the lead position.[536]

3.2.4   In Postwar Germany

On May 25, 1945 Harold Deutsch moved his R&A offices in a first airlift from Paris to the American base in Wiesbaden-Biebrich/ Germany to set up a lasting OSS Mission for and in Germany in an abandoned *Henkell Trocken* champagne factory.[537] In a "Progress Report, R&A/Paris 6 FWD 1–31 May 1945" of June 1, 1945 OSS Branch in Paris reports further that a third airlift for 23 R&A personnel of OSS from ETO staff and all divisions are scheduled to go forward from Paris and London on June 5, 1945 and that Lt. (jg) John E. Sawyer [since September 28, 1944 Deputy Chief of R&A Paris in general charge of current reporting activities[538]] has succeeded Harold C. Deutsch as Chief.

Edward Tenenbaum was not one of them, because in the pre-ceding report he is mentioned under Reporting Units, Third Army: "Lt. E. Tenenbaum, R&A analyst with P&PW DET/12th AG (Fwd), continues surveys in the Eisenach and forward territory." And in a separate Progress Report of June 1, 1945, sent from R&A/Germany, covering "Achievements" May 25–31, 1945, 1st Lt. Tenenbaum, is listed as R&A personnel on field assignments with Patton's Third Army with the task of "Reporting" as opposed to "Documents Collecting" by others on the list. "As of this date, 41 staff members have reported for permanent or temporary duty. A field staff of nine-teen responsible to this headquarters is at present operative in other parts of Germany."[539]

Among others, Tenenbaum sent a 1-page report, dated March 28, 1945, to the "Commanding Officer, PWB (G-2 Seat) Third US Army APO 403" on a supersonic fighter plane which the German air force had been testing near Frankfurt am Main until the area was taken by Third US Army. He had gathered information on this proto-type from an interview with a French forced laborer, about forty-year-old Raymond Dalmond, who was a mechanic and possessed skills in aviation. He had worked on tank motors at the *Zeppelin-Reederei* close by the airfield, where the models were tested. He could not only observe test flights, but even overhear conversations about the jet. So he knew that its motors were adapted from the German V-1 cruise missile. Other details are described. Tenenbaum's report even included a drawing of the preproduction model.[540]

With victory in Europe, all of the assignments of Tenenbaum's G-2 PWD had been accomplished, except one: "To control informa-tion services in Allied-occupied Germany."[541] Its purpose was to assist military government in controlling German thought and expression as a first step into the reeducation of Germans through control of all their information services. With the dissolution of Supreme Headquarters Allied Expeditionary Force (SHAEF) on July 13, 1945, PWD was transformed into the Information Control Division (ICD) of OMGUS with different branches such as press, publications, film, theater, music, and radio control.[542] Probably due to his radio training in Sioux Falls, South Dakota, at the beginning of his military career, Tenenbaum was attached to radio control.

This is evidenced by a letter of May 6, 1945 that Kurt Mair, director general of the *Deutsche Auslands-Rundfunk-Gesellschaft Interradio AG* sent from his seat in Oberlauterbach Castle near Rottenburg/Laaber in Lower Bavaria to "Mr. Edward A. Tenenbaum, 1st Lt., Air Corps, PWB, G-2 Section, Third United States Army." Tenenbaum had obviously met with Kurt Mair and maybe sequestrated and sealed the radio equipment that the company possessed at its station in Lower Bavaria. I realize that the letter was addressed to Tenenbaum in PWB and its date precedes the official date of transforming PWD into ICD mentioned above. But obviously wherever Third Army had broken German military resistance and taken up responsibility for civil affairs, PWD acted already on ICD principles.

In the letter Kurt Mair expresses his complaints in a very polite and also humble way to Tenenbaum. He reports that, the day before, he had come back from Mainburg where he wanted to meet the head of military government of the district of Mainburg and Rottenburg, Captain Vickersham. But

> in the meantime, the technical material of Interradio had been removed from Oberlauterbach by the 3rd Army. In view of the trusting conversations we had in Oberlauterbach Castle, I have to tell you, Dear First Lieutenant Tenenbaum, that I was very disappointed by the removal of the Interradio technical material. . . . May I ask you, Dear First Lieutenant Tenenbaum, to inform Second Lieutenants Nilson and Fleck of my above statement of opinion.[543]

Here is some background information on Nazi Germany's overseas propaganda machine via shortwave radio. Since 1943 the *Deutsche Auslands-Rundfunk-Gesellschaft – Interradio AG* organized the worldwide foreign propaganda of the Nazi regime. Its predecessor had been der *Deutsche Kurzwellensender* (KWS), founded 1933 in Berlin. In August 1943 its transmitter stations were moved to

Königs Wusterhausen outside of Berlin. With the Red Army approaching toward the end of the war, shortwave equipment was moved to alternative locations in Helmstedt for broadcasting to India and the Near East and to Landshut in Lower Bavaria for covering the Far East. The distance between Castle Oberlauterbach and Landshut is eighteen miles. Kurt Georg Kiesinger, 1966 to 1969 chancellor of the Federal Republic of Germany, was one of the three top managers of Interradio AG. During the last days of the war the trio tried to flee from the Berlin area to Landshut. Yet they never arrived there. At the end of April 1945 the Landshut station ceased broadcasting.[544] It is most likely that First Lieutenant Tenenbaum of Third US Army's PWD had arrived and forced Kurt Mair to stop radio transmissions.

After the end of the war OMGUS also recruited famous German art creatives who had fled Nazi Germany and emigrated to the USA, among them Erich Pommer, the producer of the film classics *The Cabinet of Dr. Caligari*, *Metropolis*, and *Blue Angel*, as film control officer, and Billy Wilder, famous for his comedy movies like *Some Like It Hot*, as a film consultant for ICD.[545] Wilder appears as author of two contemporaneous contributions of August 16 and 21, 1945 to a documentary of ICD's secret reports on cultural developments in Berlin July to December 1945.[546] It must have been in Berlin where Wilder was inspired to produce his film *A Foreign Affair*, acclaimed by film critics in the USA, but rejected by OMGUS as a suitable film for reeducation purposes in Germany.[547]

ICD's operation progressed through three phases:

> In the first phase, all media of public expression in Germany were shut down. This prohibition was accomplished piece-meal as the Allied armies advanced across Germany. The authority for prohibiting the operation of all German information services was provided by Military Government Law No. 191, issued under the authority of the Supreme Commander in January 1945. This was amended in June to include television broadcasts and the sale and distribution of publications and sound recordings.[548]

FIGURE 3.21 Edward A. Tenenbaum in military uniform with his wife
Jeanette Kipp Tenenbaum

After VE-Day, the end of the war in Europe, when most GIs
yearned for returning home, Tenenbaum's wife Jeanette Kipp pursued
the opposite idea. She would sacrifice her routine work in Treasury at
Washington, DC and rejoin her husband Edward in Germany. It would
be *a country to play with*, as the British economist Alec Cairncross
entitled his publication on his experience in immediate postwar negotiations on Germany's economic future.[549] The Tenenbaum couple
were young and hungry for peaceful exploration of Europe and its
different ways of life. And Kipp obviously believed in Edward's outstanding qualifications not only in finance and economics in general,
but also in the functioning of the German economy in particular. Here
is how Tenenbaum with his typical modesty and understatement
describes how their reunion in Germany came about:

> At the end of the war, my wife used her influence [in the Treasury
> Department] to get me transferred to the Finance Division of

Military Government. Since all qualified financial experts were refusing to work in Germany at the time [which is not true, the later president of American Bankers Association Joseph Dodge being a prominent counterexample], I got to be the chief US expert on the German currency reform. Thanks to the fact that I wasn't particularly sympathetic to the postwar difficulties of the German people, I was able to do a ruthless job, which turned out to be very effective. I shudder to think what would have happened if somebody who worried about individuals' problems had been in charge.[550]

The same source throws further light on Tenenbaum's character, this time also on his sense of dry, even black humor: "... the biggest job that anybody in my field could hope for fell into my lap when I was 26, more or less by accident. It's tough to be an automatic has-been so early in life. However, it's getting easier to accept, as old age creeps up on me [he was only 45 then]. Whoever thought I'd still be around for my twenty-fifth reunion? Arlington National Cemetery, here I come."[551]

Edward Tenenbaum was released from his prior assignment and transferred "to USGCC now OMGUS eff 7 July 45."[552] The transformation of USGCC into OMGUS was effective on October 1 and 15, 1945 respectively. As an OSS-trained officer and Yale-trained specialist in economics and finance with a special focus on Germany's Nazi economy Tenenbaum had a lot to investigate on financial conditions in Germany during the Third Reich and in occupation zones thereafter. Assigned to the Finance Division of OMGUS, more specifically to its Foreign Exchange and Blocking Control Branch headed since October 1945 by Jack Bennett,[553] he was strongly involved in interrogations and the making of affidavits of leading German financial managers suspicious of criminal dealings such as stealing gold from occupied countries or marketing and selling dental gold or valuables of the victims of concentration and death camps. An affidavit of November 17, 1945 taken by Edward Tenenbaum from Emil Puhl is a good example.[554] Since July 1, 1934 the latter had been director and since February 11, 1939 vice president of the Reichsbank. He had also served as a director for the Bank for International Settlements (BIS) at Basle, Switzerland. Puhl used his international reputation and his business connections in Switzerland to launder looted gold.[555] His affidavit concerned payments for electric power that Switzerland had exported to Germany during the war. On the day of their encounter formerly powerful Puhl was fifty-six and Tenenbaum, equipped with the power of US military government in Germany, had turned twenty-four exactly a week earlier. Like in so many other similar cases, the Germans involved – especially the Nazis accustomed to authoritarian rule and behavior – must have felt humiliated not only by military defeat, but also by being confronted with interrogators a generation or so younger.[556]

However, Tenenbaum also met and discussed with German financial and economic experts in political offices who were regarded as unencumbered by a Nazi past by OMGUS, like on February 1, 1946 with Ludwig Erhard and Fritz Terhalle, economics and finance ministers of Bavaria respectively. Bavaria was one of the reconstructed German states (Länder) belonging to the US zone of occupation. The meeting was probably Tenenbaum's first encounter with Erhard, because in his memo of the meeting Tenenbaum misspelled Erhard's name and referred to him as "Mr. Ehrhardt" while calling his second interlocutor correctly "Dr. Terhalle." The two Bavarian ministers discussed with Tenenbaum an unofficial memo that the finance minister had prepared with some collaboration of Erhard. Tenenbaum got the impression that of the two Erhard was the spiritus rector ("dominant factor"), yielding to Terhalle on technical and financial-theory matters, but was providing the fundamentals of policy to a large extent. On the content of the memo under discussion Tenenbaum noted that the authors are "ruthlessly critical" of the plan of Joseph Dodge, director of OMGUS' Finance Division, for decentralizing the West German banking system and further that "the strong tone of the memorandum was not carried over into the discussion, which proceeded on a very friendly basis."[557]

One of Erhard's fundamental statements was the differentiation between two phases of a change in the credit system. Of primary importance would be a currency reform. Without it there could be no stable monetary apparatus capable of credit-policy operations which would be essential for the success of the reform. This had been a lesson from ending German hyperinflation in 1923. So while Erhard agreed fully with Dodge's plan to eliminate all economic power positions, he also sided with Terhalle that elimination of economic power in the banking sector should be limited and not be "so uncompromising and unconsidered." And then Tenenbaum records Erhard with a surprising statement, later contradicted by Erhard's own price-decontrol a few days after currency reform of June 20, 1948: "In the economic sphere, for example, it will be impossible to introduce a free economy, even though the monetary prerequisites will be satisfied by the currency reform."

Already then Terhalle declared that the economic systems in the Soviet zone was so different from that in the US zone that it represented a great danger for the unity of the German economy. Erhard added that he hoped that the economic system in the US zone will be upheld until it is adopted uniformly in the three Western zones of occupation. Asked about the goal of a unified Germany, Erhard differentiated between what is ideal and what is realistically possible. In his opinion unity would stand a greater chance, if the three Western zones would unite and thereby exert greater weight vis-à-vis the Soviet zone.

> ... at least the US Zone must get together with the English
> Zone. ...] rather than slip from National Socialism to Bolshevism,
> in the hope of being able to create a basis for our existence
> somehow, we could prefer to give up the Russian Zone. Because of
> his feeling that a central administration will not work at present, he
> personally refused the American offer (by the Economics Division)

to make him a candidate for the position of State Secretary in a central department. The position is in his opinion untenable as long as there is no unity of policy among the occupying powers.[558]

Erhard's opinion presaged what two years later would become official US policy, namely a separate West German currency reform in full awareness that this would entail the East–West division of Germany.

On February 28, 1946 Headquarters US Forces, European Theater (APO 757) – specified as OMGUS – issued travel orders to First Lieutenant Edward A. Tenenbaum. He was to

> proceed on or about 1 March 1946 from his present station to
> Le Havre, France, thence by first available surface (1800-C-699)
> transportation to the United States, reporting upon arrival to the Port
> Commander, Port of Debarkation, for movement to Washington DC.
> Upon arrival thereat 1st Lt Tenenbaum will report to The Adjutant
> General, WD [War Department], for temporary duty with the
> Treasury Department for a period of approximately two (2) days, to
> carry out the instructions of the Theater Commander. Upon
> completion of this duty 1st Lt Tenenbaum will proceed to Separation
> Center No 27, Fort Meade, Maryland, for disposition under WD
> Readjustment Regulations 1–1 and 1–5 cs. 1st Lt Tenenbaum is
> relieved from further assignment and duty in this theater and
> attached unassigned to Separation Center No 27, Fort Meade, Md,
> EDCMR:[559] 2 April 1946. This is a permanent change of station.[560]

Tenenbaum arrived at the New York Port of Embarkation on Saturday, March 16, 1946. He was lodged for one night in military Camp Kilmer, New Jersey. According to his own claim for reimbursement of travel expenses and per diems, he left Camp Kilmer by train on Sunday March 17 at 9:00 and arrived in Washington, DC at 15:00 h. He probably spent the remainder of Sunday relaxing and refreshing memories of his early happy days with Jeanette Kipp in DC. The next morning, he must have reported to the adjutant general of the War Department for TDY [Temporary Duty] with the Treasury

Department. Tenenbaum didn't leave the capital until Thursday March 21, at 23:00 by bus to arrive at Separation Center No. 27 in Fort Meade MD "for disposition"[561] at 11:00 the next day. This means, Tenenbaum spent four full workdays for his TDY in the Treasury. I conjecture that he discussed currency-reform matters while the Colm-Dodge-Goldsmith (CDG) Commission was working on its currency-reform Plan in Germany.

At Separation Center No. 27 at Fort Meade MD he was discharged from active military duty in the US Army on March 23, 1946 and "temporarily" promoted to captain the same day. Tenenbaum referred to this as his "gangplank promotion."[562] As he had accrued fifty-six days of untaken leave, he reverted to inactive status fifty-six days later on May 18, 1946. Last salary payments and severance payments of 100 dollars per year for three full years of active duty were calculated in March 1946 in – according to stamp – "Fort George G. Meade Hdq., Station No. 4344" on an *Officers' Pay, Allowance, and Mileage Voucher* form. The balance of credits and debits (such as salary overpayment, dues for life insurance, and free meals) amounted to 1,191.97 dollars. It was paid out by check drawn on the US Treasury dated March 31, 1946. Tenenbaum, who had to sign the form, wished the check to be sent "to me at the following address: APT 10, 3030 Wisconsin AVE NW Washington DC." He left Fort Meade MD on April 20, 1946 by rail to New York City,[563] probably to visit his parents there. He did not directly return to Germany, but lived in his apartment 3030 Wisconsin Ave. NW, Washington, DC, until he returned to Germany to assume his position as special assistant to the financial adviser of General Clay in Berlin in August 1946.[564]

So far, the sources on Tenenbaum that I have had access to are mute on what the reason for Tenenbaum's stay in Washington, DC was, the four days with the Treasury from March 18 to 21, 1946 and the period from the second half of April to July or August 1946. For the following period he has stated in attachments to his job applications that he had worked for the General Clay's financial adviser, Jack Bennett, from August 1946 to September 1948.

After having been discharged from active duty in the US Army and put into reserve officer status, the following questions arise. Which institution took Tenenbaum on the payroll when he was active as special assistant to the financial adviser of OMGUS Berlin, charged with the preparation of currency reform in Germany? The War Department took him over from the army and footed the bill. This is evidenced explicitly by three different travel orders issued by the OMGUS Office of the Commanding General dated September 9, 21, and 30, 1946 "To: Mr. Edward A. Tenenbaum (War Dept Employee P-4) D-435254 // US Civilian named above ...."[565] It can also be concluded from the fact that in interdepartmental meetings in September/October 1947 in preparation of printing Deutschmark banknotes in the USA, he is listed as a representative of the War Department (see Section 4.2).

The second question is: Why did Tenenbaum continue to rank as a first lieutenant and not – after his "gangplank promotion" – as a reserve officer with the rank of captain throughout his tenure at OMGUS? The explanation must be that his promotion was officially announced with his discharge on March 23, 1946, the day after his last day of active duty in the army.

The third question is: Did Tenenbaum keep wearing his military uniform after he had been discharged from the army, put into reserve officer status, and assumed his function as Special Assistant for Currency Reform to the Finance Adviser of OMGUS? The answer is no, as evidenced by photos and the current practice in the five US military branches. Photos of the interned German experts together with Tenenbaum on the premises of the "Conclave of Rothwesten" from April to June 1948 (see Section 4.3) show that in contrast to Colonel Stoker, the organizer of the secret meeting, Tenenbaum appears in civilian clothes. And the current practice in the five US military branches is still that reserve officers can take their uniform home, but are allowed to wear it only when activated for further military training or military duty.

4   In Action for OMGUS and Currency Reform in Germany 1946–1948

This part of the book deals with the international political setting in which the West German currency reform of June 20, 1948 took place; the difficulties that had to be overcome; the multiple tugs-of-war between the four military governments in Germany, between them and their respective governments at home, and between currency experts of the occupying powers and German experts; Edward A. Tenenbaum's central role in planning, preparing, and organizing monetary and financial reform; and finally the economic and financial consequences of the reform.

4.1   IN THE RUN-UP TO C-DAY: GENERAL POLITICAL SETTING

Before dealing with Tenenbaum's role in planning and preparing for C-Day – as the currency-reform date was called in US military government circles[1] – I will first present an overview of the international political setting around Germany under occupation rule and its change 1945 to 1948. Subsequently, I take on two specific questions as to the exact timing of US decisions: 1.) on printing Deutschmarks in the US and 2.) on definitely giving up the chance of a joint currency reform for all four occupation zones, thereby deliberately accepting the political East–West partition of Germany.

4.1.1   International Political Setting

On May 20, 1946 Gerhard Colm, Joseph M. Dodge and Raymond W. Goldsmith (CDG) had delivered *A Plan for the Liquidation of War Finance and the Financial Rehabilitation of Germany* to General Lucius Clay. After a three-day stopover in London the two highly reputed economists Colm and Goldsmith had arrived in Berlin on March 6, 1946. As persecuted Jewish German citizens they had emigrated from Germany in 1933 and 1934 respectively and become US citizens. In Berlin they were equipped with a staff of five American economists: Horst Mendershausen, Robert Eisenberg, Lloyd Metzler, Jerome Jacobson, and Gerald Matchett.[2] Their intensive work included not only gathering statistics as well as studying literature and numerous plans for currency reform proposed by German experts. But they also consulted with financial experts of the other Allied powers, of Austria and Czechoslovakia (where currency reforms had already been implemented) and of Germany.[3]

Already since November 1945 Clay, until March 1947 still deputy military governor in Germany's US zone in charge of civil affairs, and his first financial adviser Joseph M. Dodge had been aware of the urgent need of a currency reform for putting Germany's depressed economy on its feet again. Thereby, they also aimed at reducing the need of large US financial aid to Germany. Before the end of 1945 they had asked the War Department to contact Colm and Goldsmith, bring about a temporary leave of absence from their present positions, and hire them for the job.[4] It was expressly demanded by General Clay at the outset of CDG's work that the eventual road-map to currency reform should be in accordance with the Potsdam Agreement, that is, applicable in all four zones of Germany. It was then expected that the plan would take effect in the fall of 1946.[5]

Clay, by a direct petition to Secretary of State James F. Byrnes, managed to overcome some initial resistance against the progressive capital levy and the burden-sharing provisions of the CDG Plan in Washington, DC, especially from the War Department. The plan in its original form was given the green light by telegram W-98110 of August 22, 1946[6] from the War Department to OMGUS. It reads: "At meeting this morning of Secretaries of State, War, and Navy, unanimous approval given to Colm-Dodge-Goldsmith Financial Plan as basis for American position in Quadripartite negotiation."[7] Clay introduced the CDG Plan for discussion in the Allied Control Council's Coordinating Committee on September 2, 1946. The plan appeared on the agenda of the Finance Directorate on September 7, 1946. The Soviets and the French assented immediately. By September 12, 1946 all four powers were agreed on the principles of a drastic monetary reform including the capital levy and burden-sharing provisions.[8]

OMGUS as well as War, State, and Treasury Departments were still confident that the other three Allied powers also had an interest in treating Germany "as a single economic unit" as agreed in the Potsdam Agreement of August 2, 1945. Clay writes in his memoirs: "I must admit we were more optimistic then [September 1945] with respect to the possible success of quadripartite government than was warranted by future events. By the spring of 1946 much of this optimism had gone."[9]

In addition, currency reform had become a matter of urgency for the Americans. The Congress wanted to cash in on the peace dividend. The US Army in Europe had comprised about three million men and women in uniform at the end of the war there. The GIs were brought home at an astounding pace. By late 1946, the army's strength in Europe had been reduced to 200,000 troops, and it dropped further until the outbreak of the Korean War in 1950.[10]

Futhermore, Congress wanted to see a quick way out of the very high postwar financial burden on the US taxpayer for supporting the starving German population with food as well as German industry and agriculture with raw materials and other inputs. The Americans aimed at putting the largely undestroyed industrial machinery in Germany[11] back to work so that Germany might produce and export enough to pay for its own imports. The chaotic currency conditions with an abundance of money (old Reichsmark plus Allied Military Mark) on the one side and on the other a scarcity of supply of products at frozen prices as well as a wage freeze were holding back incentives to work, produce, and invest. A currency reform that would radically reduce the huge monetary overhang was seen as a necessary condition for balancing supply and demand at noninflationary prices and for restoring incentives.

But the Soviets procrastinated because such action would make dynamic capitalist modes of production attractive also in their zone. There they stood for the imposition of a centrally planned command economy like in the Soviet Union. And until 1948 the French were unwilling to go along, because they were afraid of a rebirth of Germany's traditional economic power that would result from a successful currency reform. The prospect of receiving Marshall Plan aid and security assurances by the USA and UK that preceded the signing of the treaty creating the NATO on April 4, 1949 led to a reorientation of French policy in Germany in 1948.[12]

In January 1947 President Harry S. Truman, a Democrat, had sent former US President Herbert Hoover, a Republican, on an economic mission to Germany and Austria. This was the time of the so-called hunger-winter. Hoover's assignment was to report on the food situation. He was experienced in such matters, because he had been President Woodrow Wilson's food administrator during and after World War I. In that postwar period he had saved millions of Europeans from starvation.

After having submitted two reports to Truman on "Agriculture and Food Requirements" in Germany and Austria on February 28 and March 11, 1947 respectively, a third and final report followed on March 18, 1947 entitled "The Necessary Steps for Promotion of German Exports, so as to relieve American Taxpayers of the Burden of Relief and for Economic Recovery of Europe." I quote from this report:

> At the present time the taxpayers of the United States and Britain are contributing nearly $600,000,000 a year to prevent starvations of the Germans in the American and British zones alone. [...] policies which will restore productivity in Germany and exports with which to buy their food and relieve this drain upon us are of primary importance. // But our economic interest is far wider than this. We desperately need recovery in all of Europe. We need it not only for economic reasons but as the first necessity to peace. The United States, through loans, lend-lease, surplus supplies, and

relief, in the last two years, has spent, or pledged itself to spend, over fifteen billion dollars in support of civilians in foreign countries. Even we do not have the resources for, nor can our taxpayers bear, a continuation of burdens at such a rate. // There is only one path to recovery in Europe. That is production. The whole economy of Europe is interlinked with German economy through the exchange of raw materials and manufactured goods. The productivity of Europe cannot be restored without the restoration of Germany as a contributor to that productivity.[13]

Hoover heavily criticized the Morgenthau Plan and the elements of it that had still been contained in the Joint Chief of Staff (JCS)

FIGURE 4.1 Discussion of food and agricultural problems in Germany at General Clay's Berlin headquarters on February 7, 1947. From Left to Right: Dennis Fitzgerald, Secretary General of the International Emergency Food Council; General Lucius D. Clay; former US President Herbert Hoover on his mission as adviser of OMGUS on food problems; General William H. Draper Jr., economic adviser of Clay

FIGURE 4.2 Consultations of Secretary of Commerce W. Averell Harriman and Secretary of Agriculture Clinton P. Anderson with General Lucius D. Clay and his highest OMGUS officials in Berlin on July 3, 1947 on the economy of Western Europe. From left to right: Ambassador Robert Murphy, political adviser of Clay; Clinton P. Anderson, Secretary of Agriculture; General Lucius D. Clay, head of OMGUS in Berlin; W. Averell Harriman, Secretary of Commerce; General William H. Draper Jr., economic adviser of Clay; Jack Bennett, financial adviser of Clay

Directive 1067 "Regarding Military Government of Germany" of April 26, 1945.[14] This order spelled out the principles of American occupation policy in Germany. In its economic terms it heavily restricted OMGUS' policy leeway for raising the imploded German economy back to a self-sustaining level and thereby for relieving the American taxpayer's purse from outlays to prevent starvation among the German population. At the Potsdam Conference from July 17, to August 2, 1945 the three Allied powers USA, UK, and USSR agreed on curtailing Germany's industrial capacity, not only by dismantling existing plant and equipment for reparation purposes, but also by prescribing a "level of industry" for only peaceful uses by

Germany.[15] Its quantitative dimension was up for inter-allied negotiations. Their outcome was the first level of industry plan of March 28, 1946. It stated that German heavy industry was to be lowered to 50 percent of its 1938 level by the destruction of 1,500 listed manufacturing plants.[16] German industry altogether should not produce more than 65–67 percent of its level in 1936.[17] Although Clay knew that this was totally inadequate for Germany's economic revival, he had agreed expecting that there would soon be an upward revision.

Accompanied by his political adviser, Robert Murphy, Clay had spent the first days of November 1945 in Washington, DC to discuss a revision of JCS 1067. He presented his suggestions also in a meeting in the State Department on November 3 and had the impression that they had been received favorably. He came back from Washington confident that JCS 1067 would be revised in a few weeks. In fact, a rift had developed between Clay's opinion and experience in the Control Council that France was the culprit for noncooperation, while the State Department under the influence of George F. Kennan was already focused on the Soviet Union. Clay's memoirs are mute on this cleavage, which John H. Backer has dug out from NARA, namely Hilldring's résumé of the November 3 meeting. Nevertheless, on December 12, 1945 the US Secretary of State summarized his interpretation of the economic policy stipulations of JCS 1067 and of the Potsdam Agreement. He sent his policy position paper to the War Department, to OMGUS, and to the governments of the other occupying powers. In fact, it did point the way to some alleviations of JCS 1067's harsh stipulations.[18] But JCS 1067 was not revised until July 1947, after Hoover had reported on his mission in Germany earlier in the year. In his view the Directive was a big obstacle to German and European recovery.

Hoover's report, in essence a recast of John M. Keynes' plans for European reconstruction after World War I,[19] did actually lead to political results. On August 29, 1947 the Anglo-Saxon powers revised the level of industry plan for their Bizone, explicitly stating the same arguments that Hoover had used against the first level of industry plan. They allowed German industry on average 100 percent capacity of 1936.[20]

Clay had traveled to Washington, DC toward the end of 1945 to personally confront the departments in charge with the need of a quick revision of JCS 1067 in the direction of loosening restrictions for Germany's economy. His impression from the meetings was that it would soon be forthcoming. After nothing had budged, Clay sent a long cable to the War Department on May 26, 1946.[21] This cable is nothing less than a blueprint of further economic and political developments in Germany. Clay's points of departure: Contrary to the Potsdam Agreement and after one year of occupation the ACC had failed to establish quadripartite administrative agencies for treating Germany as an economic unit. Rather military government policies had made things worse by transforming occupation zones into:

> air-tied territories with almost no free exchange of commodities, persons, and ideas. Germany now consists of four small economic units which can deal with each other only through treaties, in spite of the fact that no one unit can be regarded as self-supporting, although British and Russian zones could become so. ... As it now stands, economic integration is becoming less each day, with Soviet and French Zones requiring approval for practically each item leaving their zones, and with the British and our zones in self defense [sic] moving in the same direction.[22]

At this point a reminder of Winston Churchill's famous Iron-Curtain speech in Fulton, Missouri, with US President Harry S. Truman present, on March 5, 1946 is useful. Although in a more political than economic sense, Churchill was the first prominent politician of the Allies to state publicly that the war alliance of the three great powers and thereby the Potsdam Agreement had fallen apart.[23]

In his long cable of May 26, 1946 Clay comes to a similar conclusion in economic policy matters. He makes the first proposal for uniting the British and American zones into the Bizone in order to create central administrations for economic policy at least on this level. "Recognizing fully the political implications of such a merger it is our belief here that even these implications would not be as serious as the continuation of the present air-tight zones. [...] we would much prefer to obtain Allied unity in the treatment of Germany as a whole."[24] While Clay did not exclude that the Soviets – in line with the stipulations of the Potsdam Agreement – might join the US–British merger project, he expressed no hope of French cooperation on this issue.[25]

At that time General Joseph T. McNarney, was serving as US commander in chief, European Command (CINCEUR) and military governor in Germany and Austria with headquarters in the former IG Farben building in Frankfurt am Main. He had succeeded General Dwight D. Eisenhower in November 1945. But his title as military governor was largely pro forma. His deputy military governors, namely General Lucius Clay headquartered in Berlin, and General Mark Clark headquartered in Vienna were in charge and in control of nonmilitary aspects of occupation policies and received their instructions directly from the War Department in Washington, DC.[26]

Probably to underline the importance that the Americans attached to the issue, it was McNarney, not Clay as usual, who on July 20, 1946, about two months after Clay's long cable, officially proposed to the ACC in Berlin the merger of all four occupation zones for matters of economic policy in accordance with the Potsdam Agreement. The British military governor Air Chief Marshal Sir William Sholto Douglas, who had succeeded Field Marshal Bernard Montgomery on May 1, 1946,[27] accepted the American proposal on July 30. The French military commander, as which he served in the French zone, Army General Marie-Pierre Koenig, rejected it on August 10, 1946. The Soviets remained aloof for a while, but signaled rejection when they noticed that their participation would be conditioned on divestiture of the Sowjetische Aktiengesellschaften (SAG) [= Soviet stock companies] they had created by expropriating about

200 larger manufacturing companies in their zone. They would have had to return to the status quo ante.[28]

Evidently, the first-best course of action, namely a common quadripartite economic and financial policy executed through central administrations responsible to and supervised by the Allied Control Council (ACC), did not materialize. The Potsdam Agreement had named the following areas for common policies: "(a) mining and industrial production and its allocation; (b) agriculture, forestry and fishing; (c) wages, prices and rationing; (d) import and export programs for Germany as a whole; (e) currency and banking, central taxation and customs; (f) reparation and removal of industrial war potential; (g) transportation and communications."[29]

All efforts of General Lucius Clay and his British counterpart, Field Marshal Bernard Montgomery, during the second half of 1945 and first five months of 1946 to establish central quadripartite agencies to execute such common policies had been in vain. Therefore, the USA and its closest ally, the UK, started to prepare for a second-best solution, the creation of the Bizone, with joint political and administrative institutions as well as a common economic policy. It was proposed by General Clay on May 26, 1946 in his long telegram to Washington[30] and negotiated since the first meeting of the *Conference on Economic Unification of the British and American Zones* on November 14, 1946 in Washington, DC.[31] On December 3, 1946 US Secretary of State James F. Byrnes and British Foreign Secretary Ernest Bevin jointly announced that the Bizone would be launched on January 1, 1947. The very same day the public relations office of OMGUS distributed the full text of the agreement by specifically pointing out in its introduction that it was designed "to make the area self-sustaining in three years. By this program it is expected not only to decrease the costs of occupation for the area but also to make possible the gradual restoration of a healthy nonaggressive German economy which will contribute materially to the economic stability of Europe."[32]

Its purpose was to create central administrations for executing common economic policies for the British and American zones for two reasons:

On the one hand, it would do away with controls between the two zones for the movement of goods and people. Bureaucracy reduction would contribute to make at least that part of Germany's economy more efficient. And on the other hand, it would save on administrative costs.

Before the agreement went into full effect, General Robertson for the British side introduced a proposal for a currency reform on the bizonal level in a meeting of the Bipartite Board on December 29, 1946. Evidently the British finance staff had informed their American colleagues about this step in advance, but had not consulted them on details of the plan. In a lengthy memo of December 28, "Subject: Financial Reform on a Bipartite Basis to the Chief of Staff," Jack Bennett recommended that Clay should oppose General Robertson's proposal, which he did. The reasons were mainly that:

- there were signs that the Soviets would cooperate in the Finance Directorate of ACC on planning a quadripartite currency reform on the basis of the American CDG-Plan,
- the bipartite and quadripartite currency reforms would be mutually exclusive, and
- the old quadripartite common currency (Reichsmark) – as long as it would exist – was an embarrassment to the Soviet zone policy of economic isolation.[33]

The Anglo-Saxons made it clear to the French and the Soviets that they were welcome to join the Bizone. But until the French finally came around to form the Trizone de facto shortly before currency reform, it had not been in the French and even much less in the Soviet interest. John Lewis Gaddis, the leading expert on the history of the Cold War, has succinctly described what Stalin's policy in Germany wanted to achieve. Stalin believed "that the Marxist–Leninist government he planned to install in eastern Germany would become a 'magnet' for Germans in the western occupation zones, causing them to choose leaders who would eventually unify the entire country under Soviet control."[34] In 1946 Stalin had defined his political aim in Germany in his own words like this: "All of Germany must be ours, that is, Soviet, communist."[35] In order "to preserve as much of Germany as possible under western rule," the Anglo-Saxon powers and belatedly also the French prepared for countermeasures, namely preferring an East–West division to the risk of losing all of Germany to communist rule.[36]

In the run-up to creating the Bizone, Clay had informed Secretary of State Byrnes in July 1946 that the ongoing communist propaganda more and more fell on fertile soil in Germany.[37] An early public statement of US policy in Germany could "nullify the effectiveness of the Communist appeal."[38] Byrnes was alarmed and convinced. The result was his famous address on Germany's economic and political future – essentially drafted by Clay – on September 6, 1946 in Stuttgart. It signaled a fundamental change in US policies in Germany. No longer would the USA be searching only for quadripartite solutions in the ACC. Byrnes made Clay's proposal for creating a Bizone and developing it into a self-government democracy public as official US policy. The latter goal was also an outgrowth of America's heritage of manifest destiny. In this tradition President Woodrow Wilson had asked Congress for a Declaration of War against Germany on April 2, 1917: "The world must be made safe for democracy."[39] Byrnes' Stuttgart address after World War II was carved from the same wood. It made clear that the USA would rather accept an East–West division of Germany with enough US troops remaining to defend the West's freedom and democracy than to put up with Soviet intransigence in the ACC. This actually had a big impact on the political mood of the Germans. They labeled it "speech of hope."[40] Clay has aptly been characterized as being "by birth and inclination an old-fashioned Jeffersonian liberal,"[41]

Two other internationally important political statements in the USA during the first half of 1947 strengthened hope in a noncommunist political and a prosperous economic future at least for the West German population. One was made by US President Harry S. Truman in a joint session of Congress on March 12, 1947 announcing the famous Truman Doctrine. The other groundbreaking statement was made by then Secretary of State George Marshall in his keynote address to Harvard students on their commencement exercises on June 5, 1947, announcing a heavily funded reconstruction program for the European economy, later called the Marshall Plan. No less important in practice for West Germany's political and economic future was a new directive to General Clay (by now US supreme military commander and governor in Germany) on July 15, 1947 from Washington, DC.[42] It finally officially superseded the restrictions on Clay's political room for maneuver in Germany. It even instructed him to care for the growth of the German economy and its exports to make it self-sustaining and as an essential contribution to the reconstruction of the European economy. Pending the treatment of all zones of Germany as an economic unit, as agreed at Potsdam, it instructed him to strive for the highest possible degree of unified economic policies, including the creation and operation of German administrative agencies for economic and financial policy fields, across zonal boundaries. It further demanded from Clay to put pressure on the ACC to adopt a common financial and currency reform and to support the removal of existing trade barriers.

4.1.2   Two Specific Questions

First question: When did the US start to pursue policies in Germany that could be interpreted as violations of the letter or the spirit of the Potsdam Agreement, especially concerning the treatment of Germany as an economic unit, and what prompted such actions?

In 1946 OMGUS began to take risks that might eventually lead to a division of Germany. The first breach of the Potsdam Agreement on Clay's part happened in the first half of 1946. Clay, then still deputy military governor, became aware of a dilemma in his policy goals. Complying with the Potsdam Agreement and cutting

Germany's industrial capacity as laid out in the level of industry plan of the ACC on March 28, 1946 contradicted his goal of cutting the financial burden of the American taxpayer from emergency aid and relief in occupied Germany.[43] On May 3, 1946 Clay unilaterally stopped the dismantling of plant and equipment in the US zone, used as reparation deliveries to the Soviet zone, whereas British military government continued to deliver such reparations to keep the Soviets from taking over all of Berlin.[44]

In his long cable to the War Department of May 26, 1946 Clay gave the reason for his decision: "In the absence of agreements essential to economic unity, we have discontinued the dismantling of reparations plants [...], as further dismantling would result in disaster if we are unable to obtain economic unity."[45]

This violation of the Potsdam Agreement was in response to the one France had practiced all along. OMGUS had pressured since the fall of 1945 to establish quadripartite central Economic administrations. Economic unity was particularly vital to the US zone which was not self-sufficient. While the British and even the Soviets had reservations as to the timing, they were in principle open to proceed. At this point only the French were adamantly opposed. On March 5, 1946 the French cabinet voted unanimously that contrary to the Potsdam stipulation that Germany should be treated as an economic unit, France would "continue its firm position on the Ruhr, the Rhineland, and the Saar."[46] Further negotiations in March and April petered out. In April 1946 OMGUS got wind of secret French efforts to win support from Germans governing the *Länder* to support French efforts to dismember Germany permanently.[47] A well-researched article in *The Commercial and Financial Chronicle* of September 12, 1946 dissected the disunity in the ACC in detail and found that it was mostly France, not the Soviet Union, that blocked decisions aimed at treating Germany as a single economic unit. Even the Soviets criticized French obstructionism. The article reports the opinion that General Draper, the head of the economics division of OMGUS, had expressed in an interview with *The Commercial and Financial*

Chronicle a week earlier in the USA while on leave from Berlin, "that the biggest mistake bearing on German administration was that the French were no party to the Potsdam Agreement yet have full vote in the Control Council. Dozens of decisions ... have been stymied by the French abstaining from voting."[48] In 1974 Jean Edward Smith published the hitherto inaccessible papers Clay had produced in Germany 1945 to 1949. In his foreword Smith mentions the following example of how the Clay Papers would contribute to a more balanced view of relations among the four occupying powers than their interpretations framed by the East–West conflict in the incipient Cold War:

> ... historians and diplomats now wrestling with problems of the cold war will be interested in Clay's cables in 1945 and 1946 which detail early attempts to achieve effective quadripartite government; attempts which foundered not because of US-Soviet hostility in Germany (where Eisenhower, Clay, Zhukov and Sokolovsky got along famously), but because of French intransigence, British suspicion, and the orders which both the US and Soviet Military Governors received from their respective capitals. // ... Many will be surprised that the cutoff of reparation deliveries from the US zone in May 1946 was not aimed primarily at the Russians but at the French.[49]

The creation of the Bizone was negotiated and agreed on in the second half of 1946 and put into practice at the start of 1947. The Soviets and the French had been invited by the US initiators, General Clay and Secretary of State James F. Byrnes, to join the fusion of administrative control and economic policy for Germany beyond zonal boundaries.[50] But they refused the offer. The Soviets saw the formation of the Bizone as another violation of the Potsdam Agreement. The last act on the course to partition of Germany, of course, was West German currency reform of June 20, 1948. Since 1946 there had been many intermediate steps, all the while the Anglo-Saxon powers kept the door open for quadripartite action. As late as December 1947, when the printing and transport of Deutschmark to Germany was in full swing, Secretary of State George Marshall had communicated to his British counterpart Ernest Bevin that he would prefer a quadripartite currency reform. It "would have the intrinsic merit of maintaining a single currency for Germany, as a whole, while preserving the rudiments of a quadripartite structure."[51] The latest instruction from the War Department to General Clay in Berlin in favor of quadrizonal currency reform dates from February 9, 1948: "Policy objective is to reach quadripartite agreement provided attainable promptly."[52]

While the Potsdam Agreement of August 2, 1945 had assigned the administration of Germany to the ACC in Berlin, it had also created the Council of Foreign Ministers. The Agreement contained a passage that the three great powers would send identical invitations to the governments of China and France to adopt the text of the Potsdam Agreement and to join in forming the council,[53] which both countries accepted. But China retreated from the council after its first meeting in London from September 11 to October 2, 1945. The Soviets disagreed with China's participation in shaping the future of Europe.

The council's permanent seat with offices and staff was established in London. The foreign ministers were mandated to meet quarterly. Then in the end the four powers were allowed to rotate their venues between their capitals.[54] The council was authorized to prepare peace treaties with the former European enemy states Italy, Romania, Bulgaria, Hungary and Finland, and to propose settlements of territorial questions open upon the end of the war in Europe for submission to the United Nations.

The council was also charged with the preparation of a peace settlement for what was left of Germany after its territorial losses. The peace treaty with Germany was to be accepted "when a government adequate for the purpose is established."[55] The four great powers and China are identical with the five veto-power nations of the UN Security Council today.

In contrast to a number of prior more successful meetings, the first foreign ministers' conference focusing on peace treaties with

Germany and Austria failed. It took place in Moscow from March 10 to April 24, 1947. The foreign ministers only decided to formally dissolve the state of Prussia, but could not agree on the main topic: peace treaties with Germany and Austria. In his closing speech Molotov sharply rebuffed Marshall's accusation that Russia had caused the failure of the conference. For the Americans this outcome induced them to plan and prepare for the eventuality of a separate bizonal currency reform.[56] The printing of Deutschmark banknotes in the USA had already far advanced when the foreign ministers again failed to agree on peace treaties with Germany and Austria at their meeting in London from November 25 to December 16, 1947.[57]

Nevertheless, after OMGUS and its Soviet counterpart had each introduced revised proposals in the second half of January, discussions on a quadripartite currency reform were resumed in the ACC on February 1, 1948. On February 11 the Council agreed to General Clay's proposal to set a time limit of sixty days for an agreement on currency reform.[58] By that time the Soviet military governor in Germany, General Vasily Sokolovsky, was certainly informed by Soviet intelligence of December 1947 that new German currency printed in the USA had been shipped to Bremerhaven. The East Berlin communist newspaper *Neues Deutschland* disclosed the news under the heading "Das neue Westgeld ist da" [= The new West German banknotes have arrived] on January 20, 1948. The article described preparations of a separate currency reform in the Bizone and even disclosed the following details: "To this we can additionally communicate that on 8 December [1947] a US steamship was unloaded at Bremerhaven, which had on board boxes of the new 'bizonal' money ... On 18 December [1947] large quantities of money were again unloaded from the US cargo ship *Madsket* and were transported by rail to Frankfurt/Main."[59] In a telegram of February 21, 1948 the final shipment of the Deutschmark notes as part of Operation "Birddog" was reported to have been unloaded from US steamship Noonday. "Therefore no necessity for you to arrange for outside storage space."[60]

In order to remove the pretext of Anglo-Saxon powers for currency reform only in the Bizone, Sokolovsky was willing to give up entrenched positions on which the Soviets had clashed with the USA, such as the location of printing new currency in Germany. The Soviets had insisted on printing by Giesecke & Devrient,[61] specialists in banknotes and securities, in Leipzig in their zone in addition to the *Reichsdruckerei* in Berlin in the American sector. Clay had not only offered quadripartite supervision for the Berlin plant, but even the transformation of the *Reichsdruckerei* into an enclave exterritorial to the US sector of Berlin and under direct quadripartite control.[62] In return the Soviets had offered quadripartite supervision of printing new currency also in Leipzig. But faced with losing all chances to extract reparations also from the Western zones instead of only from their own zone and to co-orchestrate the political future of Germany as a whole, Sokolovsky finally dropped the Soviet demand for printing currency also in Leipzig. He had previously also insisted that currency reform should be accompanied by creating a central finance agency and a German central bank. He now even signaled flexibility on these issues. However, the Soviets remained adamant on the burden-sharing provision of the Colm-Dodge-Goldsmith Plan that Clay also endorsed. But after some internal controversy about this provision, US Secretary of State George Marshall decided that burden sharing should be cut off from currency-reform legislation. Clay was embarrassed by the extent of the Soviet resolve to give ground and compromise. While taking notice of it, he set a sixty-day time limit to reach a detailed accord on currency reform in the Finance Directorate of the ACC.[63]

Robert Murphy, Clay's political adviser in Berlin (OMGUS) at the time, writes in his memoirs that the decision to pull through a bizonal instead of a quadripartite currency reform was taken after the Soviets in protest had walked out of the ACC on March 20, 1948.[64] This is the standard story of the sequence of events in almost all historical accounts. But with his walkout Marshal Sokolovsky had not been protesting against disagreements on currency-reform matters. He protested against the fact that the Western powers would not share with ACC and thus with the Soviets the results of their prior conference at London. There the three Western powers and Benelux as West Germany's neighbors had been discussing the creation of a democratic and federal West German state. The first session lasted from February 23 to March 6, the second from April 20 to June 2, 1948. The Soviets left the Control Council after their two-week efforts to be briefed on results of the first session came to nothing.[65]

Actually, it was before the USSR left the Control Council that on the part of the USA and Britain the door for a quadripartite currency reform was shut. The communist seizure of power in Prague at the end of February 1948 destroyed what was left of hopes among the Western Allies to strike a deal with the Soviets on currency reform as a step to finally treating all four occupation zones of Germany as an economic unit, as had been stipulated in the Potsdam Agreement. On March 10, 1948, Frank G. Wisner, deputy to the Assistant Secretary of State for Occupied Areas, had drafted a policy paper and sent it to Under Secretary of State Robert A. Lovett for approval of the suggested fundamental policy change regarding currency reform in Germany. Wisner argued:

> Although important points of difference continue to exist in the current quadripartite discussions, further concessions may be made by the Soviets. In brief, we may be approaching agreement in the ACC on quadripartite currency reform for all of Germany. The question arises whether this is desirable from the US standpoint, since quadripartite currency reform might enable the Soviets to frustrate further the economic recovery of western Germany by the use of obstructive and delaying tactics ... a quadripartite currency, as compared with a bizonal or trizonal currency, would deprive us of a very important monetary instrument for achieving the effective economic administration of the western zones and might impede the realization of some of the arrangements which we are now

working out on a tripartite basis. .... The progress in the negotiations in Berlin necessitates an immediate review of our position to determine whether it is still in our interest to have a quadripartite currency reform. .... currency reform on a bizonal (or tripartite) basis, instead of on a quadripartite basis, would represent a very definite move toward recognition of the East–West partition of Germany but, at the same time, an important move toward much needed economic stability in western Germany. .... it is recommended that General Clay be instructed that the policy of this government is no longer to reach quadripartite agreement on currency and financial reform in Germany.[66]

Lovett approved the policy paper the next day in concurrence with the Department of the Army which in turn instructed General Clay as suggested. Therefore, March 11, 1948 is the exact date of the final US decision on a separate currency reform in the western zones of occupation. Preparations for the founding of a West German state in 1949 followed immediately. Therefore, March 11, 1948 is also the date on which the United States decided on the political partition of Germany. British military governor, General Brian Robertson, reported to Whitehall on March 12, 1948 that Clay "is determined that the discussions [on a quadripartite currency reform] shall fail, and is instructing his men that they must look for a good opportunity and a good cause."[67]

In fact, discussions on the preparation of a quadripartite currency reform continued. There are minutes of a meeting "Allied Control Authority. Finance Directorate. Currency Printing Committee" of March 18, 1948, "Subject: Preparation of Plates and Dandy-Rolls for New Money." It is stated therein that the Finance Directorate has disapproved that the "Staatsdruckerei has begun the preparation of printing plates without quadripartite control ... it constitutes a violation of the quadripartite agreement."[68] What a hypocrisy on the part of the Anglo-Saxon powers, in view of the fact that the printing of German Mark banknotes had top secretly been undertaken in the USA since mid-October 1947, that the Deutschmarks had been shipped to Germany since December 1947. Most of it had already been stored in the cellars of the old Reichsbank building in Frankfurt am Main by March 18, 1948, the date of the above-mentioned meeting! Furthermore, the meeting had been preceded by the final decision on executing a separate West German currency reform and thus on the partition of Germany on March 11, 1948. Without an issuing authority named on the banknotes, the new currency could also have been used to implement a quadripartite currency reform in case of a four-power agreement before that date.

In his seminal study on the process of the division of Germany John H. Backer came to the following conclusion:

> instead of pinpointing any particular date or event as decisive, it is suggested that the preferred democratic strategy of incremental decision making was at work, a process which Braybrooke and Lindblom have described as decision making through small, or incremental, moves on particular problems rather than through a comprehensive long-range program. In their much discussed study[69] four typical categories of political decisions were outlined: decisions that effect large change and are guided by adequate information and understanding, decisions that effect large change but are not similarly guided, decisions that effect only small change and are guided by adequate information, and finally decisions that effect small change but are not similarly guided and therefore subject to constant reconsideration and redirection. It is the last category, provocatively labeled "disjointed instrumentalism," which seems to apply to the American occupational policies for Germany. They not only consisted – to use Braybrooke's and Lindblom's definitions – of an "indefinite series of policy moves" but actually represented "an exploratory process in which the goals of policy-making continued to change as new experience with policy threw new light on what is possible and desirable."[70]

Backer deals extensively with the many American occupation-policy moves and with missed opportunities for preserving not only economic unity in Germany, but also for winning quadripartite consent for a new German government and for the conclusion of a peace treaty with it. As to the opportunities, he spans the period from President Roosevelt's rejection of the State Department's proposal of March 10, 1945 "to strengthen the Control Council's authority over the zone commanders in order to avoid the feared partition of Germany along zonal boundaries" to the failure of the Council of Foreign Ministers conference in Moscow. According to Backer, it could have been avoided, if US diplomats had negotiated in Moscow with patience and perseverance, neither of which "is an American characteristic."[71] And as to the moves toward the division of Germany, Backer attributes a lot of influence to George F. Kennan's cable of February 22, 1946 from Moscow recommending containment policy against the threat of communism infiltrating all of Germany and maybe all of continental Europe.

But Backer is surprisingly mute on currency-reform conflicts among the four great powers. Such clashes, however, belonged to the bread-and-butter issues occupation politics had to deal with since 1945. They paved the way and led to the final decision on the part of the USA and its UK ally of dividing Germany, even nine days before Sokolovsky walked out of the ACC on March 20, 1948.

I describe one such currency conflict which took place in January 1947, about four months before the failure of the Moscow foreign ministers' conference. As will be seen, the decision that was finally reached not only antagonized the Soviets, but had also been controversial between OMGUS and War, State and Treasury Departments.

The printing of a new currency for Germany was brought to the attention of the Bureau of Engraving and Printing (BEP). "As far back as the first [month] of this year [1947] the matter was first brought to the attention of this bureau by representatives of the Military Government in Germany."[72] In January 1947 the American military government had struggled with its Soviet counterpart, where in view of quadripartite currency reform the new German currency should be printed under four-power Allied supervision, also in Leipzig in the Soviet zone or exclusively in Berlin in the traditional printing establishment for printing German currency *Reichsdruckerei* in the American sector. General Clay was inclined to agree to the currency printing also in Leipzig. State and War Departments had initially drafted a cable to Clay "approving his acceptance of the Soviet proposal that currency printing be done in Leipzig if he deemed this action necessary to break the impasse." But the Treasury Department – probably upon the advice of its BEP which in 1944 had forcefully, but in vain opposed the equipment of the Soviets with a second set of printing plates for Allied Military Mark – did not concur. It believed that "currency printing should be done under adequate quadripartite supervision which General Clay indicated could not be had in Leipzig."[73]

In order to reach a common position of the departments, a high-level meeting was called for the afternoon of January 22, 1947 in the office of the Under Secretary of State Dean Acheson. In addition to Acheson, the Under Secretary of State for Economic Affairs William L. Clayton, Assistant Secretary of State for Occupied Areas General John H. Hilldring, Assistant Secretary of War Howard C. Petersen, John C. deWilde (State Department)[74] and Andrew N. Overby (Treasury Department),[75] who wrote the minutes, were present. After deWilde had reviewed the background of the case, Clayton indicated that he shared the fears of the Treasury. Over lunch with Alvin W. Hall, director of the BEP,[76] who had shown him afterward the safeguards employed in printing currency in the bureau, Hilldring obviously had changed his mind and was now opposed to the printing in Leipzig. He also referred to the bad experience that the USA had had on finally yielding to the Soviet demand for a duplicate of the plate sets for printing Allied Military Mark currency.[77] The departments would have to expect "a searching inquiry from Congress on this subject. Mr. Peterson also apparently did not share the viewpoint of his War Department subordinates and indicated his agreement with the Treasury position."[78] General Clay was instructed accordingly. Currency printing should not take place in Leipzig, but only in Berlin with adequate safeguards and quadripartite supervision including representatives of the Soviets.[79]

This is one of the many examples of *incremental moves* on the part of the USA toward a separate currency reform in the western zones and thereby to the division of Germany. But had the Soviets accepted the American condition at this point, which after all was not unreasonable after America's bad experience with transferring duplicate plates for printing Allied Military Mark in Leipzig, they could have thwarted containment policy à la Kennan and might have kept a foothold on the productive power of the whole German economy that would be released by currency reform and thus on the West German resources for reparation payments. And the USSR would have preserved its influence on the terms of a peace treaty with a new German government formed thereafter and of military security remaining for decades under the grip of the Four Great Powers. But this trajectory is counterfactual history that serves the purpose of describing the dimension of a missed opportunity on the part of the Soviets.

Second question: How did the political process between OMGUS, War, State, and Treasury Departments develop as to the printing of Deutschmark in the USA, when exactly was the order for printing sent to the Bureau of Engraving and Printing and which conditions were attached to it?

It concerns the run-up to and the exact timing of the decision to print Deutschmark banknotes in the USA. Scholars have given different dates for the printing and shipping of the new currency to Germany. Wolfram Hoppenstedt (1997) writes that the new banknotes, printed top secretly by the American Bank Note Company, arrived in Germany from February 1948.[80] Eckhard Wandel (1980) found archival evidence that the Americans in May 1947, that is, after the failure of the Moscow conference of foreign ministers, for the first time explored the possibility of printing the new German currency in the USA, but that the Treasury, referring to time constraints, pleaded for printing either in Great Britain or in the *Reichsdruckerei* in Berlin. Wandel (1980) further contends – without providing a source – that the American Administration decided September 25, 1947 on the printing of Deutschmark in the USA and that production by the American Bank Note Company in New York and the Bureau of Engraving and Printing started in October 1947. Likewise, without giving a source, he claims that these banknotes – under strictest secrecy – were packed in 23,000 crates in New York and shipped from there to "Barcelona" for camouflage purposes, but in fact to Bremerhaven. They arrived – he continues – in the course of February to April 1948 and were transported from there into the cellars of the old Reichsbank building in Frankfurt am Main.[81]

FIGURE 4.3 Like this, D-Mark banknotes, printed in USA at the expense of the US government, were unloaded in Bremerhaven and transported by rail to Frankfurt am Main during the last quarter of 1947

I have gathered more precise information on printing and shipping the banknotes than Wandel (1980) and Hoppenstedt (1997). I was fortunate in winning the very fertile cooperation of the chief historian and archivist of the Bureau of Engraving and Printing (BEP), Hallie Brooker. Neither Wandel (1980) nor Hoppenstedt (1997) have consulted the BEP archive, which is rich in precise information on decisions on the banknote printing and shipping issue. Beyond that, files of the State Department proved to be useful to reconstruct the sequence of events and decisions.

Where to print the new currency remained a controversial matter in the ACC throughout 1947. After decision-makers in Washington, DC on January 22, 1947 had rejected the Soviet demand for also printing in Leipzig, as described above, the British and French moved away from the US position which they had originally shared. By June 1947 they were willing to accept the Soviet position that at least part of the new Mark currency should be printed in Leipzig.[82]

This prompted C. C. Hilliard, authorized by his boss in the State Department, General Hilldring, to call a State Department meeting in General Hilldring's office for June 13, 1947. "Subject: Expediting of Interdepartmental and US/UK Coordination re Monetary and Related Policy – Germany. ... The problem is to consider ways and means of expediting State-Treasury (Bureau of Engraving and Printing) War Department coordination and US/UK coordination, respectively, on the formulation and implementation of the subject policy." To underline the urgency of the matter, Hilliard listed quite a number of cables from CINCEUR (i.e., General Clay) a note from the British embassy to the Department of State of March 19 and two papers of the State-War-Navy Coordinating Committee (SWNCC) all of which were left for months or weeks unanswered or – in the case of the SWNCC papers – stuck in the coordination process between State, Treasury and War Departments. One of the cables Hilliard mentions is CC 9110 of May 11, 1947 from CINCEUR, in which General Clay requests "immediate advice of our government's views" [= Hilliard's quote from the cable] as regards printing a new German currency. Hilliard points out that this cable was still unanswered after thirty-two days.[83]

This cable from Clay two and a half weeks after the failure of the Moscow conference of the Council of Foreign Ministers documents that the American military government in Germany was the first American institution to recognize the implications for currency reform in Germany. It started to confront Washington with the eventuality of a failure of currency reform on the quadripartite level and to pressure for printing new mark currency for a bizonal currency reform outside of Germany. Decision-makers in Washington, DC obviously didn't consider the matter as urgent as Clay in Berlin. But Hilliard and General Hilldring in the State Department were the first in Washington, DC to recognize the urgency of the matter and did something about it: Hilliard first called the State Department meeting of June 13 and in his memo to General Hilldring he concluded: "It is my understanding that subsequent to the above-mentioned State Department meeting, I am to arrange for a State-Treasury-War meeting in your office on the above subject."[84]

This meeting took place on June 17, 1947 in General Hilldring's office under the chairmanship of Under Secretary of State Robert Lovett. Besides Lovett, Assistant Secretary of War Howard C. Petersen and Andrew N. Overby of the Treasury Department were present.

> It was decided to instruct General Clay to try to obtain British and French agreement to return to their original position, which is also the US position, to print the entire issue [of Deutschmark banknotes] in Berlin. If such British and French agreement were attained General Clay was to offer to place the Berlin Printing Office under full quadripartite control with entire printing to take place there. If such agreement with the British and French were not attainable then General Clay was to propose to the British and French that printing be initiated on a tripartite basis in the Berlin printing office, the Soviets to be informed of this intention and perhaps invited to send an observer. General Clay was also

informed that the State, War and Treasury Departments agree on the desirability of the printing also of a new German mark currency for bi-zonal use, in order to have such currency available in case of need.[85]

On July 18, 1947 the unsettled question of where to print a new German mark currency was further discussed in a teleconference between Clay in Berlin and Hilldring and Petersen in Washington, DC. As a result, the State Department sent an aide-mémoire to the British and French embassies in Washington asking for a return of the British and French to the original US/British/French position that the new currency "for quadripartite use" should be printed only in Berlin. By September 22, 1947 the State Department had received no responses.[86]

After the eighty-sixth meeting of the Control Council on August 11, 1947, in which the printing question was discussed, OMGUS reported its outcome in a telegram to the Secretary of State on the following day. It said that the Soviet member had reiterated the Soviet position that in view of the urgency of the matter, the Control Council should not deny itself of the large technical facilities in Leipzig in addition to the Berlin printing plant. USSR "would not object to currency printing under quadripartite control in any third or fourth place where there are facilities. Confining printing to Berlin would only increase difficulties." Clay explained that his proposal for printing the banknotes only in Berlin was based on the view that failing real quadripartite government of Germany – certainly meant as a dig at the Soviets for blocking progress in this direction at the Moscow conference of foreign ministers four months earlier – Berlin is the quadripartite center. Currency printing could best be carried out there under the necessary control. To show good faith Clay suggested placing the printing plant, the *Reichsdruckerei*, within an Allied enclave. "British member pointed out he and French could accept either Soviet or United States position." At Clay's suggestion the Control Council decided to keep the printing question on the agenda "in suspense pending reports to their governments by respective dele-gations and receipt of possible new instructions."[87]

In September 1947 Stalin nurtured Anglo-Saxon apprehensions of his ambition for a communist takeover of Western Europe by reactivating the *Comintern* under a different name. On May 15, 1943 Stalin had dissolved *Comintern*, founded in 1919, to appease its Western Allies. The *Comintern* had resolved at its Second Congress in 1920 to "struggle by all available means, including armed force, for the overthrow of the international bourgeoisie and the creation of an international Soviet republic as a transition stage to the complete abolition of the state."[88] In September 1947, following the June 1947 Paris Conference on Marshall Plan Aid, Stalin gathered a grouping of key European communist parties and set up the *Cominform*, or *Communist Information Bureau*, often seen as a sub-stitute for the Comintern. It was a network made up of the commun-ist parties of Bulgaria, Czechoslovakia, France, Hungary, Italy, Poland, Romania, the Soviet Union, and Yugoslavia.[89] This posed a real threat to the Western powers of communist takeovers in Greece, Italy, and France, where communist parties were relatively strong. And West Germany, starving in 1947, but with still low communist inclin-ations, might also fall prey to the sirens of communism for the sake of preserving a unified Germany.

The impasse in the Control Council of August 11, 1947 and the reactivation of the *Comintern* by founding the *Cominform* in September 1947 obviously launched intense activity within OMGUS and the usual Departments in Washington, DC to check out possibilities and to plan for the printing of a new German currency in the USA in order to be prepared, especially for a separate Western or for a quadripartite currency reform, in case it should be realizable after all. An office memorandum dated September 22, 1947 from Colonel Charles C. Hilliard (State Department) to his boss Charles E. Saltzman, Assistant Secretary of State, recounted the history of the mark printing issue in order to bring the latter up to date for an interdepartmental meeting in the afternoon of that same day. It reports that apparently General Draper, Under Secretary of the Army, had been "in conference" with Assistant Secretary of the Treasury Edward H. Foley and with Alvin W. Hall, director of BEP, "in recent weeks" discussing the possibilities for printing a new German mark currency, either for quadripartite or bizonal use. It seems General Draper had asked the Treasury Department to arrange for designs and dyes by BEP, the Bureau of the Mint, and the American Bank Note Company in order to be prepared.

> I am informed that General Draper had a meeting with Mr. Schomp, President of the American Bank Note Company in General Draper's office. Under instructions from General Draper, Mr. Tenenbaum, who was on temporary duty at the War Department from OMGUS, has been active in these negotiations. I am told that Mr. Tenenbaum and General Draper informed the Treasury Department at first that it was impossible to print a new German mark currency in Germany and that the US was the only practicable place for such printing. However, after the above mentioned meeting with the American Bank Note Company, it appears that the War Department changed its mind, decided to have the printing done in England, and asked the Treasury Department to cable to Secretary Snyder, in London, requesting Mr. Snyder to talk with Mr. Dalton, Chancellor of the British Exchequer, relative to printing in Great Britain. // Up to this point the Treasury Department had proceeded without advice to the State Department. I am informed that the Treasury Department had been assured that the State Department would go along on any arrangements made by War. However, when requested to cable Secretary Snyder the Treasury Department refused to proceed further without State Department agreement. Assistant Secretary Foley [War] phoned to Under Secretary Lovett [State], who advised Mr. Foley not to cable to Secretary Snyder. I am told that Mr. Lovett also advised Mr. Foley that Mr. Lovett and you [C. E. Saltzman, Assistant Secretary of State] are familiar with arrangements which are being made regarding the above subject.[90]

We know that by September 18, 1947 the bypassing of the State Department by War and Treasury Departments had ended. On that day Mr. Southard of the Treasury Department asked the State Department for approval of the following points: 1.) Preparation of designs and dyes by BEP, the Bureau of the Mint, and the American Bank Note Company. 2.) The printing of stamps for use by OMGUS in case of a sudden unilateral currency conversion in the Soviet zone. The stamps would be "affixed," glued, to all Reichsmark currency notes circulating in the US zone to protect it against the dumping of Reichsmark notes that had previously circulated in the Soviet zone.[91]

A "memorandum for the files" of October 9, 1947 by a staff member of BEP starts out with information that in September 1947 numerous conferences took place in Treasury, War, and State Departments concerning the banknote printing. The author of the memorandum then reports on the meeting of October 9, 1947 in the State Department. In attendance were: for State, Colonel Hilliard and Mr. deWilde; for Army,[92] Lieutenant Colonel Pickert; for Treasury, Mr. Schmidt, Mr. Wood and A. W. Hall; for OMGUS, Jack Bennett and Edward A. Tenenbaum.

> Mr. Bennett informed the meeting, much to the surprise of all, that the Military Government in Germany had received a cable a month or so ago to the effect that this government was actually printing the new currency. He stated that the cable came from the Army, but did not disclose who dispatched it, nor did he give any details of its contents. He was surprised to find that printing had not been undertaken, and further that work that had been accomplished was up to the designing stage only. Mr. Bennett stated that the cable referred to above was received in Germany before Mr. Tenenbaum came to America last month. I asked Mr. Tenenbaum why he did not mention that fact to us in the several conferences we had with him when he was here. He said that he was instructed to discuss certain matters with certain people, and that he had no instructions

on that matter. As the matter points up now, it develops that the American Military Government is faced with a very serious situation in that it is anticipated that the Russians may dump a new currency into the four zones without any announcement, thereby creating a collapse in the currency situation in the American and British zones. To combat any attack on the part of the Russians through a currency conversion, Mr. Bennett proposed the printing of denominational adhesive stamps the size of the American postage stamps, to be put into production immediately, and to be delivered to Germany where they could be held in readiness for application to currency in the British and American zones, as a precaution against the flooding of mark currency from the Russian zone. Mr. Bennett thought the stamp proposition could be kept in operation until the new currency was ready. It was pointed out to Mr. Bennett that under the program proposed by the Treasury it would require at least six months to produce the quantity of currency required for the conversion, and that it was very doubtful that the stamps could be kept in circulation that long without [being] counterfeited on a large scale, thereby destroying the whole arrangement.[93]

The memo further reveals that Jack Bennett was informed for the first time that the currencies required by OMGUS were broken down into three categories: One-half and One-Mark denomination would be struck off by the Bureau of the Mint, the Two- and Five-Mark notes would be printed by the Bureau of Engraving and Printing using the offset process, and all other denominations above five marks by the American Bank Note Company using the engraved process. With the designing completed, the three institutions would now be waiting for approval and further instructions. One reason why printing had not yet started was that the project from the beginning in January 1947, after Bizone had come into existence, had been classified "top secret" and that the State and Army Departments had desired that as few people as possible should be brought into the picture until the foreign ministers' conference in London in November/December 1947 would be over. Another consequence of "top secret" was:

> There had been much misunderstanding about the entire project from beginning to end, and the meeting this morning disclosed that the departments were operating at cross-purposes. As an example, the representative of the Military Government [Tenenbaum!] came to America about the middle of September and held a series of conferences on this project with explicit instructions that no one in the State Department be informed by the Treasury. It developed later that the State Department would have to be brought into the picture, and when it was, representatives of that department were very much disturbed.[94]

In the run-up to the final decision on printing the Deutschmark in the USA we know of two more "top secret" meetings in which Tenenbaum participated: on October 9, 1947 in the State Department at technical level, with Jack Bennett also present, and on October 10, 1947 in the office of William H. Draper, Under Secretary of the Army.[95] In this latter meeting OMGUS was represented by its highest echelons: besides Tenenbaum and his boss, Clay's financial adviser Bennett, also General Clay himself and his Political Adviser in Berlin Robert D. Murphy. Officials from State, Treasury, and Army Departments also participated in both meetings. The agenda of both meetings was identical:

a. Present status of US measures regarding the preparation of supplies of Deutsche Mark banknotes for eventual use in Bizone or Trizone, if quadripartite agreement on currency conversion cannot be reached in due course.
b. Coordination with the British as to these measures.
c. The preparation by the Treasury Department of a supply of special stamps for OMGUS for emergency use in Western zones in case of a currency reform in the Soviet zone prior to the availability of the Deutsche Mark banknotes to OMGUS.
d. The question of notification to the other occupying powers, and of information to the Congress and the American press about the above-mentioned US measures.

The October 9 meeting had revealed divergences of views between the representatives of the three departments that were present regarding points b, c, and d and even within the State Department between A-H [Office of the Assistant Secretary of State John H. Hilldring] and A-S [Office of the Assistant Secretary of State Charles E. Saltzman], Charles C. Hilliard reported to the participants of the October 10 meeting. Himself serving in A-S, he went on to inform them that there had been an urgent interest since January 1947 [the Bizone had come into existence at the beginning of the year] to proceed at the earliest possible moment with the printing of a new German mark currency for eventual use in a currency reform in the Bizone or perhaps a Trizone in case quadripartite reform would prove impossible to attain. For this, a joint printing project of the USA and the UK would have been preferred.

Charles C. Hilliard explained the six-week delay of the printing process, for which OMGUS seems to have blamed the State Department. He gave purely political reasons. A quadripartite currency reform in conformity with the Potsdam Agreement was under negotiation in the ACC in early 1947 and especially at the Moscow conference of the Council of Foreign Ministers in April 1947. This was not to be counteracted by preparations for a separate West German currency reform. If information about the banknote printing had leaked out to the Soviets, they could have accused the Anglo-Saxon Powers of actively pursuing the "dismemberment"[96] of Germany, argued Hilliard. The Soviets used this term, where the Western Allies spoke of "partition."

While the German population East and West was strongly in favor of preserving German unity, it would equip the Soviet side with a very powerful propaganda argument to discredit the Western Allies among the German population in general and thereby to strengthen the Communist Party in West Germany, too. The collective apprehension of the US government was succinctly described by Under Secretary of State Robert A. Lovett in a conversation with the French ambassador in Washington, DC as follows:

"The German burden must be taken off our backs ... [If Germany] did not become self-supporting it would become a cesspool into which all the evil of Europe could flow and which the Russians could easily take over."[97]

Assistant Secretary of the Treasury Foley brought the meeting up to date with the news that the American Bank Note Company had designs for banknotes ready for submission and the US Mint likewise designs and specifications for 1-mark and 50-pfennig pieces. And BEP Director Alvin W. Hall informed the meeting about supplies of paper, the time required for note printing by the engraved as well as by the photo-offset processes, and about security aspects of printing the Deutschmarks and the special stamps referred to under "c," including the problem of counterfeiting. In the following, we focus on what Clay demanded and got agreement on from this meeting.

As to point "d," Clay expressed his desire to keep the whole Deutschmark project classified as "top secret" and to deny information on it to anybody, including US Congress and especially the Soviets and the French. The meeting agreed to withhold information from the press, the public, and from the other occupying powers. But no agreement was reached on also not responding to inquiries from the Congress. Concerning point "c," the printing of special stamps for emergency use in case of currency reform in the Soviet zone before the Bizone, Clay confirmed his demand for it as an integral part of a program that OMGUS would still have to decide upon in consultation with State, Treasury, and Army Departments.

As to point "b," coordination with the British, Clay demanded that the matter of financial reform in Germany should be left in his hands. He broke the news that his counterpart in Berlin, Brian Robertson, had already informed him that London would not join the USA in the Deutschmark printing project. Therefore, there would be no need for coordination with the British on a governmental level. John C. deWilde from the State Department contradicted. Currency reform would be only one aspect of financial reform. The State

Department would want to discuss with the British at governmental level in Washington, DC overall financial reform in Germany.

Clay defended his position with efficiency arguments. He would not anticipate insurmountable difficulties when the matter would be up for settlement between the US and British military governors in Berlin. Rather an agreement could be reached promptly. Clay thereby insinuated his expectation of such difficulties and certainly delay in case of intergovernmental negotiation of the issue. As if to express the highest importance he attached to his demand, he said that he was willing to refer the entire matter of financial reform, including currency conversion, back to Washington, DC to be settled on intergovernmental level with the British.

Faced with having to take back this burden of responsibility from an experienced winning team in Berlin, deWilde backpedaled. Clay said that he would make part of the CDG Plan of 1946, which also the State Department had endorsed, the basis for an agreement with his British counterpart in Berlin. But – he added – it needed considerable modifications, especially as to the second part of the plan pertaining to the Equalization Fund.

The agreement of this meeting on point "b" reads as follows: "Mr. Saltzman reserved the State Department position, pending earliest further consideration within the State Department, of the question of further coordination with the British prior to unilateral US printing and coinage."[98] It doesn't need much interpretation to conclude that OMGUS wasn't treated benevolently by the State Department and – maybe – also vice versa, as we will see below from the proceedings of the October 13 meeting in the office of Edward H. Foley, Assistant Secretary of the Treasury.

The director of BEP, Alvin W. Hall, explained in three short identical letters of October 27, 1947 to the presidents (of the American Bank Note Company in New York City Albert L. Schomp, of the Forbes Lithograph Manufacturing Company in Boston Arthur Hitchings, and of The Tudor Press, Inc. in Boston

Harland A. Wilbur) what the Army Department's classification "Top Secret" of the Mark-printing project means:

> there will be encountered information affecting the national
> defense of the United States within the meaning of the Espionage
> Act, U.S.C. 50; 31 and 32 and its transmission or revelation in any
> manner to an unauthorized person is prohibited by law. // The
> Department of the Army has adopted the word "BIRDDOG" as a
> code and any correspondence or conversations on this project must
> always employ this code for identification purposes.[99]

It is almost needless to say that the currency printing decision on October 10, 1947 and the execution of the project were kept "top secret" vis-à-vis the German currency experts that the Bizonal government had urged the German Administration for Finance to assemble in the *Sonderstelle Geld und Kredit* (Special Agency for Money and Credit) in Bad Homburg. This is revealed in a letter of Ludwig Erhard, then chairman of the *Sonderstelle*, of October 30, 1947 to the Finance Group, Bipartite Control Office, Frankfurt/M., Taunus-Anlage 11.[100] Erhard refers to a discussion that he and vice chairman Erwin Hielscher had conducted with Colonel Stoker and Mr. Schwarz on October 15, 1947, that is, a few days after the final interdepartmental decision on the printing of Deutschmark notes in Washington, DC. A four-page memorandum about the question of banknote printing and coin minting of the *Sonderstelle* was attached. It requests information from the occupying powers whether they have already taken measures for the production of new notes and coins. In case such production has not yet been launched, the memo advocates an immediate start of the printing and minting process irrespective of the date of currency reform. It calculates the necessary volume of new money (six billion marks in notes and coins), splits up their denominations, estimates a normal production period of at least a year and a half, and discusses ways and means to overcome production bottlenecks and to shorten the production period. Finally, simply *Mark* is proposed for the new currency unit.

The German Empire (*Deutsches Reich*) had adopted this unit shortly after its foundation in 1871. It remained legal tender throughout Germany's inflation and hyperinflation 1914–1923, until the gold-backed *Reichsmark* was introduced on August 30, 1924.[101] Obviously unaware of decisions in Washington, DC, where the dice had already been cast on all of the issues that the *Sonderstelle* raised in its memo, its members had performed mental exercise, but actually they had wasted their time planning what OMGUS and Washington, DC had already conceptualized in detail.

In Washington, DC there was also a code description for the Deutschmark itself, namely "Special Army Currency." It was under this rubric that a follow-up conference to the one on October 10 was held on October 13, 1948 in the office of Edward H. Foley, Assistant Secretary of the Treasury. There the details of carrying out the printing project were determined. In attendance were: Benson E. L. Timmons (Treasury, chairing the meeting in Mr. Foley's absence); Alvin W. Hall (director of BEP), Clark R. Long (assistant director of BEP) and Henry J. Holtzclaw (staff of BEP); Jack Bennett and Edward A. Tenenbaum (listed as representatives of the Department of the Army); Albert L. Schomp (president of the American Bank Note Co.); Jerome Jacobsen and Jacob D. Beam (staff of the State Department); Dr. Frank Leland Howard (Bureau of the Mint); Clinton Tyler Wood (Office of International Finance); and Sommerfield (General Counsel).[102]

First of all, Jack Bennett outlined the requirements of the Army Department: production start at the earliest possible time, completion of the printing by December 15, 1947. He was informed that BEP could not recommend the lithographic print except as a temporary expedient, because such currency could easily be counterfeited. Dr. Howard had figures on the cost of producing coins for the lower denominations, 0.5 and 1 mark: two and a half times the cost of printing these by the lithographic process and the production period would well extend beyond the beginning of 1948. In favor of production speed the decision fell on the lithographic process without serial numbers. This would allow the notes to be printed, boxed, and shipped from the contractor's plant in contrast to the 2, 5, 20, and 50 mark denominations which would also be lithographically printed. But the latter would have to be shipped to BEP where they would be serially numbered, the printed sheets reduced to individual banknotes, and boxed for overseas shipment. The Army Department was given tentative assurance that the entire printing job would be completed by December 15, 1947, in time for the banknotes to reach Germany by January 1, 1948.[103]

On October 14, 1948 the Under Secretary of the Army sent a letter to the Secretary of the Treasury, John W. Snyder, specifying the terms of agreement between these two departments on the printing issue. A day later Acting Secretary of State, Robert A. Lovett, expressed in a letter to the Secretary of the Treasury "that the State Department is in accord with the policy expressed therein, and concurs in the request [of the Department of the Army] that your Department undertake the printing of such currency."[104] This written consent, however, was expressed ex post facto. The Secretary of the Treasury had verbally approved at 5:40 p.m. on October 14, 1947 that the BEP be authorized to start the printing project, probably following a verbal consent of the Secretary of State over the phone just prior to that. Earlier in the day, BEP had put pressure on the Treasury and Army Departments by setting 5:00 p.m. that very day as a deadline for authorization. Otherwise BEP would reject responsibility for completing the project on time.

During these critical days and hours of the launch of the Deutschmark's printing, communication by phone and cable replaced correspondence by letter. Time was too precious. In the absence of the BEP deadline

> it would have been at least a week before any written or oral instructions would have been received. ... It became necessary for this bureau to prepare a rough draft of a letter for General Draper's signature which contained all of the necessary authorization and

details sufficient for the bureau to proceed with the work. The rough draft of this letter was prepared on October 16 but the final draft was not received by the bureau until October 22.[105]

Formal written orders by the Treasury's BEP, namely by acting director Clark R. Long, to Tudor Press, Inc. for printing the 2, 5, 20, and 50 mark denominations in lithographic mode were dated October 17. Also on October 17, 1947 C. R. Long wrote two identical short letters to Tudor Press, Inc. and Forbes Lithograph Manufacturing Company: "This letter will confirm our recent arrangements made with you by telephone for the printing and processing of a special form of currency for this bureau. ... you may consider this letter as your authority to proceed with the preliminary phases of the project."[106] But we don't know when they were received by the addressees.

In a BEP memo of November 22, 1948 accounting for Marknotes delivered for each denomination and the total cost of the entire offset printing of notes, it is noted that the printing was completed on December 19, 1947. In an overview dated December 24, 1947 on the state of the project "at the close of business December 19, 1947," E.G. Shreve, assistant to the director, reported to BEP Director Alvin W. Hall that all of the offset printing had been done. Forbes Lithograph Manufacturing Company had shipped its entire lot of 0.5 and 1 Mark notes directly to the army in 12,075 boxes (each containing 40,000 banknotes, gross weight 84 pounds per box). He further noted that BEP had practically received Tudor Press, Inc.'s complete lot for serial numbering which had also been almost completely finished and that BEP had already shipped 8,142 boxes to the army for transportation to Germany. So around the end of 1947 the sum of 20,217 "Doorknob" (BEP code) boxes had already arrived in the port of Bremerhaven, which together with Bremen belonged to the American enclave in the British occupation zone, in operation "Birddog" (US Army code) or were about to arrive.[107]

Immediately following the conference and still on October 13, BEP had contacted several paper manufacturers and lithographic

To: A. W. Hall, Director   December 24, 1947

From: E. G. Shreve, Assistant to the Director

Subject: Special Army Currency, Series 1948

The following is a report at the close of business December 19, 1947.

Denomination (Marks)	Ordered	Printed Stock	Number of Notes Received by Bureau	Numbered	Shipped	Boxed for Shipment
		Forbes (thru Dec. 19)				
1/2	238,000,000	238,840,000	xxx	xxx	238,000,000	----
1	245,000,000	245,420,000	xxx	xxx	245,000,000	----
Total	483,000,000	484,260,000	xxx	xxx	483,000,000	----
		Tudor (Completed)				
2	73,400,000	74,694,480	74,225,200	73,360,000	73,360,000	----
5	128,800,000	132,044,500	130,760,210	128,800,000	128,800,000	----
20	56,350,000	57,761,400	57,495,400	56,800,000	56,800,000	----
50	42,000,000	42,771,700	42,771,700	42,000,000	42,000,000	----
Total	300,550,000	307,272,080	305,252,510	300,960,000	300,960,000	----
Grand Total	783,550,000	791,532,080	305,252,510	300,960,000	783,960,000	----

Number of Boxes			
Shipped to Date		Available for Shipment	
From Bureau	8,142	At Bureau	----
From Forbes	12,075	At Forbes	----
Total	20,217	Total	----

FIGURE 4.4 "Birddog" project money completely produced and shipped by December 19, 1947
Source: Historical Research Center of Bureau of Engraving and Printing (BEP), Washington, DC

printing establishments by phone and telegram. It turned out to be especially difficult to procure suitable paper. Most of the paper manufacturers were either booked out or lacked planchettes necessary to produce paper with fluorescent elements in it to complicate counterfeiting. BEP had to use a lot of pressure on the paper companies and the Keith Paper Company

was prevailed upon to offer every inducement to the planchette suppliers which finally resulted in their agreement to re-design their equipment and to work around the clock. With the amount of planchettes on hand at the Keith Paper Company it was possible for this concern to start production of the paper almost at once. However, sufficient planchettes could not be made available to the Parsons Paper Company until October 23, at which time the Parsons Paper Company agreed to begin manufacture of the paper.[108]

A massive quantity of paper (1,250,000 pounds) was required for the project. That meant that 3,500 pounds of planchettes were necessary. Under normal conditions it took a full year's production to reach that figure.

There was another bottleneck: ink for the colors of the various denominations, manufactured in the Ink Making Division of BEP. Many of the necessary raw materials were not on hand. In view of the urgency of the matter they were ordered by telephone. Due to the "top secret" classification of the project, all purchases of materials and services were made under the War Powers Act (Executive Order No. 9023), which greatly accelerated their procurement.[109]

Keith Paper Company at Turners Falls MA and Parsons Paper Company at Holyoke MA were involved in delivering paper. Likewise, only two unnamed planchette producers were taken under contract. The American Bank Note Company at New York City, Tudor Press, Inc. at Boston MA, Forbes Lithograph Manufacturing Company at Boston MA and the Bureau of Engraving and Printing (BEP) at Washington, DC were the four printing institutions charged by the US government to print the new German currency. BEP was responsible for coordinating the project. In addition, for banknotes of 2 Mark and upward it performed the serial-number printing and cutting the sheets into banknotes as well as the boxing and shipping them via New York to Bremerhaven.[110]

All of the above-mentioned institutions entered their contractual agreements conditioned on the consent of the trade unions to produce twenty-four hours a day and seven days a week. And the unions actually agreed to it only two years after the end of World War II. During the War, at least part of the unions had supported the cause of the Joint Boycott Council of the American Jewish Congress and the Jewish Labor Committee in boycotting trade with Germany.[111] And now during the last two and a half months of 1947, the trade unions agreed to jettison their acquired rights to normal working hours and days in order to print new currency and thereby to open the gate to prosperity for their former enemy country.

This is but one example of the magnanimous mind that is inherent in American culture of pragmatism and manifest destiny, the latter in order to instill America's ideals and values of freedom, democracy, just government and the rule of law into oppressed and unenlightened peoples. During the Nazi period, Germany's political leadership and a large majority of Germans had belonged to such peoples. I have always admired the USA for holding up the torch of liberty and enlightenment values.

BEP itself ran into a bottleneck of production capacity and space. It was still occupied with boxing and shipping Korean currency whose printing for a currency reform in Korea had not yet been completed. Nearly 2,000 boxes had still to be fabricated and filled with banknotes to be shipped. In order to get this out of the way before the new "Special Army Currency" sheets would be delivered for serial numbering, cutting into banknotes, boxing and shipping to Germany, BEP's Construction and Maintenance Division:

> was authorized to work Saturday, October 18, on the boxes for the Korean issues. ... // The Tudor Press, Inc. was likewise requested to accelerate the rate of the Korean work, which they agreed to do and the indications are, at the moment, that they will complete the Korean work approximately ten days earlier than anticipated. The numbering of the Korean issue was extended to three 8-hour shifts and two additional presses are made ready for numbering. There is a good prospect that all of the Korean notes will have been processed for shipment before the first of November. This will mean that the Korean project has been completed a month earlier than was estimated.[112]

The spatial bottleneck resulted from the commitment of BEP's auditorium for the Washington Community Chest. This was a charity institution for destitute families as well as those colored and white people actively engaged in overcoming racial segregation. It provided aid in financial as well as social-contact terms. This kind of social work was backed by the Secretary of the Treasury by putting the BEP's auditorium at the disposal of the Community Chest. But BEP now needed the auditorium as an additional production site. It contacted Assistant Secretary of the Treasury Edward H. Foley, Jr. on October 16, 1947 and informed him that unless the BEP could use the auditorium as an additional production site, BEP could not assure that the deadline for the completion of the Deutschmark printing, namely December 15, 1947, could be met. Foley answered that under the circumstances other arrangements would be made for the Community Chest.[113]

The banknote printing outside of BEP required BEP representatives to maintain the necessary records there and Secret Service guards to keep the job "top secret." The author concludes his memo of October 23, 1947:

> With the exception of the War Savings Bond project, it now appears that the production of the Special Army Currency within the period established will have been the largest single job that this bureau has ever undertaken. Everyone associated with this project up to the present moment has cooperated to the fullest extent. // Complete arrangements have also been made and proposals will be issued in the next few days for the production of the permanent currency by the American Bank Note Company. While the time element of the permanent currency is not critical at the moment, all of the many details associated with the production of this currency had to be worked out in order to obtain a final quotation for its production so that formal authorization could be given to proceed.[114]

In its letter of October 20, 1947 to the Secretary of the Treasury, the Department of the Army had requested of BEP to order intaglio mark-note printing as a stepping stone into the replacement of the provisional offset-printed mark notes by intaglio-printed currency. It would be the more counterfeit-proof permanent currency of the Bizone. As to the quantities ordered and the delivery dates in 1948, see Figure 4.4. This is mentioned in a letter of Major General, GSC, Daniel Noce, chief of the Civil Affairs Division of the Department of the Army, of June 28, 1948, that is, after West German currency reform, requesting at the expense of the Department of the Army further intaglio-printed mark banknotes: 25 million of the 10-mark denomination, 20 million of the 20-mark, 20 million of the 50-mark, and 3 million of the 100-mark denomination. "It is the desire of the Department of the Army that these currencies be produced at the earliest possible date and that every effort be made to expedite the printing and shipment of these currencies for which this department will reimburse the Bureau of Printing and Engraving."[115]

This was the last request for mark-note deliveries to West Germany at the expense of the Department of the Army. All requested notes were delivered and shipped to Germany before the end of 1948. In a letter of November 29, 1948, the new chief of the Civil Affairs Division of the Department of the Army, Brigadier General G.L. Eberle, informed BEP director Alvin W. Hall that the Department of the Army had given its approval to the *Bank deutscher Länder*, the West German central bank at Frankfurt am Main, "to have additional quantities of mark currency printed at its own expense from plates and glass plate originals employed in the production of German mark currency designated as 'Bird Dog' and 'Door Knob'." In a letter of December 1, 1948 from Albert L. Schomp, president of the American Bank Note Company, to Alvin W. Hall, director of BEP, Schomp informed Hall: "We are now in receipt of an order from the Bank deutscher Länder with additional notes, signed by Messrs. Könneker and Lenbach, to furnish them with additional notes as follows:" 73,600,000 of 10-mark denomination, 75,000,000 of 20-mark, 20,000,000 of 50-mark, and 10,000,000 of 100-mark denomination.[116] It is noteworthy that the requests especially for 10-, but also for 20-mark notes was much higher than the original provision at the US Army's expense a year earlier. By the time of the request of the Bank deutscher Länder the West German central bank had taken over from the US Army not only the provision of high-quality intaglio-processed Deutschmark banknotes, but also the footing of the bill for their production as well as offset-printed 0.5- and 1-mark notes from Forbes Lithograph Manufacturing Company.

4.2   PLANNING AND PREPARING FOR C-DAY:
TENENBAUM'S ROLE

Fritz Butschkau (from 1953 the first president of the *Deutscher Sparkassen- und Giroverband*, the central association of Germany's savings banks) had been recruited in 1946 as currency expert for the finance committee of the British Zonal Advisory Board, which consisted of German politicians. Meetings on currency-reform issues were chaired by S. Paul Chambers, chief of the Finance Division of the "Control Commission for Germany (British Element)," which was the official name for the British military government. Butschkau reports in his memoirs that when these discussions on currency questions ended, Chambers disclosed to his group of German experts "that the Americans with their currency reform planner Mr. Tennenbaum [*sic*] would make the race."[117]

Here now is the story of Tenenbaum's contributions to the unfolding of events: in decision-making on currency reform in general

FIGURE 4.5   Edward A. Tenenbaum working in his home in Berlin-Dahlem

and on the printing of Deutschmarks in particular. On November 1, 1946 OMGUS Finance Division announced in a circular letter to the Finance Division Organization that Edward A. Tenenbaum had been appointed special assistant to the director.[118] At that time Jack Bennett had headed the Division since June 9, 1946. But even before November 1946, Tenenbaum must have been working for OMGUS Finance Division in that capacity, because on September 26, 1946 he had sent a short memorandum to the Branch Chiefs of the Finance Division undersigned by him as "Special Assistant to the Director." Its subject was "Preliminary Agreement on the Establishment of a Joint German Committee for Finance" in preparation of the founding of the Bizone, the administrative and economic policy fusion of the American and British occupation zones, to be effective January 1, 1947.[119] The Agreement contained the sentence: "It is free to the other Zones to join in this Agreement."[120]

Tenenbaum himself refers to a conversation between him "representing Finance Division, OMGUS" and Ludwig Erhard, then Bavarian Minister of Economics, on February 1, 1946.[121] In Section 3.2, I have already mentioned that he had been released from his prior assignment and – effective on July 7, 1945 – transferred to US Group Control Council (USGCC) for Germany, which was transformed into OMGUS in the first half of October 1945. It was then that the Finance Division of OMGUS with several sub-branches was created. This means that Tenenbaum was attached to Finance Division of OMGUS quite a bit earlier than the date of the above-mentioned announcement.

Tenenbaum himself has solved the puzzle on his application form for government employment in Washington, DC filled out in the summer of 1948. As part of his employment history he notes that from July 1945 to February 1946 he worked as Foreign Exchange Analyst in the Finance Division of OMGUS in Frankfurt and from September 1946 to September 1948 as special assistant to the financial adviser in Berlin. Jack Bennett had been his immediate chief in both positions. But Tenenbaum has left one question unanswered: What did he do during the half year from March to August 1946? For that period, he just lists his place of residence: 3030 Wisconsin Avenue NW in Washington, DC.

I draw the conclusion that he might have been affiliated with different government institutions, like OSS, the Treasury and State Departments, the Federal Reserve Board, and the War Department, on whose payroll as P 4 he ended up while he was special assistant for currency reform in OMGUS, Berlin. I assume that the half-year period was devoted to networking, preparing, and training in German currency-reform matters whilst in personal contact with the relevant Washington institutions. In his unpublished manuscript Tenenbaum mentions that when the Allies entered German territory in late 1944 and early 1945 they were not equipped with any officially recognized plan for a German currency reform. "A plan drawn up by Professors Howard Ellis and Gottfried Haberler for the Federal Reserve Bank – 'Recommended Policies for the Allied Military Government in Germany' – received little attention."[122] It might well be that Tenenbaum used his half year in Washington, DC to prepare for his later role in OMGUS by working with the above-mentioned government institutions, especially in the Federal Reserve.

Tenenbaum also mentions that Manuel Gottlieb, his fellow economist in Finance Division of OMGUS, and other US officials had developed a rudimentary currency reform proposal by the fall of 1945. It was submitted by Tenenbaum to the ACC for discussion. "This suggested little more than revaluation of the existing banknotes and deposits at one-tenth of their face value, leaving prices unchanged, and was frankly intended as only an interim measure. Fn.: Manuel Gottlieb, 'Notes on German Inflation, Public Debt, and Remedial Programs,' mimeographed, Frankfurt 1945."[123]

Gottlieb had received his education at Harvard and later became a professor of economics at the University of Wisconsin in Milwaukee. In 1957 he published a scholarly article on the tug-of-war, the different positions of the four Allies in the ACC over currency and financial questions, and the causes for the failure of a common currency reform for all of Germany.[124]

The origin of the Finance Division of OMGUS can be traced back to August 14, 1944 when the Civil Affairs Division of Supreme Headquarters Allied Expeditionary Force (SHAEF) established a German country section including a finance division. On August 9, 1944 US Group Control Council (USGCC) had been created as a separate US institution for civil affairs policy in Germany. On November 25, 1944 it was structured into divisions, among them a Finance Division headed by Colonel Bernard Bernstein. Another organizational reform of June 29, 1945 subordinated the Finance Division to the Assistant Deputy for Trade and Finance, an office for which General Clay had managed to win the extremely successful Detroit Bank chief executive Joseph M. Dodge.[125] Perhaps the June 29 reorganization was part of a package to enhance the power of the Assistant Deputy for Trade and Finance in order to keep Dodge in Germany as part of US military government.

When USGCC was transformed into OMGUS in the first half of October 1945, the Finance Division of USGCC, became Finance Division of OMGUS with several sub-branches. Joseph M. Dodge was appointed its director and from October 1945 on also as financial adviser of OMGUS. He left these OMGUS positions in late May or early June 1946, that is, after the Colm-Dodge-Goldsmith (CDG) Plan for a quadripartite currency reform for Germany had been delivered to OMGUS on May 20, 1946.[126] His immediate successor Jack Bennett would remain in this position in OMGUS Berlin much longer than Dodge. Bennett's deputy Jo Fisher Freeman took over reduced executive functions in OMGUS on January 18, 1949.[127]

After his stint in Germany Dodge was elected president of the American Bankers Association from 1947 to 1948. As financial adviser appointed by General Douglas MacArthur, Supreme Commander for the Allied powers in the Pacific Theater of Operations, Dodge developed an economic stabilization program for Japan in December 1948, called *Dodge Line*. Dodge himself arrived in Japan in February 1949 in order to implement his plan for financial reform there.[128]

While Dodge headed the Finance Division of OMGUS, his successor Jack Bennett, as former Treasury employee also a civilian, was already part of OMGUS Finance Division. He headed the Finance Division's Foreign Exchange and Blocking Control Branch in Frankfurt from October 1945 to June 1946, before on June 9 he succeeded Joseph M. Dodge as director of the Finance Division (until March 4, 1947) and thereafter as General Clay's financial adviser in Berlin.[129] The main task of the Branch was the continuation of foreign-exchange and thus external-trade control that the government of Chancellor Heinrich Brüning had started as a consequence of the German banking crisis of July 1931. The Hitler government had expanded it to full control of external trade and foreign exchange. Tenenbaum's published Undergraduate Prize Essay of Yale University was mainly concerned with the details of this sophisticated external payment-and-trade control system of the Nazi economy.[130]

With a concrete four-power agreement on new common economic and fiscal policies for all four occupation zones in Germany pending, the Nazi economic control system had been taken over and was continued by military governments in their respective zones. This included wage and price controls that the Hitler government had introduced in 1936, when full employment had been reached in Germany and inflation had started to become a problem. The rationing-card system for food and clothing was also kept up by the occupying powers.

In view of Tenenbaum's expertise on the Nazi economy's control system, it doesn't come as a surprise that Tenenbaum was already working with Jack Bennett in OMGUS Finance Division's Foreign Exchange and Blocking Control Branch in Frankfurt. The circulars mentioned in the first paragraph of this chapter are among documents collected under that label. But in other OMGUS documents, available on microfiche in Germany's Federal Archive (*Bundesarchiv*) in Coblenz and in the Institute of Contemporary History (*Institut für Zeitgeschichte*) in Munich, I found even better proof of Tenenbaum's employment in the Control Branch, namely a memo undersigned by

"E. Tenenbaum" under two different dates in two different files. The first one dates October 27, 1945 drawn from a folder entitled "Research." The archivist's description of the folder's content is: "Foreign trade financing, foreign exchange and blocking control, suggested interim procedure for, reports and papers on." The title of Tenenbaum's two-page single-spaced memo is *Suggested Interim Procedure for Financing Imports and Exports*. Tenenbaum proposes a set of detailed procedures after enumerating four specifications that they are to meet for financing trade within Germany on the one hand and outside Germany on the other: "a. To be able to go into operation on short notice. b. To conduct imports and exports without disrupting normal economic life. c. To utilize German agencies for detailed work. d. To permit ready conversion to a permanent centralized foreign trade procedure."[131]

Tenenbaum's memo of October 27 was retyped dated October 31, 1945 and used as "Annex A" most probably to a circular letter for the Finance Division Organization and may be even beyond for other parts of OMGUS. The folder with the retyped document is entitled "War Diary." The archivist's description of the content of this folder reads: "Significant activities of the Foreign Exchange and Blocking Control Branch, summaries of."[132] Just after the founding of the Foreign Exchange and Blocking Control Branch in October 1945, its newly appointed chief Jack Bennett entrusted the task of designing the basic working procedures for the Branch to Edward Tenenbaum. This proves that Bennett highly appreciated not only Tenenbaum's deep knowledge of the Nazi external-trade system and foreign-exchange control, but also his talent for dissecting complex problems of organization and coming up with analytically structured solutions. In June 1946 Jack Bennett succeeded Joseph M. Dodge first as director of the Finance Division and later as financial adviser of OMGUS Berlin. It is reasonable to assume that Bennett played a crucial role in promoting Tenenbaum to special assistant for Germany's currency reform in his Finance Division located in Berlin.

While the Foreign Exchange and Blocking Control Branch had been working out of US military government in Frankfurt, Jack Bennett and the Tenenbaum couple must have moved to Berlin in June 1946. In handwriting Tenenbaum's office room number, "2082 Director's Building," was noted on a circular of July 17, 1947, "Subject: Amendment No. 1 under Military Government Law No. 51 'Currency.'" It was sent out by G. H. Garde, the Adjutant General of OMGUS, and addressed to the Directors of the Offices of Military Government for Bavaria, Wuerttemberg-Baden, Hesse, Bremen, and Berlin Sector.[133]

It took some time, before Tenenbaum and his wife Jeanette Kipp were assigned a large and fancy semi-detached house by Captain Pusser of the accommodation section of the OMGUS Billeting Office: Gelfertstrasse 47 A, Berlin-Dahlem.[134] This house was built in 1927–1928. Due to its beautiful expressionist-style architecture and its importance for Jewish history in Berlin, but significantly not because the Tenenbaum family had lived on the premises, this house has been officially registered to be under monumental protection since 1995. It is situated in walking distance from Tenenbaum's former office in the Director's Building, then located on Kronprinzenallee. This major street was renamed Clayallee in 1949 in honor of the organizer of the Berlin airlift. Dahlem belonged and still belongs today to the most preferred districts of Berlin.

When I looked at the house from outside, I happened to run into today's owner of the Tenenbaum semi. After telling him the reason for my interest in his house, he invited me inside and showed me all around it. He also referred me to his neighbor in the attached semi, because it was and is the neighbor's hobby to collect every information on the history of the housing complex that he could get his hands on. And, indeed, he had his files well organized on the prewar, war, and postwar history of the houses and its owners. However, he was unaware of the Tenenbaum family episode in No. 47 A. And he had no idea that the Deutschmark was introduced by Tenenbaum and not by Ludwig Erhard as almost all Germans believe.

Tenenbaum and the housing complex have their respective Jewish histories in common. Berlin-Dahlem was an agricultural estate

FIGURE 4.6 First home of the Tenenbaums in Gelfertstr. 47 A,
Berlin-Dahlem

belonging to the Prussian state. Due to high population growth in the
city of Berlin, the Prussian state felt motivated to parcel out its land
and sell it to private households and investors since 1901. By this
move the original agricultural land was multiplied in price and
became an important source of revenue for the state of Prussia. The
operation of a streetcar to Dahlem since 2005 and the construction of
the subway line from Wittenbergplatz to Dahlem, which was completed in 1913 as far as Thielplatz station, further pushed up the price
of building land in Dahlem. From 1908, the policy of Kaiser Wilhelm II
to develop Dahlem into a German Oxford also contributed to rising
prices for land.

Businessmen, especially in the apparel industry, as well as high
civil servants, judges, university professors and scientists belonged to
the wealth-owning class in Berlin. Many of them were Jewish and put
their money into buying plots of land in Dahlem and into building

mostly large and fancy detached houses there with relatively large gardens around. The land, where the Tenenbaum family would first reside, together with the adjacent lot and a larger piece on Kehler Weg 3, had originally been bought by Salo and Max Wagner, joint owners of an apparel company in Berlin, in September 1922. The German hyper-inflation had begun three months earlier. Therefore, it was a very astute investment of their money. Salo Wagner built a villa on the larger lot shortly after the land purchase. In 1927 the Wagner brothers sold the two smaller lots to Dr. Heinrich Veit Simon, an attorney at law and notary public (Gelfertstrasse 47) and to the merchant Fritz Kiefe (Gelfertstrasse 47 A). Like the Wagner brothers they were both Jewish. They immediately started building their semi-detached houses.

As this one case suggests, the share of Jewish property owners in Dahlem turned out to be disproportionally high during the inter-war period compared to the share of Jewish Germans in the popula-tion of Berlin or Germany as a whole. The persecution of Jewish citizens by the Nazis since 1933 at first drove many into exile and from 1941 finally into the death factories of the holocaust. Some felt compelled to commit suicide. Their left-behind property fell to the German Reich, which would then privatize the former Jewish real estate by selling it at low prices to particularly deserving Nazi Party members. Before the holocaust started, Salo Wagner, as well as Dr. Simon and merchant Kiefe had been forced to sell their Dahlem real estate to the Deutsche Reich. In the first half of 1941, Salo Wagner's villa was sold at a courtesy price to the Nazi mayor of Zehlendorf, of which the administrative district Dahlem was and still today is a part.

In another case a Jewish German citizen, Bianka Irma Hamburger, had been forced to sell her house in Englerallee 6. This property was sold at a price much below its real worth to the mayor of Steglitz. He was not only a devoted Nazi Party member, but also in the SS with the rank of a colonel (*Obersturmbannführer*). Salo Wagner, Dr. Heinrich Veit Simon and Fritz Kiefe all became victims of the holocaust. Most other Jewish German citizens of Dahlem suffered the same fate. Bianka Irma Hamburger and her two Jewish German citizens who had also lived in Englerallee 6 committed suicide to avoid deportation.[135]

By the end of the war, Dahlem had been stripped of its Jewish population. Nazi elite people had moved into their fancy houses. After the war they, in turn, were expropriated by the American military government (OMGUS), which set up its Berlin headquarters in the Director's Building in Dahlem. By expropriating real estate and other wealth of high-ranking Nazis, OMGUS had at its disposal a lot of houses and apartments in Dahlem for its large number of American employees to live in, and, in addition, for supplying buildings in Dahlem to the Free University of Berlin when it was founded there in 1948. When most of the American staff of OMGUS had left Berlin in tandem with the founding of the Federal Republic of Germany, the former Jewish real estate was either used for restitution of property rights of Jewish family descendants, as in the case of the Wagner, Simon, and Kiefe families. Or property rights were transferred to German authorities in West Berlin and West Germany.

I owe all this information on the Jewish history of the housing complex at the corner of Gelfertstrasse/Kehler Weg to today's owner of Gelfertstrasse 47, Wolfgang Materne. He also shared the following occurrence with me. In the morning hours of April 30, 2015, a frail-looking old lady with a walking stick was creeping around his property. He then saw the woman behind a tree from where she was trying to photograph the house without being noticed. He went out and asked her whether she needed help. She seemed relieved and told him that she had been born in this house and that she wanted to see it again before her death. He invited her inside and over a cup of tea she told him the following story:

> In April 70 years ago, the Red Army set out to storm Berlin. At the end of April [1945], the Soviet troops conquered Berlin-Dahlem. //
> Mrs. Irmgard Brova, that is the lady's name, was born in 1931 in the basement of the house at Gelfertstrasse 47, where she and her sister

lived with their mother and the house owners Simon for rent. Here she had to watch in 1941 how Katharina and Eva, the two deaf-mute sisters of the landlord, were taken away on an open truck as part of the National Socialist "racial hygiene" (euthanasia) program never to be seen again. // In the neighboring house Kehler Weg 3, a female resident went into labor when tanks rolled by. Her 5-year-old son, who was supposed to get help for his mother from neighbors, was immediately shot in the street. Later in the day, Soviet soldiers rounded up all the residents of our and surrounding houses in a garden. All the women and children had to line up in size as if for a group photo. Afterwards the soldiers shot with their Kalashnikovs several times over the heads of the people who were frozen in fear of death. But there were no final shots, probably because a Soviet jeep unexpectedly stopped in front of the house, the crew jumped out and beat the torturers half to death with their rifle butts // It remains to mention that the women were raped in rows. The old lady, our guest, told that her mother hid her and her sister in the closet before the soldiers entered the house, where the two adolescent daughters witnessed their mother's rape. // Mrs. Brova later married an American soldier, followed him to the USA and had two children with him. When they were grown up, she left her family and returned to Berlin driven by homesickness, without losing contact with her children and grandchildren. Reciprocal visits helped ease the separation.[136]

During my second visit to the Harry S. Truman Presidential Library in November 2022, I found a different address for the living quarters of Edward Tenenbaum and his family than that in Gelfertstrasse 47 A. Telephone books of all employees of the three Western military governments in Berlin, updated to March 26 and May 10, 1948 respectively, contained as Edward A. Tenenbaum's address: Föhrenweg 15 in Berlin-Dahlem.[137] This one-family villa on a large lot in a completely quiet street until today was also in walking distance from Tenenbaum's office, room number 2082, in the Director's Building of US military governor General Clay. I don't know, when the Tenenbaum family moved there. But when Tenenbaum was most engaged preparing the details of the West German currency reform in the first half of 1948, he and his family was evidently living there, when they were in town. It seems like his family had also spent time with him in military barracks at Rothwesten, where Tenenbaum was the key figure in discussions with West German currency experts to adjust the American planning for currency reform to German habits and legislative language.

Even though subordinated to Clay's financial adviser Jack Bennett, Tenenbaum was assigned important functions on the ACC level after the CDG Plan had been introduced there in early September 1946. He probably accompanied Bennett regularly to discussions of the plan in ACC committee meetings. And when Bennett – for reasons of poor health, other commitments or Tenenbaum's deeper knowledge of currency-reform issues – couldn't or wouldn't represent OMGUS on the ACC level himself, he obviously entrusted the takeover of such roles to Tenenbaum.

FIGURE 4.7 Second home of the Tenenbaums in Föhrenweg 15, Berlin-Dahlem

FIGURE 4.8 Edward
A. Tenenbaum, civil servant in
OMGUS Berlin as "special
assistant for currency reform"
at age 25

FIGURE 4.9 Jack Bennett,
financial adviser of General
Lucius D. Clay and OMGUS in
Berlin, to whom Tenenbaum,
as "special assistant for
currency reform,"
was attached

FIGURE 4.10 Edward A. Tenenbaum leaving the British sector of Berlin

In an attachment to his "Application for Federal Employment" Tenenbaum wrote that "I acted as sole US expert under the Finance Advisor, and as his alternate in quadripartite discussions in the Finance Directorate of the Allied Control Authority. (Due to illness of the Finance Advisor I was in charge of negotiations during the last few months preceding the separate currency reforms in the eastern and western Zones)."[138] This is corroborated by a letter of BICO, Joint Secretariat, Frankfurt, to the president of the Economic Council, Erich Köhler, of March 31, 1948 "Subject: Allied/German Discussion on Financial Reform. // Reference your letter of 18 February. // The delay in replying to your letter, due mainly to the illness of the US financial adviser, is regretted."[139]

With that letter Köhler is informed that the financial advisers of the Anglo-Saxon military governments demand the creation of a currency committee of not more than three or four persons "to meet with them for discussions of financial reform. ... The actual date of the meeting is not yet firm, but it is hoped that it will be in the very near future." This letter was in reaction to the resolution that the ninth plenary session of the Economic Council[140] had passed on December 18, 1947 stating that currency reform "could not be planned and executed without the responsible cooperation of German agencies." To ensure a broad German participation, Köhler, after a meeting with Generals Robertson and Clay on February 14, 1948, sent his letter of February 18 to BICO naming nine persons, including the directors of the Finance and Economic Administration, Alfred Hartmann and Ludwig Erhard.[141] After BICO's response letter of March 31, 1948, the three persons for this newly created currency committee were on April 1 nominated by President Köhler of the Economic Council: Robert Pferdmenges (CDU), Herbert Kriedemann (SPD) und Franz Blücher (FDP). Thereafter, these nominees were invited by telephone on April 3 to meet with the Anglo-Saxon military governors and financial advisers on April 5 in US OMGUS Frankfurt's headquarters, the former IG Farben building, in preparation of the so-called Conclave of Rothwesten. Compared to the time it takes today to obtain a building permit in Berlin or just a permission to chop a tree in your own garden, it is amazing how fast decisions by democratic institutions (Economic Council) could be taken at the time.

Verbatim notes of a session of the ACC's Financial Regulations Committee on December 3, 1946, with all four Allied powers represented, lists Tenenbaum as the chairman of the meeting. The following meetings of the same committee on December 9 and 17, 1946 also record Tenenbaum as chairman, while in the verbatim minutes for the same committee's session on March 17, 1947, Tenenbaum is listed as one of the four representatives of the Allied powers and his Soviet colleague as holding the chair.[142] I assume that this was one of those periods, in which Jack Bennett, Clay's financial adviser, due to his unstable health[143] was temporarily off duty and Tenenbaum had to replace him.

I have already referred to Manuel Gottlieb's account of the causes of the failure of a quadripartite currency reform in postwar Germany. Here is how Tenenbaum saw the evolution of the differences of opinion between the Allies on the issue after the CDG Plan had been introduced in the ACC on September 2, 1946:

> At first, four-power discussions gave promise of rapid agreement. Fn.: The article of Jack Bennett, "The German Currency Reform," in: The Annals of the American Academy of Political and Social Science, Philadelphia, January 1950, pages 43ff. Somewhat surprisingly, the greatest difference of opinion did not arise with the Soviets at first, but rather with the British. At that time the Labour Party had just come to power in England [actually already a year and a month earlier]. Our British colleagues in Germany – themselves mostly conservative former colonial officials – strove dutifully to promote socialist doctrines, which they did not understand or like. // While the US Military Government looked at currency reform as a way to get rid of economic controls, our British associates saw it as a chance to make controls effective, and austerity more austere. (This was at a time when butter rations were larger in Germany than in victorious England, and our British colleagues in Germany were on British rations.) The British feared a 'radical' reform, because the more farsighted saw that it would destroy the possibility of maintaining a controlled economy in Germany. ... // The French also opposed a thorough-going reform, understandably wishing that Germany should suffer from inflation at least as much as their own country, and expressing the fear that the Germans would be unnecessarily relieved of the burden of wartime debt. // The Soviets, on the other hand, at first seemed to sympathize with the American plan for a currency reform. ... Although we were often able to find common ground with Soviet technical spokesmen, we never saw evidence of a real understanding with their political commissars, who sat at their elbow, whispering, whispering as the hours of four-power negotiation went on. It seemed to be the assignment of these

political commissars to make sure that no serious agreement was reached, and they succeeded. Several times when negotiations reached a promising stage, the Soviets broke off on some minor pretext, only to renew discussions as mysteriously as they had ceased. Often we could note abrupt changes in manner and content, which must have been inspired by new instructions from Moscow. // The issue which seemed to cause the greatest difficulty, and which eventually led to the collapse of four-power negotiations, was the physical control over the printing of a new currency. ... // We may never know whether the Soviets entered the currency reform negotiations in good faith, and if so when they ceased to negotiate in good faith. But around 1947 [with the failure of the Moscow conference of foreign ministers in April 1947] it became evident that they were stalling. In the absence of a currency reform, time was on the side of the Soviets. Repressed inflation favored many Soviet interests. It facilitated the financing of their occupation, reparations and other exports (partly through a special chain of "free market" stores and operators such as Rasno-Export in which off-ration goods were sold at black market prices.) Through rigid enforcement of price controls, it helped to push private enterprises in the Eastern Zone to the wall, and thus provided justification for socialization measures. (Socialized firms were financed by government subsidies, paid in part out of extremely high excise taxes on Schnapps [= booze].) It allowed them to use Allied Military Marks, captured Reichsmarks, surplus occupation costs and other funds for clandestine purchases in the Western Zones. Huge cash reserves – variously estimated as high as RM 12 billion (Fn.: *Der Tag*, Berlin, 15 April 1948) would become worthless in the event of a currency reform. Finally, it spread dissatisfaction and creeping economic paralysis in the economies of the Western Zones, and particularly in the Ruhr. // It was clear that the continued rotting-away of the economy in our Zones could only play into the hands of the communists, and sooner or later would lead to an explosion of social disorder that would threaten our entire occupation. We had no prudent choice except to get ready for a separate currency reform.[144]

Although the British disagreed with the American CDG Plan, they had started to push for a separate currency reform in the Western occupation zones and for an end of discussions with the Soviets as early as the end of 1946. At that stage the Americans still had hope to come to terms with the Soviets on the foreign ministers' conference in Moscow planned for March/April 1947. They refused the British initiative, also because they were clearly aware that a separate currency reform of the Western Zones would turn "the de facto absence of economic unity ... [in] a de jure state of economic disunity. If we had acquiesced in such a break at the time – before the Soviets revealed their true aims – the onus for splitting Germany in two would have fallen on the West, and the Soviets might have emerged as the champions of German unity."[145]

Erwin Hielscher, who would play leading roles in the Special Agency for Money and Credit and in the so-called Conclave of Rothwesten, aiding the Western Allies in putting the finishing touches to the American plan for the Western currency reform, had already launched such a proposal at the Social Democratic Economic Experts' Conference in mid-July 1947. The official Soviet newspaper in Berlin, the *Tägliche Rundschau* of July 23, 1947 had promptly delineated the consequences:

> ... so much is clear: the realization of these plans would represent the deadly blow to the economic unity of Germany. ... As long as the unity of the currency remains assured, there are justified possibilities that a state which temporarily has fallen apart politically and economically can be put together again without difficulty. ... If the plans for a currency reform without the Soviet Zone nevertheless should take concrete form, that would undoubtedly bring with it the final and irrevocable division of Germany. ... a partial currency reform would be the first stroke of the spade in the grave of German economic unity.[146]

The Americans who had taken the lead in currency-reform policy tried to avoid being blamed for the "first stroke of the spade" in the ill-chosen pictorial comparison of the Soviet newspaper. Throughout the rest of 1947 until March 1948 they tried to reach an agreement with the Soviets on the currency-reform issue. Tenenbaum writes: "On this score, at least, my own conscience is clear: we did what we could to find a basis for keeping Germany together."[147] But Tenenbaum admits that after the failure of the Council of Foreign Ministers conference in Moscow in April 1947 the Americans warmed up and prepared for a separate currency reform in the Bizone and, if the French went along, in the Trizone. In October 1947, the printing of Deutschmark banknotes in US printing establishments at US expenses was started. However, they could have been used as well for a quadripartite as for a Western currency reform. All the while negotiations with the Soviets in ACC continued into March 1948.

FIGURE 4.11 Edward A. Tenenbaum with his daughter Anne, who was born in Berlin in 1947

Reparations from Germany was one of the main issues contested between the Soviet Union and the Anglo-Saxon Allies after the end of the War. This was also true when the Potsdam Agreement was negotiated in July/August 1945. The final settlement of the issue was postponed to the later setting of the level of industry plan. At Potsdam the Soviets wanted and were granted reparations from dismantling existing plant and equipment not only in their own, but also in Western zones of occupation. Other countries entitled to claim such reparations were organized by the three Western occupation powers into an Inter-Allied Reparation Agency (IARA) with its seat in Brussels.[148] The Agreement on its foundation entered into force January 24, 1946, after the following countries had signed it: Albania, Australia, Belgium, Canada, Czechoslovakia, Denmark, Egypt, France, Greece, India, Luxembourg, Netherlands, New Zealand, Norway, South Africa, Yugoslavia as well as the UK and the USA. The Agreement contained a percentage distribution schedule for all member countries. Excluding the highest percentages for the two Anglo-Saxon countries, which didn't claim their full share anyway, France was entitled to receive about 37 percent, by far the largest chunk of German reparations on the Agency's account.[149]

The USSR and France, the latter being afraid of a resurgence of German economic power, soon failed to honor other essential parts of the Potsdam Agreement, especially to treat all four occupation zones as a single economic unit and to insure "the equitable distribution of essential commodities between the several zones, so as to produce a balanced economy throughout Germany, and reduce the need for imports."[150] For these reasons General Clay halted reparation deliveries from dismantling existing plant and equipment of the American zone in May 1946, also to bolster West Germany's economic and export capacity and thereby relieve the American taxpayer of financial burden in the support of Germany.

Historians took it for granted that Clay's suspension of reparation deliveries from the US zone was aimed at the Soviets. Jean Edward Smith's discovery of Clay's more than 700 letters and cables in the Modern Military Records Branch of the National Archives in the summer of 1971, which had remained untouched, and his publication of those documents in 1974, changed the picture. Clay's stop of reparations was not primarily aimed at the Soviets, but at France.[151] In his book, based mainly on those documents as well as a great multitude of interviews he had conducted with Clay over several years, Smith further expounds that on the treatment of Germany as a single economic unit the American military governor had more difficulty with the French than with the Soviets. Paris demanded and against the initial opposition of Clay was conceded by Secretary of State James F. Byrnes the creation of a Saar state independent from Germany. They hoped that this move would soften French opposition to a central unified administration of Germany on a quadripartite level.[152] But it was to no avail. The French would remain adamant in their resistance to establish central economic and financial policy institutions for Germany as a whole as long as this question and a quadripartite currency reform were discussed in the ACC.

Whenever the Anglo-Saxon powers pushed ahead, for example, in creating the Bizone and preparing for currency reform, France, with its strong Communist Party that favored treating Germany as a single economic unit, felt supported in its resistance to just this by the Soviet procrastination tactics against Anglo-Saxon initiatives to fulfill the Potsdam Agreement. It felt entitled to do so as it had not been invited to the Potsdam Conference and not participated in negotiations and the signing of the Agreement. In the spring of 1948 when the dice had been cast to implement a West German currency reform in the Bizone and to prepare for the founding of a West German state, both with or without the French zone, Clay burst out in anger over French reactions in a dispatch to the War Department on January 12, 1948:

It seems always as if France and the Communists [the Soviet Union] take the same position, if for different reasons and we can only please the former by doing what the latter want. ... It is difficult to understand how the French expect the Americans and British to discuss with them arrangements which they could protest but in which they have indicated no willingness as yet to participate. In point of fact, we are getting somewhat tired here of always having the finger pointed at us for offending French pride by taking Bizonal actions without French approval, instead of having the finger pointed at the French for wanting to be a partner in planning but independent in operation.[153]

Ironically and against Soviet wishes and expectations French willingness to cooperate on currency reform and state building in West Germany was stimulated by Marshal Sokolovky's walkout of the ACC on March 20, 1948.[154] It signaled that a quadripartite solution to the German problem was dead. The French zone was now confronted with two options: either going it alone economically and politically or integrating into the Bizone. Clay and the British military governor had made it very clear to their French counterpart, General Pierre Koenig, that they would progress with a West German currency reform and the founding of a West German state no matter whether the French would participate or not. This left reluctant Frenchmen, including General Koenig, little choice but to cooperate.[155] For, doing it alone in the French zone would have been extremely costly in terms of continued high subsidies to feed the population and to keep production afloat. This way Paris would have foregone an opportunity to relieve itself of a substantial financial burden on the French budget and to profit from the benefits of the prospective revival of economic activity in the bi- or tripartite economic unit being created in West Germany.

The French had equipped the Saar with its own constitution creating democratically legitimized institutions. But all political decisions were subject to approval of a French High Commissioner. And economically the Saar was fully integrated into the French economy, its customs borders, and its currency area.[156] As the Saar question burdened French–German relations and stood in the way of deepening West European economic integration, Paris proposed a Europeanization of the Saar state with a High Commissioner from the West European Union. The French and West German governments negotiated and agreed on a Saar Statute with plans to turn the Saar into the capital of Europe subject to approval of the Saar population. But the referendum on October 23, 1955 resulted in a slightly more than two-thirds majority of the Saar citizens against the Statute. This outcome was interpreted as a vote for a return to Germany, also by Paris. It required new French–German negotiations, reaching agreement on the political reunification of the Saar with the Federal Republic of Germany on January 1, 1957. A gradual reintegration of the Saar with the West German economy followed thereafter.[157]

The French further demanded to garrison Allied troops permanently on the left bank of the Rhine including cities like Cologne and Mainz. This was actually realized, but on a temporary basis only. And they wanted to detach the industrial heartland, the Ruhr district with 13 million inhabitants, from Germany and place it under international control. However, this demand was opposed by both Anglo-Saxon powers and remained unfulfilled.[158]

After Clay's cessation of reparation deliveries to the Soviets, they concentrated on demanding reparations from current production of the Western zones. In violation of the Potsdam Agreement the Soviets had been practicing this in their own zone.

Bruce Kuklick sees the tug-of-war over reparations as a (if not the) major contributing factor to the unfolding of the Cold War and of developments leading to the division of Germany. The Russian demand for reparations clashed with the American determination to preserve a unified Germany on principles of liberal democracy and market economy and keep communism out of the whole of Germany, and if this wasn't possible, out of Western Germany.

Should the choice of the latter option be inevitable, the goal of four-power cooperation in administering the whole of Germany as an economic unit, as agreed in Potsdam, would have to be abandoned.[159] Actually, already between the war's end in Europe in May 1945 and the beginning of the Potsdam Conference in July 1945, George Kennan, Charles Bohlen, Averell Harriman and other farsighted friends had presaged that the wartime alliance with the Soviet Union would not survive the end of World War II. The ideological differences about the organization of the economy and of democracy would preclude an understanding on ruling Germany as an economic and political unit. They would inevitably not only result in the division of Germany, but also in the division of Europe.[160]

On the American side, Edward Tenenbaum played an important role in the tug-of-war over reparations. He wrote a 20-page single-spaced secret memo on October 30, 1946 entitled *Reparations From Current Production and Present Economic Policy*. This memo obviously captured the essence of the US position on the issue so well that it was retyped the following day and distributed by OMGUS Chief of Staff.[161] So it must have been considered as having been of exceptionally high quality and importance for shaping OMGUS reparations policy vis-à-vis the Soviets.

What was the situation in the East–West tug-of-war over reparations when Tenenbaum wrote his memo? In the autumn of 1946 the Americans and British were negotiating on the fusion of their respective occupation zones, the *Bizone*, becoming effective on January 1, 1947. It might well have been that this fact prompted the Soviet overtures and willingness to compromise on a deal over "more reparations from Western zones" in exchange for four-zonal economic and financial administrations. In his memo Tenenbaum refers only to the following two factors: a dire need of reparations to subdue economic difficulties in the USSR and the failure to win mass support in their own Russian zone. These "may have convinced them that it would be wise to participate in the determination of the fate of all Germany rather than seek exclusive control of a part of Germany." Whatever, Tenenbaum regards the proposed change of the Potsdam Agreement so fundamental a policy change that it requires the most careful consideration against the background of genuine US interests. He starts his memo with a summary of the new political setting:

> 1. There is now under discussion a plan for revision of the Potsdam Agreement to permit reparations deliveries from current German production. The Soviet Union, on the one hand, urgently needs immediate delivery of consumer goods to relieve internal stresses at home. The Western powers, on the other hand, the US in particular, seek economic unification of Germany as a means of reducing the costs of occupation and relief and are willing to pay some price to break the present stalemate with the Soviets in Berlin. //
> 2. An informal proposal has therefore been made by the Russians to legitimize and expand deliveries out of current German production to Russia, in return for agreement by the Soviets to the establishment of economic unity.

Tenenbaum goes on detailing the Soviet proposal under six points concerned with the resumption of capital goods reparations from the Western zones, reparations to the USSR (and Poland) and to the IARA (Inter-Allied Reparations Agency in Brussels) nations from current production in all four zones and the necessary change of the Potsdam Agreement and of the level of industry plan by decisions in the ACC, the provision of raw materials "needed for reparations out of current production will be provided by the recipient nations until Germany has a favorable trade balance and can furnish them herself." The Soviets further offered the establishment by ACC of Central German Administrative Departments, the elimination of all zonal control of economic matters (with the exception of capital goods reparations), and an agreement on a balanced import–export program for Germany as a whole to eliminate the burden on the [mainly Western] occupying powers for the importation of food and other essentials.

Subsequently the memo mentions three additions that the American side put on the bargaining table: 1.) A common budget for occupation costs and reparations for checking excesses by anyone of the occupying powers; 2.) Agreement on a currency reform: and 3.) "Political uniformity, including basic civil liberties, freedom of movement, freedom from arbitrary arrest and the right to fair and public trial, freedom for all political parties in all Zones, free interchange of newspapers between Zones, etc." (p. 1)

We don't know if the Soviets would ever have compromised on these American demands or not. In any case a deal was never struck. The main reason seems to be the following: Tenenbaum had recognized the Trojan horse in the Soviet offer. He convinced OMGUS that reparations from current production, which the Soviets practiced in their zone, also from the three Western zones would increase the financial burden of the Anglo-Saxon taxpayers, not of German producers and taxpayers. The case is clear when current production is diverted from exports to reparations, the deficit between German exports and absolutely necessary import requirements for food and other essentials would be widened and thus the bill for the Anglo-Saxon powers in support of Germany increased. After dismissing this case, Tenenbaum probes the alternative that a net expansion of production as a whole can be generated and made available for reparations.

With reference to economic theory, Tenenbaum rejects the assumption that the removal of zonal barriers by itself would lead to a substantial increase in productivity and output:

> when output is low, marginal productivities (the productivities of small increases in resources used in production) are so high that almost any increase in output is desirable, irrespective of relative efficiency. Only when output approaches full utilization of capacity

do marginal productivities drop to a point where market situations (such as the possibility of using alternative facilities available in other Zones) need very careful consideration. (p. 3)

Tenenbaum asserts that neither the zonal economic boundaries nor the level of industry plan nor reparation removals nor the lack of replacement for worn-out machinery are causing the fact that current production in the Western zones is only about one-third of existing capacity. It would not be likely, "even under the best of circumstances, that Germany will attain full utilization of the agreed level of industry for at least three to five years." (p. 4).

The most apparent limitation on current production would be the lack of coal, the basis of virtually all industrial activity in Germany. Coal production would in itself pose a question of how to increase its productivity and output.

For increasing coal and overall productivity and production in the West German economy Tenenbaum discusses three frequently suggested areas for tackling the problem: food, incentives, and organization. As to food, Tenenbaum compares food rations for coal miners and normal consumers as well as productivity levels in different zones and finds that the Soviet zone with the lowest food rations displays the highest productivity. He dismisses the thesis that food is a cause for the low productivity in coal output.

As to incentives, Tenenbaum differentiates between impediments to higher productivity from the financial situation and from the shortage of consumer goods. With a huge accumulated monetary overhang from financing Nazi war expenditure by using the money printing presses, on the one hand, and legal prices still kept at the price-stop level of 1936, on the other, the incentives were set to either not producing at all or to hoarding produced goods. The result was that those who worked could not spend their entire earnings legally. As many Germans possessed large savings they could afford not to work at all. Only currency reform would be a final solution to these financial disincentives to work.

As to the provision of more consumer goods as an incentive to increase productivity, Tenenbaum sees this as a demand for increasing support payments by the Anglo-Saxon powers for financing more imports of such goods. He becomes very explicit:

> Germany is virtually a bottomless pit insofar as possible absorption of foreign imports is concerned. ... Each additional act of charity, weakening the necessity and will for self-help, may well defeat its own purpose by making the German economy proportionally less able to take care of itself. ... To some extent, the lack of consumer goods will disappear with the introduction of the financial reform. There is ample evidence that relatively large stocks of merchandise are now hoarded throughout Germany. It may be predicted on the basis of experience in other countries (particularly Hungary) that these will come out of hiding once the value of the currency is reestablished. (pp. 8–9)

Needless to say that Tenenbaum rejects the lack-of-consumer-goods thesis for explaining the low level of productivity.

The memo's last candidate for this sort of explanation is "organization." Tenenbaum contends that the organization of the economy is normally accomplished through a functioning monetary system. But the nonperforming monetary conditions in Germany could not be repaired for some time to come. In the interim the German (and thereby the European) economy must be organized by stop-gap measures to progress on the path to a self-supporting economy. While production in the US zone ran at only one-third of industrial capacity, the share was much higher in the Soviet zone. Organization of the respective economies would explain the difference. A greater difference between food rations for normal consumers and for workers in the Soviet than in the US zone would create higher incentives to work. The same would result from a much stricter enforcement of the different categories for food rations in the Soviet zone than in the American and British zones. Also the Soviet Military Administration would enforce the fulfillment of production quotas much more seriously than the American and British authorities, and would even punish managers who did not meet their assigned quotas.

Tenenbaum criticizes that the necessities of life, particularly food, are being provided to the US and British zones as charity, without corresponding effective obligations to work:

> But true charity should be creative charity; it should seek to assist where possible in the rehabilitation of the recipient. It should not make the receiver more fortunate than the non-recipients who are self-supporting. Relief scales should not be higher than work scales. But, under present conditions it is frequently true that those who are engaged in useful occupations are at a disadvantage. They receive rations of food and other consumer items which are not really greater than those of idlers, since the idlers have the time to seek illegal supplements in the black market. A miner who works six days a week receives enough food to equalize the outflow of calories caused by his extra exertion. A miner who works four days a week receives only a little less food, and has three days to find extra food in the neighboring countryside. A voluntarily unemployed person receives a basic ration sufficient to maintain life, and has seven days out of the week to seek supplements illegally. (p. 13)

If "black market" is substituted by "illegal labor market," Tenenbaum's exposition could still today serve as a useful contribution to political discussions in Germany about the level and duration of unemployment relief payments.

Tenenbaum elaborates another example, the distribution of building materials, to show that the allocation of scarce products is not geared to the goal of increasing productivity and production in the American and British zones at all. And with his sense of black humor and comprehensive knowledge of history, both so typical for Tenenbaum, he continues:

> Only if US and British policy is in fact the reconstruction of
> German heavy industry in preparation for a war against the US and

Great Britain can present measures be explained logically.
Certainly it is not proposed to build up heavy industry in Germany
for a war against the Soviets. ... To rely on the German people to
fight against the Soviets under all future circumstances would be to
ignore the history of Russo-German relations, which shows six
sudden shifts in the last thirty years. Furthermore, the policy of the
US and Great Britain is one of peace, and the reconstruction of
German heavy industry for a war against Russia would hardly
contribute to peace. (p. 14)

Thereafter, Tenenbaum reminds the addressees of his memo of the
immediate and avowed national interests of the US and Great Britain
in the management of the German economy: 1. To reduce the costs of
occupation and relief by making Germany self-sufficient. 2.
To prevent Germany from ever again becoming a military power
capable of destroying world security. 3. To restore Germany's fundamental place in the European economy as a supplier of manufactured
goods and coal. 4. To lay the foundation for a peaceful and democratic
society in Germany by providing a reasonably adequate standard of
living and full employment. All four goals would require an increase
in German exports.

Next, he deals with the question of what type of export
Germany should specialize in. Without mentioning the term, he
answers the question along the lines of the *Heckscher-Ohlin* model,
a basic theorem in foreign trade theory. It explains what export structure is optimal for an economy depending on its relative endowment
with factors of production. Tenenbaum observes correctly that of the
three production factors, natural resources, labor, and capital,
Germany is traditionally poor (with the exception of coal) in natural
resources and, caused by the tremendous wastage during the war,
currently also in capital. But labor would be its abundant production
factor. Wartime losses in population had been overcompensated by
the influx of millions of expellees from the territories ceded to Poland
and Russia.

Thus, Germany must concentrate on exporting labor [-intensive] goods. Heavy industry requires little labor and much capital and natural resources. Light industry requires much labor, and less capital and natural resources. Thus, German exports should be based on an increase in light industry, which, with limited resources, means a decrease in heavy industry. In other words, to provide greater employment with the present limited raw materials base, emphasis must be placed on light (particularly consumer goods) industries, which require a large proportion of manpower in relation to such limited raw material resources as coal, rather than on heavy industries (such as steel production) which require little manpower and much coal. Light industries, however, require imported raw materials to a greater extent than heavy industries. This, too, means that exports must be increased. (pp. 14–15)

As a sort of statistical underpinning of previously advanced arguments, Tenenbaum then reports very interesting facts on economic developments in the US zone, such as (p. 15):

- from March to June 1946 the share of import expenditures covered by export receipts declined from 8 to 3 percent;
- from December 1945 to July 1946 US zone industrial production increased from 10 to 29 percent of existing capacity;
- in July 1946 US zone current production reached much higher percentages of the estimated 1949 level of industry in domestic heavy industries (e.g., 87 percent for gas and electric power, 73 percent for steel products, and 54 percent for cement) than in potential export industries (e.g., only 21 percent for household and decorative ceramics, 18 percent for optical goods, 17 percent for dyes, 10 percent for radio tubes, and only 2 percent for radio receivers).

The reason for the lag in export production is simple. All German industries are based on coal and its products. Coal has been allocated to the reconstruction of Germany rather than to production for export. [For example,] in the distribution of available coal tar, roofing materials and highway repair have obtained greater

> priority than the production of pharmaceuticals and dyes which
> could be used for export. ... The real value to the occupying power
> and to the German people as a whole of exports to pay for imports
> would seem to be far greater than the value of additional factory
> roofs and fewer bumps in the roads of Germany. (p. 16)

With only one-third of existing industrial capacity in use, Tenenbaum
criticizes intentions to allocate more coal to the buildup of even more
capacity as "somewhat extravagant."

> It is, of course, in the German interest to reconstruct as rapidly as
> possible, to obtain as much help as possible from abroad and return
> as little payment as possible in the form of exports. It is in the
> American interest for Germany to pay her own way as soon as
> possible ... For over 30 years Germany has lived on foreign bounty
> in the form of defaulted loans and war loot. The reliance on free
> gifts from abroad has led inevitably to war. The foreign donors
> eventually ceased supporting Germany of their own volition and
> had to be forced to continue in order to prevent collapse of the
> resulting one-sided economy in Germany. It is in the American
> interest that these habits be broken. (pp. 17–18)[162]

Tenenbaum speaks of "a curious mixture" of policy in the US and
German interest that causes inefficiency, because it becomes difficult
to set priorities with a clear aim in view. Priorities would be given to
the latest project under consideration. Therefore, virtually everything
in Germany would have priority. This would also apply in Germany's
foreign trade, made visible by the habit that each interested agency
claims that its particular import is essential.

   In conclusion Tenenbaum lists two options for paying reparations from current production: Either the US and British governments "pour even more wealth into the German economy, on the
theory that what the patient needs is more of the old prescription."
(p. 19) Or a solution that would require a number of changes to present
economic policy. The latter one – aimed at strengthening incentives

to work and produce goods for export and domestic consumption – would be less comfortable, but would hold greater prospects of acceptance by the US public, and possibly greater prospects of success. Its essential elements would be:

1. A single plan, according to unalterable and agreed principles on priorities, for the German economy as a whole.
2. Overriding priority to production of coal; next highest priority to current production for reparations and export.
3. The reparations and export plans should "not draw so much from the German economy as to prevent the manufacture of a small amount of incentive goods (such as clothing, bicycles, and miners' housing)." (p. 20, also for the following quotations in this list)
4. "Further reconstruction of any German industry should be prohibited until economic activity increases to 100 percent utilization of existing capacity."
5. Food rations of persons declared fit to work by medical authorities, but are unwilling to accept jobs offered to them by the German Labor Office, should be cut to 1,000 calories, i.e., by about one-third in the US and British zones. "With the exception of food and children's clothing, *all* consumer goods should be distributed as incentives to workers in priority industries, distribution to be dependent on satisfactory work records."
6. "Except for raw materials imported solely for the purpose of producing export goods, imports should be limited to food, fertilizer, and a minimum amount of petroleum, until such time as Germany exports enough to pay for current imports."
7. The overall plan should be revised annually. According to fixed principles, the share of current production allocated to the domestic market should be increased as industrial productivity rises.
8. "In order to restore incentives to entrepreneurs, quotas of raw materials (particularly imported raw materials) should be distributed to permit full output in plants showing the greatest efficiency, and should be withdrawn from plants whose production does not go exclusively and without delay to satisfy legal demands."

I regard this memo of Tenenbaum to be an exercise in organizing incentives for workers and entrepreneurs (or managers) in order to increase production and productivity in a centrally planned economy.

There the distribution of scarce goods is not based on monetary demand in proportion to goods supply. Money has little value when prices are fixed to avoid the inflationary manifestations of a money overhang caused by the misuse of the banknote printing press for financing public expenditure. Therefore, under such circumstances workers and managers of firms need incentives other than money earnings. Tenenbaum is well aware that for the interim period until currency reform his suggestions for creating stronger incentives would only be a second-best solution compared to the incentives provided automatically by a largely free market economy, with approximately equivalent volumes of money supply and supply of goods and services, which would result in stable prices.

Tenenbaum's focus on the restoration of production incentives, even under conditions of a fully controlled economy, in his reparations memo of October 30/31, 1946 must have increased his reputation as an economic and financial expert in OMGUS and Washington, DC departments by leaps and bounds. That he would be chosen by OMGUS to execute German monetary reform, the first-best solution for creating economic incentives, is most likely a consequence of the basic aims, the logical reasoning, and the convincing style of his reparations memo.

A more obvious, but for reasons given in Tenenbaum's memo less effective measure to increase work and production incentives is what Lucius Clay mentions in his memoirs on the doings of his military government in Germany: "Prior to 1948 wage ceilings were raised by 10–20 per cent in coal and other mining fields, building construction, building materials, textiles, clothing, manufacturing, railroads, and forestry, which permitted limited opportunity for collective bargaining."[163]

It was not his reparations memo that Tenenbaum either considered to be his best or selected as being more pertinent to the agenda of the job he was applying for. It was rather a similarly long memo, nineteen single-spaced pages, of February 15, 1948 entitled *Why We Trade for Dollars*.[164] He mentioned only this one on a four-item list of publications that he attached to his *Application for Federal Employment* of September 1948.[165] Vis-à-vis the prevailing shortage of dollars in Europe, the obligation to cover bilateral disequilibria between imports and exports of the Bizone in American currency had been much criticized not only by West German merchants, but even more by businessmen and governments of other European countries. But OMGUS kept insisting on compliance with the hard-currency rule to prevent bilateralism and discrimination as well as to further multilateralism and most-favored nation treatment. Tenenbaum's memo discusses the reasons for the US position. He starts out with:

> 1. In recent years US policy in the field of international trade has become clearly defined. It is – as any policy should be – a mixture of self-interest and idealism, of a desire to further the interests of the United States, and of a desire to further the real interests of other countries of the world. Favorable to a development of a clear and consistent policy is the fact that at present the two are identical in many ways. (p. 1)

Instead of going through all of the thirty-four points into which the memo is subdivided I here jump to the conclusion which reads like a summary of the memo:

> 32. US policy, it may be concluded, is and should be based on the belief that all these problems can be solved, not merely without abandoning the framework of free enterprise, but specifically by retaining the free enterprise system insofar as it exists or restoring it insofar as it is atrophied. The Marshall Plan is a gigantic gamble to that effect. If it proves correct, Military Government will find that present faith in multilateral policies will pay off in the form of speedier recovery of Germany. The possibility that the Marshall Plan will not be a successful gamble may also be envisaged. But US Military Government, as an organ of the US government, cannot attempt to hedge against this possibility. Bizonal Germany is, to

some extent, a testing ground for US policies. It is a yardstick by which the practicality of multilateral trade may be judged in surrounding countries, a potentially potent example which may have greater influence than we imagine on the policies of other European countries. If Military Government abandons its multilateral principles, if in particular it ceases to import and export in accordance with the principle of free convertibility of proceeds, it will in effect confess that even the US Government does not believe, that such policies are practical. Such a confession is inconceivable unless the US Government itself abandons these principles. // 33. There is no evidence that multilateral policies must fail. On the contrary, the disadvantages of bilateral trade are obvious. European countries may legitimately criticize the bizonal area for not spending in Europe the dollars it obtains from sales to Europe, though this situation is rapidly being corrected. Already the European offset accounts of the bizonal area have reached an approximate net balance: We owe as much to some countries as others owe to us. The current import program may be expected in addition to put back into European circulation a large part of our dollar income from coal sales outside the offset agreements. But no single European country has valid grounds upon which to insist that we balance our trade with it alone, rather than with Europe as a whole. It is admitted – at least in theory – that a bilateral balance with individual countries would be most unnatural under modern conditions, and would hamper the recovery of Europe. If we restore approximate balance in trade with Europe as a whole, it will likewise have to be admitted that favoritism shown to one European country would be at the expense of another, perhaps equally deserving. If we are to be criticized, therefore, it should be for our past concentration on the development of exports, to the partial exclusion of a comparable development of imports, not for attempting to follow the rules of economic sanity. // 34. We may welcome criticism of this nature, since it is in our own interests to see healthy trade develop in both directions between the bizonal area and the rest of Europe. We should, perhaps, begin to consider what price we can afford to pay as a contribution to European cooperation. Resources may be available to meet this price in connection with the Marshall Plan. But none of these considerations need lead to a system which cannot even name its price. No concern for a return to normal in Europe should lead to the abandonment of our own efforts to conduct trade in a normal manner. Therefore we trade for dollars. (pp. 18–19)

When using "We" in the quotation above, Tenenbaum identifies himself more with the long-term interests of Germans, most of them at the time governed by the Anglo-Saxon military powers, than with his US government in Washington, DC. In other words, he argues in favor of the genuine German interest in overcoming impediments to trade and thereby paving the way to a speedy economic recovery. This is probably the consequence of what he stated in his opening paragraph "that at present the two [US government and German interests] are identical in many ways." Tenenbaum shows a clear vision of the economic and political benefits of European integration and of the essential role West Germany's economic recovery would play in it.

Also with a view to his currency reform, West Germany had more luck than it deserved, not only after Germany's war mongering all over Europe, but also after organizing the holocaust, the worst crime against humanity in modern history. Tenenbaum, as the best qualified and, although Jewish, unprejudiced man was at the right time at the right place, Berlin, where OMGUS shaped Germany's economic future as part of an integrated Europe. And he should continue to do so after his return to Washington, DC and working there with the Marshall Plan administration ECA, charged mainly with the establishment of the European Payments Union.

OMGUS introduced US-style public opinion surveys in Germany on all sorts of questions in order to find out about the attitudes of the German population on occupations policies. The need for currency reform and – after it had happened – the evaluation of it and its consequences were polled. A survey of July 1, 1946 showed that 40 percent in the US zone and 52 percent in West Berlin opposed a currency reform at that time, a surprising result in view of the fact that almost all respondents were blaming the black market for the bad economic situation.[166]

But once currency reform had been instituted:

> Nine in ten termed it necessary, and over half (53%) thought that it should have taken place earlier. It tended to create an optimistic mood: Over half (54%) expected the new currency to retain its value, 58 per cent believed that they would get along better during the coming year because of the currency reform, seven in ten intended to make additional purchases, and most expected the reform either to limit (71%) or overcome (14%) the black market. There was nonetheless some dissatisfaction. It focused particularly upon the ten to one conversion ratio which, according to more than a third (35%) of the AMZON (American Zone of Occupation) Germans, treated the small savers more harshly than the rich. And 77 per cent expected – correctly, as it turned out – that the currency reform would lead to greater unemployment.[167]

While OMGUS was still hopeful to achieve a joint currency reform in all of Germany's four occupation zones and Edward Tenenbaum was preparing for such a C-Day on the basis of the CDG Plan, his and Jeanette Kipp's first child Anne Kipp Tenenbaum was born in Berlin on April 19, 1947. This fell into the period when the Council of Foreign Ministers was in session in Moscow from March 10 to April 25, 1947 negotiating about peace treaties with Germany and Austria. The American delegation, headed by Secretary of State George Marshall, including as his new adviser John Forster Dulles from the Republican Party, made a two-day stopover in Berlin, arriving March 8 to be briefed by Clay and his staff on the state of four-power negotiations in the ACC and on the position of OMGUS on shaping Germany's political and economic future.

Although Clay had asked to be excused from attending the Moscow conference, he received a cable that his attendance was desired, by Secretary of State Marshall himself. Clay flew to Moscow immediately and participated in proceedings until Marshall approved his request to return to his duties in Berlin on March 31, 1947. Beyond that, OMGUS was represented at the Moscow conference with Clay's political adviser Robert Murphy, economic experts under General William H. Draper, Clay's economic adviser, and experts in governmental affairs under General Henry Parkman and Dr. Edward H. Lichtfield. Neither Edward Tenenbaum nor his boss Jack Bennett, Clay's financial adviser, were participants of the Moscow conference. But Tenenbaum was involved in its preparation. Describing his duties as special assistant for finance and currency matters in OMGUS Berlin, he writes in an attachment to his September 1948 *Application for Federal Employment*: "preparation of recommendations as to US position at the Council of Foreign Ministers."

However, Charles P. Kindleberger was part of the American delegation in Moscow. During its two-day stopover in Berlin, he certainly met with Tenenbaum again, his fellow economist and old friend from the early days of OSS' R&A in Washington, DC in the second half of 1942 and later in the European battlefield in OSS, G-2, and syke-war (PWD) positions in General Omar Bradley's 12th US Army Group. It was here at the latest that especially Kindleberger as fellow economist integrated Tenenbaum's recommendations into the American negotiating position for the foreign minister's meeting in Moscow.

Kindleberger had returned from Germany very soon after the end of the war in Europe and immediately had begun working for the State Department. In Moscow he made a significant contribution to ward off false Soviet allegations against the Americans that they were seizing German patents for exclusive use. He impressed Clay so much that he made it into Clay's memoirs. Clay reports that Kindleberger had brought with him, "in case the occasion should arise, a letter from the Soviet commercial representative in Washington to the Secretary of Commerce thanking him for the German patent data made available to the Soviet Government ... I am sure that Marshall enjoyed reading this letter, which caught Molotov [the Soviet foreign minister] by surprise and even produced smiles on the customary poker faces of his staff."[168]

The Council of Foreign Ministers conference in Moscow ended in failure. This prompted the Anglo-Saxon powers, who for efficiency reasons had fused their occupation zones in Germany into the Bizone at the start of 1947, to prepare for a separate currency reform in case a quadripartite financial reform via the ACC in Berlin should continue to be unattainable. This was the beginning of Tenenbaum's historic role in Germany's economic and financial history, the planning, preparing and executing of West Germany's currency reform of 1948.

Section 3.2 on Tenenbaum's military service ended with my description of a trip he was ordered by OMGUS to take in March 1946 for two purposes: 1.) dealings for OMGUS in the Treasury Department in Washington, DC and 2.) release from active military duty at Separation Center No. 27 at Fort Meade MD. Tenenbaum's temporary duty in the Treasury is of interest in this chapter. Originally planned and ordered for about two days, it actually lasted four full workdays from March 18 to 21, 1946. Even with the support of expert archivists for Treasury Records at the National Archives at College Park MD, I was unable to locate documents revealing what Tenenbaum did or was assigned to do in the Treasury during those four days. In view of his assignment as financial and currency expert to OMGUS, he was probably briefed on Treasury views and plans for Germany's financial future.

Whenever OMGUS had to deal with financial questions, such as currency, fiscal, and reparation matters, Tenenbaum was involved. He wrote studies and memoranda on such issues.

He represented OMGUS in committee meetings of the ACC. He played important roles in the formation and Allied supervision of financial policies of the Bizone in practice. And due to his excellent knowledge of English, German, and French as well as some rudimentary Russian he often played the role of a liaison person with his counterparts in other military governments and with German politicians and financial experts. And he was traveling a lot between capitals of the three Western Allies and Berlin. He also shuttled between US Headquarters in Berlin and in Frankfurt am Main. The Western military governments concentrated most German political and administrative institutions in and around the latter city, while they delegated more and more of their own political power to them. OMGUS envisioned Frankfurt am Main as the future capital of a West German state. But the Federal Republic's first Chancellor Konrad Adenauer pleaded for Bonn as a provisional small-town capital. After Germany's reunification in 1990 it was decided by parliament to move the capital again to Berlin.

The above-mentioned "Preliminary Agreement on the Establishment of a Joint German Committee for Finance," which Tenenbaum had drafted and circulated, is a good case in point. In Article 1 the Agreement stipulates: *"A Joint Committee for Finance* is established. Its seat is in or near Frankfurt." The second meeting of the German Joint Committee took place on October 11, 1946 in the Reichsbank building in Frankfurt, with Tenenbaum representing OMGUS temporarily present.[169]

The same file contains a long list written November 23, 1946 with scheduled meetings of the German Joint Committee for Finance, which was abbreviated as BIXFIN, its subcommittees and working parties at Frankfurt with dates and subjects.[170] When BIXFIN and BIFIN (Bipartite Finance Control Group with only American and British members) had a joint meeting, the abbreviation for this larger group was BIGFIN. BIFIN and BIGFIN meetings were chaired by either Lt. Col. Emory D. Stoker for the USA or by Mr. J. T. Lisle for the British military government.[171] Stoker was the chief financial officer of US military government in Frankfurt am Main, while Tenenbaum was assigned to OMGUS in Berlin. One can safely assume that Tenenbaum flew in from Berlin to also participate in some of the BIFIN and BIGFIN meetings.

After the Council of Foreign Ministers conference in Moscow had not produced an agreement on peace treaties with Germany (and Austria) and thus failed in April 1947, the Anglo-Saxon occupation powers intensified planning for a separate West German currency reform. Somewhat connected to that, they transferred more and more of their political power into German hands by creating new institutions as precursors of a West German democratic Federal Republic.

The trouble for the *United Economic Area* of the US and British occupation zones, the Bizone, from January 1, 1947 was a political image problem. As long as negotiations on a quadripartite currency reform on the level of the ACC were continued, even though only formally (until the Soviets left ACC on March 20, 1948), the Western powers would face the blame for the breakdown of quadripartite negotiations and for the breach of the Potsdam Agreement in case they executed a currency reform for the Western zones only. Heinz Sauermann, a sort of secretary and insider of the CDG Commission, describes OMGUS' assessment of a way out of this political impasse:

> A fundamental change in the situation could only be expected and brought about by the fact that, in the areas where the currency reform was to be implemented, German authorities existed or were in the process of being established, to whom the implementation could be wholly or partly left.[172]

On June 25, 1947, after the failed meeting of the Council of Foreign Ministers in Moscow, the US and British military governments created the Economic Council (*Wirtschaftsrat*) as a German parliament for their United Economic Area (Bizone) with its seat in Frankfurt am Main. Its fifty-two members were elected proportionately to population size and party affiliation by the (German) members of the already existing state (*Länder*) parliaments. It was equipped with legislative powers, albeit its acts were subject to approval of the bipartite military governments. It was the forerunner of the *Bundestag*, the parliament of the Federal Republic of Germany constituted on September 7, 1949 as the outcome of the first federal elections in West Germany.

At the same time, an Executive Council (*Exekutivrat*) was created, a federal second chamber of parliament representing the eight states (*Länder*) of the Bizone with one vote each. This was obviously modeled according to the constitution of the US Senate, with two seats for each state independently of the size of its population. It turned out that the Social Democratic Party (SPD), representing the predominant anti-capitalist mood among the West German population, would have a solid majority in the federal Executive Council. But the stronger role originally envisaged for the Executive Council was not implemented, because General Clay apprehended that, otherwise, Germany could drift toward socialism.[173]

At the same time as the establishment of the Economic Council, directorates or administrations for five different political fields were created, among them both for Economic Affairs and for Finance. The respective directors were nominated by the Executive Council and elected by the Economic Council. They were each equipped with German personnel as administrative staff and with respective committees of the Economic Council. When all five directors had been elected by July 22, 1947, the directorate of all five constituted an embryonic West German government, including the forerunners of the Ministries of Economic Affairs and of Finance of the Federal Republic of Germany.

In preparation of a West German currency reform, OMGUS urged the founding of the Special Agency for Money and Credit (*Sonderstelle Geld und Kredit*) in Bad Homburg. It was to be a commission of German financial experts attached to the Administration for Finance, with Alfred Hartmann as its director. However, it was designed to be professionally independent and not bound by instructions of the Director of the Administration for Finance, the Economic Council, the Anglo-Saxon Allies, or any other institution. Its tasks were described as preliminary works concerning:

1. the elimination of the excess of money and the actual currency reform;
2. the financial reform as a whole and in this context the equalization of possessions and burdens;
3. the management of public budgets, taking into account the aforementioned reforms;
4. the planning of credit policy required thereafter.[174]

The decision by the German Economic Council to create it was taken July 23, 1947. It started its top secret mission October 10, 1947 in Villa Hansa, Kisseleffstraße 21 in Bad Homburg near Frankfurt am Main. This location was the seat of the bizonal Administration for Finance.[175] The former Bavarian Minister of Economic Affairs, Ludwig Erhard, was appointed as its head. Because the Allies had reserved all responsibilities in monetary matters for themselves, the Special Agency was obliged to submit all results of its work to the Anglo-Saxon powers of the Bizone and not to the Economic Council with its German members.

The members of the Special Agency were fully informed about the American CDG Plan of 1946.[176] Erhard knew it already from his personal discussions as Bavarian economics minister with two of its authors, Gerhard Colm and Raymond W. Goldsmith, when they consulted financial experts all over the three Western zones of occupation to test their reactions to the Plan's draft.[177] In his oral history interview, Goldsmith has disclosed that he and Colm "had really argued out the essence of the plan on the plane flying over" to Germany. "As I said, we really had the plan in essence when we came over on the plane."[178] Goldsmith mentions by name only three of the many persons they consulted: Eugen Schmalenbach in Cologne, Alfred Weber in Heidelberg, and Otto Veit who would become the first president of the *Landeszentralbank* (Land Central Bank) in Hesse. Obviously these three Germans were regarded by Goldsmith as top-notch experts. Erhard and many others, among them Erwin Hielscher, who together with Erhard would hold leading positions in the Special Agency for Money and Credit created in 1947, were not named. "I don't think we really got too much out of them. I think we assessed the psychological situation better than they did."[179] So did Charles P. Kindleberger, as we will see in a moment.

What Erhard wrote about his discussions with Colm and Goldsmith as well as with Tenenbaum on another occasion is typical of his often-practiced self-stylization in order to boost his own importance:

> During my time in Munich, I focused my intellectual work on tackling the more than overdue currency reform as quickly as possible. Shortly after the occupation, I had the opportunity to discuss the matter with some outstanding currency experts from American academic and financial circles, without being able to reach full agreement at the time. Conversely, since I was held in high esteem by them, I very soon found myself at the center of German-Allied monetary discussions.[180]

Surprisingly, the CDG Plan came under fire in the ACC less by the Soviets (and the French) than by the British.[181] In essence, the British demanded three changes to the CDG Plan: 1.) A price increase of at least 50 percent before cutting the money overhang in order to reduce the burden on public budgets from price subsidies. 2.) The British regarded the conversion rate of 10 RM to 1 DM as too drastic and deflationary. Therefore, they demanded to reduce the quantity of money by only 60 percent instead of 90 percent. 3.) The cut in the old money volume should not happen for good. Instead half of the 60 percent cut of the quantity of old money should be executed by conversion into irredeemable but transferable 2 percent government bonds and thus be blocked.[182]

Obviously, this British demand for changes to the CDG Plan prompted OMGUS to seek advice again from Gerhard Colm and Raymond Goldsmith. Colm sent his criticism of the British counterproposal directly to Jack Bennett in a letter dated November 19, 1946. Goldsmith summarized his disapproval of the changes the British had proposed in a memo to Charles Kindleberger of November 14, 1946. This memo, in turn, he attached to his letter of November 22 to Jack Bennett. Like Colm, he agreed with the judgment that Bennett had expressed in his report on the British counterproposal "Notes on the Discussions of a Currency Reform" of September 16, 1946.[183]

Maybe Goldsmith had addressed Kindleberger, head of the German desk in the State Department, in the first place, because he thought, Kindleberger would pull the strings there concerning German currency reform. In any case, Goldsmith argued, a controlled inflation prior to currency reform would be incomprehensible and psychologically fatal for the majority of the German population, as the very purpose of a currency reform would be to combat and avoid inflation. Furthermore, such a planned inflation would not be controllable. Also the much milder conversion rate proposed by the British would be inadequate to cope with the dimension of the money overhang. And finally, Goldsmith rejected the exchange of blocked old money against Reich debt securities instead of its extinction. Trade with such securities would have distorting effects and would constitute dangerous additional inflationary potential. This would not be justifiable and should be avoided in any case.[184] The OMGUS representatives in ACC followed Goldsmith's line of reasoning. They were able to largely avert the British counterproposals. This was probably due to superior power of the purse of the USA when Britain was in dire straits and needed US support for a large credit from the IMF, as Arne Weick argues.[185]

On a first name basis, Jack Bennett had a letter exchange with Gerhard Colm from December 3, 1947 until February 18, 1948. It centered around the initiative of General Clay to call on Gerhard Colm again for advice on the currency-reform planning in Germany (Colm was on leave at the time from his post on the Council of Economic Advisers in Washington, DC). General Draper, Clay's former economic adviser and at that time back in Washington, DC as Under Secretary of the Army, repeatedly exerted pressure to clear the way for Colm's desired leave of absence for the envisaged short period with OMGUS, but in the end in vain.[186]

In a more extreme form the somewhat inflationary British approach to currency reform was revitalized within OMGUS in a 6-page memo of August 5, 1947, "Subject: Removal of Price Controls" by Don D. Humphrey, deputy director of the Economics Division of OMGUS. He walked in the footsteps of Sir Paul Chambers, financial adviser of British military government, who in September 1946 had countered the American introduction of the CDG Plan for discussion in the ACC with his British proposal to simply lift price controls and let inflation run its course. But he ran into a united front of the other three powers.[187] Humphrey's opening sentence: "The Bizonal Economy is being controlled to death."[188] This simple measure, that is, removal of price controls, would make currency reform with a conversion of abundant old money into scarce new money superfluous. Open inflation should be let loose, with only a few exceptions, namely bread and potatoes as well as rents, so that "no one would be starved or evicted."

In a 15-page memo "Comments on 'Removal of Price Controls' by Dr. D. D. Humphrey" of August 15, 1947, Tenenbaum started out to admit that logically either free price inflation or a currency reform could transform a controlled economy into a market economy to restore incentives for work and production. But one of his many powerful arguments against "Dr. Humphrey's" proposal was the unconditional necessity of a restoration of confidence of the German population into its currency. An open inflation would destroy it and induce the people and businesses to get rid of their money and flee into real assets (or stable foreign currencies) as quickly as possible. Inflation would open all kinds of profit possibilities for unproductive speculators and would not provide productive companies with the necessary stable basis for calculating useful and profitable investments for the long term. "To have inflation now is to surrender our freedom of action. If we cannot do the right thing [currency reform now], we can keep from doing the wrong thing."

Another memo of August 27, 1947 by the chief of the Wages and Labor Standard Branch, Sol D. Ozer, addressed to his superior, Leo R. Werts, director of the OMGUS Manpower Division June 1946 to 1949, "Subject: Inflation – Is it the Solution of Germany's Ills?" reads in its opening statement:

> The memorandum of Mr. Don Humphrey on "Removal of Price
> Controls" is an amazing document. It is amazing not only because
> of the ideas it contains, but because of its author. Here is a man,
> very high in the councils of the administration, who after seeing
> one hopeful plan after another go awry, finally in desperation turns

to economic drunkedness – inflation – as the easy way out. The situation must indeed be serious to bring forth such advice.

Ozer further argues against Don Humphrey's proposal:

> But nowhere does Mr. Humphrey consider the really fundamental issues which prevent the recovery of Germany, namely // 1. The need for a sound currency. // 2. The need for adequate imported food to enable the Germans to work effectively. // 3. The need for adequate imported raw material to fill up the industrial pipe lines and to provide the substance for consumers' goods. // 4. The need for a few imported manufactured items to break bottlenecks as they develop in Germany's recovery.[189]

As long as the Western Allies still kept the door open for a quadripartite currency reform for all of the four occupation zones, i.e., until the end of the unsuccessful London Conference of Foreign Ministers on December 16, 1947 and even beyond into March 1948, the Anglo-Saxon powers expected from the Special Agency plans that would be compatible with a four-power agreement on currency reform. But in practice the planning had shifted toward a bizonal (or trizonal) reform.[190] The Anglo-Saxon powers saw merit in such planning. Should a currency-reform plan with input from the Special Agency be implemented in the Bizone, it would be one that originated in bizonal democratic institutions, themselves unbound by the Potsdam Agreement. This would neutralize the blame that Potsdam Agreement partners would inflict on the Anglo-Saxon powers in case of a separate currency reform based on the CDG Plan.

Tenenbaum noted that there had been

> growing political pressure for German participation, and even for full assumption of responsibility by the German authorities. ... [But] only the three military governments were able to issue laws applying to more than one Land [State]. Furthermore, we seriously doubted the wisdom of saddling the weak German government

with the enormous responsibility and onus of a currency reform. //
Finally, we had an overriding interest in the success of the reform.
Not only was it essential to our long-range goal of a democratic
Germany, but also to the reduction of the growing annual bill for
economic assistance.[191]

Tenenbaum also observed a contradiction. Currency reform would,
in fact, be dictated by military governments that were committed
and professed to introducing democracy in West Germany.
Benevolent or not, dictatorial methods ran counter "to the philosophy of General Clay. How he resolved the question in his own
conscience we do not know. Perhaps it was by the unfortunate
expedient of consulting fifty German politicians on certain technical
issues at the last minute."[192]

Together with representatives of his British counterpart Bernard
C. Cook (in the minutes of the meeting named as Mr. Schwarz und
Mr. Knoblock) Tenenbaum unofficially participated in the meeting of
the Special Agency for Money and Credit on November 20, 1947,
beginning 10:30 a.m. Due to his superior skills in finance and foreign
languages, he was the recognized authority and speaker of the
Western Allies' currency-reform experts, while Erhard, the chairman
of the Special Agency, was his main discussion partner. Tenenbaum
emphasized that he would not be speaking for military government,
but would only share his personal opinion. "If I were smart, I wouldn't
say anything at all. But at least, to be polite, I have to say
something."[193]

The exchange between Tenenbaum and Erhard on the first five
pages of the minutes revolves around the desire of the Germans to be
brought up to speed on information from the bizonal military governments, especially to be briefed on the CDG plan to avoid duplication
of effort. Erhard claims to already know the content of the plan. But he
would be under obligation not to make it accessible to others.
Tenenbaum is very reluctant to promise anything. But he offered to
make the Special Agency's wish for more information known to his

military government. He also dismissed the argument that duplication of effort should be avoided. The Special Agency should rather be left a wide-open field for developing its own ideas, unaffected by what the Allies had already planned. But he also held out the prospect of "maybe working quite closely together later." (p. 3)

The Special Agency members, in turn, agreed to the implementation of currency reform by military government laws instead of legislation by the German forerunners of full-range democratic institutions that would take over legislative powers from military governments in the future. And they agreed that such a touchy issue like a currency reform could only succeed if its concrete form would not be opened up to parliamentary debate under the influence of interest groups.

They also raised the issue whether currency reform should come second after higher production growth would have set in or whether it should come as quickly as possible. Some circles in Germany believed that only after a production surge, goods supply would suffice to meet monetary demand in a new currency at stable prices. Otherwise, the reform would be doomed to failure. But Tenenbaum and his discussion partners agreed that this fear was groundless. Currency reform would trigger production growth and stocks of hoarded goods were largely available to meet demand if the new currency would be kept scarce at conversion. However, Erhard demanded that industry should shift its output: less production goods, more consumer goods, as he would repeat time and again in articles and speeches during the following months.

The discussion turned to the necessity of founding a central bank as well as to the printing of new banknotes, the costs thereof, and the timeframe. The German experts had no clue that the printing of Deutschmarks was already in full swing in America at the expense of the US government. And Tenenbaum was silent on the subject like a tomb. Also the German experts were still of the opinion that they and the Allies were preparing a currency reform on the four-power level.

Discussion of the conversion rate and of money supply via credit creation and their interdependence follows. Erhard proposes the reintroduction of commercial bills as a credit instrument. It was suggested to start with promissory notes. These should be prolonged by commercial bills three months later. The conversion rate RM to DM became an issue. Erhard and other German experts agreed with Tenenbaum that the initial conversion rate of Reichsmarks into Deutschmarks for individuals for free disposal should not exceed 5 percent. Only the British participants in that meeting advocated a higher conversion rate.

But besides the 5 percent conversion rate for free disposal the members of the Special Agency envisioned another 15 percent conversion of Reichsmarks into Deutschmarks at the rate of 1 to 1 into blocked accounts for later availability in tandem with economic growth and for immediate use as collateral for bank credit. The proposal was driven by the strong interest of the German experts in greasing the wheels of businesses in Germany through generous credit expansion. The Germans went even further. For the 80 percent without any conversion rate, they proposed to transform those amounts into certificates, which would be valid to pay off dues resulting from burden-sharing legislation. This kind of lawmaking was expected not only on the German, but at that time also on the Allied military governments' side, to be implemented simultaneously with currency reform. The German certificates idea also purported to take the heat of burden-sharing levies off the shoulders of businesses.

The whole German program would have been a sure bank for the failure of the currency reform and, in addition, for a failure of a fair equalization of burdens between monetary and real asset owners, since businesses as opposed to households were mainly invested in real assets. Although Tenenbaum was not amused about the cornerstones of German planning, he kept his poise and diplomatically expressed his skepticism in the form of questions.

Also Erhard addressed a question to his American guest: "Have you also thought about whether we need to basically maintain the price and rationing control system that we have today, or do you think we can get back to a free enterprise system?" (p. 18). Erhard is searching out his room for maneuver that the representative of the American military government is willing to grant for his later policy of lifting controls in tandem with currency reform. Tenenbaum answered:

> It's not very easy to go back to a free market. We have experienced that in the United States. In our rich country, it's not very dangerous, but we've also had difficulties. Because you get the same difficulties, it's good to learn from experiences. // I think it is considered right by all of us that we have to go to this. How fast it will come, I don't know. We have to get rid of the excessive government controls. That's going to be the hardest thing, because people have a vested interest in seeing them remain. (p. 18)

Then, until lunch break at 12:45 p.m., issues related to the conversion rate for private debt were discussed. The German experts were not yet in agreement. Some called for at least 20 percent, others could imagine going up to 100 percent. Tenenbaum did not indicate a preference, although he could have countered the 10 percent rate that was included in the CDG Plan and was later actually implemented.

The afternoon session commenced at 2:00 p.m. and resumed discussion of the conversion rate for private debt. German experts expressed the opinion that it would be necessary to treat long-term and short-term debt differently. Tenenbaum's reaction was stoic. Thereafter, problems of absolutely necessary secrecy in the run-up to currency reform were addressed. Black market traders should thus have their opportunities for last-minute speculative transactions curtailed. Then the time for the reform in 1948 was discussed. The German experts relayed that manufacturers preferred a time during the seasonal upswing in the spring and that agricultural producers a time as close as possible to the harvest in the summer.

In response to Erhard's question whether concrete planning for the currency reform could already begin after the conference of foreign ministers of the four occupying powers currently underway in London, Tenenbaum replied, "that if we do useful work, this problem will be settled quickly, either with the Russians or without the Russians." (p. 25) Thus the Special Agency members were also attuned to the possibility of a purely West German currency reform. Furthermore, the urgent desire of the German experts to be involved in the design of the currency reform was discussed, also pointing out that this would strengthen the confidence of the German people in the new currency if Allied and German experts were to make a joint public commitment to the reform work.

The German side proposed the creation of a small council of experts who hidden from public view and under top secrecy would prepare the reform in detail together with Allied currency experts. Tenenbaum' annotated: "If you mean that not only experts for economic questions should be council members, but also experts for political matters, then I agree." (p. 28) But if the experts would be forced into general discussions with representatives of political parties, then he would have a different opinion. In that context he made the following proposal: "Once we know the date of C-day, we could open a *concentration camp* [my emphasis] 10 days before," (p. 28) where the council members could be summoned. This was actually put into practice by organizing the so-called Conclave of Rothwesten starting April 20, 1948. But instead of ten days it lasted seven weeks.

In the further course of the afternoon session, the following topics were discussed with Tenenbaum: Can occupation costs be reduced? Who will care for necessary adjustments of the price structure and of the relation between prices and wages before currency reform? Is it necessary to institute a fixed exchange rate of the new currency vis-à-vis the dollar and other hard currencies? How can the multitude of bilateral payment agreements be transformed into a multilateral payments system, which Germany with its traditionally export-oriented economy would be very interested in? What would the Marshall Plan contribute to strengthen German exports? Would decision-making on monetary and credit policy of a German central bank soon to be created be entrusted to Germans? Will monetary policy be able to meet the conflicting goals between defending the fixed exchange rate against the dollar, domestic price stability and supporting full employment? Should an easy-money or hard-money policy be pursued after currency reform? (Tenenbaum's recommendation: hard money for six months.) Will the central bank have to finance government deficits after the currency reform? Can high tax revenues also be generated via excise duties on nonessential consumer goods, such as cigarettes, so that budget deficits can be reduced? What do the discussions on the Basic Law in Herrenchiemsee promise to contribute to stabilizing public finance? In tandem with currency reform, should food rations be increased and direct taxes reduced to create incentives to increase labor productivity and production?

The session adjourned at 5:30 p.m., after Mr. Knoblock had left the meeting earlier in the afternoon. Tenenbaum, not chairman Erhard, had the last word. He held out the prospect that to eliminate the black market after currency reform, goods in demand there, especially cigarettes, would be made available from America. "We don't want to pump too much into it, of course, because otherwise we won't get to our maximum revenue [from taxing them. This is thinking in terms of the later, under President Ronald Reagan famous Laffer curve in reverse.] ... But you [the German currency experts] have more important things to deal with than tax issues."

Here is a much shorter summary on Tenenbaum's meeting with the German currency experts on November 20, 1947, by Stephen Meardon published in 2014:

> Tenenbaum dominated the meeting, emphasizing the need for
> cooperation, hearing the Germans' ideas, and pointing the way
> helpfully toward their better alignment with his own. Bureau
> Agency members wanted a higher ratio of new currency
> exchangeable for old. Tenenbaum, seeing the Colm-Dodge-

Goldsmith proposal of 10 to 100 as too lenient, said that 5 to 100 would suffice, and any more than that should be "blocked" (meaning held in account but not available for the individual's withdrawal) (Kindleberger 1997, 2–3). Erhard hoped that, absent a higher ratio, the Marshall Plan aid announced the previous summer might be siphoned off for consumption. Tenenbaum retorted that "the Marshall Plan does not mean help for consumer goods" (Ibid, 6). Erhard worried that canceling up to 80% of private debt such as mortgages, leaving "only" 20% valid, would amount to "unlawful enrichment" of homeowners. Tenenbaum was "perhaps ready to reduce all mortgages to 12 percent, and then finish with it" (Ibid., 4). One member was anxious about the adequacy of time for exchanging currency beginning C-Day. Tenenbaum said that 24 hours were enough (Ibid., 5). Tenenbaum's purport was parsimony, decisiveness, and indifference about the fine details of currency reform's distributive effects. Notwithstanding their differences, on at least one point Tenenbaum did not see fit to correct the Special Agency. Although Germans should attend to details, said Erhard, "the Allies must impose currency reform." Concurred another, "I have always felt that democracy is more tolerant than dictatorship, but with currency matters, I call for the occupation authority" (Ibid., 2). The Americans sought the semblance of German participation, the Germans the assurance of Allied leadership.[194]

While still chairman of the Special Agency for Money and Credit, Erhard published an article in *Die Neue Zeitung, Eine amerikanische Zeitung für die deutsche Bevölkerung*. It had been founded in October 1945, was subsidized by US military government, printed in Munich, and was distributed all over the US occupation zone as the official organ of OMGUS. Erhard had been a welcome guest author in that newspaper since 1946. His long article of February 8, 1948 asked for the abandonment of the previous economic policy which had favored investment over consumption industry. In view of the impending currency reform, economic and social needs would require an increase in the production of consumer goods. After C-Day the German population, equipped with the new currency, would primarily demand consumer goods. These – it is true – would be offered from large stocks hoarded by retailers. But that would by far not suffice to avoid continuing shortages and inflationary developments. These would endanger the building of trust in the new currency, which would be essential for the success of the currency reform.[195]

When the Anglo-Saxon powers had moved closer to the planning of a separate Western currency reform, they received from the Special Agency a first draft of a currency-reform bill, accompanied by an explanatory memorandum, in the last week of January 1948.[196] The second enlarged and improved draft would follow in early April.[197] The Homburg Plan wasn't approved by the Tenenbaum-Bennett-Clay team of OMGUS. It was published shortly after currency reform of June 20, 1948.[198] Like the CDG Plan it consisted of two parts, which Goldsmith described in his oral history interview in the following terms:

> First, all monetary claims, currency, mortgages, whatever it was, must be written down in the ratio of ten to one, so what had been a hundred reichsmarks became ten deutsche marks. ... [Second,] since the first step, of course, could not do anything from the point of view of social equity ... the Germans were supposed to put some levy on those people who gained by this operation and to some extent to compensate those who lost. This was called an *Ausgleichsabgabe* – equalization fund. // General Clay accepted the first part of the plan, but did not accept the second one, saying, "We are not here to introduce social reforms into Germany. If the German Government wants to do that it's all right, but I'm not going to do it." He simply regarded this equalization levy as too close to socialism. ... I'm sure that the reason he did not want to go into this second part, which we thought to be really an intrinsic part of the whole plan, was that this was against his conservative feelings.[199]

The first part of the Homburg Plan deviated considerably from the CDG Plan in detail. But in essence it was also designed to shrink the glut of money. Thus, there was the same need to compensate monetary-claim holders for their losses by way of putting levies on the gains from debt devaluation of real asset holders. Clay and his financial advisers, Jack Bennett and currency expert Edward Tenenbaum, reacted as Goldsmith has described. But I think that their motivation went beyond Clay's aversion against socialism and his conservative feelings. Hans Möller has noted that the actual currency reform without the burden-sharing part favoring real over monetary asset holders has definitely strengthened the propensity to invest and thus the reconstruction of the West German economy.[200] This ranked very high on Clay's and Washington's political agenda, namely to free the US budget from aid and relief payments to Germany.

At this point, Tenenbaum's personal opinion on West Germany's need for aid is of interest. Werner Meyer, who is himself doubtful of Tenenbaum's assessment, has filtered out the following statements from the Tenenbaum Papers:

> There were, of course, some groups of Germans who suffered severely from the food shortage. Especially very old people and some children. For the majority of Germans, their hunger was a fairy tale, born of a well-developed instinct for self-pity on the part of the Germans and compassion on the part of the Allies, for the "underdog," the weaker.... Even if the lack of food was unpleasant and uncomfortable and the food monotonous – it had a positive effect on the health of many in the end. Because they lost their excess weight.... The facts that could have burst the fairy tale of hunger were hidden both by the German food authorities and by their partners in the British and American military governments ... While the normal rations were indeed small, practically no German had to live on them. Statistics on special allotments or extra rations for certain groups were hidden – especially from visiting US

Congressmen. There was fear, Tenenbaum said, that American aid pledges would be cut short if the true facts became known.

This indicates that Tenenbaum was harder to fool than US Congressmen and that his statement at his twenty-fifth class reunion at Yale in 1967: "I got to see several interesting concentration camps and other tourist attractions and became rather hard-hearted about Germans in the process."[201] did have substance. His power of resistance to being fooled became his great asset defending a harsh currency reform against demands by German experts and even more by German politicians to soften the terms of the reform and thus running the risk of renewed inflation and failure of the whole operation.

Apart from the American refusal to legislate burden sharing in tandem with currency reform, the Homburg Plan, part 1, met with serious misgivings of OMGUS' Office of the Finance Adviser. Dated March 5, 1948 Jack Bennett sent a lengthy memo to General Clay, "SUBJECT: German Proposal on Financial Reform" with comments on and especially arguments against the first draft of the Homburg Plan. Bennett's memo is subdivided into nine points. I found an even longer undated and unsigned memo entitled "Effects of the 'Sonderstelle' Proposal" in the Tenenbaum Papers.[202] This must have been Tenenbaum's collection of arguments from which Bennett selected the most important to convince Clay of the continued inflationary danger that the implementation of the Homburg Plan would evoke. Here are some excerpts taken from the Bennett memo:

> 2. ... the plan is regarded with some favor by British representatives ... // 3. ... a. Free deposit liabilities of the banking system would be covered to more than 100 percent by cash or reserve deposits, which would result in the credit system escaping from control after the conversion. // b. Blocked or "fixed" accounts would be covered by a so-called "stabilization loan," and would be carried as a liability of the banking system in the new currency. It would thus be politically impossible to resist demands for unblocking, whether advisable or not. // c. Mortgages

or mortgage bonds would be carried over into the new currency at their nominal value. Thus, along with a large part of the private debt, they would not be written down in accordance with the devaluation of the currency. Undue enrichment would accrue to holders, and would prejudice the future savings structure of Germany to the detriment of sound monetary policies. // d. Nominal value of capital invested in bank stock would be more than covered by remaining assets, so that those who invested in the bankrupt banking system would probably come off best of all. This is neither politically nor economically desirable. // 4. The basis of the "Sonderstelle" proposal is the recognition of the Reich debt by exchange of 100 percent of Reich debt holdings [for] new claims against an equalization fund. Recognition of the Reich debt is not merely a political blunder, but is also a sure commitment to future inflation. The Reich debt, including claims against the Reich for war damages, is simply too great and too uncertain in amount to be liquidated in any way other than by repudiation. // 6. ... the Sonderstelle proposes to leave sufficient money or claims to money in the economy to make payment of an equalization levy easy, or at least not appreciably difficult. Since any equalization levy which really equalizes the gross discrepancies in Germany *must* be appreciably difficult, the Sonderstelle plan must lead to inflation if in nominal appearance it equalizes without in practice being difficult. As usual, inflation is the easy way out, the depreciation of nominally large claims to wealth until actually they can be paid easily with very little cost in terms of real wealth. // ... 9. It is therefore felt that the acceptance of the "Sonderstelle" Proposal in its present form would be contrary to our instructions and would not be in keeping with Military Government's responsibilities. ... The experience of surrounding countries shows that whatever claims are permitted to survive a currency reform measure, even in a deferred status, are eventually liquidated at the cost of the stability of the currency.[203]

Around the time OMGUS had disapproved the Special Agency's first draft of its currency-reform bill, shrewd General Clay could make use of Ludwig Erhard on a different line of confrontation. He had him transferred into a position from where his free market devotee could take the blame off OMGUS in a prospective conflict with the British over the above-mentioned "substantial relaxation or elimination of price and allocation controls" immediately after currency reform. The British, with the Labour Party in power in London, would resist a far-reaching dismantling of price and allocation controls throughout the unified economic area, the Bizone, because the UK was still practicing it widely. But if the newly founded German political institutions on the bipartite level would use their legislative powers to eliminate most price and allocation controls in the wake of currency reform, Clay's British counterpart, General Brian Robertson, would be confronted with a fait accompli.

The Anglo-Saxon powers had dismissed Johannes Semler (CSU) as director of the Administration for Economic Affairs on January 24, 1948. In an impassioned speech in front of his Bavarian CSU party colleagues assembled in Erlangen on January 4, 1948, he had used pithy words to criticize Anglo-Saxon practices in their control over bizonal economic policies. His attacks culminated in calling American corn deliveries for bread production *Hühnerfutter* in the sense of poultry feed. But it was translated as "chicken feed" with its insulting double meaning in English. Especially this had incensed General Clay. He is said to have called Semler a "damned arch liar" whose excuse for the form of his statements Clay didn't accept. He insisted on his dismissal.[204]

On March 2, 1948 Ludwig Erhard was elected by the Economic Council as his successor. He officially assumed his new duties on April 2, 1948.[205] The candidate must have been approved and he might have been even suggested by General Clay beforehand, because Clay knew that Erhard shared his and his staff's (Tenenbaum, Bennett) conviction that price regulation by bureaucrats should be abolished after currency reform in favor of the more efficient distribution of goods via the market mechanism. Erhard's deep-rooted conviction in this regard comes out very strongly in his address to the *Überseeclub* in Hamburg on December 16, 1948.[206] By this time it had been him, not the military governors, who had taken the heat when his decontrol of a portion of consumer goods was followed by considerable inflation in the second half of 1948. There were slogans in the streets of Frankfurt and other West German cities "Erhard to the gallows." There is a more serious example of the great uproar not only among the general public, the opposition parties (SPD and KPD) in the Economic Council, and the labor unions, but also in the media.

In April 1948 a young journalist of the weekly *Die Zeit*, Marion Gräfin Dönhoff, traveled from Hamburg to Frankfurt am Main to attend the first press conference of the newly installed director of the Economic Administration, Ludwig Erhard. She had a doctorate in economics. She later became *La Grande Dame* of journalism in Germany. In a long speech given to the Economic Council, the German parliament of the Bizone, on April 21, 1948 Erhard presented his economic policy program aimed at replacing administrative controls with market mechanisms shortly after currency reform.[207] Back in Hamburg Dönhoff related to her colleagues her following assessments: "If Germany were not already ruined anyway, this man with his absurd plan to abolish all price and rationing controls would certainly accomplish it. God forbid he should become economics minister one day. That would be the third catastrophe after Hitler and the dismemberment of Germany."[208]

Ludwig Erhard was informed of the impending currency reform of June 20, 1948 five days before it happened. The question is why? Evidently he was given time to fight for and convince the Economic Council to pass – after a dramatic debate during the night from June 17 to 18, 1948 – the *Leitsätze-Gesetz* (Guiding Principles Law), stipulating the principles of handling price and other market regulations after currency reform in favor of decontrol.[209] This was an enabling act authorizing Erhard in his directorial function to dismantle price and allocation controls at his will, which – as stated earlier – was entirely in line with the corresponding policy goal of OMGUS.

By permitting Erhard to exercise his powers in favor of decontrol, the OMGUS currency team reached two goals. First, British opposition to such measures could be neutralized by a formal invitation of Erhard and a reprimand by General Lucius Clay. And second, the Western powers could exonerate themselves from the unknown consequences of decontrol: unwanted inflationary or deflationary effects, which no expert at the time was able to predict with sufficient certainty. Whatever unwanted direction price developments might take, the Anglo-Saxon Allies could put the blame on the German Economic Council and on the empowered director of the Administration for Economic Affairs Ludwig Erhard, who had executed exactly what OMGUS had planned for the time after currency reform, albeit not immediately.[210]

As noted above, the dice in favor of a separate West German currency reform were cast in Washington, DC on March 11, 1948. Thereafter the two Anglo-Saxon military governments dropped all efforts aimed at a quadripartite currency reform, as demanded by the Potsdam Agreement of 1945. From then on, they concentrated their energies on devising a bizonal and, if the reluctant French could be enticed by the benefits of a common West German currency and by the Marshall Plan funds to join in, a trizonal currency reform.

In response to the War Department cable "Reurad W 95569 requesting outline of our plans on Bizonal or Trizonal currency reform," Clay sent cable CC 3335 on February 29, 1948 to the Office of Under Secretary William H. Draper of the Department of the Army.[211] Most of it must have been of Tenenbaum origin. Clay explained that they in Berlin were planning in accordance with the principles of the Colm-Dodge-Goldsmith (CDG) Plan of May 1946 that had already been approved by Washington, DC in August 1946. He described the details of the OMGUS plan for the conversion rate for individuals and businesses, of the handling of blocked accounts, annulment of the Reich's debt and replacement by Länder debt to keep financial institutions solvent, the conversion of private debt 10 to 1, "except current debts for wages, salaries, and recurrent monthly bills such as utilities." He also described the planned treatment of inter-bank liabilities. And he presented OMGUS plans for a war gains tax and a reconstruction tax on all real property, both with rather high tax rates in favor of a War Loss Equalization Fund that the CDG Plan had considered essential for an equitable sharing of the burden of war losses, mainly between holders of monetary wealth and those of real assets.

But Clay also reported to Washington in detail where current OMGUS plans deviated from CDG Plan.[212] Instead of the slow stream of revenue for the Equalization Fund resulting from the War Loss Public Mortgage of the CDG Plan with low interest and principal payments, OMGUS planned on a progressive schedule of installments for war gains and reconstruction taxes over only five years, at the end of which all dues would have been paid. The CDG approach would not provide sufficient revenue. While CDG had been mute on tax-rate questions, OMGUS planed on a substantial reduction of the very high individual and corporation income as well as property tax rates existing under quadripartite rule. These would be an unbearable burden on business after restoring sound money. A shift to high excise taxes on luxury and nonessential consumer items should produce the necessary revenue "and siphon off potential black market profits." As to price and exchange rate policy, which CDG did not address, OMGUS informed Washington of its plan to introduce immediately after currency reform a uniform conversion factor of thirty cents to one Deutschmark for exports, except coal, and imports, except food. OMGUS also reported its intention to increase immediately after C-Day coal and steel prices to cover long-term costs and to readjust legal prices to conform with these measures. And then cable CC 3335 of the Tenenbaum-Bennett-Clay team of OMGUS Berlin reads: *"After currency reform, substantial relaxation or elimination of price and allocation controls."*[213] [My emphasis]

This is exactly what Ludwig Erhard would execute as director of the bizonal Administration for Economic Affairs (*Verwaltung für Wirtschaft*) immediately after currency reform of June 20, 1948. This leads me to venture a hypothesis underpinned by circumstantial evidence of Erhard's function in currency-reform policy of the OMGUS Tenenbaum-Bennett-Clay team. Erhard served as an expedient pawn whenever OMGUS ran into difficulties with other occupying powers on the execution of its CDG currency-reform plan on the quadripartite or, with the British in Bizone, on the bipartite level.

Here is circumstantial evidence: After the introduction of the CDG Plan into the ACC in early September 1946, followed by the approval of the plan by London and Paris and the Soviet currency expert, hopes were high to come to a quick agreement for a quadripartite currency reform in the early fall of 1946. But Moscow tied its approval to other political demands, such as reparation deliveries and its participation in the control of West German industries.[214] By the time of the failure of the fourth meeting of the Council of Foreign Ministers in Moscow April 24, 1947 and even more so after the fifth meeting in London in late autumn of 1947 had also ended in disagreement on the German question, the substitute solution of the CDG Plan, a currency reform for only the West German zones, became an option to be planned for.

These efforts had made some progress

> when – less than three months before the target date for currency reform [June 1, 1948] – the US representatives suddenly received a communication from their home government which threw them into complete confusion. Issues that had been settled years before, particularly by the US Government's sponsorship of the Colm-Dodge-Goldsmith Plan [in August 1946], were suddenly reopened. The suggestion was made that we proceed with a "simple" currency reform, affecting only banknotes and bank deposits, and leaving open all problems concerning wages, prices, public and private debt, exchange rates, banking reform, and burden-sharing.

The proposed 10 to 1 conversion rate was criticized as too severe. The establishment of a uniform 30 cent exchange rate was criticized and cancellation of the Reich debt was discouraged as a radical gesture that could set a bad precedent for other countries.[215]

For the finance people in OMGUS Berlin, Tenenbaum continues, "it seemed as if the world had fallen in. We were back at the early stages of 1945. All the intervening years of discussion, experience and carefully added knowledge had been thrown away."[216] Once again General Clay's shrewdness saved the day

> by offering to transfer responsibility for the entire operation to our colleagues at the home front, suggesting that they negotiate in Washington with British and French representatives to arrive at joint instructions to the Military Governments in Germany. This offer to transfer responsibility resulted in our being left alone for a while. However we were unable to salvage any burden-sharing features, and our "radical" position on the reform was severely shaken.[217]

Tenenbaum goes on to report that although OMGUS was left alone from further intervention out of Washington,

> the incident must have rankled. In [January[218]] 1949 Jack Bennett, my immediate superior, returned to the United States. He had done more than any other man in his chosen line of work to prevent the collapse of the Western position in Europe. Nevertheless, after several decades of faithful work as a career civil servant of the US Treasury, his government no longer had a job for him. I had preceded him in the fall of 1948, and did manage to find a government position, but not one connected with either Germany in particular, or monetary problems in general. Indeed, a high State Department official refused to talk to me because he was so busy attending meetings about the German currency reform.[219]

"By the time Washington's intervention had been overcome, the Rothwesten sessions had begun." The three Western military governments were under pressure "to try to hammer out a semblance of agreement among themselves while preserving the appearance of unity in front of the Germans."[220]

When a historian sees an opportunity to check in documentary sources what he has learned from oral history or from memoirs, he should not let it pass. Even with full intention to tell the truth, memories are fallible or even distorted by story versions that politicians or media people have spread to influence public opinion. Recollections are not built on rock, but rather on sand, which may move as time goes by.

It is a historical fact that Washington's last-minute intervention into the details of a largely elaborated currency-reform concept took Clay, his financial adviser Jack Bennett, and special assistant for the reform Edward Tenenbaum completely by surprise. Since early 1946, when Clay had the Colm-Dodge-Goldsmith Commission established, whose report had been approved by War, State, and Treasury Departments in August 1946 (see Section 4.1), they had coordinated it among Allied military governments, adjusted it to changed circumstances, and fine-tuned it in Berlin for almost two years. I was lucky to find among those documents unearthed and published by Jean Edward Smith one that not only authentically reveals the serious misgivings of State and Treasury toward the reform concept in detail, but also the frustration Washington triggered in OMGUS Berlin.[221]

The message from Washington, which Clay in his answer to William H. Draper Jr., Under Secretary of the Department of the Army, referred to as a "bombshell,"[222] was contained in cable W.97929 to Clay on March 19, 1948. This was eight days after Washington had definitely decided to give up on quadripartite currency reform and a day before General Vasily Sokolovsky broke ACC apart by leaving it in protest. The War Department, as it was still called even after it was renamed Department of the Army in September 1947, informed Clay already in the introduction to the three-page cable that State and Treasury had serious second thoughts about the currency-reform plan for West

Germany, which OMGUS had informed Washington about in cable CC 3335 of February 29, 1945. They were of the opinion "that distinction can be made between measures pertinent to carrying out currency conversion as such and measures of long range character designed to rehabilitate economy of Western Germany."[223] The cable expressed further reservations in Washington, DC:

1. Regarding the proposed conversion rate of old *Reichsmark* into new *Deutsche Mark*: "View here is that the rate you propose [10 to 1] is [a] rather severe one. Your estimate of [the] impact of your conversion rate on costs and prices would be of interest to Wash[ington]." As to the blocking of 20 percent of *Reichsmarks* turned in, the Departments in DC suggested a time limit for the unblocking decision. "Four to six months should be sufficient to determine whether selected conversion ratio is likely to have deflationary effect. Any longer period is likely to allow time for development of political pressures."

2. "Your proposal for cancellation of Reich debt has been rec[eive]d with misgivings" for the following reasons:
   (A) It would be a "not necessary primary step to other measures for maintaining liquidity of banking and financial institutions; (B) Defaulted Reich debt does not constitute important inflationary threat; (C) Step of such serious import should not be taken except in consultation with appropriate German auth[oritie]s; (D) And cancellation of Reich debt would constitute [a] precedent with which this government should not be associated. For these reasons, Treasury is definitely opposed to cancellation."
   Cancellation of the Reich debt had already been part of the CDG Plan that Washington had approved in August 1946 and, as we shall see later, would be part of the West German currency reform. Clay's financial adviser Jack Bennett, who with his special assistant for the reform, Edward A. Tenenbaum, carried the main responsibility for the shape of currency reform, was not taken back into employment by the Treasury when he returned home from OMGUS in Berlin to Washington, DC. Evidently, Bennett had made himself an enemy of a rancorous Treasury by not heeding its advice on the cancellation question.

3. The authors of the cable complain that the impact of taxes on real property, namely "war gains and reconstruction taxes" on the West German

economy, "especially in view of fiscal and budgetary situation that will develop," has not been explained. They admit that it "cannot properly be estimated here." They accept the OMGUS decision that at the time of the currency reform future special tax measures should be announced. But they convey the "feeling" in Washington that the "selection and introduction of such measure should await a careful planning of their scope and character in consultation with German representatives and in relation to overall problems of the budget and tax structure. In addition, particularly re [garding] proposed tax rates of war gains and reconstruction taxes over five-year period, rates indicated would, in State and Treasury opinion, impose great difficulty arising from need to liquidate capital assets in order to meet tax liabilities."

To them it appeared unrealistic that liquidation to the required extent would take place in view of: (A) the fact "that currency conversion would eliminate present condition of excessive liquidity" and (B) the great "reluctance of owners of real property to liquidate portion of their property."

This argumentation of State and Treasury is very weak. It ignores under (A) the post-currency-reform fact of fast increasing income from rapidly growing production and sales of owners of the means of production, who belong to property owners. Thus they show themselves ignorant of the whole purpose of currency reform in Germany, namely to restore production incentives and thus to unleash entrepreneurial instincts. And under (B) they don't take into account that real property owners, whose debts had largely been canceled with worthless *Reichsmarks,* could again mortgage their property in Deutschmarks instead of selling their property to obtain the necessary liquidity for tax payments. The credit and banking system in West Germany had just been stabilized by the founding of the *Bank deutscher Länder* by the Western military governments on March 1, 1948. It was modeled after the Federal Reserve System in the USA. Its modern instruments of monetary policy would – after currency reform – determine the extent of credit and money according to the needs of a growing West German economy. The authors of cable W-97929 of March 19, 1945 seem not to have been up to date on the significance of the founding of the *Bank deutscher Länder* for credit conditions in West Germany.

4. The proposed shift in the regular tax system to more consumption and less income taxes would imply a shift from progressive income tax revenue to

rather regressive features of taxation. This is a statement worthy of Economics 101 at an American college. But again the authors concede that this might be necessary "to reflect changes in liquidity situation resulting from currency reform." But they concede "that steps should be taken in near future to accomplish this end and that there may be some value in announcing at time of currency conversion that this is being undertaken." But also this revision of tax schedules should not be linked to currency conversion, but deferred "until overall modifications of the tax structure can be worked out and agreed upon."

5. "All action should be deferred with respect to establish [a] general conversion factor or foreign exchange rate for Deutsche Mark." As the impending conversion rate and its readjustment after currency reform "cannot now be forecast, no reasonable basis exists at present for setting such rate." The authors of the cable agreed that such a rate should be set "as soon as practicable." But they doubted that this could be done before three or four months of experience after currency reform. They requested from OMGUS to keep them fully informed on all data relevant to a later decision on the foreign exchange rate for the Deutsche Mark, "as a basis for our consultation with Nat[ional] Advisory Council."

This actually meant that for at least three or four months the existing exchange rate of ten US cents to one *Reichsmark* would have been kept also for the new Deutschmark. This would have been a windfall profit, a boon for GIs and other Allied troops in Germany and thus would have contributed to the shortage of goods for Germans and to a renewed inflation. It would have ruined the success of the West German currency reform.

The exchange rate is always a key variable in opening or closing the floodgates for inflation, especially in the then existing Bretton Woods system of fixed exchange rates. As part of currency reform in West Germany it was – ignoring the wishes of cable W-97929 – expressly fixed at the rate of 30 US cents for one Deutschmark, even higher than the 25 cents CDG had proposed. This was planned to put pressure on West German production costs as well as domestic and foreign trade prices. After inflationary tendencies of the Deutschmark had subsided towards the end of 1948, this lever on prices in West Germany had served its purpose. In September 1949 the Deutschmark's exchange rate was devalued to 23.8 US cents for one Deutschmark, which was equivalent to the traditional exchange rate of the Mark and the *Reichsmark* of 4.20 to one US dollar.

Thereafter and in conjunction with the worldwide economic boom triggered by the Korean War starting in 1950, West Germany's export-led "economic miracle" took off, with very high growth rates and moderate inflation rates.

In their cable W-97929 the three Departments in Washington, DC that were involved do not seem to have been aware of the central role that the setting of the exchange rate of a currency plays in domestic stabilization measures, in contrast to Special Assistant for Currency Reform Edward A. Tenenbaum, his immediate boss Jack Bennett, and their common boss Lucius D. Clay of OMGUS in Berlin.

6. The authors of cable W-97929 requested from OMGUS to keep Washington currently posted concerning the measures outlined in Clay's cable CC 3335 of February 29, 1945. This should include "points on which important divergences of views may exist with British and French, as well as points on which tentative agreement [was] reached."

It seems that the Washington departments, especially Treasury and State, tried to keep Clay on a short leash concerning decisions on the West German currency reform. But they did not have the expertise for an informed opinion on OMGUS' plan for West Germany's currency reform. Or else they deliberately aimed at its failure, because they grudged OMGUS, General Clay, and his experts their eventual success.

This information is contained in the introduction of J. E. Smith to his publication of Document 354. While Smith must have seen cable W.97929 to Clay, because he is quoting from it, he only published Clay's immediate response, a long draft cable of March 1948 "From CLAY Personal for ROYALL." On the draft cable Clay annotated "File. Not sent. LDC." Maybe after drafting he might have had second thoughts about the wisdom of approaching Kenneth C. Royall Sr., the first Secretary of the Army this way.[224] Perhaps he took advice from Bennett and Tenenbaum or from Draper, whom he trusted ever since Draper had headed the economics division of OMGUS in Berlin before Royall made him his Under Secretary of the Army. Clay must have found more compromising means of dealing with Washington by accepting some of the State's and Treasury's demands while rejecting others.

Clay accuses State and Treasury that their "views, plans, and suggestions are in many instances in complete variance with the policy directive under which I have been acting. It is possible to presume ... that my Government has withdrawn its approval of the principles of the CDG Plan" of 1946. "You can appreciate my reluctance to proceed until this doubt concerning my policy directive is clarified." He would be left "with the imminent prospect of being faced with a separate currency reform in the eastern zone without the western powers being able to protect themselves by being able immediately to effect an agreed currency reform of their own." When asking for Washington's approval of the CDG Plan he had expressed his "firm conviction that currency reform as a means of combating inflation and providing for a stable economy was not a piecemeal operation but that for it to be effective it must include in addition to adequate reduction of currency-overhang appropriate measures of taxation that would spread the war loss." Clay states further that the War Department's cable W-98110 of August 26, 1946 had assured him of the unanimous approval of the CDG Plan by the secretaries of State, War and Navy. This had been the American position and the basis for negotiations in ACC and discussions with "our Allies" outside, also on how to proceed in executing tripartite currency reform.

Obviously because State and Treasury had called the already modified burden-sharing parts of OMGUS' current currency-reform concept into question again, Clay drew attention to the fact that in his cable CC-3335 of February 29, 1948 to William Henry Draper, Under Secretary of War under Royall from September 18, 1947, OMGUS had already informed about modifications to the CDG Plan with respect to its burden-sharing elements. He points out that this happened not only "in deference to our convictions," but also on account of OMGUS' perception that this part of the CDG Plan had been approved "with considerable doubt in the first place" and had subsequently fallen into disfavor in Washington, particularly in the Department of the Army. Clay argues against the proposed separation of currency conversion and "measures of long-range character desiring to habilitate the economy," such as burden sharing. OMGUS would turn over its legislative power to the Germans as rapidly and fully as possible. It would seem unrealistic to presume "that unless we now impose the ancillary measures as military government law, that these measures will be taken by the German legislative bodies." They might "not have the courage to impose sufficiently rigid measures to accomplish the purpose" or if they did, "the unfavorable reaction of the taxpayer would be such as to destroy the political future of those who participated in the decision." Both of Clay's alternative fears were not borne out by later West German history, possibly due to the "economic miracle" of West Germany that allowed businesses to pay their dues for burden sharing with petty cash.

State and Treasury had criticized the CDG conversion rate of 10 Reichsmark to 1 new Mark as too severe. Clay responded that the CDG commission had supported its 10 to 1 conversion proposal with plenty of collected data, which were available in Washington as well as in Berlin. Besides on CDG expertise, OMGUS would rely on its own judgment and that of German experts. "The more recent German proposals have favored a more, rather than a less, severe basis of conversion."

And as a matter of fact, the currency reform was pulled through with a final conversion rate of 10 to 0.65. Nevertheless, inflation rose its head again during the first months after currency reform on June 20, 1948 until November 1948. This led in November to the only general strike of workers in Germany's post–World War II history ever. After the reform, their wages had not been decontrolled, while consumer prices, with exceptions mainly for rent, food, and heating material, had been. Thus real wages had been squeezed for months before the labor market was also decontrolled as a result of general strike action. Although wage increases were then bargained collectively, the prior inflationary development broke off at about the same time. Why? Currency reform had initially not only entailed inflation, but also plenty of unemployment despite rapidly rising economic growth. This had resulted from productivity increases that after the introduction of the Deutschmark were even higher than the growth in production. This explains why after November 1948 substantial wage increases could coincide with a stabilization and in 1949 even with a decline of prices.

Otto Pfleiderer, who had been a member of the Agency for Money and Credit in Bad Homburg and would be also a member of the Conclave in Rothwesten, described the most important uncertainties in the planning of the West German currency reform on the fifth anniversary of the currency reform in 1953 thus:

> If we take a look back from today's perspective at the time when the currency reform was being prepared, we can hardly believe that almost all the relevant data were unknown at the time and that even the volume of currency in circulation was estimated only very roughly. All the more so, all judgments about the "correct" volume of money required for the functioning of the new currency were fraught with no less uncertainty. No one could venture a reliable judgment on the expected velocity of circulation of the new money. So there was nothing left but to take refuge, at first, in crudely arrived at orders of magnitude, which were then still corrected in the months following the currency reform – especially by the much-attacked cancellation of seven-tenths of the "fixed accounts."[225]

In planning a currency reform, the most difficult and uncertain forecasts are, first, the one for the velocity of money circulation and somewhat related to that, second, how much not only of current post-reform income, but also of left-over savings will be spent for consumption by households. First, the velocity of money, it is part of the identity equation: $M \times V = S \times P$, where M is the volume of money in circulation; V the velocity of money circulation; S the supply of goods on the market, and P the price level on an uncontrolled market. The easiest to measure is the volume of central-bank money, especially in connection with a currency reform for which currency is newly printed. The price level and its development aimed at with a currency reform is either total stability or a very mild inflation in order to avoid deflation that usually entails recession and unemployment.

The supply of goods is more difficult to estimate. In 1948 it depended especially on expectations that the new currency would retain its value. This, in turn, hinged on many factors, such as the currency conversion rate, the foreign exchange rate, the first allotment of liquidity to households and businesses, the tax rates which would more or less force businesses to speed up production and sell it in tandem with their large volumes of hoarded goods for money to remain liquid. Goods supply could also be increased by windfall assistance from abroad, for instance by Marshall Plan deliveries or when the USA would enlarge its supply of consumer goods in West Germany by delivering shoes and cookware in support of the *Jedermann-Programm* (Everyman Program) in November 1948. Ludwig Erhard had started this program earlier in cooperation with West German producers who were willing to deliver standardized goods to the market at reduced prices.[226] (More on this in Section 4.4)

But the most difficult estimate is that of the velocity of money circulation, that is, how often in a certain time period a given amount of money will be used to buy goods. In normal times of stable prices, the velocity hardly changes and can be assumed to be constant. But in uncertain times it depends on expectations of price developments. With inflationary expectations it increases, with deflationary expectations it decreases beyond the normal level. In case of pent-up demand, which was the case at the time of currency reform, an increase of money velocity is to be expected irrespective of expectations of future price developments. We do have data of expected velocity by the authors of the CDG Plan and of ex post measured velocity after the currency reform had taken place. CDG calculated their conversion rate of 10 to 1 from estimates of the volume of old currency circulating in the four zones of Germany of about 240 billion Reichsmark and of a real national output of approximately 35 billion Reichsmark. During the period 1913–1933 the volume of money in circulation had on average constituted 68 percent of Germany's national output. The 240 Reichsmark converted 10 to 1 would leave 24 billion Deutschmark. This amount, in turn, would again be about 68 percent of real national output of 35 billion.[227]

When making the conversion rate 10 to 1 a key element of their reform plan, CDG obviously assumed that the post-reform velocity of money circulation would be the same as the one in their reference period 1913–1933. It is true that by June 1948 real national output in all four zones was considerably higher than the 35 billion Reichsmark in the first half of 1946. And proportionately this would be true for the three Western zones, too. Therefore, the relation between circulating money and real output, which CDG had estimated at 68 percent in 1946, might have been only 55 percent in pre-reform 1948, implying a real output growth of one-quarter. Had prices remained stable during the six months following currency reform this would have meant that the velocity of money circulation had been 25 percent higher than on average in 1913–1933. But as prices actually rose considerably in the second half of 1948, one author reported that by fall of 1948 the velocity of money circulation had been 2.5 times higher than in 1938 and that a substantial expansion of commercial bank lending between June and December 1948 had expanded the broad money supply by a factor of more than 3.[228]

Second, it is very difficult to predict the propensity to save in a situation in which shops, as a result of currency reform, display at prices in new currency such consumer goods which before, if at all, were available only on black markets at astronomical prices in old currency or in barter trade. From hindsight it is clear that a less severe conversion rate than the actual 10 to 0.65, for example, the 10 to 1 conversion rate of the CDG Plan, would have produced a proportionately greater post-currency-reform inflationary problem. State's and Treasury's proposals of an even less severe conversion rate than

CDG's 10 to 1 might have pleased West Germans who were full of money illusions when looking at their Reichsmark saving accounts and other monetary wealth assets. But it also would have triggered an even higher inflation for the Deutschmark currency than the CDG's 10 to 1 proposal. It would thus have defeated any prospect of success for the West German currency reform of June 20, 1948. Clay refused the less severe currency conversion rate proposed by State and Treasury by pointing to the US economic policy goal in Germany, namely "to reduce or to eliminate the need for most government control by establishing a sound and stable monetary system."

State and Treasury also criticized that the plan for reform contained no time limit for the unblocking of the blocked portion of converted accounts, which at that stage of planning was to amount to 20 percent. Washington proposed six months, after which the blocked portion would be canceled. Such a time limit, Clay argued, would run counter to the aim "to give the German [monetary and fiscal] authorities maximum protection against unblocking." Without a time limit, but only with unanimous affirmative action of military governments would approval to any unblocking be given. Clay doubted that the British and French would accept the proposed time limit. But he would try to obtain their agreement.

Washington evidently also expressed great reservations against the burden-sharing part of the currency-reform plan. Evidently there were fears that the necessarily severe taxation of real wealth would hamper German economic reconstruction. Clay retorted that such taxation as provided in the CDG Plan had already been mitigated by his government and that JCS 1779, the directive to the commander in chief European Theater of July 11, 1947, explicitly committed OMGUS not only "to press for the adoption by the Control Council of a program for financial reform," but also to provide "for the equitable sharing of the costs of war and defeat."[229] Besides, high taxation on real wealth holders would exert pressure to sell hoarded inventories which would help to make currency reform a success. To further calm Washington's fears of too high tax rates in post-currency-reform

West Germany, Clay assured his counterparts that OMGUS was "aware of the fact that the present level of taxation will be unbearable immediately after the surplus of purchasing power is removed. We therefore propose to reduce certain taxes falling mostly on income, and to raise certain taxes on consumption of luxuries in order to prevent budgetary chaos."

Further, Clay had to defend his policy of setting an exchange rate for exports and imports at 30 US cents per mark, while Washington wanted to keep the previous and current rate of 10 US cents per mark. He maintained that the 30 cent rate was one of the stabilization operations of the currency reform. It was "a means of drawing internal prices into line with external prices." He could have added that the high valuation of the mark was also chosen to exert pressure on German prices via international trade.

In the cable State and Treasury had advised not to cancel the debt of the Reich arguing that it would constitute a "dangerous precedent." In response Clay even puts into question the quality of the financial expertise in the two Departments in Washington. In Berlin cancelation of Reich debt

> is considered a primary necessity if we are to restore confidence in the new currency. The Germans are well aware that the Reich debt is so great that it can never be paid except by inflation. If we leave it hanging over the heads of the German population, particularly after advocating cancellation for almost two years, they will draw their conclusions, which may differ from those drawn by Washington experts. We must remember that at about the same time the Western powers effect their currency reform, the Soviet zone may be expected to carry out a reform which will most certainly provide for cancellation of the Reich debt. Comparison of details will be inescapable. The Soviets will make political capital of any substantial change in our original proposals. If cancellation is considered dangerous precedent may I suggest that runaway inflation in a US-occupied area would be an even more dangerous precedent.

Clay wrote that he had halted ongoing discussions and coordination of details of currency reform in the three Western zones

> pending further instructions. ... I should like to say in summary that the working out of a currency reform under the existing difficult conditions in Germany cannot be accomplished by patching together little pieces from here and there. The finished pattern is most intricate and cannot hold together unless the separate pieces are fitted with scrupulous care to match one another. ... I felt in 1946 and I feel today that it would be impossible to hope for satisfactory results of negotiations with other governments here in Berlin if I am not permitted to operate under broad directives of principle, and if I must serve only as a channel of communication between my Government and the representatives of other governments involved. ... I would strongly urge that you suggest negotiations at governmental level as a more direct, expedient, and satisfactory method of arriving at agreements with our Allies. ... it would no doubt save considerable time which would otherwise be lost in the exchange of cables among Washington, London, and Paris through Berlin. Under such circumstances I would be able to make available to my Government such data as may be available to my staff here on the subject.

The most competent in Clay's staff for currency reform was, of course, Edward Tenenbaum. He certainly supported Clay with drafting the cable which was never sent to Washington, but in which OMGUS collected all its counterarguments and all of its frustration over the unexpected intervention from State and Treasury. As described in Tenenbaum's words above, Clay's offer to return responsibility for negotiations of details of the currency reform from Berlin to Washington frightened the departments. They shied away from taking responsibility. This shrewd move by Clay, as at several other moments when he offered his resignation unless his policy in Germany would be fully supported in Washington, saved the central decision-making role and room for maneuver of OMGUS in that matter.

Clay's counterpart in the State Department was Robert A. Lovett, Under Secretary of State from July 1, 1947 to 1949. During this period his boss, Secretary of State George Marshall, due to bad health, left the running of affairs mostly to Lovett. Lovett had his own opinion on General Clay. When it came to get the European countries to cooperate in launching the Marshall Plan and the French procrastinated, it has been reported about Lovett's opinion of Clay's repetitious resignation offers:

> The US Military Governor of Germany, General Lucius Clay, relentlessly sniped back at the French. Lovett finally had to remind the general firmly that policy was set in Washington, not Berlin. Clay promptly threatened to resign. This was normal procedure for Clay, who threatened to resign almost a dozen times. Accustomed to dealing with the egos of generals from his days in the War Department, Lovett carefully maneuvered to keep Clay satisfied but under control. // ... Lovett could also be withering about his own associates, especially inflated generals such as Clay.[230]

However, a few of the originally planned elements of a comprehensive currency reform had nevertheless to be sacrificed on the altar of Washington government, especially the burden-sharing provision contained in the CDG Plan and in a less severe version in OMGUS plans before the Washington intervention of March 19, 1948.[231]

In his reflections on the West German currency reform Tenenbaum admits in his unpublished book manuscript: "We recognized clearly that from the day of a bizonal or trizonal currency reform Eastern Germany would become a foreign country. The only real link between the four Zones – a common currency – would be broken, and the de facto absence of economic unity would be turned into a de jure state of economic disunity."[232]

In our three-hour interview Joan Tenenbaum Merrill, second daughter of Edward A. and Jeanette Kipp Tenenbaum, told me that her father had made sure that during the days around currency reform on June 20, 1948 her mother and her sister Anne, born in Berlin April 19, 1947, would be out of town.[233] There was a real danger that in revenge for the separate Western currency reform and the expedited preparations for transforming the Bi- or Trizone into a West German state, the Soviets would take over West Berlin.

Especially the home front had seen this danger pending over the Western sectors of Berlin ever since the communists had seized power in Prague on February 25, 1948 and the Soviets had walked out of the ACC on March 20, 1948. When Senator Henry Cabot Lodge Jr. asked Clay whether it was safe for Americans to stay in Berlin, Clay replied on March 5, 1948 that "our security arrangements in Berlin are adequate. In fact, I believe American personnel are as secure here as they would be at home. Berlin is a somewhat isolated area being surrounded by Soviet-controlled territory and this situation does provide a nervous reaction among a few American personnel but such feeling is far from universal."[234] Maybe the Tenenbaum couple was part of the "few American personnel."

In any case, also on March 5, 1948 Clay sent the following top secret message to Lieutenant General Stephen J. Chamberlin in Washington, the army's director of intelligence (G-2): "For many months, based on logical analysis, I have felt and held that war was unlikely for at least ten years. Within the last few weeks, I have felt a subtle change in Soviet attitude which I cannot define but which gives me a feeling *that it may come with dramatic suddenness*."[235]

In late February Chamberlin had visited Clay in Berlin. He had informed Clay that the army had difficulties to convince the Congress to reinstitute the draft. A strong message by Clay would be helpful in congressional testimony. So against his own judgment before and after, Clay sent an obliging message as a favor to Chamberlin. And against his own expectation, it was leaked widely in Washington and even made it into *The Saturday Evening Post*.[236] Clay's cable intensified Cold War tensions that had gradually built up since the announcement of the *Truman Doctrine* almost exactly a year earlier.

It served its purpose in Congress. However, by its publicity it also increased apprehensions of an imminent war with the Russians over the future of Berlin among Washington political and military leaders and Americans in general. And this would have consequences.

On March 17, 1948 General J. Lawton Collins, Vice Chief of Staff of the US Army, organized a top secret telephone conference with Clay to discuss the question: Should, vis-à-vis the increased danger, dependents be evacuated from Germany, Austria, and Trieste? American public opinion obviously led the Department of the Army to suggest evacuation. Clay willingly admitted that from a purely military viewpoint it would make sense. But it would be ruinous psychologically and politically.

> German people would go into despair and in Berlin into panic.
> Neighboring countries would be seriously affected and "doubting
> Thomases" would flock to Red standard. ... It was a problem of
> morale. Of good faith. I think that if we had started moving our
> dependents out we would never have had the people of Berlin stand
> firm. ... Our dependents were hostages of our good faith.[237]

But the going would soon get rougher. On March 31, 1948 the Soviets announced new regulations for the access routes to Berlin, another warning shot against the London Conference preparations for founding a separate West German state, which at that time the French also did not want. The Soviets would henceforth condition any military train and highway traffic between Berlin and the Western zones of occupation on their approval and would inspect passengers and cargo. Washington, apprehensive of war, ordered Clay to refrain from any provocation, for example, by forcing uncontrolled access to Berlin, which Clay would have favored. He informed Washington that he would organize a limited airlift in response to this Berlin blockade, which affected only the garrisons of the Western Allies. After the famous general Berlin blockade was established following West German currency reform of June 20, 1948, the Soviet measures announced on March 31, were dubbed *baby blockade* of Berlin.

On the home front, they again had increased widespread fears of a military confrontation with the Soviets over Berlin. The Pentagon was worried about the military feasibility of staying in West Berlin. And the State Department, Secretary Marshall and his Under Secretary Lovett, queried the political wisdom of it. British Foreign Secretary Ernest Bevin was at this point the only important decision-maker who shared Clay's viewpoints: a) Soviets were not planning overt military aggression in Berlin or Europe, b) Allied withdrawal from Berlin would have far-reaching psychological and political consequences and would play into the hands of the Soviet Union. He consistently refused a compromise that the Russians had offered, namely lifting the blockade in exchange for stopping preparations for the founding of a West German state along the lines of the London Conference program. Bevin had learned the lesson from Prime Minister Neville Chamberlain's failed appeasement policy ten years earlier. He gave Clay all his support to hold out in beleaguered West Berlin.

But Washington kept prodding Clay to consent to a removal of dependents of US military personnel and of civilian OMGUS employees from Berlin immediately. This was the plan General Albert Wedemeyer, the head of the army's G-3 (Operations) and a staunch supporter of the Berlin airlift, cabled to Clay on April 2, 1948. He asked for his opinion. In reply, Clay reiterated his assessment that the stoppage of American and British military trains was an attempt by the Soviets to drive the Western Allies out of Berlin. An evacuation of dependents and civilians would be regarded as a success of their policy of pinpricks.

A few days later, Secretary of the Army Kenneth Royall and General Omar Bradley, who on February 7, 1948 had succeeded Dwight D. Eisenhower as Chief of Staff of the US Army, requested a telephone conference with Clay on the same subject referring to such inquiries from Members of Congress. Bradley added that it would reduce the number of Americans to be supplied in Berlin by air. Clay reiterated his *ceterum censeo* that evacuation would play into the hands of the Soviets and would frighten the rest of Europe. He offered to let nervous dependents go home and to move unessential civilian employees from Berlin to Frankfurt. But in general OMGUS personnel in Berlin would be calm and continue to live and work normally.

However, this did not allay Bradley's fears that a military conflict with the Russians over Berlin was imminent. He had his son-in-law Hal, an Air Force officer stationed in Berlin, his daughter and their children quietly removed "from danger" to Washington. Hal was newly assigned an Air Force Pentagon staff desk job, which Hal wasn't happy about, as Bradley later conceded.

On April 9, 1948, Reuters news agency reported that the USA had proposed to come to a quick agreement on creating a West German state by immediate elections for a constituent assembly charged with the drafting of a constitution and that a quick agreement was likely. The Soviets, who had previously halted civilian rail traffic from Nuremberg and Hamburg into Berlin, reacted with threats to control the remaining rail line from Hannover to Berlin more strictly. In their telephone conference the next day the US Army Chief of Staff, General Omar Bradley, actually told Clay that he believed Berlin to be untenable. He broached the question to Clay whether the USA should announce its withdrawal from Berlin "to minimize the loss of prestige. . . . We doubt whether our people are prepared to start a war in order to maintain our position in Berlin and Vienna."

At his point with no resolve to stay firm in Berlin from the Washington side, the future of a noncommunist West Berlin, West Germany and Western Europe was hanging by a thread on Clay's own resolve and on his personal power to convince policy-makers in Washington to stand up against the Soviet threat. He advised Bradley that the USA

> should remain in Berlin unless driven out by force. . . . Why are we in Europe? . . . We have lost Czechoslovakia. We have lost Finland. Norway is threatened. We retreat from Berlin. . . . After Berlin will

come western Germany. . . . If we mean to hold Europe against communism, we must not budge. We can take humiliation and pressure short of war in Berlin without losing face. If we move, our position in Europe is threatened.

Bradley obviously tackled the Berlin question with his military mind-set only. Clay approached the same question with his broad political perview, in addition. Clay's determined position on Berlin temporarily stiffened Washington's resolve to remain in Berlin with troops, their dependents and civilian employees. While Washington did not seem to have a consistent policy concept for Germany, London had one which backed Clay's position fully. In a personal note to the Secretary of State George Marshall on April 30, 1948, Britain's Foreign Secretary Ernest Bevin wrote that the Russians were "up to every devilment" in Berlin and Vienna. But there "could be no question of letting ourselves be forced out of either city." In a foreign policy address to the House of Commons the following week, Bevin stated under applause of the House members that "We are in Berlin as of right and it is our intention to stay there." This was the first public statement of Western policy on behalf of Berlin from either of the Anglo-Saxon powers. Disenchanted with the lack of a coherent policy concept for Berlin in Washington, Clay enjoyed and was grateful for Bevin's support.

On a related matter Clay was appalled when Bradley advised him that he and British military governor Brian Robertson should not bring along any company of German officials to the impending Marshall Plan talks. Clay responded that under such circumstances he would also refrain from attending the meeting. He again asked whether Washington did have a policy for Germany at all.[238]

4.3   CAGE, CONCENTRATION CAMP, REORIENTATION CAMP, AND CONCLAVE OF ROTHWESTEN

". . . in the cage," recalls General Lucius D. Clay, US Army commander in chief and military governor in Germany, was the term used within OMGUS for the top secret confinement of eleven German monetary and financial experts. The organizing of the cage and chaperoning of its inmates was taken care of by Lieutenant Colonel Emory D. Stoker. The intellectual leader of discussions over details of currency reform was Edward Tenenbaum. The seven-week session from April 20 to June 8, 1948 aimed at "perfecting last-minute details" of monetary reform.[239] Its location was *Haus Posen* on a former German (since 1945 US) airfield next to the village of Rothwesten near Kassel. In addition to barbed wire around the whole airfield with its barracks, the building itself was surrounded by a fence with barbed wire on top and military police around, reinforced with signs warning anyone outside or inside to be shot in case of climbing the fence. On the occasion of festivities of the 50th anniversary of the currency reform on the premises of the Rothwesten site, Tenenbaum's widow, Jeanette Kipp Tenenbaum, confided to Michael Budczies, the son of Wolfgang Budczies, one of the inmates of the Rothwesten cage, that the warning signs had been placed there by order of her husband.[240]

Otto Pfleiderer, one of the interned German experts, has published a useful summary of these and other good as well as bad living and working conditions in Haus Posen on the occasion of the twenty-fifth anniversary of the currency reform.[241] He also mentions that US Army Lieutenant Colonel Emory D. Stoker had been in charge of rooming and boarding of the German experts and their staff, such as secretaries and translators. Together with J. T. Lisle, a civilian, for the UK, Lt. Colonel Stoker for the US headed the Finance Group, located in Frankfurt am Main, of the Bipartite Control Office (BICO) of the Bizone.[242]

The weekly magazine *Münchner Illustrierte* covered the tenth anniversary of the currency reform extensively in a series of articles in eight consecutive issues from June 21 to August 16, 1958. It overwhelmingly consisted of a fictitious story about a family and friends living through that period. The series starts with events happening during the night from June 14 to 15, 1948, that is, before the reform. A US Army truck runs into a tree and loses some of its load: boxes with DM notes and with forms and info sheets necessary for the currency conversion to be announced for the following Sunday, but not before June 18 at 8 p.m. Two Germans, an honest taxi driver and his customer, who had made a fortune on the black market, accidentally witness the crash and recognize that currency reform is now imminent. Although the cab driver was not at fault for the crash, he and his customer were arrested by the military police escorting the US Army truck on the spot and locked up in a prison cell so that they could not spread around in public what they had seen.

Interspersed in all eight parts of the serialized novel and printed in bold are pieces of research results and of interviews with former inmates of the cage and with its chief organizer, Lt. Colonel Stoker. Here is what was found out about Stoker's role and character:

The ten German experts [Wilhelmine Dreißig joined them days later] who arrived at Rothwesten with their escort and their chaperone, Colonel Stoker, on 20 April 1948, found a lonely, rather neglected barracks building and were horrified. // "Some of the gentlemen," reported one participant, "wanted to turn back immediately on the grounds that all this treatment was unworthy." // But there was Colonel Emory D. Stoker! The versatile man used all his charm and offered various delicacies – so that the currency reform would not be delayed once again. He served stuffed cucumbers which, to the amazement of the experts, were "swimming in butter." Thus fortified, the gentlemen went to their rooms for the night's rest, where there was only a cupboard – and an American military bed, which "outwardly made a primitive impression; but one could sleep excellently in it." // That first night, however, no one slept very long: the stuffed cucumbers in butter began to take effect. // The very next morning the work began. Colonel Stoker was a cheerful, but also relentlessly driving boss. And he was enthusiastically generous, since it was nevertheless necessary to see satisfied and industrious currency reformers at work. // Even today, the experts, almost all of whom were lean and starving, have not forgotten the delights that were available then: Danish milk, excellent coffee, white bread and unimagined quantities of cigarettes. And even shaving cream and soap, "beautiful American soap." A land of milk and honey, but without alcohol. // "We were," reported Finance Senator Dr. Dudeck, "a cohesive team that also functioned excellently on the human side. Not least thanks to the truly outstanding qualities of Mr. Stoker."[243]

While the magazine did not integrate a photo of Stoker into the currency-reform novel, despite all the praise and personal interviews with him in preparation of the story, it did so with the master of the Conclave discussions, E. A. Tenenbaum.

What is even more remarkable is the text below the picture: **"Financial genius from the USA.** [bold in original] According to the judgment of all participants, Edward A. Tenenbaum played a decisive role in the birth of the Deutsche Mark."[244]

During the whole Rothwesten internment of the German experts Stoker assumed his role of a chaperone and played it perfectly, too. However, his task, as is usual for chaperones of teenagers, was not to prevent sexual intercourse of those entrusted to his care. Rather, he had to make sure that his inmates in possible communication with family members or other outside contacts would under any circumstances keep the secret of the forthcoming currency reform. How devotedly Stoker performed his task is shown by the following recollection of the son of Conclave member Wolfgang Budczies:

Correspondence with relatives was possible, but was subject to strict censorship. Visits from outside were excluded. Outside visits were permitted only in exceptional cases and under guard. I was confirmed at Pentecost 1948. My father wanted to come to us in Bavaria for this event. This was allowed in principle, but only under the condition that Colonel Stoker had to accompany him, who – so it was told in our house – was to watch even in the bedroom that my father did not betray any secrets. Under these circumstances, my father renounced his participation in my confirmation, especially since otherwise – without the care of Stoker – his colleagues would have had to do without the experience of going to church on Pentecost, as usual on Sundays.[245]

Stoker arranged for his own festivity of the twenty-fifth anniversary of the Conclave in the spring of 1973, as Pfleiderer reports. In detail:

> 25 years later, at the invitation of Colonel Stoker, who had returned to Germany, a few former members of the "Conclave" and some of the secretaries who had been helpful there, recently saw the scene of the "Conclave" in Rothwesten again for the first time. They became painfully aware of the rich harvest of death that had been reaped in these 25 years among those with whom they had worked so intensively and confidently in the spring of 1948, and at the same time so cheerfully and curiously about what was to come. At the same time, this reunion was an occasion to remember what a strange time it was, when a few motley people sat together for weeks in an out-of-the-way corner behind barbed wire to prepare a piece of legislation of truly epochal significance, which – without the complicated procedure by which laws are usually brought about – was enacted within the shortest possible time by order of the three military governments, opening the door to the economic rise of what was to become the Federal Republic.[246]

It is remarkable that Edward Tenenbaum, the main figure in the dramatic performance at Rothwesten in the spring of 1948, was not a participant of this reunion. I would guess that former Lt. Colonel Stoker tried to win his interest in this event and invited him. But Tenenbaum did not participate. He had traveled the world in the 1950s and 1960s. At least once he had changed planes in Germany without leaving the Munich airport. In answer to some questions by Hans Möller as to different currency-reform plans discussed on the quadripartite ACC level, Tenenbaum wrote to Möller, then professor of economics at the University of Munich, on July 30, 1959: "I wish I had known sooner that you are in Munich, since I passed through there around three months ago, and would have been happy to have an opportunity to call on you."[247] However, Tenenbaum never showed an interest in spending time in Germany and in meeting with German financial experts again, such as his discussion partners, among them Möller, at the Rothwesten *concentration camp*, the term coined by him.

In his book about his family roots, covering extensively his father Wolfgang, also one of the eleven German experts of the Rothwesten camp, Michael Budczies reports that the former inmates had organized a reunion in Frankfurt am Main already for April 1949, when the success of currency reform was no longer in doubt. Tenenbaum was invited, but declined to come. Instead, he sent the following letter via Colonel Stoker, a typical example of his sense of humor:

Former Inmates of Rothwesten: // Colonel Stoker has had the kindness to send me a clipping from a German newspaper, which says that I speak and write German fluently. I hope this will not destroy your faith in a free press, and that you will permit me to address you in English, which you all understand better than I do. // On what is probably a very festive occasion, the tenth and one-half month of your liberation, may one of your former guards wish you well? To each and every one I wish good luck, and a reasonable degree of pride in the remarkable task you accomplished. Although some of you might suspect that you were merely translators, you succeeded in translating not merely English into German, but also some rather vague theories and prejudices into a remarkable practical and on the whole historically unique and successful monetary reform. // My good wishes extend to all, including those who gave extensive publicity to some off-hand remarks I may have made. Let us hope that your success does not have the same effect on your heads as wine. // If you should ever have the misfortune to need another currency reform, please do not hesitate to call on me for accommodations. // Sincerely yours, // s/d EDWARD TENENBAUM.[248]

Today the former barracks building is the site of the currency-reform museum (*Währungsreformmuseum*). The former military complex is now civilian and – like the village of Rothwesten – has been incorporated into the town Fuldatal. On April 25, 2012 the latter community named the street leading up to *Haus Posen* "Edward-Tenenbaum-Straße." This is the only public recognition that Tenenbaum has received in Germany so far.

When Tenenbaum attended a meeting of the *Sonderstelle Geld und Kredit* (Special Agency for Money and Credit) in Bad Homburg near Frankfurt am Main on November 20, 1947 he – with his often visible sense of black humor – had already presaged the necessity of assembling Special Agency members in a "concentration camp" to put the finishing touches to the currency reform shortly before it would actually be implemented (see Section 4.2, p.408). He had conceived this idea even much earlier, in the fall of 1946, after the CDG Plan had been introduced by US military government for discussion in ACC. The Plan's implementation would require extensive laws, executive orders, forms, and info sheets which should best be worked out by German experts.[249]

As history unfolded, this sort of "concentration camp" turned out to be the counter model of what the Nazis had practiced. Though the inmates were likewise in confinement and were burdened with a tremendous workload, they labored on highly useful and important tasks for shaping Germany's future. In return they received the best of food and nonalcoholic drink to keep up their morale, working spirit, and efficiency. Lt. Colonel Stoker had not only provided the best of such delicacies the US Army had in stock, but had also recruited a married couple from Tirol as excellent chefs[250] and even a barber for the looks and good feelings of his temporary prisoners, including the female secretaries and staff.

In official letters, even within military government, Edward Tenenbaum, of course, didn't use the term "concentration camp" and Lucius Clay didn't speak of "cage" for the internment of the German experts. In two written orders to Lt. Colonel Emory

D. Stoker of April 1 and 12, 1948, "Subject: Special Mission" Clay
gave instructions for "the establishment of a special political reorientation camp" to accommodate about twenty-five "important
civilians. ... The camp must be in an isolated location ... [and]
include arrangements for military personnel which will be required
as guards." In handwriting Stoker added on the empty bottom part of a
copy of Clay's written order to him of April 1, 1948: "The 'special
political reorientation camp' was actually a camp to which I brought
the leading German banker-economists as my voluntary prisoners
while the terms of the West German currency reform of 1948 were
discussed and decided, and necessary laws drafted."[251]

After Lt. Colonel Stoker had decided on *Haus Posen* at the
airfield of Rothwesten, nowadays a district of the municipality of
Fuldatal, Clay instructed him on April 12, 1948 to arrange for

> minor repairs to the building, to supply heat, light, telephone, and
> other usual building services available at Rothwesten, to supply all
> equipment, utensils, dishes, tableware and fuel which are required
> to reestablish messing facilities in the building, and to supply
> furniture, furnishings and equipment, including sheets, and
> bedding, for the purpose of providing office, conference and living
> rooms. ... [and] the immediate erection and maintenance of fencing
> in order to reduce to a minimum the need for military personnel
> which will be required as guards. ... You are also authorized, for a
> period not to exceed six months, to draw rations and other Class
> I supplies from the Sub-Post for not to exceed twenty-five persons;
> and you are not to be required to account for such supplies except to
> sign for the receipt of such supplies as are actually delivered to
> you.[252]

Almost all of the West Germans were on the brink of starvation
during winter 1947/48. The rich and tasty supply of food (and drinks)
ordered by Commander-in-Chief Lucius Clay himself and procured by
Lt. Colonel Stoker was no doubt instrumental in keeping the inmates
of the "special political reorientation camp" of "voluntary prisoners"

together, especially after they soon realized how little voice in shaping the terms of currency reform they were granted by Tenenbaum and his superiors. It has been reported that the German experts gained up to 10 kg in weight during their seven-weeks confinement in Rothwesten.[253]

Clay, his financial adviser Jack Bennett, and his special assistant for currency reform Tenenbaum had become apprehensive about a possibly impending currency reform in the Soviet zone after the Soviets had walked out of the ACC in protest on March 20, 1948. Whoever would be the second mover on currency reform, would suffer from being flooded with worthless Reichsmarks from the zone or zones with an accomplished reform. Therefore, hectic preparations for a bi- or hoped-for trizonal currency reform in West Germany were started, as not only Clay's above-cited two orders to Lieutenant Colonel Stoker show, but also what happened on April 5, 1948.

For reasons of urgency and secrecy, a meeting of the finance advisers of the bizonal military governors, Jack Bennett and Sir Eric Coats, with the three members of the just newly created currency committee of the bizonal Economic Council, Franz Blücher (FDP), Herbert Kriedemann (SPD) and Robert Pferdmenges (CDU),[254] had been arranged by telephone for that day in Frankfurt am Main.[255] The three Germans were told that they should very urgently nominate ten German experts to work out an emergency reform plan for the eventuality that the Russians beat the Western powers to the punch with a currency reform in their own occupation zone.[256] On April 8, 1948, the currency committee of the Economic Council nominated German experts and at the same time sent the currency-reform plan (the Homburg Plan)[257] of the Special Agency for Money and Credit to the bizonal military governments. The nominees were: Karl Bernard, Wolfgang Budczies, Walter Dudek, Heinrich Hartlieb, Erwin Hielscher, Hans Möller, Otto Pfleiderer, Victor Wrede. Eduard Wolf was also named, but for reasons of travel restrictions from his home town of Berlin was unable to participate. They had all been members or staff members of the Special Agency for Money and Credit in Bad

Homburg.[258] To complete the team the French military government chose and sent two additional experts: Walter Bussmann und Rudolf Windlinger.[259]

Before accepting their assignment, the nominees wanted to be informed by the bizonal authorities what their task and especially their scope of influence on the shape of currency reform would be. On April 15 (and again on their first day of confinement at Rothwesten on April 21, 1948) they were informed by the currency experts of the three Western powers, Tenenbaum, Cook, and Lefort, that their most urgent task would be a) to translate and rework the so-called interim bill, the draft of an emergency measure in case the Soviet zone would rush forward with a currency reform, and b) to discuss thoroughly with the representatives of the Western Allies all problems of currency reform in preparation of a final decision by the Allies of its principles. They pointed out, however, that the "Outlines" for principles the Western Allies had agreed on March 30, 1948, would be nonnegotiable.

The currency committee of the Economic Council had been given the same information on the nominees' task. It had responded that politically it would fully cover the German experts in all negotiations on the basis of the Homburg Plan. With these Allied declarations and the backing by the currency committee of the parliamentary German Economic Council, the nominees for the camp embarked on their work in Rothwesten with an upbeat mood hoping that they would be able to integrate as much of their Homburg Plan into the currency-reform outcome as possible.[260]

With the exception of Eduard Wolf, these men together with auxiliary personnel (from secretary to translator and from cook to barber), altogether twenty-five persons, were transported from their meeting place in Bad Homburg to their hideout under most secret circumstances in the evening of April 20, 1948. Shortly after beginning work in the "cage," the German experts asked the military governments to allow Wilhelmine Dreißig, a staff member of the Special Agency, to participate as an addition to the ten members of the assembled German expert group as keeper of the minutes of meetings.[261] It was granted.

This and the historic Conclave of Rothwesten was on the brink of not taking place at all the day following the arrival of the party in *Haus Posen* in a US Army bus with frosted glass windows after a three-hour drive in the dark. Here is the story as told by eyewitness Hans Möller:

> The first day of work of the commission of German experts, assembled and transported to Haus Posen on the airfield near the village Rothwesten the day before, came close to being the last.[262] From 9:30 to 11:00 a.m. on 21 April 1948 the experts met without military-government representatives. They discussed their bad accommodation as well as their unpleasant working conditions, and the consequences the commission should draw vis-à-vis the military governments. They even debated the question, whether under given circumstances the commission should decline to take up work. As a compromise, the commission decided that an answer to the question should be postponed until matters had been discussed with military-government representatives. In the interim the commission would refuse not only to take up work, but also the disclosure by the Allied representatives of any secret information on monetary reform in order to keep open the possibility of a withdrawal from their Conclave.

From 11:00 a.m. to 12:30 p.m., Colonel Stoker and the British financial expert Cook joined the meeting for discussions with the German experts. Erwin Hielscher, the spokesman of the commission in sessions with Allied representatives, spoke for the Germans. He said that fruitful work seemed to be very difficult for psychological reasons, because the allotted area fenced in with barbed wire and guarded by army posts was too small. Bad accommodation with insufficiently furnished rooms would not be acceptable for the commission over a longer period. He expressed doubts that the situation on the spot could be improved and suggested to seek out a new location. For all these reasons, he argued, the commission had to temporarily decline to take up work and to receive secret information on currency-reform matters until a joint discussion of the complaints would have taken place with representatives of all three military governments.

Afterward, the commission met with its female supporting staff and brought it up to date. When the secretaries and other service staff were asked whether staying seemed possible to them under the given circumstances, they answered affirmatively on the condition that the commission would likewise decide to stay on. Thereafter the commission members discussed a written statement vis-à-vis the military governments that Hans Möller had drafted. It declared that the commission would refuse to stay on unless three conditions were met: first, firm and satisfactory commitments as to completion time of work in Haus Posen; second, firm and satisfactory commitments as to the degree of participation of the commission in drawing up currency reform; and third, immediate permission to go for a walk within the outer fence of the airfield without special guards but with an obligation of absolute secrecy and of no contact whatsoever with other persons.

From 3:00 to 4:30 p.m. the commission met with representatives of all three military governments: Lt. Colonel Stoker and Tenenbaum (US), Cook (UK), and Lefort (France). Hielscher confronted the military government representatives with the demands of the German experts, who were given the following five assurances. First, work will be finished in two months at the latest, probably sooner. After finishing their work commission members will be allowed to return to their usual workplaces even before currency reform is executed. Second, living conditions in the building are to be improved as fast as possible. Furniture etc. will be procured immediately. Freedom of movement outside the inner perimeter fence cannot be granted due to the presence of German employees on the airfield. But on Sundays sufficiently long walking tours and even longer excursions with Lt. Colonel Stoker will be arranged. Third, the participation of the commission in designing currency reform is in the widest degree possible and desired. It was stated that the three military governments had reached agreement on a preliminary law for emergency use (Implementation of Financial Reform) as well as some Principles of Currency Reform. Both this law and these principles would be up for change. The attendant representatives of the three military governments declared their willingness to put all requests for modification forward to the competent bodies of their respective military governments. Fourth, sufficient contact of the German commission with the currency committee of the Economic Council (*Wirtschaftsrat*) and with representatives of the [bizonal German] Administrations for Economic and Financial Affairs [*Verwaltung für Wirtschaft, Verwaltung für Finanzen*] would be made possible as requested at any time. Fifth, finished draft laws would in any case be submitted to the currency committee of the Economic Council, if necessary with an exposition of the dissenting position of the German commission.

On the basis of these assurances, especially as to the time limitation of work in confinement, the commission members, with one exception, decided to start work immediately. Wrede asked for a reflection period of twenty-four hours. He left the session in order not to receive further secret information which would have made his immediate return to Hamburg impossible.

At this stage it was Tenenbaum who handed the emergency draft law to the commission and explained what had to be done shortly. Here we see him in his role as the spokesman of the three Allied governments and as chairman of sessions of the commission with military government participation. His role didn't change during the duration of the Conclave.

Part of the draft law were two forms, Tenenbaum explained. For capacity reasons a short-term printing of millions of them would technically be possible only in England within a period of six weeks. He asked the commission to work overnight on these forms that were already translated into German, put them into proper and customary German wording and have them ready the next morning at 8 a.m. to be transported to the printers in England by plane at 9 a.m.

FIGURE 4.12 Original table for the top-secret sessions of members of the Conclave of Rothwesten, now part of the Currency Reform Museum at the same location

From 4:30 to 6:00 p.m. the commission members read and discussed the emergency draft law and the two draft forms among themselves and later with military government representatives in order to eliminate uncertainties. The latter gave the commission an almost completely free hand for all technical details. They only insisted on unconditional delivery of the finished form at 8 a.m. the next morning. The commission worked all night, but by 6 a.m. it was done with form 1 only. Möller was assigned the task to present it to the Allied financial experts at 8 a.m., to explain it to them and discuss it with them. The Allied experts demanded a few technical changes and granted a deadline extension until 2:30 p.m. on the same day. And the commission delivered Form 1 exactly on time. However, its name would be changed to *Form A*,[263] which every citizen claiming *Deutschmark* in exchange for inflationary *Reichsmark* had to fill out at the time of currency reform. Therefore, about 40 million copies (= about 50 million West German inhabitants minus about 10 million dependent children) were due to be printed. As Form A itself states, only children who at the date of currency reform have not reached the age of eighteen years can be listed on Form A of their parents. Children beyond the age of eighteen are obliged to fill out their own Form A.

Voting rights to 18-year-olds would be granted in Germany only more than two decades later in 1970. I guess that this decision ahead of its time under Allied governments' supervision had to do with their experience of fighting the last batch of 16-year-old German soldiers. In the USA, the twenty-sixth amendment to the constitution made it happen a year later, in view of casualties young people had suffered in the Vietnam War.

On April 22 the Allied financial experts also decided that Form 2, of which only six million copies would be needed, would be printed in Germany. Thus a few extra days were gained for the commission to work on it before delivery to the printers. Presumably Form 2, eventually named Form B, was needed by businesses for their currency conversion. At the beginning of the afternoon session of the commission with the three Allied financial experts on April 22, Wrede returned and declared that he had made up his mind and would from now on participate in the commission's work.

During the evening of that day, the commission met without their Allied counterparts to discuss and decide on the organizational structure of its work. Möller was assigned the task to allocate office rooms and to manage the setup of technical equipment. Hielscher was elected as chief negotiator of the commission vis-à-vis the military governments. And Bernard was delegated to preside plenary sessions of the commission. Three working groups were formed for tasks lying ahead during the next few days: a legal team consisting of Bernard and Budczies, a team for further work on Form 2 by Hartlieb and Möller, and a team for economic questions consisting of all other commission members with Dudek as chair and Wrede as manager. It was

FIGURE 4.13 Edward A. Tenenbaum with nine of the eleven German members of the top-secret Conclave of Rothwesten. From left to right: Wolfgang Budczies, Victor Wrede, Heinrich Hartlieb, Walter Bussmann, Wilhelmine Dreißig, Otto Pfleiderer, Hans Möller, Edward A. Tenenbaum, Walter Dudek, and Karl Bernard

stipulated that the Form-2 team should until further notice join the team for economic questions.

On April 23 and 24, 1948 the working parties embarked on substantive labor on their respective tasks in morning sessions 9 a.m. to 1 p.m., afternoon sessions from 3 to 6 p.m. and even a night session on Form 2 from 8 to 11 p.m. Important procedural questions were also settled with the following results. If the commission cannot reach unanimity on decisions, it will decide by majority vote. The minutes of meetings shall not inform about the course of discussions, but simply about the results. Those in minority positions are free to write their own reports about their dissenting opinions.[264]

The mandate with which the currency committee of the Economic Council had sent the nominated experts into their confinement in Rothwesten included the following. In their discussions with the financial experts of the three Western military governments they should work out currency-reform legislation as closely as possible in conformity with the Homburg Plan. The linking of currency reform with burden equalization, envisaged in the Homburg as well as in the American CDG Plan of 1946, was emphatically demanded. Already at this point the currency committee instructed its nominees to deny any responsibility for the final reform legislation. They would merely act as financial experts without a parliamentary-political mandate and, therefore, were not legitimized to take responsibility for laws which the Western military governments would implement anyway.[265]

The experts interpreted the above-mentioned assurances as a mandate which committed them to nothing but their own evaluation standards. They were left to operate with their own intrinsic sense of duty and responsibility. In other words, they enjoyed all intellectual room for maneuver like academics in the proverbial ivory tower. The only restrictions they faced were the nonnegotiable decisions that the Allies had already taken on the essentially American reform plan based on the CDG Plan of 1946 for a currency reform for all occupation zones of Germany. Especially instructions from Washington, DC to OMGUS had limited the scope of what was negotiable at the Conclave meeting. Otto Pfleiderer, a member of the German Conclave of experts and an eyewitness of proceedings, summarized the leeway for negotiations as follows:

> The two basic decisions which had been taken under the responsibility of the occupying powers were – contrary to the original plans – first, that the currency reform should be limited to the three western occupation zones, and second, that the equalization of burdens should be separated from it and placed under the responsibility of the German authorities. Despite this drastic double restriction, there was still a great deal of room for maneuver on issues whose decision could still be considered more or less open. These were, for example, whether private debt relationships were to be converted at a ratio of 1:1 (as the German

experts suggested) or at a ratio of 10:1 (which the spokesmen for the occupying powers tended to favor); what the initial amount of new money to be issued on the day of the currency reform was to be; how the initial provision of banks and the public sector with liquid assets was to be handled, and the like.)[266]

Contrary to what has often been argued in the literature on the little scope of influence of the German experts assembled at Rothwesten, Pfleiderer's narrative shows that Tenenbaum and his two colleagues from Britain and France, Bernard C. A. Cook, and Charles Lefort, were somewhat receptive for reform-plan changes proposed by the German experts. Pfleiderer also emphasizes that especially the task to translate the substantive decisions of the Allied military governments into a legal language adequate to the German legal system for all practical purposes remained entirely within the hands of the German experts.[267]

Shortly after the start of their confinement the German experts were disillusioned about the impact that their Homburg Plan elaborated over months at the Special Agency for Money and Credit would be able to make on the final outcome of the currency-reform legislation in West Germany. Erwin Hielscher, a member of the German expert group in Rothwesten, had succeeded Ludwig Erhard as chairman of the Special Agency on March 3, 1948 after the latter had been appointed director of the Economic Administration of the Anglo-American Bizone.

As mentioned above, the German expert group assembled in Rothwesten elected Hielscher as their chairman only for meetings with the Allied experts. For internal meetings of the German group Karl Bernard, the later president of the *Bank deutscher Länder*'s central bank council, was elected chairman on account of his more diplomatic manner in conducting discussions between hawks and doves in the group's wide range of opinions. This split choice snubbed Hielscher. He was the most ardent protester against not taking the Homburg Plan with its essential burden-sharing part, but rather the

Colm-Dodge-Goldsmith (CDG) Plan of 1946 as blueprint for the separate West German currency reform. The CDG Plan had been introduced and discussed in the ACC in September 1946 as a framework for a common currency reform for all four occupation zones. Early on during the German experts' confinement in *Haus Posen,* Tenenbaum and under his leadership his British and French counterparts had made it clear to the experts that the Western Allies would adhere to the principles of the CDG Plan, especially to the conversion rate of ten old Reichsmark to one new Deutschmark.

Pfleiderer's above-quoted account of what was up for negotiations between the German and Allied experts paints a too rosy picture. Tenenbaum and Clay's American military government in the lead not only had to accept instructions from Washington to leave the burden-sharing part of the CDG Plan (and of the Homburg Plan as well) to legislative German authorities. But they also had to defend their own negotiating room for maneuver with their British and French counterparts against further restrictions from Washington. They did so successfully. The agreement between the three Western military governments on essentials of the currency reform were also not on the negotiating table with the German experts at Rothwesten. In his biography of Gerhard Colm, Wolfram Hoppenstedt lists the following principles of agreement between the Western Allies:

> Cancellation of 70 percent of old money balances; Conversion of
> 10 percent of old money balances into new money; blocking of
> 20 percent of old money balances with the proviso that German
> legislative bodies decide on the further treatment of these blocked
> amounts; cancellation of Reich debt; designation of the new money
> as "Deutsche Mark"; bank reorganization by providing banks with
> new debt securities; issue of these securities by the Länder; transfer
> of responsibility for laws concerning capital levy, equalization of
> burdens, and taxation to the Economic Council.[268]

During the first ten days of their confinement, the German experts mainly worked on information leaflets, forms, statistical data entry sheets and the like, millions of copies of which still had to be printed for the implementation of the currency reform. The more substantive work on the content of laws, details of the conversion rate, how much 1-DM-for-1-RM exchange for needy households etc. began on April 30.

It is remarkable that a day earlier Hielscher had already produced a memo in German for his colleagues and probably also for Tenenbaum and his Allied colleagues about the conditions which the currency-reform design would have to meet. As a starting point he contends that after currency reform the velocity of the circulation of money would be extremely high, when the new Deutschmark would be chasing the formerly unavailable long-wanted goods appearing on offer, because businesses would switch from hoarding goods to chasing scarce Deutschmarks.[269] He, therefore, like Tenenbaum, pleaded for a very low conversion rate. In fact, as it later turned out, the inflation that initially followed the currency reform until November 1948 was less caused by an overexpansion of money supply. As Ian Turner found out in British military government documents: "The real inflationary force came from the velocity of circulation. Whereas prior to the currency reform the velocity of circulation was lower than in the prewar period, in the post-conversion months the velocity was estimated at two and a half times the 1938 level."[270]

On April 30, 1948, the financial advisers of their respective military governors, namely Jack Bennett for General Clay, Sir Eric Coates for General Robertson, and Paul Leroy-Beaulieu for General Koenig, came to Rothwesten to confront the German experts with the unnegotiable principles enumerated above. Bennett declared that the timetable for the execution of the currency reform was extremely tight and did not allow for discussions on modifications of the principles the Allies had agreed on during the conference of the three Western powers in London.[271]

The German experts were shocked. Their mandate to integrate as much of the Homburg Plan into the Allied legislation as possible had just been washed down the drain. Hielscher reacted in protest a day later. On May 1, 1948 he wrote a letter to the director of the

Finance Administration of the Bizone, Alfred Hartmann, who, in contrast to Ludwig Erhard, was responsible for all West German contributions to the currency reform. Hielscher announced that he would resign from both his chairmanship and his membership of the German expert group from that day on in the Rothwesten "camp." Nevertheless, he would be willing to participate further in the work in the "camp."

When he revealed this to his German colleagues in a regular meeting on May 9, 1948, he was criticized by all the others for his solo run.[272] The others had decided what Walter Dudek described in his *Spiegel* article a few days after the currency conversion: "We were faced with the extraordinarily difficult question of whether we should then refuse to cooperate or rather try to make the best of the matter that was still possible from the German point of view. We chose the latter path."[273]

As if the announcements of the three financial advisers on April 30 had taken away their breath, it took the German expert group as a whole three days to react in a "crisis meeting" among themselves. They put down on paper that the three Western Allies had agreed on principles of the currency reform prior to and with disregard of the Homburg Plan. In a letter of May 4, 1948 to the three representatives of the military governments, the German experts "expressed their great disappointment that, without any reason which they could recognize as compelling, they had been kept in the dark about their actual tasks until a time when they were practically no longer free to decide whether to assume them."[274]

They demanded consultations with the currency committee of the Economic Council and with the directors of the Administrations for Finance and Economic Affairs. The Allies consented. It was most probably Lt. Colonel Stoker who made the arrangements for this meeting of the Germen experts with Blücher, Kriedemann and Pferdmenges (currency committee) as well as with Directors Erhard and Hartmann on May 11, 1948 at the Rothwesten premises. It was here where in sessions with these politicians and with the currency experts of the Allies, Tenenbaum, Cook and Lefort, the disagreements over the design of the currency reform came most openly to the fore, as the minutes of this meeting reveal.[275]

The dispute was overwhelmingly carried out between Tenenbaum who spoke for the Allies and Erhard who turned out to be the spokesman of the three German politicians of the currency committee, and, in part, of the German experts. That Hartmann, the director of the Finance Administration, who was responsible for currency-reform matters, did not assume Erhard's role, had to do not only with Erhard's engaging character, but also with the fact that Erhard had presided over most of the meetings of the Special Agency for Money and Credit which had designed the Homburg Plan for currency reform. Therefore, he was much better informed on the details of this plan than Hartmann, as were the German currency experts who had been recruited from the Special Agency. And the politicians of the currency committee were keen on and had mandated the experts to try to integrate as many elements as possible from the Homburg Plan into the final currency-reform laws of the Allies.

In a more unilateral form, the objections of the German currency experts against the currency-reform content they had been forced to design in German legal language were summarized in a common declaration of June 8, 1948, the last day of their confinement at Rothwesten, addressed to the financial advisers of the three Allied military governments.[276] Therein the authors refused any responsibility for the outcome of the currency reform, for the preparation of which they had been instrumental.

Mainly based on two documents, the minutes of the meeting of the German experts with five German politicians in the Rothwesten camp on May 11, 1948 and the German experts' last-mentioned letter of June 8, 1948, eyewitness Hans Möller has published a summary account of the contended issues. In the light of later experience with the results of currency reform he concedes, however, at the opening of his description: "Some of the things that the Allies pushed through against the declared views of the Germans later proved to be expedient solutions."[277]

Möller highlights two points as having been the most controversial: 1. The extent of the money cut, and 2. the conversion of monetary debt relations other than government debentures, which were totally devalued. Final decisions on both points were not taken during the duration of the German experts' internment in the Rothwesten camp, but between its end on June 8, and the public announcement of currency reform in the evening of June 18, 1948. In several meetings with German politicians the military governors of the Bizone and their staff gave the final touches to the reform's conditions during those days.

As to the first main point: the per capita amount of 1 to 1 conversion RM for DM on the day of currency reform. Originally, Tenenbaum had envisioned only 25 DM for per capita conversion that day (see minutes of the afternoon meeting with German politicians on May 11, 1948). The German experts wanted more and achieved the consent of the representatives of the Allies to 40 DM. During those last-minute negotiations, the members of the currency committee of the Economic Council and other German politicians, including Ludwig Erhard, demanded 50 DM. Actually, the Allies consented to 60 DM, but this in two installments of 40 DM on C-Day and additional 20 DM two months later.

This generous response of Tenenbaum and his British colleague was sort of a quid pro quo for the Allies' adamant insistence on their much more important goal of securing the stability of the new currency. The Germans demanded that the per capita amounts were not to be offset against the DM amounts resulting from the conversion of RM bank accounts into freely disposable DM accounts (initially 5 percent) at the rate of 10 to 1. Möller calculated that a consent of the Allies to the demand of the Germans would have added one to two billion DM to the circulation of money. This would certainly have had quite an inflationary effect.

On the other hand, the Germans were successful with their demand for initially freeing only 5 percent of converted RM bank accounts instead of – like in the case of private-debt conversion – a quota of 10 percent which the Allies had envisioned. However, up to 15, 20, or 25 percent – due to disagreements among the German experts – of converted old RM bank accounts should not just be left in limbo to perhaps be taken care of in the future. But the currency laws should already contain concrete decisions on how they should be handled, for example, by transforming them into non-interest-bearing new public DM bonds, with a sales ban for several years. The Allies rejected this, because they feared that strong political pressure would sooner or later develop to make these bonds interest-bearing, salable, and eligible as collateral. As restrictive as the Germans had been with their demand to allow only 5 percent of converted bank accounts as freely disposable, their proposal for an immediate final solution for converted claims beyond 5 percent would have – if taken up by the Allies – increased the danger of inflation for the new currency. Far away from the up to 30 percent of the old RM bank accounts that the Germans had proposed to convert into DM, the Allies legislated a currency conversion rate of only 10 percent, with initially five percentage points freely disposable and in the end only 1.5 percentage points in addition to the initially blocked accounts with their 5-out-of-10 percent share.

As to the second main point of contention: It has already been mentioned that recurring payments, like wages, rents and pensions, were converted 1 DM to 1 RM. The proposal of the German experts and of the Homburg Plan for private-debt conversion was also 1 to 1. The reason behind it was to avoid the debtor gains and the creditor losses from devaluation of debts. Debt devaluation would create a much larger need for action in the field of equalization-of-burdens measures. Every losing creditor and winning debtor would have to be involved. In case of a 1 to 1 debt conversion, in contrast, a wealth owner whose property had survived the war untouched and his creditor could go on with business as usual without being bothered by equalization-of-burdens measures. In case of real estate, for example, the interest payments on mortgage debt would in DM equal those in RM. And as monthly rent payments were actually converted 1 to 1, the rate of return on real-estate investment would neither increase nor decrease. No profit or loss had to be compensated for. Only those real-estate owners who suffered war damage from military actions or from expropriation, mainly in German territories east of the Oder-Neisse rivers ceded to the Soviet Union and Poland, and their creditors who lost their solvent debtors, would fall into the range of equalization-of-burdens legislation.

In 1953 Otto Pfleiderer expressed himself as having been very disappointed that the Allies remained adamant on their plan for a private-debt conversion rate of 10 to 1 and had not taken up the proposal of the German experts for a conversion rate of 1 to 1. This had been one of the few things all eleven Conclave members had agreed on. It would have avoided the occurrence of debtor gains and creditor losses, which would subject both sides of private creditor-debtor relations, that is, tens of millions of German citizens and businesses, to equalization-of-burden measures. And the 1 to 1 conversion of private debt would also have encouraged securities saving. The recent experience with the difficult and delayed German equalization-of-burden legislation had meanwhile shown "how well advised the occupying powers would have been if they had adopted the vote of the German experts on this issue."[278]

Hans Möller, however, conceded that the actual Allied debt devaluation from 100 RM to 10 DM resulted in creditor losses that were not fully compensated for through equalization-of-burden measures. On the positive side he held the view that this situation contributed to spurring investment in West Germany and thus the spectacular growth of the West German economy. And he credited the Allied refusal of the 1 to 1 debt conversion aimed at by the Germans with having saved German society an endless bickering between war-damaged debtors and their creditors, in private as well as in court. On the whole, Möller expressed a favorable opinion of

Allied decision-making in his article of 1989. In view of the eventual success of Tenenbaum's currency reform, he would have made himself a fool, if he had not done so. But keep in mind, he had signed the declaration of the German currency experts of June 8 1948, with their rejection of any responsibility for the outcome of currency reform and with harsh criticism of uncompromising Allied decisions above the head of the German experts.[279]

The term "camp" obviously remained the preferred term for the location of the German experts. It was the most neutral between the Allied expressions of "cage" or "reorientation camp," which was a fictitious denomination for camouflage reasons, and the derogatory term "concentration camp" that Tenenbaum had once used in his meeting with the members of the *Special Agency* on November 20, 1947. Maybe the German camp inmates wanted to express their disappointment about their powerlessness regarding the outcome of the currency reform and about their confinement by leaving open the allusion to a "concentration camp" of the Nazis.

When the term "conclave" had appeared for the first time in minutes of a meeting of the Special Agency for Money and Credit in Bad Homburg in March 1948 after Erwin Hielscher had succeeded Ludwig Erhard as chairman of that institution, spirits were upbeat that the elaborated Homburg Plan of the assembled German experts would be the blueprint for currency reform. But shortly after their internment in Rothwesten they were disillusioned about their role. Tenenbaum and the other experts of the Western Allies were debunking the German group mainly to experts in translation, German law and terminology, and as vicarious agents more generally. The mood went downbeat, most of all with Hielscher. He and his German expert colleagues felt better portrayed as forced laborers in a (concentration) camp than as cardinals of the Catholic Church in a conclave. The latter are ritually summoned and locked up in the Vatican in Rome until they have taken an important autonomous decision, namely the election of a new pope signaled by white smoke coming out of a chimney of the assembly room. "Conclave," in the end, turned out to be a false analogy. For the proceedings in *Haus Posen* the term is inappropriate. The term within OMGUS "in the cage" is much more apposite.

For a long time, my research hypothesis was that the term *Conclave* was coined in good faith early on during the seven-week confinement when the German experts could still be optimistic that they would strongly influence the final shape of currency reform. There were indications to substantiate this view. German experts and politicians had complained about their little say over the terms of the creation of the *Bank deutscher Länder*, the new West German central bank founded March 1, 1948. The German director of the bizonal Finance Administration, Alfred Hartmann, three members of the currency committee of the bizonal Economic Council, and Eugen Christian Hinckel, president of the Land Central Banks of Baden in the French occupation zone, met with Tenenbaum and Cook, the currency expert of the British military government, at least twice.[280] They were given assurances that the Allies expected of the German experts a significant involvement in the preparation of currency reform, that during their internment they would have the chance to confer with the members of the currency committee and that after finishing their work they would not be kept in their confinement until C-Day. Rather they would be involved in the operational implementation of currency reform from their regular offices. Finally, Tenenbaum and Cook promised that during the duration of the internment they themselves would participate in meetings of the German experts three days a week. And, indeed, they kept their promise.[281]

> During the 49 days that the conclave lasted, meetings with the representatives of the military governments took place on about 20 days, with the main work on the Allied side being done by Tenenbaum (USA), while his colleagues Lefort (France) and Cook (UK) took somewhat of a back seat. Tenenbaum, in addition to his intensive discussions with the German experts, did an immense

amount of traveling between Berlin (the headquarters of the military governments for Germany), Rothwesten, and Frankfurt (the headquarters of the bizonal agencies on the German and Allied sides) to organize the necessary coordination among the three military governments and between them and their home governments. Coordination with the French played a crucial role in this process, because the latter delayed the decision on their participation in the currency reform until the last minute.[282]

At this early stage the experts might have believed that these assurances would guarantee for them a significant role and actual decision-making power in shaping currency reform, which would justify the term "conclave." When Erwin Hielscher had asked for and was allowed by the Allies to leave the expert group and the premises on May 21, 1948 in protest of the German experts' powerlessness, the term "conclave" had for some weeks been engrained in the experts' mind, although by then their interpretation of "significant involvement" had been debunked as an illusion. But even Hielscher took the term with him and used it in a chapter title of his account of developments toward currency reform. His manuscript was finished and sent to his publisher on June 18, 1948, two days before currency reform. Hielscher obliged his publisher to come out with the booklet only about three months later, because he didn't want to disturb development opportunities of currency reform so much dependent on psychological reactions.[283] I had regarded the use of the term "conclave" by the German experts throughout their confinement as an outgrowth of their hypocrisy in order to embellish their lack of influence. Until today historians have adhered to the use of this term for the proceedings in *Haus Posen*.

So much as to my initial working hypothesis about the origin and background of the term "conclave"! On Sunday September 16, 2018, my more than one-year-old working hypothesis was shattered by an email from Anne Rüter, a professional historian and trained history teacher living in Kassel. She was then affiliated with the executive board of the *Währungsreformmuseum* in Fuldatal near Kassel. Therefore, she was also doing research on West Germany's currency reform of 1948. We have kept contact since we first met when I gave a lecture on the occasion of the seventieth anniversary of West Germany's currency reform on June 21, 2018 in Fuldatal.

On September 16, 2018 she shared with me a document of the Special Agency for Money and Credit (*Sonderstelle Geld und Kredit*) that she had found in Germany's Federal Archive in Coblenz (Z 32). In minutes of a meeting of the Special Agency on April 1, 1948 the term "conclave" had been used, where one of the participants, Director Hartlieb, summarized the result of the meeting, among them point 4: "Konklave-Beschluß: Starke Betonung der sozialen Seite und Anhörung der Sozial-Demokratie." (Decision of the Conclave: strong emphasis on social aspects and hearing of Social Democracy.)[284] In other words, the term "conclave" was not coined during the period of the seven-week confinement of the German experts in *Haus Posen* in Rothwesten starting April 20, 1948. It had been used earlier for meetings of members of the Special Agency of Money and Credit in Bad Homburg. The chairman of the Special Agency, Erwin Hielscher, had also used the term in his letter of April 16, 1948 to "Minister Franz Blücher, Essen-Bredeney, Tirpitzstr. 75," that is, four days before the secretive transport of Conclave members to the camp in Rothwesten took place: "Sie sind sicher damit einverstanden, dass ich den anderen Teilnehmern an dem Konklave von Ihrem Vorschlag Kenntnis gebe (I am sure you will agree that I should inform the other participants in the conclave of your proposal)."[285]

Here the allusion did, indeed, make sense. The members met in seclusion in Bad Homburg, where also the bizonal Administration for Finance was seated. They were obliged to renounce any public relations, a condition of the bizonal military governments attached to the permission for creating the Special Agency.[286] But their members were convinced anyway that absolute secrecy of its deliberations was essential to currency reform of whatever design. On November 20, 1947 the Agency's first director Ludwig Erhard assured the unofficially participating representatives of the American (Tenenbaum) and British (Cook) military governments: "We are eager to make sure that people take no notice of us at all."[287] Erhard himself had paved the way to the term "conclave" laden with pompous prestige when he called the Special Agency "General staff [Generalstab] for monetary and financial reform."[288]

Not only "in the cage," but also among the financial advisers of the American, British, and French military governments Tenenbaum was pulling the strings. In his unpublished book manuscript, he confessed to his influential role in shaping trizonal currency reform:

> Only the American representative [i.e., Tenenbaum] spoke all three languages: English, French, and German. Conversations between the British and French representatives passed through him, as did discussions between the Germans and the Allies. There are allegations that I took advantage of my position as interpreter to force American views on my colleagues, as well as on the Germans. At this late date [1958, when Tenenbaum wrote his manuscript] it may be safe to confess that these allegations are correct.[289]

The Soviet military governor had left the four-power ACC in Berlin on March 20, 1948. The Soviets were thus protesting the refusal of the three Western powers to inform them about decisions reached at the first session of the London Six-Power Conference launched on February 23, 1948.[290] Its first session had ended March 6. A second session would take place from April 20 to June 2, 1948. Not only the three Western Allies, but also Germany's Western neighbors – the Netherlands, Belgium, and Luxemburg – were developing plans for the creation of a federally structured West German state, based on the Western conception of democracy. The Soviets had not been invited.

On December 15, 1947 the sixth conference of the Council of Foreign Ministers of the four big Allied powers – United States, Britain, France, and the Soviet Union – in London had again ended without an agreement on a peace treaty with Germany, as had the fifth meeting in Moscow in March/April 1947.[291] The February

1948 communist takeover in Czechoslovakia strengthened the Western Allies' resolve to help create a democratic West German state as a bulwark against the penetration of communism all over the West European continent.

When the Soviets terminated their cooperation in the ACC on March 20, 1948, they expressly declared their willingness to keep on cooperating in the Council's currency-reform committees.[292] But for the Western powers the dice had already been cast in favor of progressing with a West German currency reform and eventually creating a West German state. In front of the German population the division of Germany that a separate currency reform would imply could be blamed on the exodus of the Soviet military governor from the ACC, the governing body for all four occupation zones of Germany. But, in fact, the Anglo-Saxon Allies had prepared for the division of Germany already by the decision of the US Administration on October 13, 1947 to give the order to the Bureau of Engraving and Printing for the printing of Deutschmark banknotes. Also the launching of the Six-Power Conference on February 23, 1948 in London with the aim of creating a West German state had been an unequivocal evidence of the Western powers' resolve to confront the Soviets with the division of Germany.

The March 20 walkout of the Soviets, however, immediately sparked all kinds of activities on the part of the Anglo-Saxon powers. Lucius Clay reports that after March 20, 1948: "we had no difficulty in reaching an immediate agreement with British representatives on the terms of a currency reform to be effective in the bizonal area on June 1."[293] This timetable means that the *cage-holding* of the German experts in Rothwesten was originally planned for a shorter period. But after the French government had signaled its willingness to join the bizonal area in currency reform after the end of the second session of the London Six-Power Conference on June 2, 1948, the timetable for currency reform had to be changed to June 21, 1948. It became necessary to reopen discussion with the German experts on questions that had already been settled as to the bizonal currency reform scheduled for June 1, 1948. The French government had tied conditions to its acceptance of currency reform also in its zone: a more than proportional allocation of new money to the French zone of occupation "and on the release later for investment purposes of a larger percentage of accounts blocked at time of issue. ... It became necessary to reopen these matters ... [with] the German experts."[294]

Wolfgang Budczies must have played a most constructive role during the commission's work in the "camp." In his summary article on currency reform twenty-five years after the event, Otto Pfleiderer, himself a commission member, has picked him and one more of his fellow commission members to attest them an outstanding merit for shaping the legal framework of West German currency reform. In one article he writes in 1973:

> New legal concepts, which soon became a self-evident part of
> monetary law, had to be created, such as old money, Reichsmark
> settlement account, conversion calculation, compensation claims and
> the like. The decisive merit in systematically designing the legal
> framework of the currency reform laws goes to a man who, in
> exemplary modesty, took a back seat to the matter with his person and
> whose name has remained almost unknown: Wolfgang Budczies. [295]

He was obviously a character counterpart of Ludwig Erhard. In a different article Pfleiderer also credits Karl Bernard, besides Budczies, for having coped with the difficult juridical problems in the uncharted territory of currency reform. He hints at Bernhard's rich legislative experience from his former employment in the economics ministry of the Weimar Republic.[296] Hans Möller, also one of the German experts in the "camp," has quantitatively summarized the impressive output of the German experts: 22 forms, instructions, legislative bills, executive orders, information sheets etc. Möller's detailed enumeration with individual titles would be too space-consuming to be reproduced here.[297]

Beyond what I have reported above about the main controversial points of Tenenbaum's American currency-reform plan and the

German Homburg Plan, I will not go into details of the proceedings in *Haus Posen* on Rothwesten airfield. A lot of good research has been done and published. Outstanding are long articles by Christoph Buchheim and Hans Möller.[298] The key person on the Allied side in discussions and negotiations on currency matters with the German commission, with the British and French military governments, with – mostly in the background – the head of OMGUS Finance Division, Jack Bennett, with US military governor Lucius Clay himself, and with decision-makers in Washington government departments was Edward Tenenbaum. Although the German experts initially doubted his competence in financial matters, due to his young age and lack of practical experience, they early on during the Rothwesten "conclave" dropped all their doubts. Despite all differences of opinion, he was respected, remained master of the show and pulled the strings.[299]

This is surprising in the light of some descriptions of his personality. F. Taylor Ostrander, who was chief of the price control section of OMGUS' Economics Division under Donald D. Humphrey and knew Tenenbaum personally, reminisced in a letter to Charles P. Kindleberger of April 4, 1992, when they were working on a coauthored article on the West German currency reform:[300]

> Tenenbaum was a strange, unlikable type. We used to say he "always looked like an unmade bed," but we referred more to a total habit of personality than just clothes. Don Humphrey [Ostrander's boss] once shared plane seats with him for an hour or two and later commented that he must have imbibed bitter vinegar in his mother's milk. Tenenbaum had an ugly strain of Morgenthau hatred in his make-up, and I used to say at the time that some part of his draconian aspect of M.R. [monetary reform] must have been due to this. He was also very brilliant, but was a (necessary) bear on secrecy and presumably did a very able job of carrying out the details of the currency conversion.[301]

Richard M. Westebbe, who knew Tenenbaum from having worked together on financial matters of a US aid program in Greece,

characterized Tenenbaum as "an idiosyncratic but brilliant economist" who "belonged to the group that made European integration a
necessary condition for the Marshall Plan."[302] James Warren who had
worked on the Tenenbaum team in Athens reminisced in a letter to
Tenenbaum's widow in 1986 when he was working on a piece about
the Greek "Stabilization Program of 1951/1953 of which Ed was the
author. ... I have such good memories of Ed and his brilliant leadership of what was an extraordinary turnaround" in the financial and
economic development of Greece.[303]

While we are on character descriptions, I don't want to leave
out Ostrander's observations on Jack Bennett: He "was a small-town
accountant from West Virginia who had lost a leg in World War I and
with his Veteran's status had worked up to become the Comptroller of
the Currency – a dull job at that time. He had none of the intellectual
sharpness of White or Bernstein, but began to hang around them, and
copied their Left Wing view of world events."[304]

As to Ostrander's derogatory judgment, one should know that it
might have been prompted by envy. Ostrander had proposed a wholly
different concept of bringing the excess of German Reichsmark circulation in line with the scarce supply of goods and services, namely
decontrol of prices and let inflation run its course until an equilibrium
is reached. This plan had been advanced by Ostrander and his boss
Donald D. Humphrey, deputy director of the Economics Division of
OMGUS (see Section 4.2).[305] Tenenbaum's approach, in contrast, was
a drastic reduction of money circulation by introducing a new scarce
currency, abandoning the Reichsmark altogether and trying to avoid
inflation as well as deflation. Tenenbaum's concept prevailed in
OMGUS, albeit at the price of the division of Germany. But open
inflation proposed by Humphrey and Ostrander would have had the
same consequence, because the Soviets would never have allowed
such an inflation, triggered by decontrol of prices, in their zone.
They were accustomed and interested in running a controlled instead
of a market economy. But they would have welcomed open inflation
in the Western zones as tasty food for their propaganda, as

Tenenbaum in his reply to "Dr. D. D. Humphrey" (see Section 4.2) had pointed out. Everybody involved in planning of currency reform (Tenenbaum) or open inflation (Humphrey/Ostrander) in the Western occupation zones knew that this would mean the division of Germany and expected it.

In closing this chapter, I want my readers to know about a misfortune that Otto Pfleiderer and his German "camp" colleagues had to endure after they were released from their confinement in *Haus Posen* on the Rothwesten airfield. Pfleiderer reports:

> On June 8, 1948, the experts were released from the conclave in exchange for a promise to maintain the strictest secrecy until currency reform. The drafts and similar documents for their work were burned before the dissolution of the conclave, not without a certain solemnity. // An amusing intermezzo of the 12 days remaining until the deadline of the currency reform began with the fact that the members of the conclave were promised by the spokesmen of the American military government [probably Tenenbaum, Bennett and Stoker], as a kind of reward, that they would be the first Germans to be allowed to take a look at the new notes denominated in German marks. All that was known was that these had been printed for some time and were in Frankfurt under the strict custody of the American military police. But no one in Germany knew what these notes looked like. However, when the released *conclavists* from all parts of the three western occupation zones made the then still rather arduous journey to Frankfurt, they and their American hosts had done the math without the commander in charge of the military police, who claimed that he had his orders directly from Washington, and these were not to allow any box of new money to be opened prematurely; what the American military government in Berlin said was not authoritative for him. So there was nothing left to do but, after much telephoning back and forth, to leave without having achieved anything.[306]

4.4   CURRENCY REFORM, CONSEQUENCES, AND ASSESSMENTS

4.4.1   Currency Reform

France remained hesitant and was not a safe bank for a trizonal solution. It demanded a further postponement of West German currency reform even after the Anglo-Saxon powers had granted a three-week postponement from June 1, 1948, the originally planned date for currency reform.[307] As Clay reports in his memoirs,[308] the French kept making trouble up to the last minute before C-Day on June 20. They doubted that the Anglo-Saxon plan would provide sufficient money for the French zone and demanded a higher percentage of the initially blocked accounts to be released later for investment purposes. The Anglo-Saxon Powers discussed with French representatives also their agreement on tax reductions planned for the Bizone as a necessary corollary of currency reform. The French opposed tax reductions on the grounds that these would result in inadequate revenues to meet occupation costs in their zone. The Anglo-Saxons compromised on some of the French demands "to a degree that had an immediate inflationary effect. We thought we had cleared the last obstacle to agreement. However, on June 15, the French commander in chief, General Koenig, sent us word that we must either accept the French tax proposal or he could not join us in the issue of the new currency."[309] As by paraphrasing I wouldn't be able to improve on the thrilling account by Lucius Clay of the last days immediately before currency reform, I quote further from Clay's memoirs:

> When we received this message many of the trucks were already
> loaded [with Deutschmark banknotes] and en route to the
> distribution centers. Further delay was impossible. Robertson [the
> British military governor] and I told Koenig's representatives that
> we deeply regretted the French action but had no choice other than
> to proceed in the bizonal area. I reported my decision immediately
> to the Department of the Army in a teleconference in which it was
> approved and during which I received word that General Noiret, the

French deputy, wished to see General Robertson and me. We met at my house [Im Dol 48 in Berlin-Dahlem] with our financial experts [for OMGUS Jack Bennett and Edward Tenenbaum, for British Military Government Sir Eric Coates and Bernard C. Cook] at 11 P.M. There we found that Noiret wished to negotiate but was without authority to make specific proposals. // The London agreements for tripartite fusion and international control of the Ruhr were under discussion in the French Parliament and the vote of the French Assembly was expected hourly. In our fantastic midnight negotiation Noiret would call Koenig, who was at his home in Baden, while others of his party were telephoning Paris to find out the decision of the Assembly. Finally, in the small hours of the morning, when we had made our last concession on the tax measure, we learned that the French Assembly had supported its government. Koenig accepted our final offer of compromise, and we were able to proceed trizonally.[310]

Asked in a press conference in the evening of June 15, 1948 when the currency reform would take place, Clay answered: "As yet I don't know the date of the currency reform myself."[311] Beyond protecting a top secret date with a lie, Clay may actually have spoken the truth in view of the still unsettled question, whether the French would go along with currency reform. Although already planned for June 20, a postponement might have been in the offing.

As to the actual date of the currency reform on June 20, 1948 Clay's political adviser Robert Murphy commented in his memoirs: "two years and a month after the Dodge [Colm, Dodge, Goldsmith – CDG] commission [had] declared that this reform was 'urgent.'"[312]

"On the afternoon of Friday, June 18, 1948, after the banks had closed for the week, the first announcement of the new currency law to become effective on June 20 was made by press and radio to the German people of the western zones."[313] Robert H. Lochner was the anchorman for these and other military government announcements in German. He was an American journalist whose father had been correspondent in Berlin for American media during the interwar years. So his son had grown up and finished secondary schooling in Berlin. For the US zone an official broadcast in English by Clay's financial adviser Jack Bennett on American Forces Network (AFN), Frankfurt am Main, stands out. Here is the text of Jack Bennett's announcement, in the preparation of which Tenenbaum must have played a crucial role:

> The three Military Governors of the three Western Zones have this evening announced laws for the reform of the Reichsmark currency now used by the population of these three Zones. The Reichsmark and Rentenmark notes now in circulation will be replaced by new money called the Deutsche Mark, and Germans holding ration cards will, on next Sunday and Monday, go with their ration cards to the food registration office and will receive for each member of the family 40 new Deutsche Marks upon the deposit, for each member of the family, of 60 old Reichsmarks. // During the first five days of the coming week Germans in the three Western Zones are required to deposit their remaining Reichsmarks at banks, and to fill out a declaration form showing the total of their money and bank accounts. On Friday of the coming week the terms upon which these bank accounts and money deposits will be converted into the new money will be announced. We have deliberately withheld the publication of the law covering the subsequent stages of the currency reform until after the declarations have been filed to avoid undesirable manipulation and speculation during the interim period. // The new Deutsche Marks which are to be used in this operation were printed and transported to Germany several months ago so that it would be available for quick use in the event of Quadripartite Agreement for a currency reform involving the four Zones of occupation. Unfortunately, such agreement could not be reached, despite many months of sincere and tedious effort on our part. It has proved impossible to postpone the currency reform in the Western Zones. In fact, one of the primary conditions of the

Economic Recovery Program for Europe is that the receiving countries must stabilize their currencies. Moreover, it has been amply demonstrated that aside from ERP aid, a stabilization of the currency of the Western Zones is essential to any expected boost in the production capacity of the area. // Now that Germany is to have a stable currency, and has the support of the Marshall Plan, there is no reason why we should not see immediately a great stimulation in productive activity. As is the case in any country with an inflated currency, too much man power and effort have been wasted in Germany since there has not been the incentive upon the worker to work hard in order to gain more money. Too much production has gone into non-essential types of goods which were not subject to rationing and price control, and which therefore offered to the producer the prospect of selling at fantastic Reichsmark prices. Now the German worker can expect to receive his wages in a stable currency and the manufacturer can expect to receive for his goods a money that will enable him to buy the raw materials which he needs to make more goods. // During the coming week new tax measures will be enacted by the Military Governors of the three Western Zones which will give considerable relief from the extraordinarily high taxes that have been placed on the Germans since the beginning of the Occupation. These tax relief measures will provide additional incentives since the worker and the owner may retain a greater part of his earnings. Those reductions in the tax rates are made possible as a result of the greatly increased revenues. // The currency reform law does not apply to occupation personnel. They are requested to get in touch with their nearest Finance Office or Commanding Officer for information about the details of the conversion of any Reichsmarks which they may have acquired against dollar payment. // I know that you all join with me in the hope and belief that the step which the three Military Governors have now taken will mark the definite and decisive turning point for the German economy, and that we can look forward to a period of intense and energetic activity by the Germans in the common effort to put their country on a self-supporting basis.[314]

Even before this official radio announcement of the impending currency reform to the German population – in German also over all West German radio stations at about the same time – the British military governor, General Robertson, dispatched a courteous letter of June 18, 1948 to Marshal Sokolovsky, the Soviet military governor, announcing West Germany's currency reform two days later. The letter concludes: "I can only hope that it will be possible for the Occupying Powers to agree at an early date to reintroduce a single currency for the whole of Germany as well as to take the other measures of economic unity, to which we have always attached so much importance."[315]

Ludwig Erhard is a special case. His Economic Administration of the Bizone was not in charge of currency reform. On the German side, it was rather Alfred Hartmann, the director of the Administration for Finance. But Erhard stole the show from Hartmann. In the future he would do likewise with Tenenbaum. According to Harold James, Erhard was informed by Clay about the date of the impending currency reform only in the afternoon of June 18, 1948, shortly before it was officially announced over all radio stations to the German public at 8 p.m. He was at first deeply hurt by this sign of distrust on the part of Clay. But he soon regained his composure. He realized that the fluttering coat of history was sweeping by and that he had an opportunity to hang on to its tail. He ordered his driver to take him to the *Hessischer Rundfunk* radio station in Frankfurt.[316] From there he broadcast the following message to the German people: "???"

I did my best to find it and quote it here. For the transcript I first contacted the *Stiftung Ludwig-Erhard-Haus* in Fürth, where Erhard was born. This Foundation didn't have it and referred me to the Ludwig-Erhard-Stiftung in Bonn, which Ludwig Erhard himself had founded in 1967 in order to preserve his legacy and promote the principles behind his conception of the postwar German *Social Market Economy*. These essential principles comprise that a functioning competition, not the state and its bureaucracy, should regulate the economy and protect the consumer from abuse of market power. They guarantee private property rights and freedom of contract. And they assign to the state a strong role in defending functioning competition, free market entry, and via solidly financed social expenditures redistributive corrections of socially unacceptable market outcomes.

This Foundation has collected practically all available documentary traces of Erhard's legacy. But it likewise was unable to come up with a transcript of Erhard's alleged radio message in *Hessischer Rundfunk* at Frankfurt am Main on June 18, 1948. Frustrated with these results, I finally contacted the radio station itself by email on May 13, 2020. After an evidently careful search, the archive services of the *Hessischer Rundfunk* answered by email on June 18, 2020, by chance the seventy-second anniversary of Erhard's alleged radio address on the imminent currency reform, that their extensive archival research had not produced any evidence of the occurrence of Erhard's radio address.

But Erhard's claim to fame regarding West Germany's currency reform, to which he added the decontrol of rationing and price fixing for a limited number of private household goods, was also revealed to have been a myth.[317] Heinz Sauermann, an eyewitness economist working on the staff of the German financial experts assembled at Bad Homburg as members of the Special Agency for Money and Credit and a continuing consultant to OMGUS, revealed in 1979: "the notion that Erhard insisted on immediate freedom of markets from price control against the will of the Allies is characterized by a German financial consultant to OMGUS [Sauermann] as 'legend,'" writes Charles P. Kindleberger.[318]

All the while Tenenbaum was occupied with organizing and supervising the distribution and control of Deutschmark banknote supply all over West Germany. The new currency had been stored in the cellars of the Reichsbank building in Frankfurt am Main for

C-Day in 23,000 wooden boxes weighing 1,035 tons. To camouflage their valuable content, the boxes were labeled with either "CLAY-W-OCFOFD" or "Door knobs," which in view of all the destruction of residential buildings Germany really needed. At that time the total face value of those banknotes was 5.7 billion D-Mark. On June 14 and 15, 1948, these boxes were moved from their heavily guarded storage location in Frankfurt by truck and train to West Germany's different *Landeszentralbanken* (= State Central Banks). Also under Tenenbaum's organizational responsibility, 800 military trucks transported the new currency on June 18 and 19 from there to each and every food stamp issuing point in West Germany. These were charged with the execution of the per capita currency conversion on Sunday, 20 June.[319] In his unfinished book manuscript Tenenbaum cites an article of the *Frankfurter Neue Presse* of June 27, 1948 which credits the US Army's D-Mark distribution using 800 trucks and several special trains on June 18 and 19, 1948 as the largest logistic operation since the landing in Normandy on D-Day.[320]

US and British military government laws on the reorganization of the monetary system, namely Laws Nos. 61 (Currency Act of June 18, 1948), 62 (Issue Act of June 20, 1948), 63 (Conversion Act of June 27, 1948), and 64 (Revenue Act of June 20, 1948) for reorganization of the tax schedules[321] and corresponding ordinances for the French zone came into force during those days.[322] They put into effect the currency conversion and attendant monetary and tax measures. Law No. 63, regulating the conversion of bank balances, was deliberately not made public until June 27, 1948. US financial adviser Jack Bennett explains this: RM banknotes were still in private hand after per capita and business allotments had already reduced their volume. To save them from becoming completely worthless, they had to be deposited in bank accounts by June 26 at the latest. Therefore, the terms upon which turned-in RM notes would be converted were withheld from inclusion in the laws and regulations published one week earlier.

Experience of other countries with currency reforms had shown that when the full terms of conversion were made known at the same time as the deposit of the old money and the filing of a full declaration of ownership, holders of the old money arranged to divide their holdings among their families and friends in such manner as to provide a maximum benefit to themselves contrary to the spirit of the conversion law. Thus, for example, black market operators, had they known in advance that declarations of old currency in excess of certain maxima would require examination and certification by the tax authorities and thus become subject to confiscation if illegally held, would have sought means of having some part of their funds declared by stooges.[323]

The fourth military government law on the reorganization of the monetary system, Law No. 65 (Blocked Accounts Act of October 4, 1948) in the Bizone and Ordinance No. 175 in the French zone, was also a crucial part of Allied legislation on currency reform. Actually, it was a supplement to Law No. 63, the Conversion Act, which had converted bank deposit in RM to 10 percent in DM. But only half of the converted amount, that is, only 5 percent of the original RM balance, was originally at each individual's disposal on *free accounts*. The other 5 percent had been credited to *blocked accounts*. Law No. 65 determined the share of amounts on blocked accounts that would be released from blocking, on the one hand, and would become worthless, on the other. Inflationary developments had characterized the months since currency reform. This explains why 70 percent of balances on blocked accounts were canceled, only 20 percent was transferred for each individual's disposal on his free account, and 10 percent was credited to an investment account (until 1954). By these measures the final conversion ratio for RM bank balances turned out to be not 100 RM to 10 DM, but only 100 RM to 6.5 DM.[324]

By the time of the Blocked Accounts Act in early October 1948, Edward A. Tenenbaum had changed from his position in OMGUS, Berlin, as the expert for monetary reform, to his new job in the

ERP-Administration in Washington, DC already a month or so earlier. So it was Jack Bennett alone, Clay's financial adviser, who had decided on the terms of Law No. 65. By disappointing higher expectations of the German public and currency experts alike, he acted wisely and responsibly to make sure that the DM would gain confidence and stability. Toward the end of 1948 – also due to Bennett's keeping DM purchasing power relatively scarce – inflationary developments in West Germany petered out.

According to figures published by the *Bank deutscher Länder*, the forerunner of the Deutsche Bundesbank, an estimated 135 billion RM in circulation (including bank deposits) had been canceled by April 30, 1949. On that date, as initial allotments in billions of DM 2.78 had gone to individuals, 0.47 to businesses, 2.67 to German governments (including state-owned railroad and postal systems), and 0.77 to military governments. These initial allotments sum up to 6.69 billion DM. Beyond that 5.91 billion had increased the DM volume of money from conversion of RM bank balances and 6.56 billion from credit creation. This adds up to a total of 19.16 billion DM of money in circulation by April 30, 1949, of which 6.33 consisted of banknotes and 12.83 billion DM of bank deposits.[325]

At this stage the inflationary tendencies of the second half of 1948 had subsided. Instead there were fears of deflation and depression between the end of 1948 and the start of the Korean War in June 1950, especially on the part of OMGUS and of its successor after the Federal Republic's foundation, John J. McCloy's US High Commission in Germany.[326] In May 1949 unemployment had climbed to 1.24 million person, a rate of 8.5 percent of the labor force. The USA, where due to the threatening specter of a postwar great depression Keynesianism had been enshrined in the 1946 Employment Act, urged the German authorities to stimulate the economy. But German politicians were more afraid of inflation than depression. They clung more to Neo- or – in its German version "Ordoliberalism" – than to Keynesianism.

In American eyes, there was not only a lack of fiscal stimulus to promote growth and employment, but also the monetary mantle looked too tight. The German side, however, might have taken pride in the fact that the quotation of the DM against the US dollar, which had been officially fixed at 30 US cents per DM, had recovered from its lowest quotation of 4.5 US cents in the free foreign-exchange market in Switzerland in December 1948 to about 19.5 cents in June 1949.[327] West Germany was in desperate need of gaining confidence of international foreign-exchange and capital markets in the stability of its young new currency. For the first time of many afterward, the German monetary and fiscal policy-makers found themselves on the horns of the dilemma between internal and external stability.[328]

I will not go into more specifics of currency-reform execution here, as an abundance of literature on the technical details is available.[329] But I want to point out that the West German financial reform in 1948 consisted of three elements: currency reform, tax reform, and legislation regulating burden sharing. The latter was necessary to create an equalization between economic winners and losers not only of the war, which was largely paid for by inflationary finance, but also of currency reform itself, which relieved debtors at the expense of creditors. Consequently, the original planners of currency reform on the American side (CDG Plan 1946) and on the German side (Homburg Plan 1948) treated burden sharing, just like tax reform, as an integral part to be regulated in tandem with currency legislation of the Western Allies.

Under pressure from Washington, OMGUS – against Clay's, Bennett's, and Tenenbaum's opposition and against wishes of German experts and politicians[330] – had to drop the burden-sharing part from currency-reform legislation, with one exception. The existing German legislative authorities of the Bizone, the Economic Council and the federal Länder (= states) Council, were obliged to pass burden-sharing legislation before the end of 1948. This decision was, of course, also motivated by the fact that the Western Allies did not want to be blamed by the German population for harsh tax measures that an equitable burden sharing would require. Actually, the West German authorities took only preliminary steps into burden-sharing legislation before the year ran out. Fairly close to currency reform the *Gesetz zur Sicherung von Forderungen für den Lastenausgleich – Hypothekensicherungsgesetz* (Law on Securing Claims for Equalization of Burdens – Mortgage Safeguarding Act) was passed by the Economic Council on July 9, 1948 in anticipation of further burden-sharing legislation.

Already during his discussions with the German experts at "camp" Rothwesten, Tenenbaum had insisted on the devaluation of monetary debt of private persons and businesses 10 RM to 1 DM, as also the CDG Plan had envisaged. The majority of the German experts had favored a 1 to 1 conversion, as the Homburg Plan had proposed and as currency-reform legislation would stipulate for wages, pensions, and rents. This would make burden sharing much easier, they argued. Tenenbaum didn't deny this. But he saw the inflationary danger of non-devalued private debt. And he pointed to the fact that the currency-reform laws of the Allied powers would oblige the West German legislative bodies to quickly enact measures to tax away debtors' profits for securing funds for later comprehensive German equalization-of-burdens laws. The outcome was the German Mortgage Safeguarding Act of July 9, 1948.[331]

The Western Allies had decoupled burden sharing from their currency-reform legislation. But in Law No. 61 (Currency Law) of June 18, 1948, last paragraph of the preamble, they obliged the Germans: "The task of equalizing burdens is laid on the appropriate German legislative bodies as one of the greatest urgency to be accomplished by 31 December 1948."[332] Actually, in keeping this deadline the First Equalization of Burdens Act was passed by the Economic Council on December 14, 1948.[333] General Clay and the BICO were content and more than willing to approve this law. But Washington objected and Clay for the umpteenth time offered his resignation. The Act triggered a back-and-forth tug-of-war, not only between Washington and OMGUS, but also among the Western Allies, over the First Equalization of Burdens Act, which never went into force. It was finally reshaped with few changes into the *Soforthilfegesetz*

(Emergency Relief Act). This one went into force in the Bizone on August 18, 1949.

It was only taking care of aid for urgent survival needs, like financial support for millions of refugees from lost territories in East Germany and for the victims of houses and apartments destroyed by Allied bombing in West Germany. The essence of burden sharing, the equalization of wealth, was enacted by the Federal Republic of Germany as late as August 14, 1952, with a 30-year payments schedule for equalization taxes on nominal DM wealth on June 21, 1948. Creeping inflation during the 1950s to 1970s eroded the anyhow low annual payment obligations of 1.67 percent p.a. of assessed net worth of June 21, 1948 to trivial amounts. Tenenbaum's, Bennett's, and Clay's apprehensions that a German equalization-of-burdens legislation decoupled from currency reform would be sluggish and soft under internal political and interest-group pressure were fully borne out by historical developments.[334] But I concede that the inadequate wealth equalization aided in rebuilding capital for reconstructing the German economy in the 1950s and 1960s, often called the "economic miracle." And the current distribution of income and wealth in Germany is much less unequal than in the USA.

Burden sharing was a matter of fiscal policy, just like tax policy. Fiscal policy decisions are the core of democracy in setting policy priorities. A top priority of Western Allies' policy in Germany was to instill their own preferences for democracy also in Germany with its own democratic tradition of the Weimar Republic. It is true that the Western Allies insisted on planning and executing currency reform with little say from the German side. With harsh measures they aimed at assuring success. This would put the West German economy on its own feet, thereby relieving their taxpayers at home from having to continue the transfer of massive food and other subsidies to prevent starvation, disease, and unrest. They left not only the terms of burden sharing, but also of tax reform largely to decisions by German legislative and executive institutions they had created.

The difference between burden-sharing and tax matters was that Allied currency reform legislation merely obliged the West German legislative bodies to pass a law with burden-sharing provisions before the end of 1948. In contrast, tax-policy legislation with Law No. 64, promulgated on June 22, 1948, was an integral part of currency reform enacted by the Western Allies on June 20, 1948. However, they had left it largely to German politicians to decide on the content of this law, with one exception. For cosmetic reasons they resisted the lowering of tax rates below the tax-rate schedules in their home countries. And France, anxious for revenue, insisted on higher rates than the German politicians had in mind. This resulted, for instance, in lowering income tax rates mainly for lower and middle incomes.

Walter W. Heller was an American economist born in 1915 to German parents who had emigrated to the USA. He became famous for presiding over the Council of Economic Advisers under Presidents J. F. Kennedy and L. B. Johnson and for being president of the American Economic Association. But hardly anybody knows that he had been working in OMGUS, Berlin, as the American expert for tax questions in West Germany during the run-up to currency reform. He, therefore, was an active participant in the tug-of-war over the extent of tax reductions between Allied military governments, on the one hand, and representatives of the Bizonal Economic Council, the forerunner of a West German parliament, and the *Länder* (states) finance ministers, on the other. The Anglo-Saxon powers, in principle, wanted to leave decisions over tax reform in tandem with currency reform to German legislative bodies, although they would have to enact such legislation themselves, because the bizonal German legislative bodies had no jurisdiction for the French zone. In fact, the bizonal German legislative bodies submitted their tax proposals to the Allies in the form of draft laws shortly before currency reform. In his excellent article with many details on German tax rates under German law up to 1945, ACC Law No. 12, 1946, and military government Law No. 64, 1948, Heller details to what extent the far-reaching German proposals for tax reductions were cut down before enacting Law No. 64 in the US and British zones and the equivalent by ordinance in the French zone.[335]

The total reduction of income tax rates against the prior ACC tax regime has been estimated at about 30 percent.[336] The top rate remained at 95 percent as in prior ACC Law No. 12 of February 11, 1946.[337] Its incidence, however, would not be applied at 60,000 RM as before, but only at 250,000 DM. As to corporation income tax, ACC Law No. 12 had introduced graduated tax rates of 35, 45, and 60 percent. At the request of German politicians this was changed into a unified rate of 50 percent. This was higher than the 20, later 40 percent rates that were in force in Germany during World War II and before ACC Law No. 12 was enacted. The same was true for the income tax rates of Law No. 64. But to compensate for those still high nominal tax rates, very generous depreciation allowances and tax privileges were granted, especially after the Western military governments allowed the German legislative bodies in autumn 1948 to lower the tax burden further by all other means except by lowering the tax rates. For example, reinvested profits were made completely tax-exempt. Loans to special economic sectors, such as residential construction and ship-building, were fully or partly tax deductible. And savings-bank accounts and interest on securities were granted tax privileges.[338]

For the months following currency reform a secret telegram from the Department of the Army in Washington, DC to OMGUS of July 15, 1948 announced the arrival in Frankfurt am Main of a second set of banknotes under Operation Bird Dog in boxes also labeled "Door knobs." It listed October 6, November 10, December 22, 1948, and January 26, 1949 as latest dates of delivery completion.[339] These second-set banknotes were already marked with "Bank deutscher Länder" as issuer. I assume that their face value amounted to 5.0 billion DM, which is the difference between the 5.7 billion DM delivered before currency reform and the amount of 10.7 billion DM that Ludwig Erhard often mentioned as circulating DM currency in the second half of 1948, as I report below in this chapter.[340]

In any case Hans Möller, the youngest among the German experts interned in the Rothwesten "camp," with the benefit of hindsight has published a much more detailed and reliable quantitative estimate of money supply before and after currency reform, including its composition in cash, demand and time deposits, and savings deposits. He calculated the money-supply figure put into circulation by currency-reform legislation of the Allies at 13.2 billion DM. This corresponded to 9.1 percent of the RM money supply immediately before currency reform.[341]

4.4.2   Consequences

Like all the rest of West Germans on June 20, 1948, my mother had exchanged for herself and for me 60 RM banknotes each for 40 + 40 = 80 DM banknotes and 20 + 20 = 40 DM two months later. She had lost her husband, I my father in a daylight bombing raid on the city of Münster in Westphalia in November 1944. He had been in civilian employment as executive manager of an agricultural cooperative. Besides his own accumulated savings, he had secured his family with a life insurance policy for 10,000 RM. This was a high amount at the time, considering that the average monthly pay of a worker was less than 200 RM in 1948 as well as in 1944. My mother had kept her savings inherited from her husband as well as the 10,000 RM from life insurance in our local savings and loan association, managed by a cousin of hers, in our hometown Telgte, seven miles from Münster.

Some days after currency reform she went to the bank, probably to draw cash from her savings account. On that occasion her cousin informed her that all of her deposits had been devalued by 95 percent, e.g., her life insurance amount of 10,000 RM to 500 DM. And the 80 DM she had exchanged 1 RM for 1 DM on June 20, 1948 would also be deducted from this amount. The sum of 420 DM was all that was left of her perceived small fortune of 10,000 RM. It is burned in my memory that when she came home from the bank she – an always cheerful and optimistic person, also in later life – cried as I had never seen her before. As an economist I know, of course, she was a victim of money illusion, like most of the German population at the time. Fortunately, her poise and optimism quickly returned. A year later she remarried with the best friend of my father and gave birth to three more boys during the "economic-miracle" years of the 1950s.

Let's now turn to the broader picture of currency-reform consequences. On June 20/21, 1948, the German Mark (DM) replaced the Reichsmark (RM), the remnants of the old *Rentenmark*, issued after currency reform of November 1923, and the Mark notes, which had been put into circulation as legal tender by the Allied Military Authorities, that is, the four occupying powers, after they had entered and occupied German territory. Three days later, the Soviet military government announced a currency reform in the Soviet zone of occupation, with per capita conversion of seventy marks per person starting June 24 and ending June 28, 1948. It included not only the eastern sector of Berlin, but the three western sectors as well. Faced with this possibility, the American military government was inclined to shy away from introducing the DM in West Berlin.

On December 9, 1947 Clay's financial adviser Jack Bennett had sent a top secret eight-page memo of Tenenbaum to General Clay, entitled "Berlin and Bizonal Financial Reform." Before dealing with its content, I want to share with you what Michael Wolff, who reprinted this memo in abbreviated form in his book on currency reform in Berlin, has written in praise of Tenenbaum's analytical skills:

> Tenenbaum's study impresses with its clear identification of the subject matter, a precisely conducted analysis, and clear recommendations for further action without glossing over the resulting difficulties. Tenenbaum did not confine himself to a purely financial discussion. He was fully aware of the political premises and consequences of his proposals and expressed them clearly.[342]

Tenenbaum's memo evaluated different options for monetary reform in Berlin. "To abandon Berlin finances to whatever currency system may be set up for the Soviet Zone," could not be envisaged for political reasons. On the other hand, a separate currency reform for the western sectors of Berlin would be technically most difficult. In that case he presaged a number of grave political consequences as to the free movement of persons and goods between Berlin and not only the Soviet occupation zone, but also the Western occupation zones via the *Autobahn*, railroads, and waterways. Therefore, his most desirable option was: "To agree with the Soviets on a 'neutral' quadripartite financial reform for the entire territory of Berlin"[343] And: "... a currency reform for the Western Sectors alone is not in the interest of the Western Powers."[344] But such a solution met with opposition from Germans. Michael Budczies has reported that they prevailed over the Americans' original misgivings and that also his father, Wolfgang Budczies, had a strong hand in it.[345]

In any case, eventually the DM, with a "B" stamped on it, was the outcome of the emergency currency reform in the Western sectors of Berlin, in reaction to currency reform in the Soviet zone, announced only three days after June 20, 1948. Tenenbaum, his OMGUS colleague Manuel Gottlieb, and State Department economic adviser Robert Eisenberg had previously all been in agreement that due to the division of Berlin into four occupation sectors, the city should not be split by the introduction of the DM in the Western sectors of Berlin. But while Gottlieb and Eisenberg had recommended to Clay to accept the Soviet zone mark as legal tender also in West Berlin, Tenenbaum had pleaded for a four-power currency reform in all of Berlin with the introduction of a B-Mark as a neutral solution, a special currency for all four sectors of Berlin. As history developed in its mostly unpredictable course, neither was the East German Mark introduced in West Berlin, which even Clay had been preferring over Tenenbaum's recommendation.[346] But Tenenbaum's B-Mark, DM banknotes stamped with a "B," were introduced in Berlin, though only in the Western sectors. Manuel Gottlieb's and Robert Eisenberg's efforts to avoid the currency split in the city of Berlin were all overridden by historical developments.

Ten years after currency reform Tenenbaum and his former boss Jack Bennett, then business partners in Continental-Allied Company in Washington, DC, were interviewed on their experience in the preparation of currency reform. They showed pride in their telegram address on their business cards: money-Washington. This symbolic address of their expertise would reach them. Edward Tenenbaum reported about his problems with the printing of German Mark notes in the USA at the expense of the US government in preparation of the West German currency reform:

> The money had to be printed quickly, we contacted an American printing company that usually prints securities, and found a few symbols from the typesetting box that seemed appropriate. Among them was a picture of a worker and the goddess of industry leaning on a globe. This would be a good image for the ten-mark note, we thought ... But in the highest council of the military government, frowns were raised: the symbol could be misunderstood. The globe could mean that the Germans once again want to conquer the world.

In the same interview Jack Bennett reported about negotiations with the Soviet side over the shape of a currency solution for all four sectors of Berlin:

> We had secretly flown in the money boxes to the western sectors. Then the negotiations with the Russians began; it was the purest poker game. The Soviets kept us at the negotiating table all day and ordered more and more champagne being served. They wanted to gain time to prepare their own measures and had no idea that time no longer mattered to us, since everything had been prepared in detail and we only had to press the button to carry out the West Berlin currency reform. Finally, at ten o'clock in the evening, we broke off the negotiations without any results. The next morning brought the hasty reform in the Soviet zone, but our simultaneous maneuvering pushed the value of East money down to twenty to one in favor of West money even in the first few days.[347]

After the Soviets had left the ACC on March 20, 1948, each side was on its own as to planning a currency reform for its respective occupation area. OMGUS' financial intelligence group had reported already on March 11, 1948 – exactly the same day when the dice for a separate currency reform in the Western zones had been cast in Washington, DC[348] – that new banknotes had not yet been printed in the Soviet zone, but the production of currency stamps to be glued on Reichsbank notes had been completed. This way a currency reform in the Soviet zone could be executed any time. This alarm led to emergency planning on the part of the Western powers how they should react in such a case in their sectors of Berlin, which the Soviets would certainly consider included in their currency area. Therefore, in April 1948 the financial advisers of the three Western powers charged Edward Tenenbaum, in cooperation with his French counterpart for planning currency reform, Charles Lefort, to devise an Emergency Plan for Berlin. After its completion, the British financial adviser, Sir Eric Coates, consented on April 24, 1948.

Tenenbaum and Lefort suggested to accept the inclusion of the Western sectors of Berlin into the Soviet zone currency reform to preserve the Berlin citizens' existing freedom of movement and integration into political, economic and cultural life in all four sectors. But only under the following condition. It was imperative that the Soviets assume certain guarantees for the economic and political future of the city as a whole. ... In the event that the Soviets were not prepared to assume the guarantees demanded by the West, this report recommended to the three Western military governors that the new DM (West) be introduced in Berlin. Tenenbaum jumped over his own shadow here. In his December 1947 memo, he had strongly advised against such an option. But decision-makers in Washington, DC had distanced themselves from Tenenbaum's conditional acceptance of West Berlin's inclusion into the Soviet zone currency reform.[349]

The Soviets agreed to a reactivation of the Finance Directorate of ACC and participated in a meeting of the four financial advisers on

June 22, 1948. They didn't meet the Western powers' wish for guarantees for Berlin's undivided political and economic future. Their main argument was that by their separate currency reform the Western powers had ripped apart four-power responsibility for economic and monetary policy for all of Germany and had brought about its division. Why should the Soviet part now guarantee four-power responsibility for all sectors of Berlin?

Therefore, on June 24, 1948 a currency reform for the three western sectors of Berlin was legally clad into a "Gemeinsamer Befehl der Kommandanten des amerikanischen, britischen und französischen Sektors von Berlin" (= Joint Order of the Commanders of the American, British and French Sectors of Berlin) and was made public. Before proceeding in this manner the Anglo-Saxon Allies had to break initial French resistance.[350] Here, too, the Deutsche Mark (West) was introduced. However, a "B" was stamped on or since August 1948 perforated through the banknotes. This distinction between the Berlin banknotes and the West German ones was abandoned at the end of 1953.[351] The per capita conversion one DM (West) for one RM started June 25, 1948 and lasted three days. West Berliners were entitled to 60 DM immediately, not forty plus 20 DM in two installments. Another advantage over conditions of currency reform in West Germany was that the 60 DM were not offset against the claims from the conversion of all other old RM money, which the citizens were obliged to deposit at West Berlin banks for conversion 6.5 DM for 100 RM, as it finally turned out.

Although the Western powers continued to grant legal-tender status to DM (East) besides DM (West) in West Berlin (until March 1949), their currency action triggered the blockade of all terrestrial access routes to Berlin starting June 24, 1948. Until the blockade was lifted on May 12, 1949, American and British transport aircraft, in the biggest airlift ever, supplied West Berlin with food, coal, and raw materials exclusively through the three air corridors that had been agreed with the Soviet Union years earlier when inter-allied relations were still good.

The military governments of the three Western occupation zones had legislatively implemented the currency reform without consultation with, let alone approval by Ludwig Erhard and the Economic Council. Erhard and a few hand-picked German politicians had only been informed by the Western Allies on June 15, 1948, that the currency reform would be announced on June 18 and implemented on Sunday, June 20.[352]

In order to be able to start the price reform at the same time as the currency reform, Erhard hurriedly submitted to the Economic Council on June 17 his draft of the *Gesetz über Leitsätze für die Bewirtschaftungs- und Preispolitik nach der Geldreform* (= Law on Guiding Principles for Economic Control and Price Policy after Currency Reform), also called *Leitsätzegesetz* (= Guiding Principles Act) for adoption in three readings. He and a few hand-picked like-minded staff members of the Economic Administration had been preparing it for weeks. The Economic Council was the parliamentary representation of West Germans in the Bizone with BICO-supervised legislative power in the area of economic policy. In the hall of the Frankfurt Stock Exchange, its meeting place, Erhard fought until the morning of June 18 to get it passed. And he managed to persuade a majority of the deputies to approve it.[353] The Act was an extraordinarily daring and courageous step in view of a rather anti-capitalist mood among the population. This had manifested itself even in the Ahlen party program of February 3, 1947 of the British-Zone wing of the business-oriented CDU party. This party program had demanded the socialization of German coal as well as iron and steel industries. But in the vote on the Guiding Principles Law, the CDU backed Erhard's decontrol bill. Only the representatives of the SPD and KPD voted against its adoption and thus favored the continuation of administrative controls of prices and rations.

This law, a sort of enabling act with a period of validity until the end of 1948, stipulated that the "freeing of administrative controls" and the "freeing of prices" were to be given "preference" over their fixing by the authorities.[354] The directors of the Administrations for

Economic Affairs (Ludwig Erhard) and for Food, Agriculture and Forestry (Hans Schlange-Schöningen) were authorized to implement appropriate measures by decree.

Erhard had studied in the 1920s in Frankfurt am Main with his doctoral supervisor Franz Oppenheimer. He had also followed Walter Eucken's publications. Eucken's student and friend Leonard Miksch, along with the Münster economics professor Alfred Müller-Armack, belonged to Erhard's few coworkers in the drafting of the Guiding Principles Act. It helped to spur the transition from an administratively controlled to a market-driven economy. Eucken, Miksch, Erhard, and Müller-Armack were convinced that, if the relationship between monetary demand and real supply was approximately balanced and competition was functioning, price determination via the free market was a fairer distribution system than via administrative controls with their price freezes, ration coupons and food stamps. The latter had been the practice during Nazi rule. It had also been continued by the four military governments.

Five days after currency reform, Erhard decontrolled all industrially produced finished goods by his *Decree on Pricing and Price Controls Following Currency Reform*. The Director of the Administration for Agriculture, Hans Schlange-Schöningen, did so to a much lesser extent. In addition: "Most of the economic control regulations were not prolonged and lapsed automatically on 30 June as provided for by the Economic Controls Act of October 1947."[355]

Erhard's press spokesman Kuno Ockhardt had announced these measures on Hessischer Rundfunk radio on the day of the currency reform, when people in the streets were already queuing up to be equipped with their per capita allotment of 40 DM in new currency. By this public statement Erhard wanted to make sure that shopkeepers would supply their hoarded goods when customers would come to demand them with their new currency from Monday, 21 June 1948, onward. He feared that currency reform would end in catastrophe if the demand in DM could buy as little as had been offered in exchange for RM.[356] By having Ockhardt announce his planned measures of decontrol on Sunday, Erhard also caught the Allied military governments off guard. He expected that they would not be able to act on Sunday and that due to the announced price releases the shop windows of retail traders would already be full of goods from hoarded stocks on Monday morning.

Neither had the Guiding Principles Act been discussed and confirmed in the Council of the Länder (*Länderrat*), the federal chamber of parliament and forerunner of the *Bundesrat*. Nor had the military governments approved it. While the Council of the Länder passed the law on Monday June 21, 1948, Erhard had been ordered to the headquarters of the US military government in the IG Farben building in Frankfurt am Main for that day.[357] There he was confronted by angry financial advisers and currency experts of the three Western military governors. They rightly felt they had been ignored. Furthermore, the American CDG Plan, the point of departure for the design of the 1948 West German currency reform, demanded for a transitory period "the maintenance of 'effective price control.'" The length of the period should be measured by how long the "supply of necessary goods is insufficient."[358]

Within US military government the question of decontrol of prices had been discussed already in a meeting of F. Taylor Ostrander, chief of the price control section of the OMGUS Economics Division, and Jack Bennett and Edward Tenenbaum of Clay's financial adviser's office on December 1, 1947. In his report to his boss, the acting director of the Economics Division, Ostrander reported: "Mr. Bennett raised the question whether some areas might not be released from price control upon currency reform, but we agreed that while 'flea circuses and glass eyes' might be released, on the whole it would be inadvisable to remove many controls at that time."[359] Actually, it looks like price controls on about 400 items were lifted by Erhard's solitary decision in the wake of currency reform.[360]

Erhard was asked to explain his measures and justify his actions. The British in particular were incensed because their Labour government was far from ready to end the administrative controls introduced during the war. The Americans, that is, financial adviser Jack Bennett and his special assistant for currency reform Edward Tenenbaum, also regarded Erhard's liberalization move as premature. When for hours the confrontation would not end, Erhard demanded to speak to General Clay himself.[361] The latter had, after all, promoted his political career because of his advocacy of the model of a competition-driven market economy instead of a socialist, administratively controlled planned economy. So much so, in fact, that Erhard himself noted in 1962, "For the sake of justice, I must not conceal the fact that I am, jokingly speaking, an 'American discovery,' and that without support from this side I would not have been able to carry out and get through the monetary and economic reform on a free-market basis."[362]

Clay reminded him that only the occupying powers could change administrative controls. Erhard is said to have responded, "I didn't change them, I abolished them!" To this Clay allegedly replied that all his advisers were opposed to Erhard's action. To which Erhard is reported to have replied, "You are not alone. My advisors are against it, too." Finally, Clay cut the Gordian knot: "O.k. I am not an expert, but I have the feeling you are on the right track. So keep going."[363] Christoph Buchheim summarizes: "The American Military Government in particular supported the abolition of the majority of economic controls after the currency reform."[364]

Although Erhard had blatantly violated occupation law, he was able to win Clay's approval for his free market–oriented policy. With this moral support from Clay, Erhard himself went to *Hessischer Rundfunk* radio station that evening to explain his decontrol policy in the context of currency reform to the West German population. He opened his address:

> After the mental tensions of the last days, everyday life has now taken possession of us again. Today, the German people went about their work calmly and prudently, and I believe there will have been

few among them who did not realize with a feeling of liberation that only on this day did the spook of that mass hysteria fall away from us, which had also bestowed on us this great financial swindle of price-controlled inflation. Sobered from this intoxication, we only now realize more clearly how close to the precipice we have been walking and how high time it was to tread the path of honesty and truthfulness again with the introduction of our new currency.

He further argues:

... I am only too conscious in this serious hour of responsibility before our people, and this feeling of being locked into an indissolubly common destiny also urges me to speak to you all. ... // I am not appealing to a dull, misty faith, not to the miracle of unreason, when I wish to encourage our people in their confidence in our new currency, but just the other way round I am appealing to the common sense, the insight and the power of knowledge of all of you, when I point out to you, that there can be no danger to the stability of the new money if we only apply ourselves to orderly public budget management and ensure, through an equally orderly monetary and credit policy, that the correspondence between the production of goods and the formation of purchasing power is maintained. ... Where, however, partial price increases are to be feared as a result of a massing of demand on certain requirements, such as clothing or footwear, the danger is averted by the consumption regulation and other possibilities of intervention. ... // ... So I certainly do not speak for the mass of entrepreneurs, who partly felt quite well in the compulsory economy as state pensioners, but I speak only for the capable among them, and I speak in particular again for the mass of our people, when I represent here – though consciously – the principle that the absolutely necessary selection then must not take place according to any schematic rules, but only according to the principle of performance. ... // ... But I do not know of any economic order in which this demand is better fulfilled than in a market economy, in which every individual is dependent on the mercy of the consumer, for better or worse, and which therefore, in contrast to all forms of state-controlled economy, offers the best protection against abuse of honest work of a people. ... // My Economic Administration has already announced yesterday from this place the release of various commodities and consumer goods from state control, and all preparations have been made to loosen the reins of such controls even more. The resonance that this transition to freer forms of economic dealings has found in our people only proves how thoroughly fed up they are with this state tutelage and how liberating our people feel the possibility of shaping their own destiny, which has been returned to them. We were well on the way to commanding democracy to death and to letting the basic democratic rights of our people become a chimera. Only when these rights find expression again in a free choice of occupation, in a free choice of employment and, above all, in freedom of consumption, can we expect the German people to take an active part again in the political shaping of their destiny. ... The German citizen will only regain his dignity and be able to embrace democracy from his own inner experience when he no longer needs to bend his back in any civil-servant's office. I will consider it my noble task to help him to achieve this. // But as long as I can be sure of the confidence of the Economic Council [= parliament consisting of German representatives] and of the German people, I will go down this path of dissolving the state-controlled economy with courage and determination.

In closing Erhard states in his typical melodramatic manner:

I have no political ambition, and least of all one of a party-political kind. When I return the authority granted to me into the hands of the Economic Council, I will be happy and grateful if I succeeded to have overcome all perils and to have contributed from my side to the fact that our people, working on a sound economic basis, may again feel a piece of that earthly joy of life without which it would have to wither and perish.[365]

From hindsight Erhard commented, "It was to my advantage that General Clay, probably the strongest personality in the High Commission [*sic*], backed me and covered my orders."[366]

The Guiding Principles Act carried the date of June 24, 1948. Officially it went into force in the Bizone when it was published in the *Gesetz- und Verordnungsblatt des Wirtschaftsrates des Vereinigten Wirtschaftsgebietes* (WiGBl.) on pages 59–60 as late as July 7, 1948. But encouraged by Clay's support, Erhard issued an executive order with new price ceilings on coal, electricity, gas, water, iron, rents, and some essential foodstuffs, but also with repeals of price and rationing controls on most goods as early as June 25, 1948.[367]

Even before then, the shop windows had suddenly been filled with previously hardly offered goods the very day after currency reform. This proved Ludwig Erhard's course right. Lucius Clay had previously supported Erhard's election as director of the Economic Administration because of his advocacy of a return to a free market economy and did let him have his way toward that goal now. Only a joint veto by the two Anglo-Saxon Allies could have overridden an executive order by German administrative agencies. Clay was not ready for this, as such a disavowal of Erhard's authority or maybe even his removal from his office as director of the Economic Administration would have put the instantly visible success of currency reform in jeopardy.[368] On the contrary, Clay was glad that Erhard had taken responsibility for the high-risk lifting of administrative controls, as his following statement shows:

> ... indeed, a group of West German experts including Professor Erhard had been asked to recommend any other measures which might be taken to increase its [currency reform's] effectiveness if and when it did take place. ... This [the removal of price and rationing controls] was a step which would have been difficult for the Military Governors to have taken as two of the three countries still had controlled economies. ... It did fall to my lot to ask Director Erhard the authority for his action, only to be reminded

very calmly that when he had accepted the appointment, he had been told that he was expected to exercise the authority of his office and that this was what he had done.[369]

On June 30, 1948, the Bipartite Control Office (BICO) of the Bizone approved the Guiding Principles Act.[370] Fortunately for Erhard and the future of the Social Market Economy in West Germany, it was not General Brian H. Robertson, but General Clay, who was at the time the acting governor of the Bizone.[371] Clay had probably orchestrated Erhard's summons mainly to calm the displeased military governor of the British Zone. The United Kingdom was governed by the Labour Party. Like the SPD in Germany, Labour could not yet even imagine abolishing administrative controls that had been introduced also in the UK at the start of World War II. In his memoirs, Clay pays tribute to Erhard despite and because of his insubordination: "Dr. Erhard is deserving of special mention as his advocacy of a free economy became a major issue in the first general election held in 1949. He removed many controls following currency reform, which required moral courage."[372]

The biographer of Clay, Jean Edward Smith, has revealed that on May 24, 1948 Clay had informed his counterpart and confidant in Washington, DC, Under Secretary of the Department of the Army General William H. Draper Jr., that German bureaucratic controls were stifling economic expansion and that he intended to lift them.

> But one month later, Clay had not yet acted. Erhard stepped into the policy vacuum. ... // CLAY: Robertson and I could not veto what he had done unless we both did. It took a unanimous vote between us to veto him. We never had a vote. We just let it go. I think General Robertson felt he had done his duty when he protested. I am sure he advised his government that he had protested. I am sure that his government, in defending its position before the Parliament, pointed out that they had protested. // Q [uestion]: Were you annoyed at Erhard's action? // CLAY: At first I was a little provoked that he had done this without consultation.

Later I realized that if he had consulted with us, we would probably have turned him down. Frankly, out of sympathy with Great Britain, operating under controls and a victor in the war, I would have found it very difficult to have tried to force approval. So, for me, the way it happened was the best way for it to happen.[373]

Clay's moral support for him was certainly not unknown to Erhard. Therefore, the often-encountered praise of Erhard's moral courage is only part of the anecdotal story surrounding Erhard's meeting with Clay on Monday June 21, 1948. This is also evident from a report, dated August 18, 1948, of the political adviser to the British authorities in Frankfurt, Sir Con (Douglas Walter) O'Neill, sent to the political division, British Headquarters, in Berlin and to London on Erhard's action:

> If you read again his [Erhard's] April [21, 1948] speech you will see that a very great deal of the programme he then announced has since been accomplished. Certainly an amazing transformation of the economic life of West Germany has taken place, thanks primarily of course to currency reform, but thanks also to a great extent to the *policy of relaxing controls which Erhard has pursued with consistent support and encouragement from American Military Government.* [My emphasis][374]

In the same report, that is, two months after the great reform, Con O'Neill even defended Erhard against unjustified criticism. On the allegedly inflationary developments after currency reform and Erhard's concomitant market decontrol measures he commented:

> The central fact, which Erhard's critics tend to lose sight of, is that the purchasing power of wages remains enormously greater than in the days before Currency Reform. The true standard of comparison is not between official prices now and official prices (where there were any) two months ago, but between official prices today and Black Market prices then. So regarded prices have indeed fallen.[375]

Obviously Con O'Neill found the arguments convincing that Erhard himself had used in his broadcast addressed to his critics on August 6, 1948. Erhard spoke of people "blinded by demagogy or motivated by bureaucratic obstinacy" who saw it as their duty to resist the constantly growing spirit of freedom. Price rises caused by the cutting of subsidies would not be real rises at all. Erhard admitted that a piece of clothing might have cost twelve marks before the reform and was now on offer for fifteen to eighteen marks. But the more important difference was that now it was actually available for consumers, while before the reform it was not. His critics would recommend a return to the system which had failed to equip housewives with some sewing needles, a few meters of darning-thread, and some trouser buttons. In closing: "The demand for democratic freedom will remain an empty formula so long as the basic human rights of free choice of occupation and consumption are not recognized as being untouchable and inalienable. This and nothing else is the deepest meaning of the market economy order"[376]

However, Con O'Neill's assessment of Erhard's personality and character was the opposite of flattering. He painted him as a man

> with a strong but remarkably narrow mind ... utterly lacking in any political sense ... completely devoid of tact or skill in negotiation, and frequently even spoils a good case by presenting it in a manner which is at once plaintive and aggressive ... Like the Fat Boy, whom physically he so much resembles, he asks incessantly for more; and if he gets it he appears to regard the giver not with gratitude but with contempt. ... it is difficult to hope that Erhard personally should succeed. Success in a game for such high stakes would place him in a position of almost dangerous authority: for outside the field of economic theory he is a fundamentally foolish man, rather aggressively nationalist in outlook, and no friend of us or our ideals.[377]

In an earlier report of April 30, 1948, addressed to his superiors in Berlin and in London, on Erhard's first programmatic speech to the

Economic Council on April 21, 1948 Con O'Neill had summarized his impressions as follows: Erhard's speech

> is extremely verbose and somewhat academic and theoretic [sic] in structure, but he succeeds in making himself plain enough.
> He strikes me as a man of pretty clear intelligence and fairly considerable force, though hardly a sympathetic character. He is regarded as crafty rather than straightforward. His appearance is rather against him, since he bears some resemblance, facial at least, to Göring. His small eyes and diminutive nose are almost lost in a wide expanse of gently undulating rosy flesh.[378]

This judgment should be taken with a grain of salt. As Erhard's zeal for decontrol did not conform with the British Labour Party's ongoing preference for government control of prices and rations in the UK, O'Neill's opinions unconsciously might have been shaped by what his Labour government in London expected of him. But the criteria of a British military government representative for an assessment of Erhard personality and character are nevertheless of interest.

On June 23, 1948 Paul E. Moeller, Chief Res. Br. Intelligence Division in Bavaria, sends a report "based upon personal observation and a series of interviews with various individuals selected at random" to the director of the Intelligence Division through the Office of Military Government for Bavaria. In his two-page memo subdivided into ten points he notes among others:

> 2. The first two days following the distribution of the new currency were marked by an appearance or reappearance in the shops of certain consumer goods and of considerable quantities of fresh food – fruit and vegetable. Investigators also report a noticeable change in the attitude of shopkeepers and sales personnel who suddenly became polite, considerate and solicitous. // 3. Black market prices took a nosedive reflecting the anticipated conversion rate of 10 : 1. .... // 5. Several people state they have no confidence in the new currency because it was printed in the US (implying the

Germans have no control of the amount), because it bears no signature, because it has no international value, and because the present reform will be followed by another devaluation. Reference is made to Austria. // 6. People generally agree that the reform will produce a wholesome effect upon the morale of workers. Everybody will have to work, try to make an honest mark, and turn every penny several times before spending. In this connection, fear is expressed that large numbers of people will be thrown out of work, and that wages might be cut. People in lower income brackets complain that they are unable to avail themselves of the newly created opportunity to purchase long-needed goods because food prices are too high and absorb all of their money. // ... 9. Other political implications of the reform mentioned by informants include regret that the Eastern zone is not included, and that the split of Germany has become permanent and total. Fear is expressed that the Russian reform, when it comes, will be more liberal – as it can be in view of the prior blocking of bank accounts – and that the pauperization of many people in the Western zones will drive them into the camps of extreme right or left radicalism.[379]

Point 6 deserves a comment in the light of what actually happened during the months following currency reform. Its beneficial effect on the morale and incentive of workers turns out to be fully correct. As to the fear that many people will lose their jobs, it proves to be unfounded in a surprising way. It is true that the number of unemployed in West Germany approximately doubled from 442,000 in June 1948 to 937,000 in January 1949. But during the same interval the number of employed persons increased from 14.2 to 14.9 million.[380] In other words, there were increases in unemployment as well as in employment. The latter even surpassed the former, although the January figures for employment are usually depressed by seasonal factors.

The explanation of these developments is, of course, that currency reform induced more than a million persons to give up hidden unemployment and join the official labor force, either to take up a job if possible or to receive unemployment benefits. There were push and pull factors involved in this massive restructuring of the labor market. Black- and gray-market activities or traveling the countryside for stealing of or exchanging valuables for food were no longer more lucrative than a regular job. The spectacular economic and productivity growth in the second half of 1948 offered lots of employment opportunities. The dimension of this favorable effect surprised even the Allied planners and executioners of currency reform.

At the end of the first week after the start of currency reform on June 20, 1948, Tenenbaum clipped a short newspaper article which he treated as worthy enough to be kept in his papers. Its title: *Der erste Währungssünder / verurteilt* (The first currency transgressor / sentenced). Its content:

> On the day after currency reform, when the police paid particular attention to the black marketeers doing business at Frankfurt Central Station, the twenty-five-year-old Bruno Kaschinski was arrested for selling American cigarettes. During his interrogation at police headquarters, he admitted that he was from Königsberg [East Prussia, now part of Russia and Poland] and had been roaming around without a steady job after his release from American captivity as a prisoner of war. Since April he had been living in Frankfurt from black market trading. They found 85 marks of new money in his pockets, although he had not received a head quota. He finally confessed that on Monday he had had a conversation with a gentleman who had given him 20 Deutschmarks for 1,025 marks of old money. // Kaschinski, who did not have a criminal record, was taken to the police prison the same day. Already on Thursday he stood before a summary court. After a short trial for offences against the law on currency reform, black market trading and vagrancy, County Court Judge Schilling after a short hearing gave him a verbal order of punishment, which was five weeks in prison, a fine of fifty marks and a tax rate of ten marks. The judge emphasized that after the currency reform had come into effect, no old money was allowed to be put into circulation. Whoever did not

bring it to the financial institutions in time would have to destroy it. As ordered by the law.[381]

Tenenbaum must have been very pleased to see German police and courts defending the new West German currency order, largely his creation, so forcefully and efficiently.

Erhard's action on decontrol of prices and rationing immediately following currency reform had unleashed market forces. These led to a rise of the cost of living in the second half of 1948 by 18.7 percent as compared to the first half of the same year.[382] With all the attention that has been paid to the causes of this upsurge of prices and that I will replicate in the following part of this chapter, we should keep in mind what the CDG Plan of May 1946, the blueprint of currency reform in West Germany, envisaged for price developments after an accomplished reform:

> Taking into account both these relatively stable segments of the price structure [agricultural prices and rents] and the increased costs and prices of manufactured goods, the average overall price rise may be kept to not more than about 20 percent compared to the present level of official prices, and it is expected that the increase in the cost of living may also be held to not more than 15–20 percent. This assumes, of course, that an effective system of price control is maintained for some time.[383]

In other words, the actual increase in the cost of living during the second half of 1948 as compared to the first fell exactly on the mark that Colm, Dodge, and Goldsmith had drawn as to be expected. In contrast to Tenenbaum and his British and French counterparts, the German experts locked up in camp Rothwesten were not privy to the CDG Plan and to this detail of it. I conclude from this: What Tenenbaum made look like concessions to them, was, in fact, what the American currency-reform plan allowed, and even envisaged in order to smooth the adjustment of the price structure from the administered stop-price structure to market conditions.

The price structure of a controlled economy is by definition out of line with that of a market economy, because controls are always triggered by political action against market price developments. When after a lifting of a long-term control of prices an appropriate margin for inflation is not accommodated by government and central bank authority, it would mean that a lot of prices would have to be reduced nominally to compensate for the price rises of other goods in higher demand in order to generate a market-economy commensurate price structure. As the German economy during Chancellor Heinrich Brüning's chancellorship 1930–1932 has demonstrated that general price reductions, at that time government-ordered, paved the way to unemployment, the deepest depression Germany ever experienced, and Hitler's accession to power. However, when the price-structure adjustment takes place on an inflationary trajectory, price-structure adjustment is possible without any or with few price reductions vis-à-vis price adjustments upward for products in higher demand. The CDG authors with their projection of a post-currency-reform inflation of about 20 percent and Tenenbaum were well aware of the advantages of price-structure adjustment under an inflationary trajectory. All the critics of the on average 18.7 inflation rate in the second half of 1948 versus the first half were obviously not.

The about 20 percent inflation envisaged by the CDG planners and in their trails by Tenenbaum also served as a safeguard against any post-reform deflation and depression. This fear had been particularly voiced by the British element in the ACC when the introduction of the CDG Plan in ACC was countered by a much softer currency-reform plan of the British. It had been inspired by John Maynard Keynes. Until his death of a heart attack on April 21, 1946 he had been financial *spiritus rector* of the British government.[384]

A traditionally large component of the cost-of-living basket, rent for housing didn't budge because rent control was far away from being lifted. This means prices of other items of consumption must have risen much more than the above-mentioned 18.7 percent. This is true for food prices (plus 23.2 percent) and even more for clothing (plus 29.1 percent).[385] Wages had not been decontrolled and remained administratively fixed until the Economic Council of the Bizone decided on November 3, 1948 to lift controls and reestablish collective bargaining.[386] This had de facto ended during the dissolution of the Weimar Republic in the Great Depression and de jure after the Nazis replaced the German labor unions by the *Deutsche Arbeitsfront* (German Labor Front) in 1933.

Nevertheless, the labor unions kept organizing the only general strike in West Germany ever, which took place on November 12, 1948 within the Bizone. The French occupation authorities had made such action illegal in their zone. Workers there, in contrast to those in the Bizone, remained on their jobs. The general strike was not only in protest of low wages vis-à-vis sharply increased prices for consumer goods and services, but also for democratization of economic power by codetermination, socialization of key industries, and a return to price controls with rationing as a means to create more distributive justice. As the inflation was petering out and wages were adjusted upward in new collective-bargaining agreements in the following weeks, the general strike fizzled out to nothing.[387]

Since currency reform, decontrolled prices had outperformed wage developments. What is the explanation? Evidently too much money was chasing insufficient supply of goods and services. The relation between monetary demand and real supply is traditionally expressed in the following simple formula: $M \times V = T \times P$. M is the money volume, that is, central bank money (mainly banknotes) as well as deposit money of private persons and businesses in banks. V is the velocity of its circulation of money. T is the transaction volume of goods and services, the supply, and P is the level of prices.

The most difficult to predict, especially after a structural break, such as a currency reform, is V, because it depends on the behavior of income recipients. This is shaped by their propensity to save or to consume, which in turn is influenced by their expectations of post-reform price developments. If inflationary expectations prevail, spending for consumption of households and for investment of businesses is speeded up. Should the public form deflationary expectations, consumers and investors would rather postpone the spending of money and instead increase saving. One problem is that such price expectations in either direction themselves set in motion or strengthen upward or downward spirals of price developments. Thus expectations create facts by taking the role of self-fulfilling prophesies, regardless of the money volume's influence on the price level. The formula above can be transformed into $\frac{M \times V}{T} = P$. In order to keep the price level constant, unchanged, and stable, the numerator of the fraction (the product of money volume and its velocity of circulation) in relation to its denominator (the transaction volume of goods and services) must also remain constant.

As in reality prices soared up in West Germany during the second half of 1948, the numerator of the fraction must have grown stronger than the denominator T. It is true that higher than expected economic growth increased the volume of goods and services offered on the markets and thus provided for a dampening effect on inflationary developments. But either the provision of money or the velocity of circulation or both factors together contributed more to spur inflation than the growing transaction volume could compensate for.

Christoph Buchheim favored the impact of the velocity of money over the provision of money. He found that households not only spent virtually all of their income, but also a large part of their converted deposits, as the household savings rate was negative in the second half of 1948. On the other hand, he states that the money supply was not inappropriate in itself. However, it could not be kept under control by the central bank because it was not only the result of sovereign money creation, but also of largely autonomous credit expansion, made possible by the generous initial provision of liquidity to commercial banks.[388]

Let's now turn to what Tenenbaum had to say about V and M, also with a view to his contention that the terms of the currency reform oversupplied the West German economy with liquidity "after consultation with an assemblage of over 50 German politicians, in the last days before the reform."[389] I start with V.

In his book manuscript Tenenbaum discusses the velocity of circulation V as a driver of inflation during the first five months after monetary reform extensively. It had obviously preoccupied the framers of the reform on the Allied as well as on the German side. Critics of the originally harsh conditions of the Allied monetary reform plan (i.e., the majority of German experts and politicians putting pressure on military governments to relax the restrictive terms) argued that V had been low before the reform. Because they assumed that V would remain quite stable and would not change much after currency reform, they demanded from Allied legislation to put more money into circulation than originally planned.

As against that Tenenbaum pointed out that V varies considerably with cyclical and monetary conditions, according to estimates for bank-notes alone between as little as 7 times p.a. in depressions, 12 times p.a. in prosperity, and up to 400 times p.a. just before the end of hyperinfla-tion in November 1923. This would mean that historical velocity had varied between 58 and 3,333 percent of normal (twelve times).

> The theory that the need for money was greater because velocity was lower represented an egregious confusion of cause and effect. In the first place, it took into account only the "legal" segment of the economy. Velocity in illegal transactions apparently was much higher. The black market seemed to operate more rapidly than legal markets complying with the red tape ordained by the law. We could not determine whether "average" velocity actually was low. // In the second place, low velocity of circulation was just another way of saying that a surplus of money existed, which could not be spent legally and therefore tended to lie idle. If financial reform succeeded, we expected money to resume its normal functions as the medium of exchange. Velocity would increase, just as it "normally" seemed to double during the period of recovery from depressions. // Our fear was not that velocities would remain low. On the contrary, we hoped there would be sufficient confidence in the new currency to prevent the development of excessively high velocity, particularly during the early period of money scarcity. In fact, abnormally high velocities did develop in the initial stages, as we had expected. // Even our critics had

to admit that if prewar velocities were assumed the ratio of conversion would have to be in the neighborhood of 7 : 1. Their complaint against 10 : 1 were based on the assumption that velocity might well fall as business firms and individuals sought to build up cash balances to normal levels. // The German experts were particularly fearful of the effect of tight money on business firms, and above all on the demand for investment goods. // Eventually, Erhard himself [who belonged to the German critics] must have been converted, since he declared before the reform that: "The worries over adequate provision of working capital credits to proceed with current production and to ensure marketing are understandable. However, they are not justified, since there are no objections on grounds of currency policy to the granting of short-term circulating credits (*Umschlagkredite*) and therefore (... credit ...) can be granted in the form of commercial bills. [In a footnote:] Wirtschaftszeitung, 7 May 1948."[390]

The volume of money and its development after West Germany's currency reform was also not easy to predict. As mentioned above, it consists of two parts: central bank money (mainly banknotes) as well as deposit money in banks. The banknotes' portion was relatively easy to determine, likewise deposit money in banks that would result from the conversion of old Reichsmark into new Deutschmark deposits. But that part of deposit money originating in credit policies of the banks was the uncertain part that could contribute to the difference between stable, inflationary or deflationary development of prices. Henry C. Wallich in his book *Mainsprings of the German Revival* (1955) sees the main source of the inflation surge after currency reform during the second half of 1948 in too large an expansion of credit and thus of deposit money in banks. As to his background, Wallich was born in 1914 in Berlin into a family of Jewish bankers that fled Nazi persecution by emigrating to the USA, gained a PhD from Harvard in 1944 and was long-time professor of economics at Yale (1951–1974) before serving as governor of the Federal Reserve Board from 1974 to 1986.

Here are facts and interpretations as presented by Wallich.

1948 Month	Industrial production 1936 = 100	Unemployment rate percent of labor force	Gross hourly wages 1950=100	Cost of living 1950 = 100	Currency and demand deposits billions of DM	Time and savings deposits billions of DM	Bank loans billions of DM
June	54	3.2	76.6	98	n.a.	n.a.	1.3
July	60			102	n.a.	n.a.	2.4
Aug.	65			104	n.a.	n.a.	3.2
Sept.	71	5.5	83.5	107	12.3	4.2	3.8
Oct.	76			112	13.2	3.4	4.5
Nov.	81			111	14.0	3.0	4.6
Dec.	79	5.3	88.1	112	14.3	3.2	5.2

FIGURE 4.14 Economic and monetary indicators for West Germany (Trizone), June to December 1948
Source: Henry C. Wallich, *Mainsprings of the German Revival*, New Haven: Yale UP, 1955, pp. 74–75

These data show not only the spectacular upswing of industrial production following currency reform from June to November 1948 by 50 percent, but also the rise in the cost of living from June to October 1948 by 14 percent, before the inflationary momentum petered out during the following months. Wages, still under control rose only 9 percent from June to September 1948, which created deep unrest among workers whom labor unions called to the general strike on November 12, 1948. Therefore, the upsurge of prices after currency reform was not of the type of a cost-push inflation driven by wage increases. It was a demand inflation driven by too much money or purchasing power, given perhaps the higher than expected velocity of circulation of money.

Wallich maintains that the ultimate success of currency reform in terms of monetary stability was not assured until the beginning of 1949. During the preceding months the increase in money, credit, and prices seemed to have set in motion a spiraling process that would have been in danger of getting out of hand. For monetary and fiscal policy, the second half of 1948 was a period of intense struggle against inflation, he argues. Then Wallich delves into the causes of the "too much money" drama:

The plan of the reform had been to keep business very short of funds in order to force the sale of hoarded stocks to consumers, who had been endowed with relatively generous cash allowances. To limit the use of bank credit for continued inventory hoarding, new current account credits (which in Germany ordinarily represent the bulk of short-term bank loans) had been prohibited for the first two months, leaving bills (a more formal and less flexible type of credit) as the only major form of bank financing. Despite these restrictions expansionary forces gained the upper hand. // The reliance that the authors of the reform had placed on hoarded stocks proved a sound speculation. The initial monetary tightness – ten days after the reform the total money supply (currency and demand deposits) did not exceed 6 billion D-Mark – brought these stocks out in volume. But business showed a surprising capacity for getting along temporarily with next to no cash balances. Very soon, moreover, various inflationary factors began to make themselves felt. Bank credit rose from almost zero at the time of the reform to 5.2 billion in December; the conversion of the old [Reichsmark] balances provided large additional amounts; and the second installment of the 60 D-Mark per capita allowance became payable [in August 1948]. All this combined to lift the money supply to 12.3 billion in September and 14.3 billion in December [see Table 4.14. ERP (European Recovery Program) goods, which had been counted upon to help meet the situation, came in disappointingly slowly. The tax cuts which accompanied the currency reform produced initial [public] deficits. Personal saving was very small, since pent-up consumer demand was intense. The upward trend of prices led to renewed inventory hoarding. The fate of the new currency seemed to hang in the balance.[391]

While during the second half of 1948 still controlled wage increases lagged behind the galloping inflation rate and far behind productivity increases, business profits exploded. In as much as they were reinvested, they had been made tax-free. Businesses were able to self-finance most of their investments. Due to demand inflation in the absence of cost-push, their liquidity status emerged so favorably that the initially vital pressure to sell their hoarded products vanished into thin air. In addition, the business liquidity glut helped to escape restrictive credit policies by which the *Bank deutscher Länder* (BdL), West Germany's central bank founded in February 1948, began in October 1948 to counteract the inflationary boom.

Wallich lists the following monetary policy measures: 1.) The BdL made use of its new monetary policy instrument with which the Western Allies had equipped it; it raised minimum reserves commercial and savings banks had to keep with the central bank from 10 to 15 percent of their deposits. 2.) It stopped discounting bank acceptances with the exception of those that financed exports and the public storage of foodstuffs and specific raw materials. 3.) With a few exceptions in special cases, the BdL ordered all banks to limit their total loan volume to the level of October 31, 1948. Wallich concedes that these restrictions contributed somewhat to the halt of inflation around the end of 1948. But in his judgment the main share was provided by the following four factors: "(1) the growing gap between prices and consumer purchasing power created by [relative] wage stability; (2) the end of the influx [into the volume of money] of [into DM] converted [RM-] balances; (3) the emergence of budget surpluses resulting from rising revenues due to higher national income; and (4) the incipient downturn in world markets."[392]

So far I have presented an assessment of post-reform inflationary dynamics by an expert scholar, not by a political actor on the scene or himself involved in shaping the terms of introducing the Deutschmark in West Germany. I will now also report what Ludwig Erhard and Edward A. Tenenbaum had to say about the causes of those galloping inflation rates during the second half of 1948. For Erhard's view I draw on his address in his famous debate with Erik Nölting , SPD economics minister in North Rhine-Westphalia, in the tent of Circus Althoff in Frankfurt am Main on November 14, 1948.[393] Tenenbaum's opinion is taken from his unfinished and never-published book manuscript "Die Deutsche Mark."[394] Both conceded that by the rate or concomitant measures of currency conversion reform-makers had provided too much purchasing power that could at first not be met by enough real supply of goods and services to keep prices stable.

In his verbose manner, Erhard informed his audience several times that 10.7 billion Deutschmarks (DM) had been created in the process of converting RM into DM (as central bank [banknotes] and deposit money in commercial and savings banks). He maintained that their owners wanted to use these marks as soon as possible for consumption. This is only partly true in so far as DM-owners were not businesses, which would use their liquid funds rather for investments than for consumption. But Erhard was, of course, right in asserting that the real supply of decontrolled consumer goods was insufficient to absorb the purchasing power in the hands of consumers without price increases.

Erhard did not blame the conversion rate for having over-equipped consumers. But he rather criticized failures in tax-policy measures. In his view they had been too favorable for the business sector. Tax measures included not only a substantial reduction of the very high postwar individual income tax rates and a partial lowering of corporation income tax rates. But also and more importantly, they introduced extremely generous depreciation allowances and tax privileges, as I have mentioned above. These provisions as well as the decoupling of burden-sharing legislation from currency reform allowed the business sector to accumulate excess liquidity. The reason: Had burden-sharing legislation been an integral part of currency reform like tax reform with Law No. 64 which both the CDG Plan of May 1946 and the German experts' Homburg Plan of April 1948 had envisaged, it would have been financed by immediate special taxes on businesses. Not only Tenenbaum, Bennett, and Clay in OMGUS, but also the German experts and politicians would have preferred this to the actual decoupling and postponing ordered by Washington. This course of events, in turn, freed businesses from the need to sell off their inventories in order to stay liquid. Instead of the mere 3 percent tax actually levied on business inventories on the day of currency reform, Erhard told his audience that he had repeatedly endeavored to have the tax rate raised to 25 percent.[395] This would have put pressure on owners of hoarded goods to throw them on the market and thereby dampen the upward trend of prices.

While Erhard conceded that he had been unsuccessful with his tax-policy proposal that he had advanced for the First Equalization of Burdens Bill, he pointed to the success of two of his other anti-inflation policy initiatives: 1.) For goods in especially short supply, such as shoes and clothing, Erhard's economic administration had organized the *Jedermann* (Everyman) production program shortly after currency reform. These utility items were manufactured to simple specifications at low costs and were sold at low fixed prices. 2.) He also pressured the Allied authorities to deviate from their decartelization principles into allowing industrial firms to fix and control the retail prices of their products. Although this was also at odds with Erhard's belief in competition rather than price fixing as markets' regulator, it helped to eliminate speculative price excesses at the time. Erhard added that imported goods also had to be sold at fixed prices. He pointed out to his audience that, therefore, more than half of consumption goods were still subjected to price controls. Erhard also mentioned STEG goods. They were items sold in German stores in the post-reform period of 1948/49 that were originally intended for American troops. On the basis of two contracts for the takeover of American army goods after currency reform, they were sold by the *Staatliche Erfassungs-Gesellschaft für öffentliches Gut* (STEG) through retailers at moderate prices. Essentially, these were articles of daily use as well as clothing, and also vehicles. For the rest, he appealed to his audience, they should let market forces of supply and demand find the necessary price equilibrium.[396]

Erhard fought against the blaming of price rises and other unfavorable developments like shortages on his economic policy.

They [the price increases] were "in fact nothing other than the conse-
quential effects of a currency reform that was not entirely flawlessly
constructed,"[397] he argued. Erhard was still critical of the design of
the currency reform and assigned responsibility for it to the decision-
makers of the Western Allies. In this, he was in line with the German
monetary experts whom Tenenbaum and his British and French counterparts had assembled at the so-called Conclave of Rothwesten for
consultation and support in preparation of the reform. At the end of
their seven-weeks confinement, they had distanced themselves by
letter to the Western military governments from any responsibility
for the outcome of the currency reform, which had been designed
according to mainly American plans, not the Homburg Plan proposed
by the German currency experts.

Edward A. Tenenbaum, like Erhard, admits to over-equipment
of the West German economy with liquidity that created the inflationary environment of the second half of 1948. But as to its cause,
Tenenbaum contends ten years later, when he wrote his book manuscript, it "resulted largely from the success of German politicians and
experts in putting pressure on military government to change our
plans."[398] He states:

> It was known then [20 June 1948] and for some time thereafter as
> "the Allied currency reform." German leaders took some pains to
> point out that many of their proposals and objections had been
> overridden by the Military Governments. // Some months later,
> when success of the experiment was assured, the name changed.
> Today, a decade later, the events of 20 June 1948 are known as "the
> German currency reform." The fact of Allied sponsorship is in the
> process of being forgotten. A prominent West German leader
> [Ludwig Erhard] even has begun to suggest that the "German"
> currency reform succeeded despite the opposition of the Western
> Military Government. [in a footnote Tenenbaum cites a "Fortune
> article on Erhard" without further specification. It must have been
> published in 1958 or earlier.][399]

Most of the German experts who had designed the Homburg Plan and from whom the members of the Conclave were recruited, regarded the 10 percent conversion rate of the American CDG Plan of 1946 as too severe. It would depress the German economy and lead to unemployment. Erwin Hielscher was an exception. He had adopted the much stricter views of Max Schönwandt, the author of the German *Konstanzer Plan* of October 3, 1945.[400] He agreed with Tenenbaum's 5 percent conversion rate assessment. He left the Conclave in protest against the more generous monetary-supply views of his German colleagues early. It is true that the Homburg Plan nominally adopted the 10 percent conversion rate for immediate exchange of RM into DM. But it would park an additional 10 percent of RM holdings in blocked DM accounts which were reserved for conversion at an appropriate later time. Tenenbaum describes the main difference between his American/Allied plan and the Homburg Plan of the German experts as follows:

> Our proposal was for conversion of only 5% of the old money claims. We had reached the conclusion that the original Colm-Dodge-Goldsmith proposal of 10%, far from being too severe, was not severe enough. We came to the conclusion (similar to Schönwandt's) that the "right" rate of conversion was as close to no conversion at all as one could come. The greater the amount of new money issued at the time of the original conversion, the less control the central bank would have over the supply of money. The "right rate" definitely was not a rate which might satisfy all actual needs for money, since that would destroy the possibility of reducing money supply if money demand decreased, or if additional money had to be issued to cover an emergency budget deficit. There was no way to know with any precision how much money was in circulation in the Western Zones, and how much would be turned in for exchange. Finally, we could only guess what the velocity of circulation would be after the reform.[401]

On which points did Tenenbaum and the other Allied currency-reform experts yield to demands of the German Conclave members and of the over 50 German politicians that Clay allowed to voice their opinions on the imminent monetary and financial reform? Clay felt uneasy about the dictatorial implementation of the currency reform by the three Western Allies. He was keen on implanting democratic decision-making procedures in Germany. By inviting the over 50 West German politicians for last-minute consultations, he satisfied his ambition to cloak the reform program in an appearance of West German political codetermination.

The Allied plan discussed at the Conclave had stipulated the 5 percent conversion rate that Tenenbaum mentions above. Under pressure from German experts and politicians it was raised to eventually 6.5 percent. The Allied plan as presented to the Conclave members had provided for a 1-to-1 conversion amount as low as 25 DM per capita.[402] This conformed to Erwin Hielscher's notion of an indeed painful, but deep cut into the inflated RM-liquidity. Hans Möller has distinguished between representatives of a "mild" or "radical" currency reform.[403]

The "mild" majority of the German experts first induced Tenenbaum and his two Allied colleagues to push the 1-to-1 conversion amount up to 50 DM. The Special Agency for Money and Credit had already early on in the process of developing the Homburg Plan decided that the per capita exchange RM into DM should be "at least 50 DM."[404] This amount was even increased to 60 DM by a last-minute concession on the part of Tenenbaum and his British and French colleagues shortly before the end of the Conclave.[405]

This was part of a deal. The German experts had demanded that their per capita conversion amount of "at least 50 DM" 1 to 1 should not be offset against the claims from the conversion of all other old RM money on bank accounts plus RM cash to be deposited there for conversion, 6.5 DM for 100 RM, as it eventually turned out. But Tenenbaum and his British and French counterparts insisted on the offsetting part. In exchange, they were willing to raise the per capita amount to 60 DM instead of 50 DM or only 25 DM, as initially envisaged in Allied planning. The German experts of the Special Agency for Money and Credit and of the Rothwesten camp gave primacy to social aspects of monetary reform with equalization of burden as an integral part, which was decoupled from the reform on Washington, DC's insistence. For the Americans, in contrast, an end to inflation and putting the West German economy back on its track of growth and development was of prime importance, as Jack Bennett stated in his analysis of the first draft of the Homburg Plan for General Clay on March 5, 1948. For them a raising of the per capita amount was a small concession to the Germans' social concerns, compared to the more generous overall conversion rate that the Germans wanted to allow for and to the inclusion of an equalization-of-burden scheme into the currency-reform legislation itself. Jack Bennett judged that the Homburg Plan, if realized, would lead to another inflation.[406]

In exchange for 60 RM, 40 DM were handed out on June 20, 1948 and 20 DM followed two months later. In order to keep businesses afloat with their wage and other payment obligations, these were also equipped with 60 DM in exchange for 60 Reichsmark per employee. This generosity contributed to the over-endowment of business with liquidity that Henry C. Wallich's quote above speaks of.

The German inmates of the camp in Rothwesten had been released on June 8, 1948. For June 14,[407] 15 and 16, 1948, General Clay and his British counterpart General Robertson had invited the most important German politicians in charge of economic and monetary policy matters, the directors of the Finance and Economic Administrations, Alfred Hartmann and Ludwig Erhard respectively, the president of the Land Central Bank of Baden-Württemberg Karl Bernard, members of the currency committee of the Economic Council and others, to these top secret meetings with the military governors of the Bizone. Of course, the latter's expert personnel, like Tenenbaum and his boss Jack Bennett, were also present. The meetings took place in room 130 of the former German chemical giant IG

Farben headquarters, which the US Army had taken over as its Frankfurt headquarters for military government.

Karl Bernard reported about the first meeting that the three Western Allies had not yet reached an agreement on the details of the currency reform. As described in Section 4.1, the French were still procrastinating and demanding further concessions. In the second session General Clay wanted to hear the Germans' opinion once again on some key issues, for example the level of the initial per capita conversion amount. Should it be 30 DM or 60 DM paid out in two installments? On this, in turn, depended the percentages of disbursement and blocking of the money that was stuck in bank accounts. Because Clay had to attend another important appointment, there were only eight minutes available to discuss the question with him, Karl Bernard noted. Here the opposites became again visible. Erhard spoke out in favor of 60 DM. Bernard was opposed to this, saying that, from a monetary point of view, a per capita conversion amount of 60 DM would hardly be justifiable.

Another controversial issue on that day was the exchange rate of the DM versus the US dollar. Should it be 1 DM = 30 US cents, as Clay and Tenenbaum wanted, or should the DM value at only 10 US cents, as favored by Washington, DC? On this question Tenenbaum and Clay eventually prevailed over Washington. Asked by a German politician whether the time for currency reform had now come, Clay still answered somewhat evasively that he believed yes. But only in the evening or the following morning would he get the final word. And indeed, in another meeting on June 16, the politicians of the Bizone learned from the mouth of the British military governor, General Sir Brian Robertson, that the currency reform would be officially announced on Friday evening, June 18, via radio and press for June 20, 1948.[408]

Other too generous concessions of the Allies in the field of tax reform seem to have come about under pressure from those German politicians the Allied military governors met with on June 15 and 16: too generous depreciation allowances and tax privileges for businesses and investors of the sort mentioned above.

In a wider political sense one consequence of currency reform was a few days later the separate currency reform in the Soviet zone and East and West Berlin cementing the division of Germany and the formation of the Trizone in the western part of Germany. Around that time OMGUS was still habituated to refer to Germans as *indigenous people*. For example, in a letter of the Finance Branch of the Office of Military Government for Bavaria in Munich to OMGUS in Berlin of June 19, 1948, Subject: *Wage Payment to Indigenous Personnel of the US Forces after the Currency Reform*, the term is used throughout the letter.[409] German pride was hurt, somewhat mirroring residual beliefs that Germans belonged to a *master race*. In the second half of 1948 this led to the composition of one of the most successful carnival songs ever by Karl Berbuer, in an English translation called *The Trizonesia Song*. The refrain in its original German version is more telling: *Wir sind die Eingeborenen von Trizonesien* (We are the indigenous people of Trizonesia).[410]

After having been played on radio stations all over Germany for months, the song still resonates in my ears today. Catholic regions in Germany celebrated their carnival during its season then. As always it had started on November 11, 1948 at 11:11 a.m. and reached its climax the week before Ash Wednesday on March 2, 1949. I had grown seven years old on January 23, 1949. The popularity of the song did have extraordinary political consequences. General Clay issued a special order to all OMGUS branches in the US zone to stop using the term *indigenous* for German personnel employed by US Forces and for German citizens in general.

4.4.3   Assessments

"A currency exchange is not a currency stabilization," Tenenbaum warned not only his colleagues in military government, but even more West German politicians, central bankers, and interest groups.[411] To protect his newly born baby, *the Deutsche Mark*, he kept writing memos about the conditions for success and the dangers that would lurk around many corners. He called to mind that economic history was replete with failed currency reforms and pointed to such examples in the more distant (assignats in the French revolution) and post–World War II past (Japan and Austria). In another memo of July 4, 1948, two weeks after the birth of the DM, entitled "The Preservation of the Deutsche Mark," Tenenbaum mentions that the Western powers have made three expensive promises [under pressure from the Germans] that might endanger the stability of the DM:

> a. By 20 August, an additional 800,000,000 Deutsche Marks must be placed in circulation, 20 Marks per person living in the Western Zones to complete the 60-Mark per-head payment. //
> b. By 20 September, subject to any last-minute possibilities of finding an alternative solution, an additional five percent of all money turned in or declared must be converted into Deutsche Mark. A reasonable, if somewhat premature estimate of the amount involved is 3,500,000,000 Deutsche Marks. // c. In Berlin the Western powers have fallen into the same trap as the Soviets, and have allowed the terms of the Western Sector currency reform to be influenced by political considerations. The cost of campaign promises to the Western Sectors of Berlin is not yet clear. What is clear, however, is that these promises were made at the expense of the Deutsche Mark currency as a whole.[412]

He further argues that experience during the period of price and rationing control in Germany since 1936 had clearly shown "that controls are almost inevitable as long as the currency is unsound." It would be "perhaps less obvious, but no less true, that the elimination of controls is inevitable if the currency remains sound, and that the maintenance of controls will in itself cause the currency to be inflated. Controls function so poorly and with so much friction that they must have the lubricant of surplus purchasing power in order to keep them from breaking down." As a concrete example to substantiate this point, he describes the current crisis in the "food wholesaling industry," in which controls were kept in force after currency reform. Warehouses would be bulging with imported sugar, whose sale would be prohibited by the rationing authorities, "yet storage costs cannot be paid until the goods are moved. The alternatives will soon be either a substantial relaxation of rationing or the granting of inflationary credits to maintain frozen stockpiles of food." There were no other options "wherever controls are maintained in the face of a sound money. Either the controls go or the sound money must be made unsound by inflation in order to pay for them."

In a broader sense, Tenenbaum described two dangers that the new currency would face: 1.) a hang-over from the past, namely a lack of confidence in the stability of the DM, the refusal or failure to abandon controls, and "the refusal to believe that the new money will perform the function for which money exists." And 2.) "the possibility of deteriorating the public currency for private profit or for reasons of state." The answer to both problems would be an "unyielding" credit policy. It would determine "whether the Germans build houses or wear shoes, whether they export coal or spend their resources on pleasure trips to Bavaria, whether they are prosperous according to their own wishes, or driven to extreme politics by the will of a minority, whether free enterprise will grow roots or fail. Most significant of all, it can determine these things whether the German people as a whole like it or not."

It is no wonder that monetary economist Tenenbaum sings the praises of credit (= monetary) policy. But concomitantly he demands prudent fiscal policies as a guarantor of stable money.[413] It would have been a surprise if he, a believer in Keynesianism, would not equally have stressed this point to pave the way for a safe and sound future for his newly born creature, the DM.

On July 9, 1948, not even three weeks since C-Day, Maurice N. Altaffer, American Consul General in Bremen, sent a confidential report to the Secretary of State in Washington, DC "Subject: Developments Since Currency Reform." It is stamped as received there on July 29, 1948.[414] Here are excerpts from his report:

"The subject has, of course, been one of pre-eminent interest to the German press as well as to the individual German, and for some days crowded even the Berlin crisis from the headlines." As to the effects on the German economy:

> the most pronounced is at least the temporary reversal of the post-war German norm of acute shortage of consumer goods in relation to circulating currency; and the popular mood ... appears to range from mitigated hopefulness mixed with considerable trepidation to gloomy and resigned pessimism. // No one expected that the drastic devaluation of assets involved in currency reform would be popular as such or easy to take. Perhaps not so expected has been the intensity of criticism, the negative attitude shown by a great part of the German public and many of its leaders, even by some of those who might well have been counted upon to give strong support. When reduced to essentials, this criticism seems to be directed not so much at the fact of currency reform ... or even at its implications in general, but ... In the psychological hothouse of contemporary Germany extraneous or secondary considerations are often blown up beyond all proportion until they become near obsessions which blind to salutary results achieved.

Thereafter, the Consul General quotes Wilhelm Kaisen, the mayor of Bremen, characterized as one of those German leaders with a more positive opinion: "While we do not particularly like the form which currency reform actually took, it was admittedly necessary and will undoubtedly achieve many desirable results. It is therefore our duty to support it and to carry out its administration as far as possible." But the memo's author remains unsure whether "this sensible and realistic viewpoint is sufficiently widespread to counteract the negativism, and in some cases defeatism, which appears to have set in among many groups." He reports that "responsible observers" have informed him that apparently in the important areas of the Rhineland and Ruhr this mood is particularly prevalent.

> There appears to be general agreement among Germans that the
> public relations end of currency reform was badly handled. Apart
> from individual efforts by the press and last-minute radio speeches
> by officials, there was no organized educational campaign to
> prepare the German public for the shock of currency devaluation, to
> show why it was required, and how, while it might work hardship
> in the short run, it would operate to the general advantage in the
> long run. . . . the comment is frequently made that this [the need for
> secrecy as to timing and details] should not have precluded the
> giving of more thought and effort towards the enlisting of popular
> support and understanding for a measure the ultimate success of
> which is so dependent on favorable reaction on the
> psychological level.

That currency reform had been almost entirely an Allied measure,
since practically all suggestions made by German experts had
allegedly been rejected by Allied officials, would be perhaps the most
common German complaint. German participants in the secret pre-
reform discussions had apparently started a "whispering campaign,"
abetted by many German politicians, about how high-handedly their
advice had been treated "by what they considered to be relatively
inexperienced and technically unqualified Allied personnel." These
tales were apparently meeting with wide credence among Germans
and might lead to the myth which, if currency reform turns out to be
unsuccessful, will enable German experts and politicians to disclaim
responsibility.

> A name which in recent weeks has achieved a sort of notoriety
> throughout Germany among intellectual and political circles, as
> the bête noir of the pre-currency reform discussions, is that of Mr.
> Edward A. Tenenbaum, Special Assistant to the Finance Adviser,
> OMGUS. His comparative youth has apparently made him the
> specific target for criticism involving the charge of inexperience.
> A popular current joke is to the effect that now the Germans
> can again enthusiastically sing their beloved folk song:

> 'O Tannenbaum, O Tannenbaum, Wie gruen sind deine Blaetter!'
> (O Fir Tree, O Fir Tree, how green are your leaves (sheets of paper or banknotes)!)

The report continues with the information that various political leaders, including Dr. Konrad Adenauer, the head of the CDU party for the British zone, "have brought to the attention of the Consulate ... the disastrous reduction in the funds of the political parties which will be available for the use in any elections to be held in connection with the political reorganization of Western Germany."

The report concludes with a listing of numerous specific criticisms of currency reform "heard on all sides," such as the new Deutschmark banknotes would have an unfamiliar size and shape, and would lack any authenticating signature. Charges were made

> that the various regulations were badly drafted to the extent that some cannot even be understood by the officials supposed to administer them. One important criticism, made by local officials of JEIA [Joint Export Import Agency] as well as by German manufacturers and exporters, is that the arbitrary 30 cent rate set for the export mark is having the net effect of pricing many items of German manufacture out of the world market. While some mutterings have been heard that the whole thing is nothing but a plot to eliminate German competition, the general feeling among Bremen business men is that the establishment of the 30 cent rate was in good faith and represents simple [sic] a case of overvaluation in terms of Germany's internal price structure. They express the belief that devaluation must and will follow in due course.[415]

It is true that the Deutschmark was devalued by a decision of Adenauer's first cabinet, which had just been formed, on September 21, 1949, retroactively effective from September 19, by 20.6 percent in relation to the US dollar. From then on, one DM would cost 23.8 instead of 30 US cents. Calculated in reverse one US dollar that – significantly influenced by Tenenbaum – had been fixed for foreign trade purposes of the Anglo-Saxon occupation zones through JEIA at 3.33 RM and had been kept unchanged with currency reform in DM, would from then on be valued at 4.20 DM. This had been the familiar traditional exchange rate of the Mark before World War I and again of the RM after the currency reform that had ended hyperinflation in 1923.

This DM external value adjustment was part of a general realignment of exchange rates under the Bretton Woods system of fixed exchange rates supervised by the IMF. It was triggered by a devaluation of the British pound by 30 percent on September 18, 1949. Due to its significantly lower devaluation rate against the US dollar, the DM was in fact revalued vis-à-vis the British pound and most other European currencies. Those European governments had chosen devaluation rates equal or closer to the British one than the devaluation rate of the newly formed West German government under Chancellor Konrad Adenauer with his economics minister Ludwig Erhard. Especially Adenauer was afraid that a higher devaluation rate would lead to price increases at home. This would burden the inflation-damaged population and voters of the nascent Federal Republic with fear and mistrust in the new government.[416]

In fact, the exchange rate is a powerful, often overlooked tool in the arsenal of anti-inflation instruments. Not only Adenauer and Erhard, but also Tenenbaum knew this. The 30 US cents valuation of the DM was regarded as a gross overvaluation by most of German export industry. As we have seen above, only few recognized that it favored foreign competitors in order to put pressure on price level developments in West Germany after currency reform. The exchange rate helped to prevent an acceleration of price increases during the second half of 1948. With a lower exchange rate already then, currency reform would probably have ended in failure. The high external valuation of the DM was a key factor in the reform's eventual success, alongside with the exceptionally high growth rates of industrial productivity and production as well as the above enumerated economic policy initiatives to counter inflation.

In October 1945 a Public Opinion Survey Unit had been established within OMGUS, headquartered at first in Bad Nauheim, but soon transferred to Bad Homburg.[417] Between October 26, 1945 and September 12, 1949 seventy-two OMGUS surveys were undertaken in the American zone of occupation (AMZON), in its exclave Bremen, including the port of Bremerhaven, and in the American sector of Berlin. These surveys resulted in 191 summarizing reports on specific subjects. The reports were distributed widely in OMGUS. In his memoirs General Clay mentions his appreciation of the public opinion surveys: "We had much faith in these polls."[418] They obviously played quite a role in shaping American occupation policies.

The Report No. 133 of August 10, 1948, entitled *Reactions Toward Currency Reform in the US Zone of Germany*, based on 500 people in the American zone and 100 in Bremen, interviewing dates of July 21 to 25, 1948, contradicts the report of the American Consul General in Bremen to the State Department.

> One month after the currency reform ... One-half of the AMZON respondents asserted that their food supply had increased during the previous weeks and almost eight in ten made this claim in Bremen. // Almost everyone (90 per cent in AMZON and 96 per cent in Bremen) thought that the currency reform had been necessary and 53 per cent even felt that it should have come sooner. In AMZON, only a third of the respondents were satisfied with all the regulations implementing it, with the most frequent criticism concerning the effect of the ten to one conversion rate on small savings accounts.[419]

Actually the conversion rate ended up to be only 6.5 instead of 10 percent.

The Soviet occupation zone followed the Western occupation zones with its own currency reform for its zone and all four sectors of Berlin on June 24, 1948. This was also the start of the terrestrial traffic blockade of road and waterways from the Western zones to West Berlin. At that time the Soviet authorities had to tackle a smaller problem than the three Western zones. As one of its first actions already in 1945 the Soviet military government had blocked all deposits in banks and saving institutions. Somewhat later it devalued them 10 to 1 and transformed the 1-part into a forced loan to itself. Thus old deposits had already been fully taken care of and had vanished for all practical purposes.

This helped to shape the conversion terms more favorably for low-income people in the Soviet currency area than in West Germany. It also served propaganda purposes in the East–West conflict, readily adopted by West Germany's Communist Party and by critics of separate currency reforms which would cement the division of Germany. In the Soviet zone 70 RM per capita were exchanged one for one for Deutsche Mark East. And for new savings after the blocking of old accounts in 1945 the conversion rate would also be 1 for 1 up to 100 RM. For saving amounts between 100 and 1,000 RM, that is, the next 900 RM, it would be 1 DM East for 5 RM. Loans to farmers resulting from land reform were also revalued at a rate of 5 RM to 1 DM East. Only for savings accounts beyond 1,000 RM a conversion rate of 1 to 10 applied. "For the revalorization of amounts on current account of State, Reich, communal and other people-owned enterprises preferential conditions provide a rate of 1 to 1. ... Wages, salaries, pensions, scholarships and prices remain unchanged."[420]

In terms of social equity this kind of currency conversion looked much better than the West German conditions, especially for small savers. But the fact that, for lack of newly printed banknotes, currency reform in the Soviet zone and in all sectors of Berlin started out with the old Reichsmark notes with only a coupon glued on it, which was easy to forge, did not contribute to confidence in the new money. Moreover, due to the more generous terms of conversion than in West Germany, the monetary overhang in the Soviet zone and Berlin remained high. While, as a result of the currency reform in West Germany, citizens there ended up with only 6.5 percent of their former RM cash and bank deposits, it amounted to 21 percent in the Soviet zone and Berlin.[421] For that reason alone a lifting of price and ration controls in the Soviet zone would have triggered an at least three times higher inflation rate than the 18 percent that occurred in the Western zones in the second half of 1948. This might have triggered a three times higher level of protest against the outcome of the Soviet military government's currency reform than against the inflationary consequences of currency reform in the three West German zones.

Not least for these reasons, the whole apparatus for controlling the economy with price freezes and rationing remained in place in the Soviet zone and Berlin. The price of it was the absence of an explosion of productivity and production growth like in West Germany and the continuing problem of money facing the familiar shortage of supply, except in the Western sectors of Berlin. There, after the end of the city's blockade and the foundation of the Federal Republic in 1949, market conditions adjusted to those in West Germany. The tracking of developments after the two currency reforms in West and East Germany 1948, with their differently shaped social conditions, could contain empirical answers to the following perennial question. What promotes human well-being more: equality of income or income growth with less equality, but more advancement of income for all?

Back to the public opinion survey:

> Slightly more than half thought that the new Mark would retain its value during the coming year. Well over half (58%) of the AMZON residents as well as 66 per cent of the Bremen residents expected to be better off during this time period. ... the better educated and upper socioeconomic groups were more inclined than their counterparts to take an optimistic view. ... A fairly large majority (71 per cent in AMZON and 73 per cent in Bremen) felt that the currency reform would cut down the extent of the black market. ... Huge majorities felt that the currency reform would increase unemployment, as was indeed the case.[422]

German observers of effects of currency reform also noted the sudden reappearance of material goods on legal markets, where supply and demand were booming. Suppliers were released from price controls, while their confidence in the future value of money resurged. Therefore, their incentive for hoarding goods instead of selling them for old *Reichsmarks*, which had been expected to be devalued since the end of the war, was reversed by introducing the Deutschmark and dismantling price controls. Consumers, on the other hand, with their huge pent-up demand, experienced that their new money could actually buy goods that they had not seen on offer for years. A new incentive to work hard and thus earn wages and salaries in the new scarce currency with proven purchasing power replaced the prior disincentive to do so because earnings in *Reichsmarks* were less valuable than time spent dealing on black or gray markets or traveling to rural areas to procure food. The introduction of the Deutschmark unleashed suppliers' and consumers' hunting instinct for money and material goods.

However, the reverse side of the coin was that all sorts of services fell out of favor, such as taxis and other means of transportation as well as the hotel business and gastronomy. And especially the demand for intellectual and cultural life and its expressions plummeted. It had previously flourished for lack of material goods. The publication of many journals and magazines was discontinued and their publishing houses often went broke. Theater, opera, and concert performances, shows of cabaret and circus artists, and especially those traveling, faced empty seats. This has been described as the *Crisis of Culture* that started with currency reform. "It demonstrated that much of what had been perceived as a great spiritual change and new consciousness, as a moral reconstruction during life in ruins, had actually been only the result of deprived materialism."[423]

In the second half of 1948, highly reputed economist Günter Keiser wrote a memo about the causes of price increases and the problem of wages.[424] Before the reform, he had been employed by the Special Agency for Money and Credit (*Sonderstelle Geld und Kredit*). From there he changed into the *Verwaltung für Wirtschaft* (Economic Administration) after Ludwig Erhard, up to then chairman of the Special Agency, had been elected by the Economic Council (*Wirtschaftsrat*) on March 2, 1948 to be the director of the Economic Administration. Keiser was still working there when he wrote the memo.

He is puzzled by the unexpected price rises vis-à-vis stable and partially even declining wages due to the discontinuation of part of the above-tariff bonuses. He asks why consumer purchasing power is still sufficient to allow for inflationary tendencies. He starts out with the often neglected fact that subsidies for raw materials and for their import have been cut and a number of administered prices, such as transport rates, have been hiked in conjunction with currency reform. He also points out that decontrolled prices have risen only when compared to controlled prices before the reform. In fact, however, the reference point should be the average of pre-reform controlled prices and prices on the illegal black market. Viewed from this angle, inflation would only be apparent, not real. Keiser excludes that inflation, as perceived by consumers, was driven by rising production costs. Economies of scale, improvements in work performance, and the cessation of uneconomic compensation transactions on gray markets had rather created reductions in production costs.

He then turns to the volume of money. Had it been overexpanded? He dismisses the argument that the amounts of per capita conversion 1to1 for private persons and businesses had played a major role in the expansion of purchasing power that allowed businesses to mark up their prices. Instead he holds the following factors accountable: 1.) The obligation imposed on businesses to pay all wages for the whole month of June 1948 in new DM currency. This had motivated businesses to ask banks for credit which would be transformed into purchasing power in the hands of wage earners. 2.) The equipment of the German public and of the occupation authorities with a sum of about three billion DM, two-thirds of which pumped into money circulation by government expenses. 3.) The withdrawal of money from bank accounts already converted in DM without a compensatory buildup of new savings. 4.) The banks had been so well equipped with liquidity that limiting factors for credit-drawing by businesses, except for high interest rates, were absent. Therefore, banks' liquidity dissipated into businesses all over.

Despite these origins of a possibly too large monetary mantle for securing price stability, Keiser was reluctant to hold the 4.5 billion DM in cash balances held in Germany as the main driving force behind price increases. Instead, his main culprit was the unusually high velocity of circulation of money since currency reform. Producers and consumers showed little propensity to hold money. After many years of deprivation, a preference for consuming and holding goods instead of saving and holding money had surfaced. In as much as this behavior led to price increases, it would feed itself by accelerating the circulation velocity of money and thereby inflation.

So far, Keiser had dealt with the proximate causes of the post-currency-reform price rises. He then devoted more than half of his seven-page memo to what he saw as the remote cause: the extraordinary quick and large change in the distribution of income between wages and profits. While productivity of labor and capital on the supply side and the hunger for goods and purchasing power on the demand side were exploding during the second half of 1948, wage income remained under control and tended rather to shrink than to grow in tandem with productivity and overall economic growth. The result was an explosion of profits or – in tax terms – of unearned as opposed to earned income, such as wages and salaries. Keiser saw the post-reform price increases as a prototype of a profit inflation. Accordingly, he demanded not only restrictive monetary policies for credit to businesses and fiscal policy tax measures, but also the decontrol of wages and a careful adjustment of wages in order to correct the highly skewed income distribution and return to a balanced growth of wage and profit incomes.

I have found another assessment of the causes of inflationary developments during the second half of 1948, after currency reform, from an informed eyewitness. The book of Oskar Liebeck contains observations up to and including January 1949. This means that the author could not take into account the stable, even declining price trend in West Germany in 1949. Had he published his book a year later on the basis of observations up to January 1950, his assessment of failure or success of the currency reform would certainly have been quite different. But his observations on price developments and their causes until January 1949 are most revealing of what Germans with economic knowledge, including Ludwig Erhard, might have thought about the currency reform "dictated by the Allied military govern-ments." Here is Liebeck's account:

> Despite all the crises and the undoubted distress in which the German people still find themselves, I see the economic problems with which we entered the year 1949 as, at their core, a monetary problem – despite the currency reform that has taken place. One can even say that the difficulties, which without doubt were the effect of the muddled monetary relations before the currency reform, have remained the same due to the incorrectly performed reform and continue to be money-related. . . . // It is true that at first every owner of goods entered the new monetary epoch with only 40 D-Marks for himself and his family. But after a very short time the picture changed completely. A few months after the introduction of the new D-Mark, there were already not inconsiderable groups of entrepreneurs who did not know what to do with the abundance of D-Marks. Likewise, there was already a not insignificant black market, which drew considerable sums of D-Marks uncontrollably to itself. . . . // The hunt for goods of all kinds as well as the hoarding of goods remained at first almost as strong as in the Reichsmark era. The general opinion was almost that the currency reform had been a blow in the water, and one spoke at times of a second currency reform. . . . This brings me to the criticism of the currency reform: // . . . Basically, I would like to say: Too many D-Marks were put into circulation, and the distribution of money developed inorganically. Compared with the last pre-war figures and in view

of the low production, a maximum of three billion D-Marks should have been issued in the united Western zones, which could then have been successively increased to about five billion D-Marks as soon as production approached the normal peacetime level. I must confess that I was horrified when I heard on the radio that they intended to put up to ten billion D-Marks into circulation. //
To this two to three times inflated D-Mark cash issued was added the disastrous credit creation by commercial banks. Circumventing the ban on open lending, the banks rediscovered the instrument of promissory notes [Solawechsel]. ... // Apart from the excessively large initial circulation and the banks' credit creation, the way in which money was issued was also flawed. One serious error was that all employers were forced to pay in D-Marks the full amount of wages and salaries, not yet due by June 20, retroactively from June 1. This was not possible in most cases, despite the 40 DM bridging allowance for employers per head of their workforce. The banks therefore had to step in with promissory note loans. // The 40 DM bounty (a sum of 15 DM would have been more appropriate) and the retroactively paid wages and salaries now rushed into the existing stocks of goods. The hunger for goods increased the velocity of circulation of money extraordinarily, so that the stocks of goods in the stores etc. were used up in a short time. Naturally, with this excessive demand in relation to possible production, prices rose. The fact that production also increased across the board and that many more goods were still offered for sale than during the Reichsmark era is the real "miracle of the D-Mark."[425]

In contrast to Edward Tenenbaum, who returned to the USA in early September 1948, his boss Jack Bennett stayed on until toward the end of January 1949. On October 1, 1948 he published an article on the "Impact of Currency Reform" in *Monthly Report* No. 37 of the US military governor. It was reprinted in the *Information Bulletin* of OMGUS on October 5, 1948. Bennett admits that currency reform brought difficulties and hardships to certain sectors of the population, such as small savers. But he calms his readers by informing them that the correction of those hardships "has been made a responsibility of German legislative bodies which have been directed in the Currency Reform Law to enact by Dec 31 [1948] an Equalization of Burdens Tax." And in a small paragraph he concedes that a "rising trend in the price of many goods, in particular those in great demand, such as textiles, shoes, household articles, and fruit, is apparent." And as to its causes he continues: "The price increases were created by the far-reaching decontrol in the wake of currency reform, by legal price increases of basic materials such as coal and iron, by the need of adaption to world market prices for imported raw materials, and in certain cases by the failure of current production to equal consumer demand."[426]

Yet, for the overwhelming part the article reads like a success story of the currency reform, which at this early stage could not be taken for granted at all. Bennett's praise of shop windows full of goods that had been missing for a long time on Monday June 21, 1948, the return of incentives to work and produce, the high growth in productivity, the collapse of the black market, the psychological effect of creating optimism for the future is not beside the point. This is also true for his criticism of the Communist Party in West Germany:

> They concentrated their initial propaganda on the attempt to draw unfavorable comparisons between the execution of the currency reform in the western zones and that in the Soviet Zone. Later they focused their propaganda upon the subject of price increases which they labored to exploit as a medium for the creation of social unrest. // On the subject of the basic and visible differences in effect between the currency reform in the western zones from that in the Soviet Zone, they have maintained silence. In contrast to the western zones with their shops filled with goods of many descriptions, returning travelers from the Soviet Zone brought back with them a different picture. // Shops in the Soviet Zone, they stated, were as bare of goods during July as during May. The

exorbitant prices of former times, however, continued unchanged. The food supply was equally inadequate and vegetable shortages even during the peak period of the season were reported. // They described the consumer supply picture prevailing in the western zones versus the Soviet Zone as a study in direct contrast.[427]

But to tell a success story in the stage of turmoil and public unrest in West Germany before currency reform success is empirically validated, is wishful thinking, in this case that of Jack Bennett. Confidence in the new currency was by far not yet assured. Inflation in the second half of 1948 was close to galloping. Talk about the need of a second currency reform was widespread.

The goodbye article for Jack Bennett in the *Information Bulletin* of OMGUS of January 25, 1949 also contains Bennett's then current assessments of the results of the West German currency reform. When interviewed for the article he maintained "that every sign indicates the Deutsche mark is serving its purpose and commanding respect and confidence."[428] He admits that much discontent is expressed over high prices. But "Nine years [he means either the period from the beginning of price and wage controls in Germany in 1936 to the end of World War II 1945 or the period from the beginning of World War II in 1939 to the year of currency reform in 1948] of demand cannot be met by the production of one year. Consequently, prices will be high until increased production can absorb the demand." The article also reports: "Denying rumors that a new currency reform is planned, Mr. Bennett declared there is no reason or justification for such action because the Deutsche mark is serving its purpose and upholding the functions of the German economy." Furthermore, the article quotes Bennett with the following statement in which he concedes weaknesses of the currency reform: "The remedy for any weakness as that developed in the currency is to remove the cause. The Bank deutscher Länder has the weapons and the power to control the currency and to take steps to prevent excess currency from getting into the German economy."[429] Here is

Bennett's clear admission that the terms of the currency reform had led to an excess supply of liquidity in the West German economy, which in turn caused high price increases during the second half of 1948.

In all modesty, let me in this concluding part of this chapter make a calculation that – if I would have had a voice in shaping the terms of the currency reform – would have prevented excess liquidity in Deutschmarks, which caused the inflationary problems during the half year following currency reform. According to historical statistics published by the Bundesbank in 1976, about 59.1 billion in old cash money (Reichsmark and Rentenmark) was circulating in Germany according to their last available official Reichsbank figure of March 7, 1945. The Bundesbank's estimate for cash circulation at the end of the war two months later was 73 billion RM.[430] After German unification had made accessible documents formerly locked up in East Germany's state archive, a new study, published 1997, found an official Reichsbank figure for March 31, 1945 (59.5 billion RM) and a precise amount of Reichsmark banknotes (7.5 billion RM) added to cash circulation from the end of March to the war's end on May 8, 1945.[431] So instead of the Bundesbank's estimate of 73 billion RM the precise amount based on official Reichsbank statistics is 67 billion RM.

The author then uses detailed subtractions and additions to that volume of cash in circulation for the period up until currency reform. Some developments and measures led to a reduction of this amount already during the war on account of war damage by bombing and loss of German territory. On the other hand, the Allies inflated cash circulation in Germany by printing and spending Allied Military Mark, which was declared legal tender side-by-side with the Reichsmark. Its total issue has been estimated rather reliably at 12.0 billion mark. So at the time of the two currency reforms in West and East Germany, the author's calculations result in 65.0 billion RM and Allied Military Mark of cash in circulation to be converted into DM West or East. The data on converted RM cash balances recorded during the implementation of the two currency reforms corroborate the author's calculation. They amounted to 62.4 billion RM.[432]

It is true that the four powers constituting ACC were united in legislating drastic tax increases early on by ACC Law No. 3 of October 20, 1945 and even more so by ACC Laws Nos. 12–17 of February 1946.[433] The result were high income tax rates progressing up to 95 percent and graduated corporation income tax rates of 35, 45, and 60 percent, in tandem with the elimination of tax exemptions and deductions. In addition, turnover and other indirect tax rates were, increased. This policy served for enough revenue to balance the budgets of the soon reconstituted *Länder* (states). But due to these confiscatory tax rates as well as the continuing elimination of market mechanisms by price controls and rationing, black- and grey-market activities were more rewarding than regular jobs or entrepreneurial activities. Therefore, the sluggish development of the economy persisted and revenue was not high enough to generate the aspired high surpluses in order to siphon off purchasing power and thus reduce cash circulation to any meaningful degree. I have found one informed estimate that up until currency reform eight to ten billion RM had been drawn out of money circulation by budget surpluses in the Western zones of occupation, especially in the US zone.[434]

I assume that by June 20, 1948 the issue of Allied Military Mark more or less compensated for reductions in Reichsmark cash circulation from the above-mentioned territorial developments and ACC tax measures. Therefore, I think that it is justified to estimate cash circulation in the four occupation zones and in Berlin at a worth of about 60 billion Reichsmark just prior to currency reform.[435] In 1936, when full employment had been reached in Germany and before price and wage controls had been introduced on November 26, cash circulation amounted to a little more than 6 billion RM.[436] This relationship explains why already the CDG Plan of May 1946 planned on a general conversion rate of 10 DM for 100 RM.

The majority of German currency experts assembled in the Special Agency for Money and Credit at Bad Homburg and from

April 21, 1948 for seven weeks at the Conclave of Rothwesten considered that rate as too strict. However, in view of the very high capacity-utilization differences of the German economy between 1936 and the first three postwar years even this rate was too generous to avoid an inflationary start of the new currency. Industrial production of the Bizone during the first half of 1948 had crawled up to only 55 percent of its level in 1936.[437] Another indicator for 1946 was lagging even more behind its level of 1936, namely the social product in prices of 1936. In 1946 it amounted to only 48.6 percent of its 1936 level.[438] It is, therefore, safe to assume that the supply of goods and services to meet monetary demand after currency reform would only amount to about 50 percent of its level in 1936. Therefore, a conversion rate of 5 DM for 100 RM, as advocated by Edward Tenenbaum and Erwin Hielscher, would have been appropriate. Hielscher left the Rothwesten camp early in protest not against Tenenbaum, but against the majority of his colleagues who would not follow his and Tenenbaum's plea for the strict five- instead of the too generous 10 percent general conversion rate.

My hypothesis of the currency reform's initial oversupply of the DM-economy with liquidity can also be supported by the controversially discussed terms of the per capita conversion 1 DM for 1 RM on June 20, 1948 for 40 RM and two months later for another 20 RM. Excluding Berlin and the Saar region, the latter being under French tutelage and equipped with French currency, the number of inhabitants in the West German currency reform area was roundabout 46 million. Each one, including babies and children, was entitled to exchange 60 RM 1 for 1 into DM. This means that sixty times 46 million, which equals 2.76 billion of the new currency was handed out this way. In addition, employers were entitled to exchange one for one 60 RM into 60 DM for each of their employees. There were roundabout 14 million employees in West Germany at the time of currency reform.[439] This means that 14 million times 60 DM, which equals 840 million DM, was exchanged 1 RM for 1 DM into the hands of businessmen. Together with the per capita exchange for every citizen the total one for one exchange amounted to 3.6 million DM.

Had this amount not been included into the eventual general conversion rate of 6.5 DM for 100 RM, but exempt from the conversion rate for all other funds in cash and bank accounts, as currency reform in the Soviet zone and Berlin arranged for, the 1-for-1 conversion of 3.6 billion would hardly have reduced the roundabout 60 billion RM of circulating cash that were to be diminished at least into 6 billion DM according to the CGD Plan and to even half of that according to Tenenbaum's, Hielscher's, and Bernard's and equally my calculations. Offsetting the 1-for-1 per capita amounts against total DM claims resulting from the eventual 6.5 DM for 100 RM conversion of monetary cash claims, simple rule of three, reduced the approximately 60 billion RM claims by roundabout 55 billion RM. Tenenbaum's insistence on this offsetting part of 1-for-1 currency conversion, against strong demands by West German currency expert to let 1-for-1 pass without offsetting,[440] was the key decision for the eventual success of the West German currency reform. It rendered Tenenbaum's concessions on the amount of 1-to-1 per capita conversion – 25, 50, or 60 DM for RM, the latter amount as granted by the Western Allies in a last-minute concession to the inmates of the Rothwesten camp – practically irrelevant. Probably for propaganda reasons, the planners of monetary reform in the Soviet zone ignored the dimension and importance of offsetting 1-to-1 conversions against their general conversion rate of 1 DM (East) for 10 RM.

In his memo of July 4, 1948 "The Preservation of the Deutsche Mark," Tenenbaum had recognized the inflationary potential created by the terms of the currency reform, in his opinion due to expensive promises that the Western powers had made to German politicians demanding concessions.[441]

In closing let me state that the discussants in the contemporary and current literature about inflation during the second half of 1948 in West Germany, that is, after the currency reform executed by the Western Allied military governments on June 20, 1948, are mostly unaware of the function of the 20 percent inflation forecast of the CDG Plan, namely to facilitate the price-structure adjustment from controlled to market-economy requirements without deflation and depression, as discussed above. Maybe a timely communication at least of this element of the American currency-reform plan would have somewhat calmed doubts and widespread apprehensions of failure of the reform among the German public.

Last, but not least, some general remarks as to the contributions of Colm and Goldsmith with their CDG Plan of May 1946 for a common currency reform of all four Allied powers in Germany, on the one hand, and of Tenenbaum's work in OMGUS thereafter for two years on implementing a currency reform. At first he was still involved in bringing about the reform on the four-power level. But since the failure of the Moscow conference of foreign ministers in April 1947, his work input went more and more into preparation of a bizonal or, if politically possible, a trizonal West German currency reform. Colleagues with whom I have discussed Tenenbaum's central role in decision-making on the terms of the West German currency reform have tried to downplay his achievements by arguing that Colm and Goldsmith had delivered the blueprint which Tenenbaum only executed. They argued with the idiom that Colm and Goldsmith had been the chefs and Tenenbaum the waiter. Others have talked of Tenenbaum as a currency technician.

One is as far off the mark as the other. I have mentioned above that F. Taylor Ostrander, Tenenbaum's colleague on the staff of OMGUS in Berlin, had envied Tenenbaum's currency-reform success. In reaction to an article in IMF's magazine *Finance & Development* on currency reform, when the introduction of the DM in East Germany was on the political agenda, Ostander wrote on May 26, 1990:

> I would criticize the Fin & Dev article on two grounds: // A. They
> talk almost as though the Colm-Goldsmith proposals had
> themselves been legislated into German law. I don't believe that

was the case. Finance Division's nose must have been sorely out of joint that the C-G Mission had been set up outside their jurisdiction, and the likes of Tannenbaum [*sic*] et al. wanted to make it from there on *their* Reform. And the group of German experts they kept secluded behind Secrecy walls somewhere were no doubt allowed to put in their own ideas – up to a point. // ... It is my strong impression ... that much of what C-G proposed didn't get done. // B. It seems to me the Fin & Dev authors (and many others) don't give adequate importance to the fact that Germany's vastly successful currency reform was carried out by a ruling occupying military power. That, under Gen. Clay, this tended to be largely wise and benevolent is overwhelmed by the brute fact this is *not* a democratically worked out reform, but basically was imposed from above and outside the democratic process. The "wise doctor" and his "this medicine is the best thing for you" was basic to its success. // Of course, there was also a further factor in Military Gov't's role. We know that many of the "Commies" and perhaps most of the "Morgenthau-ites" that got into Mil. Gov't were in Finance Division. ... many of the latter were influenced by, if not chosen by, Harry White and his crowd in Treasury. (I have always said that Eddie Bernstein wrote "the White Plan" and we know that Harry White wrote "the Morgenthau Plan.") Therefore, there was a definite ingredient of "be tough to the Krauts" mixed into this "wise old doctor's" prescriptions as they emerged from that Division. Certainly Tannenbaum [*sic*] had a generous dose of this.[442]

After all, Tenenbaum's reform deviated not only in scope, but also in detail of such issues as conversion rate (finally 100 RM to 6.5 DM instead of the C-G ratio of 100 RM to 10 DM) and in many other details. The old recipe of the original chefs was rewritten by Tenenbaum to suit the new challenge of a West German currency reform under a completely different political setting than the one the CDG Plan had been designed for. In this context Ostrander's claim to fame in his same memo might be of interest:

I would claim that it was *my* personal relation to Raymond Goldsmith (through our association as "Co-Directors" of the Defense Finance Division in Henderson's Price Stabilization Div. of the Nat'l Defense Advisory Board in 1940–41) and my admiration for Gerhart [*sic*] Colm (I used to say in Washington before going overseas that Colm and Goldsmith were the only two German refugee economists who made successful and important contributions to economic policy in F.D. R.'s Administration, and Gerhart [*sic*] was ahead of Raymond on the *policy* side) that resulted in Clay's asking just these two to do their study. When Raymond came to Berlin just after you joined our office there in early 1946, you sat in on the preliminary discussions of Clay's cable suggesting their names and function.[443]

The last sentence might contain a clue to whom Ostrander had originally sent his memo of May 26, 1990. It was years later that he sent it to Charles P. Kindleberger.

5 From OMGUS to Civil Service in Washington, DC and for Europe 1948–1953

Before I embark upon Edward Tenenbaum's professional career in Washington, DC in the following Section 5.1, I will start with the circumstances of the move of the Tenenbaum family from Berlin to the Washington, DC area in September 1948, their short-term addresses there, and their purchase of agricultural land and forest, including a sort of farmhouse for living, at the outskirts of Washington, DC toward the end of 1948. I will also track some of their private family matters and the encroachment of urban living into the Tenenbaum's rural hideout.

5.1 ECA, MSA, AND IMF IN WASHINGTON, DC 1948–1952

The Tenenbaum couple and their first child Anne returned to the USA, more precisely to Washington, DC, in late August or early September 1948, depending on whether they crossed the Atlantic by plane or by boat, in the latter case probably from the port of Le Havre in France. But before they left Europe, Tenenbaum himself, if not accompanied by his wife and daughter Anne, spent five nights in the first-class Hôtel des Champs-Elysées, Rue Balzac, in Paris from August 13 to 18, 1948, as the hotel bill in the Tenenbaum Papers shows. He used the reverse side of the bill to take handwritten notes in preparation of his application for employment with the European Cooperation Administration (ECA) in Washington, DC. This means he was not using the hotel bill for reimbursement purposes in case he had been traveling to Paris in a last OMGUS mission. Therefore, it can be assumed that the Paris trip was for private pleasure using up vacation days that he had accumulated during his service for OMGUS in Berlin. In any case, he continued drafting parts of his "Application for Federal Employment" in handwriting on stationery of Hotel Raleigh "on famous Pennsylvania Avenue at 12th St., Washington 4, DC" Obviously, he, with or without his family, stayed there upon arrival in Washington, DC, before moving into c/o Stuart, 8425 Woodcliff Court, Silver Springs, Maryland, from September to October 1948, from where his job application was sent off.[1]

Tenenbaum has listed Fairhaven, Maryland, as his address from October to November 1948. In November 1948 the Tenenbaums settled down on premises on Route 3, today Bennett Road, in Herndon, Virginia, well outside DC limits.[2] Between their arrival in Washington, DC and their move to Herndon, the Tenenbaum couple must have purchased the house there with 24 acres of wood and agricultural land around it. Son Mark Tenenbaum gave me a ride out there, when I met him in Washington, DC on November 10, 2018. It was way out of the center of Herndon and more of a rural than residential area.

During the following years the family kept growing. The Tenenbaum couple would procreate a son, a second daughter, and as a late offspring a second son: Mark Jon (born October 11, 1949), Joan Kipp (born December 22, 1950) and Charles Berish (born January 23, 1956).[3] Judging from where the Tenenbaum family lived and worked when these children were born, their birthplaces must have been in Washington, DC or in Fairfax County, close by their new home in Herndon VA. In a flash of inspiration just before finishing my manuscript for this book and by then knowing Edward Tenenbaum's mentality and dry humor quite well, I noticed that the naming of his son Mark in 1949 might have been inspired by his giving birth to the German Mark in 1948.

Teenager Edward had already shown a preference for pastoral over urban living in his prize-winning contribution to Ecolint's essay contest, class of 1938 in Geneva (see Section 3.1, pp. 115–117). After the family's return to Washington, DC from Tenenbaum's special assignment in General Clay's US military government in Berlin, he and his wife Jeanette Kipp had used their savings to buy a big chunk of agricultural land in Herndon VA. According to information provided orally by Anne Toohey, the oldest child of the Tenenbaums, in a conversation on January 24, 2018 in Washington, DC, the purchase amounted to only 13 acres. But her two siblings, Mark Tenenbaum and Joan Tenenbaum Merrill, in interviews on October 29 and November 10, 2018 respectively, informed me independently of each other that the original purchase covered 24 acres, of which 11 acres were later sold.

The Tenenbaums settled there after tearing down most probably an old farm house and building a new home. In *Yale's Twenty-Fifth Yearbook Class of 1942* Edward Tenenbaum describes in 1967 his investment in land in the following terms: "I also moved to the country, and started tearing down a house and raising a family. My friends thought I was crazy, and my reputation has only been redeemed seventeen years later by the rise in real estate prices, and the encroachment of suburbia on our rural hideaway. Also my family turned out to be pretty nice."[4]

What had happened? In 1965 or 1966 ("seventeen years later"), that is, shortly before *Yale's Twenty-Fifth Yearbook Class of 1942* was published in 1967, the Tenenbaum couple had sold the 11 acres of their original 24-acre purchase to Gulf Reston, Inc. or, if earlier, to the original developer of Reston, Virginia, Robert E. Simon, a real estate entrepreneur. Simon had launched the community on his fiftieth birthday on April 10, 1964 and named it using his initials for the first three letters. He ran into financial difficulties early on and Gulf Oil helped him out with a then huge loan of $15 million. But as by 1967 the financial situation hadn't improved, Gulf forced Simon out and Gulf Reston, Inc. took over the management of the community and continued to purchase land for developing the city.

Reston VA was and is adjacent to Herndon's Eastern side. Simon had planned and developed Reston from scratch since 1964 as an alternative to traditional urban living. It was to be an example of the then modern Garden City movement. Neighboring Herndon on its Western side, *Dulles International Airport* had been under construction since September 2, 1958 and was opened by President

John F. Kennedy on November 17, 1962. In a sort of pincer movement from West and East of Herndon, developers had driven real estate prices there up on a big scale, resulting in large windfall profits to real estate owners. Needless to say that the large margin between the selling price and the entry price seventeen years earlier provided the Tenenbaum couple with pennies from heaven up to the amount of a small fortune, just at the time when three of their kids were already in college or would enter college soon.

From October 1948 to July 1950, Tenenbaum was employed by ECA, 806 Connecticut Avenue NW in Washington, DC, the agency for the execution of the Marshall Plan.[5] Founded in April 1948, it was headed by Paul G. Hoffman and reported to both the State Department and the Department of Commerce. Tenenbaum narrowly missed crossing paths with Charles P. Kindleberger again, who had left his position as Chief of the German Desk in the State Department in the summer 1948 to take up a professorship of economics at MIT. Obviously, Tenenbaum with his expertise on West Germany's economy kept working in this field.

The *Official Register of the United States 1950* covers: "Persons occupying administrative and supervisory positions in the legislative, executive, and judicial branches of the Federal Government, and in the District of Columbia Government, as of May 1, 1950." Under ECA it lists Edward A. Tenenbaum as "Assistant Chief (Finance), European Trade Policy Branch," which was part of the Fiscal and Trade Policy Division. directed by James A. McCullough, who was thus Tenenbaum's boss. The 8th Congressional District of the State of New York is noted as Tenenbaum's legal residence, although he and his family already lived in Herndon VA, Route 3, which is today named Bennett Road. The Register's purpose is to inform the general public on annual compensation of every higher employee in the federal government's civil service. Tenenbaum's was $8,800 per year. This was what most assistant chiefs were paid, while his boss James A. McCullough drew the exceptionally high salary for a division director of $15,000. Tenenbaum's $8,800 p.a. in 1950 amounts to a value of $111,000 in 2023. For a civil servant twenty-eight years of age this is an extraordinarily high salary.[6] The now online accessible original questionaires of the US Census of April 1950 for the Tenenbaum family in Herndon VA contain income data for 1949. For that year, E. A. Tenenbaum reported a salary of $7,432, together with fifty-two weeks of work. That is, he did not allow himself a vacation. For the week immediately preceding the Census interrogation, he stated his weekly working time as fifty-eight hours, including unpaid work on family farm or business.

During his ECA employment Tenenbaum got involved in planning and designing the European Payments Union (EPU). It was created on September 19, 1950 by all eighteen members of the Organization for European Economic Cooperation (OEEC) who participated in the Marshall Plan. It entered into force, retroactively, on July 1, 1950. It facilitated the convertibility of European currencies by setting exchange rates that were deemed to reflect the reality of each country's economic situation. On a day-to-day basis it acted as a multilateral European clearing house. In preparation of its creation a working committee which studied the problem was set up. "Included were John Hulley, H. van Buren Cleveland, Theodore Geiger, and Walter Stettner of the ECA and Albert Hirschman of the Federal Reserve Board. Other active contributors, as thinking matured, included James McCullough, Arthur Smithies, and Edward Tenenbaum."[7]

Tenenbaum's expertise on German currency, finance, and economy remained an asset in the execution of the Marshall Plan. This is evidenced by the following story in the weekly of the *Deutscher Gewerkschaftsbund* (DGB, German Labor Union Federation) *Welt der Arbeit* (World of Work) of February 24, 1950. Like all eighteen governments participating in the European Recovery Program (ERP), Franz Blücher, federal minister for the Marshall Plan and vice chancellor in Chancellor Konrad Adenauer's first cabinet 1949–1953, had been asked in late 1949 to deliver a projection of expected economic development in West Germany until the end of the ERP in 1952 to the

OEEC in Paris. This was to serve coordination and planning purposes. Blücher's ministry delivered its projection for West Germany in mid-December 1949. The report estimated an average number of 1.8 million unemployed for 1952. Investment would have to be curbed until then to avoid an overexpansion of consumption.

Especially these two points were sharply criticized in some German media, by labor unions, and especially by the head of the Marshall-Plan office in Frankfurt am Main, Mr. Hanes, in his 100-page report. Even the *Financial Times* in London ran an article on this critic of economic policy in West Germany. Hanes' critical report reached Washington, DC before Blücher came for an official visit in late January or in February 1950. Washington was not amused, strongly criticized Blücher, asked for immediate changes in economic policies to avoid the high number of unemployed in 1952, and informed its High Commissioner in Germany, John McCloy. The latter presented the German government with an official memorandum containing the harshest criticism of West German economic policy and thus first and foremost of Federal Minister of Economics Ludwig Erhard. The author of this memo was Edward Tenenbaum, which the mentioned journal of the labor unions made public.[8] Inside the article the reader is informed that Erhard surely knew that within Frankfurt circles Tenenbaum had been identified as the originator of the High Commissioner's memo for some time. Was Erhard of such vindictive character that this episode explains why he kept concealing Tenenbaum's outstanding importance for creating the foundation for Erhard's Social-Market policy and for Germany's spectacular economic resurrection during the 1950s and 1960s? In any case, under pressure from Washington, DC, from the High Commissioner in Germany, and from Edward Tenenbaum with specific demands for change, Erhard made economic-policy adjustments. The actual number of unemployed in 1952 turned out to be 1.65 million instead of 1.8 million as projected at the end of 1949.[9]

Fortunately, Tenenbaum was well organized and so are his papers. He kept job descriptions of his different postwar jobs and copies of the forms of his applications for employment, in which he was asked for many details of his past employments. He even kept the mostly handwritten drafts of text in preparation for filling out the forms.

5.1.1   ECA from October 1948 to July 1950

Here is how Tenenbaum described his duties while working in Washington, DC after his return from Germany in the late summer of 1948.

> Title: Acting Chief, European Trade Policy Branch. // Superiors: Mr. James A. McCullough, then Director, Fiscal and Trade Policy Division, now ... // Mr. Richard M. Bissell, jr., then Deputy Administrator, Economic Cooperation Administration, now ... // Duties: 1. Development of policies on European Payments Union, economic integration, and related matters. Assisted in representation of ECA at U.S. National Advisory Council Staff Committee (top working party on international financial affairs in U.S. Government). // 2. Advised on implications for Marshall Plan of foreign exchange, export and import controls and methods of circumventing (such as trading in blocked currencies, "clearing currencies" and "cheap sterling," over- and under-invoicing, barter compensation, and foreign exchange bonuses, commodity shunting, etc. // Salary: $7,600 per annum (beginning) – $8,800 per annum (final).[10]

In the same document, as part of his job description of his prior employment by OMGUS Berlin, Tenenbaum states that his annual salary there had amounted to $6,250 (beginning) – $9,200 (final, including $1,840 overseas differential). At ECA in Washington, DC he lost, of course, his overseas differential. But even his beginning annual salary, all the more his final, was higher than that he was paid at the end of his OMGUS employment in Berlin, when he was the key person managing the West German currency reform of June 1948.

Shortly before Tenenbaum left ECA for employment by IMF, Tenenbaum and his boss, Melville E. Locker, director of the Fiscal and Trade Policy Branch, signed a job description for Tenenbaum on May 2 and 3, 1950. It listed Tenenbaum's tasks as follows:

1. Develops general ECA policies and procedures in connection with the removal of barriers to payments and to the movement of capital. . . . 2. Is responsible for projects involving the removal of barriers to payments among the entire group of Western European countries. . . . 3. Formulates policy with respect to the use of ECA funds in connection with plans for removing barriers to payments among Western European countries and for determining conditions governing the use of such funds. . . . 4. Determines relation of plans for removal of barriers to payments and for movement of capital among Western European countries to other objectives of U.S. policy in fields of international finance. . . . 5. Is responsible for the coordination and negotiation with other agencies of the U.S. government, foreign governments, and international agencies on policies relating to the economic unification of Western Europe. . . . 6. As assigned, assumes full responsibility for the operation of the branch in the absence of the branch chief.[11]

Obviously, his duties also included informing the American business world about the purpose and functioning of the European Payments Union (EPU), for which he carried responsibility within ECA. A newspaper article in Richmond VA announced a meeting with him: "Edward A. Tenenbaum, chief of the European trade policy branch of the European Cooperation Administration, will discuss the operation of the European payments plan between Western European countries at a meeting of the Richmond Export–Import Club at 12:30 P. M. today [28 June 1950] at Hotel Rueger."[12] One can assume that Richmond wasn't the only place where he gave a talk about the topic.

This proves that Tenenbaum was one of those Americans in the State Department's Marshall Plan organization who were assigned responsibility for promoting the economic integration and unification of Western Europe.[13] Without the American stick and carrot policy at the start European economic, monetary, and progressively political integration, the stage the European Union has reached now would not have been attained.[14]

5.1.2 IMF from July 1950 to May 1951

From July 24, 1950 to May 1951 Tenenbaum worked for the IMF as an economist on the regular staff on multiple currency practices in the Exchange Restrictions Department, Grade 16-1 with an annual salary of $7,850.[15] This was nominally about $1,000 less than he had made on his job with ECA. But as IMF income is tax-free, this was probably a rise in his net income.

Despite my great efforts I was unable to obtain any information on Tenenbaum's work for the IMF, neither from IMF's personnel department nor from its archivist. It is, therefore fortunate that the Tenenbaum Papers contain a long description of his IMF duties, dated April 1, 1951, obviously as part of his application for a return to ECA, with its successor MSA already in the making. Tenenbaum records:

> As an economist in the Exchange Restriction Department
> [Director: Irving Friedman] my duties have included: // (a) Initiation
> and supervision of a research project undertaken by six professional
> staff members over a period of four months, including substantive
> and editorial guidance, maintenance of relations with other
> Departments of the Fund concerned with the study, development
> and exploitation of appropriate tools of analysis. The study, entitled
> "Regional Clearing and Convertibility" concerns the theoretical
> and practical implications of regional clearing systems such as the
> EPU. // (b) Participation in formulation of Fund policy on recent
> word-wide economic developments (e.g., improvement in balance
> of payments of soft-currency countries, impact of rearmament on
> world economy), the European payments union, broken cross-rates,
> methods of furthering programs towards convertibility, etc.

Includes advising Director of Exchange Restrictions Department, participation in preparation of Fund Annual Report on Exchange Restrictions, preparation of memoranda on particular subjects, representation of Department in intra-Fund working parties and committees, attendance at meetings of Fund Staff Committee and Board of Executive Directors. // (c) Independent research on the restrictive system, economic conditions and policy problems of Belgium-Luxembourg, leading to recommendations as to Fund policy on the possibility of restoring "full convertibility of the Belgian franc. // (d) Maintenance of liaison with certain US Government agencies, particularly ECA; advising Director of Department on problems of liaison with OEEC, the US Economic Commission for Latin America, etc.; advising Director in evaluating applicants for employment."[16]

In a different description of his jobs for application purposes Tenenbaum reports an IMF salary of $8,800 p.a., including income tax and other benefits. The Edward A. Tenenbaum Papers actually contain a few of the memos he wrote for the IMF.[17]

5.1.3 ECA/MSA from May 1951 to April 1952 in Washington, DC

After the end of his US government appointment in Athens (see Section 5.2) and his return home to Herndon VA, Route 3, in June 1953, Tenenbaum obviously prepared another application for employment with several attachments containing descriptions of his former jobs. One of these covers his activities for MSA after he quit his employment with IMF to return to ECA in May 1951, which in October 1951 officially became MSA. He describes his position and duties in Washington, DC before leaving for his MSA Mission to Athens in early April 1952 as follows:

Title: Economic Adviser Office of Assistant Director for Europe. // Superior: Mr. Melville E. Locker, Special Assistant to Assistant Director for Europe, now Assistant to Deputy Director for Mutual

Security, MSA, Washington D.C. // Duties: General supervision of work on the European Payments Union (EPU), special country problems of a financial nature (e.g., Belgian balance of payments difficulties and inflation in Greece), development of policies for financing European military effort (such as administration of "offshore procurement" and "infrastructure" funds), review of policies for investment guaranties; economic adviser to Samuel Welldon, head of special mission to initiate financial reforms in Greece. // Salary: $10,800 per annum.[18]

I will quote the second part of this attachment on Tenenbaum's position and duties during his MSA Mission in Athens in Section 5.2. As to inflation in Greece, Tenenbaum wrote a memo on October 25, 1951 entitled "Requirements for a Currency Reform in Greece."[19] He starts out from a lesson of many inflations in the past that progressive price increases, if not stopped, erode confidence in the currency. This by itself fuels higher inflation, which in turn undermines confidence in the currency even more. If not halted, this interaction develops into a vicious circle. It reaches a point where regular anti-inflation monetary and fiscal measures no longer suffice, as the authorities executing them are no longer trusted by the population. In that situation, only drastic action can put an end to the vicious circle, such as new political institutions and a wholly new currency. He also mentions that strong vested interests who profit from an ongoing inflation must be overcome. "Greece today seems to be somewhere in the middle of this process. The end is not clearly in sight. ... But the beginning of the circle is long past and there is no easy turning back. As usual there are strong vested interests in the continuance of inflation." He names the advocates of the grossly oversized "investment program," of which probably half of such expenditures in the long run will turn out to have been wasted. He also identifies the "farm bloc." Its interest in granting price subsidies in tandem with supporting a rationing program would "make the farmer's lot better, and inflation worse.

To end inflation, the 'farm bloc' must be forced to cease spending other people's money."

Tenenbaum continues with a big-bang attack on fellow Americans who work in the US embassy and other US missions in Athens:

> The "investment program" interest and the "farm bloc" interest (as well as a multitude of other pro-inflation interests) are strongly represented within the U.S. agencies operating in Greece. Perhaps the numerical majority of U.S. citizens employed in Greece do not really want inflation to end. With it must end many of their present functions, and many of their present jobs. In this, as in so many respects, Greece is not really a special case. The same was true of U.S. Military Government in Germany before the currency reform of 1948, and on a smaller scale is true in many other ECA countries. // Thus, any attempt to end inflation in Greece will be opposed not only by all Greeks (for lack of faith that it will succeed), not only by the special interests in Greece which actually profit by inflation, but also by a large part of the U.S. missions to Greece. Until that final crisis in which inflation (before the final crisis makes an end imperative) requires U.S. leadership such as never has been exercised, and is not now visible. // ... Put baldly, the fundamental requirement for success of any technical proposal to end inflation is: a person or persons in authority who will stand up to the tremendous moral, political and financial pressures for a continuance of inflation.

Only if this prerequisite would be fulfilled, would Tenenbaum advocate a currency reform for Greece, probably with his successful West German currency reform of 1948 in the back of his mind. Tenenbaum identifies wage-earners and salaried employees as the only group benefiting immediately from a successful currency stabilization. Their real earnings would increase almost overnight. But he also lists the losers: last but not least, unemployment hidden by inflation would become open unemployment. All businessmen would suffer, because either their profits would be reduced to normal proportions or because uneconomic enterprises that had been kept in business only due to inflation would go bankrupt. The government, "faced with problems of transition (from the grotesque abnormality of inflation to the forgotten normality of no inflation), most likely will fall into a panic." And farmers would be among the losers. Tenenbaum argues further: Until the disadvantages of ending inflation would not be accepted, there would be no use in trying to have a currency reform in Greece. It would result in "a terrible failure. Since unwillingness to accept them still seems to prevail in US missions to Greece, currency reform should not be encouraged."

Nevertheless, Tenenbaum also lists advantages of ending inflation in Greece, "as intelligent decision cannot be made on the basis of disadvantages alone." The first purpose would be to keep Greece out of the hands of communism, an American foreign-policy aim since the announcement of the Truman Doctrine in March 1947. He argues: "Inflation, as always and everywhere, leads to social injustice which breeds communism. Lenin is supposed to have said … that "the best way to destroy the capitalist system is to debauch the currency." The second advantage Tenenbaum lists is: "the free enterprise system cannot function to the reasonable satisfaction of all concerned without reasonable monetary stability." Third, two of many unfortunate consequences of inflation would be "(1) Inflation causes hoarding of goods and (2) inflation results in tremendous economic inefficiency." They would disappear with the restoration of price stability. Fourth, "A currency reform makes it possible for a country to cease to depend on foreign aid, something which usually is not possible as long as inflation continues." Tenenbaum sums up: "US authorities in Greece can continue to enjoy their proclivities for inflation, provided they exercise sufficient moderation to avoid forcing the inevitable crisis. The Greek people, and we, will suffer the consequences. Let us at least spare them and us the consequences of a premature currency reform which we will not allow to succeed."[20]

This concise, 3.5-page memo, which I consider to have been one of Tenenbaum's best ever, was probably the reason why Tenenbaum became an economic adviser of Samuel A. Welldon (1883–1962). Welldon was a graduate of Harvard College and Harvard Law School. His main job was chairman of the executive board of the First National Bank of the City of New York. He also served as director of several of the largest American companies.

American plans to reduce economic aid to Greece mainly for investment purposes, without curbing Greek military contributions to the NATO Alliance, ended up in resistance, tension, and controversy not only between the US representatives in Athens and the Greek government, but also among and between leading MSA and US embassy personnel up to ambassador John Emil Peurifoy. In order to break the deadlock, MSA in Washington decided to send a delegation, chaired by the highly reputed Wall Street banker Samuel A. Welldon, to Greece, including Edward Tenenbaum as his economic adviser who previously had worked for the Greek desk of MSA in Washington, DC, and Francis Lincoln, Office of Greek, Turkish and Iranian Affairs, State Department in Washington, DC. They arrived in Athens in early April 1952, where Welldon would remain until early May 1952 and Tenenbaum until June 1953.

The two Ivy-League graduates evidently operated on the same wavelength. In his report Welldon recommended a harsh currency reform for Greece, that is, the Tenenbaum proposal shaped according to what he had accomplished in Germany. Their common four weeks in Athens was the beginning of a friendship. At the time of their arrival Roger Lapham, former Republican mayor of San Francisco, was the head of the ERA/MSA Mission to Greece from 1951 to 1952. He had fallen out of favor with his superiors at the MSA Greek desk in Washington, DC. To the great relief of Tenenbaum, he was replaced by Leland Barrows who would serve on that mission from 1952 to 1954.[21] Barrows later became a career diplomat in the State Department. Still under Republican President Eisenhower he was hesitantly appointed US ambassador to

Cameroon in 1960. Like Tenenbaum he had been affiliated with the Democratic Party.[22]

The tension between the Greek desk of MSA/Washington, on the one hand, and MSA/Athens still headed by Roger Lapham and the US embassy in Greece, on the other, is well readable between the lines of a letter of May 12, 1952 by ambassador John E. Peurifoy to John Kenney, deputy director of MSA /Washington, and of Kenney's answer of May 29, 1952. Peurifoy is concerned about what recommendations the MSA's Welldon Mission might write in its report. And Kenney takes responsibility for telegrams out of MSA/Washington whose content displeased Peurifoy, even met with "condemnation." At the end of his letter Kenney writes with Lapham's dismissal already in mind:

> Of course, one of our principal problems in Greece was to strengthen Roger's [Lapham] hand and provide him with competent personnel. To this end I have, at Roger's request, agreed to the transfer of Barrows as Deputy Chief and Tenenbaum as Economic Advisor. . . . // I do appreciate the interest you have taken in my problems and hope that we are progressing on the way to solutions.[23]

Because Welldon and Tenenbaum trusted each other amicably, they could exchange their views on developments and US personnel in Athens without diplomatic reservations.[24] Shortly after his return to New York in early May. Welldon wrote a letter to Tenenbaum, dated May 7, 1952. Since the report of the Welldon delegation had caused some political turmoil and confusion in Greece, Tenenbaum waited with his answering letter until June 30, 1952, when he had gathered a clearer view of the situation. He then reported to Welldon:

> Sufficient time has now elapsed to permit me to write down a few impressions with some hopes of accuracy. // In the first place, I am happy to report that your fears as to the Economic Policy Committee and as to myself have proven groundless. I attribute this not so much to myself as to the wholehearted cooperation and

skillful support of Lee Barrows for the program we are undertaking. I don't know how well you came to know him before you left, but I hope you know me at least well enough to realize that in nature I am not exactly uncritical of other people. Nevertheless, I have only the highest praise for the tact and single-mindedness with which he has pursued our common objective. This, needless to say, has not been entirely simple in his present position.[25]

5.2   FOR MSA IN ATHENS 1952–1953: GREEK CURRENCY REFORM

ECA was superseded by MSA (Mutual Security Agency) when the US Congress had passed the Mutual Security Act on October 10, 1951. Until then, Edward Tenenbaum, who in May 1951 had changed his employer from IMF to ECA, was again a civil servant in Washington, DC. There he worked on financial problems of Greece, unless he was out of town on official trips to Europe. Taken over by the newly founded MSA in October he tackled the same questions, first in Washington, DC, certainly with some business trips to Athens. He moved there with his family in April 1952.

In the Tenenbaum Papers I found a document of July 28, 1952 from the Office of the Chief of the MSA Mission in Athens, who at that time was already Leland Barrows, with a revised position description for a special economic adviser for MSA – Special Mission to Greece "Incumbent: Edward A. Tenenbaum."[26] It is a description of Tenenbaum's qualifications and tasks. But it also let's one read between the lines that there were unsettled frictions between the powers of the US embassy and the MSA Mission in Greece. The embassy resented that Tenenbaum had already tried to have new drachmae banknotes printed outside of Greece.[27] The revised position description granted to Tenenbaum far-reaching powers of communication with the highest echelons of Greek government. But it also made clear that the incumbent as economic adviser would be subject to orders by the chief and the deputy chief of the MSA Mission.

However, the author of the job description admitted that the chiefs of the mission didn't have any expertise in economic matters. The whole thing reads like a piece of the tug-of-war going on between the mission and the US embassy when MSA wanted Tenenbaum to take currency, economic, and maybe military-aid matters in hand on the spot in Athens as financial adviser to the Greek government.

In any case, this document proves that Edward Tenenbaum and his family did not arrive in Athens before 1952. Actually they arrived in early April 1952, as a memo of April 21, 1952 from Tenenbaum to ambassador Frederick L. Anderson, US ambassador to NATO, "Subject: Interim Report on Greek Operation" proves. It states in its first sentence: "We have now spent about two and a half weeks in Athens." In this memo Tenenbaum already reports some improvement in the very strained relations between the Greek government and US representatives in Greece. He also confirms their common prior impression that detailed intervention by the US Mission had been carried too far. He had arrived with a new offer to the Greeks: "responsibility for their own affairs. In return, at least as long as the novelty of our approach lasts, they seem ready to offer us more than the usual amount of cooperation."[28] In an eight-page letter of June 19, 1952 to Fotis Makris, general secretary of the Greek labor unions, Tenenbaum had explained his approach toward stabilizing the Greek currency and asked for labor's share in support of anti-inflation measures.[29]

On June 30, 1952 Tenenbaum wrote to his boss and colleague Melville Locker, MSA Office of assistant director for Europe in Washington, DC. As this letter reveals a lot about Tenenbaum's personality, especially his humorous side, I quote from it:

> Dear Mel: // Naturally, this letter really is to Cecilia, who, unlike you, at least writes to me from time to time. So I'll start over again. // Miss Cecilia Albaugh //MSA/Washington // Dear Cecilia: // Many thanks for your letter of June 18 and particularly for the part which says that the government may owe me more money. . . . // Life here is extremely interesting, for men. My wife has her German

housekeeper now, and as a result hasn't got too much to do. Of course, she always can run down to the PX and Commissary to spend my money. On the other hand, even with the tremendous salary I now earn, that doesn't take all day, because both worthy institutions follow tradition by closing for inventory all the time. // ... please forward the attached letter to Welldon, and anybody else who might conceivably be interested. Also give my regards to Mel, if he still has the time to receive them. // Platonic affection,[30]

The Tenenbaum family returned to the USA in June 1953, "because his appointment was not renewed."[31] As we will see in more detail at the end of this chapter, Tenenbaum himself had asked already in February for the expiration of his contract on June 15, 1953. This latter date was shortly before MSA was abolished on August 1, 1953.

Back in Washington, DC Tenenbaum evidently prepared a new application for employment. In an attachment he described his position and duties on his MSA Mission to Athens from early April 1952 to June 1953 as follows:

> Title: Special Economic Adviser and Director, Finance and Program Division, MSA Mission to Greece. // Superior: Mr. Leland C. Barrows, Chief, MSA Mission ... // Duties: Director of Division charged with planning and budgeting U.S. aid and use of American bargaining power to obtain policies leading to Greek economic recovery. Supervised 20 American and 50 Greek employees. Under the general direction of the Mission Chief, helped to introduce policy and attitude changes which permitted a reduction of U.S. economic aid from $180 million in 1951–52 to $20 million (requested from Congress) in 1953–54. ... // Salary: $12,700 per annum plus oversees allowances.[32]

By the time of the Tenenbaums' return home, the stabilization program for the Greek currency and economy had successfully been implemented. However, it deviated from Tenenbaum's plan shaped according to his West German currency reform of 1948, including the introduction of a new currency, new drachma, with new banknotes, which had already been printed in the UK. Thus Tenenbaum wanted to avoid another devaluation of the old drachma.

On July 31, 1952 he had drafted a 16-page memo "Comparison of Simple Devaluation with a Currency Reform," in which under different sub-headings he listed the advantages and disadvantages of each alternative. He came to the conclusion that a currency reform was the best cure for the Greek economy's inflation and other weaknesses.[33] Tenenbaum's arguments for his preferred solution, however, failed to convince Greek economic-policy makers. In fact, the last step in implementing the stabilization program was a substantial devaluation, as we will see. Why it did not lead to further inflation, contrary to Tenenbaum's expectations, is well described in a study by Apostolos Vetsopoulos. He summarizes that

> this measure [devaluation] was needed in order to boost exports of
> Greek agricultural products, since their prices were high in the
> international market, to balance imports-exports, to attract
> investments of foreign capital, to increase invisible receipts, such as
> tourism, and to balance the national budget. The Stabilization
> Program was successful because it was built upon the foundation of
> physical and social reconstruction which was carried out by means
> of American aid and administered by the American Missions.[34]

What was the political background of Tenenbaum's departure from his post in Athens? Elections on September 9, 1952 on the basis of a proportional voting system had resulted in a fragmented party composition in Greek parliament. This made coalition building difficult and unstable. The American ambassador to Greece, John Emile Peurifoy, and a number of his American supporters, in the embassy and also in the State Department, argued that implementation of the stabilization program needed a strong and stable majority in Greek parliament. In order to achieve that, Peurifoy demanded a change in the voting system to majority voting. The two strongest parties agreed. They brought about the change in the voting system. A new election on

November 16, 1952 on that basis resulted in a spectacular victory for the conservative party *Greek Rally*: 239 seats out of the total of 300. Its leader Field Marshal Alexandros Papagos formed a strong government with Spyros Markezinis as powerful finance and government coordination minister. This was the end of the prior center government.[35] This political change and the implementation of the stabilization program somewhat deviant from Tenenbaum's design would signal to Washington, DC in 1953 that the new Greek government didn't need – or should I say want – Tenenbaum anymore. After having contributed to the stabilization of the Greek currency, the drachma, Tenenbaum had fallen in disgrace among the political elites in Athens. He had to leave his post, because not only the new Greek government, pushed by business interest groups and labor unions,[36] but also quite a few fellow Americans in the embassy and the State Department had opposed his harsh anti-inflation policy. Not quite as powerfully as in West Germany in 1948, Tenenbaum had nevertheless contributed to lay the foundation for Greece's *economic miracle* during the following two decades and thus for political freedom and democracy until a military junta took power from April 1967 to 1974.

Here is the story in more detail. When in October 1944 the German *Wehrmacht* withdrew from its more than three-year occupation of Greece and bitter fighting with Greek resistance, the Germans had destroyed Greece's infrastructure, such as ports and harbors, railroads, bridges, roads, and electric power, had stripped agriculture of its cattle, had devastated many fruitful cropping areas, and had demolished industrial plant and equipment. On this breeding ground of famine and chaos the country was stricken by civil war immediately after World War II hostilities had ended. Communists, supported by Yugoslavia and not directly by the Soviet Union, were fighting an authoritarian regime in Athens. The latter was backed financially and militarily by the USA and the UK. Greece had become a bone of contention in the incipient Cold War. It was the only state in the Balkans that should and would not turn communist. Especially for the USA this was of enormous strategic importance.

In 1947 the UK itself needed financial aid from the USA. It urged the Washington government to step in on a big scale to secure Western strategic positions in the Mediterranean and to contain the spread of communism there. This prompted President Truman to announce the Truman Doctrine to a joint session of Congress on March 12, 1947. He specifically asked for $400 million of military and economic aid for Greece and Turkey, $300 million of which was to be allotted to Greece, and to support the dispatch of American civilian and military personnel and equipment to those countries.[37]

> Truman justified his request on two grounds. He argued that a Communist victory in the Greek Civil War would endanger the political stability of Turkey, which would undermine the political stability of the Middle East. This could not be allowed in light of the region's immense strategic importance to US national security. Truman also argued that the United States was compelled to assist "free peoples" in their struggles against "totalitarian regimes," because the spread of authoritarianism would "undermine the foundations of international peace and hence the security of the United States." In the words of the Truman Doctrine, it became "the policy of the United States to support free peoples who are resisting attempted subjugation by armed minorities or by outside pressures."[38]

Congress quickly and fully acted on Truman's request. On June 5, 1947 Secretary of State George Marshall would announce at Harvard Commencement Exercises the manifold larger financial and economic aid program for Europe, the European Recovery Program (ERP), the so-called Marshall Plan. The flow of ERP funds to Europe, including West Germany after its currency reform of June 20, 1948, started in the second half of that year. It ended four years later. The Mutual Security Agency (MSA) took over its key functions in October 1951, that is when Tenenbaum with his expertise in currency reform and financial matters had become active to work on such problems in Greece from his desk in Washington, DC. On June 23, 1951, ECA, which would soon be succeeded by MSA, had more or less forced the Greek government to agree on "Principles of Program Agreement ... which it will observe in reorganizing and expanding the existing system of rationing distribution of basic foods."[39]

On August 1, 1951, while still in Washington, DC, Tenenbaum sent an office memo to his ECA boss James A. McCullough, "Subject: Buying Finance Ministers." Besides showing his ability to analytically dissect a problem, it also contains examples of his typical black humor. The question he treats is: How can the US government make use of its foreign aid to European countries to share in the military built up against the threat from communist countries? In contrast to the past when US aid was partially allowed to end up in the pockets of finance ministers instead of the purses of the people, we must win the cooperation of the European people "to keep the Iron Curtain from rolling forward," he argued. In general, he considered European governments to be weak. They

can only be strengthened by forcing them to actions (or by taking actions ourselves, but letting them have the credit) which meet the needs of the average European. // Our "programming" of dollar aid has not been ideal in this respect. There is great room for improvement, and particularly for concentration of our bargaining power on the few things that really matter. But "programming" has been better than nothing. The alternative – "free dollars" in return for a military effort of a given size – means reducing our influence on the internal affairs of European governments to precisely nothing. (If it doesn't mean that it is pointless). // We may get guns that way. But which one of the "weak governments" can be called upon to shoot them, in the right direction? Being ready to shoot is a far greater test of the strength of a government than producing guns (or spare parts). Any doubt on this score should have been settled long ago, by the fate of the very expensive Maginot line, built by a succession of weak governments. Some of these weak governments even had buyable Finance Ministers.[40]

Some months before Tenenbaum's arrival in Athens, where he officially served as director of finance and program division, and of his studying the currency problem of Greece on the site, he had sent a secret message to Paul R. Porter, the chief of the ECA and MSA US aid program for Greece, dated July 13, 1951, "Subject: The Pesmasoglu Proposals." Pesmasoglu was the governor of the National Bank of Greece, the biggest commercial bank in the country. Through his proposals he wanted American money to sustain the bank. The bank was finally merged with the bank of Athens in 1955. Tenenbaum's message to Porter reads:

> Attached are two memoranda concerning the Pesmasoglu
> proposals. The first (unclassified) analyses Mr. Pesmasoglu's plan
> for an IBRD [International Bank for Reconstruction and
> Development] loan to Greece, in the form of dollar bonds to be sold
> in Greece for drachmae. It comes to the conclusion that the plan is
> technically unworkable, and would not contribute substantially to
> ending inflation. It is written in such a way that it might be sent to
> Mr. Pesmasoglu for his consideration. // The second (classified
> Secret) discusses the need for a currency reform in Greece, and
> suggests a program which might prove feasible. I would recommend
> against sending this to Mr. Pesmasoglu or giving it wide
> distribution either in Washington or in Greece. Any leak of news
> that ECA is considering such a step – however informally – could
> easily produce an economic crisis in Greece. // I do not know
> whether the time to raise this question has arrived, nor whether the
> Pesmasoglu proposals provide an opportunity to do so. However,
> one thing seems clear: Greece will never recover social and
> economic stability, will never be able to move out of the "U.S.
> Ward" class, until a radical reform of the monetary system is
> introduced and succeeds. For this, no time is better than the present
> (with the possible exception of the past).[41]

Tenenbaum progressed at ERA/MSA in Washington, DC with his planning of a Greek currency reform by writing a one-and-a-half-page memo, classified "Secret," on August 10, 1951. It is entitled "Summary of a Proposal to End Inflation in Greece." It contains all essential components for a successful currency reform. The memo displays the severity of measures he had planned. It looks like when writing this blueprint, he drew on his experience with currency reform in West Germany in 1948, including mistakes that had resulted there from political compromising with Washington, DC, among the Western Allies as well as with West German financial experts and politicians. As in contrast to Germany 1948, Greece had its own government and powerful interest groups, such as labor unions and business organizations, the severity of proposed measures already carried the germ of Tenenbaum's later falling from grace. Here is what he had in mind:[42]

> When severe inflation continues for long enough in any country, a point is reached where normal means are insufficient to overcome it. The extraordinary means of a currency reform then must be considered. That point seems to have been reached in Greece. // The basic technique of a currency reform is to reduce the amount of money in circulation, not just until its total real value is equal to the amount required to maintain normal operation of the economy, but initially well below that amount. The result is to produce a breathing spell, time and room within the monetary system to undertake adjustment of inflationary pressures. // The three prerequisites of a currency reform are: // a. The will and political ability to undertake radical measures to end inflation. // b. The ability to avoid further inflation; in particular this means the ability of the government to balance its expenditures by tax revenues, and of central monetary authorities to prevent undue expansion of private bank credit, after the reform takes place. // c. A clear understanding of the techniques and consequences of currency reform. // The following is a proposal of a currency reform for Greece, intended more as an illustration than as a fully developed plan: // 1. The reform might begin with an announcement that the National Bank no longer is able to stabilize the market for gold sovereigns. In the ensuing panic, the Bank would secretly bid up the rate (as quickly as possible) to 100,000 drachmae

per dollar of gold content. // 2. To stem the panic, the government and Bank would be "forced" to intervene with a currency reform. They would announce creation of the "new drachma," with an exchange rate of (e.g.) one "new drachma" per U.S. dollar. (A "new drachma" currency already would have been printed). // 3. Old drachmae as a rule would be converted into new drachmae at the rate of 100,000 to one. This would have the effect of reducing the real value of the money supply (taking the present black-market rate of 16,000 drachmae per dollar as the standard of comparison) to 16.5% of its present value. Conversion of the existing money supply would result in issuance of 37 million "new drachmae." // 4. If properly handled, the reform could bring hoarded gold sovereigns into the hands of the National Bank. (There would be certain technical difficulties to be overcome, such as rules of the IMF.) We may estimate that 140 million "new drachmae" would be issued to buy up $100 million in hoarded gold. // 5. As a simple and reasonable social measure, each person in Greece should have an initial allowance of new currency, regardless of his holdings of old currency. At 5 "new drachmae" per person that would require 37 million "new drachmae." // 6. The government also should receive an initial allowance, of perhaps 13 Million "new drachmae." // 7. In addition, some room must be left for expansion of credit to business in the first few weeks after the reform. We arbitrarily assume an amount of 50 million "new drachmae." // 8. The total would be 277 million "new drachmae." This is somewhat more than the equivalent of the prewar money supply (167 million "new drachmae") and than the equivalent of the present money supply (224 million "new drachmae"). Within this wide margin of error which must prevail in any such planning, however, it seems to be a reasonably satisfactory amount. // 9. In addition to the pure conversion operations, a number of other measures may be either necessary or desirable. The most necessary may be some reorganization of the banking system, to ensure strict control of new credit after the reform.

Before his arrival in Athens Tenenbaum had worked out a detailed plan on currency and thereby economic stabilization in Greece, as is documented in a secret telegram from the US ambassador in Athens, John Emile Peurifoy, to the Secretary of State of December 8, 1951:

> Greatly appreciate valuable advice of Tenenbaum concerning stabilization plans. I pointed out that political difficulties may delay timing but otherwise deem program highly necessary. Mission [MSA] and Emb[assy] in general agreement major outlines this program but in view of importance effect on entire Greek economy, I wld [would] appreciate review of all plans by limited (repeat limited) number of very senior State, Treasury and ECA officials. // I stress security precautions because of dangers of premature disclosure and need for speed of review so that econ [omic] and political preparations may be made here.[43]

Tenenbaum's new drachmae plan was not made public. It was choked to death by the US embassy.[44] However, the support he received from the Greek government in itself turned into a stabilizing factor. Between the second half of February and June 1952, "the decrease in the price of gold sovereigns for the first time in the interwar and postwar periods showed the determination of the American planners and Greek government to implement an economic policy which supported the stabilization of the Greek currency."[45]

What was the economic, fiscal, and monetary background of Tenenbaum's coming into play? Bilateral treaties for the aid program had been signed in June 1947, which granted American administrators of the aid program rights to control Greek economic and fiscal policies in order to bring the partially corrupt elites running the Greek government back on the rails of good government and democratic values. The personnel of the first American Mission for Aid to Greece (AMAG) arrived in July and the first cargo in the port of Piraeus in August 1947. With American military aid the civil war was brought to an end in September 1949. But the task of improving economic conditions in Greece and balancing the Greek economy was continued until midyear of 1954.[46]

At the outset of the program, the American proconsuls found the Greek economy suffering from large twin deficits, namely imbalances in the government budget and in the balance of current account.[47] Given the state of emergency the Bank of Greece accommodated these policies by granting plenty of credit to the government as well as to private business at relatively low interest rates. At the same time the Bank of Greece sold gold sovereigns, a policy that the Americans didn't like and that did not prevent high inflation as a result of credit expansion. It was especially painful for the poorer classes of society whose members could not meet their daily needs even if they worked for wages. Weak or even also corrupt labor unions were unable to match wage increases with price increases. This condition drove many desperate Greeks into the arms of the communist side in the civil war. Therefore, economic aid was as important as military aid to finish civil war.

A few figures will best illustrate the dimension of the problems at the outset and the accomplishments of the aid program (Truman Doctrine plus Marshall Plan) for Greece. In 1948, the first full year of American aid, Greece's balance on current account was deeply in deficit (All dollar figures here and further down are nominal values of the time. To get an approximate idea of the dimension in current (2023) purchasing power, multiply by about 12.6!).

In order to phase out the need for foreign aid and to put this balance into equilibrium the program aimed at lifting the productivity and production of the Greek economy with massive investments. From the first year of the aid program 1947/48 to the phase-out year 1953/54 an aggregate total of $609 million in investment and development expenditures had been spent. Productivity and production, especially in agriculture, increased so much that import substitution occurred and exports could be increased, both on a massive scale. Here are the data for agricultural production and productivity in 1953 as compared to prewar 1938/39.

The yearly development of US aid to Greece is shown with the following data on aid-allotment of Marshall Plan Assistance and on investment and development expenditures undertaken by the Truman Doctrine and Marshall Plan aid in millions of US dollars.

	Millions of US dollars
1.Foreign exchange outlays for	
a) imports	451.0
b) invisibles	18.7
Total	467.7
2. Foreign exchange earnings from	
a) exports	87.4
b) invisibles (mainly remittances from abroad)	57.5
Total	146,9
Balance on Current Account	minus 322.8

FIGURE 5.1 Greece's balance on current account in 1948
Source: See note 46

Crop	Production	Yield per hectare
Wheat	+90%	+50%
Corn	+20%	+30%
Cotton	+100%	+60%
Potatoes	+200%	+65%

FIGURE 5.2 Agricultural production and productivity 1953 compared to 1938/39
Source: See note 46

Fiscal Year	Marshall Plan/MSA Assistance	Investment/Development
Expenditures		
1947/48		53.5
1948/49	271.8	92.7
1949/50	282.4	131.1
1950/51	281.9	148.2
1951/52	179.0	86.5
1952/53	80,0	51.3
1953/54	21.0	45.8

FIGURE 5.3 Annual US aid to Greece 1947/48 to 1953/54
Source: See note 46

As one can see from these figures, fiscal year 1950/51 was the peak of the development phase. This was also true in terms of personnel in that year:

> there were 181 American specialists, advisors, and controllers and agents-of-change not only in all the mayor sub-sectors of agriculture and mining and industry; roadbuilding and ports and harbors; electric power and civil aviation – but also in civil service organization and method, in governmental decentralization, in labor union organization, in banking legislation and the progressive income tax, in public health and social security administration.[48]

At the same time the American Marshall Plan, the mission in Athens employed forty-eight Greeks as interpreters, special assistants, typists, drivers, and two as legal advisers.[49] Already in 1952, the Greek economy not only had overcome the dislocations of World War II and the civil war, but was already operating well above prewar levels. Here is where the indices of National Consumption/ Economic Activity had increased in 1952 as compared to 1938/39.

In 1950/51 recovery of the Greek economy had been well under way. But one problem still had to be tackled: inflation. It is true that hyperinflation in the Phillip D. Cagan[50] sense during the last phase of German occupation had been ended when the Government-in-Exile returned. In its currency reform 50 billion old drachmae were exchanged for one new drachma, which in turn was pegged to the dollar at 150 drachmae = $1.[51] But galloping inflation continued.

Sector	Percentage change
Consumption of wearing apparel	+37%
Energy consumption	+45%
Transportation	+107%
Metal working	+30%
Construction activity	+46%

FIGURE 5.4 Increase in consumption and economic activity 1952 compared to 1938/39
Source: See note 46

By the time bilateral agreements on the terms of the Truman Doctrine had been signed (June 1947) the exchange rate had deteriorated to 8,300 drachmae = $1. The inflow of American aid slowed devaluation somewhat. But the problem of high inflation remained. By mid/late 1951 the peg had effectively fallen to 20,000 drachmae = $1.

During the first third of the nineteenth century, Greece, supported by the three big powers Great Britain, France and Russia, had fought its war of independence from the Ottoman Empire. It became a kingdom in 1832. As such, it developed a tradition of unstable financial conditions with often recurring outbursts of high inflation.[52] As a protective shield against currency debasement, the Greek citizenry had made the exchange of their drachma currency for British gold sovereigns part of their national culture, had hoarded those gold coins, and used them for ritual decorations of wedding gowns, and for the Greek Orthodox custom of Vasilopita (New Year's cake) with the lucky coin inside.

> The daily quotations for the sovereign became the barometer by which goods were priced – for example olive oil and cotton. Dowries were established in sovereigns. Savings were held in sovereigns. An insurance policy was a cache in sovereigns. Major transactions, such as the purchase and sale of real estate, were of course negotiated in sovereigns. The gold sovereign was also a registry for domestic political and international events; it was not only limited to just economic functions. When the Truman Doctrine was announced, the price of the sovereign fell. When Berlin was placed under Soviet blockade, it rose. When the Communist party in Italy was defeated in the important elections of the Spring of 1948, the sovereign price fell. When guerrilla attacks within Greece increased, so did the gold price. The outbreak of the Korean War forced the price up, as did the Chinese crossing of the Yalu River later that year (1950).[53]

The prewar national stock of gold sovereigns has been estimated at about two million pieces some of it held centrally by the Bank of

Greece. When inflation picked up speed in 1941 after the Germans had occupied the country and made use of the note printing press, the Greeks lost confidence in their drachma currency. They demanded payment for goods in gold sovereigns. Therefore, the British government supported Greek resistance groups against the German occupants by supplying not only weapons, but also an estimated two million more gold sovereigns to Greece. The German occupants also realized that gold sovereigns could buy what drachmae no longer could. They supplied an estimated one million of those gold coins. During the first year (1944/45) after the end of German occupation the Bank of Greece sold 150,000 pieces to the public. After the USA had supplied the Bank of Greece (see the quotation below), net sales of gold coins to the public amounted to two million pieces in 1946. When the Truman Doctrine was announced and AMAG started its work in 1947, confidence in the drachma currency increased and the Bank of Greece's net sales of gold sovereigns went down to 0.4 million in 1947, in 1948 to 0.9 million, and in 1949 to 0.5 million. But when thereafter economic recovery was well under way and prices, therefore, were under upward pressure, the Bank of Greece's net sales of gold sovereigns to the public climbed to 1.8 million pieces in 1950, and to 1.5 million in 1951.

The balance on current account was still negative. Therefore, what source enabled the Bank of Greece to pay out such huge amounts of gold sovereigns, each of which with a gold content of a little more than $8 at then current valuation? Most of the British gold sovereigns had accumulated in the Federal Reserve Bank of New York due to World War II transactions. AMAG had to arrange for the Bank of Greece to purchase these gold coins and to ship them to Athens by air. As James C. Warren, Jr., reports:

> We had to do so because we were stuck ... with the policy (which had been established in 1946) whereby the Greek Central Bank would meet all demand for gold at a specified ceiling price, a ceiling price established to give some credibility to the notion that the

national currency, the drachmas, had a certain backing or validity.
It was, in other words, a gold exchange standard. The sovereign was
the safety valve for an overheated economy in a nervous corner of
the Balkans. // In each year of the American major presence in
Greece, from 1947 through 1952, we had authorized the exportation
of gold sovereigns from New York and their importation and sale by
the Bank of Greece, 5 million of them in all. We swallowed hard and
rationalized the action as a kind of insurance premium: expensive,
indeed unconscionably wasteful, but worth it by comparison with
the feared alternative. // If a run on the Central Bank's gold stock
were to start, the Cabinet would panic and we, the Americans, were
fearful of a financial collapse. The Greek public had concluded that
the only reason to hold the drachmas, even if only temporarily, was
the implicit promise in the Greek/U.S. compact to keep open the
gold window – to exchange paper drachmas for gold upon demand
and at an open market price which had an established ceiling, or
maximum, price. Had that gold window closed . . . we fully expected
that by nightfall all tangible goods throughout the country would
disappear from sight and there would not be a store in all of Greece
that would be selling its merchandise for drachmas. The price of the
sovereign would go through the roof, and with it the price of
everything else, including those basics for the least well off: olive
oil, wheat flour and dried salted codfish. The price/wage spiral
would then go totally out of control. Loans, frequently (and
illegally) underpinned by a gold clause, would be called, driving the
sovereign price still higher. Worst of all, we reasoned, that timid
and tentative confidence in the future, that fragile sense that there
were better days to come – which we had worked so hard to
nurture – would be utterly shattered and, with it, all our hopes and
plans for reconstruction and development, the cornerstone of our
presence in Greece. // And so we paid the price, disgusted and
hating ourselves for so doing. We allowed scarce and precious
foreign exchange balances to be frittered away in the importation of
sterile gold.[54]

During the four months from November 1950 to February 1951 the run for gold sovereigns surpassed the one during the whole year of 1946: 2.3 million versus 2.0 million pieces. It was an expression of repudiation of paper drachmae by the Greek population. An unexpected new run occurred already during September and October 1951 and not as expected as late as December 13th, when salaries were paid out which each year led to increased demand for gold coins. The October/September run required that Washington be asked to agree to gold sovereign exports to Athens in order to maintain the openness of the Bank of Greece's gold window. Washington consented in a telegram at the end of October 1951, but in especially strong language tied it to a condition: the inauguration of a stabilization program for the drachma currency. Thus, on October 29, 1951 Greece's Currency Stabilization Program was launched.

Why now and not after the earlier and stronger run on the Greek Central Bank from November 1950 to February 1951? On October 10, 1951 the Mutual Security Act had become effective with President Truman's signature. It dissolved the Economic Cooperation Administration (ECA) under its director Paul G. Hoffman whose top management experience in the American automobile industry had qualified him for the job. ECA's functions were integrated into the Mutual Security Agency (MSA). Under this umbrella economic aid as well as military and technical support were integrated. In order to secure the passage of the bill in Congress original appropriations for foreign economic aid were reduced. With the intensity of the Cold War growing and the Hot War in Korea in full swing, most of the funds were now devoted to military support.

Since May 1951 Edward Tenenbaum had been involved in working on the Greek monetary problem, at first out of Washington, DC. He, who had so successfully stabilized the West German currency in June 1948, was probably recruited for the job as a reaction to the four-months record demand for gold sovereigns at the Bank of Greece from November 1950 to February 1951. This flight from paper drachmae into gold also meant higher inflation. The successful efforts of AMAG to put the Greek economy on its feet would be incomplete without stabilizing the currency. It might well have been Tenenbaum who demanded the strong language by his colleagues at the Greek desk of MSA in Washington, DC. The end-of-October-1951 telegram contained blunt messages like "irrevocably the last (repeat last) time gold will be sold." Henceforth the "containment of inflation" should have "highest priority." It was noted in the cable that the growth in Greek national production "had not been attended by a comparable decline in requirements for external resources." It reprimanded that there was "increasing evidence of hoarding," which would be "indefensible under the letter and spirit of the Mutual Security Act." Another message two weeks later brought home the same new priority-setting: "Regardless of intrinsic merits of any given program, it must be discarded, or at least shelved, as long as its implementation has a net inflationary effect."[55]

This was the strongest backing Washington could provide for Tenenbaum's task, namely to put the currency house of Greece in order. By the same token, it was especially the second message that triggered resistance among the division heads of ECA, each with his own sectoral program that was now put into question. The very able mission chief, Paul R. Porter, battled with Washington for months until in a cable of March 11, 1952 he finally caved in: "Having received his directives, the Mission Chief has donned his firechief's hat, has sharpened his hatchet, and is now set to tear down as much of the house of Greece (which American aid has helped to erect) as is necessary to stamp out the fire-devil of inflation."[56]

However, the battle between division heads and the officers of the Greek desk of the Mutual Security Agency (MSA) back home continued until May 1952. The division heads regarded the Greek-desk personnel as bean counters ignorant of the real needs of Greece and without an appreciation of the successes the aid program meant for the future of the country. The US ambassador in Athens and his superiors in the State Department took the side of the division heads and tried to scuttle the currency stabilization program. The ambassador even tried to have the officers at the Greek desk of MSA fired. But Tenenbaum in Athens and his colleagues at MSA's Greek desk in Washington stood firm. Despite all the resistance, also from Greek politicians, the stabilization program was not called off, if only because congressional interest in savings on foreign economic aid programs in a country where these obviously had made for a successful economic recovery prevailed.

In order to comprehend how the Stabilization Program worked, some information on the implementation of Marshall Plan and MSA aid is necessary. First, before the aid under the Truman Doctrine started to flow, the Greek government had subjected itself under US control by AMAG in the following fields:

> Members of the American mission have advised the Greek government on such matters as government organization and procedure, budgetary and fiscal controls, programming and control of imports, various measures for stimulating exports, formulation of a wage-price policy, and laying out reconstruction and development programs. // Greek imports are controlled by a Foreign Trade Administration of the National Economy which is staffed by Americans. Americans are employed in the Ministry of Finance. The Greek government has established by law a Greek-American Committee on Government Organization composed of top officials to work with members of the mission on administrative methods and techniques.[57]

The tool for control was especially the release of counterpart funds that domestic businesses in the sixteen ERP countries had to pay in for the acquisition of foreign exchange, namely dollars, to finance imports. Every expenditure of such funds in European countries was dependent on the assent of ECA and since December 31, 1951 of MSA.

> On several occasions, the ECA or the embassy would intervene, using the threat of aid reduction, to force the respective Greek government to comply with their suggestions. ... // This

interventionist approach can best be interpreted through the control of two powerful tools which were at the core of the Marshall Plan initiative – the release of counterpart funds and the appropriation of drawing rights. The counterpart fund was an account at each national bank created specifically to contain the proceeds from the local sale of ERP-supplied goods. Foreign aid was in the form of loans and grants, but, more importantly, as merchandise sent from the United States and sold to the respective countries that had applied for it. Main responsibility for this undertaking was held by the OEEC which operated as the institutional liaison between ERP countries and the U.S. Government. Following a coordinated, but often heated, debate, the OEEC would decide the amount allocated to each country based on requirement studies submitted by the participating states. The ECA would then arrange for the transfer of those goods (as indicated in the requirements studies) to their European recipients. The American supplier was paid in dollars, which had been credited against the appropriated ERP fund, while the European recipient of the goods had to pay for them in the local currency, which was then deposited in the respective counterpart account of each country. It was from this account that the money to pay for national reconstruction and modernization efforts, as decided between the ECA Mission and the government in each participating capital, would come. // The second method of economic assistance provided by the United States was less direct, and involved the intra-European exchange of goods rather than their shipment from the United States. The "drawing rights," as they were commonly called, allowed nations that participated in the ERP to purchase consumer and industrial products in Europe rather than the United States or the dollar region."[58]

The Marshall Plan aimed at European integration. Therefore, the Organization of European Economic Cooperation (OEEC) was founded on April 16, 1948 in Paris to promote European cooperation in the distribution of Marshall Plan funds. Under the OEEC's aegis the European Payments Union (EPU) was agreed on in September 1950, effective retroactively from July 1, 1950. Its purpose was to convert bilateral into multilateral trade relations, to abolish quantitative restrictions on trade, and to promote the return to convertibility of national currencies. Of course, Greece was a member of both organizations from the beginning. As James C. Warren, Jr., who himself at the time headed AMAG's import office in Athens, reports that 42 percent of Marshall Plan aid to Greece was given in the form of grants in European currencies, like French francs or Italian lira.[59] Of all sixteen European participants in ERP, Greece received the highest per capita allotment.[60]

Admonitions from Washington to stop inflation and the flight of the Greek population from paper drachmae into gold coins, to balance the budget and the current account had been plentiful from the start of the US engagement in Greece. But these had been of no avail. The Stabilization Program pursued mainly by Tenenbaum after the alarming cable of October 29, 1951 from Washington to ECA in Athens should make a big difference. The Greek desk in Washington, namely Frank Mahon according to the oral history interview of James Warren, invented the so-called *Inflationary/ Deflationary Balance Sheet*. It was a tight corsage for the further development of the Greek money supply resulting from monetarist-school thinking, which conformed to Tenenbaum's position.[61]

Aggregates of the Greek economy that impacted on the money supply were quantitatively tracked on a monthly, quarterly, semi-annual and annual basis according to the following diagram of a balance sheet.

The changes, denoted with the Greek symbol Δ, on the left side take paper drachmae out of circulation, for example, because the importer has to buy foreign exchange from the Central Bank to pay for imports. The changes on the right side do the opposite, for instance because the exporter sells his payment in foreign exchange to the Central Bank in exchange for paper drachmae. The balance sheet total

Deflationary		Inflationary
Δ Imports		Δ Exports
Δ Government Tax Revenue		Δ Government Expenditures
Δ Bank Credit Contraction		Δ Bank Credit Expansion
Δ Gold Sovereign Sales		Δ Counterpart Fund Releases as balancing item
Δ Balance Sheet Total	=	Δ Balance Sheet Total

FIGURE 5.5 Inflationary/deflationary balance sheet to improve on monitoring money supply
Source: See note 46

is capped by the authorities of MSA in tandem with the Greek Government and Central Bank. It could and should be expanded from period to period according to the real growth rate and a tolerable inflation rate of the Greek economy. If not, deflationary forces would prevail and the release of counterpart funds that helped finance investment and development programs in Greece would dry up, e.g., from an increase of Greek exports which in itself constituted a goal of American policy in Greece.

In the past (1946 to early 1952) the Central Bank's sales of gold sovereigns that were supplied by the Fed of New York at the expense of the US government had been the principal means of counteracting the inflationary increase of the money supply, essentially without success. The open gold window had rather been an invitation for flight out of paper drachmae, thus had contributed to build up inflationary expectations further, while perpetuating hoarding of gold by the Greek population at the expense of the American taxpayer.

Early 1952 was the last time the US supplied gold sovereigns to Greece. The other items of the balance sheet were from then on required to play their roles in checking inflation. Tenenbaum and his MSA colleagues would make sure that they did this more effectively than the costly gold sales had done. Greek politicians, businessmen, and the Greek population had seen how domestic investment of counterpart funds had worked economic miracles for them and had built their future on it. It now lied in Greek hands to determine the volume of counterpart funds by focusing its own credit, fiscal and trade policies on goals which the Americans wanted them to pursue. The application of the inflationary/deflationary balance sheet turned out to be the most powerful lever for American influence on shaping Greek economic policy. And – in contrast to the gold sales – it did work, indeed. The currency was relatively stabilized without suffocating economic activity.

Quite the contrary, Greece experienced the highest economic growth rate of all European countries during the postwar boom. It is true that the introduction of the inflationary/deflationary balance sheet as economic policy guideline gradually since late 1950 had stymied real economic growth to only 1.0 percent in 1951 despite the ongoing Korea boom worldwide. But from 1952 to 1973 the average real growth rate of Greek GDP (in 1970 prices) was 7.2 percent p.a.[62] During the same period from 1952 to 1973 the average real growth rate of the West German economy (in 1962 prices) was 6.0 percent p.a.[63]

What had happened? The immediate most powerful effect of the introduction of the inflationary/deflationary balance sheet came about through a turnaround in inflationary expectations. James C. Warren, Jr., reports about its most spectacular symptom:

> the December 1951/January 1952 gold sovereign panic came to an end in February and reversed itself with such speed that the public, by March, 1952 was selling sovereigns back to the Bank of Greece at a price of 180,000 drachmas per unit, sovereigns which they had purchased less than two months earlier at the maximum ceiling price of 226,500.[64]

For the business world the most painful measure had been that the Bank of Greece after very high expansions of credit (in percentage p. a. 1949: 63; 1950: 34; 1951: 22) under pressure from the American proconsuls, most likely especially from Tenenbaum, engineered a contraction of credit by 4 percent in 1952. Together with tax increases, mainly income and corporation income taxes, this state of affairs forced merchants and manufacturers to protect their liquidity by selling their goods in order to maintain their cash flow. Wholesale prices in 1952 not only stabilized, but even fell slightly during the course of the year. The import volume of goods fell, because their hoarding in anticipation of inflation ceased. Foreign exchange earnings not only from exports increased, but also from emigrant remittances while capital flight through black channels out of Greek currency into other currencies not only slowed down, but actually reversed itself.

Georgios Kartalis, who had served in the 1950–1952 Nikolaos Plastiras center-left cabinets as finance and government coordination minister, had closely cooperated with Tenenbaum in planting these fruits of the Stabilization Program. In the fall of 1952 – with US backing – Greece decided on a constitutional change from proportional voting, the outcome of which had been fragmented party constellations in parliament and fragile coalition governments, to majority voting, in which small parties never stand a chance. After a new election on this basis on November 16, 1952, the center-left government was succeeded by a conservative right-wing government with Field Marshal Alexandros Papagos as prime minister. His party *Greek Rally* had won 239 of 300 seats in parliament. Spyros Markezinis not only took over the powerful Finance and Government Coordination Ministry from Kartalis. In contrast to his predecessor, Markezinis regarded Tenenbaum's radical currency-reform plan, with the introduction of newly printed drachmae and declaration of worthlessness of the old currency, as too harsh politically against especially vested business interests that had supported him during the election campaign. The successful West German precedent in June 1948 did not convince him otherwise. He wanted to get rid of Tenenbaum in Athens. In cooperation with the US embassy, which had always regarded Tenenbaum as a rival in executing American power on the Greek government, Tenenbaum's influence was neutralized, which led to his return to Washington, DC in June 1953.

During the first few months of 1953 all the disadvantages plagued the Greek economy that Tenenbaum had listed in his ground-breaking memo of October 25, 1951 "Requirements for a currency reform in Greece."[65] In early March 1953, the Greek newspaper *Apogevmatini* published a well-informed article, describing its content under two titles, as we will see in a moment. Its first part is devoted to government measures to cope with the economic crisis which had resulted from anti-inflation measures. Its second part covers the differences between Tenenbaum and the US embassy. The Tenenbaum papers contain a contemporary translation of the article into English. I quote some text passages:

> THE GOVERNMENT SEEKS A WAY OUT OF THE ECONOMIC
> CRISIS WHICH THE CENTER CREATED WITH ITS ANTI-
> INFLATIONARY POLICY // DISAGREEMENTS EXIST
> BETWEEN THE AMERICAN EMBASSY AND THE MISSION AS
> TO THE MEASURES TO BE TAKEN // ... // It should be noted
> that, as we are in a position to know, the greatest difficulties are
> met with coming to an understanding with the competent
> Americans. ... The policy of a rigid anti-inflation, regardless of its
> results, is an inspiration of the retiring economic adviser of the
> Mission, Mr. Tenenbaum. ... // It appears, however, that a
> difference in outlook exists between the American Embassy and the
> Mission as to the policy to be followed. The Mission has not yet
> been persuaded that an excessive anti-inflationary policy must be
> abandoned, while the Embassy, accepting the views of its economic
> adviser, Mr. Turkel, inclines in favor of the strengthening of
> production and trade by a conservative granting of sufficient
> credits. On the other hand, Mr. Constanzo, a [American] member
> of the Currency Committee, although rejecting the views of
> Mr. Tenenbaum, hesitates to accept the suggestions of Mr. Turkel
> who even reaches the point of supporting that an increase in the

currency circulation for the sake of production and recovery does not contain any danger of inflation.[66]

But Markezinis also took credit for the good results of the painful measures that Kartalis had put through. The final test of success came when the drachma was again devalued on April 9, 1953, this time by decree of Markezinis, to 30,000 drachmae equalling $1 in exchange for lifting all import restrictions. Jeanette Kipp Tenenbaum has described in a personal reminiscence letter of April 4, 2000 to James C. Warren, that the powerful minister explained at a dinner that he had chosen the devaluation date, "because his stars were in the right place in the sky, and if this hadn't been, the whole thing would have been a disaster!" Mrs. Tenenbaum was dumbfounded (More details in Section 6.2).[67]

Until then the official exchange rate had been 15,000 drachmae to $1, but due to multiple exchange rates the average effective exchange rate had been about 20,000 drachmae to $1. The devaluation had been well prepared by Kartalis' rigorous stabilization policy during the preceding year and a half. Therefore, the public regarded this devaluation as credible in contrast to all the others that had taken place since World War II. As the yearly figures presented in Figure 5.3 show, Marshall Plan and MSA Assistance for Greece in fiscal year 1953/54 had petered out to 21 million US dollars from its peak of 282 million dollars in fiscal year 1950/51. And personnel of the American Aid Mission had dropped from its peak of 181 persons in 1950/51 in annual steps to 169, to 134, to 62 and to 11. American aid and personnel had become superfluous. By mid-1954 the Greek economy could stand on its own feet.[68]

James C. Warren, Jr., Aid Mission member in Athens, does not name Americans involved in aid and development operations in Greece in his article, with one exception: Paul R. Porter, the mission's chief. He remains mute about the essential role Edward Tenenbaum played in stabilizing the Greek monetary and economic situation. Instead, he praises the great contribution of Georgios

Kartalis for the implementation of the Stabilization Program. Warren reports that Kartalis like almost all Greek politicians strongly opposed the Stabilization Program, especially because it was aimed at cutting US aid, increasing direct taxation, tightening credit, and stopping business on black markets. It was feared that its austerity nature would cause deflation, economic depression, and the return of large unemployment and poverty. But Kartalis was not only a shrewd politician, but had intellectual capabilities far beyond his fellow politicians. He realized that Greek opposition could not win against the united phalanx of American defenders of the Stabilization Program, composed by the Greek desk in Washington's State Department and the MSA planners in Washington, DC as well as its mission members in Athens, with Tenenbaum as the driving force for a successful monetary stabilization. Therefore, he changed sides and became its Greek advocate. Once he understood the logic of it, he fell for its intellectual elegance and understood what no one else in Greek parliament seemed to be able to understand. Warren calls him an "intellectual snob." And the *inflationary/deflationary balance sheet* "became for him a kind of theoretician's *palouki* (club) with which he could knock about his opponents and make them feel small. He would just ride over them."[69]

Without being a snob, Tenenbaum must have been his closest intellectual partner and friend among all of the Aid Mission's American members. As a European counterpart to Tenenbaum's status as best-of-his-class economist at Yale, Kartalis, born 1908, had studied economics until 1933 at the best European universities for economics during the interwar period: ETH Zürich, University of Munich, University of Leipzig, London School of Economics, University of Kiel.[70] He might have actually been behaving like a snob. But in economic-policy matters, he was definitely better educated than any other Greek politician.

In an interview that Harry B. Price conducted in Athens on December 15, 1952 (i.e., after Tenenbaum, aided by Kartalis, saw his

Stabilization Program in Greece implemented), Tenenbaum summarized his mission accomplished thus:

> The reorientation ["with a view to the time when aid would be
> drastically curtailed"] ... was a bit rough. We applied some basic
> rules. We looked at the balance of payments. We looked at the
> deficit. Investments were overexpanded. Credit was expanding
> rapidly. We cut down the credit through Treasury representations.
> We succeeded in reducing investments and, more important, in
> helping the government to really deal with its budget. The result
> has been a basic improvement in the balance-of-payments position
> before the longer-range investments came into production. And the
> level of aid has been sharply reduced.[71]

In his letter to Samuel A. Welldon of June 30, 1952, three months after
his arrival in Athens, Tenenbaum described his main Greek political
cooperation partner as follows:

> Minister Kartalis appears to be achieving real and substantial
> progress towards balancing the budget. Admittedly, there will be
> room for doubt whether the plans he approves actually can be
> carried out, given political and economic realities in Greece.
> However, a courageous attempt will have been made, which
> permits us to believe that fulfillment is possible if not certain. //
> However, Kartalis will require encouragement he now lacks. He has
> at least (and certainly not exclusively) one failing: he is impatient
> and impetuous. He cannot, in my humble, to some extent
> prejudiced, but honest opinion, hold out over a long pull. He must
> be able to envisage some concrete results soon, or he will be unable
> to hold out against the mounting pressure (some from his own
> immediate family) which now surround him. // I will admit
> cheerfully that he is not the only influential person in Greece, of
> course. Therefore, he is not absolutely essential to the success of
> our plans. However, it seems clear to me that he is the main
> influential person in the present cabinet of Greece who might

possibly understand and sympathize with U.S. monetary and economic policy in Greece. ... we either must buck up the chief advocate of financial and economic stability in the present government or must face serious setback and many months of delay. Either of these would be fatal to the enterprise.[72]

In a letter to Welldon of September 5, 1952, for confidentiality reasons sent via an MSA colleague in Washington, DC, Tenenbaum reports that he had been invited to Kartalis home. This is an expression of their high mutual esteem. There he had gathered the following impressions: "I found the Minister quite reasonable and I am sure we can rapidly come to an agreement with him." But political difficulties would prevent this. Especially the US embassy would not want an agreement at the moment. It would hope that the Greek government would resign shortly and new elections would follow. Nevertheless, Tenenbaum expressed optimism that from his point of view a reasonably satisfactory economic program for the year could be agreed on, "if these political difficulties ever can be overcome."[73]

Of course, Tenenbaum on the spot in Athens, also gathered and reported his impressions of Markezinis. In a letter to Samuel A. Welldon of January 23, 1953, he wrote:

At the moment, I believe Markezinis may be toying with the idea of delaying action [on the Stabilization Program] until he can go to Washington and obtain some kind of official and open US Government blessings. ... // My own view is that we should not engage our own government's prestige or money in the operation at present. We do not have to in order to get action, since Markezinis is eager to go ahead on his own. Markezinis probably would find the additional prestige of open US blessings politically useful. However, his present political strength, with full support from Papagos and a huge majority behind him, seems more than adequate. // Finally, I am afraid a public commitment by the US Government might encourage his tendency towards extremism and strong-arm tactics. At any rate, it would remove the potential check-rein of our disapproval, since we would have to allow him to go to great lengths to protect our prestige as well as his own. In my opinion a loan might be a useful device to bolster the government's prestige after it has succeeded in doing the right thing for long enough to ensure success. It would then come as a reward for good performance, rather than as our blank-check endorsement of the government's future policies.[74]

Tenenbaum talked about Markezinis more bluntly in a letter of February 21, 1953 to Francis Lincoln, Office of Greek, Turkish and Iranian Affairs in the State Department in Washington, DC. Lincoln had been his colleague in the Samuel A. Welldon delegation to Athens in early April 1952. He had not stayed in Athens like Tenenbaum, but had returned to his State Department position in Washington, DC. Tenenbaum wrote:

> Dear Francis, // ... It seems to me that the situation here has become quite difficult. To put it bluntly, we have a screwball on our hands, in the person of Markezinis. He is, of course, extremely able. Unfortunately, however, he is (a) economically illiterate and (b) highly erratic. The business of telling the newspapers he will go to Washington before he received an invitation is only a sample of the type of thing he does all the time. // The Ambassador is just beginning to wake up to this fact, and as far as I can tell from my worm's-eye view hasn't yet decided what he can do about it if anything. It's a little hard to push Markezinis out without making our support of the Rally Party look pretty silly. In the meantime, the greatest concern to a worm like myself is whether Markezinis can be prevented from going off half-cooked in the monetary field. ... // I have no positive recommendation to make, except that the US Government should be most careful with Markezinis if and when he goes to Washington.[75]

In his letter to Welldon of February 17, 1953 Tenenbaum already took stock of their work for Greece. The Americans would leave Greece about where the country was when they started. "except that a certain amount of financial stability will have been introduced, and the US aid will have been cut substantially. . . . I think we can say with a certain amount of pride that the 'Welldon Team' saved the US taxpayer $100 million in eighteen months, and saved Greece (temporarily) from some of its worst faults." In his frustrated state of mind Tenenbaum doubted that they had accomplished any long-lasting improvements. "However we have managed to harden Uncle Sam's generous heart somewhat. If that sticks perhaps his Greek nephews may be forced to try to solve some of their long-run problems as best they can." Tenenbaum also reports that in doing his job "a certain amount of personal friction developed, particularly between members of the Embassy staff and myself. . . . Unfortunately, many months ago it reached the point where the Embassy stopped inviting me to official cocktail parties." On the one hand, it had been a very good thing for his liver, he continued to write, but, on the other, it had not improved his standing in the rather small community of Greek and American officials. . . . "As always, I am prepared to admit that the fault probably lies on both sides. Nevertheless, I don't intend to dignify the accusations which have been made against me by trying to defend myself." What a fine self-portrait of his character! In conclusion, he goes on:

> I feel that my usefulness here now is limited. Therefore, this
> morning I requested termination of my contract by June 15. I gave
> as a reason my small boy's need for specialized medical attention
> (which is true). I am not entirely sure what I will do next. However,
> I am coming to the conclusion, after ten years of trying, that
> I probably am not the type the government needs. Perhaps now that
> so many businessmen are entering the government [with
> Republican President Dwight D. Eisenhower having entered the
> White House] I may be able to find an opening in the field of private
> business. Alternatively, I may try to retire to some convenient
> payroll (such as the I.M.F.) and write a book. // Your friend Kartalis
> sends his regards. . . . // With best wishes, I remain // Sincerely
> yours, // Edward A. Tenenbaum.[76]

6 Life and Fate as a Businessman and Family Man 1953–1975 and Beyond

After Tenenbaum's mission to Greece by the Mutual Security Agency (MSA) had ended, he, his wife Jeanette Kipp, and their three children left Athens in June 1953 and returned to Washington, DC. He surely contributed somewhat to stabilizing the Greek currency. But his plan for stopping galloping inflation by bringing about a thorough and harsh currency reform in Greece had failed. He had been convinced that a financial reform shaped after the West German one of June 20, 1948, including the printing and introduction of new banknotes, would be the only way to restore confidence in the Greek currency and thereby to stop inflation. In Washington, DC, Tenenbaum didn't return to his former employers, neither to the IMF nor to US civil service. He became a businessman and founded Continental-Allied Company, a firm providing financial services worldwide. His former boss in OMGUS Berlin, Jack Bennett, became a partner of the company.

6.1 BUSINESSMAN

Sometime in the second half of 1953 after his return from Greece, he founded the Edward A. Tenenbaum Co. in Washington, DC. In February 1954, he announced to the press the formation of a partnership named Continental-Allied Company, Inc. (first address: 1823 Jefferson Place NW) with his former boss in Berlin, Jack (short for Andrew Jackson) Bennett who had been General Clay's financial adviser in US military government in Germany during the preparation and execution of the 1948 currency reform. The description of the company's purpose reads: "it will accept commissions for international and United States investments, exports and imports,

FIGURE 6.1 First Continental-Allied Company seat, 1823 Jefferson Place NW, Washington, DC

consultation and advice in financial, economic and trade matters, as well as public relations."[1]

But to my surprise I found publications issued by Continental-Allied Company, Inc. in WorldCat and the Library of Congress where the author or coauthor is named as Jack F. Bennett. I then found out that Jack Franklin Bennett was an economist like Tenenbaum, was quite a prolific writer, especially on monetary subjects and outside Continental-Allied Company, Inc. He was the son of Jack (Andrew Jackson) Bennett.

Like his father he was also called Jack Bennett. He was born January 17, 1924, a little more than two years later than Edward Tenenbaum. In 1941 he graduated from Woodrow Wilson High School in Washington, DC and in 1944 with a BA from Yale University in the war-shortened class of 1945. He then served as a US Navy Lieutenant (jg) on destroyer USS Boggs in the Pacific. From 1946 to 1947 he worked alongside his father in US military government in Berlin. After his return from Germany he earned a PhD in economics from Harvard University in 1951. Starting August 14, 1951 he worked in the State Department serving in different functions as a civil servant of the federal government, including the Fairness Committee on Mutual Security which focused on US foreign economic policy. In 1955 Jack Franklin Bennett joined the Standard Oil Company of New Jersey.[2] For a while I had assumed that the son Jack Franklin of former financial adviser of OMGUS in Berlin and not his father Jack Bennett had entered into partnership with Tenenbaum.

The last above-mentioned information, however, had cast doubts on my hypothesis, because Bennett's spell as a partner of Edward Tenenbaum lasted longer, probably until 1960, as we will see below. WorldCat lists a book authored by Jack Bennett entitled *Small Business in Liberia: Development of Private Enterprise in an Underdeveloped Country: A Background Study*, and a book coauthored by Jack F. Bennett, Edward A. Tenenbaum, and Sol D. Ozer entitled *Industrial Finances of Israel*. They were published by Continental-Allied Co. in Washington, DC in 1956 and 1958 respectively. And for 1959 (however, with a question mark) the Library of Congress catalog records a book coauthored by Jack F. Bennett and Edward A. Tenenbaum titled *Indonesian Industrial Financing*, authored by Jack Bennett and Edward A. Tenenbaum, likewise published by Continental-Allied Co. I came to the conclusion that in cataloging the latter two publications, librarians have obviously been searching for a middle initial for Jack Bennett for symmetry reasons, found the F. for Jack Franklin in his many publications on monetary subjects and added it to Bennett's name, although the authors themselves never specified a middle initial for Bennett on the title pages of studies issued by Continental-Allied Company.

My doubts about the identity of Jack Bennett were eventually removed for good by Tenenbaum's son Mark. When I asked him for his childhood impressions of his father's partner, he remembered that Jack Bennett had the appearance of an elderly gentlemen, clearly older than his father. In fact, he was about twenty years older than Edward Tenenbaum. I found this and other information on Jack Bennett in two obituaries.[3] He died of pneumonia at the age of eighty-six in a hospital in Chapel Hill NC on March 8, 1988. He had lived there since he had moved in 1965 from Chevy Chase, a fancy and rich neighborhood in Northwest Washington, DC or the adjoining Maryland area. Jack Bennett was born and grew up in Vienna GA. After finishing his education, he worked as a commercial banker in Macon GA during the 1920s. In 1930 he was employed by the US Treasury Department as a receiver of banks that the Great Depression pushed into bankruptcy. During World War II he was transferred to the Office of Foreign Funds Control.

Together with other financial experts from the Treasury he was sent to Europe in July 1945, on loan for half a year to support US military government in sorting out financial problems in the American zone of occupation and beyond in Germany. He was recalled by Treasury in December 1945. General Lucius Clay, then US deputy military governor, arranged with the Treasury Department an extension of his work for OMGUS. In June 1946 he was made the successor of Joseph M. Dodge as director of the Finance Division of OMGUS, which was later renamed the Office of the Finance Adviser.[4] In his book manuscript Tenenbaum complained about the fact that Treasury refused to reemploy Jack Bennett after he had returned to Washington, DC in January 1949. It did so probably to settle old scores from disputes between Treasury and OMGUS over monetary and fiscal policy in West Germany.

From 1949 to 1952 Bennett served in Ethiopia, ruled at the time by Emperor Haile Selassie, and as its representative in the World Bank and the IMF in Washington, DC. The obituaries report that thereafter he worked as a private financial consultant in Washington, without mentioning his partnership with Edward Tenenbaum in Continental-Allied Company, Inc.

Evidently while he was still working with Tenenbaum, he became President Dwight D. Eisenhower's economic representative in South Korea. Later, probably during the early 1960s after having left Continental-Allied Company, he served as regional director of the US foreign aid program for the Near East and South Asia and as director of the Agency for International Development (AID) mission in Ceylon. He retired in 1963, which is quite early. The reason was probably poor health which had already plagued him during his activity as finance adviser of OMGUS in Berlin. Therefore, Tenenbaum as his Special Assistant for Currency Reform, often had to deputize for his boss in Allied Control Council and its committee meetings in Berlin, in OMGUS and BICO internal consultations and external meetings with representatives of German institutions located in Frankfurt am Main or the *Länder* of the American zone of occupation. Even at the Conclave of Rothwesten Jack Bennet had taken a backseat behind the master of the show Edward A. Tenenbaum.

The obituary in the *Washington Times* also reports on the honors Bennett was awarded: the [US] Army Medal for Exceptional Civilian Service, the Order of the White Lion of Czechoslovakia, and the Star of Ethiopia. He was also granted the title of a grand officer of the Order of Orange-Nassau of the Netherlands. It is also reported that his marriage to Mary Eloise Franklin, who obviously gave birth to their son Jack Franklin Bennett, ended in divorce. But obviously there was a second marriage; the obituaries report that Andrew Jackson Bennett is survived by his wife Myrtle McInnis Bennett.

Given Jack Bennett's several orders of merit, Edward Tenenbaum's opinion on the work ethic of his closest partner on the jobs during more than two years in US military government in Germany and during about six years in Continental-Allied Company in Washington, DC might be more realistic. In our interview on October 29, 2018 Tenenbaum's daughter Joan told me: "I do know that the Jack Bennett who was in Washington was kind of lazy and my father did everything. That's what he said."

And for how long did Jack Bennett belong to the team of Continental-Allied Company? There are also two letters and a memorandum of Jack Bennett on stationery of Continental-Allied Company, Inc. addressed to Mr. Fred Clayton, USOM to Afghanistan, c/o American Embassy, Kabul, Afghanistan of December 23 and 24, 1958. Jack Bennett is named as president and Edward A. Tenenbaum as executive vice president of the company. That is also the case on stationery Tenenbaum used for a letter dated February 26, 1960, however, with the addition of Ray C. Burrus as vice president of engineering. I come back to that letter below. On the other hand, I have come across two publications of Continental-Allied Co., Inc. in 1960 on which Jack Bennett no longer appears as a coauthor: Edward A. Tenenbaum/James S. Taylor, *An Economic Strategy for Morocco* (182 pp. mimeographed) and Edward A. Tenenbaum, *Industry for B. G.* [British Guiana].[5] I conclude that Jack Bennett left the company in 1960.

Continental-Allied Company, Inc. was first located at 1823 Jefferson Place NW in Washington 5 DC. In June 1958 the address of the company was Second National Bank Building, 1333 G Street NW, Washington, DC.[6] In early 1960 the company had moved to "1319 F Street NW in Washington 4 DC." This is evidenced by the head of a covering letter of February 26, 1960 that Edward A. Tenenbaum addressed and sent to Mr. Edward W. Sheridan, chief of US Operations Mission to British Guiana, Georgetown, Demerara, British Guinea. Attached was the just finished 93-page study (Washington, DC: Continental-Allied Company, Inc., 1960) *Industry for B.G.* [British Guiana] by Edward A. Tenenbaum "and members of the staff of Continental-Allied Company Incorporated."

Here is the unusual story of how I obtained the letter. It was one of those fortunate coincidences when during an online search for the study in Google Books and WorldCat I detected the publication in only two libraries, one in the Harvard and the other one in the University of Wisconsin Library System. In an online photo of the study's title page, the latter library had part of the head of the covering letter stick out of the brochure. On Sunday, November 24, 2019, two days after my email request for the complete covering letter,

FIGURE 6.2 Second
Continental-Allied Company
seat, Second National Bank
Building, 1333 G Street NW,
Washington, DC

I received the scans from Wisconsin's Memorial Library in perfect
condition. This is proof of what technical progress has already made
possible and how much further it might advance wherever *man and
machine* use their respective capacities and keep pushing the frontiers
of human achievements further out.[7]

The study was prepared for AID/Washington, Contract No.
ICA-504-3. AID stands for Agency for International Development.
For this contract Tenenbaum's address was not noted as that of
Continental-Allied Company, Inc., but "P. O. Box 88, Herndon VA
22070."[8] This conforms to Tenenbaum's home address in Herndon
VA. Thus he might have wanted to keep his company financially out
of this contract, perhaps because it was in turmoil with Jack Bennett
leaving and other partners not yet officially installed or because it was
in the process of moving from its location in G Street to F Street.

A year and a half later the *Letter of Transmittal* of August 20,
1961, contained as the first part of the booklet, to the "International

Cooperation Administration [ICA], Washington 25, DC" for submitting the about 150-page brochure *Helping Honduran Industry: A Diagnostic Study* stated the same address in its letterhead. But a president and vice presidents were no longer listed there. By that time Bennett and Burrus had obviously left Continental-Allied Company. As the signatures under the *Letter of Transmittal* show there had been a major change in the leadership of the company. Edward A. Tenenbaum signed as president, James Spear Taylor as vice president, and Henry Kirkpatrick as engineer. In their opening statement the three mention that their study was based on a two-month stay of the undersigned team in Honduras, "assisted by Dr. Joseph Pincus (on loan from ICA)."[9] An equally long study *Credit for Bolivia's Private Sector: Report to The Government of Bolivia and US Aid Mission/La Paz*, (Washington, DC: Continental-Allied Company, Inc., 1962) also starts out with its *Letter of Transmittal* of April 6, 1962 addressed to "US Aid Mission c/o American Embassy La Paz, Bolivia." The letterhead shows nothing but the company's name and address and is signed exclusively by "Edward A. Tenenbaum President."

As a typical example of Tenenbaum's general approach to such studies, to problems addressed and solutions proposed, I quote excerpts from his covering letter of April 6, 1962. The report would be based on

> a three-week survey in Bolivia by the undersigned. ... // With so little time at our disposal, our report suffers from more than the usual quota of errors and omissions. ... Unfortunately, the time for careful study of Bolivia's problems no longer exists. Time is not marching on in Bolivia, it is running out. // ... In summary our conclusions are as follows: // All underdeveloped countries are short of skills, markets and capital; Bolivia is shorter than most. It is the poorest country in South America. It has suffered from a flight of both capital ... and skilled manpower. ... Savings are at the phenomenally low rate of 1% gross national product. The country depends for new investment on foreign credit, coming mainly from

foreign governments and through the Bolivian government. // This
has resulted in a disproportion between public and private
investment. Credit for the private sector is extremely scarce. The
great scarcity of credit makes it impossible for commercial banks to
provide developmental financing. There is therefore a need for
specialized development banks, not only as temporary channels for
foreign resources, but also to stimulate savings within the Bolivian
economy. ... // International lending agencies want to help Bolivia.
But Bolivia has a shortage of institutions that can employ money
effectively. In the past, makeshift agencies have been set up under
foreign technicians as channels for foreign lending. However, it has
not been possible to provide enough foreign technicians to run large-
scale credit programs in Bolivia. // The only satisfactory solution for
the long run is to build up independent Bolivian institutions, strong
enough to dispense with foreign supervision. In particular, there is a
need for a thorough reform of the government's Agricultural Bank
and Mining Bank. // Like most government-owned development
banks, these suffer from political pressures and a lack of
responsibility on the part of borrowers. Reform programs for these
institutions, outlined in Chapter II, would involve:

Thereafter, Tenenbaum lists five concrete reform proposals.

A second company, Continental-Allied Air Inc., had been established on the same business premises, probably upon the arrival of
Jack Bennett as a partner of Continental-Allied Company, Inc. in early
1954. On stationary of the Continental-Allied Air Inc. Jack Bennett is
listed as president and Edward Tenenbaum as vice president and
treasurer. The scope of activity of this company is described as
"Aviation Finance, Aircraft Sales, and Airlines Consultants."[10]

Here is what Jeanette Tenenbaum remembered in
1981 about Continental-Allied Company, Inc.: "He [Edward] had a
small economic consulting company after Greece and probably hit
more countries than I can remember now – and I remember more
than 40."[11] Continental-Allied Company has left many footprints of

its activities beyond its existence: self-published studies and brochures. Quite a number of them are listed in the Library of Congress
catalog:

- Jack F. Bennett/Edward A. Tenenbaum, *Indonesian Industrial Financing* /
  authored by Jack Bennett and Edward A. Tenenbaum, 162 pp, 1959 (?).[12]

And the following publications of Continental-Allied Company, Inc.,
Washington, DC, with Edward A. Tenenbaum as author:

- *Israel's Industrial Finances – A Second Look*: report to the Government of
  Israel and USA – International Cooperation Administration, 206 pp., 1960.
- *Helping Honduran Industry*: a diagnostic study, 132 pp., 1961.
- *Credit for Bolivia's Private Sector*: report to the Government of Bolivia and
  US Aid Mission/La Paz, 149 pp., 1962.
- *Tanganyika Five Year Industrial Plan*: report under contract AIDafe-
  160, 1964.
- *Ivorian Small Enterprise Development Program*: report, 9 pp., 1966.
- *Industrial Progress for Laos*: report under contract AIDfe-150, 298 pp.,
  1966.[13]

Evidently, Tenenbaum was also involved in solving financial and
currency problems in inflation-ridden Iran after a change in government there which was favorable for the USA. The Tenenbaum
Papers contain quite a thick folder with memos, reports, and statistical infos on the Iranian economy from August 1953, when probably
shortly thereafter Tenenbaum started working on Iran's financial
problems. He even proposed an elaborate banking and currency
reform law.[14]

However, Continental-Allied Company was not only active in
missions abroad, but also within the United States. Here is an
example:

On Saturday, 6 August 1966, the *Augusta Chronicle* of Augusta,
Georgia, published an article entitled "S.C. counties are selected
for OEO test." It reports: The US Office of Economic Opportunity
(OEO) has selected four Central Savannah River Area counties,

namely Allendale, Barnwell, Bamberg, and Hampton, all in the
Salkehatchie area, for an experimental technical assistance
program. Wilbur Free, director of the Salkehatchie Community
Action Council Inc. in Allendale, had informed the press that
"the OEO will provide around $600,000 to the council in the next
year to meet expenses of child care, civic beautification and other
projects in the area. // The director said a Washington, D.C.,
economic consultant, Edward A. Tenenbaum, will start the
program. He has met with mayors, town councilmen and other
officials in Allendale, Bamberg, Denmark, Barnwell, Blackville,
Hampton and Varnville. // Tenenbaum is helping the officials to
apply for available government funds for public housing,
neighborhood centers, water and sewerage installations and
similar facilities. // "Results so far are encouraging," Free said.
"We have found a great need for these projects, and we are
working on some things that should help to meet it." // The
program, first in South Carolina, will be closely followed by OEO
in Washington and may lead to important improvements in
helping needy rural areas throughout the country. // Free said the
government recognizes that many of its programs have not
reached small towns because they lack experts in cutting red tape.
// Free said, "Mr. Tenenbaum is a red tape expert and we're
hoping that he will help us get results. // Tenenbaum is an
internationally known specialist in economic development and
president of Continental-Allied Co. Inc., a management
consulting firm with offices in Washington. // He is being assisted
here by Mrs. Henrietta M. Canty, field representative for South
Carolina from the OEO regional office in Atlanta."[15]

In a short biographical note on Edward A. Tenenbaum the US
National Archives catalog reports not only that he worked as an
economist with OMGUS on the German currency reform, but also
"with the Office of Economic Opportunity (OEO) and the Agency for
International   Development   (AID)   during   the   Johnson

Administration."[16] As we saw above, Tenenbaum's cooperation with AID – bypassing Continental-Allied Company – had already taken place in 1960 during Dwight D. Eisenhower's presidency and before first John F. Kennedy and then Lyndon B. Johnson succeeded him. AID was and is officially responsible for foreign aid, but unofficially it also served and serves spy and covert-action purposes, when diplomacy reaches its limits and where the conflict does not justify military action. The Office of Economic Opportunity (OEO), in contrast, serves domestic purposes. It was the agency responsible for most of the programs of President Lyndon B. Johnson's War on Poverty, which was part of the US Great Society legislative agenda.

In its issue no. 9 of March 1, 1964 the German weekly *Stern* published part 4 of its series "Unser Nachbar Amerika" [= Our Neighbor America]. This part was entitled "USA. Eierköpfe und Texashüte" [= USA. Eggheads and Texas Hats]. In it the Germans were reminded that they owe the introduction of the Deutschmark on June 20, 1948 to the three Allied Western military governments

FIGURE 6.3 Third Continental-Allied Company seat, 1319 F Street NW, Washington, DC

and especially to one American financial expert, Edward
A. Tenenbaum. The author was Hans Habe, a Jewish Austro-
Hungarian journalist and novelist, who had fled from Vienna to
France when Germany had annexed Austria in 1938 and from
France via Lisbon to the USA when Germany had occupied France
in 1940. In 1941, he had assumed American citizenship. In 1942 he
had been drafted into the US Army and, like Tenenbaum, had served
in Psychological Warfare. He had moved to Germany after the end of
the war in order to support American military government in
founding new newspapers, such as *Die Neue Zeitung*, of which he
became its first editor. In 1964 he had traveled to Washington, DC to
interview "the father of the DM [German Mark]" and elsewhere
within the USA to collect material and photos for his article. As this
interview and Habe's comments in it reveal quite a bit of
Tenenbaum's personal traits, I quote from it extensively:

> I made the acquaintance of a man in Washington, who, as no other,
> was responsible for the fortunate development of West Germany
> after 1948 – the former second lieutenant Edward A. Tenenbaum
> "the father of the DM [German Mark]." // Tenenbaum, at that time
> scarcely twenty-six years old, carries through the currency reform
> (one DM equals ten RM) against strong resistance. ... // We are
> seated in the drawing room of my hotel facing each other.
> Tenenbaum, a big man with broad shoulders, still extraordinary
> young looking. The head: a mixture of an intellectual and a
> sportsman – a typical American combination. He answers my
> questions with sympathetic candour. // "It was pure chance that
> involved me in the financial management of the Military
> Government," he said. "I was then a lieutenant in the 4th Tank
> Division. My wife worked in the U.S. Treasury. I hoped she might
> come to Germany, and asked to be transferred to the Revenue
> Office." ... He laughs; his eyes and almost each word are full of
> humor, – his predominant characteristic. // "Excuse my tactless
> question. You are a Jew. What was your reason for saving
> Germany?" // "I was neither for sentiment nor resentment, but

I thought about things rationally. // [...] When we arrived in Germany," Tenenbaum continues, "it was an *undeveloped* country. In such a situation a country cannot act normally, particularly when the country is essentially not *undeveloped*. Thus, it was essential to establish a normal economic situation. For that there were only two alternatives: Charity or Self-Support. I could not see why we should treat Germany charitably. It was wiser to lead Germany to her own prosperity." // "Did you find any help from German economic experts?" // "There was a division of views both on the part of the Germans, as well as the Americans. However, I succeeded. Maybe because I was so young, ingenuous and inexperienced. I succeeded in putting aside all pertinent objections, for I absolutely believed in the currency reform. I had also the full assistance of an experienced German economist by the name of Dr. Ludwig Erhard." // "Are you satisfied with the German development?" Tenenbaum paused. // "Yes, more or less. People with millions of intelligent technicians do not require to create *miracles*, of that I was sure. It was only necessary to *provide* a chance for them, though, I think, it would have been wiser and sounder for the country, if the prosperity would develop at a somewhat slower tempo. By way of example, it took some fifteen years until the wages conformed to the prices. This could have been achieved in a better way." // "Did the Federal Government ever appreciate your advice?" // 'The Federal Government can manage without my advice. I work with eighteen governments – I have just arranged a loan for Nicaragua, – but not for Germany. I consider it right. The work is done." // "Do you think that the German currency is absolutely solid?" // "Absolutely." // Edward Tenenbaum has never been in Germany since his return to the United States. He has never received any award from Germany. "I never thought about it." He has four children (the oldest was born in Berlin), and is satisfied with his life. // Before departing he tells me casually that his father was President of the Committee, formed after Hitler's emergence, which organized the boycott against German goods.[17]

FIGURE 6.4 Edward A. Tenenbaum in his office in Washington, DC 1964

FIGURE 6.5 Jack Bennett as Tenenbaum's partner in Continental-Allied Company 1954–1960

6.2   FAMILY MAN AND BEYOND

At the age of sixteen, Edward Tenenbaum had already shown a predilection for bucolic life in his prize-winning essay at *Ecolint* in Geneva, Switzerland (see Section 3.1). The purchase of twenty-four acres of land out in the woods in Herndon VA along Route 3, which is now called Bennett Road, near but not contiguous to Washington, DC, is an expression of the same fondness for living in a rural setting. In my interview with son Mark I asked him why his parents were interested in living in the countryside. His answer: "For some peace from the city. ... And some land, have a garden, a cat, have ponies! That's how we live. We don't want to live down here [in downtown Washington, DC where our interview took place]." And in my interview with Joan she simply said: "They wanted to bring up their children in the country." When I asked whether she had liked to grow up in the country, Joan replied: "I didn't know any different. It was where I lived. It wasn't a choice. But there are wonderful things about living in the country: I had a pony. I remember riding through some field of flowers when I was really little and they were like up to here and they were all like beautiful colors. Lovely memories!"

The contract was concluded shortly after Edward, Jeanette, and their first child Anne had returned to Washington, DC from his special assignment in US military government in Germany. And the parents seem to have been successful in instilling their penchant not only into daughter Joan, but also into their sons. A newspaper for the Metro Area of Washington, DC gave Mark and Charles Tenenbaum, then eleven and five years, prominence on a photo with explanatory notes that reported on *The Future Farmers of America Clubs' junior fair* at the Floris School in Fairfax County on August 4 to 5, 1961.[18] Evidently the fair was organized as a sort of beauty contest for young ponies, goats and the like. It even included a greased-pig race. The photo that Edward contributed in 1967 to the twenty-fifth yearbook of his class of 1942 at Yale is pointing in the same direction. It doesn't show his family or a portrait of himself as almost all of his classmates had selected. Instead it pictures his son Mark holding a young cow on a leash in front of a stable.[19]

In my interview with Mark on November 10, 2018, I asked him whether this was an example of his father's sense of black humor and how he, Mark, would explain it. Here is his answer:

> He had a very strange kind of humor which people often didn't understand. They thought it was dumb. I wouldn't say that it's black humor. I mean somebody would rather say that maybe he was kidding. ... He was a realist. He just was very vocal, he said some funny things. He was a funny person when he felt like talking. I think he was realistic. ... If you went through the yearbook and you looked to some of the other people and the way they show their families, some of them were really nice excepts [meaning "exceptional persons"]. But some of them I didn't fancy. They showed their children as examples of how they progressed from Yale to being captain of industry. Although I didn't grow up in a good neighborhood, but now look at my beautiful kids. Some of them were like that. And I think that's the kind of where my father's humor was aimed at, especially with the photo of the cow and me.

In our interview on October 29, 2018, Joan contributed another typical example of her father's humor, which I would now call dry humor:

> The CIA was always visiting him [in his office at Continental-Allied Company] to see if he knew anything because he traveled all over the world to his places. One time they came and they showed him an aerial photo of something, I think it was Thailand, somewhere like that. And there were all these white spots, all these square white spots on the ground. And they asked: "Mr. Tenenbaum, do you know what this is?" He looked down and said: "I don't know, laundry?" He was a funny guy. He used to make fun of all those super serious spies. ... He was a joker. Everything was funny. He was like a stand-up comic.

Ed Tenenbaum's son, Mark (top),
cow (bottom)

FIGURE 6.6 Instead of posting a happy-family photo at his 25th Yale reunion, Tenenbaum chose this 1965 photo of his teenage son Mark holding a cow on a leash in front of a barn

A few months after Mark and Charlie's prominent participation in the junior fair in August 1961, their grandfather and Edward's father, Dr. Joseph L. Tenenbaum, died in a Brooklyn hospital on December 10, 1961. Mark had turned twelve years old on October 11, 1961. In my interview with him on November 10, 2018 he told me that he had met his grandfather Joseph a few times and got along with him fine. "During the last of my summer vacations [in grade school] I stayed with him and his [second] wife Sheila in New York ... I don't remember meeting my grandmother Otilia [Joseph's first wife]. I don't know anything about her education, or when she died." Mark was quite surprised to learn that his grandmother Otilia Tenenbaum was highly educated with a PhD from the University of Vienna. She died in 1975 in New York at the age of eighty-four, when Mark was twenty-five or twenty-six. This means that neither Mark nor his parents had tried to keep up personal contacts between grandchildren and grandmother Otilia.

This was different as to grandmother Myrtle Kipp, Jeanette's mother. Mark told me in our interview: "I knew my mother's adoptive mother because she lived with us for a while at an older age." He believed to remember that his mother's adoptive father, Warren Kipp, had died between the late 1950s and 1962. But he did have no idea when his mother's adoptive mother, Myrtle Kipp, died. Here are the facts: She died at the age of seventy-eight on November 23, 1965 "in St. Anthony Hospital after a long illness. Born Sept. 10, 1887, in Chambersburg, Pa., daughter of Mr. and Mrs. William Cave. Lived forty-eight years in Rockford, coming from Indiana. Married to Warren Kipp. He died in 1959." Son William, Rockford, and daughter, Mrs. Jeanette Tenenbaum, Herndon VA, two sisters and four brothers, six grandchildren and three great-grandchildren are mentioned in the obituary.[20]

Mark didn't spare his parents what so many other teenage college students inflicted on their families as part of the 1968 movement protesting the Vietnam War. As an eighteen-year-old student of the private Methodist American University in Washington, DC, Mark and five fellow students were arrested on campus on April 4, 1968 in a raid by federal narcotics agents and District Police on charges of violating federal marijuana laws. A two-month undercover investigation, in which college officials cooperated, had preceded the raid. From each of the arrested US Commissioner Sam Wertleb demanded bail in exchange for their release: $1,000 for possession only and $2,000 for possession and sale. In 2023 purchasing power this would amount to about $8,740 and $17.480 respectively. I would call these amounts draconian. Mark's trial was to take place on April 18, 1968 before Commissioner Wertleb.[21] However, Mark's conflict with the law in those turbulent times for college students in protest and in search for antiauthoritarian ways of living did probably not put Edward's "pretty nice" family under real strain.

Mark had started his college education in September 1967. In 1970 he transferred to the equally private George Washington

University (also in Washington, DC), from where he graduated in 1972. Mark's older sister, Anne had studied Library Science and finally became a prominent employee of the Library of Congress. She published a number of genealogical research guides. Joan was educated at Cornell University Medical College, Ithaca NY, to become a practicing MD and a professor of medicine at the University of Oklahoma.

On March 14, 1969, a Friday, Edward's and Jeanette's family was hit by the heaviest stroke of fate a family can suffer: losing a child. Their youngest son Charles Berish was "struck by car" on a street in Herndon VA. Charles Berish was delivered to Fairfax Hospital in Falls Church VA, but he was DOA, (i.e., dead on arrival). The MD signing the official Certificate of Death of the Commonwealth of Virginia on March 17, 1969 testified that Charles Berish had died the moment of the accident. The kid had just turned to be thirteen years old on January 23, and was a seventh-grade student in the Herndon Schools. As to the cause of death the MD noted for immediate cause (A): "Severed cervical spinal cord" due to (B): "Multiple severe traumas."[22] As Charles's older brother Mark told me in our interview November 10, 2018, this heavy blow to the Tenenbaum family traumatized his parents, so much so that it also affected their health. Mother Jeanette developed a nervous condition. "My mom was pretty broken up and went through a hell of a time. She never got over it and ended up with a form of a shaking disease," another expression for Parkinson disease. Her husband Edward, who had always been less able than his wife to show emotions (Joan: "He was really more of a closed-up guy.") developed high blood pressure and a heart problem.

But this wasn't the last heavy blow for the Tenenbaum family. On October 14, 1975 Edward and Jeanette were driving through Dillsburgh PA and crashed. A Washington, DC newspaper (*Evening Star*) reported three days later: "Edward A. Tenenbaum, 53, an economist who was the American manager of German currency reform after World War II and later a consultant to underdeveloped countries, died Tuesday in an automobile accident near Harrisburg, Pa. ... His wife, Jeanette Kipp, also was injured in the accident and is in critical

Economist E. A. Tenenbaum Dies at 53 in Pa. Car Crash

Edward A. Tenenbaum, 53, an economist who was the American manager of German currency reform after World War II and later a consultant to underdeveloped countries, died Tuesday in an automobile accident near Harrisburg, Pa. He lived on Centreville Road in Herndon.

His wife, Jeannette K., also was injured in the accident and is in critical condition in a Camp Hill, Pa., hospital.

At the time of his death, Tenenbaum was operating his own economics consulting firm, Continental Allied Co., and a greenhouse business, Dulles Winter Garden, both in Herndon.

He was a summa cum laude graduate of Yale University and served as captain in the Air Force during World War II.

After the war he was named special assistant to the finance adviser of occupied West Germany and, in 1948, became American manager of the German currency reform.

He later worked as an economist for the Agency for International Development in Greece.

Tenenbaum opened his own economics consulting firm in 1954 and for the last two years had been consultant to the International Bank of Reconstruction and Development in Europe and Asia.

He leaves his wife; three children, Mrs. Ann K. Toohey of Kalamazoo, Mich., Joan K., of New York City, and Mark J., of Falls Church, and a brother, Robert, of Ithaca, N.Y.

FIGURE 6.7 Newspaper article on Edward A. Tenenbaum's fatal car accident on Route 15 in Dillsburg near Harrisburg, PA on October 14, 1975

condition in a Camp Hill, Pa., hospital." [23] In a letter of May 26, 1981 to an old friend, Jeanette described the circumstances of his death in the car crash there: "We were together on a short trip to Pennsylvania in 1975 and a truck jumped the median and hit us head-on. He was 53!"[24] She didn't mention that she had also been seriously injured.

I wanted to double check and find out more details about this fatal accident. So, I just called the Carroll Township Police Department in charge of Dillsburg PA, a small town with about 2,500 inhabitants, almost 100 percent white and living off agriculture, particularly growing pickles. The person who answered my call, was female, Lori Snider, by good fortune, as it turned out, a records clerk for that police station. I told her I was calling from Berlin/Germany with a very unusual request. I would be in the process of writing a biography of an American military officer in World War II, Edward A. Tenenbaum, who as a financial and economic expert trained at Yale was hired by American military government in Germany after the War. As a first lieutenant of the reserve, aged twenty-six, he was the key person for designing, managing and implementing currency reform in West Germany in June 1948 which introduced the Deutschmark. I informed her that E. A. Tenenbaum, at the age of 53, was killed and his wife Jeanette seriously injured in a car crash at Dillsburg PA on October 14, 1975.

She was very friendly and responsive. She doubted that they would be having any IT-based information on car accidents as far back as 1975, but she would look for it. She proposed that I call back half an hour later. By that time, she would have checked the IT resources available to her. Thirty minutes later I called again, only to find out that her initial doubts had been confirmed. She had found no trace of the accident online. But she was expecting a colleague coming in at 4:30 p.m., an officer who had already been active in the 1970s and was still taking care of the records of Carroll Township Police Department, Gene Baptisti. She would inform him of my request and gave me the telephone number under which I should call him at 5:00 p.m. (11:00 p.m. Berlin time). I called and reached him at 5 p.m. He had made a search in the records available to him without result. But he, the Records Officer of Carroll Township Police Department, told me that he knew a Dillsburg citizen who had for years gathered information on the many fatal accidents on Route 15 in York County PA that is passing through Dillsburg. He would contact him for me. On his request I gave him my email address.

This person was Douglas A. Boelhouwer, a retired Division Chief of Nonpublic and Private School Services of the Pennsylvania Department of Education and a Dillsburg citizen since August 1969.[25] He and other concerned citizens had for decades demanded from responsible state, county and township authorities an improvement of traffic safety on the relatively short strip (8.9 miles) of Route 15 through York County PA. But nothing substantial had changed and the strip has remained a hotspot of fatal accidents until today. In 2017 Boelhouwer published online the *1974–2016 Report of US Route 15 Fatal Crashes York County, Pennsylvania*. He distributed it to PA governor Tom Wolf, his Secretary of Transportation, Leslie S. Richards, two other responsible officials of the Department of Transportation (DOT) in

PA's capital Harrisburg, to Will Clark, Chief of the Transportation Planning Division of the York County Planning Commission, to PA State Senator Michael Regan and PA State Representative Dawn Keefer, to John Richardson, president of the Dillsburg Borough Council, Bruce R. Trostle, chairman of Carroll Township Supervisors, and Kevin Cummings, chairman of Franklin Township Supervisors. For decades Boelhouwer had tried to promote public awareness of the exceptionally high and rising death toll on Route 15 in York County PA and to engage the authorities in remedial action, in vain. He summarized the root of the problem in his covering letter to Governor Wolf sending his round-about 60-page report of February 2017 as attachment:

> State, County and Local officials have been working on the complex problem for more than 30 years because local communities can't come to agreement how to fix the problem with solutions suggested by Penn DOT. Little progress has been made but the number of fatalities, traffic congestion and non-fatal accidents continue to rise. The most serious is the loss of life. This has to stop. There has been a 200% increase in fatalities on the 8.9 measured miles of US Rt. 15 in York County in the past 12 years.[26]

Boelhouwer reports that US Route 15 on its short York County strip is crossed by sixteen intersections where the crashes usually occur. He informed me that in his list of accidents there was none for 1975. But he would consult the archive of the local newspaper, the Dillsburg *Weekly Bulletin*, again. Besides police records he had used the paper to establish his list. Then for a number of weeks he remained silent. I thought that he had dropped the case. But he finally informed me that Marie Chomicke, the current publisher of the Dillsburg *Weekly Bulletin*, for lack of own archival material that far back, had referred him to the Northern York County Historical & Preservation Society. There the administrative assistant Ethan Walker found a detailed art-icle of the *Weekly Bulletin* on the Tenenbaum accident in an archive binder for 1975. He emailed it to Doug Boulhouwer on March 19, 2018 who, in turn, immediately forwarded it to me.

In addition to the Tenenbaum crash the article reports on a second fatal accident two days later on Route 15.[27] Boelhouwer's successful search not only contributes to completing his list of fatal accidents on Route 15 in York County PA. But it also provides in detail all information on the Tenenbaums' car crash that I had hoped for.

I quote from the article:

> Edward A. Tennenbaum [*sic*!], 54 [in fact he was still 53], Herndon, Va., was pronounced dead at the scene of an accident Oct. 14 on Rt. 15 near Siddonsburg Road, by Deputy Coroner Marion Rider. // Police reported the Tennenbaum [*sic*] vehicle was traveling south when it was struck head-on by a pick-up truck driven by Marlin A. Dieffenderfer, 43, Hummelstown RD 4. The pickup was traveling north. Police said another car, identified only as a brown sedan, forced the pickup across the medial strip and into the Tennebaum [*sic*!] car. // The brown sedan left the scene, and police are still investigating the accident. Anyone with information about the sedan is asked to contact the Carroll-Franklin Police Department at 911 or 766-0249. // Tennebaum's [*sic*] wife, Jeanette, 56, was listed in guarded condition at Holy Spirit Hospital upon admission. Lee E. Deibert, Sacramento, Pa. and Berry E. Deibert, his 23-year old son, were passengers in the Diffenderfer [*sic*!] pickup. The son received multiple facial fractures and was taken to Holy Spirit Hospital. His father received lacerations. // A third vehicle, a pickup driven by Charles E. Wolf, East Berlin RD 2, struck the Tennebaum [*sic*] car in the rear during the collision. // Total damage has been set at $10,700 [equals $60,600 in 2023 dollars]. // Carroll-Franklin Police Department was assisted by the upper Allen and the Pa. State Police and the Dillsburg Rescue squad and ambulance. The Dillsburg Fire Department stood by.[28]

In our interview I asked Joan whether her mother had suffered more from losing her son Charles or from losing her husband. Joan: "My mother did much better with him [Edward] dying than with her son dying. She said she missed him and all that. But she wasn't like when Charlie died, she did not go on."

By the time of their father's death Edward's and Jeanette's remaining three children were adults and had left home. Anne Kipp had married James Benjamin Toohey of Kalamazoo, Michigan, on August 7, 1971 in an Episcopal church in Herndon, Fairfax County VA.[29] They established their home in Kalamazoo MI. Joan Kipp, at the age of thirty, married Charles Merrill in 1981.[30] And they lived in New York City thereafter. Mark Jon never married and lives on a farm in the countryside near the Washington, DC area, thus following in the footsteps of his father.

In 1981 Jeanette described Edward's activities during the three years preceding his death:

> By 1972 he [Edward] was sick of the type of work [running his Continental-Allied Company., Inc.] he was doing – closed the Washington office – then consulted for the World Bank. In his spare time he built us three greenhouses for me to run. He died 2 days after he got the furnaces working + all the automatic controls installed.[31]

She also informs her friend that

> I stayed in Virginia until 1979 and then sold part of the property (at a nice profit, of course) and moved to Michigan to be near one daughter [Anne] and her children. I will be in New York soon to preside at the wedding of another daughter [Joan], who will enter Cornell Medical college in the fall. [32]

Edward Tenenbaum had been a member of the Democratic Party.[33] Being a native of New York City he probably read the *New York Times*. His wife definitely read the *New York Review of Books*, also after having moved to Kalamazoo. In reaction to Robert L. Heilbroner's review of Rose and Milton Friedman's book *Free to Choose*,[34] she wrote a letter to the editors praising Heilbroner's competent dealing with the Friedmans' "bad scholarship." As to the origins of West Germany's economic revival in 1948 she expressed concern "not just with their omissions of fact, but with their blatant untruths." She blames the Friedmans for crediting West Germany's currency reform of 1948 to Ludwig Erhard. "This is pure fiction." Instead it had been the work of the Western military governments, dominated by the USA, whose director of its Finance Division, Jack Bennett, announced it. "My late husband, Edward Tenenbaum, his assistant in charge of currency reform, sat at his side. Erhard was not present." Because in 1948 a West German government did not yet exist, the Friedmans erred in calling Erhard "German Minister of Economics," Jeanette Kipp stated. I quote the following part of her letter to the editors in full, because she – with her own sound knowledge of economics and finance – had been a contemporary witness of the currency reform that her husband had planned for the Western occupation zones and had executed while they both lived family life with their first child Anne in Berlin-Dahlem, first in Gelfertstrasse 47A and later in Föhrenweg 15:

> The currency reform was in effect dictated to the German people by the Tri-zonal Military Government. German participation was welcomed, and the many plans they submitted were carefully studied. It was a group of German financial experts who wrote the laws of currency reform under Allied direction at Rothwesten. Although Erhard was closely identified with one of the prominent German plans, he was not a member of this group, and his actual participation in currency reform was minor. In any case, the power of decision was reserved by the Allies, and the final product predominantly reflected the opinions of the Americans.

> The Friedmans picture Erhard as battling military government bureaucracy in an uphill fight to bring a free economy to Germany. This is nonsense. They quote Erhard as saying he announced the currency reform and lifted "almost all" price controls on a weekend so the military authorities could not countermand his orders.

We know he did not announce the currency reform. What Erhard actually did that weekend was to lift price controls on selected consumer items, a far cry from "almost all." Furthermore, the minor flap which ensued had little to do with his lifting controls, and much to do with his having exceeded his authority. Indeed, the Americans looked to the currency reform as a vehicle to relax controls, as opposed to the British, who wanted to tighten them. American opinion prevailed; which was fortunate for the revival of the German economy.

The Friedmans' whole book is a diatribe against government interference and bureaucracy, yet in Germany after World War II the remarkable reconstruction of the economy could not have occurred without a sound currency and massive aid from the Marshall Plan, both accomplishments of the US bureaucracy so despised by the Friedmans. It was upon this basis that Ludwig Erhard was able to make his impressive contributions to the German "economic miracle." It seems impossible that the Friedmans were unaware of the vital role played by their own government in halting the inflation and introducing a sound currency in Germany. One is led to believe that the historic facts did not conform to the Friedmans' theories and prejudices, so they changed the facts to suit themselves, a dangerous practice which casts doubts on their abilities as scholars.

J. Kipp Tenenbaum, Kalamazoo, Michigan[35]

As a senior scholar of economics and finance trained on solid foundations of empirical and historical research, I can only concur with the essence of J. Kipp Tenenbaum's eyewitness report. Kipp Tenenbaum beats Milton (and Rose) Friedman by a wide margin as to the truth about West Germany's currency reform of 1948.

Her harsh criticism of Milton (and Rose) Friedman was noticed by James C. Warren, Jr., an old friend of the Tenenbaums from their common Marshall Plan/Mutual Security Agency (MSA) missions to Greece in the early 1950s.

In a letter of recommendation of December 6, 1954 Edward had described Warren's function there as chief of the Import Branch within the Program Division, of which Edward was the director. Warren had worked there during one year, closely observed by his superior Edward Tenenbaum. The following wording of the letter contains – in my view beyond the usual niceties of such letters – a real appreciation of Jim Warren's capabilities and proven performance:

> I have no hesitation in recommending him as an outstanding employee, who combined high intelligence, energy, initiative and an unusual ability to get along with people. Mr. Warren developed the first careful study of Greece's import requirements in the modern history of that country. His study played an important part in helping to reduce the aid requirements of that country from around $180 million to around $20 Million per annum. It involved not merely the ability to apply theoretical economic principles, but also the understanding of practical industrial and commercial problems of an entire nation.

> Outside the office, Mr. Warren distinguished himself by his sympathy and interest in the Greek people. He undertook to learn the difficult language of that country, and to explore many parts which lie off the beaten path, acting as an unofficial ambassador of good will.

> Although he entered the Mission as a relatively junior employee, and did most of his work during a period when the size and scope of the Mission was declining, Mr. Warren rapidly became one of its most valuable employees. His work showed reliability, resourcefulness and integrity. I would have no hesitation in hiring him for our own firm [Continental-Allied Company, Inc., still a start-up after having been founded in early 1954], if our present level of activities permitted.

> Edward A. Tenenbaum[36]

It was this James Warren, then living in Auburn, Maine, to whom Jeanette Kipp had confided in a nutshell the course of her life since the Greek Mission had ended. Above I have already quoted from her first letter of May 26, 1981 to him, after Jim had read Jeanette Kipp's piece in the *New York Review of Books* and resumed contact. They kept in touch over the years. On July 5, 1986 Jim wrote a letter from an address in New York to her who was still living in Kalamazoo MI: "Dear Kipp, This is a voice out of the distant past!" With the fortieth anniversary of the Truman Doctrine and the foreign aid program to Greece coming up in 1987, he had started to work "on a serious piece of writing about the Greek economic assistance program – But, in particular about the Stabilization Program of 1951 / 53 of which Ed was the author," he informed her. He also reported that he had already consulted the National Archives in Washington, DC and Suitland, Maryland. He asked Jeanette whether he could consult her in a telephone conversation and whether it was true that she had donated Edward's papers to the National Archives. In closing he wrote: "And it would be nice to see you and to reminisce about those adventurous days. I have such good memories of Ed and his brilliant leadership of what was an extraordinary turnaround. Do let me know if all of this sounds good to you. All the best, Jim."[37]

The next letter I found dates April 9, 2000 from J. Kipp, then living at 11128 Saffold Way, Reston VA, to Jim. She thanked him for having sent his paper about "Frank, Victor + Ed," which he had published in a book on people involved in the Greek mission.[38] She would certainly look up the book because she remembered a number of people, among them expressly Paul R. Porter. He was – as Warren describes him – the "mission chief of tough, demanding, mid-western, LaFollette/liberal/New Deal persuasion and galvanic, reformist energy," with

181 American specialists, advisors, and controllers and agents-of-change not only in all the major sub-sectors of agriculture and mining and industry; roadbuilding and ports and harbors; electric power and civil aviation – but also in civil service organization and

method, in government decentralization, in labor union
organization, in banking legislation and the progressive income tax,
in public health and social security administration.[39]

Warren also states that "June 30, 1954, then, essentially marks the
end of the American proconsular role in Greece, and the end of
America's reformist, New Deal adventure in and for Greece."[40]

J. Kipp Tenenbaum writes in the above-mentioned letter to Jim
Warren further that Paul R. Porter and his wife Hilda used to live right
around the corner from where she had moved to in Reston VA and
that she is anxious to see Porter's articles. In that letter she also shares
with Jim Warren a reminiscence of a dinner just after devaluation of
the Greek currency. She and Edward were sitting across the table from
Spyros Markezinis and his wife. He was the Minister of Finance and
Government Coordination then, a powerful figure in Greek economic
policy. Jeanette Tenenbaum recalls that Markezinis

> was expounding at great length about how the devaluation was set
> for a particular day because his stars were in the right place in the
> sky, and if this hadn't been, the whole thing would have been a
> disaster! Then his wife explained that astrology was very important
> to him. I can't remember saying anything at all in reply, but
> I imagine I must have been sitting there with my mouth wide open!

The last paragraph of J. Kipp's letter is also very revealing about the
way in which her husband Edward Tenenbaum was sidelined and
eventually withdrawn from his mission: "Thanks again – it certainly
brought back the past – especially the last months when everyone was
mad at Ed + we stopped being invited to those awful parties (Ed said
we were put on the S – list as punishment, which was a delight to us
since we were then free in our last days there to roam around Greece
and ignore the social life.) Very best wishes, Kipp"[41]

Jeanette Kipp Tenenbaum died at the age of ninety-one on
January 8, 2011. She was buried next to her husband in Arlington
National Cemetery.[42] She had been his great love as well as his
inspirer, best friend and companion through thick and thin.

In my interviews with the Tenenbaums' children Joan (October 29, 2018) and Mark (November 10, 2018) I asked for their parents' religious life. Joan answered: "We weren't Jewish ... I mean we were and we weren't. We were Jewish from the point that we were not ashamed to be Jewish. ... We didn't celebrate any Jewish holidays, we celebrated Christmas." In preparation of Christmas Dad would cut a fancy Christmas tree in their surrounding forest and Mom would decorate it with Christmas ornaments that she had brought back from Berlin. Her adoptive mother wasn't really of Jewish origin, Joan said, "and my father didn't really care and they were both kind of atheists." Joan thought that her grandfather Joseph had probably been practicing Jewish religion, but nobody else in the family. Mark shared this opinion. He even made the point that all of Edward's and Jeanette's children were not Jewish. It would be true that Edward was. But to be Jewish your mother must have been Jewish. And Jeanette Kipp definitely was not. From Joan I received the information that her mother was adopted from a Catholic hospital. This would fit with Mark's observation that "by the looks of it" she had Irish roots. But Mark also shared with me what Mary Pierce had told him. She was a lawyer and his mother's best friend. The Pierces with their kids were also the closest other family the Tenenbaum kids grew up with. As a newborn, Jeanette "was found in a basket in a train station, and it was just typically what Irish people did back then," Mary Pierce had told him. Joan's and Mark's stories could both be true. If not-yet-named baby Jeanette was found in a basket in a train station and if somebody found her who knew that child suspension was practiced more by Catholics with Irish roots than by other religious or native groups, he or she would bring the newborn to a Catholic hospital. And anyway, Catholic hospitals had and have a tradition of offering baby hatches.

Because who you are best friends with also sheds light on your own character, I think it's worth to report here what Joan told me about Mary Pierce in our interview: "Oh, she was an interesting character. She went to community college and she went with a judge. She never had to go to law school and got to be a lawyer anyway. So she was a very interesting woman. Pulled herself up by the bootstraps, really."

FIGURE 6.8 Grave plaque at Arlington Cemetery

7   Conclusion

Tenenbaum's role as father of the West German currency reform was kept under the carpet in Germany even by people who knew about his decisive role. This fact inspired me to write this biography, mainly in order to shatter the general belief that Ludwig Erhard merits credentials for this. Therefore, let's start this final chapter with a review of Tenenbaum's currency-reform contributions and achievements. He himself has listed them in his CV for his application for his assignment in Athens to stabilize the Greek currency and economy:

> German currency reform, including // a. Physical arrangements (printing of new currency, preservation of secrecy, distribution and control of banknote supply, procedure for exchange operation, preparation of forms, publicity, etc.) // b. Legal arrangements (preparation and promulgation of laws and administrative ordinances covering treatment of money supply, public and private debt, banking, social security system, insurance companies, etc.) // (1) Aims, prerequisites, and timing of currency reform, // (2) Proper rate of exchange between old currency (and monetary claims) and new, // (3) Provisions for hardship cases, // (4) Provisions for recapture of speculative and black-market profits held in the form of money, // (5) Public finance and banking policies in immediate post-reform period.[1]

Not only journalists, caricaturists, biographers and contemporary historians, but also Erhard himself and his respective ghost writers have with their publications contributed to the myth that Ludwig Erhard was the doer of the currency reform in 1948. But the mythmaking around Erhard's person as the father of the currency reform would have failed, if the German experts had come out with the truth more strongly than they did. With them, Edward A. Tenenbaum had spent seven weeks in the so-called Conclave of Rothwesten working out the details of implementing the American currency reform plan agreed with Washington, DC as well as the British and the French Allies. The same was true of the many Germans with economic and monetary policy responsibilities in state governments, bizonal administrative agencies, the state central banks, and the Bank deutscher Länder, as well as with the forerunner of the Bundestag, the Economic Council, with its committees and advisory councils.

The Germans were not only crushed militarily. The end of the war also revealed the inhumane breaches of civilization with which the criminal Nazi regime had led the German "Volksgenossen" into a moral abyss. Perhaps the latter were only able to regain their own self-respect and dignity by perceiving the most important setting of the course for the economic and political resurgence of the Federal Republic, the currency reform of 1948, not as an act of mercy by the victorious powers, but as a merit of their charismatic and popular compatriot Ludwig Erhard.

Lucius Clay was wise enough to take into account this mass psychological disposition of the German population. He promoted Erhard's economic policy career by having him appointed economics minister in Bavaria and later chairman of the Agency for Money and Credit in the Bizone. Given the quality of US intelligence at the time, it is hardly possible to assume that this was done in ignorance of Nazi-conformist views, from which Erhard had only turned away in the face of imminent German military defeat with his 1944 memorandum "War Financing and Debt Consolidation." In it, he departed from his previously held Nazi-conformist economic policy views, namely, a centralized control economy subject to primary political objectives, including by means of price controls and ration coupons, cartels and compulsory membership in *Reichsgruppen* (Reich Groups) of economic sectors and branches in the service of the political leadership. Perhaps under the influence of his commissioner for the memorandum, the *Reichsgruppe Industrie*, which started planning for

Germany's postwar economic order in 1943, he transformed himself into a proponent of a "free market economy," the peacetime economic model practiced in the United States. Clay and his political associates and advisers most certainly knew about Erhard's turncoat past. And his subservience to the leadership of the American military government was evident at the latest after city commander of Fürth, Captain Cofer, had made Erhard's letter of May 24, 1945 available to them. In the run-up to C-Day of West German currency reform, the Americans were determined not to abandon their Colm-Dodge-Goldsmith (CDG) currency reform plan for all four occupation zones, drafted in the first half of 1946, in favor of German ideas as contained in the Homburg Plan of the Agency for Money and Credit.

General Clay was at least on a par with the fox of all foxes, Konrad Adenauer. Neither of them was interested in socialist experiments. Erhard had offered himself to the American military government in May 1945, after he had changed from a far-reaching supporter of National Socialist economic policy to an advocate of the free market economy. Clay recognized the usefulness that Erhard's "new clothes," coupled with his skillful rhetoric, could unleash, in sending him into the political arena of West Germany. Erhard's task was to battle against Germans infected with socialism all the way into the CDU camp and, at the same time, against the Labour-ruled British. Adenauer, after all, agreed with this assessment when he promoted Erhard in CDU circles to the best of his ability, even though Erhard shunned membership in the CDU party.

Reading Siegfried Lenz's novel "Der Überläufer" (The Defector), about a soldier in the German Wehrmacht who defected to the Red Army toward the end of World War II, strengthened me in the following assumption. During the first two postwar decades, it seems to have been mentally impossible for the people of defeated Germany – still infected by Nazi antisemitism – to recognize and appreciate the fact that the basis of West Germany's resurgence, the currency reform of 1948, was owed to Edward A. Tenenbaum, son of Jewish Austrians who had emigrated to the United States in 1920. Moreover, the first draft of May 1946 for an all-German currency reform, the CDG plan, which

Tenenbaum adapted to suit the restricted West German currency reform, had also been prepared by two emigrated German citizens of Jewish origin on behalf of General Clay and his then financial adviser Joseph Dodge. Gerhard Colm had been a professor at the Kiel Institute for the World Economy until his dismissal due to "legislation to restore German civil service" of April 7, 1933 and his subsequent emigration to the United States. Raymond W. Goldsmith had graduated from the French Gymnasium in Berlin under the name Raimund Wilhelm Goldschmidt. He had received his doctorate from Berlin University in 1928 with a dissertation on *Das deutsche Großbankkapital in seiner neueren Entwicklung* (Berlin: Ebering, 1928). He then worked as an employee of the Statistisches Reichsamt in Berlin until he pursued postdoctoral work in 1933–1934 at the London School of Economics, followed by emigration to the United States.

Siegfried Lenz had offered his anti-war novel, completed in 1951, to his publisher Hoffmann und Campe in Hamburg for publication in early 1952. He received it back for editing. Lenz revised it. Nevertheless, his editor refused to publish it for political reasons. "The story of a young soldier who defects from the Wehrmacht to the Red Army toward the end of the war simply did not fit into the restorative climate of the early Adenauer era," one reviewer wrote.[2] The manuscript of the novel only resurfaced in the Lenz Papers after his death in 2014. With a 64-year delay, Hoffmann and Campe published the novel in February 2016, by which time Tenenbaum had been dead for a good forty years and Erhard for almost thirty-nine.

Another example of how antisemitism in West German society persisted after World War II is the case of Philipp Auerbach. He had survived concentration and death camps Auschwitz and Buchenwald.

> Active in the care of victims of the Nazi regime, he was the most important Jewish official in Germany after WW II and very quickly the most controversial and, for some people, the most hated Jew in the entire country. Like no other, he organized for Jews who had survived the Holocaust to leave Germany. ... His office did not function according to the principles of Prussian or Bavarian

officialdom. That was not even possible after the war, there was no
infrastructure anymore, there was a lack of money. Even the
bookkeeping was complicated. Auerbach was also not high-handed;
he decided, for example, that people should pay a percentage to his
authority when it gave them contracts: When an architect was
awarded a contract to restore a Jewish cemetery, Auerbach told him
he thought a small portion of the fee should be donated. This
money he used to support the people who came to his office asking
for help. This, of course, was not in accordance with the rules of
correct official conduct. Auerbach quickly came under suspicion of
pocketing the money himself. Unjustly, by the way.[3]

After his arrest in 1951, Auerbach was put on trial in 1952 for alleged
bribery, embezzlement and corruption. He was found guilty by three
judges, who had joined the NSDAP and SA at different times, and was
sentenced to two and a half years in prison. The following night,
Auerbach took his own life.

In the case of Tenenbaum the question remains why he himself did
not resist the concealment and forgetting of his key role in preparing,
shaping and enforcing the currency reform of 1948, especially when
Ludwig Erhard was increasingly claiming Tenenbaum's credit for himself. The answer lies in the fundamentally different characters of the two.

Tenenbaum was characterized by a quick grasp of the issues,
networked thinking, and a meticulous approach to work. In his
personal environment, he was considered a brilliant mind, but
idiosyncratic and insufficiently determined in protecting his
personal interests. ... When General Clay's financial advisor, Jack
Bennett, once expressed concern that the currency reform might go
down in history as a German achievement, Tenenbaum replied
laconically, 'Who cares who gets the credit.'[4]

Tenenbaum lived the wisdom of the Roman general Cato the Elder:
Esse quam videri (More being than appearing), that is, perform much
and stand out little. In Erhard's case, the emphasis was obviously on
standing out even in areas in which he had achieved little.

Notes

I INTRODUCTION

1 This is the title of the best twentieth-century war novel I have read: Vasily Grossman, *Life and Fate*.

2 As of late, I am not the only one with this kind of approach to a biography. See Dean Reuter/Colm Lowery/Keith Chester, *The Hidden Nazi. The Untold Story of America's Deal with the Devil*, Washington, DC: Regnery History, 2019. This is a biography of SS General Hans Kammler. He had helped build the death camp at Auschwitz and had perfected the slave labor system in secret and underground wonder-weapon production. Philippe Sands, *The Ratline. Love, Lies and Justice on the Trail of a Nazi Fugitive*, London: Weidenfeld & Nicolson, 2020. This is a biography of SS General Otto Baron von Wächter. After World War II he had escaped searches for him from quite a few states for four years. He died unexpectedly in July 1949 after three months in Rome shortly before his final escape to safety in Argentina via the Vatican-organized "Ratline" would have occurred.

3 "Stenographischer Bericht der Sitzung vom 20.11.47. Beginn: 10:30 Uhr." In Bundesarchiv Koblenz Z 32/7. Kindleberger had obtained his copy either from Jeanette Kipp Tenenbaum directly or from the Tenenbaum Papers, box 5, folder: Germany – Currency Reform – Memoranda (9 of 9). HSTPL. The creation of the *Sonderstelle* in Bad Homburg near Frankfurt am Main was decided by the Economic Council of the Bizone on July 23, 1947. But its actual work started not until October 10, 1947 with its first meeting. For the history and work of the *Sonderstelle* see Arne Weick, *Homburger Plan und Währungsreform. Kritische Analyse des Währungsreformplans der Sonderstelle Geld und Kredit und seiner Bedeutung für die westdeutsche Währungsreform von 1948*, St. Katharinen: Scripta mercaturae, 1998, pp. 37–62. Michael Brackmann, *Vom totalen Krieg zum Wirtschaftswunder. Die Vorgeschichte der westdeutschen Währungsreform 1948*, Essen: Klartext, 1993, pp. 244–249.

4 Robert Nef/Bernhard Ruetz, "Starkes Stück. Wie der jüdische US-Offizier Edward A. Tenenbaum vor 60 Jahren den Deutschen zur D-Mark verhalf,"

Jüdische Allgemeine, June 19, 2008. Online: www.juedische-allgemeine
.de/allgemein/starkes-stueck/ (Accessed February 3, 2020).

5 Charles P. Kindleberger/F. Taylor Ostrander, "The 1948 Monetary Reform
in West Germany," in Marc Flandreau/Carl-Ludwig Holtfrerich/Harold
James (eds.), *International Financial History in the Twentieth Century.
System and Anarchy,* Cambridge: Cambridge University Press, 2003,
pp. 169–195.

6 Email of May 8, 2020 by Julia Plötzgen, archivist of the town of Telgte.

7 Oral testimony by Irwin Collier, a student of Kindleberger's classes at MIT
and my successor on the chair for economics and economic history at the
John F. Kennedy Institute for North American Studies at the Free
University of Berlin.

8 Hans Möller, "Die westdeutsche Währungsreform von 1948," in Deutsche
Bundesbank (ed.), *Währung und Wirtschaft in Deutschland 1876–1975,*
Frankfurt am Main: Fritz Knapp, 1976, p. 445.

9 Erwin Hielscher, *Der Leidensweg der deutschen Währungsreform,*
Munich: Richard Pflaum, 1948.

10 Ibid., pp. 38–39. My translation.

11 The other chairman, Karl Bernhard, president the German expert group in
internal meetings, was elected by his peers, because they regarded him
more flexible and capable of bridging the different views of Conclave
colleagues than Hielscher. The latter, in turn, was offended by this choice,
because he had been Ludwig Erhard's successor as chairman of the Special
Agency on Money and Credit since early March 1945 and nine of the
eleven members of the Conclave had been selected from that Agency.

12 Möller, "Die westdeutsche Währungsreform von 1948," pp. 433–483, the
quote on p. 446. My translation.

13 Ibid., p. 449. My translation.

14 Otto Pfleiderer, "Die Geburtsstunde der Deutschen Mark vor 25 Jahren.
Die politische Grundsatzentscheidung trafen die Westmächte.
Erinnerungen an das Konklave von Rothwesten, das die Währungsreform
vorbereitete," in *Stuttgarter Zeitung,* June 19, 1973, p. 12. This article and
two preceding drafts with correction marks have been made available to
me by the Historical Archive of the Deutsche Bundesbank in Frankfurt am
Main, Otto Pfleiderer Papers, file number N 1/36.

15 My translation from Michael Budczies, *Meine Familie. Geschichte und
Geschichten,* Limburg: C. A. Starke, 1999, pp. 162–163.

2 LUDWIG ERHARD, WHO TOOK CREDIT FOR EDWARD A. TENENBAUM'S SUCCESS

* The overwhelming part of this chapter was originally written in German. It was translated by Charlie Zaharoff.

1 Bundesarchiv/Institut für Zeitgeschichte (eds.), *Akten zur Vorgeschichte der Bundesrepublik Deutschland 1945–1949*, 5 vols., Munich: Oldenbourg, 1989.

2 Christoph Weisz (ed.), *OMGUS-Handbuch: Die amerikanische Militärregierung in Deutschland 1945–1949*, Munich: Oldenbourg, 1994.

3 Theodor Eschenburg (ed.), *Jahre der Besatzung 1945–1949*, Stuttgart: Deutsche Verlags-Anstalt, 1983. Wolfgang Benz's contribution to this volume "Währungsreform und soziale Marktwirtschaft" deals with Ludwig Erhard, the ideological background of his social-market-economy concept, and his decontrol of price fixing and rationing immediately after currency reform, while currency reform itself is treated only in passing.

4 Hans-Ulrich Wehler, *Deutsche Gesellschaftsgeschichte, vol. 4: Vom Beginn des Ersten Weltkriegs bis zur Gründung der beiden deutschen Staaten, 1914–1949*, Munich: Beck, 2003.

5 Henry C. Wallich, *Mainsprings of the German Economic Revival*, New Haven: Yale University Press, 1955.

6 Christoph Buchheim, "The Establishment of the Bank deutscher Länder and the West German Currency Reform," in Deutsche Bundesbank (ed.), *Fifty Years of the Deutsche Mark: Central Bank and the Currency in Germany since 1948*, Oxford: Oxford University Press, 1999, pp. 55–100.

7 Helmut Schmidt's diploma thesis, University of Hamburg 1949, deposited in the archive of the city state of Hamburg.

8 Helmut Schmidt, *Men and Powers: A Political Retrospective*, New York: Random House, 1989, p. 130. See also: Helmut Schmidt, "Aus Anlaß des 25. Jahrestages der Währungsreform am 20 Juni 1948," in *Pressemitteilungen und Informationen / SPD* 21,192 (1973), pp. 1–2. In it, Schmidt describes how he personally experienced the currency reform at that time as a student of economics.

9 Robert Nef/Bernhard Ruetz, "Wer war der Vater der Deutschen Mark?" In *Reflexion* 46 (2002), p. 9. The same authors also published: "Der Manager der Währungsreform 1948: In Vergessenheit geraten [Edward

Tenenbaum]," in *Frankfurter Allgemeine Zeitung*, December 31, 2001, p. 18.

10 Otmar Emminger, *D-Mark, Dollar, Währungskrisen: Erinnerungen eines ehemaligen Bundesbankpräsidenten*, Stuttgart: DVA, 1986, p. 23.

11 Summary of Alfons Kössinger's memoirs in the communal archive of Roggenburg, where he grew up. Online: www.roggenburg.de/nr.-108-109-ein-tragisches-und-ein-spektakulaeres-ereignis (Accessed March 19, 2022).

12 Otto Pfleiderer, "Fünf Jahre Deutsche Mark. Die Währungsreform von 1948," in *Stuttgarter Nachrichten*, June 20, 1953.

13 For the date see Alfons Kössinger, *Die Entstehung und der Werdegang des Museums "Währungsreform 1948,"* Kassel: Kasseler Bank, n.d., pp. 6–7. See also "Der Schwere Abschied," in *Der Spiegel 18/1998*. Online: www .spiegel.de/politik/der-schwere-abschied-a-6489008d-0002-0001-0000-000007870431 (Accessed March 19, 2022).

14 "'Symbol für Freiheit und Wohlstand.' Festakt in der Paulskirche: Kohl und Tietmeyer würdigen die Deutsche Mark," *Frankfurter Allgemeine Sonntagszeitung*, June 21, 1998.

15 "50 Jahre Deutsche Mark. Festakt der Deutschen Bundesbank. Rede des Bundesbankpräsidenten am 20. Juni 1998 in der Paulskirche in Frankfurt am Main." Online: www2.hu-berlin.de/linguapolis/ConsIV99-00/ Tietmeyer.htm (Accessed March 19, 2022).

16 Quotations from Nef/Ruetz, "Wer war der Vater der Deutschen Mark?" Reflexion, passim. See also Robert Nef/Bernhard Ruetz, "Edward A. Tenenbaum. Wie der jüdische US-Offizier Edward A. Tenenbaum vor 60 Jahren den Deutschen zur D-Mark verhalf," *Jüdische Allgemeine*, June 19, 2008. Online: www.juedische-allgemeine.de/allgemein/starkes-stueck/ (Accessed March 19, 2022).

17 Werner Meyer, *Abschied von der Mark. Die Geschichte unserer Währung*, Düsseldorf: Patmos, 1998. In 2001, a revised edition of the book was released in paperback with a different title (*Mythos Deutsche Mark. Zur Geschichte einer abgeschafften Währung*), and a second in 2005 with another change of title (*20.6.1948. Währungsreform – Das neue Geld ist da*), again revised and supplemented with substantial photographic material.

18 Email from the municipality of Fuldatal to the author on July 5, 2017.

19 Massimo Bognanni/Sven Prange, *Made in Germany. Große Momente der deutschen Wirtschaftsgeschichte*, Frankfurt: Campus, 2016, pp. 142–154.

20 This is the translated draft of the telegram in the archive of the Ludwig-Erhard-Stiftung, Bonn, Nachlass Erhard, Allg. Korrespondenz 1971–1975.

21 Quoted from Werner Meyer, *Mythos Deutsche Mark. Zur Geschichte einer abgeschafften Währung*, Berlin: Aufbau Taschenbuch, 2001, p. 56.

22 Ludwig Erhard, "20. Juni 1948 – Ende und Anfang," *Zeitschrift für das gesamte Kreditwesen* 26,12 (1973) (June 15), pp. 526–528, here p. 526.

23 Ludwig Erhard interviewed by Günter Gaus, telecasted April 10, 1963, in Günter Gaus, *Zur Person. Porträts in Frage und Antwort*, Munich: Feder, 1964, pp. 101–115, here p. 110. Online: www.rbb-online.de/zurperson/ interview_archiv/ludwig_erhard.html (Accessed June 8, 2021).

24 An English translation of Ludwig Erhard, *Wohlstand für Alle*, was published in numerous editions under the title *Prosperity through Competition*, 3rd ed., London: Thames & Hudson, 1962.

25 Luise Gräfin Schlippenbach, *Im Wandel stets dabei: Eine Zeitzeugin erinnert sich 1922–1997*, Munich: Allitera, 2005, p. 51.

26 All publications written and edited by Karl Hohmann and by Horst Friedrich Wünsche fall into this category. Hohmann was not only managing director (1974–1980) and chairman (1980–1991) of the Ludwig Erhard Foundation, but had also been head of Chancellor Ludwig Erhard's Office (1963–1966). Wünsche had been Erhard's sole research associate from 1973 until Erhard's death in 1977. Thereafter, he was employed by the Ludwig Erhard Foundation and moved up the career ladder to become its managing director from 1991 to 2007. Other examples of hagiographic or apologetic books include Jess M. Lukomski, *Ludwig Erhard. Der Mensch und der Politiker*, Düsseldorf: Econ, 1965. Gerhard Schröder et al. (eds.), *Ludwig Erhard. Beiträge zu seiner politischen Biographie. Festschrift zum fünfundsiebzigsten Geburtstag*, Berlin: Propyläen, 1972. Willi Schickling, *Entscheidung in Frankfurt. Ludwig Erhards Durchbruch zur Freiheit. 30 Jahre Deutsche Mark. 30 Jahre Soziale Marktwirtschaft*, Stuttgart: Seewald, 1978. Volkhard Laitenberger, *Ludwig Erhard: Der Nationalökonom als Politiker*, Göttingen: Muster-Schmidt, 1985. Schlippenbach, *Im Wandel stets dabei*. Ulrich Horstmann (ed.), *Ludwig Erhard Jetzt*, Munich: FinanzBuch, 2015. Thies Claussen, *Ludwig Erhard. Wegbereiter unseres Wohlstands gestern und heute*, Munich: Bayerisches

Staatsministerium für Wirtschaft, 2019. The Bavarian State Ministry of Economic Affairs, where Thies Claussen worked as state secretary, is an explicit supporter of the Ludwig Erhard Zentrum in Fürth. This publication contains a short bibliography. However, there are no notes.

27 The exceptions: Dieter Mühle, *Ludwig Erhard. Eine Biographie*, Berlin (East): Dietz, 1965. Ludolf Herbst, "Krisenüberwindung und Wirtschaftsneuordnung: Ludwig Erhards Beteiligung an den Nachkriegsplanungen am Ende des Zweiten Weltkrieges," *Vierteljahreshefte für Zeitgeschichte* 25 (1977), pp. 305–340.

28 A concise résumé up to his death has been published by Klaus Hildebrand, "Ludwig Erhard 1897–1977," in Lothar Gall (ed.), *Die Grossen Deutschen unserer Epoche*, Berlin: Propyläen, 1985, pp. 368–378. The article is mute on Erhard's commissioned work for top leaders of the SS, who were responsible for expropriating and deporting not only Jews but also the indigenous non-German population in occupied areas that were to be annexed to the German Reich. Erhard delivered assessments of economic implications of such policies, especially for the Saar and Lorraine on the Western border and the Western part of Poland in the East, as we will see in more detail below. More information on Erhard's life is contained in Karl Hohmann, "Aus dem Leben Ludwig Erhards: Die Jahre bis 1945," *Orientierungen zur Wirtschafts- und Gesellschaftspolitik 1982*, 1, pp. 50–60. Meike-Marie Thiele, "Ludwig Erhard kennenlernen, Zeitgeschichte erleben und Soziale Marktwirtschaft verstehen: Die Dauerausstellung des Ludwig Erhard Zentrums," in Das Ludwig Erhard Zentrum (ed.), *Ludwig Erhard: Der Weg zu Freiheit, Sozialer Marktwirtschaft, Wohlstand für Alle*, Bielefeld: Kerber, 2018, pp. 162–255.

29 Daniel Koerfer, *Kampf ums Kanzleramt. Erhard und Adenauer*, Munich: Benevento, 2020, p. 27.

30 Hohmann, "Aus dem Leben Ludwig Erhards," pp. 50–60, here p. 54.

31 Ibid., pp. 50–60. These four articles are reprinted in Karl Hohmann (ed.), *Ludwig Erhard: Gedanken aus fünf Jahrzehnten. Reden und Schriften*, Düsseldorf: Econ, 1988, pp. 21–47.

32 These passages – except where otherwise annotated – are based on Koerfer, *Kampf ums Kanzleramt*, pp. 21–30. Andreas Metz, *Die ungleichen Gründerväter. Adenauer und Erhards langer Weg an die Spitze der Bundesrepublik*, Konstanz: Konstanz University Press, 1998, pp. 28–35.

Hohmann, "Aus dem Leben Ludwig Erhards," pp. 50–60. Lukomski, *Ludwig Erhard*, pp. 28–34. Claussen, *Ludwig Erhard*, pp. 11–31. For Erhard's motives in his voluntary dismissal from the Nuremberg Institute in mid-1942, see: Laitenberger, *Ludwig Erhard*, p. 34. For the date of the bankruptcy filing, see: Ulrike Herrmann, *Deutschland, ein Wirtschaftsmärchen: Warum es kein Wunder ist, dass wir reich geworden sind*, 2nd ed. Frankfurt am Main: Westend, 2019, p. 56.

33 Ludwig Erhard interviewed by Günter Gaus, telecasted April 10, 1963, in Gaus, *Zur Person*, pp. 101–115, here pp. 107–108.

34 Metz, *Die ungleichen Gründerväter*, pp. 50, 62.

35 Volker Hentschel, *Ludwig Erhard. Ein Politikerleben*, Munich: Olzog, 1996, p. 42.

36 Koerfer, *Kampf ums Kanzleramt*, p. 118.

37 Ibid.

38 Quotations from Hentschel, *Ludwig Erhard*, p. 43.

39 Quotations and this paragraph in general from ibid.

40 Laitenberger, *Ludwig Erhard*, pp. 54–55. Koerfer, *Kampf ums Kanzleramt*, p. 118. Herrmann, *Deutschland, ein Wirtschaftsmärchen*, p. 70.

41 Both Hentschel, *Ludwig Erhard*, p. 42, and Koerfer, *Kampf ums Kanzleramt*, p. 118, use this wording.

42 Rich archival sources on the activities of the Special Agency for Money and Credit are accessible in the German Federal Archive in Coblenz in Record Group Z 32, with fifty-eight file units. The genesis of the currency problem and of the Special Agency for Money and Credit is vividly described in Herbert Alsheimer, *Ludwig Erhard: Der Weg unseres Landes aus den Trümmern des Krieges*, Bad Homburg: Taunus Sparkasse, 1997, pp. 35–63.

43 The ten most important experts are named in Alsheimer, *Ludwig Erhard*, p. 63.

44 For the establishment and work of the *Sonderstelle*, see: Metz, *Die ungleichen Gründerväter*, pp. 61–63.

45 Anthony J. Nicholls, *Freedom with Responsibility. The Social Market Economy in Germany, 1918–1963*, Oxford: Clarendon, 1994, p. 206.

46 Arne Weick, *Homburger Plan und Währungsreform. Kritische Analyse des Währungsreformplans der Sonderstelle Geld und Kredit und seiner Bedeutung für die westdeutsche Währungsreform von 1948*, St. Katharinen: Scripta Mercaturae, 1998, pp. 63–64.

47 Bundesarchiv/Institut für Zeitgeschichte (eds.), *Akten zur Vorgeschichte der Bundesrepublik Deutschland 1945–1949*, vol. 4, part 1, pp. 32–34. Gerold Ambrosius, *Die Durchsetzung der sozialen Marktwirtschaft in Westdeutschland 1945–1949*, Stuttgart: DVA, 1977, pp. 155–156.

48 Schlippenbach, *Im Wandel stets dabei*, p. 51.

49 "Engineer of a 'Miracle,'" in *Time Magazine*, October 28, 1957, pp. 21–24, here p. 21.

50 Hans Möller, "Die westdeutsche Währungsreform," in Deutsche Bundesbank (ed.), *Währung und Wirtschaft in Deutschland 1976–1975*, Frankfurt am Main: Knapp, 1976, pp. 448–449.

51 Ludwig Erhard interviewed by Günter Gaus, telecasted April 10, 1963, in Gaus, *Zur Person*, pp. 101–115, here p. 107. Also cited in Mühle, *Ludwig Erhard*, pp. 22–23 and note 22 on p. 171.

52 Laitenberger, *Ludwig Erhard*, p. 24.

53 Ludwig Erhard, "Herrn Schachts 'Grundsätze,'" in *Das Tagebuch* 1932, issue 34, pp. 1300–1306. It is reprinted in Hohmann (ed.), *Ludwig Erhard: Gedanken aus fünf Jahrzehnten*, pp. 30–36. For a summary and discussion of this article, see Mühle, *Ludwig Erhard*, pp. 23–27.

54 As quoted in Mühle, *Ludwig Erhard*, pp. 23, 26–27. Erhard's scathing review of Schacht's book is also dealt with in Hentschel, *Ludwig Erhard*, pp. 19–21.

55 Archiv der Ludwig-Erhard-Stiftung, Bonn, Erhard Papers IV, 14, as quoted in Koerfer, *Kampf ums Kanzleramt*, p. 108. This reminiscence of 1933 is no proof that, thereafter, Erhard did not make a U-turn on Nazi economic-policy doctrines, as Koerfer seems to assume.

56 Ludwig Erhard, "Marktverbände und Fertigindustrie an der Jahreswende," in *Die deutsche Fertigware* 1934, Heft 1, S. 3. As quoted in Karl Heinz Roth, "Das Ende eines Mythos. Ludwig Erhard und der Übergang der deutschen Wirtschaft von der Annexions- zur Nachkriegsplanung (1939 bis 1945), part 1: 1939 bis 1943," in *1999. Zeitschrift für Sozialgeschichte des 20. und 21. Jahrhunderts* 10 (1995), issue 4, pp. 53–93, summary p. 164 for the first quote and for the others p. 57. On the latter page, Roth also exploits other articles Erhard published during the 1930s before Hitler started the war. They also confirm Erhard's agreement with Nazi policies of economic concentration, cartelization, elimination of competition, as well as price controls and rationing.

57 Roth, "Das Ende eines Mythos," p. 97. For further publications since
    1933 in which Erhard outs himself as an endorser of Nazi economic
    policies, see 77–78.

58 Hentschel, *Ludwig Erhard*, pp. 25–26. See also: Manfred Görtemaker,
    *Geschichte der Bundesrepublik Deutschland: Von der Gründung bis zur
    Gegenwart*, Munich: Beck, 1999, pp. 142–143. He shares Hentschel's view
    of Erhard's political stand in the prewar Nazi years.

59 Herbst, "Krisenüberwindung und Wirtschaftsneuordnung," pp. 305–340.
    here pp. 314–316. For these issues, Herbst relies on Ludwig Erhard,
    "Einfluß" der Preisbildung und Preisbindung auf die Qualität und die
    Quantität des Angebots und der Nachfrage," in Georg Bergler/Ludwig
    Erhard (eds.), *Marktwirtschaft und Wirtschaftswissenschaft, Eine
    Festgabe aus dem Kreise der Nürnberger Schule zum 60. Geburtstage von
    Wilhelm Vershofen*, Berlin: Deutscher Betriebswirte Verlag, 1939,
    pp. 47–100. And on Ludwig Erhard, "Die Marktordnung," in Karl
    Theisinger (ed.), *Die Fiihrung des Betriebes, Festschrift zum 60.
    Geburtstag von Wilhelm Kalveram*, Berlin: Industrieverlag Spaeth &
    Linde, 1942, pp. 274–282.

60 Mühle, *Ludwig Erhard*, pp. 27–53.

61 Horst Friedrich Wünsche, *Ludwig Erhards Gesellschafts- und
    Wirtschaftskonzeption. Soziale Marktwirtschaft als Politische Ökonomie*,
    Stuttgart: Bonn Aktuell, 1986, p. 29.

62 Hohmann (ed.), *Ludwig Erhard: Gedanken aus fünf Jahrzehnten*.

63 Roth, "Das Ende eines Mythos," pp. 64–66.

64 Laitenberger, *Ludwig Erhard*, p. 33.

65 Archive of the Institut für Zeitgeschichte in Munich, ED 120–122, folio
    8–26.

66 Metz, *Die ungleichen Gründerväter*, pp. 34–35. Similarly Laitenberger,
    Ludwig Erhard, p. 33.

67 File of the *Reichskommissar für die Festigung deutschen Volkstums*, in
    Bundesarchiv Berlin-Lichterfelde, R 49/3537.

68 Ibid., folio 6. Bürckel performed functions of the *Reichskommissar für die
    Festigung deutschen Volkstums* in his territorial rule.

69 Ibid., folio 1–2.

70 Ibid., folio 7.

71 If not otherwise annotated, the following paragraphs are based on Koerfer,
    Kampf ums Kanzleramt, pp. 34–64.

72 "Haupttreuhandstelle Ost und Treuhandstellen." Online: https://portal
.ehri-project.eu/units/de-002429-r_144 (Accessed May 24, 2021). It is a
description of archival records, mainly available in the Bundesarchiv
Berlin-Lichterfelde.

73 Erhard "went through this Hitler dictatorship with a strange mixture of
inner distance, naiveté, and opportunism, often grossly underestimating
the murderous brutality of the regime or, in occupation areas – especially
in the East – where he must undoubtedly have come across its traces,
studiously looking the other way." Koerfer, *Kampf ums Kanzleramt*, p. 96.

74 See his letters to the Reich Commissariat for the Consolidation of German
Nationhood – both to SS Lieutenant General Greifelt and Councilor Schaefer
and to the Reich Commissioner himself, Reichsführer-SS Himmler, at the
address Berlin-Halensee, Kurfürstendamm 143/145 und 142/143 (to
Himmler). Bundesarchiv Berlin-Lichterfelde R 49/893, folio 1, 3–5.

75 The complete list of addressees as an attachment to Ludwig Erhard's letter
to the mayor of Nuremberg, Dr. W. Eickemeyer, of October 27, 1941 can be
found in the archive of the Institut für Zeitgeschichte in Munich, ED
120–122, folio 17–20.

76 Herrmann, *Deutschland, ein Wirtschaftsmärchen*, pp. 62–63.

77 Christian Gerlach, "Ludwig Erhard und die ‚Wirtschaft des neuen
deutschen Ostraums.' Ein Gutachten aus dem Jahr 1941 und Erhards
Beratertätigkeit bei der deutschen Annexionspolitik 1938–43," in *Beiträge
zur nationalsozialistischen Gesundheits- und Sozialpolitik* 13 (1997),
pp. 241–276.

78 Roth, "Das Ende eines Mythos," pp. 64–69.

79 Ibid., p. 61.

80 Quoted from Herrmann, *Deutschland, ein Wirtschaftsmärchen*, p. 63.

81 Quoted from ibid.

82 "Vermerk über eine Besprechung mit den Vertretern des Instituts für
Wirtschaftsbeobachtung der deutschen Fertigware, Nuremberg, 4. Juni
1942." Bundesarchiv Berlin-Lichterfelde R 49/893, folio 54.

83 Brief Erhard an den Reichskommissar für die Festigung deutschen
Volkstums, z.Hd. Herrn Regierungsrat Schaefer, vom 8. Juni 1942.
Bundesarchiv Berlin-Lichterfelde R 49/893, folio 56.

84 Numerous critical comments on Erhard's preliminary report, Erhard's
correspondence with Himmler's office, including his letters requesting the
assignment, and the terms of reference for the supplementary report, "The

Economy of the New German East," [*Die Wirtschaft des neuen deutschen Ostraumes*], assuming that all Poles would be expelled from it, are contained in the following file: Bundesarchiv Berlin-Lichterfelde R 49/ 893, passim.

85 Ralf Ptak, *Vom Ordoliberalismus zur Sozialen Marktwirtschaft. Stationen des Neoliberalismus in Deutschland*, Opladen: Leske & Buderich, 2004, pp. 82–87.

86 Ibid., p. 89.

87 Roth, "Das Ende eines Mythos," p. 93.

88 Walter J. Mueller, "Confidential Security Information. Biographical Data on Ludwig Erhard, from HICOG, Germany, 27 May 1952." National Archives at College Park MD, RG 263 Records of the Central Intelligence Agency. Second Release of Name Files Under the Nazi War Crimes and Japanese Imperial Government Disclosure Acts, 1936–2002, Entry ZZ-18, box 32, p. 4 of the document.

89 As quoted in Maja Brankovic, "Erhard und die NS-Zeit," in *Frankfurter Allgemeine Zeitung*, November 15, 2020, p. 20.

90 Koerfer, *Kampf ums Kanzleramt*, pp. 102–103.

91 Archive of the Institut für Zeitgeschichte in Munich, ED 120–122, folio 7, to which folios 8–28 were attached. Apparently, this OSI research was initiated in Fürth only after Erhard had been appointed Bavarian Minister of Economics on October 3, 1945.

92 I do not heed the warning against a misinterpretation of the letter as a prototype of a self-denazification certificate in Koerfer, *Kampf ums Kanzleramt*, p. 108. The content of the letter is more than clear on Erhard's white-washing attempt.

93 The Archive of the Ludwig-Erhard-Stiftung in Bonn holds Erhard's German draft of this letter to Captain Cofer, with handwritten corrections and additions, under call number NE 746A.

94 Erhard in his preface to a collection of his articles, interviews, speeches, and other statements in Ludwig Erhard, *Deutsche Wirtschaftspolitik. Der Weg der Sozialen Marktwirtschaft*, Düsseldorf: Econ, 1962, p. 8.

95 Letter of Dr. Ludwig Erhard to the US Military Government, Captain Cofer, Fürth / Bay. of May 24, 1945, in Archive of the Institut für Zeitgeschichte in Munich, ED 120–122, folios 3–6.

96 Herbst, "Krisenüberwindung und Wirtschaftsneuordnung," pp. 305–340.

97 Ibid., p. 339.

98 Ludwig Erhard, *Kriegsfinanzierung und Schuldenkonsolidierung*, Frankfurt am Main: Propyläen, 1977, p. 202.

99 Herbst, "Krisenüberwindung und Wirtschaftsneuordnung," p. 539.

100 Ludolf Herbst, *Der Totale Krieg und die Ordnung der Wirtschaft. Die Kriegswirtschaft im Spannungsfeld von Politik, Ideologie und Propaganda 1939–1945*, Stuttgart: DVA, 1982, pp. 176–177.

101 Claussen, *Ludwig Erhard*, p. 28. Alfred C. Mierzejewski, *Ludwig Erhard. A Biography*, Chapel Hill: North Carolina University Press, 2004, p. 14. Roth, "Das Ende eines Mythos," pp. 92–123 with summary pp. 248–249, here p. 100.

102 "formierte Gesellschaft." Online: formierteGesellschaftausdemLexikonwissen.de (Accessed March 19, 2021).

103 Gerhard Schröder, "Zur Einführung," in Schröder et al. (eds.), *Ludwig Erhard*, pp. 13–17, here p. 15.

104 He had subdivided his 144-page book of 1947 into two parts: "I. Die Bewährungsprobe der Wirtschaftslenkung" ("The Test of Economic Governance") and "II. Soziale Marktwirtschaft" ("Social Market Economy"). He had thus introduced the term in West Germany's political circles. Alfred Müller-Armack, *Wirtschaftslenkung und Marktwirtschaft*, Hamburg: Verlag für Wirtschafts- und Sozialpolitik, 1947, p. 59. The author had been a Nazi Party member since 1933. During that year he published a sixty-two-page booklet titled *Staatsidee und Wirtschaftsordnung im neuen Reich*, Berlin: Junker & Dünnhaupt, 1933. In footnote 1 on pp. 11–12, he states that he had already recognized the "emergence of a new historical activism" at his first encounter with fascism in Rome in 1924. And on p. 19 he writes: "Only in National Socialism does historical feeling, which has always been one of the most innate elements of the German spirit, take on the form in which it acquires the power to shape history." (I thank my colleague and friend Gerd Hardach for this reference.) Like many former Nazis, Müller-Armack joined the CDU early after the war. From 1940 to 1950 he was Professor of Economics at the University of Münster and from 1950 to his retirement in 1970 at the University of Cologne. In 1948 he was appointed to the newly founded Scientific Advisory Board of Erhard's Economic Administration of the Bizone, the forerunner of the Scientific Advisory Board of Erhard's Federal Ministry of Economics after 1949, in which he remained a member. In 1952 Erhard appointed him head

(*Ministerialdirigent*) of the Economics Ministry's department for economic policy and in 1958 the Ministry's State Secretary (*Staatssekretär*) for European Affairs. Konrad Adenauer Foundation, History of the CDU, Significant Figures, Alfred Müller-Armack. Online: Konrad-Adenauer-Stiftung-GeschichtederCDU-AlfredMüller-Armack(kas.de) (Accessed August 16, 2021).

105 Lucius D. Clay, "Glückwunschadresse," in Schröder et al. (eds.), *Ludwig Erhard*, pp. 39–41, here p. 41.

106 Walter J. Mueller, "Confidential Security Information. Biographical Data on Ludwig Erhard, from HICOG, Germany, 27 May 1952." National Archives at College Park MD, RG 263 Records of the Central Intelligence Agency. Second Release of Name Files Under the Nazi War Crimes and Japanese Imperial Government Disclosure Acts, 1936–2002, Entry ZZ-18, box 32, p. 7 of the document. A photostatic copy of Mueller's typewritten 8-page bio of Erhard is also contained in RG 319 Office of the Assistant Chief of Staff for Intelligence, G-2, Entry A1 134-B, box 186, folder "Ludwig Erhard," fols. 75–82, here fol. 81.

107 Erhard, "20. Juni 1948 – Ende und Anfang," pp. 526–528, here p. 528.

108 Hohmann, "Aus dem Leben Ludwig Erhards," pp. 50–60.

109 Karl Hohmann, *Ludwig Erhard (1897–1977). Eine Biographie*, herausgegeben von der Ludwig-Erhard-Stiftung e.V. Bonn, Düsseldorf: ST-Verlag, 1997. Online: www.ludwig-erhard.de/wp-content/uploads/ Biographie.pdf (Accessed August 8, 2021).

110 Horst Friedrich Wünsche, "Zu jüngsten Falschmeldungen, die Ludwig Erhard verunglimpfen." Publication of the Ludwig-Erhard-Stiftung, August 31, 2018. Online: www.ludwig-erhard.de/orientierungen/zu-juengsten-falschmeldungen-die-ludwig-erhard-verunglimpfen/?pdf=8495 (Accessed August 10, 2021).

111 Günter Keiser, "Zur Vor- und Frühgeschichte der D-Mark," in *Zeitschrift für das gesamte Kreditwesen* 25 (1973), pp. 530–536, here p. 530.

112 Johannes Bähr/Christopher Kopper, *Industrie, Politik und Gesellschaft. Der BDI und seine Vorgänger 1919–1990*, Göttingen: Wallstein, 2019, p. 162.

113 Michael Brackmann, *Vom totalen Krieg zum Wirtschaftswunder. Die Vorgeschichte der westdeutschen Währungsreform 1948*, Essen: Klartext, 1993.

114 Michael Brackmann, "Erhards doppelter Coup," in *General-Anzeiger Bonn*, 18 June 2018, pp. 10–11. Michael Brackmann, "70 Jahre

Währungsreform – Aus den Trümmern zum Wirtschaftswunder," in *Handelsblatt*, June 20, 2018, pp. 10–11.

115 This trace of the intellectual origin of the 1948 reforms has also been treated by Bernhard Löffler, *Soziale Marktwirtschaft und administrative Praxis. Das Bundeswirtschaftsministerium unter Ludwig Erhard*, Wiesbaden: Steiner, 2002, esp. pp. 58–59.

116 Karl Günther Weiss, *Wahrheit und Wirklichkeit: der Weg aus den Weltkriegen in die Soziale Marktwirtschaft und eine künftige Weltordnung*, Homburg-Saarpfalz: Ermer, 1996, pp. 541, 564–565, 569.

117 Ibid., p. 541.

118 Heinz Boberach, "Ohlendorf, Otto," in *Neue Deutsche Biographie* 19 (1999), pp. 485–486. Online: www.deutsche-biographie.de/sfz73260.html (Accessed August 11, 2021). For Ohlendorf's vita see also: David Kittermann, "Otto Ohlendorf – Gralshüter des Nationalsozialismus," in Ronald Smelser/Enrico Syring (eds.), *Die SS: Elite unter dem Totenkopf*. Paderborn: Schöningh, 2000, pp. 379–393. Christian Ingrao, *Hitlers Elite. Die Wegbereiter des nationalsozialistischen Massenmordes*, Berlin: Propyläen, 2012, passim. Reprint: Bonn: *Bundeszentrale für politische Bildung*, 2012.

119 Weiss, *Wahrheit und Wirklichkeit*, pp. 570, 575, 577; 590.

120 Ibid., pp. 580, 666, for the rediscovery of Erhard's *Kriegsfinanzierung und Schuldenkonsolidierung*, p. 656. See also Meyer, *Mythos Deutsche Mark*, pp. 21–23.

121 Ohlendorf was not the only Nazi who preferred a competition-based market economy with its performance incentives for private initiative over a state planned economy. Statements by Hitler himself bear this out. A command economy was considered necessary only for the organization of armament and especially for the wartime economy. After the end of the war, under market-based conditions, a strong state was to "enforce the primacy of politics also in the area of economic policy measures in order to ensure economic and social stabilization internally." In this respect, the economic policy concept of the Nazis was close to the ordoliberalism of the Freiburg School, which was formed during the Nazi era. For a finely differentiated and well documented account of this: Ptak, *Vom Ordoliberalismus zur Sozialen Marktwirtschaft*, pp. 62–72, here p. 67.

122 Weiss, *Wahrheit und Wirklichkeit*, pp. 570–571.

123 Ibid., p. 649.

124 Ibid., p. 667.

125 Ibid., p. 649.

126 Ptak, *Vom Ordoliberalismus zur Sozialen Marktwirtschaft*, p. 207.

127 Daniel Koerfer, "Ludwig Erhard – Fundamentaloptimist und Vater der Sozialen Marktwirtschaft," in Ludwig Erhard Zentrum (ed.), *Ludwig Erhard. Der Weg zu Freiheit, Sozialer Marktwirtschaft, Wohlstand für Alle*, Bielefeld: Kerber, 2018, pp. 60–75, here p. 69.

128 Weiss, *Wahrheit und Wirklichkeit*, p. 552.

129 Thiele, "Ludwig Erhard kennenlernen," pp. 162–255, here p. 198.

130 Ptak, *Vom Ordoliberalismus zur Sozialen Marktwirtschaft*, p. 79.

131 "Memorandum to the Office in Charge. Subject: Erhard, Ludwig." National Archives at College Park MD, RG 319 Office of the Assistant Chief of Staff for Intelligence, G-2, Entry A1 134-B, box 186, folder "Ludwig Erhard," fol. 67–68.

132 "Subject: Letter of Appreciation of 21 October 1946," National Archives at College Park MD, RG 319 Office of the Assistant Chief of Staff for Intelligence, G-2, Entry A1 134-B, box 186, folder "Ludwig Erhard," fol. 60.

133 Ludwig Erhard interviewed by Günter Gaus, telecasted April 10, 1963, in Gaus, *Zur Person*, pp. 101–115, here pp. 107–108.

134 Hentschel, *Ludwig Erhard*, pp. 21–24.

135 Koerfer, *Kampf ums Kanzleramt*, p. 31.

136 Letter of Dr. Ludwig Erhard to the US Military Government, Captain Cofer, Fürth / Bay. of 24 May 1945, in Archive of the Institut für Zeitgeschichte in Munich, ED 120–122, folio 3.

137 Ludwig Erhard Zentrum (LEZ), *Ludwig Erhard. Der Weg zur Freiheit, Sozialer Marktwirtschaft, Wohlstand für Alle*, Bielefeld: Kerber, 2018, p. 199.

138 Länderrat des Amerikanischen Besatzungsgebiets (ed.), *Statistisches Handbuch von Deutschland 1928–1944*, Munich: Ehrenwirth, 1949, p. 473.

139 Volker Caspari/Klaus Lichtblau, *Franz Oppenheimer. Ökonom und Soziologe der ersten Stunde*, Frankfurt am Main: Societäts-Verl., 2014, chapter XIV "Von der Emeritierung bis zur Auswanderung," pp. 151–164.

140 Hohmenn, "Aus dem Leben Ludwig Erhards," pp. 50–60, here p. 57, note 45.

141 My translation from Ludwig Erhard, "Zu meiner Denkschrift 1943/44,"
in Erhard, *Kriegsfinanzierung und Schuldenkonsolidierung*, pp. vii–xiii,
here p. x. In Vershofen's correspondence, Koerfer detected evidence of
another Goerdeler visit to the Nuremberg Institute on February 21, 1941,
concerning a new order for the Institute from the Robert Bosch electric
company, which had employed Goerdeler as a consultant. Koerfer, *Kampf
ums Kanzleramt*, p. 90. Erhard was probably not in town, as he might
have been working in SS General Bürckel's so-called *Westmark* on that
day. Otherwise, he would certainly have mentioned his second personal
encounter with Goerdeler in Nuremberg on that occasion.

142 Erhard, "Zu meiner Denkschrift 1943/44," p. xii. For Goerdeler's lecture
on Erhard's invitation in Nuremberg see ibid., p. x. Laitenberger, *Ludwig
Erhard*, p. 37.

143 A pathbreaking biography of Carl Goerdeler has been written by Gerhard
Ritter, *Carl Goerdeler und die deutsche Widerstandsbewegung*,
Stuttgart: DVA, 1954. More recently Goerdeler's daughter has published
Marianne Meyer-Krahmer, *Carl Goerdeler. Mut zum Widerstand: eine
Tochter erinnert sich*, rev. ed., Leipzig: Leipzig University Press, 1998.

144 Inge Marßolek, *Die Denunziantin. Die Geschichte der Helene Schwärzel
1944–47*, Bremen: Temmen, 1993, pp. 32–35, 38–42.

145 Ibid., pp. 52–89. See also "Helene Schwärzel," in Wikipedia. Online:
https://de.wikipedia.org/wiki/Helene_Schw%C3%A4rzel (Accessed
September 13, 2021). The story of Helene Schwärzel's denunciation of
Goerdeler has also been subject of the German movie *Die Denunziantin*,
which came out in May 1993.

146 Erhard, "Zu meiner Denkschrift 1943/44," pp. vii–viii.

147 Ibid., pp. xii–xiii.

148 Ibid., p. xii.

149 His attempts at promoting Nazi ideology via the *Reichsgruppe Industrie*
are documented in Bähr/Kopper, *Industrie, Politik und Gesellschaft*,
p. 104. His attempt at securing a postwar career as press and
communication spokesman for the Federation of German Industries (BDI)
ended in 1951. The BDI kept him on the payroll, but relegated his
employment to its Cultural Circle (*Kulturkreis*) of the German Economy.
Ibid., p. 193.

150 Ludwig Erhard interviewed by Günter Gaus, telecasted April 10, 1963, in
Gaus, *Zur Person*, pp. 101–115, here p. 108.

151 Ulrike Herrmann, *Kein Kapitalismus ist auch keine Lösung. Die Krise der heutigen Ökonomie oder Was wir von Smith, Marx und Keynes lernen können*, Frankfurt am Main: Westend, 2016, pp. 211–212.

152 Herrmann, *Deutschland, ein Wirtschaftsmärchen*, pp. 53–80.

153 Don D. Humphrey, "Epilogue," in John H. Backer, *Winds of History. The German Years of Lucius DuBignon Clay*, New York: Van Nostrand Reinhold, 1983, pp. 292–293.

154 "Bekenntnis der Professoren an den deutschen Universitäten und Hochschulen zu Adolf Hitler und dem nationalsozialistischen Staat," p. 134. Online: Bekenntnis der Professoren an den Universitäten und Hochschulen zu Adolf Hitler und dem nationalsozialistischen Staat; überreicht vom Nationalsozialistischen Lehrerbund Deutschland-Sachsen : Nationalsozialistischer Lehrerbund, Deutschland-Sachsen: Free Download, Borrow, and Streaming : Internet Archive (Accessed March 20, 2021).

155 Bundesarchiv Berlin-Lichterfelde, R 49/893, folio 87–88.

156 Bähr/Kopper, *Industrie, Politik und Gesellschaft*, pp. 160–161. For Erhard's close relations with top managers of big indusry see also Herbst, "Krisenüberwindung und Wirtschaftsneuordnung," pp. 305–340, here pp. 321–322. For the broad scholarly discussion since 1939 of war finance, debt consolidation, and a return to market-economy conditions after the war, see ibid., pp. 309–314. For Erhard's involvement in the planning of the transition from a wartime to peacetime economy since 1944 by RI and RWM, see ibid., pp. 327–337. And Wolfgang Schumann, "Nachkriegsplanungen der Reichsgruppe Industrie im Herbst 1944. Eine Dokumentation," in *Jahrbuch für Wirtschaftsgeschichte* 13 (1972), Part 3, pp. 259–296.

157 Roth, "Das Ende eines Mythos," pp. 92–123.

158 Koerfer, *Kampf ums Kanzleramt*, p. 72.

159 Quoted from Metz, *Die ungleichen Gründerväter*, pp. 50, 62. For more information on this probably first parliamentary committee of inquiry in all of West Germany see ibid., pp. 57–60.

160 Sebastian Haffner, "Fall Seebohm – Fall Erhard," in the weekly *Stern Hamburg* 17 (1964), issue no. 23 (June 2), pp. 6–7, here p. 7.

161 Heinz Reintges, *Wendezeiten. Im Strom des Jahrhunderts. Im Dienst der Industrie. Im Bann der Kohlenpolitik*, Essen: Glückauf, 1989, p. 130.

162 Ibid., pp. 220–221. As to the functions of Burckhardt und Reintges: ibid., pp. 66–67, 69.

163 Hans-Peter Schwarz, *Die Ära Adenauer. Gründerjahre der Republik 1949–1957*, Stuttgart: Deutsche Verlags-Anstalt, 1981, p. 41.

164 Mierzejewski, *Ludwig Erhard*, p. 90.

165 Walter J. Mueller, "Confidential Security Information. Biographical Data on Ludwig Erhard, from HICOG, Germany, 27 May 1952." National Archives at College Park MD, RG 263 Records of the Central Intelligence Agency. Second Release of Name Files Under the Nazi War Crimes and Japanese Imperial Government Disclosure Acts, 1936–2002, Entry ZZ-18, box 32, p. 7 of the document. A photostatic copy of Mueller's typewritten 8-page bio of Erhard is also contained in RG 319 Office of the Assistant Chief of Staff for Intelligence, G-2, Entry A1 134-B, box 186, folder "Ludwig Erhard," fols. 75–82, here fol. 81.

166 National Archives at College Park MD, RG 319 Office of the Assistant Chief of Staff for Intelligence, G-2, Entry A1 134-B, box 186, folder "Ludwig Erhard," fols. 46–50, 51–52, 58–59, 73.

167 "Subject: Dissension in High Government Circles." National Archives at College Park MD, RG 319 Office of the Assistant Chief of Staff for Intelligence, G-2, Entry A1 134-B, box 186, folder "Ludwig Erhard," fol. 35.

168 "Subject: Possible Resignation of the Federal Minister of Economics, Prof. Dr. Ludwig Erhard. Special Team Report # 80." National Archives at College Park MD, RG 319 Office of the Assistant Chief of Staff for Intelligence, G-2, Entry A1 134-B, box 186, folder "Ludwig Erhard," fol. 34.

169 United States Department of Justice. Federal Bureau of Investigation, Washington, DC, 11 December 1957, "Ludwig Erhard." National Archives at College Park MD, RG 263 Records of the Central Intelligence Agency. Second Release of Name Files Under the Nazi War Crimes and Japanese Imperial Government Disclosure Acts, 1936–2002, Entry ZZ-18, box 32.

170 "Dispatch of 10 June 1963 from Chief, EE to Chief of Base, Frankfurt; Chief of Base, Bonn; Chief of Station, Germany; Subject: Derogatory allegation re CASPHERE." National Archives at College Park MD, RG 263 Records of the Central Intelligence Agency. Second Release of Name Files Under the Nazi War Crimes and Japanese Imperial Government

Disclosure Acts, 1936–2002, Entry ZZ-18, box 32. Identity-2 is Dr. Elsie Kuehn-Leitz, sister of the owner of the Leitz Company for cameras and other optical instruments. Identity-3 is her former husband Dr. Kurt Hermann Kuehn, who had been Erhard's collaborator on planning the economic integration of the German-occupied territories in the East.

171 "Research Aid: Cryptonyms and Terms in Declassified CIA Files. Nazi War Crimes and Japanese Imperial Government Records Disclosure Acts." Online: www.archives.gov/files/iwg/declassified-records/rg-263-cia-records/second-release-lexicon.pdf (Accessed April 27, 2022).

172 National Archives at College Park MD, RG 263 Records of the Central Intelligence Agency. Second Release of Name Files Under the Nazi War Crimes and Japanese Imperial Government Disclosure Acts, 1936–2002, Entry ZZ-18, box 32.

173 Lukomski, *Ludwig Erhard*. Jess M. Lukomski, *Erhard*, Milan: Della Volpe, 1966.

174 For this and the previous two quotations see National Archives at College Park MD, RG 263 Records of the Central Intelligence Agency. Second Release of Name Files Under the Nazi War Crimes and Japanese Imperial Government Disclosure Acts, 1936–2002, Entry ZZ-18, box 1–145. Online: https://catalog.archives.gov/id/640446 (Accessed May 14, 2022).

3 EDWARD A. TENENBAUM'S FAMILY ROOTS, ADOLESCENCE, AND MILITARY EXPERIENCE UNTIL 1946

1 In Social Security Administration records (NARA RG 47) Robert F. Tenenbaum assumed different last names, namely Tannenbaum (July 30, 1975) and Tannebaum (August 27, 1984), while he kept listing Otilia and Joseph Tenenbaum as his mother and father. See online: https://aad.archives.gov/aad/display-partial-records.jsp?f=5138&mtch=5&q=Robert+Tenenbaum&cat=all&dt=3080&tf=F (Accessed November 13, 2019). This might indicate that he wanted to cut off his identification with his father's and mother's family and activities. For Robert F. Tannenbaum's death see online: https://aad.archives.gov/aad/display-partial-records.jsp?f=5058&mtch=1&q=Robert+F.+Tannenbaum&cat=all&dt=3020&tf=F (Accessed November 14, 2019).

2 Online: https://de.findagrave.com/memorial/74863780 (Accessed November 14, 2019).

3 Ibid.

4 For these and most of the following biographical details see the article "Joseph Tenenbaum," in *Who is Who in America* 18–31 (1934–1935 to 1960–1961). Also article "Dr. Joseph L. Tenenbaum Dies; Urologist, Zionist and Author," in *New York Times*, December 11, 1961, p. 31. Article "Joseph Tenenbaum, Urologist, Author," Online: http://prabook.com/web/person-view.html?profileId=1085245# (Accessed November 11, 2017). Joshua Fogel, "YOYSEF-LEYB TENENBOYM (JOSEPH TENENBAUM) (May 22, 1887–December 10, 1961)," posted October 26, 2016 in Yiddish Leksikon. Online: http://yleksikon.blogspot.de/2016/10/yoysef-leyb-tenenboym-joseph-tenenbaum.html (Accessed December 11, 2017). Article "Tenenbaum, Joseph," in *The Universal Jewish Encyclopedia*, vol. 10, New York: Universal Jewish Encyclopedia Co., Inc., 1948, p. 197.

5 See article "Treaty of Saint-Germain 1919," in *Encyclopaedia Britannica*. Online: www.britannica.com/event/Treaty-of-Saint-Germain (Accessed November 26, 2017).

6 Biographical note, Joseph Tenenbaum Papers (RG-21/1987.081), United States Holocaust Memorial Museum Archive, Washington, DC. Online: https://collections.ushmm.org/search/catalog/irn554130 (Accessed October 7, 2019).

7 Since 1919 Lemberg belonged to the newly created Polish state and renamed Lwow. Since the early days of World War II it was part of the area of Poland which due to the Hitler-Stalin-Pact, signed on August 24, 1939, had been annexed by the Soviet Union after the German armed forces had defeated Poland. Lemberg was called Lvov under Soviet rule. After Germany's attack on Russia it became part of *Generalgouvernement Poland*. With the advance of the Red Army toward Germany it belonged again to Soviet territory and was again named Lvov. Since 1991 it is part of Ukrainian territory under the name of Lviv. As to the different names for the city see online: https://ome-lexikon.uni-oldenburg.de/orte/lemberg-lviv/ (Accessed January 21, 2019).

8 "Lemberg (Lviv, Lwow, Lvov). Die Hauptstadt Ostgaliziens. Städte und Regionen der Ukraine," Online: www.dreizackreisen.de/Lemberg-Lvov-Lwow-Lviv-Leopolis-Galizien-Westukraine (Accessed December 26, 2017).

9 For the dates see Thomas Childers, *The Third Reich. A History of Nazi Germany*, New York: Simon & Schuster, 2017, pp. 2–3.

10 See article "Adolf Hitler in Wien," Online: www.was-war-wann.de/personen/adolf_hitler_wien.html (Accessed November 11, 2017). For further details see Brigitte Hamann, *Hitlers Wien: Lehrjahre eines Diktators*, 3rd ed., Munich: Piper, 1999, pp. 496–512. Ralf Georg Reuth, *Hitlers Judenhass. Klischee und Wirklichkeit*, Munich: Piper, 2009, pp. 21–49 esp. pp. 29–30. Using mainly Hamann's findings Reuth criticizes that the early biographers of Hitler, namely Allan Bullock, Joachim Fest and Ian Kershaw, have followed Hitler's own account in *Mein Kampf* that his years in Vienna were, indeed, the seedbed of his antisemitism. For a careful weighting of evidence lending itself to ambivalent interpretations see Childers, *The Third Reich. A History of Nazi Germany*, pp. 2–13. The author reaches the conclusion "that there is no documented evidence of Hitler making anti-Semitic remarks or displaying anti-Semitic attitudes while in Vienna." (p. 12). Pioneering the use of a wealth of primary sources of the List Regiment in which Private Hitler served as a dispatch runner throughout World War I, Thomas Weber, *Hitler's First War. Adolf Hitler, the Men of the List Regiment, and the First World War*, Oxford: Oxford University Press, 2010. The chapter *Epilogue* (esp. p. 346) shows that Hitler's radicalization did not take place during World War I either, but thereafter. Most of his comrades were patriotic and politically conservative, but at the same time open for developing parliamentary democracy further, as had already happened before and toward the end of World War I and in a leapfrogging manner with the foundation of the Weimar Republic in 1919. The latest book adds little to Brigitte Hamann's findings: Hannes Leidinger/Christian Rapp, *Hitler. Prägende Jahre. Kindheit und Jugend 1889–1914*, Salzburg: Residenz, 2020.

11 Sven Felix Kellerhoff, "Adolf Hitler war im Ersten Weltkrieg ein Feigling," in *Die Welt* 16.09.2010. Online: www.welt.de/kultur/article9673138/Adolf-Hitler-war-im-Ersten-Weltkrieg-ein-Feigling.html (Accessed November 27, 2017).

12 Thomas Weber, *Becoming Hitler: The Making of a Nazi*, Oxford: Oxford University Press, 2017, pp. 109–110.

13 Weber, *Hitler's First War*, pp. 11–12. More on Weisberger's artistic achievements, connections with famous artists in Munich and abroad, and international travels see his biography online: www.kettererkunst.de/bio/AlbertWeisgerber-1878-1915.php (Accessed September 25, 2019).

14 Klaus Reinhardt, *Die Wende vor Moskau. Das Scheitern der Strategie Hitlers im Winter 1941/42*, Stuttgart: DVA, 1972.

15 For further details see Weber, *Hitler's First War*, pp. 255–296, 340–344.

16 Social Security death index. Online: www.genealogybank.com/doc/ssdi/news/112D17FD403F8E3F?h=49&fname=&lname=Tenenbaum&fullname=&rgfromDate=01/01/1970&rgtoDate=01/01/1980&formDate=&formDateFlex=exact&dateType=range&kwinc=&kwexc=&page=3 (Accessed January 7, 2020).

17 Tenenbaum's entry in *Yale Yearbook, Class of 1942*, p. 569.

18 Online: https://phaidra.univie.ac.at/detail_object/o:104996 (Accessed March 5, 2020).

19 Ibid.

20 Ibid.

21 Ibid.

22 Ibid.

23 "Tenenbaum, Joseph," in *Who's Who in America*, vol. 20 (1938–1939), p. 2447. "Tenenbaum, Joseph," in Isaac Landman (ed.), *The Universal Jewish Encyclopedia*, vol. 10, New York: Universal Jewish Encyclopedia Co., 1948, p. 197.

24 Online: http://prabook.com/web/person-view.html?profileId=1085245 (Accessed December 10, 2017).

25 Joshua Fogel, "YOYSEF-LEYB TENENBOYM (JOSEPH TENENBAUM) (May 22, 1887–December 10, 1961)," posted 26 October 2016 in Yiddish Leksikon. Online: http://yleksikon.blogspot.de/2016/10/yoysef-leyb-tenenboym-joseph-tenenbaum.html (Accessed December 11, 2017).

26 www.libertyellisfoundation.org/passenger (Accessed December 30, 2017). Search for Joseph Tenenbaum and Otylia (this spelling) Tenenbaum separately. They traveled on the same vessel to New York, but at different dates.

27 The size of the steamship was 11,146 gross tons. It could carry 1,114 passengers, of which 446 first class, 116 second class and 552 third class (steerage passengers).

28 "Tenenbaum, Joseph L. (1887–1961)." Encyclopedia.com. Online: encyclopedia.com/religion/encyclopedias-almanacs-transcripts-and-maps/ tenenbaum-joseph-l (Accessed March 14, 2023).

29 This paragraph is based on Carole Fink, *Defending the Rights of Others. The Great Powers, the Jews, and International Minority Protection, 1878–1938*, Cambridge: Cambridge University Press, 2004, especially pp. 101–121.

30 A letter by the Medical Advisory Board, 175 East Broadway, New York of 26 March 1930 was addressed to "Dr. J. Tenenbaum, 2 East 77 Street, New York City." Joseph Tenenbaum Papers, 1908–1990. This address was used by different senders in the following years, too. On microfiche: RG-21.001.01, fiche 1 to 3 of 3. Archive US Holocaust Memorial Museum (USHMM), Washington, DC. This obviously was the correct postal address.

31 *Who's Who in America* was and is a biennial publication. It only lists living Americans. Therefore, his entry in vol. 31 (1960–1961) was the last one.

32 The obituary in the *New York Times* also refers to this address.

33 "Investigation Data Request, Economic Cooperation Administration, Form ECA-1, Rev. 12–48," in Edward A. Tenenbaum Papers, box 8, folder: Personnel File. HSTPL.

34 Online: http://prabook.com/web/person-view.html?profileId=1085245 (Accessed December 10, 2017).

35 Biographical note, Joseph Tenenbaum Papers (RG-21/1987.081), United States Holocaust Memorial Museum Archive, Washington, DC. Online: https://collections.ushmm.org/search/catalog/irn554130 (Accessed October 7, 2019).

36 The titles in English: *Our question of peace, from a Zionist* and *The Jewish pogrom in Lemberg, November 1918–January 1919.*

37 Title in English: *The Jewish question in Poland.*

38 I collected the titles from the Joseph Tenenbaum entries in *Who's Who in America* 18 (1934–1935) to 31 (1960–1961). And from Joshua Fogel "YOYSEF-LEYB TENENBOYM (JOSEPH TENENBAUM) (May 22, 1887– December 10, 1961)," posted 26 October 2016 in Yiddish Leksikon. Online: http://yleksikon.blogspot.de/2016/10/yoysef-leyb-tenenboym-joseph-tenenbaum.html (Accessed December 11, 2017).

39 Biographical note, Joseph Tenenbaum Papers (RG-21/1987.081), United States Holocaust Memorial Museum Archive, Washington, DC. Online: https://collections.ushmm.org/search/catalog/irn554130 (Accessed October 7, 2019).

40 Article "Dr. Joseph L. Tenenbaum Dies; Urologist, Zionist and Author," p. 31.

41 Ray H. Abrams, "Review of Joseph Tenenbaum, *The Riddle of Woman*," in *The Annals of the American Academy of Political and Social Science* 192 (1937), p. 251.

42 Laura Lou Brookman, "Women Loom As Future's Stronger Sex. Dr. Tenenbaum Says Man's Dominance Threatened By Feminine Rise," in *Sandusky Star Journal* (Ohio), 20 November 1936, p. 13 (Accessed March 13, 2020 via newspaperarchive.com).

43 Carol Bird, "A Riddle. What Will America Do About Its Women?" In *Sunday Journal and Star* (Lincoln, Nebraska), March 21, 1937, p. 44 (Accessed March 13, 2020 via newspaperarchive.com).

44 The school and the NYC department of education currently reveal this about Stuyvesant High School history: "Stuyvesant High School was founded in 1904 as a 'manual training school for boys.' ... Incoming ninth and tenth graders are selected by an examination that is open to all residents of New York City. Stuyvesant has served as a premier school for the development of talent in science, mathematics and technology. From its inception, it has been a school which serves an immigrant population. The school was housed in the same 15th Street building for almost ninety years. In September 1992, a multi-million dollars building was completed in Battery Park City for Stuyvesant High School. Four Nobel Laureates, as well as a host of leaders in science, mathematics, government, law, the arts, and music, are included among the graduates. With our outstanding record of academic achievement and our commitment to excellence, we feel that Stuyvesant High School merits the national recognition it has continued to maintain." Online: http://stuy.enschool.org/apps/pages/index.jsp?uREC_ID=126631&type=d&pREC_ID=251657&hideMenu=1 (Accessed December 9, 2017). A more objective assessment of Stuy's high school rank can be derived from the most recent US News and World Report ranking. Currently Stuy is ranked thirteenth of 522 public high schools in New York City, twenty-first in STEM high schools and seventy-first in public high schools nationwide. Online: www.usnews.com/

education/best-high-schools/new-york/districts/new-york-city-public-schools/stuyvesant-high-school-13092 (Accessed December 16, 2017).

45 Online: www.tandfonline.com/doi/abs/10.1080/02783190903386561?src=recsys&journalCode=uror20 (Accessed December 10, 2017).

46 Online: https://en.wikipedia.org/wiki/Stuyvesant_High_School#Original_building (Accessed December 10, 2017).

47 See online: https://en.wikipedia.org/wiki/The_Spectator (Stuyvesant_High_School) (Accessed April 18, 2018).

48 Email of Anne Toohey, born Tenenbaum, to me of August 30, 2017.

49 Email of the archivist of Ecolint, Alejandro Rodriguez-Giovo, to Christel McDonald January 17, 2018.

50 Online: https://en.wikipedia.org/wiki/International_School_of_Geneva (Accessed January 13, 2018).

51 Email of the archivist of Ecolint, Alejandro Rodriguez-Giovo, to Christel McDonald January 17, 2018.

52 École Internationale de Genève, *Journal Annuel*, Juin 1938, p. 36. Courtesy of teacher and archivist of Ecolint, Alejandro Rodriguez-Giovo.

53 See Section 6.2.

54 According to the Ecolint register for 1937, Tenenbaum arrived at the school on September 14, 1937, was enrolled as the 991st student since the founding of the school in 1924 and left in July 1938. A photo of the register page was made available to me courtesy of Alejandro Rodriguez-Giovo.

55 Tenenbaum's entry in *Yale Yearbook, Class of 1942*, p. 569.

56 "Cubs Endorse Prom, Suggest Glenn Miller," in *Yale Daily News*, November 29, 1939, p. 1.

57 "Glenn Miller Calls US Colleges Hothouses For Budding Songs, Bands," in *Yale Daily News*, December 17, 1940, p. 1.

58 "Captain Glenn Miller Rehearses Air Force Band in Woolsey Hall," in *Yale Daily News*, April 21, 1943. For other activities of Glenn Miller on Yale campus see: "Air Corps Band to Give Concert. Glenn Miller to Conduct; Entertainers Make Debut," *Yale News Digest* no. 39 October 2, 1943, p. 1. "Glenn Miller Featured on WOCD Interview," *Yale News Digest* no. 58 November 30, 1943, p. 1.

59 James Aiken Fisher/Mark McDonald Lindsey/Frank Arnott Sprole (eds.), *A History of the Class of 1942 Yale University*, New Haven: Yale University Press, 1942 (= *Yale Yearbook 1942*), p. 569.

60 "Student Allocations to nine College Units Announced," in *Yale Daily News*, March 6, 1939, pp. 1, 3.

61 "Yale Awards 13 Prizes for High Freshman Marks," in *The Boston Globe*, October 6, 1939, p. 2 (Accessed via newspapers.com June 9, 2019).

62 Fisher/McDonald Lindsey/Sprole (eds.), *Yale Yearbook 1942*, p. 569.

63 "Yale Graduates Numbered 607," *The Waterbury Democrat*, Waterbury, CT, vol. LX, issue 132, June 8, 1942, p. 5. The article appeared a day before graduation ceremonies at Yale.

64 "PBK Announces Recent Election of 37 Seniors. Eight Chosen From Sheff; Twenty-Nine Selected In Yale College," in *Yale Daily News*, November 14, 1940, p. 1. "Sheff" is Yale's attached *Sheffield Scientific School*.

65 "Phi Beta Kappa Chooses Ewald 1942 President," in *Yale Daily News*, October 17, 1941, p. 1. In an email from Manuscript and Archives at Yale, I was informed that the class of 1942 comprised 453 BA students.

66 "University Notices," in *Yale Daily News*, No. 108, February 17, 1940, p. 6.

67 "Students Needed in Warden Jobs," in *Yale Daily News*, No. 68, December 10, 1941, pp. 1–2.

68 *Yale Yearbook 1942*, pp.170–172.

69 Yale University Library, call number: Yen +A11 1942–44.

70 *Yale Yearbook 1942*, p. 569.

71 "P.U. Issues Call for Membership," in *Yale Daily News*, No. 6 of September 6, 1939, pp. 1, 3.

72 Ibid.

73 "Fifty-Six Receive P.U. Membership," in *Yale Daily News*, No. 14 of October 10, 1939, pp. 1, 5.

74 "Resolution for Cash and Carry Plan Defeated in Political Union, 52-34," in *Yale Daily News*, No. 16 of October 12, 1939, pp. 1, 6.

75 Ibid., pp. 1, 6.

76 The students of Smith College, until today only for women on the undergraduate level, were favored by Yale undergraduates as mates for dancing, flirting, and the like. But there is evidence in *Yale Yearbook Class of 1942* that female high school students of the area also stood a good chance for the affection of a Yale undergraduate.

77 ASU, "where beliefs vary from liberal to radical," had been fighting American participation in the Olympic Games in Germany in 1936 on the

grounds of "the extent of discrimination in Germany both in and out of sports." Source: "Conference Reaffirms National A.S.U. Stand," in *Yale Daily News*, No. 126 of March 9, 1936, pp. 1, 3.

78 "Smith's Toni Grose Tells Yale A.S.U. She Is Glad They Are Dubbed 'Red'," in *Yale Daily News*, No. 89 of January 26, 1940, p. 1.

79 "The Yale Political Union," in *Yale Yearbook 1942*, pp. 114–115.

80 Stephen H. Norwood, *The Third Reich in the Ivory Tower. Complicity and Conflict on American Campuses*, New York: Cambridge University Press, 2009, p. 74.

81 Richard Breitman, "Review of Stephen H. Norwood, Third Reich in the Ivory Tower, and Michaela Hoenicke Moore, "Know Your Enemy. The American Debate on Nazism, 1933–1945," in *American Historical Review* 116 (2011), pp. 197–199.

82 Thomas Wolfe, *The Web and the Rock*, Garden City: Sun Dial Press, 1940 and Thomas Wolfe, *You Can't Go Home Again*, Garden City: Sun Dial Press, 1942.

83 Michaela Hoenicke Moore, *Know Your Enemy. The American Debate on Nazism, 1933–1945*, Cambridge University Press, 2010, p. 76.

84 Ibid., p. 69.

85 Ibid., p. 71, footnote 94. Full of evidence on these issues, including Ernst Hanfstaengel's uncontested Hitler salute at the twenty-fifth reunion of his class of 1909 in June 1934, which is presented with photos in Norwood, *The Third Reich in the Ivory Tower*, esp. chapter 2, pp. 36–74. Hanfstaengel was a supporter of Hitler's party since the early 1920s, besides his prestige as a Harvard graduate, he also contributed financial means.

86 John Krueckeberg, "Review of M. Hoenicke Moore, Know Your Enemy," in *Literature & History* 20 (2011), pp. 106–107.

87 Hoenicke Moore, *Know Your Enemy*, p. 266.

88 Dan A. Oren, *Joining the Club. A History of Jews and Yale*, New Haven: Yale University Press, 1985, p. 109. "Rabbi Newman Speaks at Kohut Anniversary," in *Yale Daily News*, No. 72 of January 8, 1937, p. 1.

89 Dan A. Oren, "The Founding of the B'Nai Brith Hillel Foundation at Yale University," in Jonathan D. Sarna (ed.), *Jews in New Haven*, vol. 2, New Haven: Jewish Historical Society of New Haven, 1979, p. 61.

90 Ibid., pp. 57–59.

91 Oren, *Joining the Club*, p. 109.

92 "History of Jewish Life at Yale." Online: https://slifkacenter.org/about/history-of-jewish-life-at-yale/ (Accessed March 3, 2021).

93 Oren, *Joining the Club*, p. 109.

94 Ibid., pp. 109–110.

95 Ibid., p. 109.

96 One example of a six-man panel discussion on "What are the Vocational Opportunities Today" was announced for February 11, 1941 under "Mere Mention," in *Yale Daily News*, No. 106 of February 11, 1941, p. 3.

97 Oren, *Joining the Club*, p. 109.

98 Oren, "The Founding of the B'Nai Brith Hillel Foundation at Yale University," p. 61.

99 "Kohut Forum Hears Dr. Louis I. Newman," in *Yale Daily News*, No. 83 of January 20, 1939, p. 1.

100 "J. G. Rogers Relates German Experiences," in *Yale Daily News*, No. 28 of October 26, 1939, p. 1.

101 Ibid.

102 "Kohut Forum to Convene," in *Yale Daily News*, No. 118 of February 29, 1940, p. 1.

103 "Tepfer to Speak at Kohut Forum," in *Yale Daily News*, No. 96 of January 28, 1942, p. 2.

104 "Rudin Probes Causes of Present Conflict," in *Yale Daily News*, No. 28 of October 24, 1940, p. 5.

105 Ibid., p. 5.

106 Oren, "The Founding of the B'Nai Brith Hillel Foundation at Yale University," p. 62.

107 "Rev. Tittle Will Open Yale Peace Conclave," in *Yale Daily News*, No. 146 of April 18, 1936, p. 1.

108 "J. H. Nichols Speaks on Student Pacifism," in *Yale Daily News*, No. 124 of March 6, 1936, p. 3.

109 "Eli Peace Council Will Stage Rally," in *Yale Daily News*, No. 146 of April 22, 1937, pp. 1, 5.

110 Ibid.

111 "Annual Rally Held by Peace Council," in *Yale Daily News*, No. 147 of April 23, 1937, p. 1.

112 "The Ivy League," in *Yale Daily News*, No. 151 of April 28, 1937, p. 4.

113 "Isolation Policy of the United States Strongly Rejected by Elis in Poll," in *Yale Daily News*, No. 144 of April 20, 1937, p. 1. For more results of the

poll, e.g., on the students' willingness to take up arms for different purposes, see ibid.

114 "Eli Peace Council Will Stage Rally," pp. 1, 5.

115 "Peace Council Plans Revised Organization. Delegates from Activities Selected for Positions," in *Yale Daily News*, No. 124 of March 7, 1940, p. 5.

116 "A. J. Muste Speaks on Non-Intervention," in *Yale Daily News*, No. 144 of April 20, 1939, p. 3.

117 Ibid.

118 *Yale Yearbook 1942*, p. 34.

119 Ibid., p. 393.

120 John T. Pigott Jr., "Class Oration," in *Yale Yearbook 1942*, p. 38.

121 See Chapter 3, pp. 245–273.

122 For details see below pp. 406–462.

123 *Yale Yearbook 1942*, p. 569.

124 Email of Joan Tenenbaum Merrill to me of September 24, 2018.

125 *Yale Yearbook 1942*, p. 481.

126 Email of Joan Tenenbaum Merrill to me of September 25, 2018.

127 Available online: www.youtube.com/watch?v=VINCt6eLEMo (Accessed September 28, 2018).

128 Email of Joan Tenenbaum Merrill to me of September 24, 2018.

129 Email of Joan Tenenbaum Merrill to me of September 25, 2018.

130 "Samoa" online: https://de.wikipedia.org/wiki/Samoa#Verwaltungsgliederung (Accessed October 3, 2018).

131 As to the German role in Samoa see online: Article of July 8, 1914: Nikolaus Doll, "Das Paradies leidet unter seinem deutschen Erbe" www.welt.de/wirtschaft/article129912197/Das-Paradies-leidet-unter-seinem-deutschen-Erbe.html (Accessed October 3, 2018) and article "Deutsch-Samoa" https://de.wikipedia.org/wiki/Deutsch-Samoa (Accessed October 3, 2018).

132 *Yale Yearbook 1942*, p. 569.

133 Ibid., p. 173.

134 Ibid., p. 34.

135 "Tenenbaum, Samford, Willets Receive Heber Dickerman Prize in Economics," in *Yale Daily News*, April 27, 1942, p. 1. The other two first prizes were awarded for the best essay of the Yale College as a whole and of the Sheffield Scientific School.

136 "Dean's Honor List of Upperclassmen For Half-Year," in *Yale Daily News*, February 18, 1942, p. 5.

137 Edward Tenenbaum, *National Socialism Vs. International Capitalism*, New Haven: Yale University Press and London: Humphrey Milford/ Oxford: Oxford University Press, 1942, p. XI. The book has been reprinted as a paperback in 2011.

138 See Section 4.4.

139 "The Yale Bookshelf," in *Yale Alumni Magazine*, vol. 6, no. 7, February 1943, p. 23.

140 Rita Davidson, "Review of Edward Tenenbaum, National Socialism Vs. International Capitalism," in *American Political Science Review* 37 (1943), pp. 375–376.

141 Registration Card. Online: www.fold3.com/image/695784217 (Accessed March 3, 2021). Registrar's Report. Online: www.fold3.com/image/ 695784218 (Accessed March 3, 2021).

142 Yale History Timeline: 1940–1949. Online: https://guides.library.yale .edu/c.php?g=296074&p=1976343 (Accessed January 7, 2018).

143 Robert W. Winks, *Cloak and Gown: Scholars in the Secret War, 1939–1961*, New York: William Morrow, 1987.

144 Yale History Timeline: 1940–1949. Online: https://guides.library.yale .edu/c.php?g=296074&p=1976343 (Accessed January 7, 2018).

145 Ibid.

146 This information is taken from a form of Edward A. Tenenbaum's "Application for Federal Employment" with which he applied successfully for a job with ERCA immediately after he had returned from Germany in September 1948. His provisional address at that time was c/o Stuart, 8425 Woodcliff Court, Silver Springs MD. Edward A. Tenenbaum Papers, box 8, folder: Personnel File. HSTPL.

147 "Investigation Data Request, Economic Cooperation Administration, Form ECA-1, Rev. 12–48," in Edward A. Tenenbaum Papers, box 8, folder: Personnel File. HSTPL.

148 AAF had succeeded the US Army Air Corps (AAC) on June 20, 1941 and would exist until September 18, 1947 as part of the army before becoming independent as US Air Force the following day. Online: https://en.wikipedia .org/wiki/United_States_Army_Air_Forces (Accessed July 21, 2018).

149 "Investigation Data Request, Economic Cooperation Administration, Form ECA-1, Rev. 12–48," in Edward A. Tenenbaum Papers, box 8, folder:

Personnel File. HSTPL. See also: Obituary "E.A. Tenenbaum, Overseas Economist, Dies," in *The Washington Post*, October 31, 1975, p. A24. Article "Edward A. Tenenbaum," in Everipedia. Online: https://everipedia .org/wiki/Edward_A._Tenenbaum/ (Accessed December 27, 2017).

150 This appears as the subtitle of an official short history of OSS, issued by the successor agency CIA: Michael Warner, *The Office of Strategic Services. America's First Intelligence Agency*, Washington, DC: Public Affairs CIA, 2002.

151 Kermit Roosevelt (ed.), *War Report of the OSS*, Washington, DC: Government Printing Office, 1947, Reprint with a New Introduction by Kermit Roosevelt, New York: Walker, 1976, p. 5.

152 Corey Ford, *Donovan of OSS*, Boston: Little, Brown, 1970, pp. 19–20.

153 Douglas Waller, *Wild Bill Donovan. The Spymaster who Created the OSS and Modern American Espionage*, New York: Free Press, 2011, pp. 14–18 with more detailed information on his career as attorney and his social and private life in Buffalo.

154 Ford, *Donovan of OSS*, p. 11.

155 Waller, *Wild Bill Donovan*, pp. 22–23. Waller contends that "Wild Bill" originated during Donovan's service in France. For more details of Donovan's war experience in Europe see ibid., pp. 21–31. He returned to the USA in April 1919 with less than half of his regiment's men as had departed to Europe in late October 1917.

156 Waller, *Wild Bill Donovan*, p. 35. For a complete long list of Donovan's *Decorations and Awards* for World War One and World War Two service by the USA, seven European countries and China see Ford, *Donovan of OSS*, pp. 345–346.

157 Ibid., pp. 71–72.

158 For details of Donovan's first mission to Britain see: Waller, *Wild Bill Donovan*, pp. 59–61.

159 Ford, *Donovan of OSS*, p. 89.

160 William L. Langer, *In and Out of the Ivory Tower. The Autobiography of William L. Langer*, New York: Neale Watson Academic Publications, 1977, p. 180.

161 For details of Donovan's second mission and its purposes see: Waller, *Wild Bill Donovan*, pp. 63–66.

162 Ernst C. Stiefel/Frank Mecklenburg, *Deutsche Juristen im amerikanischen Exil (1933–1950)*, Tübingen: Mohr, 1991, p. 149.

163 Online: www.cia.gov/library/readingroom/docs/CIA-RDP84-00022R000200100014-7.pdf (Accessed March 16, 2019).

164 Roosevelt's original document is accessible online: www.cia.gov/library/readingroom/docs/CIA-RDP13X00001R000100080007-9.pdf (Accessed January 11, 2019). The executive order is reprinted in Ford, *Donovan of OSS*, pp. 335–336.

165 Langer, *In and Out of the Ivory Tower*, p. 187.

166 Ibid., p. 182.

167 This paragraph, including the quote, relies on the *Introduction* to Nelson Douglas Lankford (ed.), *OSS Against the Reich. The World War II Diaries of Colonel David K. E. Bruce*, Kent, OH: Kent State University Press, 1991, pp. 1–15.

168 Arthur Schlesinger, Jr., "The London Operation: Recollections of a Historian," in George C. Chalou (ed.), *The Secrets War. The Office of Strategic Services in World War II*, Washington, DC: NARA, 1992, p. 64. Complete article pp. 61–68.

169 David K. E. Bruce, "The National Intelligence Authority," in *Virginia Quarterly Review* 22 (1946), p. 363.

170 William Phillips, *Venture in Diplomacy*, Boston: Beacon, 1953, p. 335. Quoted from R. Harris Smith, *OSS. The Secret History of America's First Central Intelligence Agency*, Berkeley: University of California Press, 1972, p. 1.

171 Charles A. Lindbergh, *Wartime Journals*, New York: Harcourt, Brace, Jovanovich, 1970, p. 573. Quoted from Harris Smith, *OSS. The Secret History of America's First Central Intelligence Agency*, p. 1.

172 Quoted in Waller, *Wild Bill Donovan*, subtitle to the photo of the OSS building between pp. 180–181. The quote seems to have originated in Drew Pearson's daily column "Washington Merry Go-Round" for December 3, 1941, i.e. a few days before the Japanese attack on Pearl Harbor. See Harris Smith, *OSS. The Secret History of America's First Central Intelligence Agency*, p. 1 and 387, note 1.

173 Langer, *In and Out of the Ivory Tower*, pp. 181–183.

174 Robert Murphy, *Diplomat among Warriors*, London: Collins, 1964, p. 74.

175 Ibid., pp. 88, 94, 100.

176 For sources not specifically noted, the last two paragraphs rely on Murphy, *Diplomat among Warriors*, pp. 45, 70, 71, 74, 80, 85, 87, 94.

177 Ibid., p. 96. For the whole account of Murphy's assignment and his encounter with the president, see ibid., pp. 93–100.

178 Ibid., p. 99.

179 Ibid., p. 117.

180 Ibid., pp. 130, 141.

181 Ibid., p. 138. For the twenty months in Algiers see ibid., p. 183.

182 Ibid., pp. 231, 250.

183 Ibid., pp. 276, 279–281.

184 For sources not specifically noted, the last three paragraphs rely on Roosevelt (ed.), *War Report of the OSS*, pp. XIII, 93–95. And on Murphy, *Diplomat among Warriors*, pp. 92–129. See also Langer, *In and Out of the Ivory Tower*, pp. 183, 188.

185 Ford, *Donovan of OSS*, p. 155. For the clandestine radio-communication network between the different US consulates in French North Africa, which OSS had provided, and Eddy's unconventional warfare activities in preparation for the Allied Force invasion see ibid., pp. 155–161.

186 Murphy, *Diplomat among Warriors*, pp. 141–158.

187 Listed, but not reprinted in Roosevelt (ed.), *War Report of the OSS*, pp. XXIII–XXIV.

188 "Military Order Establishing the Office of Strategic Services, June 13 1942." Online: https://books.google.de/books?id=7CfeAwAAQBAJ&pg= PA283&lpg=PA283&dq=Military+Order+Establishing+the+Office+of +Strategic+Services,+June+13+1942&source=bl&ots=LBC24j3F_F&sig= ACfU3U32S3CexYDUz_-_dLmrgIjySSidBA&hl=de&sa=X&ved= 2ahUKEwiP2OjU0Y7hAhUPwcQBHeVPCpgQ6AEwCXoECAMQAQ#v= onepage&q=Military%20Order%20Establishing%20the%20Office% 20of%20Strategic%20Services%2C%20June%2013%201942&f=false (Accessed March 19, 2019). Reprinted in Ford, *Donovan of OSS*, p. 337.

189 Ibid., p. 174.

190 Ibid., p. 314.

191 Alfred H. Paddock, Jr., *US Army Special Warfare: Its Origins. Psychological and Unconventional Warfare, 1941–1952*, Washington, DC: National Defense University Press, 1982, p. 40.

192 Langer, *In and Out of the Ivory Tower*, p. 184.

193 Stiefel/Mecklenburg, *Deutsche Juristen im amerikanischen Exil (1933–1950)*, pp. 150–151. As to Dorn's career see Walter L. Dorn,

Inspektionsreisen in der US-Zone. Notizen, Denkschriften und Erinnerungen aus dem Nachlass, translated and edited by Lutz Niethammer, Stuttgart: DVA, 1973, pp. 8–13.

194 Ford, *Donovan of OSS,* p. 111.

195 Winks, *Cloak and Gown 1939–1961,* p. 113. Tim B. Müller, *Krieger und Gelehrte. Herbert Marcuse und die Denksysteme im Kalten Krieg.* Hamburg: Hamburger Edition, 2010, p. 38.

196 Roosevelt (ed.), *War Report of the OSS,* p. 116.

197 Barry M. Katz, *Foreign Intelligence. Research and Analysis in the Office of Strategic Services 1942–1945,* Cambridge, MA: Harvard University Press, 1989, pp. 80–81. Müller, *Krieger und Gelehrte,* p. 38. For a summary description of OSS' different branches see: Christof Mauch, *The Shadow War against Hitler. The Covert Operations of America's Wartime Secret Intelligence Service,* New York: Columbia University Press, 1999, pp. 12–18.

198 Robin W. Winks, "Getting the Right Stuff: FDR, Donovan, and the Quest for Professional Intelligence," in Chalou (ed.), *The Secrets War,* p. 20.

199 Online: www.cia.gov/news-information/featured-story-archive/2010-featured-story-archive/oss-research-and-analysis.html (Accessed December 9, 2018).

200 Martin Bowman, *B-17 Flying Fortress Units of the Eighth Air Force,* Part 2, Oxford: Osprey, 2002, pp. 49, 52. There are quite a few more and more frequent reports on similar bombing missions on oil installation on pp. 52–69.

201 Richard Overy, *The Bombing War. Europe 1039–1945,* London: Allen Lane/Penguin, 1913, p. 370.

202 Walt W. Rostow, "The London Operation: Recollections of an Economist," in Chalou (ed.), *The Secrets War,* pp. 48–60, here p. 53. As Rostow cited, the data were taken from official German sources and were published in the *US Strategic Bombing Survey,* table 41, p. 179.

203 Richard Overy, *The Bombers and the Bombed. Allied Air War over Europe, 1940–1945,* New York: Viking, 2014, pp. 202–203, and the description of a photo with a B-17 attacking Ludwigshafen between pp. 194 and 195.

204 George C. Marshall, *General Marshall's Report. The Winning of the War in Europe and the Pacific. Biennial Report of the Chief of Staff of the*

United States Army July 1, 1943 to June 30, 1945 to the Secretary of War, New York: Simon & Schuster, 1946, p. 31.

205 Albert Praun, *Soldat in der Telegraphen- und Nachrichtentruppe*, Würzburg: author's edition, 1965, p. 246.

206 "Messerschmitt Me 262," Wikipedia online: https://de.wikipedia.org/wiki/Messerschmitt_Me_262 (Accessed September 28, 2020).

207 Arthur Harris, *Bomber Offensive*, London: Collins, 1947, p. 220. Quoted from Rostow, "The London Operation," p. 58.

208 Walt W. Rostow, *Pre-Invasion Bombing Strategy. General Eisenhower's Decision of March 25, 1944*, Austin: University of Texas Press, 1981, p. 78.

209 Adolf Galland, *The First and the Last*, New York: Holt, 1954, Bantam Edition 1978, pp. 208–210; quoted from Rostow, *Pre-Invasion Bombing Strategy*, pp. 78–79.

210 Langer, *In and Out of the Ivory Tower*, p. 184.

211 Charles P. Kindleberger, *The Life of an Economist. An Autobiography*, Cambridge, MA: Basil Blackwell, 1991, p. 72.

212 Classification stands for first and second priority for drafting.

213 All information and quotes are from the 4-page copy of "Affidavit to Support Claim for Occupational Deferment." In NARA at College Park MD, RG 226 Records of the OSS, OSS Personnel Files, 1941–1945, box 769: Tenenbaum, Edward to Terry, James R., folder: Tenenbaum, Edward, Lieutenant (Army). See also: Memorandum from James B. Opsata, Chairman Deferment Committee, to Dr. William L. Langer, Subject: Deferment of Edward A. Tanenbaum [*sic*] of October 30, 1942. In ibid.

214 Stiefel/Mecklenburg, *Deutsche Juristen im amerikanischen Exil (1933–1950)*, pp. 150–152. As to Dorn's career see Dorn, *Inspektionsreisen in der US-Zone*, pp. 8–13.

215 Interoffice Memorandum from Walter L. Dorn to Robert L. Wolff of October 13, 1942. In NARA at College Park MD, RG 226 Records of the OSS, OSS Personnel Files, 1941–1945, box 769: Tenenbaum, Edward to Terry, James R., folder: Tenenbaum, Edward, Lieutenant (Army).

216 Letter of James B. Opsata, OSS Acting Executive Officer, to the chairman of Local Board No. 42 of the Selective Service System, 1632 York Avenue, New York NY, of October 17, 1942. In NARA at College Park MD, RG 226 Records of the OSS, OSS Personnel Files, 1941–1945, box 769:

Tenenbaum, Edward to Terry, James R., folder: Tenenbaum, Edward, Lieutenant (Army).

217 The OSS Executive Office's receipt stamp shows October 27, 1942. In a letter from James B. Opsata, OSS Director of Personnel, to Edward W. Bourne, Government Appeal Agent, Local Board No. 42 in New York City of November 20, 1943, the receipt of the denial letter is dated as October 17, 1942. This must have been a typo. Both letters in NARA at College Park MD, RG 226 Records of the OSS, OSS Personnel Files, 1941–1945, box 769: Tenenbaum, Edward to Terry, James R., folder: Tenenbaum, Edward, Lieutenant (Army).

218 Letter of Edward W. Bourne, Government Appeal Agent of the Selective Service System, Local Board No 42, 1632 York Avenue, New York NY to James B. Opsata, Acting Executive Officer, Office of Strategic Services, Washington, DC of November 17, 1942 "Re: Edwin Adam Tanenbaum" [sic]. In NARA at College Park MD, RG 226 Records of the OSS, OSS Personnel Files, 1941–1945, box 769: Tenenbaum, Edward to Terry, James R., folder: Tenenbaum, Edward, Lieutenant (Army).

219 NARA at College Park MD, RG 226 Records of the OSS, box 3: Entry NM-54 34 Reports on Industrial Resources of the Axis Powers, 1942–1943 (end) THRU Entry NM-54 29 Reports Prepared by the Economic Division of the Office of the Coordinator of Information 1941–1942, folder: # 100–200 Industrial Resources. See also: RG 226 Records of the OSS, OSS Personnel Files, 1942–1962, box 405: Kin-Cade, A. THRU King, G, folder: Kindleberger, Charles P., Term.

220 Edward A. Tenenbaum Papers, box 8, folder: Personnel File. HSTPL.

221 OSS Personnel File of Charles P. Kindleberger in NARA at College Park MD, RG 226, box 405. See also Kindleberger, The Life of an Economist, pp. 66, 212. Charles P. Kindleberger, Marshall Plan Days, Boston: Allen & Unwin, 1987, p. 163.

222 Kindleberger, The Life of an Economist, p. 66.

223 For a good description of its organization, assignments, and working methods see: Katz, Foreign Intelligence, pp. 103–113.

224 Ibid., pp. 99, 109.

225 Kindleberger, Marshall Plan Days, p. 163.

226 NARA at College Park MD, RG 226 Records of the OSS, OSS Personnel Files, 1942–1962, box 405: Kin-Cade, A. THRU King, G, folders: Kindleberger, Charles P. Arrival date February 28, 1943 is mentioned in

Walt W. Rostow, "Preface," in Charles P. Kindleberger, *The German Economy, 1945–1947: Charles P. Kindleberger's Letters from the Field*, Westport CT: Meckler, 1989, p. VII.

227 It is strange that British economic historian Richard Overy in his publications on the bombing war of World War II mentions neither Chandler Morse nor Charles Kindleberger as head of EOU, but only Colonel Richard D. Hughes. It is true, the latter was the initiator and strong supporter of EOU as well as the US Air Force's liaison person to whom EOU reported, but not the immediate head of EOU. Overy correctly mentions that Hughes had formerly been a British officer who acquired US citizenship in the early 1930s. Overy, *The Bombing War*, p. 349. See also Overy, *The Bombers and the Bombed.*

228 Katz, *Foreign Intelligence*, p. 114. On pp. 114–124 the book contains a good summary of EOU activities, including a photo of a casual get together after work. More recent summaries of EOU's origin and activities are contained in Rostow, "The London Operation," pp. 48–60. Mauch, *The Shadow War against Hitler*, pp. 94–97; and in an article focused on economists: Mark Guglielmo, "The Contribution of Economists to Military Intelligence during World War II," in *Journal of Economic History* 68 (2008), pp. 109–150, specifically on EOU pp. 132–137.

229 Kindleberger, *The Life of an Economist*, p. 72. In a slightly different version also quoted in Katz, *Foreign Intelligence*, p. 114.

230 William Casey, *The Secret War against Hitler*, Washington, DC: Regnery Gateway, 1988, p. 78.

231 Katz, *Foreign Intelligence*, p. 114. Widewing, Wydewing, or Wyde Wing was the codename for US Eighth Air Force Headquarters at Bushy Park, Teddington, 15 miles (24 km) west-southwest of London. See Oral History of Rutgers University, The Wartime Diaries of Captain Edward C. Piech, USAAF, 1942–1944, chapter six, entry for February 24, 1944, footnote 24. Online: The Wartime Diaries of Captain Edward C. Piech, USAAF, 1942–1944 [Chapter 6: January 6, 1944 to April 14, 1944] (rutgers.edu) (Accessed January 25, 2021).

232 Casey, *The Secret War against Hitler*, pp. 78–79. Katz, *Foreign Intelligence*, pp. 113–114. Kindleberger, *The Life of an Economist*, pp. 74–75. Rostow, "The London Operation," pp. 48–60, for the development of EOU's doctrine pp. 49–50, for the empirical testing of the doctrine as applied in air force practice pp. 50–55.

233 Walt W. Rostow, "Waging Economic Warfare from London. The Enemy Objectives Unit." Online: www.cia.gov/library/center-for-the-study-of-intelligence/kent-csi/vol35no4/html/v35i4a06p_0001.htm (Accessed May 25, 2019), in section "Some Final Observations."

234 Kindleberger, *Marshall Plan Days*, p. 165.

235 Kindleberger, *The Life of an Economist*, pp. 69–70.

236 "Letter #170, Major C. P. Kindleberger, 0-925563, G-2 HQ, 12th Army Group, APO 655, Postmaster, NYC, Somewhere in Germany 19 April 1945" to his wife Sarah, in Kindleberger, *The German Economy, 1945–1947*, pp. 200–205. In his *Marshall Plan Days*, Kindleberger mixes a few things up where he refers to this trip (p. 165). But there he names the journalist who accompanied the two officers on this trip: *Time-Life* reporter William Walton.

237 Rostow, "The London Operation," pp. 48–60; quotation on p. 49. Rostow, "Waging Economic Warfare from London."

238 Katz, *Foreign Intelligence*, pp. 80–81. For the roles of Mason and Morse see pp. 98, 114.

239 See Kindleberger's cover letter of June 19, 1944, headed "G (Air) Branch, 21st Army Group Headquarter, 2 TAF," where he had served "during this past month," addressed to Lt. Col. A. A. Part, GS (I) sending his *Interim Report on the Rail Movement of German Reserves*, in Rostow, *Pre-Invasion Bombing Strategy*, Appendix F, pp. 122–123.

240 In the second half of 1945 Sibert, then head of G2 of all US Forces in the European Theater (USFET) and a stern anti-communist like Reinhard Gehlen, managed to have the *Organization Gehlen* founded and financed by US Congress. While the old guard of Gehlen's secret service had been working for Hitler's Armed Forces, it would henceforth serve the intelligence needs of the US Army. *Organization Gehlen* would in 1956 be transformed into West Germany's Federal Intelligence Service (*Bundesnachrichtendienst*), with Gehlen as president until his retirement in 1968. See Winfried Meyer, "Spione, Trickser und ein General," in *Der Tagess*piegel March 1, 2016. Online: www.tagesspiegel .de/gesellschaft/spionage-gehlen-beschliesst-sich-den-amerikanern-anzubieten/13022802-3.html (Accessed November 21, 2019).

241 Tenenbaum's entry in *Yale Yearbook, Class of 1942*, p. 569.

242 Katz, *Foreign Intelligence*, pp. 83–84.

243 For a short vita of Jürgen Kuczynski see: Agnieszka Brockmann, "Robert René Kuczynski (1876–1947), Jürgen Kuczynski (1904–1997)," in Günter Benser, Dagmar Goldbeck, Anja Kruke (eds.), *Bewahren, Verbreiten, Aufklären. Archivare, Bibliothekare und Sammler der Quellen der deutschsprachigen Arbeiterbewegung. Supplement*, Bonn: Friedrich-Ebert-Stiftung, 2017, pp. 49–61, here pp. 51–55. Online: http://library.fes .de/pdf-files/adsd/14092-20180323.pdf (Accessed January 25, 2021). For an extensive treatment of Jürgen Kuczynski's life and his Bourgeois-Marxist role in the GDR see: R. S.-Axel Fair-Schulz, "Loyal Subversion. East Germany and Its Neo-Humanist Marxist Intellectuals," PhD dissertation State University of New York at Buffalo, Dept. of History. Proquest Dissertations Publishing, 2004. 3141270, pp. 79–228. Online: https://search.proquest.com/docview/305080600?pq-origsite=primo (Accessed February 11, 2021).

244 Rebecca Grant, "The Long Arm of the US Strategic Bombing Survey." Online: www.airforcemag.com/article/0208bombing/ (Accessed January 30, 2021).

245 Walter Isaacson/Evan Thomas, *The Wise Men. Six Friends and the World They Made. Acheson, Bohlen, Harriman, Kennan, Lovett, McCloy*. New York: Simon & Schuster, 1986, pp. 207–208.

246 Jürgen Kuczynski, *Memoiren. Die Erziehung des J.K. zum Kommunisten und Wissenschaftler*, 2nd ed., Berlin/Weimar: Aufbau-Verlag, 1975, pp. 401–402.

247 Rainer Fremdling, "Zur Bedeutung nationalsozialistischer Statistiken und Statistiker nach dem Krieg – Rolf Wagenführ und der United States Strategic Bombing Survey (USSBS) – On the Significance of Nazi-Statistics and –Statisticians after the War," in *Jahrbuch für Wirtschaftsgeschichte / Economic History Yearbook 57(2016)*, pp. 589–613, here p. 591, footnote 6.

248 Kuczynski, *Memoiren. Die Erziehung des J.K. zum Kommunisten und Wissenschaftler*, pp. 403–415. On Kuczynski's role in USSBS and especially in Bad Nauheim see Fremdling, "Zur Bedeutung nationalsozialistischer Statistiken und Statistiker nach dem Krieg," pp. 589–613.

249 Sophia Dafinger, *Die Lehren des Luftkriegs. Sozialwissenschaftliche Expertise in den USA vom Zweiten Weltkrieg bis Vietnam*, Stuttgart: Steiner, 2020, p. 60.

250 Rostow, "The London Operation," pp. 48–60, here pp. 55–56.

251 Jürgen Kuczynski, *Ein linientreuer Dissident. Memoiren 1945–1989*, Berlin/Weimar: Aufbau-Verlag, 1992, pp. 18–27.

252 Ibid., p. 28. My translation.

253 Oscar W. Koch/Robert G. Hays, *G-2 Intelligence for Patton*, Atglen, PA: Schiffer, 1990, pp. 7, 93–94.

254 See the praise for Koch's G-2 in Robert S. Allen, *Lucky Forward. The History of Patton's Third US Army*, New York: Vanguard, 1947, pp. 48–54, 68, 373. Colonel Allen had served as assistant chief in General Oscar Koch's G-2 for Patton's Third Army. Denny G. Hair, *Secrets Hidden. Nazi Terror Camps, Stolen Gold, and a Secret Weapon*, Houston, TX: Third Army Publishing, 2018, p. 204.

255 During World War II Third Army Headquarters – like other US Armies and Army Groups – was equipped with five General Staff sections: "G-1 (Personnel), G-2 (Intelligence), G-3 (Operations), G-4 (Supply), G-5 (Civil affairs or military government)." Allen, *Lucky Forward*, pp. 4–5. The personnel strength of Third Army Headquarters was about 450 officers and 1,000 enlisted men, much less than other headquarters. See ibid, p. 47.

256 Robert Hays, *Patton's Oracle Gen. Oscar Koch, as I Knew Him. A Biographical Memoir*, Savoy, IL: Lucidus Books. A division of Herndon-Sugarman Press, 2013, p. 119.

257 Ibid., p. 146.

258 George S. Patton, *War As I Knew It*, Boston: Houghton & Mifflin, 1995, p. 186, footnote 1.

259 Ibid., p. 91.

260 Kevin M. Hymel, *Patton's Photographs. War As He Saw It*, Dulles, VA: Potomac Books, 2006, p. 53. American Kennel Club, "Once Upon a Dog: General Patton and Willie." Online: www.akc.org/expert-advice/lifestyle/once-upon-a-dog-general-patton-and-willie/ (Accessed July 21, 2020). Denny G. Hair, *The Images Uncovered. The Story of Patton and His Third Army, Hidden in Print for 75 Years*, Houston, TX: Third Army Publishing, 2015, p. 15.

261 Harry H. Semmes, *Portrait of Patton*, New York: Paperback Library, 1970, p. 195.

262 Marshall, *General Marshall's Report*, 31. The source of other information in this paragraph is ibid., pp. 30–31.

263 Ibid., pp. 37, 42 respectively. The best account of WW II in Western Europe by a military historian is Rick Atkinson, *The Guns at Last Light. The War in Western Europe, 1944–1945*, New York: Henry Holt, 2013.

264 Patton, *War As I Knew It*, pp. 92–97, 104, 117, 119–120, 126, 131, 152, 191.

265 Martin Blumenson/Kevin Hymel, *Patton. Legendary Commander*, Washington, DC: Potomac Books, 2008, p. 78.

266 Patton, *War As I Knew It*, p. 250.

267 Hymel, *Patton's Photographs*, p. 95.

268 Blumenson/Hymel, *Patton. Legendary Commander*, p. 70.

269 Patton, *War As I Knew It*, p. 252.

270 Blumenson/Hymel, *Patton. Legendary Commander*, p. 84.

271 Ibid., p. 86.

272 Koch/G. Hays, *G-2 Intelligence for Patton*, pp. 68–71, 76–77.

273 Martin Blumenson (ed.), *The Patton Papers 1940–1945*, Boston: Houghton Mifflin, 1974, pp. 494–511.

274 Ibid., p. 510.

275 Allen, *Lucky Forward*.

276 The successful breaking of the German military communication code transmitted by the *Enigma* and other German ciphering machines throughout most of WW II was called ULTRA. It was accomplished with the aid of mainframe early computers at the top secret Government Code and Cipher School at Bletchley Park, England. There, about 7,000 experts worked with computer pioneer Alan Turing. On a daily basis ULTRA secrets were communicated to top military leaders of the Western Allies. This essential contribution to the defeat of Germany became public knowledge only after the following publication: Frederick W. Winterbotham, *The Ultra Secret*, London: Weidenfeld & Nicolson, 1974.

277 Hair, *Secrets Hidden*, p. 204.

278 Casey, *The Secret War against Hitler*, p. 32.

279 Katz, *Foreign Intelligence*, note 33, pp. 223–224. On p. 121 a photo of six EOU members, including Kindleberger, is displayed. A not quite fully complete list of EOU members is contained in Appendix B of Rostow, "The London Operation," pp. 48–60, here p. 59.

280 These controversies are summarized in Rostow, *Pre-Invasion Bombing Strategy*, pp. 3–87. And more succinctly in Rostow, "Waging Economic Warfare from London." See also: "Oral History Project. Interview with

Charles P. Kindleberger," in NARA at College Park MD, RG 263 Records of the Central Intelligence Agency, Center for the Study of Intelligence History Office, OSS Oral History Project Transcripts, box 2, folder: Charles P. Kindleberger.

281 Rostow, "The London Operation," pp. 48–60, here p. 48. Kindleberger, *The Life of an Economist*, p. 70.

282 Kindleberger, *Marshall Plan Days*, p. 162. For his engagement during the first period see also: Kindleberger, *The Life of an Economist*, p. 71.

283 Kindleberger, *The Life of an Economist*, pp. 211–215 for his vita, pp. 130–131 for the dates of his move to MIT, and pp. 112–130 for his work in the State Department.

284 Kindleberger describes his military service in his autobiography *The Life of an Economist*, p. 212.

285 Kindleberger, *The German Economy, 1945–1947*, p. IV. For more details of Kindleberger's transport to France and his experience in G-2 12th US Army Group see ibid., pp. 90–102.

286 OSS Personnel File of Charles P. Kindeberger, in NARA at College Park MD, RG 226 Records of the OSS, OSS Personnel Files, 1942–1962, box 405: Kin-Cade, A. THRU King, G, folder: Kindleberger, Charles P., Term.

287 Kindleberger, *The Life of an Economist*, p. 102.

288 *Yale Yearbook Class of 1942 at 25*, New Haven CT 1967, pp. 311–312.

289 Article "Miss Jeanette Kipp to Be Wednesday Bride. Will Be Wed to Pvt. Edward A. Tenenbaum in Sioux Falls, SD," in Rockford Register – Republic, Tuesday, March 30, 1943, p. 6. Online via Genealogy Bank (Accessed December 15, 2017). Kipp's place of birth is not mentioned in the article, but in the application form for government employment in Washington, DC that Edward Tenenbaum had filled out sometime after July 1950. "Investigation Data Request, Economic Cooperation Administration, Form ECA-1, Rev. 12–48," in Edward A. Tenenbaum Papers, box 8, folder: Personnel File. HSTPL. See also: "Jeanette Kipp To Wed Pvt. Tenenbaum," *Morning Star (Rockford IL)*, March 31, 1943, p. 4.

290 Interview with Joan Tenenbaum Merrill October 29, 2018.

291 Jeanette's parents are listed under separate addresses in Rockford, i.e. they lived separately. This was certainly true of Dr. Joseph and Otilia Tenenbaum, because two months earlier Joseph had married Sheila Schwartz, his second wife. See above.

292 Online: https://t311.wordpress.com/2014/05/28/a9-july-12-1973-national-personnel-records-center-fire/ (Accessed July 21, 2018).

293 Eugene Price, "Seymour Johnson Air Force Base," reported in 2006 on the history of the base: "Seymour Johnson Field, Goldsboro, was activated on 12 June 1942 as Headquarters, Technical School, Army Air Forces Technical Training Command. The following year it also assumed responsibility for preparing Air Corps personnel for deployment overseas as replacements and became the home of the Seventy-fifth Training Wing, which conducted a pretraining school for aviation cadets." Online: www.ncpedia.org/seymour-johnson-air-force-base (Accessed June 21, 2018).

294 "Special Orders No. 96 by Headquarters, Technical School / Army Air Forces Technical Training Command (AAFTTC) / Yale University, New Haven, Conn.," dated April 5, 1944, pp. 1, 5. In NARA at College Park, MD, RG 226 Records of the OSS, OSS Personnel Files, 1941–1945, box 769: Tenenbaum, Edward to Terry, James R., folder: Tenenbaum, Edward, Lieutenant (Army).

295 "Special Orders No. 96 by Headquarters, Technical School / Army Air Forces Technical Training Command (AAFTTC) / Yale University, New Haven, Conn.," dated April 5, 1944, pp. 1, 5. In NARA at College Park MD, RG 226 Records of the OSS, OSS Personnel Files, 1941–1945, box 769: Tenenbaum, Edward to Terry, James R., folder: Tenenbaum, Edward, Lieutenant (Army). A copy of the same document was provided by the National Personnel Records Center in St. Louis MO on March 2, 2018 after I had asked for Edward A. Tenenbaum's *Final Pay Voucher*. For the same information see also "War Department Pay and Allowance Account" for the month of May concerning Edward A. Tenenbaum. In NARA at College Park MD, RG 226 Records of the OSS, OSS Personnel Files, 1941–1945, box 769: Tenenbaum, Edward to Terry, James R., folder: Tenenbaum, Edward, Lieutenant (Army).

296 For the seventeen weeks of officer candidate training see online: https://en.wikipedia.org/wiki/Officer_Candidate_School_(United_States_Army)#World_War_II_era (Accessed July 16, 2018).

297 "ETO Card on Tenenbaum, Edward A., 1st Lt., serial number 0870114, AC Branch" of May 28, 1946. In NARA at College Park MD, RG 226 Records of the OSS, OSS Personnel Files, 1941–1945, box 769: Tenenbaum, Edward to Terry, James R., folder: Tenenbaum, Edward, Lieutenant (Army).

298 Copies of Tenenbaum's *Final Pay Voucher*. They were sent to me by the National Personnel Records Center in St Louis MO on March 2, 2018.

299 Tenenbaum's *Final Pay Voucher*. "comm." could mean commissioned (officer) or (in) command.

300 This is corroborated by Tenenbaum's own statement on an application form for government employment in Washington, DC sometime after July 1950. Asked for his employment history, he states for the period December 1942 to April 1944: Private and 2nd Lieutenant US Army Air Forces at "Sioux Falls, Goldsboro, New Haven." "Investigation Data Request, Economic Cooperation Administration, Form ECA-1, Rev. 12–48," in Edward A. Tenenbaum Papers, box 8, folder: Personnel File. HSTPL.

301 OSS Special Orders No. 83 of April 8, 1944. In NARA at College Park MD, RG 226 Records of the OSS, OSS Personnel Files, 1941–1945, box 769: Tenenbaum, Edward to Terry, James R., folder: Tenenbaum, Edward, Lieutenant (Army).

302 Interview with Joan Tenenbaum Merrill October 29, 2018.

303 Noted on OSS, Special Orders No. 111 of May 11. In NARA at College Park MD, RG 226 Records of the OSS, OSS Personnel Files, 1941–1945, box 769: Tenenbaum, Edward to Terry, James R., folder: Tenenbaum, Edward, Lieutenant (Army).

304 OSS, Travel Orders, Shipment IJ-900-CN to Personnel Concerned of June 14, 1944. In NARA at College Park MD, RG 226 Records of the OSS, OSS Personnel Files, 1941–1945, box 769: Tenenbaum, Edward to Terry, James R., folder: Tenenbaum, Edward, Lieutenant (Army).

305 Ibid.

306 Ibid.

307 Ibid.

308 OSS, Subject: Manner of Performance Rating. In NARA at College Park MD, RG 226 Records of the OSS, OSS Personnel Files, 1941–1945, box 769: Tenenbaum, Edward to Terry, James R., folder: Tenenbaum, Edward, Lieutenant (Army).

309 "Certificate" of Edward A. Tenenbaum, 2nd Lt., Air Corps, Washington, DC, June 24, 1944. Source: NARA at College Park, MD, RG 226 Records of the OSS, OSS Personnel Files, 1941–1945, box 769: Tenenbaum, Edward to Terry, James R., folder: Tenenbaum, Edward, Lieutenant (Army).

310 Headquarters and Headquarters Detachment, Office of Strategic Services, 24th and F Streets, N.W., Washington 25, DC Source: NARA at College Park, MD, RG 226 Records of the OSS, OSS Personnel Files, 1941–1945, box 769: Tenenbaum, Edward to Terry, James R., folder: Tenenbaum, Edward, Lieutenant (Army).

311 "ETO Card on Tenenbaum, Edward A., 1st Lt., serial number 0870114, AC Branch" of May 28, 1946. In NARA at College Park MD, RG 226 Records of the OSS, OSS Personnel Files, 1941–1945, box 769: Tenenbaum, Edward to Terry, James R., folder: Tenenbaum, Edward, Lieutenant (Army).

312 Letter containing "Special Orders, Number 100" by HQ & HQ Detachment, Office of Strategic Services, ETOUSA, to APO 887, US Army of July 18, 1944. Source: NARA at College Park, MD, RG 226 Records of the OSS, OSS Personnel Files, 1941–1945, box 769: Tenenbaum, Edward to Terry, James R., folder: Tenenbaum, Edward, Lieutenant (Army).

313 For a summary of the establishment of PWD as a joint American–British unit under General Robert A. McClure in February 1944, its purpose, tasks, and activities see Earl F. Ziemke, *The US Army in the Occupation of Germany 1944–1946*, Washington, DC: Center of Military History US Army, 1975, pp. 173–175. For the establishment and tasks of the German Country Unit in London see ibid., pp. 80–83.

314 Katz, *Foreign Intelligence*, p. 125.

315 All quotes from Schlesinger, Jr., "The London Operation," pp. 61–68.

316 This is explained in Special Orders No. 96 by Headquarters, Technical School / Army Air Forces Technical Training Command (AAFTTC) / Yale University, New Haven, Conn., dated April 5, 1944, p. 1. In NARA at College Park, MD, RG 226 Records of the OSS, OSS Personnel Files, 1941–1945, box 769: Tenenbaum, Edward to Terry, James R., folder: Tenenbaum, Edward, Lieutenant (Army).

317 "Army Air Forces Training Command." In Wikipedia. Online: https://en .wikipedia.org/wiki/Army_Air_Forces_Training_Command (Accessed July 23, 2018).

318 "Report of Physical Examination" of Edward A. Tenenbaum. In NARA at College Park MD, RG 226 Records of the OSS, OSS Personnel Files, 1941–1945, box 769: Tenenbaum, Edward to Terry, James R., folder: Tenenbaum, Edward, Lieutenant (Army).

319 *The Psychological Warfare Division Supreme Headquarters Allied Expeditionary Force. An Account of Its Operations in the Western European Campaign 1944–1945*, Bad Homburg, Germany, October 1945, pp. 21, 23.

320 Ibid., p. 47.

321 Nat Frankel/Larry Smith, *Patton's Best: An Informal History of the 4th Armored Division*, New York: Hawthorn Books, 1978, pp. 116–117.

322 Ronald Schaffer, "American Military Ethics in World War II. The Bombing of German Civilians," in *Journal of American History* 67 (1980), pp.318–334, quotation on p. 324.

323 For a concise summary of the battle and the German losses in equipment and men see Marshall, *General Marshall's Report*, pp. 44–45. For a detailed description of the Battle of the Bulge see Patton, *War As I Knew It*, pp. 193–229. And the chapter in Charles B. MacDonald, *The Last Offensive* (Office of the Chief of Military History US Army), Washington, DC: GPO, 1973, pp. 22–54.

324 The date and hour is from "The Story of the 87th Infantry Division, chapter: Across the Moselle and into Coblenz." Online: www.lonesentry.com/gi_stories_booklets/87thinfantry/ (Accessed September 8, 2019). See also Peter Brommer, "Koblenz und der Mittelrhein zwischen Zerstörung und Wiederaufbau." Online: www.regionalgeschichte.net/bibliothek/texte/aufsaetze/brommer-koblenz.html#a31 (Accessed April 17, 2019). Originally published in Kurt Düwell/Michael Matheus (eds.), *Kriegsende und Neubeginn. Westdeutschland und Luxemburg zwischen 1944 und 1947* (= Geschichtliche Landeskunde 46), Stuttgart: Franz Steiner, 1997, pp. 107–138. A summary of the fighting for the conquest of old-town Coblenz is contained in *An Historical and Pictorial Record of the 87th Infantry Division in World War II 1942–1945 Golden Acorn*, Baton Rouge, LA: Army & Navy Publishing Co., 1946, pp. 37–38. Stefan Michels, *Sturm am Mittelrhein. Die deutschen Rückzugskämpfe im Vorderhunsrück und dem Rhein-Mosel-Dreieck sowie das Kriegende im Rhein-Lahn-Kreis im März 1945*, Aachen: Helios, 2013, pp. 89–90. And with photos in Willi Wagner, *Krieg in der Heimat. Die Endphase des 2. Weltkrieges im Mosel-Rhein-Hunsrück-Raum*, Simmern/Hunsrück: Stadt Simmern, 1995, pp. 185–190. The official military history of the conquest of Coblenz is contained in MacDonald, *The Last Offensive*, pp. 249–251.

325 Willi K. Michels, *Die Heimat in Scherben. Kriegsende an Rhein und Mosel 1945*, Coblenz: Mittelrhein-Verlag, 1985, p. 63.

326 Cited in Michels, *Sturm am Mittelrhein*, p. 83. And in Hans-Joachim Mack, *Die Kämpfe im Rhein-Mosel-Gebiet und um Koblenz im März 1945*, Coblenz: Görres-Verlag, 1990, pp. 13–14.

327 As to US Army patrol activity across the Moselle around Coblenz on or after March 13 see Frank L. Culin, *Stalwart and Strong. The Story of the 87th Infantry Division*, Paris: Information and Education Division USFET, 1945, chapter: "Across the Moselle and into Koblenz." Online: www.lonesentry.com/gi_stories_booklets/87thinfantry/ (Accessed September 8, 2019). Wagner, *Krieg in der Heimat*, pp. 185–190. Wagner relies heavily on the above source.

328 Peter Neu, "Bevor Koblenz fiel. Amerikanische Geheimberichte vor der Eroberung der Stadt Koblenz im März 1945," in *Landeskundliche Vierteljahrsblätter* 29 (1983), p. 21.

329 Michels, *Die Heimat in Scherben*, p. 70. My retranslation from the German translation of the report.

330 Mack, *Die Kämpfe im Rhein-Mosel-Gebiet und um Koblenz im März 1945*, pp. 19–20. For the more general picture in that area see Marshall, *General Marshall's Report*, p. 47.

331 Neu, "Bevor Koblenz fiel. Amerikanische Geheimberichte vor der Eroberung der Stadt Koblenz im März 1945," p. 23.

332 Culin, *Stalwart and Strong. The Story of the 87th Infantry.*

333 The patrol's original report can be found in NARA at College Park MD, RG 407, file 212, box 11471, p. 97, as cited in Michels, *Sturm am Mittelrhein*, p. 95. These parts of the report are quoted in a German translation. A German translation of these and other parts of the patrol's report are also quoted in Neu, "Bevor Koblenz fiel. Amerikanische Geheimberichte vor der Eroberung der Stadt Koblenz im März 1945," pp. 23–24. The above-mentioned summarizing intelligence report of March 14, 1945 quotes extensively from it. See Michels, *Die Heimat in Scherben*, p. 72.

334 Mack, *Die Kämpfe im Rhein-Mosel-Gebiet und um Koblenz im März 1945*, p. 20.

335 After-Action Report Third US Army August 1, 1944–May 9, 1945, vol II: Staff Section Reports. In NARA at College Park, Series: WW II Operations Reports, RG 407 Records of the Adjutant General's Office, 1917–, Entry Number 427 [A1], box 1571 D, 3rd Army 103-0.3 17410, p. G-2 CLXXXV.

336 Stephen M. Rusiecki, *In Final Defense of the Reich. The Destruction of the 6th SS Mountain Division "North,"* Annapolis, MD: Naval Institute Press, 2010, especially pp. 54–71.

337 "Message Attachments to G-2 Journal of Hqs 87th Inf Div FROM 152345A Mar 45 TO 160740 Mar 45," NARA at College Park MD, RG 407 Records of the Adjutant General's Office, 1917–, World War II Operations Reports, 1940–45, 87th Infantry Division, 387-2.2 March 1945 to 387-2.2 April 1945, box 10775, Entry 427, HM 2007, folder: March 1945.

338 *An Historical and Pictorial Record of the 87th Infantry Division in World War II*, p. 37.

339 "First Yank Patrol to Reach Coblenz Directed by Lt. Edward Tenenbaum," in *Rockford Morning Star*, Sunday, April 22, 1945, p. 10.

340 If I remember correctly, I saw a copy of the article in NARA at College Park MD, RG 226 Records of the OSS, OSS Personnel Files, 1941–1945, box 769: Tenenbaum, Edward to Terry, James R., folder: Tenenbaum, Edward, Lieutenant (Army).

341 "Culin's Patrol Is Alert on Mission. Scouting Assignment Carried Out on Moselle River." *Tucson Daily Citizen*, April 19, 1945, p. 7. See also the article with identical content except the quoted part: "Placer County Sergeant Explains How Tiger Patrols Operate." *The Press-Tribune* (Roseville, California), April 18, 1945, p. 7.

342 John M. O'Connell, Jr., "Victory Bound." *The Bangor Daily News* (Bangor, Maine), March 31, 1945, pp. 1, 4. These details had already been reported two days after the event by the *Baltimore Sun* of 18 March 1945 in an article entitled "Patton at Nahe River at Two Points behind German Forces in Saar."

343 March 7, 1945 is the date recorded by the city archive of Coblenz for the blow-up of the Adolf Hitler Bridge. www.schaengel-geschichten.de/als-die-europabruecke-noch-nicht-europabruecke-hiess/ (Accessed August 25, 2019). Michels (*Sturm am Mittelrhein*, p. 83) reports that the blow-up occurred on March 8, 1945, after the blow-up of two other Mosel bridges had taken place on March 7. According to him other bridge blow-ups in Coblenz followed on March 9 and 11. Because Michels differentiates between blow-up dates, whereas the city archive of Coblenz dates all of them on March 7, I give his dates more credit than the undifferentiated dating of the city archive. After reconstruction, the

former Adolf Hitler Bridge was called *Neue Brücke* (New Bridge) and has been in use again since 1954. In 1974 its four lanes were doubled by building a twin bridge adjacent to it. On October 7, 1991 the bridge was officially named *Europabrücke* (Europe Bridge).

344 Erich Ludendorff and Paul von Hindenburg were the two commanding generals of the German troops fighting the Allies in France 1916 to the end of the War. Reactionary Ludendorff sided with Hitler in the famous beer hall putsch in Munich November 8 and 9, 1923.

345 The official history of the US Army in World War II devotes a whole chapter to the Remagen Bridge. See MacDonald, *The Last Offensive*, pp. 208–235. For the story of the Remagen Bridge from a German perspective see Michels, *Die Heimat in Scherben*, pp. 99–109.

346 Frankel/Smith, *Patton's Best*, p. 123.

347 Patton, *War As I Knew It*, pp. 266–267, 273. Based on that source the story is also reported in Wagner, *Krieg in der Heimat*, pp. 292–293. For more information on the Rhine crossings at Oppenheim and Nierstein and all others of the Allied Armies see *The US Army Campaigns of World War II: Central Europe*, pp. 9–12. Online: https://history.army.mil/html/books/072/72-36/CMH_Pub_72–36.pdf (Accessed November 20, 2019). For details of General Manton S. Eddy's XIIth Corps that executed the Rhine crossing at Oppenheim see: George Dyer, *XII Corps Spearhead of Patton's Third Army*, Headquarters XII US Army Corrps, 1947, pp. 360–268. For Patton's personal account of the planning for and execution of the Rhine crossing see: Blumenson (ed.), *The Patton Papers 1940–1945*, pp. 659–661, based on Patton's diary and letters to his wife Beatrice.

348 Patton, *War As I Knew It*, pp. 289–290.

349 Ibid., p. 291.

350 These far-reaching consequences are pointed out in Dieter Zeigert, *Hitlers letztes Refugium? Das Projekt eines Führerhauptquartiers in Thüringen 1944/45*, Munich: Utz, 2003, p. 115. The following paragraphs are based on information from this source (pp. 115–119), unless I cite other sources.

351 The full name is spelled out in Hair, *Secrets Hidden*, p. 121. Also in Dean Reuter/Colm Lowery/Keith Chester, *The Hidden Nazi: The Untold Story of America's Deal with the Devil*, Washington, DC: Regnery History, 2019, p. 380, note 35. As against that, Zeigert (*Hitlers letztes Refugium?*,

p. 115) has deliberately changed the name to *Arms* and is mute on his first name. And Third Army G-2 chief Oscar W. Koch who eyewitnessed the interrogation and related the story doesn't mention the name at all. See: Koch/G. Hays, *G-2 Intelligence for Patton.*

352 Praun, *Soldat in der Telegraphen.* Unfortunately, Arntz is not mentioned in this book with Praun's memoirs.

353 Ibid., p. 245.

354 NARA at College Park MD, RG 165, Entry 79, P-File, C.S.D.I.C. (UK)-Report S.I.R. 1593 of April 1, 1945. Quoted and cited from Zeigert, *Hitlers letztes Refugium?*, pp. 116 and 260 for endnote 307.

355 This account of the German officer's interrogation is based on Koch/Hays, *G-2 Intelligence for Patton*, pp. 116–118. Based on this source it is retold in Hair, *Secrets Hidden*, pp. 122–125.

356 Hair, *Secrets Hidden*, p. 125.

357 On the change of strategy with full backing from Washington (General Marshall and the Joint Chiefs of Staff as well as President Roosevelt himself), but with quite some reservations by the British see: Hair, *Secrets Hidden*, pp. 161–171.

358 Frankel/Smith, *Patton's Best*, pp. 127–128.

359 Reuter/Lowery/Chester, *The Hidden Nazi*, p. 380, note 35. As the authors didn't cite the source of this information from NARA more precisely, they obviously had gained access to this file as to others with similarly incomplete quotations via the Freedom of Information Act.

360 Frankel/Smith, *Patton's Best*, p. 128.

361 For detailed research results on S-III see: Zeigert, *Hitlers letztes Refugium?* pp. 116–161.

362 Hair, *Secrets Hidden*, pp. 126–128. See also Koch/Hays, *G-2 Intelligence for Patton*, pp. 114–116.

363 Rainer Karlsch, *Hitlers Bombe. Die geheime Geschichte der deutschen Kernwaffenversuche*, Munich: DVA, 2005. Rainer Karlsch (ed.), *Für und Wider "Hitlers Bombe": Studien zur Atomforschung in Deutschland*, Münster: Waxmann, 2007.

364 Reuter/Lowery/Chester, *The Hidden Nazi*, p. 239. On this page the authors start reporting on the German submarine U-234 leaving a German-controlled port in Norway on March 25, 1945 with designs and samples of Germany's most modern weapons' technologies. It was officially "bound for Japan in a last-gasp effort to fortify Japan with

German technology and make sure the German tech did not die with the Third Reich." U-234 surrendered to the Americans off the Newfoundland coast, after it had been spotted, but was not attacked by US warplanes. It also contained more than a 1,000 pounds of uranium oxide in very valuable containers for enriched uranium. The authors unearthed evidence that this uranium material went straight into the Manhattan Project. They claim that this German uranium material was integrated for use in the American uranium bombs dropped over Hiroshima and Nagasaki. For the U-234 story see Reuter/Lowery/Chester, The Hidden Nazi, pp. 239–243. The authors present this as part of the American deal with the "Lord" (Hans Kammler) of German secret-weapons development: The US Army Counter Intelligence Corps (CIC) orchestrated his alleged suicide at the end of the War. They put him through the usual PW-interrogation process in Europe and later served for his undercover survival, but not in the USA. Against the standard rule that every SS officer belonged to a terrorist organization committing crimes against humanity, Kammler and his subordinate SS officer Wernher von Braun were spared a trial at the Nuremberg Court. Von Braun with his team was even privileged to continue his missile projects in the USA. The authors provide "very powerful" circumstantial evidence that CIC arranged for Kammler's escape with false ID papers in 1947 from American custody in Europe to South America via the illicit *Ratline*. The latter had been organized by European and Latin American Catholic circles to protect war criminals and Nazi collaborators in occupied countries from prosecution. Ibid., pp. 315–326. "Kammler had American help in escaping to safety in South America after the CIC and OSS-CIA exhausted his usefulness in interrogation." Ibid., p. 315. The most recent publication on the Ratline is Philippe Sands, *The Ratline. Love, Lies and Justice on the Trail of a Nazi Fugitive*, London: Weidenfeld & Nicholson, 2020. This book is more of a biography of Otto Gustav von Wächter, born July 8, 1901 in Vienna, than a systematic study of the Ratline, its organization, and its users. The latter purpose is better served by Gerald Steinacher, *Nazis on the Run: How Hitler's Henchmen Fled Justice*, Oxford/New York: Oxford University Press, 2011. And for the Vatican's controversial organizer and middleman, also for the US secret service CIC, of the Ratline, the Austrian-born Bishop Alois Karl Hudal, a stern anti-communist like the Nazis, who previously had aimed at and believed in a reconciliation of Christianity and National Socialism, see Johannes Sachslehner, *Hitlers Mann im Vatikan. Bischof Alois Hudal. Ein dunkles Kapitel in der Geschichte der Kirche*, Vienna: Molden, 2019. It was recently detected that Bishop Hudal was subordinated to CIC's top postwar agent in Rome Karl Hass. The latter had been a highly decorated SS Major who had worked for the Nazi Secret Service SD (*Sicherheitsdienst*). CIC recruited him, on the one hand, to support its hunt for the most wanted Nazis and Italian Fascists and, on the other, to link up with such persons and try to recruit them for CIC to assist in the Cold War against Communisms in the Soviet sphere of influence. See: Sands, *The Ratline*, chapter 41 "Los Angeles," pp. 246–250. The US *Nazi War Crimes Disclosure Act of 1998* triggered the declassification of about eight million pages of documents. Intelligence records, such as from CIC, OSS, and from cooperation with British Secret Services, such as MI5 (domestic security service to catch the enemy's spies) and MI6 (foreign intelligence service with its network of "own" spies abroad). These files were among the most valuable to shed new light on old questions. Newly revealed documents prove that – shortly before he went there – OSS' representative in Bern, Switzerland, Allan Dulles, knew more and earlier (June 1942) than historians have known so far that Jews were not only persecuted, but systematically exterminated. This information was based partly on British intelligence reports from Warsaw and on eyewitness accounts of OSS informants on mass shootings in the Baltic states. The files not only reveal that officers in the German Foreign Intelligence Service, like Admiral Wilhelm Canaris' *Abwehr* and the SD Foreign Intelligence of the SS, in general displayed little professional quality. They likewise demonstrate the CIC's many blunders and misjudgments as well as the little use from Nazi criminals taken on CIC's payroll and its white-washing power. Norman J. W. Goda/Richard Breitman, "Conclusion," in Richard Breitman et al., *US Intelligence and the Nazis*, Cambridge University Press, 2005, pp. 443–460.

Back to Otto von Wächter: He was educated in Catholic faith by his parents and became a conservative nationalist and anti-Semite like his father Josef, a highly decorated, with hereditary nobility honored Austrian professional military officer of World War I. Otto had started his career by joining in 1923 the precursor of the Nazi Party in Austria, dropped out a year later and joined the real Nazi Party in Austria again in

1930. By then professionally attorney at law, he defended Party comrades in court actions. He had become a member of the SS already in April 1932. He finished his career with the rank of a general of the SS (*Gruppenführer*) as one of the deputies of Hans Frank. The latter was governor general of the German-occupied Polish territories. For murder of 4 million persons Frank was sentenced to death and hanged in Nuremberg in 1946. In November 1939 Wächter had become governor of the district of Krakow in Frank's dominion. In 1942 Frank had appointed him governor of the district of Galicia with its capital Lemberg, today's Lwiw in the Ukraine. In August 1942 Frank had come to Lemberg and delivered a speech to his fellow Nazi ideologists there, in which he gave the go-ahead for the extinction of Jews there as elsewhere. Galicia in general and Lemberg in particular were home to large Jewish communities. Wächter, who executed this crime against humanity in Galicia, was also accused at the Nuremberg trials for mass murder by shooting and other modes of executions of more than 100,000 men, women and children. But he managed to remain untraceable. After hiding in the mountains he somehow managed to be lodged in a monastery in Italy on the waiting list for the Ratline to Catholic South America. However, in July 1949 he died in a hospital in Rome, where he had been brought by two monks for treatment of his jaundice infection under a false identity. It wasn't the Ratline that protected him from prosecution by human justice authorities, but death which he himself had inflicted on so many other human beings. In his case though it is only his youngest son Horst who sticks to the belief that his father had been murdered, too, by poison. Philippe Sands, *The Ratline. Love, Lies and Justice on the Trail of a Nazi Fugitive*, London: Weidenfeld & Nicholson, 2020, pp. 21–62.

365 Kesselring, who had commanded the German troops in Italy in their defensive operations, was called to see Hitler the day after the Remagen Bridge had been captured intact by US troops. Hitler appointed him successor of Field Marshal Gerd von Rundstedt as commander-in-chief for all German military forces on the Western Front as of March 11, 1945.

366 Quoted from Hair, *Secrets Hidden*, p. 199.

367 Ulrich Brunzel, *Hitlers Geheimobjekte in Thüringen. Ein Buch zur Aufdeckung weißer Flecken in der Geschichte des Freistaates Thüringen*, 16th ed., Zella-Mehlis/Meiningen: Heinrich-Jung-Verlagsgesellschaft, 2013. For the location of the thirteen most important sites see a map in

ibid., p. 90. On S-III, the tunnel system under construction, see also Dankmar Leffler, *MUNA Crawinkel. Die Luftmunitionsanstalt I/IV Crawinkel und ihr militärisch geprägtes Umfeld*, without publishing location: Dankmar Leffler author's edition, 2015. On S-III and German nuclear research in Stadtilm see also Gerhard Rembt/Günter Wermusch, *Rätsel Jonastal. Die Geschichte des letzten "Führerhauptquartiers,"* Berlin: Links, 1992. On S-III and Führer headquarters *Olga* see also Klaus-Peter Schambach, *Tatort Jonastal. Ermordet für das Führerhauptquartier in Thüringen im Außenkommando S III des KL Buchenwald*, 2nd ed., Zella-Mehlis/Meiningen: Heinrich-Jung-Verlagsgesellschaft, 2011.

368 According to official US records Hans Kammler committed suicide in Bohemia on May 9, 1945. But recently Frank Döbert/Rainer Karschl, "Hans Kammler, Hitler's Last Hope, in American Hands," in *The Cold War International History Project Working Paper Series of the Woodrow Wilson International Center for Scholars*, ed. by Christian F. Ostermann and Charles Kraus, No. 91, Washington, DC, 2019) with documents newly discovered in the British National Archives advanced the thesis that Kammler sold his valuable military knowledge to the US forces. After some months in American PW camps in Europe for interrogation he probably lived on in arranged hiding in the USA. Documents in NARA that could shed further light on Kammler's cooperation with and survival in the USA have so far remained classified. See also a recent biography of Hans Kammler, including the American cover-up of Kammler's survival by Reuter/Lowery/Chester, *The Hidden Nazi*.

369 Zeigert, *Hitlers letztes Refugium?* p. 174.

370 "Alsos Mission," Online: *Wikipedia* (Accessed September 24, 2020). In more detail from the eyewitness Samuel A. Goudsmit, *Alsos*, New York: Henry Schuman, 1947.

371 Reuter/Lowery/Chester, *The Hidden Nazi*, p. 231.

372 Ibid., pp. 232–233.

373 Wikipedia "Rheinbote." Online: https://en.wikipedia.org/wiki/Rheinbote (Accessed November 2, 2020). Reuter/Lowery/Chester, *The Hidden Nazi*, pp. 258–259.

374 Zeigert, *Hitlers letztes Refugium?* p. 174.

375 The whole story of the Allen mission is extensively documented in chapter 31 of Hair, *Secrets Hidden*, pp. 211–234.

376 Allen, *Lucky Forward*, p. 367.

377 Ibid, p. 368.

378 MacDonald, *The Last Offensive*, p. 376. Allen, *Lucky Forward*, p. 369. With many details on the course of US advance and discoveries in that region: Zeigert, *Hitlers letztes Refugium?* pp. 165–173.

379 MacDonald, *The Last Offensive*, pp. 377–378. Zeigert, *Hitlers letztes Refugium?* p. 44. Praun, *Soldat in der Telegraphen*, p. 244.

380 More details in Zeigert, *Hitlers letztes Refugium?*

381 "The Edward and Joseph Tenenbaum papers." Online: https://collections .ushmm.org/search/catalog/irn559430 (Accessed October 23, 2019).

382 "Translation from German. Hans Habe in Conversation with Mr. Edward A. Tenenbaum (Excerpts from an article in the periodical 'Stern', Hamburg, March 1, 1964)." Edward A. Tenenbaum Papers, box 5, folder: Germany – Currency Reform – Memoranda (9 of 9). HSTPL.

383 For details of the "horror camp" and the reaction of German civilians and a German District Military Surgeon, who were forced to attend a memorial service at the "gruesome open-pit ghat" of the camp, as well as for a description of the purpose and the state of completion of the tunnel system see Allen, *Lucky Forward*, pp. 369–372. An original documentary of the forced labor and concentration camp is available online: www .youtube.com/watch?v=8FASm1SupaE (Accessed May 18, 2019). A fact-oriented summary of the history of the camp, of the atrocities committed therein, and of its liberation is provided by Geoffrey P. Megargee (ed.), *Encyclopedia of Camps and Ghettos 1933–1945*, vol. 1, part A, Bloomington: Indiana University Press, 2009, pp. 402–405. From that source we know that by March 29, 1945 the number of inmates had climbed to 11,700 and that besides Combat Command B of the Fourth Armored Division members of the US 602nd Tank Destroyers' Battalion and the 89th Infantry Division were participating in the liberation.

384 MacDonald, *The Last Offensive*, p. 378.

385 Blumenson/Hymel, *Patton. Legendary Commander*, p. 69.

386 Ziemke, *The US Army in the Occupation of Germany 1944–1946*, p. 232. A somewhat less fact-based but more docudrama-fiction-like description of the same events is contained in Frankel/Smith, *Patton's Best*, pp. 130–131.

387 Quoted from "16 Photographs At Ohrdruf," Online: http://16photographs .com/kzs3.html (Accessed October 30, 2019).

388 Patton, *War As I Knew It*, pp. 292–293.

389 Barbie Zelitzer, *Remember to Forget. Holocaust Memory Through the Camera's Eye*, Chicago University Press, 1998, p. 91.

390 With documents, photos and text all three subjects are covered by Hair, *Secrets Hidden*, pp. 181–265. For a more concise treatment of the subjects see Hair, *The Images Uncovered*, pp. 125–138.

391 Patton, *War As I Knew It*, p. 291.

392 Ziemke, *The US Army in the Occupation of Germany 1944–1946*, p. 228.

393 This paragraph is based on Patton, *War As I Knew It*, pp. 287–288.

394 Ibid., p. 292.

395 Ziemke, *The US Army in the Occupation of Germany 1944–1946*, p. 229.

396 Ibid., pp. 229–230.

397 Ibid., pp. 230–231.

398 Ibid., p. 230, note 10. The 19 IARA nations were: Albania, Australia, Belgium, Canada, Czechoslovakia, Denmark, Egypt, France, Greece, India, Luxembourg, Netherlands, New Zealand, Norway, Pakistan, South Africa, UK, USA, and Yugoslavia. Special Report of the Military Governor, OMGUS, November 1948, "Three Years of Reparations" (A Survey), Reprinted in James K. Pollock/James H. Meisel/Henry L. Bretton (eds.), *Germany Under Occupation. Illustrative Materials and Documents*, Ann Arbor, MI: George Wahr, 1949, pp. 64–67, here p. 64.

399 Hajo Holborn, *American Military Government. Its Organization and Policies*, Washington, DC: Infantry Journal Press, 1947, p. 201. See also: Ziemke, *The US Army in the Occupation of Germany 1944–1946*, p. 230, note 10.

400 Josef Henke/Klaus Oldenhage, "Office of Military Government for Germany (US)," in Christoph Weisz (ed.), *OMGUS-Handbuch. Die amerikanische Militärregierung in Deutschland 1945–1949*, Munich: Oldenbourg, 1994, pp. 101–102.

401 Ziemke, *The US Army in the Occupation of Germany 1944–1946*, pp. 197–200. For the establishment and the bumpy start of MFA&A within the military hierarchy see ibid., pp. 53–57.

402 As quoted in Ziemke, *The US Army in the Occupation of Germany 1944–1946*, pp. 197–198.

403 Lothar Pretzell, *Das Kunstgutlager Schloss Celle 1945 bis 1958*, Celle: Pohl, 1958, p. 10.

404 Ziemke, *The US Army in the Occupation of Germany 1944–1946*, pp. 270–272.

405 A detailed description of the history, production, and (labor) conditions in
    Mittelwerk and *Mittelbau-Dora* is contained in Brunzel, *Hitlers
    Geheimobjekte in Thüringen*, pp. 127–146.

406 Ziemke, *The US Army in the Occupation of Germany 1944–1946*, p. 235.
    See also: Frank Baranowski (2016), "Das Muster-Untertagelager. Der
    Umbau des Kaliwerkes Bernterode zu einem Munitionsdepot des
    Heeres." Online: www.rabaranowski.de/bernterode_kaliwerk_muna/
    (Accessed October 6, 2020).

407 Megargee (ed.), *Encyclopedia of Camps and Ghettos 1933–1945*, p. 295.
    There is a reference to: "Collection 4th Armored Division, 604-2.2-Daily
    Reports, June 1944–May 1945, which includes the report of US Army
    member Paul Bodot, who as a scout of the 4th Armored Division of the
    Third US Army entered the camp." In NARA at College Park MD.

408 Walter Bartel, "Das internationale antifaschistische Aktiv befreite das
    Konzentrationslager Buchenwald," in Nationale Mahn- und
    Gedenkstätte Buchenwald (ed.), *Buchenwald*, journal no. 10/1979, 57pp.,
    here testimony by Paul Bodot/Emmanuel Desard, appendix pp. 34–38.
    A somewhat shortened version with some important details left out is
    published in Walter Bartel et al., *Buchenwald. Mahnung und
    Verpflichtung. Dokumente und Berichte*, 4th ed., Berlin: VEB Deutscher
    Verlag der Wissenschaften, 1983, pp. 629–630. The original in French was
    published in *Le Serment. Bulletin de l'Association Francaise
    Buchenwald-Dora et Commandos*, no. 120 (January–February 1978),
    pp. 16–17.

409 David A. Hacket, *The Buchenwald Report*, Boulder, CO: Westview, 1999,
    p. 332. For a more complete timeline of what happened on April 11,
    1945 in and around Buchenwald see ibid., pp. 4–5 of the introduction and
    pp. 331–334 with a documentary report on the course of events on April
    11, 1945. A very authentic description of the unfolding of events in April
    1945 in concentration camp Buchenwald, especially for the dramatic day
    of April 11, is contained in the secretly written diary of the German
    inmate Ernst Thape. He, born 1892, had been a member of the Social
    Democratic Party (SPD) since 1910. He was a metalworker by training.
    After having spent the period of World War I in Zurich/Switzerland, he
    returned to Germany in 1922 and became an editor of the *Magdeburger
    Volksstimme*, an SPD newspaper. After the Nazis outlawed the printing
    of the paper in tandem with their burning of the *Reichstag* building in

Berlin, Ernst Thape became unemployed. His Swiss wife's seamstress skills provided for their livelihood. A few days before the outbreak of World War II the *Geheime Staatspolizei* (Gestapo) took him into "protective custody" and without trial sent him to Buchenwald in September 1939. There he lived until his release in May 1945. Then he initially supported the union of the Communist Party with the SPD for the new Socialist Union Party (SED) in the Soviet occupation zone. But during the Berlin Blockade 1948–49 he was fed up with the communists and moved to West Germany. There he became a press speaker of Social Democratic prime minister of Lower Saxony Hinrich Wilhelm Kopf in Hanover. Manfred Overesch, "Ernst Thapes Buchenwalder Tagebuch von 1945," in *Vierteljahreshefte für Zeitgeschichte* 29 (1981), pp. 631–672, here pp. 635–636.

410 Hackett, *The Buchenwald Report*, p. 332.

411 "Edward Tenenbaum Egon Fleck Preliminary Buchenwald Report." Online: https://archive.org/details/ EdwardTenenbaumEgonFleckPreliminaryBuchenwaldReport/page/n7, p. 4 (Accessed November 25, 2020).

412 Mel Mermelstein, *By Bread Alone. The Story of A-4685*, Huntington Beach, CA: Auschwitz Study Foundation, 1983, pp. 207, 218–219.

413 Ibid., p. 207.

414 Ibid., p. 205.

415 Ibid., p. 206.

416 All information on the vita is collected from Mermelstein, *By Bread Alone*, passim. Some of the general information on concentration camps and the arrest and transportation of Hungarian Jews to Auschwitz has been collected online.

417 "Edward Tenenbaum Egon Fleck Preliminary Buchenwald Report." On p. 6 the report mentions that the 78 SS men were "mostly captured by the camp inmates in the woods, a few found sneaking off disguised as inmates." See also Overesch, "Ernst Thapes Buchenwalder Tagebuch von 1945," pp. 631–672, here pp. 651, note 40.

418 Hackett (ed.), *The Buchenwald Report*, p. 334.

419 For example: Günter Kühn/Wolfgang Weber, *Stärker als die Wölfe*, Berlin: Militärverlag der DDR, 1976. Walter Bartel/Nationale Mahn- und Gedenkstätte Buchenwald (eds.), *Buchenwald: Mahnung und Verpflichtung. Dokumente und Berichte*, 4th ed., Berlin: Deutscher

Verlag der Wissenschaft, 1983. Klaus Drobisch, *Widerstand in Buchenwald*, 4th ed., Berlin: Dietz, 1989.

420 Drobisch, *Widerstand in Buchenwald*, p. 193.

421 This is confirmed by inmate and eyewitness Bruno Bettelheim, *Surviving and Other Essays*, New York: Knopf, 1979, pp. 294–295.

422 Overesch, "Ernst Thapes Buchenwalder Tagebuch von 1945," pp. 649–650, note 38. Mermelstein, *By Bread Alone*, p. 207. See also Hackett (ed.), *The Buchenwald Report*, pp. 5 and 22 of Hackett's introduction. Robert H. Abzug, *Inside the Vicious Heart. Americans and the Liberation of Nazi Concentration Camps*, New York/Oxford: Oxford University Press, 1985, p. 48.

423 Hackett (ed.), *The Buchenwald Report*, p. 333.

424 Ibid.

425 "First American liberators arrive at Buchenwald." Online: www .scrapbookpages.com/Buchenwald/Liberation6.html (Accessed February 7, 2018).

426 *Yale Yearbook Class of 1942 at 25*, New Haven CT 1967, p. 312.

427 See documents of the two Declarations of Intention on Fold3 for Egon Fleck www.fold3.com/image/10925678 and for Hedwig Fleck www.fold3 .com/image/7692912 (Accessed January 13, 2019).

428 Fleck's draft registration document as well as the date and place of his death taken from Social Security records are also available online on Fold3 (Accessed January 13, 2019). For Fleck's OSS activity see his OSS personnel file at NARA at College Park MD, RG 226, Entry 224, box 239.

429 Stefan Heymann aus Mannheim, in Hackett (ed.), *The Buchenwald Report*, pp. 325–331, here 330.

430 Overesch, "Ernst Thapes Buchenwalder Tagebuch von 1945," pp. 631–672, here pp. 646–650.

431 Ibid., pp. 631–672, here p. 639 note 21, 653.

432 "Edward Tenenbaum Egon Fleck Preliminary Buchenwald Report."

433 Overesch, "Ernst Thapes Buchenwalder Tagebuch von 1945," pp. 631–672, here p. 639. My translation.

434 Hackett (ed.), *The Buchenwald Report*, p. 332. For the name of the senior camp inmate see: ibid., p. 4.

435 Ibid., p. 332.

436 "Edward Tenenbaum Egon Fleck Preliminary Buchenwald Report."

437 Overesch, "Ernst Thapes Buchenwalder Tagebuch von 1945,"
pp. 631–672, here p. 651. My translation.
438 For a fact-oriented summarizing account of the atrocities in Buchenwald
since its foundation at the beginning of July 1937 see Megargee (ed.),
Encyclopedia of Camps and Ghettos 1933–1945, pp. 290–295.
439 Patton, *War As I Knew It*, pp. 298–299.
440 Ibid., pp. 300–301.
441 Hackett, *The Buchenwald Report*. Book review online: http://go
.galegroup.com/ps/retrieve.do?tabID=T003&resultListType=RESULT_
LIST&searchResultsType=SingleTab&searchType=
AdvancedSearchForm&currentPosition=1&docId=GALE%
7CA16848712&docType=Book+review%2C+Brief+article&sort=
RELEVANCE&contentSegment=&prodId=AONE&contentSet=GALE%
7CA16848712&searchId=R2&userGroupName=fub&inPS=true
(Accessed July 14, 2018).
442 These men were PWs still wearing their original uniform of Allied
armies. See Niethammer (ed.), *Der gesäuberte Antifaschismus*, p. 181,
note 30.
443 "Edward Tenenbaum Egon Fleck Preliminary Buchenwald Report."
444 Ibid.
445 It was Eugen Kogon. See: Hacket, *The Buchenwald Report*, p. 102, note
53. In 1946 Kogon published his famous analytical study on the SS
concentration camp system. In 1950 it first came out in an English
translation under the title *The Theory and Practice of Hell*, New York:
Farrar, Straus and Cudahy.
446 "Edward Tenenbaum Egon Fleck Preliminary Buchenwald Report."
447 Reprint of *The Dungeon Democracy* in Christopher Burney, *Solitary
Confinement and The Dungeon Democracy. A Classic of Prison
Literature and the Triumph of the Human Spirit*, London: Macmillan
Paperback, 1984, pp. 217–232.
448 Ibid., p. 206.
449 Ibid., p. 227. Kogon presents a full version of the short letter. But its
content deviates from Burney's quoted excerpts. Compare Eugen Kogon,
The Theory and Practice of Hell, New York: Berkley Books Paperback,
1998, p. 284.
450 Reprint of *The Dungeon Democracy* in Christopher Burney, *Solitary
Confinement and The Dungeon Democracy. A Classic of Prison*

Literature and the Triumph of the Human Spirit, London: Macmillan Paperback, 1984, pp. 217–218.

451 Hacket, *The Buchenwald Report*, p. 102, note 53.

452 Burney, "The Dungeon Democracy," p. 217.

453 Kogon mentions explicitly that some of his confidants saved Burney's life by hiding him in a cavity under Block 56 in the Small Camp. Kogon, *The Theory and Practice of Hell*, pp. 281–282.

454 Ibid., p. 282.

455 Burney, "The Dungeon Democracy," p. 148.

456 Ibid., pp. 149–150.

457 "Edward Tenenbaum Egon Fleck Preliminary Buchenwald Report."

458 Ibid., p. 5.

459 Ibid., p. 6.

460 Ibid.

461 Ibid.

462 Ibid., p. 7.

463 Burney, "The Dungeon Democracy," p. 162.

464 "Edward Tenenbaum Egon Fleck Preliminary Buchenwald Report," p. 7.

465 Ibid., p. 7.

466 Ibid., p. 8.

467 Ibid.

468 Ibid., p. 9.

469 An exception was Jorge Semprún, born December 10, 1923. With his family he had fled Madrid in 1936, i.e. early in the Spanish Civil War, first to Geneva and from there to Paris, where he studied philosophy. In 1941 he joined the communist resistance group in France and in 1942 the Communist Party in Spain. In 1943 the Gestapo arrested him in Paris. After its infamous interrogations and tortures, Semprún was transported to Buchenwald, where he arrived in January 1944. The German communists actually assigned him to the Labor Office (*Arbeitsstatistik*). This means they shared their power over life and death of ordinary inmates with him. But this also means that they cared to the utmost for his survival. After Buchenwald's liberation he returned to Paris where he lived until he died on June 7, 2011. Online: www.stiftung-ettersberg.de/stiftung/jorge-semprun-der-initiator/ (Accessed December 1, 2020).

470 "Edward Tenenbaum Egon Fleck Preliminary Buchenwald Report."

471 Ibid., p. 10.

472 Ibid., p. 11.
473 Bettelheim, *Surviving and Other Essays.*
474 Kogon, *The Theory and Practice of Hell.* First English edition 1950. Original edition in German 1946.
475 Jorge Semprún, *The Long Voyage,* London: Weidenfeld & Nicolson, 1964. Original edition in French 1963. Jorge Semprún, *What a Beautiful Sunday.* New York: Harcourt, Brace, Jovanovich, 1982. Original edition in French 1980.
476 Ibid., p. 12.
477 Annette Hinz-Wessels, "Das Robert Koch-Institut im Nationalsozialismus." Online: www.rki.de/DE/Content/Institut/ Geschichte/Dokumente/Erinnerungszeichen_Broschuere.pdf?__blob= publicationFile (Accessed December 23, 2020). The RKI was Germany's lead institution in tracing and combating the Covid-19 pandemic in 2020 to 2022.
478 "Edward Tenenbaum Egon Fleck Preliminary Buchenwald Report," pp. 12–13.
479 Christopher Burney reports in his *Dungeon Democracy* that Marcel Michelin had been sent to Buchenwald by the Gestapo "for resistance activities in which, among other things, he had ordered the destruction of a large stock of rubber in order to prevent it from falling into German hands. Michelin was a man of over sixty, and would have been automatically exempt from transport by the SS for that reason, but he was a capitalist and therefore condemned as an enemy of mankind. There were several attempts to send him away, but they were thwarted, until finally he was slipped into the confusion of a big departure for Ohrdruf. The medical formalities were by-passed, protests ignored. Indeed his executioners worked almost too suddenly for his friends to have time to protest. He left. Three weeks later he died." Burney, *The Dungeon Democracy*, pp. 168–169. Marcel Michelin was born in Paris on April 12, 1886 and died in Ohrdruf on January 21, 1945. See: "Marcel Michelin." Online: https://fr.wikipedia.org/wiki/Marcel_Michelin (Accessed December 23, 2020).
480 "Edward Tenenbaum Egon Fleck Preliminary Buchenwald Report," p. 13.
481 Ibid., p. 14.
482 Ibid.
483 Ibid.

484 Ibid., pp. 14–15.

485 Ibid., p. 15.

486 Ibid., p. 2.

487 Documented in Kogon, *The Theory and Practice of Hell*, pp. 279, 281–282.

488 Burney, "The Dungeon Democracy."

489 Ibid., p. 243.

490 Norbert Guterman, "Seven Books on Nazi Atrocities," in Commentary, July 1946. Online: www.commentarymagazine.com/articles/norbert-guterman/seven-books-on-nazi-atrocities/ (Accessed January 4, 2021). Post-1945 political developments in continental Europe proved Burney's judgment wrong.

491 *Kirkus* Reviews, Issue: 1 April 1946. Online: www.kirkusreviews.com/book-reviews/a/christopher-burney/dungeon-democracy/ (Accessed January 4, 2021).

492 Kenneth Waltzer, "Block 66 at Buchenwald: The Clandestine Barracks to Save Children." Online: www.fold3.com/page/286022387-buchenwald/stories (Accessed April 10, 2019).

493 "Edward Tenenbaum Egon Fleck Preliminary Buchenwald Report."

494 This paragraph is based on Kogon, *The Theory and Practice of Hell*, pp. X–XIII.

495 "Issue Regulations; The Bronze Star." Online: www.amervets.com/replacement/bs.htm#isr (Accessed July 11, 2018). The exclusion of aerial flight participation was simply due to the fact that a medal for similar achievements in aerial flight had already been introduced at an earlier date.

496 "J. Russell Forgan Dead at 73; Banker Was Official of OSS," in *The New York Times*, February 1, 1974. Online: www.nytimes.com/1974/02/01/archives/j-russell-forgan-dead-at-73-banker-was-official-of-oss-won-many.html (Accessed July 10, 2018). Forgan had graduated from Princeton University with a BA degree.

497 APO stands for Army Post Office. APO 757 was the number for Headquarters US Forces European Theater.

498 NARA at College Park MD, RG 226 Records of the OSS, OSS Personnel Files, 1941–1945, box 769: Tenenbaum, Edward to Terry, James R., folder: Tenenbaum, Edward, Lieutenant (Army).

499 NARA at College Park MD, RG 226 Records of the OSS, OSS Personnel Files, 1942–1962, box 405: Kin-Cade, A. THRU King, G, folders: Kindleberger, Charles P., Major (Army).

500 NARA at College Park MD, RG 226 Records of the OSS, OSS Personnel Files, 1942–1962, box 405: Kin-Cade, A. THRU King, G, folders: Kindleberger, Charles P., 0925563.

501 "ETO Card on Tenenbaum, Edward A., 1st Lt., serial number 0870114, AC Branch" of 28 May 1946. In NARA at College Park MD, RG 226 Records of the OSS, OSS Personnel Files, 1941–1945, box 769: Tenenbaum, Edward to Terry, James R., folder: Tenenbaum, Edward, Lieutenant (Army).

502 Kathy Peiss, *Information Hunters. When Librarians, Soldiers, and Spies Banded Together in World War II Europe*, Oxford University Press, 2020, esp. chapter 3 for establishing T-Forces, pp. 68–92. For the term *Target Force* see the report by Frederick B. Alexander Jr. cited in endnote 3 on p. 230. In a leading position, Alexander was involved in T-Force operations of the Sixth US Army Group in Southern Germany. I am most indebted to Kathy Peiss for paving my way to Tenenbaum reports on his T-Force activity in NARA at College Park MD.

503 Brian N. MacPherson, "Kings and desperate men: The United States Office of Strategic Services in London and the Anglo-American relationship, 1941–1946," PhD dissertation, University of Toronto (Canada), ProQuest Dissertations Publishing, 1995, p. XIII.

504 Winks, *Cloak and Gown 1939–1961*, p. 244.

505 His obituary online: www.mn-ww2roundtable.org/harold-c-deutsch-obituary/ (Accessed January 4, 2020).

506 From Harold C. Deutsch to Colonel D. K. E. Bruce "Progress Report, R&A/Paris, 28 September–15 October 1944." NARA at College Park MD, RG 226 Office of Strategic Services, Entry NM 54 1: Research and Analysis Branch, Office of the Chief: General Correspondence, 1942–46, box 31, folder 1.

507 Greg Bradscher, "A Finding Aid to Records at the NARA at College Park. For the Interagency Group on Nazi Assets Directed by Stuart E. Eizenstat, Under Secretary of Commerce." Online: 1997–2001.state.gov/regions/eur/nginv.pdf (Accessed January 6, 2020). This quantification conforms to the figure of "almost 13,000 men and women" employed by OSS at its peak in late 1944. See Warner, *The Office of Strategic Services*, p. 9.

508 NARA at College Park MD, RG 226 Office of Strategic Services, Entry A1 146: Miscellaneous Washington Files Budget, WASH – R&A – OP – 7, 319.1 – Europe-Africa Division Out-Post Letter (NO1) THRU 319.1 – Progress Reports – ETO, box 92.

509 Ibid.

510 Ibid.

511 NARA at College Park MD, RG 226 Office of Strategic Services, Entry NM 54 1: Research and Analysis Branch, Office of the Chief: General Correspondence, 1942–46, box 31, folder 1.

512 Quoted from Peiss, *Information Hunters*, p. 85.

513 Ibid., pp. 78–79. Quotations are taken from there.

514 Ibid., p. 232, endnote 26. As source Peiss cites Rubint's OSS Personnel File.

515 NARA at College Park MD, RG 226 Office of Strategic Services, Entry A1 146: Miscellaneous Washington Files Budget, WASH – R&A – OP – 7, 319.1 – Europe-Africa Division Out-Post Letter (NO1) THRU 319.1 – Progress Reports – ETO, box 92.

516 Ibid.

517 Ibid.

518 This date for Tenenbaum's departure from London to France is also officially noted in OSS ETO, US Army (Main), APO 413, R&A Branch, "Progress Report, 16 November to 30 November 1944. Activities of the Branch as a Whole" of November 30, 1944. NARA at College Park MD, RG 226 Office of Strategic Services, Entry NM 54 1: Research and Analysis Branch, Office of the Chief: General Correspondence, 1942–46, box 31, folder 1.

519 NARA at College Park MD, RG 226 Office of Strategic Services, Entry A1 146: Miscellaneous Washington Files Budget, WASH – R&A – OP – 7, 319.1 – Europe-Africa Division Out-Post Letter (NO1) THRU 319.1 – Progress Reports – ETO, box 92.

520 Many of the documents in German and their translations into English that Tenenbaum collected in Brussels are contained in Edward A. Tenenbaum Papers, box 1, folders: Belgium – Germany Fiscal Policy Toward, 1941–1942 and Belgium – Germany Fiscal Policy Toward, 1943–1944. HSTPL.

521 NARA at College Park MD, RG 226 Office of Strategic Services, Entry A1 146: Miscellaneous Washington Files Budget, WASH – R&A – OP – 7, 319.1 – Europe–Africa Division Out-Post Letter (NO1) THRU 319.1 – Progress Reports – ETO, box 92.

522 Ibid.

523 OSS ETO, US Army (Main), APO 413, R&A Branch, "Progress Report, 16 November to 30 November 1944. Activities of the Branch as a Whole"

of 30 November1944. NARA at College Park MD, RG 226 Office of Strategic Services, Entry NM 54 1: Research and Analysis Branch, Office of the Chief: General Correspondence, 1942–46, box 31, folder 1.

524 NARA at College Park MD, RG 226 Office of Strategic Services, Entry A1 146: Miscellaneous Washington Files Budget, WASH – R&A – OP – 7, 319.1 – Europe–Africa Division Out-Post Letter (NO1) THRU 319.1 – Progress Reports – ETO, box 92.

525 Ibid.

526 For the history and functions of IDC see: Winks, *Cloak and Gown 1939–1961*, pp. 101–110. Thomas R. Barcus/Verner W. Clapp, "Collecting in the National Interest," *Library Trends* 3 (1955), pp. 337–355.

527 For a complete list of APO numbers in WW II see online: www .7tharmddiv.org/docrep/Location%20of%20APOs%201942-1947.pdf (Accessed January 13, 2020).

528 NARA at College Park MD, RG 226 Office of Strategic Services, Entry A1 146: Miscellaneous Washington Files Budget, WASH – R&A – OP – 7, 319.1 – Europe–Africa Division Out-Post Letter (NO1) THRU 319.1 – Progress Reports – ETO, box 92.

529 Ibid.

530 For all information and citations from Tenenbaum's second report from Brussels: Ibid.

531 "Secret for OSS Use Only, La Roche, Belgium, 12 December 1944, FROM: Edward A. Tenenbaum, 2nd Lt., AC, ATTENTION: Lt (jg) Just Lunning, Chief, German Unit (Tempo), R&A/London, TO: Harold Deutsch, Chief, R&A/Paris." NARA at College Park MD, RG 226 Office of Strategic Services, Entry NM 54 1: Research and Analysis Branch, Office of the Chief: General Correspondence, 1942–46, box 31, folder 1.

532 Ibid.

533 Ibid.

534 While in his letter to Deutsch of December 10, 1944 Tenenbaum had used "Krafft" for the spelling of the captain's last name, he spelled him "Craft" in his third weekly report of December 12, 1944. I have retained the spelling Captain "Krafft" throughout my text.

535 NARA at College Park MD, RG 226 Office of Strategic Services, Entry NM 54 1: Research and Analysis Branch, Office of the Chief: General Correspondence, 1942–46, box 31, folder 1.

536 OSS Detachment (Main), APO 413 US Army, "Memo From Harold Starr To Lt. Philip Bastedo" of March 9, 1945. NARA at College Park MD, RG 226 Office of Strategic Services, Entry NM 54 1: Research and Analysis Branch, Office of the Chief: General Correspondence, 1942–46, box 31, folder 1.

537 Katz, *Foreign Intelligence*, p. 86.

538 From Harold C. Deutsch to Colonel D. K. E. Bruce "Progress Report."

539 "Progress Report, R&A Paris & Forward, Activities of the Branch as a Whole," dated May 1 for the period 16–30 April and dated June 1, 1945 for the period May 1–31, 1945. And "Progress Report, R&A/Germany, Activities of the Branch as a Whole," dated June 1 for the period May 25–31, 1945. NARA at College Park MD, RG 226 Office of Strategic Services, Entry NM 54 1: Research and Analysis Branch, Office of the Chief: General Correspondence, 1942–46, box 31, folder 1.

540 Edward A. Tenenbaum Papers, box 6, folder: Germany – Economic Situation, 1944–45. HSTPL.

541 Erwin J. Warkentin (ed.), *The History of US Information Control in Post-war Germany: The Past Imperfect*, Newcastle upon Tyne: Cambridge Scholars Publishing, 2016. Previous online version: "History of the Information Control Division OMGUS 1944 to June 30, 1946," 2010, p. 3. www.erwinslist.com/Files/History%20I.pdf (Accessed September 6, 2019).

542 For its history until June 30, 1946 see Warkentin (ed.), "History of the Information Control Division OMGUS 1944 to June 30, 1946."

543 Edward A. Tenenbaum Papers, box 6, folder: Germany – Economic Situation, 1944–45. HSTPL. My translation. Like during their mission in Buchenwald Tenenbaum was also here accompanied by Egon Fleck, who was not a military, but a civilian employee as mentioned above.

544 "Deutscher Kurzwellensender." Wikipedia online: https://de.wikipedia .org/wiki/Deutscher_Kurzwellensender (Accessed April 16, 2020).

545 Cora Sol Goldstein, "Before the CIA: American Actions in the German Fine Arts (1946–1949)," in *Diplomatic History* 29 (2005), pp. 747–778, as to Pommer and Wilder, p. 751.

546 Brewster S. Chamberlin, *Kultur auf Trümmern. Berliner Berichte der amerikanischen Information Control Section Juli bis Dezember 1945*, Munich 2010, *Inhaltsverzeichnis*.

547 Christina Riley, "Billy Wilder's A Foreign Affair: Marlene Dietrich's Star Persona and American Interventionist Strategies in Postwar Berlin," in *Bright Lights Film Journal*, April 30, 2012. Online: https://brightlightsfilm.com/billy-wilders-a-foreign-affair-marlene-dietrichs-star-persona-and-american-interventionist-strategies-in-postwar-berlin/#.YDrCQ9wxlPY (Accessed February 27, 2021).

548 Warkentin (ed.), "History of the Information Control Division OMGUS 1944 to June 30, 1946," p. 6.

549 Alec Cairncross, *A Country to Play With: Level of Industry Negotiations in Berlin 1945–46*, Wiltshire: Smythe, 1987.

550 *Yale Yearbook Class of 1942 at 25*, p. 312.

551 Ibid, p. 313.

552 Sequel to "ETO Card on Tenenbaum, Edward A., 1st Lt., serial number 0870114, AC Branch" of 28 May 1946. In NARA at College Park MD, RG 226 Records of the OSS, OSS Personnel Files, 1941–1945, box 769: Tenenbaum, Edward to Terry, James R., folder: Tenenbaum, Edward, Lieutenant (Army).

553 Henke/Oldenhage, "Office of Military Government for Germany (US)," pp. 1–142, p. 106.

554 The original document is available online: www.fold3.com/image/304760058?terms=Tenenbaum,%20Edward%20A. (Accessed October 5, 2018).

555 Emil Puhl, in Wikipedia. Online: https://en.wikipedia.org/wiki/Emil_Puhl and https://de.wikipedia.org/wiki/Emil_Puhl (Accessed April 18, 2018).

556 This had already been a problem during the Weimar Republic when the American S. Parker Gilbert was stationed in Berlin from October 1924 to May 1930 as Reparation Agent to supervise and enforce Germany's commitments under the Dawes Plan. Gilbert was thirty-two when he arrived and thirty-seven when he left. The old guard of Reichsbank leaders and German finance ministers felt not only offended by the control power over their monetary and fiscal policies which Gilbert possessed, but also by his relatively young age.

557 "Meeting with Dr. Terhalle, Bavarian Minister of Finance, and Mr. Ehrhardt [*sic*], Bavarian Minister of Economics, 1 February 1946," Abijah U. Fox Papers, box 8, folder: Military Government for Germany – Finance

Division – Translations re German Banks. HSTPL. The memo with "the strong tone" had been written for OMGUS by Fritz Terhalle in cooperation with Ludwig Erhard in preparation of the personal meeting with Tenenbaum on February 1, 1946. It is contained in ibid. This meeting was part of Tenenbaum's major assignment, still as 1st lieutenant US Army Air Corps, to hold exploratory talks with German officeholders in the different states of the US occupation zone about their views on banking decentralization being pushed by Joseph Dodge. For Tenenbaum's memo of February 6, 1946 "Banking Decentralization," covering results of the whole tour, see ibid. On the issue also: Craig Dee Scott, "Money Talks: The West German Currency Reform of 1948." PhD Dissertation Graduate School, University of Wisconsin at Madison, 1995, p. 285.

558 Abijah U. Fox Papers, box 8, folder: Military Government for Germany – Finance Division – Translations re German Banks. HSTPL.

559 EDCMR stands for Estimated Date of Completion Mid-Range.

560 Tenenbaum's *Final Pay Voucher*. Document provided by National Personnel Records Center in St Louis MO on March 2, 2018.

561 Order by the Assistant Adjutant of the New York Port of Embarkation, First Lieutenant J. E. Hoskinson, addressed to the Adjutant General at Washington, DC. Tenenbaum's *Final Pay Voucher*. Document provided by National Personnel Records Center in St Louis MO on 2 March 2018.

562 *Yale Twenty-Fifth Yearbook. Class of 1942*. New Haven, CT: Yale University Press, 1967, p. 311.

563 All the information and quotes in this paragraph are from Tenenbaum's *Final Pay Voucher*. Documents provided by National Personnel Records Center in St Louis MO on March 2, 2018.

564 In an *Investigation Data Request* from of ECA, where Tenenbaum was required to list his *Dates and Places of Residence for Last 10 Years*, Tenenbaum noted his residence at 3030 Wisconsin Ave. NW. Washington, DC, for the period March to August 1946. Edward A. Tenenbaum Papers, box 8, folder: Personnel File. HSTPL.

565 Edward A. Tenenbaum Papers, box 8, folder: Personnel File. HSTPL. When Tenenbaum left his OMGUS job and thereby the War Department payroll in September 1948, his employment classification was P-6 and his earnings were $9,200 per annum. Ibid.

4 IN ACTION FOR OMGUS AND CURRENCY REFORM IN GERMANY 1946–1948

1 E.g., by Jack Bennett, "Financial Stabilization after Currency Reform," 10-page memo, written by Edward A. Tenenbaum, sent to General Clay March 24, 1948, in IfZ Archive RG 260 / OMGUS, on microfilm. Provenance OMGUS FINAD, shipment 2, box 103, folder 1. A copy, identifying Tenenbaum as author, is contained in Edward A. Tenenbaum Papers, box 3, folder: Germany – Background Data on Monetary Problems (2 of 2).

2 John H. Backer, *Priming the German Economy. American Occupation Policies 1945–1948*, Durham, NC: Duke University Press, 1971, p. 91, note 3. In their covering letter to General Clay, with their final report of May 20, 1946 attached, Colm, Dodge and Goldsmith thank these five persons "for their great help."

3 Lucius D. Clay, *Decision in Germany*, Garden City, NY: Doubleday, 1950, p. 209. For a useful summary of the content of the CDG Plan see Backer, *Priming the German Economy*, pp. 91–93.

4 How exactly Clay and Dodge came to choose Colm and Goldsmith is told in Wolfram Hoppenstedt, *Gerhard Colm. Leben und Werk (1897–1968)*, Stuttgart: Steiner, 1997, pp. 194–205.

5 Gerhard Colm/Joseph M. Dodge/Raymond W. Goldsmith, "A Plan for the Liquidation of War Finance and the Financial Rehabilitation of Germany," in *Zeitschrift für die Gesamte Staatswissenschaft* 111 (1955), Preface, pp. 204–206. The Plan with its covering letter of May 20, 1946, signed by Gerhard Colm, Joseph M. Dodge and Raymond W. Goldsmith, a 3-page summary, a 5-page draft law and the list of seventeen appendices are contained as original documents in Abujah U. Fox Papers, box 8, folder: Military Government for Germany – Plan for the Liquidation of war finance – financial rehabilitation of Germany (folder 1). HSTPL.

6 With "August" or "late August" Clay and Gottlieb date Washington's approval imprecisely. Clay, *Decision in Germany*, p. 210. Manuel Gottlieb, *The German Peace Settlement and the Berlin Crisis*, New York: Paine-Whitman, 1960, p. 112 and endnote 29 p. 235. See also Manuel Gottlieb, "Failure of Quadripartite Monetary Reform," in *Finanzarchiv*, Neue Folge, 17 (1957), pp. 398–417. This article is a condensed version of chapter VI of Gottlieb's book, but with fuller documentation.

7 Office of Military Government for Germany (US), AG Cable Control, Incoming Message REF NO W-98110 of 22 August 1946. Edward A. Tenenbaum Papers, in HSTPL.

8 Gottlieb, *The German Peace Settlement and the Berlin Crisis*, p. 112.

9 Clay, *Decision in Germany*, p. 72.

10 Kevin Conley Ruffner, "The Black Market in Postwar Berlin. Colonel Miller and an Army Scandal," in *Prologue* 34 (2002), pp. 170–183.

11 *US Strategic Bombing Survey*, 2 vols., Washington, DC: GPO, 1945.

12 Beate Neuss, *Geburtshelfer Europas? Die Rolle der Vereinigten Staaten im europäischen Integrationsprozeß 1945 – 1958*, Baden-Baden: Nomos, 2000. Gerd Hardach, *Der Marshallplan. Auslandshilfe und Wiederaufbau in Westdeutschland 1948–1952*, Munich: DTV, 1994. John Killik, *The United States and European Reconstruction: 1945–1960*, Edinburgh: Edinburgh University Press, 2022.

13 Online: www.trumanlibrary.org/whistlestop/study_collections/marshall/large/documents/index.php?documentdate=1947-03-18&documentid=5170&pagenumber=1 (Accessed April 28, 2018), pp. 1–2.

14 Directive JCS 1067 to General Eisenhower is reprinted in FRUS 1945, vol. III, Washington, DC: GPO, 1968, pp. 484–503. James K. Pollock/James H. Meisel/Henry L. Bretton (eds.), *Germany Under Occupation. Illustrative Materials and Documents*, Ann Arbor, MI: George Wahr, 1949, pp. 76–91. And in Hajo Holborn, *American Military Government. Its Organization and Policies*, Washington, DC: Infantry Journal Press, 1947, pp. 157–172. The previous JCS "Directive for Military Government in Germany Prior to Defeat or Surrender" was sent to General Eisenhower on April 28, 1944. It is reprinted in Holborn, American Military Government, pp. 135–143.

15 For the political and economic agreements reached at the Potsdam Conference, partly more restrictive than the US Directive JCS 1067, see: "Report on the Tripartite Conference of Potsdam. August 2, 1945," It is reprinted in Holborn, American Military Government, pp. 195–205.

16 Online: https://en.wikipedia.org/wiki/Allied_plans_for_German_industry_after_World_War_II (Accessed April 28, 2018).

17 Manfred Overesch, *Deutschland 1945–1949. Vorgeschichte und Gründung der Bundesrepublik. Ein Leitfaden in Darstellung und Dokumenten*, Königstein/Taunus: Athenäum, 1979, p. 127.

18 "Statement on American Economic Policy towards Germany. December 12, 1945." It is reprinted in Holborn, *American Military Government*,

pp. 215–222. Clay, *Decision in Germany*, pp. 72–73. John H. Backer, *Winds of History. The German Years of Lucius DuBignon Clay*, New York: van Nostrand Reinhold, 1983, pp. 92–94. Backer had himself served in the Economics Division of Clay's OMGUS.

19 John M. Keynes, *The Economic Consequences of the Peace*, New York: Harcourt, Brace and Howe, 1920. And initiated, coordinated and edited by Keynes: *Manchester Guardian Commercial. Supplement: Reconstruction in Europe* 1922–1923.

20 For details on which industries were allowed to produce more or less of 100 percent see Overesch, *Deutschland 1945–1949*, p. 127.

21 The "almost" full text of cable CC 5797212- is quoted in Clay, *Decision in Germany*, pp. 73–78. It is also printed in Jean Edward Smith (ed.), *The Papers of General Lucius D. Clay. Germany 1945–1949*, vol. 1, Bloomington: Indiana University Press, 1974, pp. 212–217. A summary is contained in John Gimbel, *The American Occupation of Germany. Politics and the Military, 1945–1949*, Stanford: Stanford University Press, 1968, pp. 56–57.

22 Clay, *Decision in Germany*, pp. 73–74.

23 Text of the speech online: http://historyguide.org/europe/churchill.html (Accessed June 7, 2018).

24 Clay, *Decision in Germany*, p. 78.

25 Ibid., p. 77.

26 Jean Edward Smith, *Lucius D. Clay. An American Life*, New York: Henry Holt, 1990, p. 396.

27 Douglas served as British military governor in Germany from May 1, 1946 to October 31, 1947. He was the successor of Field Marshal Bernard Montgomery. Douglas' successor was General Sir Brian Hubert Robertson, who served from November 1, 1947 to September 21, 1949. With the founding of the Federal Republic of Germany on the latter date, he kept on serving as British High Commissioner in Germany until June 24, 1950. "Allied-occupied Germany" Online: https://en.wikipedia.org/wiki/Allied-occupied_Germany#Military_governors_and_commissioners (Accessed May 3, 2018).

28 Overesch, *Deutschland 1945–1949*, p. 128.

29 Text of the Potsdam Agreement II, 14. Online: http://avalon.law.yale.edu/20th_century/decade17.asp (Accessed May 5, 2018).

30 Clay, *Decision in Germany*, p. 78.

31 FRUS, vol. V (1946), Washington, DC: GPO, 1969, pp. 635–647 for documents on the negotiation of the Agreement.

32 NARA at College Park MD, RG 260 OMGUS FINAD, on microfiche IfZ Munich and BArch Coblenz, OMGUS, shipment 11, box 284, folder 4.

33 Edward A. Tenenbaum Papers, box 4, folder: Germany – Currency Reform – Memoranda (5 of 9). HSTPL.

34 John Lewis Gaddis, *The Cold War. A New History*, New York: Penguin, 2005, p. 22.

35 Vladimir O. Pechatnov/C. Earl Edmondson, "The Russian Perspective," in Ralph B. Levering/ Vladimir O. Pechatnov/Verena Botzenhart-Viehe/C. Earl Edmondson (eds.), *Debating the Origins of the Cold War: American and Russian Perspectives*, New York: Rowman & Littlefield, 2002, pp. 85–151. The quote is from p. 109.

36 Gaddis, *The Cold War*, p. 24.

37 The newly founded conservative party, the Christian Democratic Union (CDU) in the state of North Rhine-Westphalia (British zone) reacted to this mood by drafting a new party program and adopting it as its *Ahlener Economic and Social Program* during the "hunger winter" on February 3, 1947. It starts out with the statement that the economic system of capitalism failed to serve the vital public and social interests of the German people. Content and goal of the necessary social and economic reorganization could no longer be the capitalistic strife for profit and power, but only the well-being of our people. Online: www .geschichte.nrw.de/artikel.php?artikel[id]=45&lkz=de (Accessed June 7, 2018).

38 Clay, *Decision in Germany*, p. 78. On the exchange between Clay and Byrnes in the run-up to Byrnes' Stuttgart address see Paul Y. Hammond, "Directives for the Occupation of Germany: The Washington Controversy," in Harold Stein (ed.), *American Civil-Military Decisions. A Book of Case Studies*, Birmingham: University of Alabama Press, 1963, pp. 311–464, here p. 441.

39 The text of Woodrow Wilson's address to Congress online: http:// historymatters.gmu.edu/d/4943/ (Accessed June 7, 2018).

40 For the content of Byrnes' address see the full text online: www.cvce.eu/ en/obj/address_given_by_james_f_byrnes_stuttgart_6_september_1946- en-17a77af6-adcd-41b7-a724-5c7d98a08f76.html (Accessed June 7, 2018). As to the "speech of hope" see Reinhold Weber, "Rede der Hoffnung,"

Online: www.byrnes-rede.de/byrnes_rede_kontext.html (Accessed June 7, 2018).

41 Delbert Clark, *Again the Goose Step*, Indianapolis, IN: Bobbs-Merrill, 1949, p. 36. As quoted in Backer, *Winds of History*, p. 19.

42 Reprinted in Pollock/Meisel/Bretton (eds.), *Germany Under Occupation*, pp. 91-99.

43 In 1946 Congress had appropriated large funds for Government Aid and Relief in Occupied Areas (GARIOA) in line with JCS 1067's explicit permission to take measures "to prevent 'such disease and unrest as would endanger the forces of occupation' in occupied Germany. Congress stipulated that the funds were only to be used to import food, petroleum, and fertilizers. Use of GARIOA funds to import raw materials of vital importance to the German industry was explicitly forbidden." Online: http://military.wikia.com/wiki/GARIOA (Accessed April 29, 2018).

44 Carolyn W. Eisenberg, *Drawing the Line. The American Decision to Divide Germany, 1944-1949*, Cambridge University Press, 1996, p. 379. For a more differentiated and detailed view of American reparation policies in the complex web of interdependencies between the goals of a unified economic policy for Germany, agreement on its postwar levels of industry, development of German export capacities to liberate the country from Allied support, the dismantling of war plants and equipment, and reparation commitments and expectations see the historical account: Special Report of the Military Governor, OMGUS, November 1948, "Three Years of Reparations" (A Survey), Reprinted in Pollock/Meisel/Bretton (eds.), *Germany Under Occupation*, pp. 64-67.

45 Clay, *Decision in Germany*, p. 74. Different explanations for Clay's dismantling halt are discussed in Gimbel, *The American Occupation of Germany*, p. 57-61.

46 Gimbel, *The American Occupation of Germany*, p. 52.

47 Ibid., pp. 52-53.

48 "Aims Toward Germany Widely Divergent," in *The Commercial and Financial Chronicle*, September 12, 1946, pp. 1377, 1405. For the report on the original interview a week earlier see Herbert M. Bratter, "Report Progress on Implementing Potsdam Economic Provisions," in *The Commercial and Financial Chronicle*, September 5, 1946, pp. 1267, 1289.

49 Smith, "Foreword," *The Papers of General Lucius D. Clay*, pp. xxv-xxxvii, here p. xxvii. The relationship bonded in friendship after the war between

the two top military commanders, Eisenhower and Zhukov, who had defeated Germany are also evidenced in Walter Isaacson/Evan Thomas, *The Wise Men. Six Friends and the World They Made. Acheson, Bohlen, Harriman, Kennan, Lovett, McCloy.* New York: Simon & Schuster, 1986, p. 318.

50 Clay, *Decision in Germany*, pp. 131, 166.

51 Eisenberg, *Drawing the Line*, p. 379.

52 Quoted in Tab "A" II. Discussion (= Annex to a Memorandum by Frank G. Wisner March 10, 1948), in FRUS 1948, vol. II: Germany and Austria, p. 881.

53 Text of the Potsdam Agreement I, B. Online: http://avalon.law.yale.edu/ 20th_century/decade17.asp (Accessed May 5, 2018). For extensive documentation of the preparation, proceedings, and agreement of the Potsdam Conference see FRUS 1945, vol. II: The Conference of Berlin (The Potsdam Conference).

54 Smith, *Lucius D. Clay*, p. 371. Robert Murphy, *Diplomat among Warriors*, London: Collins, 1964, p. 367.

55 Text of the Potsdam Agreement I, A (3). Online: http://avalon.law.yale .edu/20th_century/decade17.asp (Accessed May 5, 2018). "Council of Foreign Ministers." Online: https://en.wikipedia.org/wiki/Council_of_ Foreign_Ministers (Accessed April 23, 2018). "Council of Foreign Ministers." Online: www.britannica.com/topic/Council-of-Foreign-Ministers (Accessed April 23, 2018).

56 This is also the position in John H. Backer, *The Decision to Divide Germany. American Foreign Policy in Transition*, Durham, NC: Duke University Press, 1978.

57 On the outcome of the Moscow Conference see "Fourth meeting of the Council of Foreign Ministers, Moscow, March 10 to April 24, 1947. Report by Secretary Marshall, April 28, 1947." Online: http://avalon.law.yale.edu/ 20th_century/decade23.asp (Accessed June 3, 2018). For more details negotiated at the Moscow conference of foreign ministers see: "Council of Foreign Ministers, Moscow, 1947," in *The International Law Quarterly* 1 (1947), pp. 341–348. On the outcome of the London Conference see "Fifth meeting of the Council of Foreign Ministers, London, November 25–December 16, 1947. *Report by Secretary Marshall, December 19, 1947.*" Online: http://avalon.law.yale.edu/20th_century/decade24.asp (Accessed June 3, 2018). Both CFM conferences are extensively

documented in FRUS 1947, vol. II, pp. 1–576 (Moscow conference), 676–830 (London conference).

58 A useful short summary of the unfolding of decisions and negotiations on the currency issue since the failure of the London conference of the Council of Foreign Ministers on December 16, 1947 until March 7, 1948 is contained in Tab "A" II. Discussion (= Annex to a Memorandum by Frank G. Wisner March 10, 1948), in FRUS 1948, vol. II: Germany and Austria, pp. 881–882.

59 My retranslation of the quote in German in Werner Meyer, *20.6.1948. Währungsreform – Das neue Geld ist da*, edited by Karl-Otto Saur, Augsburg: Weltbild, 2005, p. 14. The original quote in German: "Wir können hierzu ergänzend mitteilen, dass am 8. Dezember in Bremerhaven ein US-Dampfer entladen wurde, der Kisten des neuen ‚bizonesischen' Geldes an Bord hatte ... Am 18 Dezember wurden von dem US-Frachter, Madsket' erneut größere Geldsendungen in Bremerhaven ausgeladen und von dort mit der Bahn nach Frankfurt am Main transportiert."

60 "Incoming Message from HQ Dept of the Army from Chief of Finance to EUCOM for COL: William Brey, Foreign Exchange Depository – Reurad S-1527." Online: Page 23 – US, OMGUS – Foreign Exchange Depository Group, 1944–1950 – Fold3 (Accessed February 6, 2024). The documents on the preceding pages contain very interesting information on the arrangements made for railroad transfer of "Birddog" money from Bremerhaven to Frankfurt am Main, the sort of equipment of guards with arms, and the request for bricklayers to brick up all windows of the basement of the Reichsbank building in Frankfurt am Main for security reasons. The dates of the documents also reveal that most of the new money had arrived by the end of December 1947.

61 Helmut Kahnt/Michael H. Schöne/Karlheinz Walz, *50 Jahre Deutsche Mark 1948–1998. Die Geschichte der deutschen Nachkriegswährungen in Ost und West*, Regenstauf: H. Gietl, 1998, p. 44. The authors name the following printing houses that would also have been suited for the banknote printing job: Hanseatische Druckanstalt in Hamburg, Enßlin & Laiblin in Reutlingen, and Westermann in Braunschweig.

62 Clay, *Decision in Germany*, p. 209.

63 Eisenberg, *Drawing the Line*, pp. 380–381.

64 Murphy, *Diplomat among Warriors*, p. 383.

65 For Sokolovsky's declaration during the 20 March ACC meeting see Royal Institute of International Affairs, *Documents on International Affairs 1947–1948* (ed. by Margaret Carlyle), Oxford University Press, 1952, pp. 574–575 (in English). Ministerium für auswärtige Angelegenheiten der UdSSR (ed.), *Die Sowjetunion und die Berliner Frage (Dokumente)*, Moskau: Ministerium für Auswärtige Angelegenheiten der UdSSR, 1948. For a view of the Soviet side on the ACC walkout see Viktor N. Belezki, *Die Politik der Sowjetunion in den deutschen Angelegenheiten in der Nachkriegszeit 1945–1976*, Berlin: Staatsverlag DDR, 1977, pp. 81–82.

66 FRUS 1948, vol. II: Germany and Austria, pp. 879–880.

67 Quoted from Eisenberg, *Drawing the Line*, p. 382, footnote 77.

68 NARA at College Park, RG 260 OMGUS, Records Regarding Financial Policy & Advising, box 32, folder: 10th Meeting Currency Reform.

69 David Braybrooke/Charles E. Lindblom, *A Strategy of Decision Policy: Evaluation as a Social Process*, New York: Free Press, 1963.

70 Backer, *The Decision to Divide Germany*, pp. 171–172.

71 Ibid., pp. 172–173, 176.

72 "Memorandum for the Files" of October 9, 1947 by a staff member of BEP (signature illegible), who forwarded it also to A. W. Hall, director of BEP. Document provided by Hallie Brooker, Lead Curator, Historical Research Center of BEP, by email attachment of April 5, 2018.

73 For both quotations: "Memorandum for the Files" of January 22, 1947, sent by its author A. N. Overby (Treasury) to W. Glenville Hall, financial secretary to the Treasury. Document provided by Hallie Brooker, Lead Curator, Historical Research Center of BEP, by email attachment of April 5, 2018.

74 John C. deWilde was the deputy chief of the State Department's Division of German and Austrian Economic Affairs (GA). See Charles P. Kindleberger, *Marshall Plan Days*, Boston: Allen & Unwin, 1987, p. 182, 172 and endnote 43 on p. 203. deWilde's name is spelled in different ways in minutes and memos that I cite. As Kindleberger was chief of GA, i.e., his boss from 1945 to 1948, I take his spelling as correct and use it.

75 Andrew N. Overby, born 1909, joined the Treasury Department in 1946 and moved up the career ladder to assistant secretary of the Treasury from 1952 to 1957, serving at the same time under presidential appointment as executive director of the International Bank for Reconstruction and Development. See his obituary in the *New York Times*

708 NOTES TO PAGES 332–337

online: www.nytimes.com/1984/05/01/obituaries/andrew-overby-banker-dies-at-75.html (Accessed May 19, 2018).

76 Back in 1944, the decision to equip the Soviets with a set of plates for printing Allied Military Mark "was taken at the highest governmental level, although over the strenuous objection of the head of the Bureau of Engraving and Printing," namely Alvin W. Hall. Kindleberger, *Marshall Plan Days*, p. 182.

77 For details on that "bad experience" see chapter 5 of Vladimir Petrov, *Money and Conquest. Allied Occupation Currencies in World War II*, Baltimore: Johns Hopkins Press, 1967, pp. 107–131.

78 "Memorandum for the Files" of January 22, 1947, sent by its author A. N. Overby (Treasury) to W. Glenville Hall, financial secretary to the Treasury. Document provided by Hallie Brooker, lead curator, Historical Research Center of BEP, by email attachment of April 5, 2018.

79 For a short summary of the results of this meeting see: Office Memorandum from C. C. Hilliard to Mr. Saltzman (both A-S) of September 22, 1947, "Subject: Printing of a New German Mark Currency." NARA at College Park, RG 59 Dec. File 862.515/6-1247, Entry 1945–49, box 6788.

80 Hoppenstedt, *Gerhard Colm*, p. 223.

81 Eckhard Wandel, *Die Entstehung der Bank deutscher Länder und die deutsche Währungsreform 1948*, Frankfurt am Main: Knapp, 1980, pp. 128–130.

82 Office Memorandum from C. C. Hilliard to Mr. Saltzman (both A-S) of 22 September 1947, "Subject: Printing of a New German Mark Currency." NARA at College Park, RG 59 Dec. File 862.515/6-1247, Entry 1945–49, box 6788.

83 Office Memorandum from C. C. Hilliard (A-S) to General Hilldring (AH) of 12 June 1947, "Subject: Expediting of Interdepartmental and US/UK Coordination re Monetary and Related Policy – Germany." NARA at College Park, RG 59 Dec. File 862.515/6-1247, Entry 1945–49, box 6788.

84 Ibid.

85 Office Memorandum from C. C. Hilliard to Mr. Saltzman (both A-S) of 22 September 1947, "Subject: Printing of a New German Mark Currency." NARA at College Park, RG 59 Dec. File 862.515/6-1247, Entry 1945–49, box 6788.

86 Ibid.

87 Incoming telegram no. 1933 from Berlin to Secretary of State of August 12, 1947. Department of State, Division of Communication and Records, Telegram Branch. Document provided by Hallie Brooker, lead curator, Historical Research Center of BEP, by email attachment of April 5, 2018.

88 Harold Henry Fisher, *The Communist Revolution: An Outline of Strategy and Tactics*, Stanford: Stanford University Press, 1955, p. 13. Quoted from https://en.wikipedia.org/wiki/Communist_International#Successor_ organizations (Accessed May 19, 2018).

89 Online: https://en.wikipedia.org/wiki/Communist_ International#Successor_organizations (Accessed May 19, 2018).

90 Office Memorandum from C. C. Hilliard to Mr. Saltzman (both A-S) of 22 September 1947, "Subject: Printing of a New German Mark Currency." NARA at College Park, RG 59 Dec. File 862.515/6-1247, Entry 1945–49, box 6788.

91 Ibid.

92 The Department of War had been renamed by the National Security Act of 1947 Department of the Army on September 18, 1947.

93 "Memorandum for the Files" of October 9, 1947 by a staff member of BEP (signature illegible), who forwarded it also to Alvin W. Hall, director of BEP. Document provided by Hallie Brooker, lead curator, Historical Research Center of BEP, by email attachment of April 5, 2018.

94 Ibid.

95 "Department of State, Memorandum of Conversation, Date October 13, 1947, Subject: Printing by the US of a New German Mark Currency for Bizonal Use." In NARA at College Park, RG 59 Dec. File 862.515/10-1347, Entry 1945–49, box 6788.

96 FRUS 1948 vol. II, passim.

97 "Memorandum of Conversation, by the Under Secretary of State (Lovett)" of May 21, 1948. In FRUS 1948 vol. II, pp. 270–272 with the quote on p. 272.

98 "Department of State, Memorandum of Conversation, Date October 13, 1947, Subject: Printing by the US of a New German Mark Currency for Bizonal Use," p. 5 of the memo. In NARA at College Park, RG 59 Records of the Department of State, Civil Affairs Division, Dec. File 862.515/10-1347, Entry 1945–49, box 6788.

99 Three identical letters from A. W. Hall, director of BEP, to the three mentioned presidents of printing establishments of October 27, 1947.

Documents provided by Hallie Brooker, lead curator, Historical Research Center of BEP, by email attachment of April 5, 2018.

100 Institut für Zeitgeschichte, Munich, Nachlass Hans Möller, ED 150/21, "Technische Durchführung der Währungsreform."

101 Already the introduction of the *Rentenmark* on November 15, 1923 had stopped hyperinflation. It had not been legal tender, but the par between *Rentenmark* and *Mark* was legally fixed 1 to 1 billion. The main reason for the stability intermezzo of the *Rentenmark* was the fact that the *Rentenmark* and the old *Mark* currency were kept in short supply, while the population regained confidence in the new currency.

102 A memo under the heading "Special Army Currency," dated October 23,1947, comprises five single-spaced typewritten pages. It starts with minutes of the October 13 meeting and then describes the hectic activities thereafter. Document provided by Hallie Brooker, lead curator, Historical Research Center of BEP, by email attachment of April 5, 2018. The function of a "Legal Counsel" has been described as follows: "there are hundreds of local, general, and international laws that corporations and government departments need to be aware of. The general counsel role mainly exists to help organizations understand those laws and steer clear of legal issues." Josh Fechter, "General Counsel Job Description: Roles and Responsibilities." Online: https://corporatecompliancehq.org/general-counsel-job-description/ (Accessed July 4, 2022).

103 Memo "Special Army Currency" of October 23, 1947.

104 Letter of October 15, 1947. Document provided by Hallie Brooker, lead curator, Historical Research Center of BEP, by email attachment of April 5, 2018.

105 Memo under the heading "Special Army Currency," dated October 23, 1947. Document provided by Hallie Brooker, lead curator, Historical Research Center of BEP, by email attachment of April 5, 2018. William Henry Draper Jr. (1894–1974) was at the time the Under Secretary of the Army.

106 Copies of the four "Bureau of Engraving and Printing Miscellaneous Orders" to Tudor Press, Inc. of October 17, 1947 for each of the four denominations and of the two letters were provided by Hallie Brooker,

lead curator, Historical Research Center of BEP, by email attachment of April 5, 2018.

107 Copies supplied by Hallie Brooker, lead curator, Historical Research Center of BEP, by email attachment of April 5, 2018, attachment 5b.

108 Memo "Special Army Currency" of 23 October 1947.

109 Ibid. The number of the Executive Order is listed on the form for Purchase Orders of BEP to Forbes Lithograph Manufacturing Co. of November 13, 1947, American Bank Note Company of December 4, 1947 and Tudor Press, Inc. of December 8, 1947. Copies were supplied by Hallie Brooker, lead curator, Historical Research Center of BEP, by email attachment of 5 April 2018.

110 As the one-half and one-mark notes were not to be serially numbered, Forbes Lithograph Manufacturing Company was not only made responsible for printing them, but also for boxing and shipping them via New York to Bremerhaven. Memo "Special Army Currency" of October 23, 1947.

111 Edward Tenenbaum's father Joseph had been a key person in organizing it and had chaired the Joint Boycott Council. See Section 3.1, pp. 111, 138.

112 Memo "Special Army Currency" of 23 October 1947.

113 Ibid.

114 Ibid.

115 Letter from Civil Affairs Division to Alvin W. Hall, Director of BEP, of June 28, 1948. Copy provided by Hallie Brooker, lead curator, Historical Research Center of BEP, by email attachment of April 5, 2018, attachment 6.

116 Copies of those letters provided by Hallie Brooker, lead curator, Historical Research Center of BEP, by email attachment of April 5, 2018, attachment 7 and 8.

117 Fritz Butschkau, *Erinnerungen. Wenn's ums Geld geht ...*, Düsseldorf: Econ, 1972. p. 51. My translation.

118 Letter of November 1, 1946, Subject: Announcement of Staff Appointments, from OMGUS Finance Division to Finance Division Organization signed by J. B. A. Robertson, Administrative Officer. Online: www.fold3.com/image/303611069 (Accessed April 18, 2018). Even such internal letters would carry the Army Post Office (APO) number, in this case APO 742 for Berlin Headquarters, including OMGUS.

119 Letter of September 26, 1946 from OMGUS Finance Division to Branch Chiefs signed by Edward A. Tenenbaum. Online: www.fold3.com/image/ 303616137 (Accessed September 13, 2018).

120 Attachment to the letter of September 26, 1946 "Preliminary Agreement on the Establishment of a Joint German Committee for Finance." Online: www.fold3.com/image/303616144 (Accessed September 13, 2018).

121 Unfinished book manuscript of Edward A. Tenenbaum "The German Mark," chapter 12, p. 62, footnote 87. Edward A. Tenenbaum Papers, boxes 2 and 3, 5 folders: *The German* Mark Book Draft. HSTPL.

122 Ibid., chapter 13, p. 2. Edward A. Tenenbaum Papers, box 2, folder: *The German Mark* Book Draft (2 of 5). HSTPL.

123 Ibid., chapter 13, p. 5. Edward A. Tenenbaum Papers, box 2, folder: *The German Mark* Book Draft (2 of 5). HSTPL.

124 Gottlieb, "Failure of Quadripartite Monetary Reform," pp. 398–417. See also chapter VI in Gottlieb, *The German Peace Settlement and the Berlin Crisis*, pp. 101–122.

125 Josef Henke/Klaus Oldenhage, "Office of Military Government for Germany (US)," in Christoph Weisz (ed.), *OMGUS-Handbuch. Die amerikanische Militärregierung in Deutschland 1945–1949*, Munich: Oldenburg, 1994, pp. 1–142, here pp. 105–106.

126 See Section 4.1.

127 Henke/Oldenhage, "Office of Military Government for Germany (US)," pp. 1–142, here pp. 105–107.

128 Article on Joseph Dodge in Wikipedia. Online: https://en.wikipedia.org/ wiki/Joseph_Dodge (Accessed September 14, 2018).

129 Henke/Oldenhage, "Office of Military Government for Germany (US)," pp. 1–142, here pp. 105–107, 784. Numerous reorganizations of the Finance Division are listed there.

130 Edward Tenenbaum, *National Socialism vs. International Capitalism*, New Haven: Yale University Press, 1942.

131 NARA at College Park MD, RG 260 (OMGUS). On microfiche in IfZ Munich and BArch Coblenz, OMGUS, shipment 11, box 341, folder 7, Provenance: OMGUS FINAD.

132 NARA at College Park MD, RG 260 (OMGUS). On microfiche in IfZ Munich and BArch Coblenz, OMGUS, shipment 11, box 350, folder 9, Provenance: OMGUS FINAD.

133 Edward A. Tenenbaum Papers, box 5, folder: Germany – Currency Reform Memoranda (8 of 9). HSTPL.

134 One page of handwritten exchange between Tenenbaum asking for the exact address in Gelfertstrasse and Captain Pusser disclosing the street number. Edward A. Tenenbaum Papers, box 8, folder: Personnel File. HSTPL.

135 This and numerous other examples of factual expropriation of Jewish property owners in Dahlem are described in Christian Simon, *Dahlem. Zwischen Idylle und Metropole*, Berlin: be.bra, 2016, pp. 93–96.

136 Memo of Wolfgang Materne, dated April 30, 2015. My translation.

137 J. Anthony Panuch Papers, box 10, folder: Berlin Telephone Directories, 1948–49. HSTPL.

138 Edward A. Tenenbaum Papers, box 8, folder: Personnel File. HSTPL.

139 BArch Z 3/720.

140 For the creation of the Economic Council by Proclamation No. 5 of June 9, 1947 as well as documents on prior agreements between the bizonal partners, in English and in German translations, as well as for organizational charts of the Economic Council see J. Anthony Panuch Papers, box 12, folder: Economic Council – Proclamation and Organizational Charts. HSTPL.

141 BArch Z 3/720.

142 Verbatim Notes, Financial Regulations Committee, of meetings on December 3, 9, and 17, 1946 and on March 17, 1947. Edward A. Tenenbaum Papers, box 3, folder: Germany – Currency Reform – Memoranda (1 of 9). HSTPL.

143 Meyer, *20.6.1948. Währungsreform*, pp. 42–43.

144 Unfinished book manuscript of Edward A. Tenenbaum "The German Mark," chapter 13, pp. 8–13. Edward A. Tenenbaum Papers, box 2, folder: *The German Mark* Book Draft (2 of 5). HSTPL.

145 Ibid., chapter 13, p. 14. Edward A. Tenenbaum Papers, box 2, folder: *The German Mark* Book Draft (2 of 5). HSTPL.

146 Ibid., chapter 13, pp. 14–15.

147 Ibid., chapter 13, p. 15.

148 See "Memorandum relating to Inter-Allied Reparation Agency (October 15, 1945)." Online: www.cvce.eu/content/publication/2003/10/29/d653ef3e-ed28-4be0-b5e6-a8f1225b70f8/publishable_en.pdf (Accessed October 13, 2019).

149 "Reparation from Germany, Establishment of Inter-Allied Reparation Agency, and Restitution of Monetary Gold." Online: www.loc.gov/law/help/us-treaties/bevans/m-ust000004-0005.pdf (Accessed October 13, 2019). For statistics of IARA accounts for the end of 1948, including percentages of agreed claims and actual allocations, see: "German Industrial Reparation in 1948 as Reported by the Inter-Allied Reparation Agency: Excerpts from Report of the Secretary General for the Year 1948," in US Department of State (ed.), *Germany 1947–1949. The Story in Documents*, Washington, DC: GPO, 1950, pp. 381–385.

150 Clay, *Decision in Germany*, p. 122.

151 Smith (ed.), *The Papers of General Lucius D. Clay*, xxvii (Foreword), pp. 203–204 (Document 115), and especially pp. 218–223 (Document 123).

152 Smith, *Lucius D. Clay*, pp. 371–372.

153 Smith, *Lucius D. Clay*, pp. 460–461. For the original of the quotation from two documents of 12 January 1948 see: Smith (ed.), *The Papers of General Lucius D. Clay*, pp. 534, 538.

154 Sokolovsky's declaration and explanation for the walkout during the ACC meeting on March 20, 1948 is published in English in Carlyle (ed.), Royal Institute of International Affairs, *Documents on International Affairs 1947–1948*, pp. 574–575. And in German in Ministerium für Auswärtige Angelegenheiten der UdSSR (ed.), *Die Sowjetunion und die Berliner Frage: Dokumente*, pp. 19–21.

155 Smith, *Lucius D. Clay*, p. 478. How difficult the French were on joining the Bizone and on Clay's and Robertson's plans for forming a West German government in 1949, is described in the secret telegram CC 3687 of April 1, 1948 from Clay to Draper. See Document "360. Implementation of London Conference Decisions," in Smith (ed.), *The Papers of General Lucius D. Clay*, pp. 608–611.

156 "Wiederaufbau und Autonomie. Der Saarstaat 1945–1955." Online: www.saarland.de/SID-6933B334-4B77FCE3/122957.htm (Accessed October 16, 2019).

157 "Saarstatut und Volksabstimmung 1955. Das Ende eines Experiments." Online: www.saarland.de/SID-3402A24E-80213FBD/122958.htm (Accessed October 16, 2019).

158 As to the French claims see Smith, *Lucius D. Clay*, pp. 371–372.

159 Bruce Kuklick, *American Policy and the Division of Germany. The Clash with Russia over Reparations*, Ithaca, NY: Cornell University Press, 1972, esp. pp. 226–235.

160 Isaacson/Thomas, *The Wise Men*, p. 286 and passim.

161 NARA at College Park MD, RG 260 (OMGUS). On microfiche in IfZ Munich and BArch Coblenz, OMGUS, shipment 3, box 176-3, folder 12, Provenance: OMGUS COS (= Chief of Staff). This memo dates October 31, 1946. The same memo less well typed and dated October 30, 1946, is available on microfiche in IfZ Munich and BArch Coblenz, OMGUS, shipment 2, box 74, folder 7, Provenance: OMGUS FINAD.

162 This argument that Germany had to go to war in 1939 to prevent an internal economic (and thus political) crisis was later advanced by British historian Timothy W. Mason, "Innere Krise und Angriffskrieg 1938/1939," in Friedrich Forstmeier/Hans-Erich Volkmann (eds.), *Wirtschaft und Rüstung am Vorabend des Zweiten Weltkrieges*, Düsseldorf: Droste, 1975, pp. 158–188. See also Adam Tooze, *The Wages of Destruction. The Making and Breaking of the Nazi Economy*, London: Allen Lane/Penguin, 2006/2007.

163 Clay, *Decision in Germany*, p. 298.

164 Edward A. Tenenbaum Papers, box 4, folder: Germany – Currency Reform – Memoranda (4 of 9). HSTPL.

165 Edward A. Tenenbaum Papers, box 8, folder: Personnel File. HSTPL.

166 Anna J. Merritt/Richard L. Merritt (eds.), *Public Opinion in Occupied Germany. The OMGUS Surveys, 1945–1949*, Urbana: University of Illinois Press, 1970, pp. 21–22, and Report No. 32 (December 10, 1946) pp. 118–121, here p. 120.

167 Merritt/Merritt (eds.), *Public Opinion in Occupied Germany*, pp. 21–22, and Report No. 133 (August 10, 1948) pp. 251–252.

168 Clay, *Decision in Germany*, p. 151 for the quotation. My whole story of the Moscow conference of foreign ministers is based on pp. 146–152 of Clay's memoirs. See also Wolfgang Krieger, *General Lucius D. Clay und die amerikanische Deutschlandpolitik 1945–1949*, Stuttgart: Klett-Cotta, 1987, pp. 225–229.

169 See first page of the minutes. Online: www.fold3.com/image/303616173 (Accessed September 15, 2018).

170 The document is online: www.fold3.com/image/303616207 (Accessed September 15, 2018).

171 Minutes of several BIGFIN meetings in late 1946 and early 1947 can be found in NARA at College Park MD, RG 260 OMGUS, Records Regarding Financial Policy & Advising, box 32, folder: Meeting of

Chairmen of Bizonal Committee. The same folder contains a letter of BIFIN to the Bipartite Finance Committee of November 15, 1946, signed by "J. T. Lisle, Principal Control Officer, British Element, Chairman." It informs that Dr. Mattes is chairman of BIXFIN and Dr. Kriege his deputy. It also lists German Executive Committees for the following policy fields: economy BIXECO, transport BIXTPT, and commerce BIXCOM.

172 Heinz Sauermann, "Der amerikanische Plan für die deutsche Währungsreform," in *Zeitschrift für die Gesamte Staatswissenschaft* 111 (1955), p. 196. My translation.

173 "Wirtschaftsrat des Vereinigten Wirtschaftsgebietes," Online: Wirtschaftsrat desVereinigtenWirtschaftsgebietes–Wikipedia (Accessed July 18, 2021).

174 Arne Weick, *Homburger Plan und Währungsreform. Kritische Analyse des Währungsreformplans der Sonderstelle Geld und Kredit und seiner Bedeutung für die westdeutsche Währungsreform*, St. Katharinen: Scripta Mercaturae, 1998, p. 41.

175 Ibid., pp. 41–42. Herbert Alsheimer, *Ludwig Erhard. Der Weg unseres Landes aus den Trümmern des Krieges – Spuren des Wirkens in Frankfurt am Main-Höchst und Bad Homburg von der Höhe*, Bad Homburg: Taunus-Sparkasse, 1997, pp. 53–54.

176 Volker Hentschel, *Ludwig Erhard. Ein Politikerleben*, Munich: Olzog, 1996, p. 49. Weick, *Homburger Plan und Währungsreform*, pp. 30, 58.

177 Volkhard Laitenberger, *Ludwig Erhard. Der Nationalökonom als Politiker*, Göttingen: Muster-Schmidt, 1986, p. 57.

178 HSTPL, Oral History Interview with Raymond W. Goldsmith by Richard D. McKinzie, June 25, 1973, pp. 5, 20. Online: www.trumanlibrary.gov/library/oral-histories/goldsmth#36 (Accessed July 24, 2021).

179 Ibid., pp. 18–20.

180 Ludwig Erhard, "20. Juni 1948 – Ende und Anfang," in *Zeitschrift für das gesamte Kreditwesen* 26 (1973), pp. 526–528, here p. 526.

181 A fine summary of the differing starting positions of the four members of the ACC on currency-reform issues and their modifications under pressure to compromise and reach agreement on a plan, first on the quadripartite and after its failure on the tripartite level, is Ian Turner, "Great Britain and the Post-War German

Currency Reform," *The Historical Journal* 30 (1987), pp. 685–708. His article is mainly based on original British military government documents. For more general approaches to British policy goals in Germany see: Ian D. Turner (ed.), *Reconstruction in Post-War Germany. British Occupation Policy and the Western Zones 1945–55*, Oxford: Berg, 1989. Joseph Foschepoth/Rolf Steininger (eds.), *Die britische Deutschland- und Besatzungspolitik 1945–1949*, Paderborn: Schöningh, 1985.

182 "The British Counterproposal for German Currency Reform." Memo from Raymond W. Goldsmith to Charles Kindleberger of November 14, 1946. NARA at College Park MD, RG 260 (OMGUS). On microfiche in IfZ Munich and BArch Coblenz, OMGUS, shipment 2, box 92, folder 8. Arne Weick is wrong in citing this memo as having been sent from Kindleberger to Goldsmith. See Weick, *Homburger Plan und Währungsreform*, p. 34.

183 Edward A. Tenenbaum Papers, box 3, folder: Germany – Background Data on Monetary Problems (2 of 2). HSTPL.

184 "The British Counterproposal for German Currency Reform." Memo from Raymond W. Goldsmith to Charles Kindleberger of November 14, 1946, Gerhard Colm's letter of November 19, 1946 to Jack Bennett, and Goldsmith's covering letter to Jack Bennett of November 22, 1946. In NARA at College Park MD, RG 260 (OMGUS). On microfiche in IfZ Munich and BArch Coblenz, Z 45-F (OMGUS), 2/92/8. See also Weick, *Homburger Plan und Währungsreform*, p. 34.

185 Weick, *Homburger Plan und Währungsreform*, p. 35.

186 Gerhard Colm Papers, box 22, folder: German currency reform mission 1946–1954. Library of Congress Manuscript Division.

187 Turner, "Great Britain and the Post-War German Currency Reform," pp. 685–708, here p. 695.

188 Edward A. Tenenbaum Papers, box 4, folder: Germany – Currency Reform – Memoranda (3 of 9). HSTPL.

189 This and the foregoing quotations are taken from different documents contained in Edward A. Tenenbaum Papers, box 3, folder: Germany – Currency Reform – Memoranda (1 of 9). and box 4, folder: Germany – Currency Reform – Memoranda (3 of 9). HSTPL.

190 Weick, *Homburger Plan und Währungsreform*, p. 43.

718 NOTES TO PAGES 404–413

191 Unfinished book manuscript of Edward A. Tenenbaum "The German Mark," chapter 13, pp. 17–19. Edward A. Tenenbaum Papers, box 2, folder: *The German Mark* Book Draft (2 of 5). HSTPL.

192 Ibid.

193 42-page single-spaced verbatim minutes of the meeting of the Special Agency for Money and Credit on November 20, 1947, p. 1. Edward A. Tenenbaum Papers. In HSTPL. Also contained in BArch Z32/7, folio 41–82.

194 Stephen Meardon, "On Kindleberger and Hegemony: From Berlin to MIT and Back," in *History of Political Economy* 46 (2014), suppl. 1, pp. 351–374. Online: https://doi.org/10.1215/00182702-2716235 (Accessed January 21, 2022).

195 An English translation of Erhard's article is available in NARA at College Park MD, RG 260 (OMGUS). On microfiche in IfZ Munich and BArch Coblenz, OMGUS, shipment 2, box 102, folder 12, Provenance: OMGUS FINAD. Also in Edward A. Tenenbaum Papers, box 3, folder: Germany – Currency Reform – Memoranda (1 of 9). HSTPL.

196 The explanatory memo in German, in fact a summary of the Agency's currency-reform plan of January 24, 1948, nine pages long with two appendices of three pages each, is contained in the Edward A. Tenenbaum Papers, box 4, folder: Germany – Currency Reform Memoranda (3 of 9). HSTPL.

197 Sauermann, "Der amerikanische Plan," pp. 197–198.

198 Verwaltung für Finanzen des Vereinigten Wirtschaftsgebiets, *Entwurf eines Gesetzes zur Neuordnung des Geldwesens (Homburger Plan)*, Heidelberg/Berlin/Göttingen: Springer, 1948. Preface of June 30, 1948.

199 HSTPL, Oral History Interview with Raymond W. Goldsmith by Richard D. McKinzie, June 25, 1973, pp. 8–9. Online: www.trumanlibrary.gov/ library/oral-histories/goldsmth#36 (Accessed July 24, 2021).

200 Hans Möller, "Die Geldreform: ihre wirtschaftliche und politische Bedeutung," in *Zeitschrift für das gesamte Kreditwesen* 26 (1973), pp. 536–542, here p. 538.

201 *Yale Twenty-Fifth Yearbook*, p. 312.

202 "Effects of the 'Sonderstelle' Proposal." Edward A. Tenenbaum Papers, box 3, folder: Germany – Background Data on Monetary Problems (2 of 2). HSTPL.

203 The original of the memo is in NARA at College Park MD, RG 260 (OMGUS). On microfiche in IfZ Munich and BArch Coblenz, OMGUS, shipment 2, box 91, folder 3, Provenance: OMGUS FINAD. It is printed in the appendix to Peter Hampe (ed.), *Währungsreform und Soziale Marktwirtschaft. Rückblicke und Ausblicke*, Munich: Olzog, 1989, pp. 116–118.

204 For more details see: Wolfgang Benz, "Vorform des 'Weststaats': die Bizone 1946–1949," in Theodor Eschenburg (ed.), *Jahre der Besatzung 1945–1949* (Geschichte der Bundesrepublik Deutschland, vol. 1), Stuttgart: Deutsche Verlags-Anstalt, 1983, pp. 404–405.

205 For details of German politics behind Erhard's election see: Alfred C. Mierzejewski, *Ludwig Erhard. A Biography*, Chapel Hill: North Carolina University Press, 2004, pp. 60–62.

206 Ludwig Erhard, "Die neue Marktwirtschaft." Online: www.ueberseeclub .de/resources/Server/pdf-Dateien/1922-1959/vortrag-1948-12- 16Professor%20Dr.%20Ludwig%20Erhard.pdf (Accessed February 17, 2020).

207 Ludwig Erhard, "Der Weg in die Zukunft. Rede vor der 14. Vollversammlung des Wirtschaftsrates des Vereinigten Wirtschaftsgebiets, Frankfurt a. M., 21. April 1948," The speech is reprinted in Karl Hohmann (ed.), *Ludwig Erhard: Gedanken aus fünf Jahrzehnten: Reden und Schriften*, Düsseldorf: Econ, 1988, pp. 95–119.

208 Marion Gräfin Dönhoff, *Von Gestern nach Übermorgen. Zur Geschichte der Bundesrepublik Deutschland*, Hamburg: Knaus, 1981, pp. 149–150. Also quoted in Daniel Koerfer, "Ludwig Erhards Kampf für die Soziale Marktwirtschaft." Online: www.ludwig-erhard.de/erhard-aktuell/forum/ ludwig-erhards-kampf-fuer-die-soziale-marktwirtschaft/ (Accessed February 17, 2020). My translation.

209 The text of the Guiding Principles Law is reprinted in Alsheimer, *Ludwig Erhard*, pp. 29–33.

210 The imbroglio with Erhard's rush-ahead, undercover supported by General Clay, but disapproved by British military government is discussed in Mierzejewski, *Ludwig Erhard*, pp. 69–70.

211 NARA at College Park MA, Record Group 165, Entry (NM-84) 466 Records of the War Department, General and Special Staff. Civil Affairs Division. Top Secret Incoming and Outgoing Messages, 1943–1949, box 21.

212 Colm/Dodge/Goldsmith, "A Plan for the Liquidation of War Finance and the Financial Rehabilitation of Germany," pp. 204–243.

213 Cable CC 3335, p. 9. NARA at College Park MA, Record Group 165, Entry (NM-84) 466 Records of the War Department, General and Special Staff. Civil Affairs Division. Top Secret Incoming and Outgoing Messages, 1943–1949, box 21.

214 Sauermann, "Der amerikanische Plan," p.196.

215 Edward A. Tenenbaum's book manuscript "The German Mark," chapter 13, pp. 20–21. Edward A. Tenenbaum Papers, box 2, folder: *The German Mark* Book Draft (2 of 5). HSTPL.

216 Ibid., chapter 13, p. 21.

217 Ibid.

218 "Finance Adviser Ends MG Service," in OMGUS *Information Bulletin*, 25 January 1949, p. 10.

219 Edward A. Tenenbaum's book manuscript "The German Mark," chapter 13, pp. 21–22. Edward A. Tenenbaum Papers, box 2, folder: *The German Mark* Book Draft (2 of 5). HSTPL

220 Ibid., chapter 13, p. 22.

221 Smith (ed.), *The Papers of General Lucius D. Clay*, Document "354. Currency Reform," pp. 589–596.

222 Smith, *Lucius D. Clay*, p. 482.

223 "Top Secret Eyes Only cable W.97929." NARA at College Park MD, RG 165 Records of the War Department, General and Special Staffs, Army CAD Messages, Nov. 1942–July 1949, SOP/Eyes Only, Nov. 1942–Dec. 1943, Nov. 1946–May 1949, box 14, folder: Eyes Only. Collection Name: TS Incoming / Outgoing Messages. Without the expert support by NARA archivist Eric van Slander I would never have found this document. If not otherwise cited, this is also the source of the following quotations.

224 Kenneth C. Royall Sr. became the first Secretary of the Army after the Department of War, headed by him since July 1947, was renamed Department of the Army in September 1947.

225 Otto Pfleiderer, "Fünf Jahre Deutsche Mark. Die Währungsreform von 1948," in *Stuttgarter Nachrichten*, June 20, 1953.

226 Ludwig Erhard, "Die neue Marktwirtschaft," Lecture at the *Überseeclub* in Hamburg on December 16, 1948. Online: www.ueberseeclub.de/resources/Server/pdf-Dateien/1922-1959/vortrag-1948-12-16Professor%20Dr.%20Ludwig%20Erhard.pdf (Accessed February 14, 2020).

227 Figures as reported in Sauermann, "Der amerikanische Plan," p. 200.

228 Michael L. Hughes, "Hard Heads, Soft Money? West German Ambivalence about Currency Reform, 1944–1948," in *German Studies Review* 21 (1998), pp. 309–327, here p. 319. See also: Christoph Buchheim, "Die Währungsreform 1948 in Westdeutschland," in *Vierteljahrshefte für Zeitgeschichte* 36 (1988), pp. 189–231, here pp. 227–231. Turner, "Great Britain and the Post-War German Currency Reform," pp. 685–708, here pp. 705–706.

229 "1947 Directive to the Commander in Chief of the US Forces of Occupation (JCS 1779)," in US Department of State (ed.), *Germany 1947–1949. The Story in Documents*, Washington, DC: GPO, 1950, pp. 33–41, here p. 39.

230 Isaacson/Thomas, *The Wise Men*, pp. 420–421.

231 It is amazing that Smith in his biography of Clay only mentions the dispute about the currency exchange rate, 10 or 30 US cents to the mark. See Smith, *Lucius D. Clay*, pp. 482–483.

232 Tenenbaum's book manuscript "The German Mark," chapter 13, p. 14. Edward A. Tenenbaum Papers, boxes 2 and 3, 5 folders: *The German Mark* Book Draft. HSTPL.

233 Interview in New York City on October 29, 2018.

234 As quoted in Smith, *Lucius D. Clay*, p. 466.

235 Ibid.

236 Ibid., p. 467.

237 This is what Clay told his biographer Smith in an interview. Ibid., pp. 469–470.

238 The foregoing pages, quotations included, rely on ibid., pp. 471–477. The political and military tug-of-war between Clay and Bradley over giving up West Berlin is also treated in William Stivers/Donald A. Carter, *The City Becomes a Symbol. The US Army in the Occupation of Berlin, 1945–1949*, Washington, DC: US Army Center of Military History, 2017, pp. 214–216.

239 Clay, *Decision in Germany*, p. 212.

240 Michael Budczies, *Meine Familie. Geschichte und Geschichten*, Limburg: C. A. Starke, 1999, p. 163.

241 Otto Pfleiderer, "Die Geburtsstunde der Deutschen Mark vor 25 Jahren. Die politische Grundsatzentscheidung trafen die Westmächte. Erinnerungen an das Konklave von Rothwesten, das die Währungsreform vorbereitete," in *Stuttgarter Zeitung*, June 19, 1973, p. 12.

242 Henke/Oldenhage, "Office of Military Government for Germany (US),"
pp. 1–142, here p. 56.

243 Hans Hellmut Kirst, "Dann aßen wir wieder Schnitzel," in *Münchner
Illustrierte*, June 28, 1958, pp. 16–21, here pp. 20–21.

244 Hans Hellmut Kirst, "Dann aßen wir wieder Schnitzel," in *Münchner
Illustrierte*, July 19, 1958, pp. 8–12 and 38–39, here p. 10.

245 Budczies, *Meine Familie*, p. 163. My translation.

246 Pfleiderer, "Die Geburtsstunde der Deutschen Mark vor 25 Jahren," p. 12.
My translation.

247 "Letter of Edward A. Tenenbaum to Prof. Dr. Hans Möller of July 30,
1959." In Edward A. Tenenbaum Papers, box 3, folder: Background Data
on Monetary Problems (2 of 2). HSTPL.

248 Budczies, *Meine Familie*, pp. 171–172. In this German book Tenenbaum's
letter is printed in its original English version.

249 Memo of E. A. Tenenbaum to K. V. Hagen of December 17, 1946, in
NARA, RG 260, C11/D1/S1, box 17. As cited in Hoppenstedt, *Gerhard
Colm*, p. 227, note 3.

250 Pfleiderer, "Die Geburtsstunde der Deutschen Mark vor 25 Jahren," p. 12.

251 Written order of Lucius Clay to Lieutenant Colonel Emory D. Stoker of
April 1, 1948, in Historical Archive of the Deutsche Bundesbank (HA
BBK) B 330/6153/1.

252 Written order of Lucius Clay to Lieutenant Colonel Emory D. Stoker of
April 12, 1948, in HA BBK B 330/6153/1.

253 Werner Meyer, *Mythos Deutsche Mark. Zur Geschichte einer
abgeschafften Währung*, Berlin: Aufbau Taschenbuch, 2001, p. 83. Without
further specification Meyer mentions an article in *Der Spiegel* as source.

254 Hans Möller, "Die westdeutsche Währungsreform von 1948," in
Deutsche Bundesbank (ed.), *Währung und Wirtschaft in Deutschland
1876–1975*, Frankfurt m Main: Fritz Knapp, 1976, p. 446. Reinhold
Schillinger, *Der Entscheidungsprozess beim Lastenausgleich 1945–1952*,
St. Katharinen: Scripta Mercaturae, 1985, p. 99.

255 "Wirtschaftsrat, Telefonische Mitteilung Schmidt für Dr. Dörr von Mr.
Klare, BICO, 3.4.48, 11 Uhr, betr. Besprechung mit den Herren
Militärgouverneuren. Dr. Klare teilt mit, dass die Herren Minister a.D.
Franz Blücher, Essen // Herbert Friedemann, Hannover // Dr. Robert
Pferdmenges, Köln // Dir. Hartmann, Bad Homburg // zu einer äußerst
wichtigen Besprechung mit den Herren Militärgouverneuren am Montag,

den 5. April, 14:30 Uhr, Hochhaus, Zimmer 621 (Büro Mr. Klare) gebeten werden. Mr. Klare bittet uns, die Herren sofort zu benachrichtigen." BArch Coblenz Z 3, 516, folio 142. For the date see also Möller, "Die Geldreform," pp. 536–542, here p. 536.

256 Möller, "Die Geldreform," pp. 536–542, here p. 536.

257 Till Crazius, *Die Währungsreform von 1948: Vorbereitung, Durchführung und Folgen (bis 1952)*, Hamburg: Diplomica, 1997, p. 32.

258 Weick, *Homburger Plan und Währungsreform*, pp. 48, 52 for a list of members and staff members.

259 For accounts of the selection of the financial experts assembled "in the cage" in Rothwesten and of their seven-weeks proceedings in *Haus Posen* see Erwin Hielscher, *Der Leidensweg der deutschen Währungsreform*, München: Richard Pflaum, 1948, pp. 20–37. Möller, "Die westdeutsche Währungsreform von 1948," pp. 445–452. Buchheim, "Die Währungsreform 1948 in Westdeutschland," pp. 189–231, here pp. 212–217. Wandel, *Die Entstehung*, pp. 106–118. Hoppenstedt, *Gerhard Colm*, pp. 227–237.

260 Weick, *Homburger Plan und Währungsreform*, pp. 68–69. See also Wandel, *Die Entstehung*, p. 108.

261 Möller, "Die Währungsreform von 1948," pp. 55–77, here p. 62, fn 11. Accordingly, Dreißig did not have a vote in the German experts' decisions on their positions in the tug-of-war with Tenenbaum and the other currency experts of the Western Allied powers over the terms of the currency reform.

262 The following account of proceedings in *Haus Posen* is based on a sort of diary that was kept by Hans Möller. IfZ Archive ED 150/10. Papers of Hans Möller.

263 For an original of Form A see online: www.archivverlag.de/dokumente/ waehrungsreform/ (Accessed January 13, 2022).

264 End of reporting from the diary that was kept by Hans Möller. IfZ Archive ED 150/10. Papers of Hans Möller.

265 Möller, "Die westdeutsche Währungsreform von 1948," pp. 433–483, here p. 446. Möller's eyewitness account is taken up by Hoppenstedt, *Gerhard Colm*, p. 228. And by Michael Budczies [son of Rothwesten member Wolfgang Budczies], *Meine Familie*, p. 162.

266 Pfleiderer, "Die Geburtsstunde der Deutschen Mark vor 25 Jahren," p. 12. My translation.

267 Ibid.

268 Hoppenstedt, *Gerhard Colm*, pp. 230–231. My translation. See also Buchheim, "Die Währungsreform 1948 in Westdeutschland," pp. 189–231, here p. 212.

269 Erwin Hielscher summarized some of his views on currency conversion in a 7-page untitled memo of April 29, 1948. Edward A. Tenenbaum Papers, box 3, folder: Germany – Background Data on Monetary Problems (2 of 2).

270 Turner, "Great Britain and the Post-War German Currency Reform," pp. 685–708, here p. 705.

271 Following a resolution of the Economic Council of December 18, 1947 demanding German participation in the planning of currency reform, Jack Bennett, certainly with advise from Tenenbaum, had already expressed himself reluctant to let the Germans play an important role. In a memo to Clay of February 10, 1948 he judged their Homburg Plan as "highly inadequate and socially and politically indefensible." He proposed the following course of action: "The US and UK military governments could agree on the principles of a currency reform, and then obtain German advice and assistance in working out the details. This is the policy we are now following. It avoids, in particular, any tendencies to make the Germans the arbiter or court of appeal for settlement of the known differences in policy between the two military governments on this important matter. It also seems more likely to permit the French to be drawn in to discussion at an early moment." The original of the memo is in NARA at College Park MD, RG 260 (OMGUS). On microfiche in IfZ Munich and BArch Coblenz, OMGUS, shipment 2, box 91, folder 3, Provenance: OMGUS FINAD.

272 Minutes of the plenary session with E. A. Tenenbaum and C. Lefort on Sunday May 9, 1948. HA BBK B 330/6153/1-1.

273 Walter Dudek, "Eine *Spiegel* Seite für Walter Dudek." *Der Spiegel* 1948, issue 26 (June 25, 1948), p. 18.

274 IfZ Archive Munich, ED 150: Papers of Hans Möller. As quoted in Hoppenstedt, *Gerhard Colm*, p. 231. My translation.

275 The minutes of this meeting in their original German version are available in the Historical Archive of the Deutsche Bundesbank in Frankfurt am Main and in Papers of Hans Möller IfZ Archive ED 150. They have been printed in the appendices of Wandel, *Die Entstehung*,

pp. 182–187. Hampe (ed.), *Währungsreform und Soziale Marktwirtschaft*, pp. 119–124.

276 The common declaration of eight of the German experts has been published in the appendices of Wandel, *Die Entstehung*, pp. 188–191. Hampe (ed.), *Währungsreform und Soziale Marktwirtschaft*, pp. 124–127.

277 Möller, "Die Währungsreform von 1948," pp. 55–77, here p. 63. My translation.

278 Pfleiderer, "Fünf Jahre Deutsche Mark."

279 This is the end of my reporting from the article by Möller, "Die Währungsreform von 1948," pp. 55–77.

280 Möller, "Die westdeutsche Währungsreform von 1948," p. 445, without giving a precise date speaks of "meetings with representatives of Military Governments." Hoppenstedt, *Gerhard Colm*, p. 228, mentions two such "preparatory meetings."

281 Möller, "Die westdeutsche Währungsreform von 1948," p. 446.

282 Ibid., p. 446. My translation.

283 Hielscher, *Der Leidensweg der deutschen Währungsreform*, Vorwort (= preface).

284 BArch Coblenz, Z 32/11, folio 123.

285 BArch Coblenz, N 1080/354 (Franz Blücher Papers), folio 183. Blücher was finance minister of the state of North Rhine-Westphalia 1946–1947 and a member of the Economic Council and its currency committee 1947–1949, before he served in Konrad Adenauer's cabinet as minister and vice-chancellor after the foundation of the Federal Republic of Germany in 1949.

286 Weick, *Homburger Plan und Währungsreform*, pp. 42–43.

287 My translation from "Wir sind emsig darauf bedacht, dass man von uns überhaupt keine Notiz nimmt." Minutes of the 18th meeting of the Sonderstelle Geld und Kredit of November 20, 1947, p. 24. In BArch Coblenz Z 32/7, folio 64. Quoted from Weick, *Homburger Plan und Währungsreform*, p. 43.

288 Ferdinand Fried, "Das Drama von der Deutschen Mark," in *Die Welt*, June 21, 1958. Reprinted in Ludwig-Erhard-Stiftung, *Materialien zur Wirtschafts- und Währungsreform 1948*, Bonn: Ludwig-Erhard-Stiftung, 1978, chapter 7, without page numbers.

289 Unfinished book manuscript of Edward A. Tenenbaum "The German Mark," chapter 13, pp. 22–23. Edward A. Tenenbaum Papers, box 2, folder: *The German Mark* Book Draft (2 of 5). HSTPL.

290 Hoppenstedt, *Gerhard Colm*, p. 222. Online: Wikipedia "London Six-Power Conference" https://en.wikipedia.org/wiki/London_Six-Power_ Conference (Accessed April 22, 2018).

291 Elke Kimmel, "Zusammenarbeit und Gegensätze bis 1947," in Bundeszentrale für politische Bildung (ed.), *Dossier Der Marshallplan – Selling Democracy*. Online: Zusammenarbeit und Gegensätze bis 1947 | bpb (Accessed September 8, 2021).

292 Möller, *"Die westdeutsche Währungsreform von 1948,"* p. 445.

293 Clay, *Decision in Germany*, p. 212.

294 Ibid.

295 Otto Pfleiderer, "Vor 25 und vor 50 Jahren: Wendepunkte der deutschen Geldgeschichte," in *Zeitschrift für das gesamte Kreditwesen* 26 (1973), issue 12, pp. 543–549, here p. 548. My translation.

296 Pfleiderer, "Die Geburtsstunde der Deutschen Mark vor 25 Jahren," p. 12.

297 Möller, "Die westdeutsche Währungsreform von 1948," pp. 433–483, here pp. 451–452.

298 Buchheim, "Die Währungsreform 1948 in Westdeutschland," pp. 189–231. Christoph Buchheim, "The Establishment of the Bank deutscher Länder and the West German Currency Reform," in Deutsche Bundesbank (ed.), *Fifty Years of the Deutsche Mark. Central Bank and the Currency in Germany since 1948*, Oxford University Press, 1999, pp. 55–100. Möller, "Die westdeutsche Währungsreform von 1948," pp. 433–483.

299 Hielscher, *Der Leidensweg der deutschen Währungsreform*, pp. 38–39.

300 Published as: Charles P. Kindleberger/F. Taylor Ostrander, "The 1948 Monetary Reform in Western Germany," in Marc Flandreau/Carl-Ludwig Holtfrerich/Harold James (eds.), *International Financial History in the Twentieth Century. System and Anarchy*, Cambridge University Press, 2003, pp. 169–195.

301 Letter of F. Taylor Ostrander to Charles P. Kindleberger of 4 April 1992. Charles P. Kindleberger Papers, box 18, folder 2. HSTPL. See also Michalis M. Psalidopoulos, "Desperate Survivors. American economists in Greece, 1947–1953," unpublished manuscript.

302 Richard M. Westebbe, "The Marshall Plan: A personal perspective," unpublished manuscript. Quoted from Michalis M. Psalidopoulos, "Desperate Survivors. American economists in Greece, 1947–1953," unpublished manuscript.

303 Letter of James C. Warren to J. Kipp Tenenbaum of July 5, 1986. James C. Warren Papers, box 15, folder: Tenenbaum, Edward. HSTPL.

304 Letter of F. Taylor Ostrander to Charles P. Kindleberger of April 4, 1992. Charles P. Kindleberger Papers, box 18, folder 2. HSTPL.

305 "A monetary reform which can be put into effect immediately – a proposal by Don D. Humphrey and F. Taylor Ostrander for a currency reform and simultaneous price and wage adjustment i.e., inflationing the Reichsmark, memo [of September 11, 1947] to General Clay." BArch Z 45-F (OMGUS), 3/152-3/32.

306 Pfleiderer, "Die Geburtsstunde der Deutschen Mark vor 25 Jahren," p. 12. My translation.

307 See two telegrams between the US ambassador in London, Lewis W. Douglas, and the Secretary of State in Washington, DC of May 22 and 29, 1948. In FRUS 1948 II, pp. 904–905. See also Murphy, *Diplomat among Warriors*, p. 383.

308 Clay, *Decision in Germany*, p. 212.

309 Ibid., pp. 212–213.

310 Ibid., p. 213.

311 "Währungsreform-Konferenzen in Frankfurt am Main," *Der Tagesspiegel*, 16 June 1948.

312 Murphy, *Diplomat among Warriors*, p. 383.

313 Jack Bennett, "The German Currency Reform," in *The Annals of the American Academy of Political and Social Science* 267 (1950), pp. 43–54, here p. 49.

314 "Text for talk by Mr. Jack Bennett, Finance Adviser to the Military Governor (US) over AFN, Frankfurt, Friday 18 June 1948." Edward A. Tenenbaum Papers, box 5, folder: Germany – Currency Reform – Memoranda (7 of 9). HSTPL. The same folder contains many of the currency-reform laws, executive orders, and implementation leaflets in English.

315 This letter, which in the same wording was sent by Generals Koenig and Clay, to whom Sokolovsky's answering letters of June 19 and 22 were addressed, a document "Proclamation to the German people on Western currency reform by Marshal Sokolovsky, 19 June 1948," and a letter of June 23, 1948 from General Robertson to Marshal Sokolovsky announcing the introduction of the new currency into the Western sectors of Berlin are published in Carlyle (ed.), Royal Institute of

International Affairs, *Documents on International Affairs 1947–1948*, pp. 575–582. My quotation is from p. 576. The letters and the document were also published in German early on in Ministerium für Auswärtige Angelegenheiten der UdSSR (ed.), *Die Sowjetunion und die Berliner Frage: Dokumente*, pp. 19–33. Clay's letter to Sokolovsky of June 18 and Sokolovsky's answer to Clay of June 20, 1948 can also be found in NARA at College Park MD, RG 260 (OMGUS). On microfiche in IfZ Munich and BArch Coblenz, OMGUS, shipment COS, box 3, folder 1.

316 Harold James, "Die D-Mark," in Étienne Francois/Hagen Schulze (eds.), *Deutsche Erinnerungsorte*, vol. 2, Munich: Beck, 2001, p. 437, for this paragraph. James is not only wrong on the date of Erhard's radio address, but also on the date of Erhard being informed by Clay's military government about the upcoming currency reform. This took place already on June 15, 1948 (see below), not "in the afternoon of 18 June 1948." Harold James seems to have fallen prey to the story that Smith reported in his biography *Lucius D. Clay*, pp. 484–485. Unfortunately, James didn't reference Smith's biography of Clay. In any case, Smith's story of Clay's meeting with Erhard and Erhard's broadcast on June 18, 1948 are fiction.

317 Ulrike Herrmann, *Deutschland, ein Wirtschaftsmärchen. Warum es kein Wunder ist, dass wir reich geworden sind*, 2nd ed., Frankfurt am Main: Westend, 2019, p. 41.

318 Charles P. Kindleberger, *A Financial History of Western Europe*, London: Allen & Unwin, 1984, p. 416. He cites Heinz Sauermann, "On the economic and financial rehabilitation of Western Germany (1945–1949)," in *Zeitschrift für die gesamte Staatswissenschaft* 135 (1979), pp. 301–331, here p. 316.

319 Anne Rüter/Dietmar Bittner/Hans-Hermann Trost, *70 Jahre Konklave und Währungsreform 1948–2018. 25 Jahre Museum Währungsreform 1948*, Fuldatal-Rothwesten: Museumsverein Währungsreform 1948, 2018, pp. 47–48, 53–54.

320 Unfinished book manuscript of Edward A. Tenenbaum "The German Mark," chapter 13, p. 16. Edward A. Tenenbaum Papers, box 2, folder: *The German Mark* Book Draft (2 of 5). HSTPL.

321 Although all military government laws after March 20, 1948, when the Soviets had walked out of ACC, were no longer ACC laws, the American

and British powers united in the Bizone kept numbering their laws in the sequence practiced by ACC.

322 The text in English of these laws, including No. 65 of October 4, 1948 (Blocked Accounts Act or "supplementary conversion law" stipulating the final 6.5 percent conversion rate) are published in "Banking and Currency," in US Department of State (ed.), *Germany 1947–1949. The Story in Documents*, Washington, DC: GPO, 1950, pp. 492–518. The texts in German of these laws and ordinances as well as their amendments and changes have been collected in Rudolf Harmening (ed.), *Währungsgesetze. Vorschriften zur Neuordnung des Geldwesens in der Bundesrepublik und in Berlin(West)*, Munich: Beck, 1955. A detailed legal commentary on the most complicated and interpretative currency law, the Conversion Law, was already published in 1949: Hermann Reinbothe/Alfons Wetter/Heinz Beyer, *Umstellungsgesetz. Gesetz Nr. 63. Drittes Gesetz zur Neuordnung des Geldwesens*, Stuttgart: Schäfer, 1949.

323 Bennett, "The German Currency Reform," pp. 43–54, here p. 49.

324 Buchheim, "The Establishment of the Bank deutscher Länder and the West German Currency Reform," pp. 55–100, here pp. 92–93. For the text of the Blocked Accounts Law, see Harmening (ed.), *Währungsgesetze. Vorschriften zur Neuordnung des Geldwesens in der Bundesrepublik und in Berlin(West)*, pp. 360–362. Many more details of West (and East) German currency reform, including for West Germany monthly data on the circulation of money, on industrial production, and price indexes until the end of summer 1949 are presented in the excellent article by Fritz Grotius, "Die europäischen Geldreformen nach dem zweiten Weltkrieg," Part II: "Der Ablauf der Reformmaßnahmen in den einzelnen Ländern // 7. Deutschland." In *Weltwirtschaftliches Archiv* 63 (1949), pp. 276–289.

325 Walter W. Heller, "Tax and Monetary Reform in Occupied Germany," In *National Tax Journal* 2 (1949), pp. 215–231, here p. 216.

326 Carl-Ludwig Holtfrerich, "Monetary Policy under Fixed Exchange Rates (1948–70)," in Deutsche Bundesbank (ed.), *Fifty Years of the Deutsche Mark. Central Bank and the Currency in Germany since 1948*, Oxford University Press, 1999, pp. 307–401, here pp. 331–334.

327 Heller, "Tax and Monetary Reform in Occupied Germany," pp. 215–231, here p. 217.

328 For later dilemma situations see Holtfrerich, "Monetary Policy under Fixed Exchange Rates (1948–70)," pp. 307–401, here pp. 362–375, 384–390.

329 For example: Otto Pfleiderer, "Währungsreform in Westdeutschland (1948)," in *Enzyklopädisches Lexikon für das Geld-, Bank- und Börsenwesen*, 3rd ed., 2 vols., Frankfurt am Main: Knapp, 1967/68, pp. 1771–1779. Möller, "Die westdeutsche Währungsreform von 1948," pp. 433–483. Buchheim, "The Establishment of the Bank deutscher Länder and the West German Currency Reform," pp. 55–100. Weick, *Homburger Plan und Währungsreform*.

330 Schillinger, *Der Entscheidungsprozess beim Lastenausgleich 1945–1952*, pp. 98–107. See also Bennett, "The German Currency Reform," pp. 43–54, here p. 49.

331 Schillinger, *Der Entscheidungsprozess beim Lastenausgleich 1945–1952*, p. 119.

332 "Banking and Currency," in US Department of State (ed.), *Germany 1947–1949. The Story in Documents*, Washington, DC: GPO, 1950, pp. 492–500, here p. 492.

333 Schillinger, *Der Entscheidungsprozess beim Lastenausgleich 1945–1952*, p. 133.

334 "Lastenausgleichsgesetz," in Wikipedia (Accessed February 20, 2022). For more details on the sluggish German decision-making see: Schillinger, *Der Entscheidungsprozess beim Lastenausgleich 1945–1952*, pp. 135–145, 274–282.

335 Heller, "Tax and Monetary Reform in Occupied Germany," pp. 215–231.

336 Klaus Franzen, *Die Steuergesetzgebung der Nachkriegszeit in Westdeutschland (1945–1961)*, Bremen: Klamroth, 1994, p. 36.

337 A complete list of income tax rates and quarterly advance tax payments is contained in Einkommensteuertabelle für vierteljährliche Vorauszahlungen mit den amtlichen Einkommensteuerbeträgen (laut Gesetz Nr. 12 des Alliierten Kontrollrates vom 11. Februar 1946) mit Erläuterungen, Berlin-Schmargendorf: Archiv und Kartei, 1946. The brochure is also available in NARA at College Park MD, RG 59 Dec. File 862.5123/4-1146, Entry 1945–49, box 6788.

338 For these and further tax changes as well as for the political process preceding Law No. 64 see first of all the mostly neglected, but excellent article of the public finance expert, who had been personally involved in

preparing currency reform as one of the eleven German experts summoned within the cage of Rothwesten, Wilhelmine Dreißig, "Steuerpolitik im Zusammenhang mit der Währungsreform," in Walter A. S. Koch/Hans-Georg Petersen (eds.), *Staat, Steuern und Finanzausgleich. Probleme nationaler und internationaler Finanzwirtschaften im zeitlichen Wandel. Festschrift für Heinz Kolms zum 70. Geburtstag*, Berlin: Duncker & Humblot, 1984, pp. 171–199. See also the works of Jens van Scherpenberg, *Öffentliche Finanzwirtschaft in Westdeutschland 1944–1948*, Frankfurt am Main: R. G. Fischer, 1984, esp. pp. 351–360. Franzen, *Die Steuergesetzgebung der Nachkriegszeit*, esp. pp. 26–38. For an overview of the tax changes in a newspaper article at the time of enactment see "Lohn- und Einkommensteuer gesenkt," in *Frankfurter Neue Presse*, June 23, 1948, p. 1.

339 OMGUS Incoming Message of July 15, 1948 for OMGUS Finance Adviser from Department of the Army, REF NO WX-85735, in NARA RG 260/ OMGUS, microfilmed shipment 2, box 174, folder 3–6.

340 For details of currency shipments from the US to West Germany and their transport from Bremerhaven to Frankfurt am Main see "Records relating to Operation 'Birddog' and 'Doorknob' 1948–1950 (A1, Entry 590)," in the finding aid NARA Digital Publications DN 1924 "Records of the Foreign Exchange Depository Group of the Office of the Finance Adviser, OMGUS, 1944–1950," prepared by Onaona Miller Guay, pp. 10–32. Online: www.fold3.com/publication/839/omgus-foreign-exchange-depository-group (Accessed August 9, 2022).

341 A lot more interesting details have been calculated by Hans Möller in his appendix to "Die Währungsreform von 1948 und die Wiederherstellung marktwirtschaftlicher Verhältnisse," in Hampe (ed.), *Währungsreform und Soziale Marktwirtschaft*, pp. 55–77, here, p. 76.

342 Michael W. Wolff, *Die Währungsreform in Berlin 1948/49*, Berlin: Walter de Gruyter, 1991, p. 21. My translation.

343 The memo is reprinted in abbreviated form in ibid., pp. 297–299, here pp. 297–298. See also Meyer, *Mythos Deutsche Mark*, pp. 129–132.

344 As quoted in Wolff, *Die Währungsreform in Berlin 1948/49*, p. 23. Wolff devotes his pages 21–26 to a detailed presentation of the content of Tenenbaum's memo.

345 Budczies, *Meine Familie*, p. 172.

346 Stivers/Carter, *The City Becomes a Symbol*, pp. 216–218.

347 For both quotations see the identical articles of George Wronkow, "Geburtsstunde der Deutschen Mark. Zwei Amerikaner arbeiten als 'Währungsärzte,'" in *Berliner Morgenpost*, June 15, 1958, p. 1. George Wronkow, "Die Sowjets fuhren immer neuen Champagner auf ...," in *Münchner Merkur*, June 20, 1958, p. 1. George Wronkow, "Gold ist gut für Manschettenknöpfe, aber für das Geld ...? Die amerikanischen Väter der Deutschen Mark äußern sich über ihr Kind," in Kölner Stadt-Anzeiger, June 20, 1958, p. 1. For Tenenbaum's and Jack Bennett's correspondence with Wronkow in 1958 see Edward A. Tenenbaum Papers, box 3, folder: Germany – Background Data on Monetary Problems (2 of 2). HSTPL.

348 See above pp. 328–329.

349 Wolff, *Die Währungsreform in Berlin 1948/49*, pp. 30–31, 41.

350 Ibid., p. 77.

351 Ibid., p. 79. Frank Zschaler, "Die vergessene Währungsreform. Vorgeschichte, Durchführung und Ergebnisse der Geldumstellung in der SBZ 1948," in *Vierteljahrshefte für Zeitgeschichte 45* (1997), pp. 191–223.

352 Hentschel, *Ludwig Erhard*, p. 69.

353 For the dramatic proceedings of the night session, as well as the arguments and partisan makeup of proponents and opponents, see: Andreas Metz, *Die ungleichen Gründerväter. Adenauers und Erhardts langer Weg an die Spitze der Bundesrepublik*, Konstanz: Uni-Verlag Konstanz, 1998, pp. 126–128. An English translation of the law is available in IfZ Archive RG 260 / OMGUS, on microfilm. Provenance OMGUS FINAD, shipment 2, box 142, folder 6.

354 Willi Schickling, "Ludwig Erhards große Tat," in Karl Hohmann (ed.), *Ludwig Erhard. Erbe und Auftrag. Aussagen und Zeugnisse*, Düsseldorf: Econ, 1977, pp. 353–360. Ludwig Erhard, *Wohlstand für Alle*, paperback edition, Gütersloh: Signum, 1962, pp. 15–16. The first edition was published in Düsseldorf: Econ, 1957.

355 Buchheim, "The Establishment of the Bank deutscher Länder and the West German Currency Reform," pp. 55–100, here p. 95.

356 Kuno Ockhardt, "Der Vater des Wohlstandes," in Gerhard Schröder et al., *Ludwig Erhard: Beiträge zu seiner politischen Biographie. Festschrift zum 75. Geburtstag*, Propyläen, 1972, pp. 575–585. Metz, *Die ungleichen Gründerväter*, pp. 127–129. Ludwig Erhard, "Das deutsche Volk vor Schaden zu bewahren," TV interview teleasted April 10, 1963, in Günter

Gaus, *Zur Person. Porträts in Frage und Antwort*, Munich: Feder, 1964, pp. 101–115, here p. 112. Online: Sendung vom 10.04.1963 – Ludwig, Erhard | rbb (Accessed January 13, 2022).

357 Kathrin Zehender, "2. Parteitag der CDU der britischen Zone in Recklinghausen. Programmatische Neuorientierung in der Wirtschafts- und Sozialpolitik," p. 4. Online: www.kas.de/de/web/geschichte-der-cdu/ kalender/kalender-detail/-/content/2.-parteitag-der-cdu-der-britischen- zone-in-recklinghausen-programmatische-neuorientierung-in-der- wirtschafts-und-sozialpolitik (Accessed March 9, 2021).

358 Weick, *Homburger Plan und Währungsreform*, pp. 29, 33.

359 NARA at College Park MD, RG 260 (OMGUS). On microfiche in IfZ Munich and BArch Coblenz, OMGUS, shipment 3, box 133-3, folder 3, Provenance: OMGUS ED Dir Off.

360 See the article "400 Waren freigegeben," in *Die Welt,* 22 Juni 1948. Edward A. Tenenbaum Papers, box 5, folder: Germany – Currency Reform – Newspaper clippings (2 of 2). HSTPL.

361 Jess M. Lukomski, *Ludwig Erhard. Der Mensch und Politiker,* Düsseldorf: Econ, 1965, pp. 93–94.

362 Erhard in his preface to a collection of his articles, interviews, speeches, and other statements in Ludwig Erhard, *Deutsche Wirtschaftspolitik. Der Weg der Sozialen Marktwirtschaft,* Düsseldorf: Econ, 1962, p. 8. My translation.

363 Lukomski, *Ludwig Erhard,* p. 94. My translation. See also: Franz Thoma, "Der Ökonom, der ein Wunder schuf," in Hohmann (ed.), *Ludwig Erhard: Erbe und Auftrag,* pp. 152–158, here p. 153.

364 Buchheim, "The Establishment of the Bank deutscher Länder and the West German Currency Reform," pp. 55–100, here p. 95.

365 Ludwig Erhard, "Der neue Kurs (Rundfunkansprache am 21. Juni 1948)," in Erhard, *Deutsche Wirtschaftspolitik,* pp. 62–68.

366 Ludwig Erhard, *Wohlstand für Alle,* paperback edition, Gütersloh: Signum, 1962, p. 16.

367 Metz, *Die ungleichen Gründerväter,* p. 129.

368 Ibid.

369 Lucius D. Clay, "Glückwunschadresse," in Gerhard Schröder et al. (eds.), *Ludwig Erhard. Beiträge zu seiner politischen Biographie,* pp. 39–41, here pp. 40–41.

370 Manfred Görtemaker, *Geschichte der Bundesrepublik Deutschland: Von der Gründung bis zur Gegenwart*, Munich: Beck, 1999, p. 152.

371 Anthony J. Nicholls, *Freedom with Responsibility. The Social Market Economy in Germany, 1918–1963*, Oxford: Clarendon, 1994, p. 217.

372 Clay, *Decision in Germany*, pp. 92–93.

373 Smith, *Lucius D. Clay*, pp. 485–486.

374 NARA London, FO/1049/1432, as cited in Nicholls, *Freedom with Responsibility*, p. 221, note 34.

375 Ibid., p. 221.

376 Ludwig Erhard, "Zur Kritik an der neuen Ordnung," in Hohmann (ed.), *Gedanken aus fünf Jahrzehnten*, pp. 127–133. My translation.

377 NARA London, FO/1049/1432, cited in Nicholls, *Freedom with Responsibility*, p. 221.

378 Ibid., p. 210.

379 Microfilmed OMGUS FINAD files in Intitut für Zeigeschichte, Munich, shipment 2, box 174, folder 3–6.

380 Figures are taken from Wolfram Bickerich, *Die D-Marl. Eine Biographie*, Berlin: Rowohlt, 1998, p. 126.

381 "Der erste Währungssünder / verurteilt," in *Frankfurter Rundschau*, Friday June 25, 1948, p. 3. Edward A. Tenenbaum Papers, box 5, folder: Germany Currency Reform – Newspaper Clippings. HSTPL.

382 Statistisches Bundesamt (ed.), *Bevölkerung und Wirtschaft 1872–1972*, Stuttgart: Kohlhammer, 1972, p. 250, where only for 1948 consumer price index numbers are presented semi-annually. Based on 1938 =100 the index numbers for West Germany (without Berlin and the Sarre) for the first half of 1948 is 141.8 and for the second half 168.3. This amounts to an increase of 18.7 percent.

383 Colm/Dodge/Goldsmith, "A Plan for the Liquidation of War Finance and the Financial Rehabilitation of Germany," pp. 204–243, here p. 234.

384 Buchheim, "Die Währungsreform 1948 in Westdeutschland," pp. 189–231, here, p. 205.

385 Statistisches Bundesamt (ed.), *Bevölkerung und Wirtschaft 1872–1972*, p. 250.

386 *Gesetzblatt der Verwaltung des Vereinigten Wirtschaftsgebiets* 1948, p. 117, as cited in Rudolf Stucken, *Deutsche Geld- und Kreditpolitik 1914–1963*, 3rd edition, Tübingen: Mohr/Siebeck, 1964, p. 209.

387 For an extensive treatment of the general strike and its origins in the Bizone see Uwe Fuhrmann, *Die Entstehung der 'Sozialen*

Marktwirtschaft' 1948/49. Eine historische Dispositivanalyse, Konstanz: Konstanz University Press, 2017, pp. 233–252.

388 Buchheim, "Die Währungsreform 1948 in Westdeutschland," pp. 189–231, here p. 229.

389 Unfinished book manuscript of Edward A. Tenenbaum "The German Mark," chapter 13, p. 32. Edward A. Tenenbaum Papers, box 2, folder: *The German Mark* Book Draft (2 of 5). HSTPL.

390 Ibid.

391 Henry C. Wallich, *Mainsprings of the German Revival*, New Haven: Yale University Press, 1955, pp. 73–74.

392 Ibid., pp. 76–78.

393 "Im Streitgespräch mit Erik Nölting. Kundgebung der SPD im Zirkus Althoff, Frankfurt a. M., 14. November 1948," in Hohmann (ed.), *Ludwig Erhard. Gedanken aus fünf Jahrzehnten*, pp. 166–181.

394 Unfinished book manuscript of Edward A. Tenenbaum "The German Mark," chapter 13. Edward A. Tenenbaum Papers, boxes 2 and 3, 5 folders: *The German Mark* Book Draft. HSTPL.

395 The motivation for and failure of Erhard's surprise proposal of this drastic one-time levy on all business inventories in connection with drafting the First Equalization of Burdens Bill, which was passed in the Economic Council on December 14, 1948, but due to Allied vetoing never went into force, is discussed in Schillinger, *Der Entscheidungsprozess beim Lastenausgleich 1945–1952*, pp. 127–131.

396 Erhard's arguments have been aptly summarized by Nicholls, *Freedom with Responsibility*, pp. 225–230. For these and a number of other anti-inflation measures during the second half of 1948 see Fuhrmann, *Die Entstehung der 'Sozialen Marktwirtschaft' 1948/49*, pp. 165–230.

397 "Im Streitgespräch mit Erik Nölting, Kundgebung der SPD im Zirkus Althoff, Frankfurt a. M., 14. November 1948," in Hohmann (ed.), *Ludwig Erhard. Gedanken aus fünf Jahrzehnten*, pp. 166–181, here p. 166.

398 Unfinished book manuscript of Edward A. Tenenbaum "The German Mark," chapter 13, p. 2. Edward A. Tenenbaum Papers, box 2, folder: *The German Mark* Book Draft (2 of 5). HSTPL.

399 Ibid.

400 Max Schönwandt, "Konstanzer Plan," in Hans Möller (ed.), *Zur Vorgeschichte der Deutschen Mark. Die Währungsreformpläne 1945–1948*, Tübingen: Mohr, 1961, pp. 109–115. Schönwandt's original 14-page explanatory memorandum of September 14, 1945 to his

currency-reform bills can be found in Edward A. Tenenbaum Papers, box 4, folder: Germany – Currency Reform – Memoranda (2 of 9). HSTPL. Erwin Hielscher summarized some of his views on currency conversion in a 7-page memo without title of April 29, 1948. Edward A. Tenenbaum Papers, box 3, folder: Germany – Background Data on Monetary Problems (2 of 2).

401 Unfinished book manuscript of Edward A. Tenenbaum "The German Mark," chapter 13, pp. 23–24. Edward A. Tenenbaum Papers, box 2, folder: *The German Mark* Book Draft (2 of 5). HSTPL. On January 18, 1948 Jack Bennett sent Tenenbaum's memo "The 'Right Rate of Conversion'" to General Clay. Edward A. Tenenbaum Papers, box 3, folder: Germany – Currency Reform –Memoranda (1 of 9). HSTPL.

402 Hampe (ed.), *Währungsreform und Soziale Marktwirtschaft*, p. 121. The amount appears in reprinted minutes of a Rothwesten Conclave plenary session of May 11, 1948, with the German expert inmates of the camp, a few German politicians, including Ludwig Erhard, and the three currency experts of the three Western military governments.

403 Hans Möller, *Zur Vorgeschichte der Deutschen Mark. Die Währungsreformpläne 1945–1948*, Tübingen: Mohr/Siebeck, 1961, p. 12.

404 Minutes of the sixth meeting on October 17, 1947. BArch Coblenz, Z 32/1, folio 48.

405 Fried, "Das Drama von der Deutschen Mark," chapter 7 without page numbers. For details see Buchheim, "Die Währungsreform 1948 in Westdeutschland," pp. 189–231, here pp. 214–215.

406 Jack Bennett, finance adviser of OMGUS, Memo to General Clay of March 5, 1948, Subject: German Proposal of Financial Reform [= preliminary version of Homburg Plan], NARA RG 260, reprinted in original English in Hampe (ed.), *Währungsreform und Soziale Marktwirtschaft*, pp. 116–118.

407 The meeting on June 14, its subject, and participants are documented with sources in Wilhelmine Dreißig, "Steuerpolitik im Zusammenhang mit der Währungsreform," in Koch/Petersen (eds.), *Staat, Steuern und Finanzausgleich*, pp. 178–179.

408 This whole paragraph is based on Meyer, *Mythos Deutsche Mark*, pp. 90–91. See also the richly illustrated edition of the same author: Meyer, *20.6.1948 Währungsreform*, p. 55.

409 NARA at College Park MD, RG 260 (OMGUS). On microfiche in IfZ Munich and BArch Coblenz, OMGUS, shipment 2, box 174, folder 4.

410 The lyrics of the song in German as well as an English translation and a link to the original performance of the song are online: https://lyricstranslate.com/de/trizonesien-song-trizonesia-song.html (Accessed October 9, 2019).

411 Opening sentence in E. A. Tenenbaum's undated memo "Financial Stabilization After Currency Conversion." Edward A. Tenenbaum Papers, box 3, folder: Germany – Background Data on Monetary Problems (2 of 2). HSTPL.

412 Edward A. Tenenbaum, memo of July 4, 1948 "The Preservation of the Deutsche Mark." Edward A. Tenenbaum Papers, box 3, folder: Germany – Background Data on Monetary Problems (2 of 2). HSTPL.

413 Ibid.

414 Report No. 408 from The Foreign Service of the USA, American Consulate, Bremen, Germany, 9 July 1948 to "The Honorable Secretary of State, Washington. Confidential." NARA at College Park, RG 59 General Records of the Department of State, Civil Affairs Division, Decimal Files 862.515/7-948.

415 Ibid.

416 "Neuer Wechselkurs der DM." Kabinettsprotokolle. 3. Kabinettssitzung 21 September 1949. Online: Kabinettsprotokolle Online "1. Neuer Wechselkurs der DM" (2.3.1:) (bundesarchiv.de) (Accessed November 21, 2021).

417 Frederick W. Williams, "Foreword," in Merritt/L. Merritt (eds.), *Public Opinion in Occupied Germany*, p. xvii.

418 Clay, *Decision in Germany*, p. 283.

419 Merritt/Merritt (eds.), *Public Opinion in Occupied Germany*, pp. 251–252.

420 Charles E. Bancroft, "Subject: Currency Reform / Extract from National-Zeitung 23 June 1948." Edward A. Tenenbaum Papers, box 5, folder: Germany Currency Reform – Newspaper Clippings. HSTPL.

421 Frank Zschaler, "Die vergessene Währungsreform. Vorgeschichte, Durchführung und Ergebnisse der Geldumstellung in der SBZ 1948," in *Vierteljahrshefte für Zeitgeschichte* 45 (1997), pp. 191–223, here p. 209. Wolff, *Die Währungsreform in Berlin 1948/49*, pp. 68–72.

422 Merritt/Merritt (eds.), *Public Opinion in Occupied Germany*, p. 252.

423 Hermann Glaser, *Kulturgeschichte der Bundesrepublik Deutschland. Zwischen Kapitulation und Währungsreform 1945–1948*, Munich: Carl Hanser, 1985, p. 332.

424 Günter Keiser, "Die Ursachen der Preissteigerung und das Lohnproblem." IfZArch ED 150/23 Nachlass Hans Möller. Unfortunately, the document carries no date. But its content reveals that it must have been written in the second half of 1948.

425 Oskar Liebeck, *Vernunft statt Tradition. Das Wesen der Demokratie*, Stuttgart: Franz M ittelbach, 1949, pp. 118–120. My translation.

426 Jack Bennett, "Impact of Currency Reform," in *Information Bulletin* [of OMGUS] October 5, 1948, pp. 18–21, here p. 21. Online: http://digicoll .library.wisc.edu/cgi-bin/History/History-idx?type=turn&entity=History .omg1948n145.p0022&id=History.omg1948n145&isize=text (Accessed January 17, 2022).

427 Bennett, "Impact of Currency Reform."

428 "Finance Adviser Ends MG Service," in *Information Bulletin* [of OMGUS] 25 January 1949, p. 10.

429 Ibid.

430 Deutsche Bundesbank (ed.), *Deutsches Geld- und Bankwesen in Zahlen 1876–1975*, Frankfurt am Main: Knapp, 1976, pp. 4, 14.

431 Frank Zschaler, "Die vergessene Währungsreform. Vorgeschichte, Durchführung und Ergebnisse der Geldumstellung in der SBZ 1948," in *Vierteljahrshefte für Zeitgeschichte* 45 (1997), pp. 191–223, here p. 195.

432 Ibid.

433 Franzen, *Die Steuergesetzgebung der Nachkriegszeit*, pp. 26–29.

434 Wilhelmine Dreißig, "Steuerpolitik im Zusammenhang mit der Währungsreform," in Koch/Petersen (eds.), *Staat, Steuern und Finanzausgleich*, p. 175. Eduard Wolf, "Geld- und Finanzprobleme der deutschen Nachkriegswirtschaft," in Deutsches Institut für Wirtschaftsforschung (ed.), *Die deutsche Wirtschaft zwei Jahre nach dem Zusammenbruch. Tatsachen und Probleme*, Berlin: Nauck, 1947, pp. 195–262, here pp. 215–217. Hans-Peter Ullmann, *Der deutsche Steuerstaat. Geschichte der öffentlichen Finanzen vom 18. Jahrhundert bis heute.* Munich: Beck, 2005, p. 180.

435 This conforms to an early estimate of cash circulation of 65.1 billion RM for the end of 1946. See the study of the German monetary expert, who was nominated for the Conclave meeting, but due to travel restrictions from Berlin could not participate: Wolf, "Geld- und Finanzprobleme der deutschen Nachkriegswirtschaft," pp. 195–262, here p. 221.

436 Länderrat des Amerikanischen Besatzungsgebiets (ed.), *Statistisches Handbuch von Deutschland 1928–1944*, Munich: Ehrenwirth, 1949, p. 505.

437 Werner Abelshauser, *Wirtschaftsgeschichte der Bundesrepublik Deutschland 1945–1980*, Frankfurt am Main: Suhrkamp, 1983, p. 34.

438 Deutsches Institut für Wirtschaftsforschung (ed.), *Die deutsche Wirtschaft zwei Jahre nach dem Zusammenbruch*, pp. 195–262, here pp. 268–269.

439 In December 1947 the number of employees in the three Western zones of occupation amounted to 13.4 million. See Charlotte Arnold, "Der Arbeitsmarkt in den Besatzungszonen," in Deutsches Institut für Wirtschaftsforschung (ed.), *Wirtschaftsprobleme der Besatzungszonen*, Berlin: Duncker & Humblot, 1948, pp. 36–64, here p. 36. For the average of 1949 13.5 million employees have been recorded. See Heiner R. Adamsen, "Faktoren und Daten der wirtschaftlichen Entwicklung in der Frühphase der Bundesrepublik Deutschland 1948–1954," in *Archiv für Sozialpolitik* 181 (1978), pp. 217–244, here p. 237. Employment in the second half of 1948 went down by about 0.5 million. In a summer month, such as June, employment is usually higher than in a winter month or than the average for a whole year.

440 Weick, *Homburger Plan und Währungsreform*, pp. 100–103 for the discussion among the German monetary experts on the 1-to-1 per capita conversion.

441 Details above pp. 520–522.

442 F. Taylor Ostrander, "First thoughts on a discussion of Germany's 1948 currency reform and its (possible) relevance to today's two-Germany unification and the monetary turmoil sure to come in USSR and Eastern Europe," dated May 26, 1990. Charles P. Kindleberger Papers, box 11, folder: F. Taylor Ostrander, 1992. HSTPL.

443 Ibid.

5 FROM OMGUS TO CIVIL SERVICE IN WASHINGTON, DC AND FOR EUROPE 1948–1953

1 Edward A. Tenenbaum Papers, box 8, folder: Personnel File. HSTPL.

2 Tenenbaum himself listed these addresses on "Investigation Data Request, Economic Cooperation Administration, Form ECA-1, Rev.

12–48." Edward A. Tenenbaum Papers, box 8, folder: Personnel File. HSTPL.

3 *Yale Twenty-Fifth Yearbook. Class of 1942*, New Haven, CT: Yale University Press, 1967, p. 311.

4 Ibid., p. 312.

5 "Investigation Data Request, Economic Cooperation Administration, Form ECA-1, Rev. 12–48," in Edward A. Tenenbaum Papers, box 8, folder: Personnel File. HSTPL.

6 United States Civil Service Commission, *Official Register of the United States 1950*, Washington, DC: Government Printing Office, 1950, title page and for Tenenbaum and his director McCullough p. 555. Online: https://books.google.de/books?id=n8khAAAAMAAJ&pg=PA555&lpg= PA555&dq=harlan+cleveland+and+tenenbaum&source=bl&ots= y09LHWV5Sr&sig=ACfU3U1pOAR-VHYGEeNu0dBTw24mCBF0mA& hl=en&sa=X&redir_esc=y#v=onepage&q=harlan%20cleveland%20and% 20tenenbaum&f=false (Accessed June 23, 2021). See also Tenenbaum's CV with which he applied for his ECA/MSA appointment on Greek fiscal and monetary matters, while he was still working for the IMF. Edward A. Tenenbaum Papers, box 8, folder: Personnel File. HSTPL.

7 Harry B. Price, *The Marshall Plan and Its Meaning*, Ithaca, NY: Cornell University Press, 1955, pp. 124–125, fn. 14.

8 Alfons Montag, "Eine tolle – jedoch wahre Geschichte. Verfaßte Mr. Tennenbaum [sic] die Kritik der Hochkommission am deutschen OEEC-Memorandum?" In *Welt der Arbeit*, February 24, 1950, p. 3. My colleague Gerd Hardach made me aware of this article.

9 Statistische Bundesamt, *Bevölkerung und Wirtschaft 1872–1972*, Stuttgart: Kohlhammer, 1972, p. 148. The Korean War might also have played a role in bringing unemployment down.

10 [Attachment] "III. Economic Cooperation Administration." Edward A. Tenenbaum Papers, box 8, folder: Personnel File. HSTPL.

11 Edward A. Tenenbaum Papers. box 8, folder: Personnel File. HSTPL.

12 "Tenenbaum to Address Export-Import Club," *Richmond Times Dispatch*, June 28, 1950, p. 3.

13 Tenenbaum's many memoranda on trade and currency aspects of West European integration are contained in Edward A. Tenenbaum Papers, box 1, folders: European Economic Cooperation 1–3 of 4. box 2, folder: European Economic Cooperation 4 of 4. HSTPL.

14 Beate Neuss, *Geburtshelfer Europas? Die Rolle der Vereinigten Staaten im europäischen Integrationsprozeß 1945–1958*, Baden-Baden: Nomos, 2000.

15 See the form of the IMF "Advice of Personnel Action" attached to Tenenbaum's CV with which he applied for his ECA/MSA appointment on Greek fiscal and monetary matters, while he was still working for the IMF. Edward A. Tenenbaum Papers, box 8, folder: Personnel File. HSTPL.

16 Edward A. Tenenbaum, "Duties at International Monetary Fund," April 1, 1951. Edward A. Tenenbaum Papers, box 8, folder: Personnel File. HSTPL.

17 Edward A. Tenenbaum Papers, box 7, folder: International Monetary Fund – Memoranda. HSTPL.

18 [Attachment] "V. Mutual Security Agency." Edward A. Tenenbaum Papers, box 8, folder: Personnel File. HSTPL.

19 In Edward A. Tenenbaum Papers, box 6, folder: Greece – Economic Aid To (2 of 3). HSTPL.

20 Ibid.

21 For this paragraph and the controversial bickering inside of American institutions and between these and Greek government representatives see Michalis M. Psalidopoulos, "Desperate Survivors. American economists in Greece, 1947–1953," unpublished manuscript, pp. 28, 65–73. I am deeply indebted to the author for having shared his unpublished manuscript with me and for several fruitful personal meetings and exchanges in 2018 and 2019, while he represented Greece and some other countries at the IMF in Washington, DC. The manuscript is the author's translation into English of his book which has been published in Greek.

22 "Leland Barrows, Oral History Interview – 2/4/1971." Online: www .jfklibrary.org/sites/default/files/archives/JFKOH/Barrows,%20Leland% 20J/JFKOH-LJB-01/JFKOH-LJB-01-TR.pdf (Accessed July 30, 2022).

23 James C. Warren Papers, box 1, folder: American Embassy, Athens Greece 1952–54. HSTPL. This folder contains many documents exemplifying the prevailing tension, also with the Greek government and central bank.

24 Tenenbaum collected memos, reports, and letters of Welldon, while they were working on that mission together in Athens. Edward A. Tenenbaum Papers, box 10, folder: Welldon, Samuel A. – Chronological File, 1952. HSTPL.

25 "Letter of Edward A. Tenenbaum, Athens, to Samuel A. Welldon, New York, June 30, 1952." Edward A. Tenenbaum Papers, box 6, folder: Greece – Economic Aid To (3 of 3). HSTPL.

26 Edward A. Tenenbaum Papers, box 6, folder: Greece – Economic Aid To (2 od 3). HSTPL.

27 From a comment of Michalis Psalidopoulos on an earlier version of this chapter, sent to me by email on August 22, 2022.

28 Edward A. Tenenbaum Papers, box 10, folder: Welldon, Samuel A. – Chronological File, 1952. HSTPL.

29 Edward A. Tenenbaum Papers, box 6, folder: Greece – Economic Aid To (2 of 3). HSTPL.

30 Edward A. Tenenbaum Papers. box 6, folder: Greece – Economic Aid To (3 of 3). HSTPL.

31 Psalidopoulos, "Desperate Supervisors," p. 47; for the return date p. 44. Psalidopoulos asserts that the Tenenbaums had arrived in Athens in May 1951. This is not correct, as Tenenbaum's memos written in Washington, DC during the 1950s show.

32 [Attachment] "V. Mutual Security Agency." Edward A. Tenenbaum Papers, box 8, folder: Personnel File. HSTPL.

33 "Comparison of Simple Devaluation with a Currency Reform," undated. HSTPL. Edward A. Tenenbaum Papers, box 6, folder: Greece – Economic Aid To (2 of 3).

34 Apostolos Vetsopoulos, "'The Economic Dimensions of the Marshall Plan in Greece, 1947–1952: The Origins of the Greek economic miracle," PhD Diss. University of London, 2002, pp. 338–339. Available online ProQuest Number: U642335.

35 For the results of the elections and the delay in forming the new government see: ibid., pp. 285, 337.

36 A number of documents by business circles and labor unions can be found in National Archives at College Park MD, RG 59, Entry A 1205-N, box 5402.

37 The leading administrator of the American aid to Greece under the Marshall plan since 1949 reports a different distribution of the $400 million Truman Doctrine aid, namely $250 million for Greece and $150 million for Turkey. Paul R. Porter, "Greece's Vital Role in the Triumph of the Democracies," in Eugene T. Rossides (ed.), *The Truman Doctrine of Aid to Greece: A Fifty-Year Retrospective*, New York: The Academy of Political Science, 1998, pp. 170–173, here p. 171. The official summary account of American aid programs to Greece, in contrast, speaks of $300 million. See: US Operations Mission in Greece (ed.), *The American Aid*

Programs in Greece. A Summary Account of the American Economic Aid Programs to Greece from 1947 to the Spring of 1954, Athens, July 1954, p. 1. World War II developments and the communist postwar threat in Greece that triggered the Truman Doctrine is also described on the same page.

38 US State Department. Office of the Historian, "The Truman Doctrine, 1947." Online: https://history.state.gov/milestones/1945–1952/truman-doctrine#:~:text=With%20the%20Truman%20Doctrine%2C%20President,external%20or%20internal%20authoritarian%20forces.&text=Truman%20asked%20Congress%20to%20support%20the%20Greek%20Government%20against%20the%20Communists (Accessed August 2, 2020).

39 "Principles of Program Agreement of June 23, 1951." National Archives at College Park MD, RG 59, Entry A 1205-N, box 5405.

40 Edward A. Tenenbaum, Office memo to James A. McCullough of August 1, 1951, "Subject: Buying Finance Ministers." Edward A. Tenenbaum Papers, box 3, folder: Germany – Currency Reform – Memoranda (1 of 9). HSTPL.

41 Message of July 13, 1951 from Edward A. Tenenbaum to Paul R. Porter, at that time US Special Representative in Europe for the Marshall Plan, 1949–1950 chief of ECA Mission to Greece, dated July 13, 1951, "Subject: The Pesmasoglu Proposals." National Archives at College Park MD, RG 469, Entry (UD) 359, box 3, Folder "Currency Reform." This folder also contains the two enclosures: Tenenbaum's single-spaced 18-page comments on the Pesmasoglu proposals as well as his secret double-spaced 20-page memo "Ending Inflation in Greece," It also contains a memo "What Our Position on Greece Means."

42 Edward A. Tenenbaum, Secret memo of August 10, 1951: "Summary of a Proposal to End Inflation in Greece." National Archives at College Park MD, RG 469, Entry (UD) 359, box 3, Folder "Currency Reform." This folder also contains a memo of November 23, 1951 "Provisional Estimate of Currency Required by Greece" in preparation of printing new drachma currency in the USA through BEP like in the West German case or in the UK.

43 National Archives at College Park MD, RG 59, Entry A 1205-N, box 5404. Also in RG 469, Entry (UD) 359, box 3, Folder: "Currency Reform." For earlier Greek currency reforms before 1951 see: George Politakis, *The Post-War*

Reconstruction of Greece. A History of Economic Stabilization and Development, 1944–1952, New York: Palgrave Macmillan, 2017.

44 Information provided in a comment of Michalis Psalidopoulos on an earlier version of this chapter, sent to me by email on August 22, 2022.

45 Vetsopoulos, "'The Economic Dimensions of the Marshall Plan in Greece, 1947–1952," p. 304. Available online ProQuest Number: U642335.

46 James C. Warren, Jr., "Origins of the 'Greek Economic Miracle,': The Truman Doctrine and Marshall Plan Development and Stabilization Programs," in Eugene T. Rossides (ed.), *The Truman Doctrine of Aid to Greece: A Fifty-Year Retrospective*, New York: The Academy of Political Science, 1998, pp. 76–105, here p. 77. Where not otherwise noted, the information in this section relies on that article. Warren had been part of AMAG and had worked with Tenenbaum. He spent almost all of his professional life as a consultant for companies doing business in Greece. For details see the contributor list in ibid., p. 195.

47 For data see: U.S. Operations Mission to Greece, *Greece Statistical Data Book, vol. 1* (1955–56), [Worldcat reports: Place of publication not identified]. National Statistical Service of Greece (ed.), *Statistical Yearbook of Greece*, since 1954 annually, Athens: National Printing Office. Online: http://dlib.statistics.gr/portal/page/portal/ESYE/categoryyears?p_cat=10007369&p_topic=10007369 (Accessed August 16, 2020).

48 Warren, Jr., "Origins of the 'Greek Economic Miracle,'" pp. 76–105, here p. 79.

49 Paul R. Porter, "Greece's Vital Role in the Triumph of the Democracies," in Eugene T. Rossides (ed.), *The Truman Doctrine of Aid to Greece: A Fifty-Year Retrospective*, New York: The Academy of Political Science, 1998, pp. 170–173, here p. 172.

50 Phillip D. Cagan, "The Monetary Dynamics of Hyperinflation," in Milton Friedman (ed.), *Studies in the Quantity Theory of Money*, Chicago University Press, 1956, pp. 25–117.

51 For a study of specifically the Greek hyperinflation see: Michael Palairet, *The Four Ends of the Greek Hyperinflation of 1941–1946*, Copenhagen: Museum Tusculanum Press, 2000.

52 Carmen M. Reinhart/Kenneth S. Rogoff, *This Time Is Different. Eight Centuries of Financial Folly*, Princeton University Press, 2009, p. 186 for (hyper)inflation data since 1834.

53 Warren, Jr., "Origins of the 'Greek Economic Miracle,'" pp. 76–105, here p. 90.

54 Ibid., pp. 76–105, here pp. 90–91.

55 Ibid., pp. 76–105, here p. 94.

56 Ibid., pp. 76–105, here p. 95.

57 "American Aid to Greece. A document from the CQ Researcher archives." Online: https://library.cqpress.com/cqresearcher/document.php?id= cqresrre1949020900 (Accessed August 12, 2020).

58 Stelios Zachariou, "Implementing the Marshall Plan in Greece: Balancing Reconstruction and Geopolitical Security," in *Journal of Modern Greek Studies* 27 (2009), pp. 303–318, here pp. 309–310. Online: www .researchgate.net/publication/236755370_Implementing_the_Marshall_ Plan_in_Greece_Balancing_Reconstruction_and_Geopolitical_Security (Accessed August 11, 2020).

59 Warren, Jr., "Origins of the 'Greek Economic Miracle,'" pp. 76–105, here p. 96, fn. 21.

60 Barry Machado, *In Search of a Usable Past: The Marshall Plan and Postwar Reconstruction Today.* Lexington, KY: The George C. Marshall Foundation, 2007, pp. 59, 70.

61 Psalidopoulos, "Desperate Supervisors," pp. 37, 79.

62 Computed from data in Brian R. Mitchell, *European Historical Statistics 1750–1975*, 2nd rev. ed. London: Macmillan, 1980, p. 830.

63 Computed from data in Deutsche Bundesbank, *Deutsches Geld- und Bankwesen in Zahlen 1876–1975*, Frankfurt am Main: Fritz Knapp, 1976, p. 7.

64 Warren, Jr., "Origins of the 'Greek Economic Miracle,'" pp. 76–105, here p. 98. As to income tax increases see ibid., p. 97, fn. 22. See also: 16-page lecture manuscript with statistical annexes, author not revealed. It could have been Paul R. Porter, former US Mission Chief in Athens who later lived in Florida. But it could also have been James C. Warren's lecture, given at Gainesville, Florida, April 18, 1990, entitled "The American Economic Aid Program in Greece 1947–54." James C. Warren Papers. box 1, folder: American Economic Aid Program in Greece 1947–52. HSTPL. For the spectacular results of the application of the Inflationary/Deflationary Balance Sheet in terms of price developments and economic growth see esp. pp. 14–16.

65 For details see above pp. 557–559.

66 In Edward A. Tenenbaum Papers, box 6, folder: Greece – Economic Aid To (2 of 3). HSTPL. The article's publication date is given as March 9, 1953, the date of the translation as March 3, 1953. From this sequence I conclude that the newspaper was obliged to at least inform the embassy and the mission, if not to ask for their consent before publishing articles dealing with economic- and monetary-policy questions. The two handwritten names at the top of the translation, Tenenbaum and Turkel, support my conjecture.

67 A portrait of Markezinis and many examples of his strained relations with Tenenbaum are contained in Psalidopoulos, "Desperate Supervisors." On Markezinis' astrological justification for the timing of the drachma's devaluation, Psalidopoulos commented: "The IMF had decided about the date two months earlier. Markezinis says rubbish." Email of August 22, 2022 to me.

68 The spectacular broad-based economic and social development, which never before had happened in Greek history, is the subject of the book by William H. McNeill, *The Metamorphosis of Greece since World War II*, Chicago University Press, 1978.

69 Warren, Jr., "Origins of the 'Greek Economic Miracle,'" pp. 76–105, here p. 102, fn. 28.

70 Online: Georgios Kartalis – Wikipedia (Accessed April 24, 2022).

71 Quoted from Price, *The Marshall Plan and Its Meaning*, p. 279.

72 "Letter of Edward A. Tenenbaum, Athens, to Samuel A. Welldon, New York, June 30, 1952." Edward A. Tenenbaum Papers, box 6, folder: Greece – Economic Aid To (3 of 3). HSTPL.

73 "Letter of Edward A. Tenenbaum, Athens, to Samuel Welldon, through Mr. Victor Sullam, MSA, Washington, DC, September 5, 1952." Edward A. Tenenbaum Papers, box 6, folder: Greece – Economic Aid To (1 of 3). HSTPL. See also Tenenbaum's memo about conversations with Kartalis of September 5, 1952. Edward A. Tenenbaum Papers, box 7, folder: Greece – Economic Problems. HSTPL.

74 "Letter of Edward A. Tenenbaum, Athens, to Samuel A. Welldon, New York, 23 January 1953." Edward A. Tenenbaum Papers, box 6, folder: Greece – Economic Aid To (2 of 3). HSTPL.

75 "Letter of Edward A. Tenenbaum, Athens, to Francis Lincoln, Office of Greek, Turkish and Iranian Affairs, State Department, Washington, DC, 21 February 1953." Edward A. Tenenbaum Papers, box 6, folder: Greece – Economic Aid To (2 of 3). HSTPL.

76 "Letter of Edward A. Tenenbaum to Samuel A. Welldon of 17 February 1953." Edward A. Tenenbaum Papers, box 6, folder: Greece – Economic Aid To (2 of 3). HSTPL.

6 LIFE AND FATE AS A BUSINESSMAN AND FAMILY MAN 1953–1975 AND BEYOND

1 *Evening Star* (Washington, DC), Wednesday, February 24, 1954, p. 24.
2 Jack Franklin Bennett's obituary in *The Washington Post* of April 28–29, 2010. And "Jack Franklin Bennett" in The Department of State (ed.), *Biographic Register. May 1, 1954*, Washington, DC: Department of State Publication 5553, 1954, p. 45. Online: www.google.de/books/edition/The_Biographic_Register/ZHti9LWgXx8C?hl=en&gbpv=1&dq=Jack+Franklin+Bennett+OMGUS&pg=PA46-IA13&printsec=frontcover (Accessed January 21, 2022).
3 "Andrew Jackson Bennett, 86, reformed W. German currency," in *Washington Times* March 9, 1988, p. 16. "Jack Bennett, 86, Dies; Government Economist," in *New York Times* March 12, 1988, p. 10.
4 "Finance Adviser Ends MG Service," in *Information Bulletin* [of OMGUS] 25 January 1949, p. 10.
5 See online: https://books.google.de/books?id=e9jx2CRp0d0C&q=Edward+A.+Tenenbaum+Industry+for+B.G.&dq=Edward+A.+Tenenbaum+Industry+for+B.G.&hl=de&sa=X&ved=0ahUKEwjC5Jf-5f3lAhULa1AKHZ98AjgQ6AEILDAA (Accessed November 22, 2019).
6 Fred Clayton Papers. Online: http://qalabist.com/?cat=13 (Accessed October 23, 2019) for December. For June see a letter dated June 30, 1958 of Werner Prym, journalist of *Münchner Illustrierte*, to Miss Myrtle M. Watson, who worked in Tenenbaum's and Bennett's office as typist and secretary. Her initials accompany those of Bennett on the two letters and those of Ray C. Burrus, an employed technical expert, on the memorandum. Prym thanked her for having sent a photo of Tenenbaum for a series of articles that *Münchner Illustrierte* was running on America, including Tenenbaum's central role in West Germany's currency reform ten years earlier. In: Edward A. Tenenbaum Papers, box 3, folder: Germany – Background Data on Monetary Problems (2 of 2). HSTPL.
7 I am deeply indebted to Michael Enyart, Director of the Business Library, and Rebecca Payne, Memorial Library, who in their field have delivered

proof of why the University of Wisconsin at Madison is an institution with a reputation of excellence.

8 See online item 392: https://books.google.de/books?id= YjUbAAAAMAAJ&pg=PA106&dq=Edward+A.+Tenenbaum,+Industry +for+B.+G.&hl=de&sa=X&ved=0ahUKEwjR4a- GnfzlAhVFMewKHUfZDZ8Q6AEIMzAB#v=onepage&q=Edward%20A .%20Tenenbaum%2C%20Industry%20for%20B.%20G.&f=false (Accessed November 21, 2019).

9 *Helping Honduran Industry: A Diagnostic Study*, Washington, DC: Allied-Continental Company, Inc., 1961.

10 See Edward A. Tenenbaum's letter of recommendation on behalf of James C. Warren of December 6, 1954 "TO WHOM IT MAY CONCERN," in James C. Warren Papers, box 15, folder: Tenenbaum, Edward. HSTPL.

11 Letter of Jeanette Kipp Tenenbaum to James C. Warren Jr. of May 26, 1981, in James C. Warren Papers, box 15, folder: Tenenbaum, Edward. HSTPL.

12 Washington, DC: Continental-Allied Co. [1959?]. The question mark stems from the Library of Congress catalog.

13 WorldCat lists ten publications by Continental-Allied Company, not all identical with the ones listed here. Online: http://worldcat.org/identities/ lccn-n80139314/ (Accessed October 16, 2018).

14 Edward A. Tenenbaum Papers, box 8, folder: Iran – Monetary Reform. HSTPL.

15 "S. C. counties are selected for OEO test," in: *Augusta Chronicle* (Augusta, GA), August 6, 1966, p. 16. (Accessed July 17, 2021).

16 "Tenenbaum, Edward Adam, 1921–1975. Person Authority Record." Online: https://catalog.archives.gov/id/10571069 (Accessed February 4, 2020).

17 "Translation from the German," probably by Hans Habe and sent to Edward Tenenbaum, as part of the article "USA. Eierköpfe und Texashüte." Part 4 of the article series "Unser Nachbar Amerika" [Our Neighbor America] in the weekly *Stern* Hamburg 17 (1964), issue no. 9 (February 25), pp. 40–52. Tenenbaum photo p. 46. The translation of the interview in: Edward A. Tenenbaum Papers, box 5, folder: Germany – Currency Reform – Memoranda (9 of 9). HSTPL.

18 "Big Day in the Lives of Ramona and Danny Dee," in: *Evening Star* Washington, DC Metro Area, August 5, 1961, p. 24.

19 *Yale Twenty-Fifth Yearbook Class of 1942*, New Haven, CT, 1967, p. 310.

20 "Complete Obituaries," in: *Register-Republic (Rockford IL)*,
November 24, 1965, p. 15. Online: www.genealogybank.com/doc/
obituaries/image/v2:135D854BCB3CDE11@GB3OBIT-
1377A03084114089@2439089-13775DFE775FA75A@14-
17569D246BE804CC@?h=144&fname=&lname=Kipp&fullname=&
kwinc=&kwexc=&rgfromDate=&rgtoDate=&formDate=&formDateFlex=
exact&dateType=range&processingtime=&addedFrom=&addedTo=&
page=9&sid=djndodidfxcfhgovbdcskfbsxxlfwhsa_wma-gateway001_
1652902943923 (Accessed May 18, 2022).

21 "Six Students Get Bond on Drug Charge," in: *Evening Star* Washington,
DC, April 5, 1968, p. C-2.

22 Commonwealth of Virginia – Certificate of Death, State File Number 69
009104 (Accessed via Ancestry.com January 29, 2018).

23 "Economist E. A. Tenenbaum Dies at 53 in Pa. Car Crash." *Evening Star*
Washington, DC, Friday October 17, 1975, p. 46. See also: "E.A.
Tenenbaum, Overseas Economist, Dies," in: *The Washington Post*,
October 31, 1975, p. A24. The death notice in the same issue of The
Washington Post informs that the fatal accident happened at Dillsburg PA
and that memorial service will take place at 2 p.m. on Saturday,
November 1, 1975, at Green Funeral Home, 721 Elden St., Herndon VA.
Ibid. See also the identical death notice in: *The Washington Star*,
31 October 1975, p. B-7. For the burial on Arlington National Cemetery in
Arlington County VA see online: www.findagrave.com/cgi-bin/fg.cgi?
page=gr&GRid=97198542 (Accessed August 23, 2017).

24 Letter of Jeanette Kipp Tenenbaum to James C. Warren Jr. of May 26, 1981,
in James C. Warren Papers, box 15, folder: Tenenbaum, Edward. HSTPL.

25 Email of March 2, 2018 from him to me, in which he promised to search
again in the Dillsburg Weekly Bulletin for a report on the Tenenbaum
accident on October 14, 1975.

26 Online: http://robbywerner.com/RTE15.pdf (Accessed March 5, 2018),
p. 5.

27 "Fatalities mar week," in: *The Weekly Bulletin*, Wednesday, October
22, 1975.

28 Ibid. I have searched for the difference between "critical" (used in the
Evening Star article of October 17, 1975) and "guarded" condition (used in
The Weekly Bulletin article of October 22, 1975). I found the following
information in an online discussion: "there is an American Hospital

Association set of guidelines for these terms, which if used around the USA should mean the same, but they caution that using the term 'Serious' may not really mean the same to everyone ..." A police officer with more than twenty years of experience at local, state, and federal levels writes: "Not certain of the precise meanings, but 'critical' is worse than 'serious' and 'serious' is worse than 'guarded'." Online: www.quora.com/Whats-the-difference-between-critical-serious-and-guarded%E2%80%9D-condition-terms-used-to-describe-injured-crime-or-accident-victims?utm_medium=organic&utm_source=google_rich_qa&utm_campaign=google_rich_qa (Accessed April 9, 2018).

29 According to a marriage return form of the Commonwealth of Virginia, State File No. 71 031354, accessible through ancestry.com.

30 See the next quote from a letter of Jeanette Kipp Tenenbaum to James C. Warren Jr. of May 26, 1981, in James C. Warren Papers, box 15, folder: Tenenbaum, Edward. HSTPL.

31 By email of September 21, 2018, Edward and Jeanette Kipp Tenenbaum's oldest son, Mark Jon Tenenbaum, informed me that he had "helped in part to build the greenhouses. We started in 1973 and a lot of the layout and preconstruction work was done by me and my father."

32 Letter of Jeanette Kipp Tenenbaum to James C. Warren Jr. of May 26, 1981, in James C. Warren Papers, box 15, folder: Tenenbaum, Edward. HSTPL.

33 *Yale Twenty-Fifth Yearbook Class of 1942*, p. 311.

34 Robert L. Heilbroner, "The Road to Selfdom," in: *New York Review of Books* 27, no. 6 of April 17, 1980.

35 J. Kipp Tenenbaum, "Free to choose?" In: *New York Review of Books*, 27, no. 18 (November 20, 1980). Online: www.nybooks.com/articles/1980/11/20/free-to-choose-1/ (Accessed March 8, 2018).

36 Letter of Edward A. Tenenbaum on behalf of James C. Warren of December 6, 1954 "TO WHOM IT MAY CONCERN." James C. Warren Papers, box 15, folder: Tenenbaum, Edward. HSTPL.

37 Letter of James C. Warren Jr. of July 5, 1986 to Mrs. J. Kipp Tenenbaum in Kalamazoo MI, in James C. Warren Papers, box 15, folder: Tenenbaum, Edward. HSTPL.

38 James C. Warren, Jr., "Origins of the 'Greek Economic Miracle:' The Truman Doctrine and Marshall Plan Development and Stabilization Programs," in: Eugene T. Rossides (ed.), *The Truman Doctrine of Aid to*

Greece: A Fifty-Year Retrospective, New York: The American Academy of Political Science, 1998, pp. 76–105.

39 Ibid., p. 79. The Paul R. Porter Papers, like the James C. Warren Papers and the Edward A. Tenenbaum Papers are located in the HSTPL.

40 Warren, Jr., "Origins of the 'Greek Economic Miracle'," p. 103.

41 Letter of Jeanette Kipp Tenenbaum to James C. Warren Jr. of April 4, 2000, in James C. Warren Papers, box 15, folder: Tenenbaum, Edward. HSTPL.

42 See online: www.findagrave.com/cgi-bin/fg.cgi?page=gr&GRid=97198547 (Accessed August 23, 2017).

7 CONCLUSION

1 Tenenbaum's CV with which he applied for his appointment in Greece, while he was still working for the IMF. Edward A. Tenenbaum Papers, box 8, folder: Personnel File. HSTPL.

2 Christoph Schröder, "'Der Überläufer.' Stechmücken statt Pathos," in: Zeit Online April 7, 2020. "Der Überläufer": Stechmücken statt Pathos | ZEIT ONLINE (Accessed March 21, 2021).

3 Annett Heide, "Dieser Mann hat ein Denkmal verdient," interview with Hans-Hermann Klare (author of the book *Auerbach. Eine jüdisch-deutsche Tragödie oder Wie der Antisemitismus den Krieg überlebte*, Berlin: Aufbau-Verlag, 2022), in: *Der Tagesspiegel*, February 16, 2023, pp. 16–17.

4 Robert Nef/Bernhard Ruetz, "Wer war der Vater der Deutschen Mark?" In: *Reflexion* 46 (2002), p. 9.

Acknowledgments

FOR RESEARCH AND OTHER SUPPORT:

Archivists of the Harry S. Truman Presidential Library at Independence, MO:
  Sam Rushay
  Randy Sowell
  Jim Armistead
  Laurie Austin

Research Consultants of National Archives at College Park, MD:

  Thomas McAnear (especially for RG 59 State Dept.)
  David A. Langbart (for RG 59 State Dept.)
  Paul Brown (for RG 260 OMGUS, RG 226 OSS, and RG 165 War Dept.)
  Suzanne Zoumbaris (for RG 260 OMGUS, RG 226 OSS, RG 165 War Dept.,
    and miscellaneous RGs 407, 43, 263, 226)
  James Schwarz (for RG 260 OMGUS)
  Eric van Slander (for military records, esp. a top secret cable from War
    Dept. to OMGUS)
  Robin E. Cookson (for military records, esp. Operation Reports)

Curators and Historians in Other US Government Institutions:

  Hallie Brooker, Lead Curator of the files of the Bureau of Engraving
    and Printing
  Kevin Ruffner, Historian of the CIA
  William McAllister, Chief of the Special Projects Division at the State
    Department Office of the Historian
  Pamela D. Campbell, Digital Preservation Specialist and Archivist Federal
    Reserve Bank of St. Louis

US Embassy in Berlin:

Ambassador Amy Gutmann
Katrin Jordan-Korte
Leonard C Purrington
Sigurd M. Nietfeld

Staff of Manuscripts & Archives (MSSA) of the Sterling Memorial Library at Yale University, New Haven, CT, especially:

Genevieve Coyle
Judith Schiff

Institute for New Economic Thinking (INET), New York City, especially:

Thomas Ferguson, Director of Research, who accompanied and supported my project in various ways and suggested that I publish my book in his series with Cambridge University Press

The Three Living Tenenbaum Children:

Anne Kipp Toohey
Joan Tenenbaum Merrill
Mark Jon Tenenbaum

Newspaper Portals:

Genealogybank.com
newspaperarchive.com

Museum Währungsreform 1948 Fuldatal-Rothwesten:

Bernd Niesel (†)
Hans-Hermann Trost
Anne Rüter

Archive of the University of Vienna:

Manuela Bauer

Archive of the Institut für Zeitgeschichte, Munich:

Klaus Lankheit

The State Archive of Hamburg:

Susanne Schmidt (and her agents in Hamburg), who allowed me to access the economics diploma thesis of her father Helmut Schmidt, Germany's former chancellor, on currency reforms

Archive of the Ludwig-Erhard-Stiftung, Bonn:

Andreas Schirmer

Municipal Archive Coblenz:

Michael Koelges

Colleague Historians with a Strong Interest in My Project:

Christel McDonald, Arlington, VA, who supported my research over the years most of all.
Kevin M. Hymel, Arlington, VA
Kathy Peiss, University of Pennsylvania
Thomas Childers, Media, PA
Stephen A. Schuker, Washington, DC
Michalis Psalidopoulos, The American College of Greece, Athens
Alejandro Rodriguez-Giovo. École Internationale (Ecolint), Geneva
Gerd Hardach, Berlin (†)
Dieter Lindenlaub, Leipzig
Wolfgang Materne, hobby historian for the housing complex in which the Tenenbaum family first lived in Berlin 1946

Colleagues of the J. F. Kennedy Institute for North American Studies (JFKI) and of the Free University of Berlin (FUB) at Large, especially:

Jeremias Gayer
Jessica Gienow-Hecht
Irwin Collier
Max Steinhardt

Kerstin Brunke

Marie Bergeron

As well as the extremely cooperative library staff of the FUB, in particular:

Medea Seyder, head of the JFKI library, and its staff

Manuela Hainke , interlibrary loan staff

Franziska Bauer, librarian of the social science library

Karin Reese, head of the economics library

Kerstin Conrad, librarian of the economics library

Gerold Streif, librarian of the economics library (who even searched for
    publications relevant to my project)

Cambridge University Press for Its Diligent Work in the Production of My Book:

Robert Dreesen

Sable Gravesandy

Laura Blake

Hemalatha Subramanian

Fiona Cole

Trent Hancock (for his fine work on the index)

For Translation and Copy-Editing:

Charlie Zaharoff, Berlin

Deepl.com

For Financial Support:

Fritz Thyssen Stiftung, Cologne

Truman Library Institute, Kansas City, MO

Institute for New Economic Thinking (INET), New York

Abbreviations

Edward A. Tenenbaum: "Apart from combat troops, the T-Force includes [...] more alphabetical abbreviations than all of Washington."[1]

//	denotes a paragraph within a quotation
AAF	US Army Air Forces
AAC	US Army Air Corps
AAFTTC	Army Air Forces Technical Training Command
ABC	Atomic, Biological, and Chemical (weapons)
AC or A.C.	Air Corps
AC of S	Assistant Chief of Staff
ACC	Allied Control Council
AG	Army Group or (in German) Aktiengesellschaft (= stock company)
AID	Agency for International Development, Washington DC
AMAG	American Mission for Aid to Greece
AMZON	American Zone (of Occupation in Germany)
APO	US Army Post Office
ASU	American Student Union
AUS	Army US
A/C	Aviation Cadet

---

[1] Edward A. Tenenbaum, after having been assigned to T-Force of 12th Army Group, described in his report of December 12, 1944 from La Roche, Belgium, their function, tools, and characteristics. "Secret for OSS Use Only, La Roche, Belgium, 12 December 1944, FROM: Edward A. Tenenbaum, 2nd Lt., AC, ATTENTION: Lt. (jg) Just Lunning, Chief, German Unit (Tempo), R&A/London, TO: Harold Deutsch, Chief, R&A/Paris." NARA at College Park MD, RG 226 Office of Strategic Services, Entry NM 54 1: Research and Analysis Branch, Office of the Chief: General Correspondence, 1942-46, Box 31, folder 1.

A-H	Office of the Assistant Secretary of State John H. Hilldring
A-S	Office of Assistant Secretary of State (Charles E. Saltzman/C. C. Hilliard)
BA	Bachelor of Arts
BArch	Bundesarchiv (= Archive of the Federal Republic of Germany)
BDI	Bundesverband der Deutschen Industrie (= Federation of German Industries)
BdL	Bank deutscher Länder, West Germany's central bank founded in February 1948, forerunner of the Deutsche Bundesbank
BEP	Bureau of Engraving and Printing of the Treasury Department
BEW	US Board of Economic Warfare
BICO	Bipartite Control Office (of the Bizone)
BIFIN	Bipartite Finance Control Group / Panel
BIGFIN	Meetings of BIFIN and BIXFIN together
BIRLS	Beneficiary Identification and Records Locator Subsystem (e.g., of the US Department of Veterans Affairs)
BIXFIN	(German) Joint Committee for Finance
BRD	Bundesrepublik Deutschland (= Federal Republic of Germany)
CAFT	Combined Advanced Field Team
CDG Plan	Colm, Gerhard/Dodge, Joseph M./Goldsmith, Raymond Plan of 1946 for quadripartite currency reform in Germany
CDU	Christlich Demokratische Union Deutschlands (= political party)
C.d.Z.	Chef der Zivilverwaltung
CFM	Council of Foreign Ministers
CIA	Central Intelligence Agency

CIC	Counter Intelligence Corps of the US Army
CID	Central Information Division of OSS
CIG	Central Intelligence Group
CINCEUR	Commander in Chief Europe, US Army
CIOS	Combined Intelligence Objective Subcommittee
COI	Coordinator of Information (July 1941–June 1942 preceding OSS)
Col.	Colonel
COS	Chief of Staff
Cpl	Corporal
CQ	Congressional Quarterly
CSU	Christlich-Soziale Union (= CDU sister political party in Bavaria)
DC	District of Columbia
DDP	Deutsche Demokratische Partei (= political party)
DDR	Deutsche Demokratische Republik (= German Democratic Republic)
DGB	Deutscher Gewerkschaftsbund (German Labor Union Federation)
DNVP	Deutschnationale Volkspartei (= political party)
DOT	Department of Transportation
DP	Deutsche Partei (= political party)
DPs	Displaced Persons
DS	Detached Service
ECA	European Cooperation Administration, Washington DC (Marshall Plan)
Ecolint	École Internationale in Geneva, Switzerland
EDCMR	Estimated Date of Completion Mid-Range
EEIS	Enemy Equipment Intelligence Service
EM	Enlisted Military
EOU	Economic Objectives Unit
EPU	European Payments Union
ERA	European Recovery Act (Marshall Plan)

ERP	European Recovery Program
ETO	European Theater of Operations
ETOUSA	European Theater of Operations US Army
FDP	Freie Demokratische Partei (= political party)
FFI	Forces Françaises de l'Intérieur
Fin & Dev	Finance and Development Magazine of the IMF
FINAD	Finance Adviser (of OMGUS)
Fn.	Footnote
FO	Foreign Office, London
fol.	Folio refers to page of archival material
FRUS	Foreign Relations of the United States (official document collection)
Fwd	Forward
G-2	Intelligence staff of US Army units
GA	Office of German and Austrian Economic Affairs, State Department
GDR	German Democratic Republic
Gestapo	*Geheime Staatspolizei* (=Secret State Police)
GPO	Government Printing Office, Washington, DC
GI	Government Issue (= popular term for members of US Armed Forces in WW II)
HA BBK	Historical Archive of the Deutsche Bundesbank, Frankfurt am Main
HG	Headquarters Group
HICOG	US High Commission for Germany, Bonn
HQ	Headquarters
HSTPL	Harry S. Truman Presidential Library, Independence MO
HTO	Haupttreuhandstelle Ost (= Main Trustee Office East)
IARA	Inter-Allied Reparations Agency, Brussels
IBRD	International Bank for Reconstruction and Development, also called World Bank
ICA	International Cooperation Administration

ICD	Information Control Division of OMGUS
IDC	Interdepartmental Committee for the Acquisition of Foreign Publications
IMF	International Monetary Fund, Washington, DC
IR	Intelligence Report
JEIA	Joint Export Import Agency
Kapo	*Kameradschaftspolizei*, privileged KL inmates, selected by the SS leadership, for self-administration of the camp
KGB	Russian abbreviation for "Committee for State Security" of the USSR
KL	Konzentrationslager (concentration camp)
km	kilometers
KPD	Kommunistische Partei Deutschlands (= Germany's Communist Party)
LCVP	Landing Craft, Vehicle, Personnel
LEZ	Ludwig Erhard Zentrum
LoN	League of Nations
Lt.	Lieutenant
Lt. (jg)	Lieutenant junior grade in the US Navy
MFA&A	Monuments, Fine Arts, and Archives (sub-branch of the Economics Division of OMGUS)
MII	Military Intelligence Interpretation (of 4th Armored Division)
MP	Military Police
MSA	Mutual Security Agency, Act, or Assistance
NARA	National Archives & Records Administration (US)
NATO	North Atlantic Treaty Organization
Nazi	Nationalsozialistisch/Nationalsozialismus
NCO	Non-Commissioned Officer (*Unteroffizier* in German)
NKDW	People's Commissariat for Internal Affairs of the USSR, also operating as a secret service active in the Soviet occupation zone of Germany

NPRC	National Personnel Records Center, St. Louis MO
NRW	Nordrhein-Westfalen (= the state of North Rhine-Westphalia)
NS	Nationalsozialistisch/Nationalsozialismus
NSDAP	Nationalsozialistische Deutsche Arbeiterpartei
NYC	New York City
OCS	Officer Candidate School
OEEC	Organization for European Economic Cooperation
OEO	Office of Economic Opportunity
OKW	Oberkommando der Wehrmacht (= German Armed Forces High Command)
OMGUS	Office of Military Government for Germany (US)
ORA	Organisation de Résistance de l'Armée
OSI	Office of Special Investigations
OSO	Office of Special Operations
OSS	Office of Strategic Services (June 1942–September 1945)
OTIC	Ordnance Technical Intelligence Team
OWI	Office of War Information
P&PW DET	Publishing & Political Warfare Detachment, 12th US Army Group
p.a.	per annum, annually
PC	Peace Council (at Yale University and elsewhere)
Pfc	Private first class
PU	Political Union (at Yale University and elsewhere)
PW or P/W	Prisoner of War
PWB	Psychological Warfare Branch
PWD	Psychological Warfare Division
R&A	Research & Analysis branch (of COI and OSS)
RCN	Reconnaissance
RCT	Regimental Combat Team (infantry regiment with their own artillery, engineers, medical, and tanks)
RD	Road
REIMAHG	Reichsmarschall Hermann Göring

Reurad	Reply (or Response) to your radio (= telegram)
RG	Record Group
RI	Reichsgruppe Industrie
RKI	Robert Koch-Institut
RM	Reichsmark
SAG	Sowjetische Aktiengesellschaft
SC	South Carolina
SD	Sicherheitsdienst (Secret Service of the SS)
SED	Sozialistische Einheitspartei Deutschlands
SHAEF	Supreme Headquarters Allied Expeditionary Force
SI	Secret Intelligence branch of OSS
SOE	Special Operations Executive (= British agents in German-occupied Europe)
SOP	Standard Operating Procedure
SOS	Save Our Souls
SPD	Sozialdemokratische Partei Deutschlands (= political party)
SS	Schutzstaffel (as military units Nazi elite troops)
SS	Steamship
SSN	Social Security Number
STEG	Staatliche Erfassungs-Gesellschaft für öffentliches Gut (= state acquisition company for public property)
SWNCC	State-War-Navy Coordinating Committee
T-Force	Target Force
TD or TDY	Temporary Duty
TIIC	Technical Industrial Intelligence Committee (of the US Navy)
T/O	Theater of Operations
UK	United Kingdom
UNRRA	United Nations Relief and Rehabilitation Administration
UP	University Press
USFET	US Forces European Theater

USGCC	US Group Control Council (Germany; World War II)
USHMM	US Holocaust Memorial Museum
USSR	Union of Soviet Socialist Republics
USSBS	US Strategic Bombing Survey
USSTAF	US Strategic Air Forces
VE-Day	Victory in Europe Day
WD	War Department
WiGBl	Gesetz- und Verordnungsblatt des Wirtschaftsrates des Vereinigten Wirtschaftsgebietes
WW	World War
ZDF	Zweites Deutsches Fernsehen

Index

Milton Keynes UK
Ingram Content Group UK Ltd.
UKHW040909261024
450121UK00002BA/15

9 781009 492805